GUIDE TO THE PLANTS OF THE
WALLOWA MOUNTAINS
OF NORTHEASTERN OREGON

To
Susan
whose confidence, encouragement
and unflagging interest
have made this
flora
possible

A PATHFINDER BOOK REPRINT EDITION
Complete and Unabridged

Printed in the United States of America

ISBN: 979-8-8691-8971-4

GUIDE TO THE PLANTS OF THE WALLOWA MOUNTAINS OF NORTHEASTERN OREGON

by

Georgia Mason

Special Publication
of the
Museum of Natural History
University of Oregon
Eugene, Oregon
December 1975

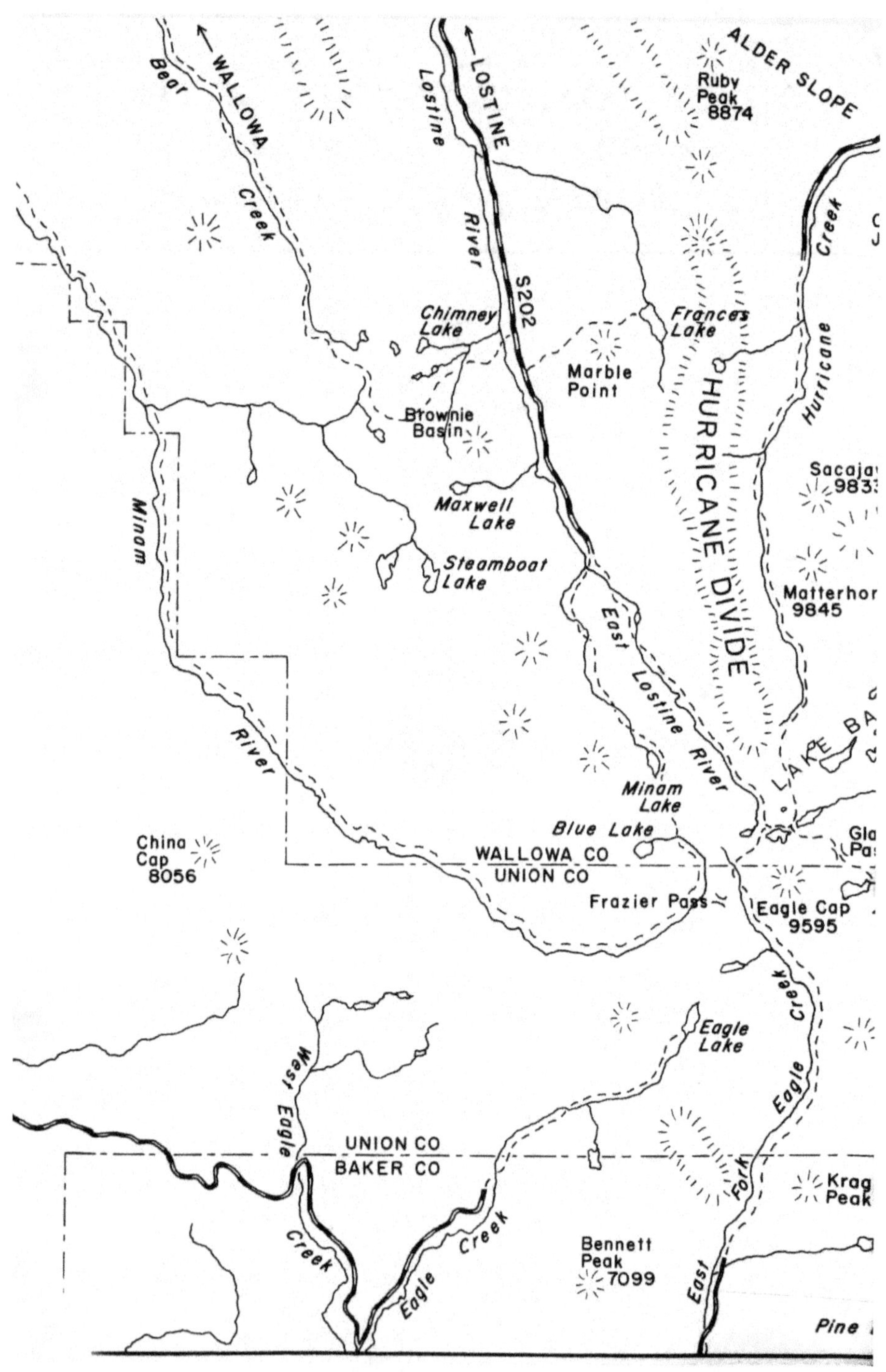

Bear
WALLOWA
Creek
Lostine
LOSTINE
ALDER SLOPE
Ruby Peak 8874
Lostine River
S202
Chimney Lake
Frances Lake
Hurricane Creek
HURRICANE DIVIDE
Marble Point
Brownie Basin
Maxwell Lake
Sacaja 983
Minam
Steamboat Lake
Matterhor 9845
East Lostine River
LAKE BA
Minam Lake
Blue Lake
China Cap 8056
WALLOWA CO
UNION CO
Gla Pa
River
Frazier Pass
Eagle Cap 9595
Eagle Creek
Eagle Lake
West Eagle
UNION CO
BAKER CO
East Fork
Krag Peak
Creek
Eagle Creek
Bennett Peak 7099
Pine

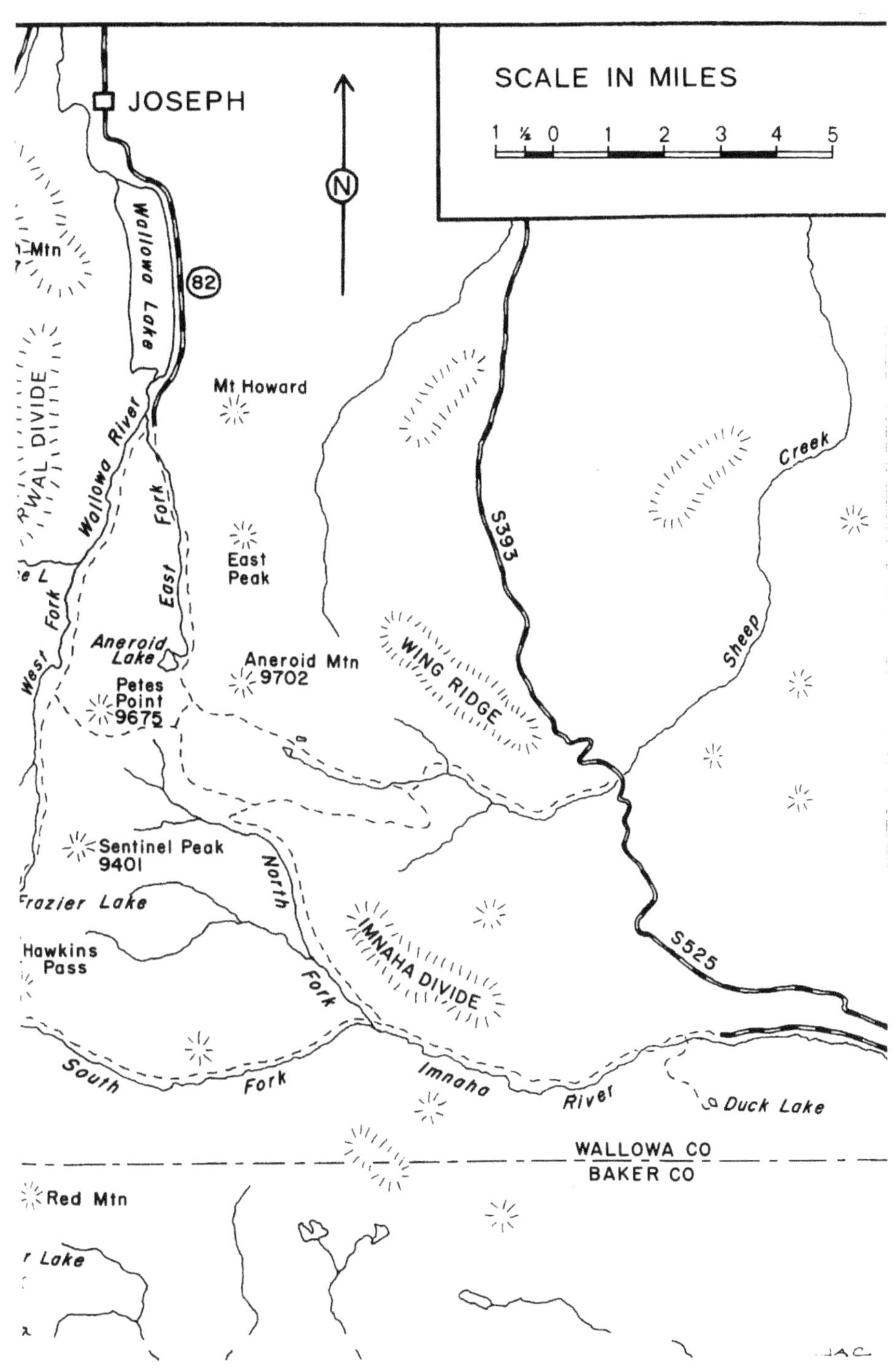

JOSEPH
N
SCALE IN MILES
1 ½ 0 1 2 3 4 5
Wallowa Lake
82
Wallowa River
RWAL DIVIDE
West Fork
East Fork
Mt Howard
East Peak
Aneroid Lake
Petes Point 9675
Aneroid Mtn 9702
WING RIDGE
S393
Creek
Sheep
Sentinel Peak 9401
Frazier Lake
Hawkins Pass
North Fork
IMNAHA DIVIDE
S525
South Fork
Imnaha River
Duck Lake
WALLOWA CO
BAKER CO
Red Mtn
Lake
e L
Mtn
JAC

CONTENTS

Guide to the Plants of the Wallowa Mountains of Northeastern Oregon

by

GEORGIA MASON

INTRODUCTION AND ACKNOWLEDGEMENTS

This first published record of plants growing in the Wallowa Mountains is based mostly on my own collections over a period of 11 years. Earlier William C. Cusick who lived in the nearby town of Union collected extensively from 1896 to 1910. Records exist of several taxa which apparently have not been collected again since his time. Other collectors of whom I know who have deposited specimens in herbaria which I have visited include: William H. Baker, Lincoln Constance, Ray J. Davis, LeRoy E. Detling, Carl English, Serge Head, A. R. Kruckeberg, Lilla Leach, Bassett Maguire, Marion Ownbey, Morton E. Peck, Carl W. Sharsmith and Dennis W. Woodland.

The locations, ecological data and elevations given are those for which some Wallowa Mountain record exists and may or not be true elsewhere. Such data are not to be interpreted to mean that the conditions given are the only conditions for a taxon in our mountains; it may grow higher or lower, in more sun or less, in valleys as well as on slopes, in bogs as well as on drier soil. It is also possible that not all plants of the region have been seen or collected.

I welcome any additions or suggestions which would help to make our knowledge of the vegetation of the Wallowas more complete.

In the preparation of this work many people have helped. For permission to go through their collections and study specimens from the Wallowa Mountains I am grateful to the Curators of the Herbaria of the University of Idaho at Moscow, Washington State University at Pullman and Oregon State University of Corvallis. The late Dr. LeRoy E. Detling gave me access to the facilities of the Herbarium of the Museum of Natural History of the University of Oregon at Eugene during his curatorship. Thanks are due also to Dr. Donald J. Pinkava and Elinor Lehto of Arizona State University for use of the herbarium facilities at Tempe during 1967-1970.

I have deposited numerous specimens at all the herbaria mentioned, and at others, but the most nearly complete collections are to be found at the Museum of Natural History of the University of Oregon at Eugene and at Oregon State University at Corvallis.

For their kindness and expertise in the determinations of my specimens my deep appreciation is due to: Dr. Rimo C. Bacigalupi for Saxifragaceae, *Orobanche* and Scrophulariaceae; Dr. Rupert C. Barneby for *Astragalus* and *Oxytropis*; Dr. Katherine Beamish for *Dodecatheon*; Dr. Lyman Benson for *Ranunculus*; Dr. Kenton L. Chambers for *Agoseris* and *Microseris*; Dr. Robert Clausen for *Botrychium* and *Sedum*; Dr. Lincoln Constance for Hydrophyllaceae and Umbelliferae; J. O. Coolidge for *Polygonum*; Dr. Herbert F. Copeland for Ericaceae; Dr. Arthur Cronquist for the Com-

1

positae; Dr. Ray J. Davis for Portulacaceae; Dr. Lauramae Dempster for *Galium*; Dr. David B. Dunn for *Lupinus*; Dr. Joseph Ewan for *Delphinium*; Dr. Charles Feddema for certain Gramineae; Dr. Leslie A. Garay for Orchidaceae; Dr. John M. Gillett for *Gentiana* and *Trifolium*; Dr. G. J. Goodman for *Eriogonum*; Dr. Lawrence R. Heckard for *Phacelia*; Dr. Fred J. Hermann for Cyperaceae and Juncaceae; Dr. C. Leo Hitchcock for *Draba*; Carlos Jativa for Labiatae; Dr. LaRea D. Johnston for *Callitriche* and other aquatics; the late Dr. G. N. Jones for *Amelanchier, Sambucus* and *Symphoricarpos*; Dr. A. R. Kruckeberg for *Silene*; Dr. Charles T. Mason for Gentianaceae; Dr. Herbert L. Mason for Polemoniaceae; Dr. Mildred E. Mathias for Umbelliferae; Dr. Fred G. Meyer for *Valeriana*; the late Dr. Conrad V. Morton for *Lycopodium, Selaginella* and Polypodiaceae; the late Dr. Philip A. Munz for Onagraceae; Dr. Marion Ownbey for *Allium, Calochortus and Castilleja*; Dr. C. L. Porter for *Potamogeton*; Dr. Reed C. Rollins for Cruciferae; Dr. Jason R. Swallen for Gramineae; Dr. T. M. C. Taylor for *Isoetes*; Dr. Warren H. Wagner for *Botrychium*; Dr. Herbert A. Wahl for *Chenopodium*; Dr. George H. Ward for *Artemisia*; Dr. William A. Weber for *Helianthus, Helianthella, Balsamorhiza* and *Wyethia*; Mr. Ralph R. Wilson for Salicaceae and Gymnospermae and Dr. Dennis W. Woodland for *Urtica*.

Most of the illustrations were done from herbarium specimens by David Eric Cole. A number were done by John A. Christy and others.

THE WALLOWA MOUNTAINS

The rugged Wallowa Mountains of the Wallowa-Whitman National Forest lie east of La Grande in northeastern Oregon. The main mass is in the southwest corner of Wallowa County with some portions extending into Union and Baker Counties. The present study has concentrated mostly on that portion of the Wallowa Mountains designated as the Eagle Cap Wilderness Area, an area of roughly 350 square miles dominated by the mountain called Eagle Cap which rises to an elevation of 9595 feet. From this peak and the lakes huddled at its base four major streams and their forks flow in a north to north-westerly direction: the Minam River, the Lostine River, Hurricane Creek and the Wallowa River. They join the Grande Ronde River which eventually empties into the Snake River to the east. The valleys they have helped to create are long, steep-walled and often narrow except for those of the Lostine which are wider and more U-shaped. Two streams originate east and south of Eagle Cap and eventually empty into the Snake River: one is Eagle Creek which probably accounts for the earlier local name of "Eagle Creek Mountains" for the southern part of the Wallowa Mountains, the other is the Imnaha River which, fed by several forks and creeks, first flows east and then turns north to meet the Snake River near the Washington border.

Besides Eagle Cap other high peaks in the Wilderness Area are: Chief Joseph Mountain, Aneroid Mountain, Petes Point, Sentinel Peak, Sacajawea (9833 feet) and the tallest, the Matterhorn (9845 feet) with a gleaming limestone dome at its peak. Though rugged, all are accessible to the hiker.

The lowest elevation included in the area of study is 4500 feet, the elevation of Wallowa Lake, a deep glacial lake surrounded on three sides by moraines. From here trails lead into the high country. Other usual points of entry are at the end of the Hurricane

Creek Road west of Joseph, Sheep Creek Road east of Joseph, the Lostine River Road south of Lostine, Bear Creek Road south of Wallowa and Eagle Creek Road east of Medical Springs.

Trails throughout the area are well maintained by the Forest Service and campgrounds of varying degrees of improvement have been established, especially in the Lake Basin where recreational use is the heaviest.

Included in the study but separated from the main mountain mass is a ridge east of the Eagle Cap Wilderness boundary. This region is composed of timbered slopes rising to about 6000 feet with two or three peaks up to about 8000 feet. Little Sheep Creek, Gumboot Creek and Lick Creek flow through it on their way to the Imnaha River. Access is from the Imnaha Highway east of Joseph.

Pronunciation of the word "Wallowa" varies: the Indians of the Nez Perce Tribe who lived in Wallowa Valley and around Wallowa Lake and sent smoke signals from the top of the presently called Howard Mountain (formerly Signal Peak) pronounced it whale-AWAY; visitors often pronounce it wah-LOH-uh; the local pronunciation is wahl-OW-uh with a broadening of the OW syllable. This last is the one I have used over the years.

Geological History
by Dennis W. Woodland
Curator, McGill University Herbarium

The peaks of the Wallowa Mountains rise to an elevation of nearly 10,000 feet above the plateau of northeastern Oregon. The mountains are bounded by river valleys on three sides: the Wallowa on the north, the Grande Ronde on the west and the Powder to the south. The Snake River Canyon and the state of Idaho are found to the east.

The oldest rocks in the area are altered greenish lava flows and tuff beds which were extruded probably during the Permian Period in a similar manner as the Columbia River basalts. These 3000- to 5000-feet-thick layers are found along the Imnaha and Snake rivers in the southeast region and around Wallowa Lake along the northern edge of the range. Following erosion resulting from an uplift, the land area sank below sea level and was covered by salt-water deposits of lime and clay which later became metamorphosed into limestones and sediments during the Triassic.

During the Jurassic the earlier deposited layers were pushed up from the sea and became folded and eroded. As the folding continued, underlying granitoid magma (molten rock) pushed its way upward through the green layers. This intrusion of granodiorite formed a dome-like elevation in the surrounding plateau. During the later part of the intrusion large deposits of mineral ore were emplaced primarily in the southern part of the Wallowas.

Extensive erosion which occurred from the time of the intrusion to the Miocene Epoch removed much of the sedimentary rock and folds overlying the granodiorite and reduced the area to a plain.

In Miocene time the Columbia River lava flow appeared and basalts from this flow were extruded from long fissures over most of the area. Erosion has removed much of this flow but basalt dikes can be easily seen throughout the area.

The elevation of the range as a large horst or block to its present height occurred

3

during post-Miocene time. Gentle upwarping and extensive faulting occurred throughout the area but was most extensive in the northern portion of the range. The steep north escarpment of Chief Joseph Peak follows a fault line. Other faults probably account for the Grande Ronde Valley and Eagle Creek may flow along such a fracture.

Erosion from water which has lasted to the present from late Miocene or early Pliocene times cut deep V-shaped valleys and canyons into the plateau leaving mountains of almost uniform height. During the Pleistocene period the mountains were heavily glaciated with alpine glaciers radiating from the central region of Eagle Cap Mountain. All the large canyons (Eagle Creek, Imnaha, Lostine, Minam, Hurricane, Pine and the East and West Forks of the Wallowa) of the drainage system contained large glaciers which developed their present U-shapes. Smaller alpine glaciers fed ice and neve to the larger valley glaciers. One such area, the Lake Basin, is a hanging valley containing eleven named lakes of cirque or paternoster origin. Glacial striae are most common along with numerous glacially polished bluffs indicating much ice movement in the past. The Wallowa Lake moraines probably contain more glacial till than all the other moraines in the area combined and are the most outstanding glacial features in the region. They also give a good estimate as to the immensity of the glacier which formed them.

The Vegetation

Wallowa Lake is surrounded on the east, west and north by moraines. The most imposing is the East Moraine rising to an elevation of about 5200 feet and drier than the West Moraine. A few Ponderosa Pine trees grow on its mostly grassy sandy slopes. Cattle are pastured on the crest and the east slope; bridle trails are maintained on the south and west slopes. Early in the summer it is usually covered with *Balsamorhiza sagittata, Phacelia linearis, Clarkia pulchella*, Lupines and other sun-loving plants.

The West Moraine supports more of a mixed forest.

Plants commonly found on one or both moraines include *Arnica sororia, Antennaria anaphaloides, A. rosea, Arenaria congesta, Arctostaphylos uva-ursi, Bromus brizaeformis, B. carinatus, B. tectorum, Calamagrostis rubescens, Castilleja* spp., *Chrysanthemum leucanthemum, Geranium viscosissimum, Helianthus annuus, Luzula campestris, Polygonum majus, Valeriana edulis, Verbascum blattaria, V. thapsus* and *Zigadenus* spp.

From Wallowa Lake at about 4500 feet the thickly timbered slopes rise steadily southward to tree-line (about 7-8000 feet) where the trees are noticeably thinned out, still blanketing the slopes and lining the ridges, hovering close to the streams and the lakes but leaving openings in the forest as they tend to collect into small groups. In some locations along the way *Pinus contorta* (Lodgepole Pine) forms large dense stands, in others *Picea engelmannii* (Engelmann's Spruce) shuts out the sun and produces a dark dank forest in which vegetation is restricted to a few plants.

The mixed woods of the lower elevations include *Abies grandis* (Grand Fir), *Alnus sinuata* (Alder), *Juniperus* spp., *Pinus contorta, P. ponderosa, Populus* spp. (Cottonwood and Quaking Aspen), *Pseudotsuga menziesii* (Douglas Fir), *Salix* spp. (Willows), *Sambucus* spp. (Elderberry) and *Symphoricarpos* spp. (Snowberry). These give way gradually at higher elevations to *Abies lasiocarpa* (Alpine Fir), *Larix occidentalis* (Larch), *Picea engelmannii, Pinus albicaulis* (White Bark Pine) and *Tsuga mertensiana* (Hemlock).

Other common plants include *Arceuthobium* spp., *Botrychium* spp., *Calypso bulbosa*, *Campanula rotundifolia*, *Carex dioica* var. *gynocrates*, *Ceanothus velutinus*, *Cercocarpus ledifolius*, *Cheilanthes gracillima*, *Cryptogramma crispa*, *Cystopteris fragilis*, *Habenaria* spp., *Listera* spp., *Lonicera utahensis*, *Pachistima myrsinites*, *Potentilla fruticosa*, *Pyrola* spp., *Ribes* spp., *Vaccinium* spp. and many more, some in the dry rocky open meadows, others along the shady watercourses.

At about 7200 feet a fairly level bench or valley appears to flatten out abruptly and extend for about 8 to 10 miles southward with occasional dips and rises up to as much as 7800 feet. The surface is deeply eroded by glaciation and the action of the various rivers and creeks which run through it following the northerly descending slope of the land.

This is the open lush zone of the alpine and sub-alpine meadows bordering the numerous lakes of the Lake Basin huddled at the northern base of Eagle Cap and at the foot of the Matterhorn, Petes Point, Sentinel Peak, Marble Point and other summits. This is where avalanches from above pile up and snow fields lie late. The soil is rich and deep. Water is plentiful. Lake borders are frequently boggy. The sun is strong and the trees uncrowded. Snow may fall during any month of the year. The growing season is short, from about the first week of July to about the end of August, but the height of the summer flowering occurs between the middle of July and almost to the middle of August.

Plants common to this belt include *Allium validum, Arnica cordifolia, A. mollis, A. parryi, Carex illota, Cassiope mertensiana, Castilleja chrysantha, C. rhexifolia, Dodecatheon* spp., *Isoetes bolanderi, Juncus drummondii, J. mertensianus, Gaultheria humifusa, Gentiana calycosa, Kalmia polifolia* var. *microphylla, Ledum glandulosum, Monardella odoratissima, Pedicularis* spp., *Penstemon* spp., *Phyllodoce empetriformis, Polemonium pulcherrimum, Ranunculus* spp., *Salix barclayi, S. commutata, Sparganium angustifolium, Vaccinium caespitosum, Veronica cusickii* and *Zigadenus elegans.*

Above this belt rise the exposed rocky summits and peaks of the Matterhorn, Sacajawea, Chief Joseph Mountain, Eagle Cap, Petes Point, Sentinel Peak, Aneroid Mountain and others with top elevations between 9500 and 9845 feet. Here also are a number of hidden lakes, visited by the few and thus more likely to preserve their natural environment. Generally the rocky slopes are steep, unstable, unprotected. The soil is shallow and often sandy or gritty. Moisture is lost quickly. The vegetation is sparse, tends to be hairy, to have shortened stems or to sprawl over the ground, and to take advantage of any depression, crack, crevice or other shelter.

Although timberline in the Wallowa Mountains is roughly at about 8000 feet it sinks as low as 7100 feet near Frazier Lake and rises up to about 9000 feet in other places. The few trees of *Pinus albicaulis* (White Bark Pine) and *Abies lasiocarpa* (Alpine Fir) which inhabit this region of rocks exhibit the effects of strong winds, avalanches, deep persistent snow fields and other extremes of mountain weather. They tend to collect into small groups and to become drawfed, twisted, one-sided.

Besides the trees plants usually found in this zone include *Androsace septentrionalis, Astragalus kentrophyta, Campanula scabrella, Carex foetida* var. *vernacula, C. nigricans, C. pyrenaica, Castilleja fraterna, C. rubida, Claytonia megarhiza, Crepis nana, Draba lemmonii* var. *cyclomorpha, D. lonchocarpa, D. oligosperma, D. paysonii, Dryas octopetala, Erigeron simplex, Epilobium anagallidifolium, Eritrichium nanum, Gilia* *congesta, Hulsea algida, Ivesia gordonii, Lewisia pygmaea, Oxyria digyna, Oxytropis viscida, Phoenicaulis cheiranthoides, Salix arctica, S. nivalis, Saxifraga bronchialis* var. *austromontana, S. caespitosa, S. oppositifolia, Sedum lanceolatum, Silene acaulis, Sitanion hystrix, Smelowskia calycina, Townsendia montana* and *Trisetum spicatum.**

From its source on Eagle Cap (9595 feet) East Eagle Creek flows in a southerly direction for about 8 miles in its descent to an elevation of about 5000 feet in our area. The vegetation of this southern exposure of the Wallowa Mountains differs from that of the north-facing mass discussed above. There are several lakes at about the 7200 to 7800 foot level but the slopes generally tend toward dryness. Plants of this Eagle Creek drainage include *Acer douglasii, Abies grandis, Alopecurus aequalis, Agrostis scabra, Carex brunnescens, C. jonesii, C. limnophila, C. microptera, Eriogonum* spp., *Gentianella simplex, Gnaphalium palustre, Juncus balticus, J. howellii, Polemonium occidentale, Polygonum* spp., *Lupinus* spp., and *Scirpus microcarpus.*

East of Eagle Cap and barely within the eastern border of the Wilderness Area is the region through which flow Sheep Creek, Lick Creek and Gumboot Creek which eventually join the Imnaha River at about 4400 feet elevation.

Except for a few peaks up to about 8000 feet the crest is fairly level at about 6000 feet and supports grazing by cattle and sheep during the short summer. Logging of *Pinus contorta, Pinus ponderosa* and *Pseudotsuga menziesii* is carried on almost the year around. The soil is of heavy stony reddish clay moistened by occasional springs.

Common plants of the region include *Allium madidum, Antennaria luzuloides, Artemisia rigida, A. tridentata, Brodiaea douglasii, Deschampsia danthonioides, Floerkea proserpinacoides, Orogenia linearifolia, Perideridia bolanderi, Phlox longifolia, Polygonum bistortoides, P. kelloggii, Primula cusickiana, Purshia tridentata, Spergularia rubra, Trifolium cyathiferum, T. macrocephalum* and *Wyethia helianthoides.*

USE OF THE KEYS

Keys are presented to help in the determination of the generic and specific name of a particular plant. They are arranged in numbered pairs of characters which oppose each other, requiring a decision before going on to the next numbered pair where again a decision must be made. It is good practice to study both choices of each pair before coming to a decision for two reasons: the differences may be very small and require careful reading of the data presented; then too it is easy to see a feature of a plant when it is there but it is not so easy to recognize when the feature is reduced, obsolete, inconspicuous or missing. A succession of decisions through the numbered pairs of the key should provide a tentative determination which should then be followed up by reading

---

* I have not found either *Kobresia bellardii* collected by William C. Cusick in 1900 or *Senecio porteri* also collected by him in 1889 with the note "very little seen." Both are believed to be from "alpine summits" in the locality of Ice Lake, the Matterhorn or Sacajawea or "near Keystone Creek." The exact location of Keystone Creek remains unknown. Though Cusick gives elevations for it ranging from 5000 to 8000 feet no such creek exists. Adam Creek is there but it is not Keystone Creek. One explanation has been suggested: that it might have been associated with a Keystone Mine in the past and both have disappeared. The presence of a deep prospector's hole at the summit of the Matterhorn lends support to the idea that there was mining activity in the past, though old-timers do not know of either a mine or a creek by that name.

the detailed description in the text and consulting the illustration if there is one. The keys have been simplified as much as possible so that they may be used by the average person without constant reference to the Glossary. The descriptions are of a more technical nature.

It should be kept in mind that keys are man-made and subject to personal interpretation and so may not "work" the first time or two. Keys to *Carex* and the grasses are especially difficult.

In the text the families are arranged in a modified Englerian taxonomic order but within each family the genera and species are arranged alphabetically.

KEY TO THE FAMILIES OF VASCULAR PLANTS OF THE WALLOWA MOUNTAINS

Plants not producing seeds or flowers; reproduction by spores ....**PTERIDOPHYTA**
Plants producing seeds and flowers or seed-bearing cones ....**SPERMATOPHYTA**
    Ovules not enclosed in an ovary, often borne on the surface of a scale; plants without
    true flowers..**GYMNOSPERMAE**
    Ovules enclosed in an ovary; plants with true flowers....................................**ANGIOSPERMAE**
        Leaves usually parallel-veined; flower parts generally in 3's, rarely 2 or 4, never 5;
        vascular bundles scattered irregularly through the stem; seed
        leaf 1...MONOCOTYLEDONEAE
        Leaves usually with divided veins; flower parts mostly in 4's or 5's; vascular
        bundles in layers encircling the stem; seed leaves 2 ......................DICOTYLEDONEAE

PTERIDOPHYTA   Ferns and Fern Allies

Plants with a life cycle of two generations, separate even in maturity: the Gametophyte, the small, sexual, inconspicuous phase produced from the spores produced by the conspicuous, asexual Sporophyte, usually differentiated into root, stem and leaf. Flowers and seeds none.

1. Stems jointed, angled or ribbed, hollow; leaves reduced to toothed sheaths at the nodes; sporangia in cone-like spikes at the tips of the stems and branches ............................EQUISETACEAE
1. Stems not jointed; leaves from scale-like to large and broad
    2. Stems and branches rather long, covered with short scale-like overlapping leaves; sporangia borne in or near the leaf axils
        3. Spores all of one size..LYCOPODIACEAE
        3. Spores of two sizes..SELAGINELLACEAE
    2. Stems usually very short, not branched; leaves very narrow or expanded
        4. Leaves with an expanded blade; land plants; spores all of one size, the sporangia borne on the under surface of the leaves or on specialized leaf portions
            5. Leaves with 2 conspicuously different portions, the fertile spore-producing portion usually above the sterile blade portion, both on a common stalk from the base ..................................OPHIOGLOSSACEAE
            5. Leaves either fertile and the sporangia borne on the under leaf surface, or the fertile leaves entirely separate from the sterile ones on the same plant ....POLYPODIACEAE
        4. Leaves narrow, scarcely leaf-like, the base expanded and bearing the sporangia; spores of 2 sizes; aquatic plants..ISOETACEAE

SPERMATOPHYTA   Seed Plants

Plants with the two generations combined, the gametophyte dependent on the older sporophyte. Seeds produced.

Ovules not enclosed in an ovary, often borne on the surface of a scale; plants without true
flowers..GYMNOSPERMAE
Ovules enclosed in an ovary; plants with true flowers..ANGIOSPERMAE

GYMNOSPERMAE   Coniferous Plants

Trees or shrubs usually woody, with narrow scale-like or needle-like, deciduous or evergreen leaves; true flowers missing; stamens several to many, spirally arranged in small deciduous cones; ovules and seeds naked, often paired, borne on spirally arranged scales forming cones at maturity, or solitary.

Leaves scale-like, opposite or whorled; ovulate cones small, fleshy (ours), the scales
few..CUPRESSACEAE
Leaves needle-like, in small bunches of 2 to 5, or many and borne on short lateral branches;
ovulate cones woody, the scales many, spirally arranged..PINACEAE

ANGIOSPERMAE   Flowering Plants

Herbs, shrubs and trees; true flowers present, these consisting of stamens and pistils usually surrounded by 2 sets of modified leaves, the corolla and the calyx, together constituting the perianth, or sometimes one set or both missing or modified; stamens usually with 2 pollen sacs supported by a stalk, the filament; pistils with an enlarged base, the ovary, containing the ovules and seeds, and the style supporting the pollen-receiving stigma at its tip.

Leaves usually parallel-veined; flower parts generally in 3's, rarely 2 or 4, never 5; vascular
bundles scattered irregularly through the stem; seed leaf 1........................MONOCOTYLEDONEAE
Leaves usually net-veined; flower parts mostly in 4's or 5's; vascular bundles in layers
encircling the stem; seed leaves 2...DICOTYLEDONEAE

MONOCOTYLEDONEAE   Plants with 1 cotyledon

Leaves usually parallel-veined; flower parts generally in 3's.
1. Plants rooted and growing in water or very wet places; perianth when present inconspicuous
    2. Ovary superior; flowers mostly clustered
        3. Flowers in globose heads; pistillate flowers with 3 to 6 perianth parts........SPARGANIACEAE
        3. Flowers in spikes, small clusters, or solitary; perianth parts if present 4, not
           united...POTAMOGETONACEAE
    2. Ovary inferior; vegetative parts all underwater; flower solitary....................HYDROCHARITACEAE
1. Plants not aquatic though sometimes growing in wet places and swamps
    4. Perianth parts always present, usually in 2 sets, rarely 1
        5. Ovary inferior
           6. Perianth regular; stamens 3...IRIDACEAE
           6. Perianth irregular; stamens usually 2, rarely 1......................................ORCHIDACEAE
        5. Ovary superior
           7. Perianth segments not united, usually brown or greenish; fruit a capsule...JUNCACEAE
           7. Perianth segments mostly united but if not then white or colored; fruit
           a capsule or berry ....LILIACEAE
    4. Perianth missing, sometimes replaced by bracts or bristles of varying numbers
        8. Flowers mostly perfect, in the axils of dry bracts, arranged in spikes or spikelets; grasses or grasslike
           9. Leaves 2-ranked; stems (culms) mostly hollow, terete, swollen at the
           nodes; fruit a grain or caryopsis...GRAMINEAE
           9. Leaves 3-ranked; stems (culms) usually filled with pith, terete or triangular, not swollen at the nodes; fruit an achene.................................CYPERACEAE
        8. Flowers mostly imperfect, the staminate separate from the pistillate, in heads or a long terminal spike; none grasslike

10. Flowers in roundish unisexual heads; pistillate flowers with 3 to 6 perianth parts..SPARGANIACEAE
10. Flowers in crowded spikes, the staminate above the pistillate flowers; plants tall with very long leaves ....TYPHACEAE

DICOTYLEDONEAE   Plants with 2 cotyledons

Leaves usually with divided veins; flower parts mostly in 4's or 5's

1. Petals separate and free from each other, or missing*
    2. Calyx and corolla both missing, or if present vestigial or obsolete
        3. Trees or shrubs; flowers unisexual, at least the staminate in catkins; leaves alternate
            4. Fruit a capsule or dry berry; seeds minute, with a coma...........................SALICACEAE
            4. Fruit not a capsule; seeds winged nutlets in a woody or thin-scaled cone..BETULACEAE
        3. Herbs or subshrubs; flowers perfect or unisexual
            5. Plants parasitic on trees, usually branching; fruit a 1-seeded berry....LORANTHACEAE
            5. Plants not parasitic
                6. Plants aquatic, living in the water or on drying mud
                    7. Leaves whorled, dissected and toothed; fruit a nutlet..CERATOPHYLLACEAE
                    7. Leaves mostly opposite, not dissected or toothed; fruit flattened..CALLITRICHACEAE
                6. Plants terrestrial, not growing in water
                    8. Inflorescence of small unisexual flowers in a modified involucre, in all appearing flower-like (*Euphorbia*)............EUPHORBIACEAE
                    8. Inflorescence not as above; flowers in spikes; leaves with 3 leaflets (*Achlys*)...BERBERIDACEAE
    2. Calyx at least present, or calyx and corolla both present
        9. Flowers with a calyx but without petals
            10. Calyx long, conspicuously colored or white and corolla-like, or large, or with both characters; vines or herbs; achenes in heads (*Anemone, Clematis*)..RANUNCULACEAE
            10. Calyx very short, green or colored
                11. Trees, shrubs, or subshrubs
                    12. Style and stigma 1; ovary 1-celled, 1-seeded; leaves simple, entire or toothed
                        13. Flowers perfect; stamens many, opening by slits; shrubs; fruit dry (*Cercocarpus*)... ROSACEAE
                        13. Flowers imperfect or perfect; shrub with leaves silvery or red-spotted beneath; fruit fleshy (*Shepherdia*)...............ELAEAGNACEAE
                    12. Styles and stigmas 2 or 3 or more
                        14. Flowers perfect; perianth white or colored (*Eriogonum*)..POLYGONACEAE
                        14. Flowers perfect or not; perianth not white or colored
                            15. Ovary superior; shrub 1-3 meters tall; fruit a fleshy drupe or berry (*Rhamnus*).......................................RHAMNACEAE
                            15. Ovary inferior; plant a subshrub (*Galium* spp.) .... RUBIACEAE
                11. Annual or perennial herbs
                    16. Stamens attached to the hypanthium, surrounding the ovary but not joined to it (perigynous)
                        17. Stems leafless; basal leaves simple and shallow-lobed (*Heuchera*).. SAXIFRAGACEAE

---

* Petals slightly united in certain species of Portulacaceae, Caryophyllaceae, Fumariaceae, Crassulaceae, Malvaceae and Leguminosae.

      17. Stems leafy; stipules present; leaves compound
        (*Sanguisorba*) ....ROSACEAE
   16. Stamens attached to the receptacle and free from the ovary
    (hypogynous) or attached to the ovary and appearing to grow
    from it (epigynous)
      18. Ovary inferior
        19. Leaves opposite or whorled (*Galium*) ....RUBIACEAE
        19. Leaves alternate, entire; plants partially parasitic
         (*Comandra*) .... SANTALACEAE
      18. Ovary superior
        20. Fruit a capsule
         21. Capsules opening by valves; leaves opposite,
          nodes swollen (*Arenaria, Sagina*) .... CARYOPHYLLACEAE
         21. Capsules loculicidally dehiscent; plants low an-
          nuals with whorled leaves (*Mollugo*) ....AIZOACEAE
        20. Fruit otherwise than a capsule
         22. Sepals falling at flowering time; leaves alternate
          or basal; sepals 2 to 5, often petal-like; petals 5 or
          more when present................................. .............RANUNCULACEAE
         22. Sepals not falling off at flowering time; fruit an
          achene or a utricle
          23. Fruit an achene
           24. Flowers perfect with a colored perianth;
            achenes 3- or 4-angled, or lenticular....POLYGONACEAE
           24. Flowers perfect or unisexual, or both;
            perianth never colored; achenes flattened
            or ovoid; leaves with stinging hairs.........URTICACEAE
         23. Fruit a utricle; stipules usually present
          25. Calyx herbaceous.............................CHENOPODIACEAE
          25. Calyx thin, dry and papery, not herba-
           ceous.................................. ...................AMARANTHACEAE
9. Flowers with both calyx and corolla
   26. Leaves with sensitive glandular hairs for trapping insects; small bog
   plants ....DROSERACEAE
   26. Leaves not adapted to trapping insects
      27. Corolla or calyx, or both, irregular
        28. Calyx with sepals showy and colored, as well as the petals, and
        often with modifications in shape; pistils 2 to 5; fruit of clus-
        tered follicles (*Aconitum, Aquilegia* and *Delphinium*).........RANUNCULACEAE
        28. Calyx with sepals small and regular and if colored inconspicu-
        ous; petals with different shapes, or spurred, or otherwise
        modified
         29. Flowers butterfly-shaped; stamens 10 ....LEGUMINOSAE
         29. Flowers not butterfly-shaped; stamens fewer than 10
          30. Capsule 2-valved, or an indehiscent nutlet; leaves
           much lobed and cleft.... .... FUMARIACEAE
          30. Capsule 3-valved; leaves entire or lobed or cleft but
           not as much as above ....VIOLACEAE
  27. Corolla regular, the petals all alike or essentially so
     31. Ovary completely inferior, or if half-inferior the ovary not
     fused the entire length of the calyx
       32. Ovary completely inferior
        33. Fruit a berry, drupe or pome, juicy or fleshy
         34. Leaves opposite, simple with entire margins . ...CORNACEAE
         34. Leaves alternate, compound, or if simple the
          margins serrulate, toothed or lobed

35. Fruit a berry; hypanthium produced above the ovary; shrubs often with spiny stems..GROSSULARIACEAE

35. Fruit a pome; hypanthium not produced above the ovary; shrubs or trees, mostly without spines (*Sorbus Amelanchier, Crataegus*) ....ROSACEAE

33. Fruit not a berry, drupe or pome; dry

36. Fruit a many-seeded capsule; petals in most species showy and rather large; inflorescence mostly few-flowered

37. Stems and leaves rough-hairy; sepals and petals 5 or more................................LOASACEAE

37. Stems and leaves hairless or soft-hairy; sepals and petals normally 4........................ONAGRACEAE

36. Fruit at maturity splitting into 1-seeded divisions; petals small; inflorescences many-flowered in UMBELLIFERAE

38. Fruit of 4 divisions; aquatic plants with much divided submerged leaves (*Myriophyllum*) ................................HALORAGIDACEAE

38. Fruit of 2 divisions; leaves if submerged not divided into many narrow segments as above; stems and leaves with an odor................UMBELLIFERAE

32. Ovary half-inferior; fruit of separate follicles, or a non-circumscissile capsule

39. Leaves mostly basal; stem leaves few when present (except in species of *Saxifraga*); herbaceous perennials or rarely annuals ................................SAXIFRAGACEAE

39. Leaves opposite; plants shrubs or trailing vines....HYDRANGEACEAE

31. Ovary superior, either clearly visible or inside the floral tube, free from it

40. Stamens normally more than twice as many as the petals (in some species 10 or less)

41. Stamens united in a tube around the pistil; stipules present; flowers large................................MALVACEAE

41. Stamens separate, or in clustered bundles, or if united at all, not as above

42. Plants aquatic; leaves large, entire, floating on the surface of the water (*Nuphar*) ................NYMPHAEACEAE

42. Plants not aquatic, except RANUNCULACEAE species with leaves not as above; sepals differing from the petals

43. Sepals falling off early; petals the same number as sepals, rarely more................RANUNCULACEAE

43. Sepals not falling off at anthesis

44. Plants trees or shrubs; carpels 3 to many; stipules present in most genera; fruit a fleshy drupe or of follicles mostly 3-6 mm long................................ROSACEAE

44. Plants annual herbs or perennial herbs which may be woody-based or woody-branched and cushion-forming

45. Sepals 2 (*Lewisia* spp.) ........PORTULACACEAE

45. Sepals as many as petals or more
  46. Fruit of 2 to 5 follicles; flowers
      large, solitary..............................PAEONIACEAE
  46. Fruit not as above
    47. Stamens attached to the
        floral tube, surrounding the
        ovary...ROSACEAE
    47. Stamens attached to the
        receptacle, below the ovary
        and free from it, usually
        united at the base; leaves
        all opposite...........................HYPERICACEAE
40. Stamens few, usually 5 or 10, not more than twice as many
  as the petals
  48. Plants shrubs or trees
    49. Fruit winged, seed-like; leaves opposite, simple,
        palmately lobed (3 leaflets in a variety of *Acer
        glabrum*)...ACERACEAE
    49. Fruit not winged and seed-like
      50. Leaves simple or reduced to scales
        51. Stamens opposite the petals, 4 or 5;
            petals mostly hooded ....RHAMNACEAE
        51. Stamens alternate with the petals, 10 or
            less; petals not hooded ... .CELASTRACEAE
      50. Leaves divided into leaflets, persistent; fruit
          a sessile berry (*Berberis*).........................BERBERIDACEAE
  48. Plants herbs, annual or perennial
    52. Leaves divided, trifoliate, or variously pinnately
        or palmately dissected
      53. Petals and sepals 5 (3 in *Floerkea*) ; stamens
          often 10
        54. Style persistent on the fruit, long, either
            curved or coiled..............................GERANIACEAE
        54. Style not persistent on the fruit, arising
            from the base of the ovaries; leaves pin-
            nately dissected................................LIMNANTHACEAE
      53. Petals and sepals 4; stamens 6 ....CRUCIFERAE
    52. Leaves simple, entire or the margins sometimes
        serrulate or crenulate
      55. Carpels free or joined at the base; fruit
          follicles; plants succulent or fleshy; stamens
          as many or twice as many as petals ...........CRASSULACEAE
      55. Carpels united; fruit a capsule
        56. Flowering stems leafless; flowers soli-
            tary; plants of moist places; staminodia
            always present, lobed or gland-fringed
            (*Parnassia*) ....SAXIFRAGACEAE
        56. Flowering stems leafy; staminodia if
            present not as above; seeds produced at
            the base of the capsule or along its core
          57. Stamens clearly united into a ring
              at the base.......................................LINACEAE
          57. Stamens free or nearly so; capsule
              completely 1-celled or incompletely
              2- to 5-celled at the base

58. Sepals 2; stems never with swollen nodes; seeds usually few......................PORTULACACEAE

58. Sepals normally 5; stems usually with swollen nodes; seeds usually many....................CARYOPHYLLACEAE

1. Petals usually united at the base, forming a corolla tube and a lobed limb; stamens mostly inserted on the corolla tube

59. Plants parasitic or saprophytic, non-green

60. Corolla regular, petals free or fused; filaments free or united only at the base; plants of coniferous forests (*Hypopitys, Pterospora*)........................ERICACEAE

60. Corolla irregular, 2-lipped........................OROBANCHACEAE

59. Plants not parasitic or saprophytic, or, if partially so, then having chlorophyll and colored green

61. Ovary superior

62. Corolla regular, lobes equal in length, tube not spurred or unsymmetrical

63. Stamens 5 or fewer

64. Fruit of paired or single follicles much longer than the flowers; plants with milky juice........................APOCYNACEAE

64. Fruit a capsule, a berry, or of 2 to 4 free nutlets; plants without milky juice

65. Stamens as many as corolla lobes and opposite them (staminodes sometimes present); some genera with the corolla so deeply parted as to be free petals; calyx herbaceous; seeds few to many........................PRIMULACEAE

65. Stamens alternate with the corolla lobes, of the same number or fewer; corollas not deeply parted

66. Fruit a circumscissile capsule, not 2-lobed; corolla thin and dry and membranous; herbs........................PLANTAGINACEAE

66. Fruit if capsular, not circumscissile

67. Fruit of 2 to 4 nutlets (or 1 by abortion); leaves alternate (rarely whorled or opposite); inflorescences mostly coiled........................BORAGINACEAE

67. Fruit not of nutlets; anthers opening by longitudinal slits; fruit a capsule

68. Style 3-parted; ovary 3-celled; capsule opening by 3 valves........................POLEMONIACEAE

68. Style, ovary and capsule not as above

69. Rhizome long and thick; perennials of lakes and bogs at high elevations........................MENYANTHACEAE

69. Rhizome if present not long and thick; habitat not as above; herbs; ovary and capsule not 2-lobed

70. Stem leaves when present opposite (except *Verbascum*)

71. Capsule 1-celled; flowers often showy; stamens 4 or 5........................GENTIANACEAE

71. Capsule 2-celled; stamens 2 or 4 (5 in *Verbascum*)........................SCROPHULARIACEAE

70. Stem leaves alternate; inflorescence branches usually coiled; corollas lobed........................HYDROPHYLLACEAE

63. Stamens at least twice as many as corolla lobes (petals united only at the base in some genera; see also CRASSULACEAE and MALVACEAE); anthers opening by pores or tubes........................ERICACEAE

62. Corolla irregular, 2-lipped or spurred, the lobes evidently unequal

72. Plants aquatic with dissected leaves bearing minute bladders on the many narrow segments (except *Pinguicula* of bogs, with entire basal leaves)..**LENTIBULARIACEAE**
72. Plants not aquatic
    73. Fruit of 4 nutlets; stems and leaves aromatic in most genera; ovary 4-celled and -lobed..**LABIATAE**
    73. Fruit a several- to many-seeded capsule opening by valves or pores..**SCROPHULARIACEAE**
61. Ovary inferior
    74. Stamens free, 2 to 5; leaves opposite (alternate in **CAMPANULACEAE**)
        75. Stipules present, leaf-like in *Galium* so the leaves appear whorled.......**RUBIACEAE**
        75. Stipules missing (except in *Sambucus* in **CAPRIFOLIACEAE**)
            76. Fruit a berry, drupe, or often a modified achene (dry, 3-celled and 1-seeded fruit in *Linnaea*)
                77. Plants shrubs or woody vines (*Linnaea* a creeping evergreen herb)..**CAPRIFOLIACEAE**
                77. Plants annual or perennial herbs; flowers irregular, the tube usually spurred or unsymmetrical at the base................**VALERIANACEAE**
            76. Fruit a capsule, with valve-like openings or dehiscing by splitting between the ribs..**CAMPANULACEAE**
    74. Stamens with either filaments or anthers or both parts completely or partially fused; leaves alternate (sometimes opposite or completely basal in **COMPOSITAE**)
        78. Individual flowers small, collected into a head on a receptacle and surrounded by a calyx-like involucre, the whole seeming to be a flower; flowers without sepals..**COMPOSITAE.**
        78. Individual flowers if in heads not collected and arranged as above; sepals present
            79. Fruit a juicy berry; stamens opening by pores (*Vaccinium*); (see also *Gaultheria* with fleshy calyx)..**ERICACEAE**
            79. Fruit a capsule, rupturing irregularly; stamens opening by slits; flowers perfect; herbs..**CAMPANULACEAE**

LYCOPODIACEAE   Club-moss Family

Evergreen herbs, often moss-like, erect or trailing; stems leafy, the branches alternate or dichotomous; leaves small, simple, 2- to many-ranked, usually overlapping; sporangia in the leaf axils or in cone-like terminal spikes; spores minute, uniform, smooth or sculptured.

Lycopodium L.

Perennial evergreen plants; aerial branches rising from a prostrate or creeping main stem; leaves closely arranged in 4 to 16 ranks; sporangia (ours) aggregated into terminal spike-like cones on the fertile branches; spores yellow, numerous.

Cones solitary at the tips of the erect branches; leaves of the branches spreading or turning downward, 6-10 mm long ....*L. annotinum*
Cones mostly more than one at the tips of the erect branches; leaves only 2-3 mm long ....*L. sitchense*

Lycopodium annotinum L.   Stiff Club-moss

Stems often 2 m long, prostrate, creeping above the ground and rooting, and also sending up numerous simple or forked branches 5-30 cm tall; leaves 5- to 8-ranked, serrate, spine-tipped, 6-10 mm long; cones sessile, solitary at the tips of the branches, 1.5-3.5 cm long.
Moist shade of coniferous woods, at about 6000 feet.

Lycopodium sitchense Rupr.   Alaska Club-moss

L. sabinaefolium Willd. var. *sitchense* (Rupr.) Fern.

Main stems creeping on or near the ground, 10-40 cm long; aerial branches erect, dichotomously-branched, forming close tufts near the ground, the sterile 3-10 cm tall, the fertile up to 15 cm tall with one or more terminal cones at the tip; leaves entire, 5-ranked, 2-3 mm long; cones sessile or peduncled, one or more per branch, 1-2.5 cm long.
Moist meadows and forest openings, at and above about 8000 feet.

SELAGINELLACEAE   Selaginella Family

Depressed or creeping leafy terrestrial plants, ours moss-like; stems branched; leaves minute, scale-like, 4- to many-ranked, all alike or of two kinds; sporangia in terminal cones, the lower ones usually containing 1 to 4 large megaspores and the upper ones filled with numerous smaller reddish or orange microspores, or the sporangia mixed together.

Selaginella Beauv.

Characters of the family.

Selaginella wallacei Hieron.   Wallace's Selaginella

Moss-like evergreen mat-forming plants; main stems leafy, prostrate, up to 20 cm long with many crowded erect branches; leaves minute, scale-like, thick and firm, crowded, ciliate or entire, spirally arranged: cones numerous, quadrangular, sessile, 1-3 cm long; megaspores usually 4, yellow or orange; microspores numerous, reddish or orange.
Among rocks and on open rocky slopes, 4000 to 9000 feet.

ISOETACEAE   Quillwort Family

Small aquatic or terrestrial monoecious or dioecious perennials, the stem corm-like with branched roots below and a cluster of grass-like annual leaves above; the outer leaves often sterile, the next inner ones expanded at the base and enclosing megasporangia, the next inner enclosing microsporangia at their bases and the innermost ones with a rudimentary sporangium.

Isoetes L.

Characters of the family.

Leaves 3 to 10, soft and narrow, mostly 2-5 cm long, the sterile outer ones missing ....*I. bolanderi*
Leaves mostly 1 to 30, firm with membranous margins, 5-12 cm long, the sterile outer ones
  usually present..*I. howellii*

Isoetes bolanderi Engelm.   Bolander's Quillwort

Perennial, usually submersed; leaves 3 to 10, mostly 2-5 cm long, soft and narrow, tapering to a fine point, without outer sterile strands; sporangia rounded or oblong, covered less than halfway by the velum extending down from above; megaspores white or cream-colored with scattered tubercles sometimes merged to form ridges; microspores smaller, numerous, spiny.
In shallow water of mountain lakes, pools or ponds, or washed up on their shores, 7200 to about 7600 feet.

Isoetes howellii Engelm.   Howell's Quillwort

Amphibious plant; leaves firm, many, mostly 5-12 cm long, sometimes up to 30 cm long; outer sterile strands usually 4; sporangia oblong, covered less than halfway by the velum from above; megaspores white, sometimes marked with spots scattered or merged to form ridges or wrinkles; microspores smooth or spiny.
In shallow water of mountain lakes, pools and ponds and the drying mud bordering them, 7100 to 8600 feet.

EQUISETACEAE   Horsetail Family

Perennial rush-like plants with blackish rhizomes rooting at the nodes; aerial stems annual or perennial, jointed, cylindrical, the internodes usually hollow; leaves scale-like, in sheathing whorls at the nodes, their tips (teeth) free or connate, persistent or deciduous separately or in groups; sporangia borne in terminal cone-like spikes; spores uniform, minute and numerous, each with 4 elaters.

Equisetum L.

Characters of the family.

1. Aerial stems annual; cones mostly blunt or rounded at the tip (sometimes slightly sharp-pointed in *E. laevigatum*)
     2. Stems of 2 kinds: the fertile stems flesh-colored and appearing before the green, much-branched sterile ones; stems solid ....*E. arvense*
     2. Stems all alike, green and hollow, the central cavity more than half the diameter of the stem...*E. laevigatum*
1. Aerial stems perennial; cones sharp-pointed
     3. Stems slender, 3- to 12-angled; central cavity half the diameter of the stem or less, or the stem not hollow...*E. variegatum*
     3. Stems robust, 16- to 48-angled; central cavity more than half the diameter of the stem..*E. hyemale*

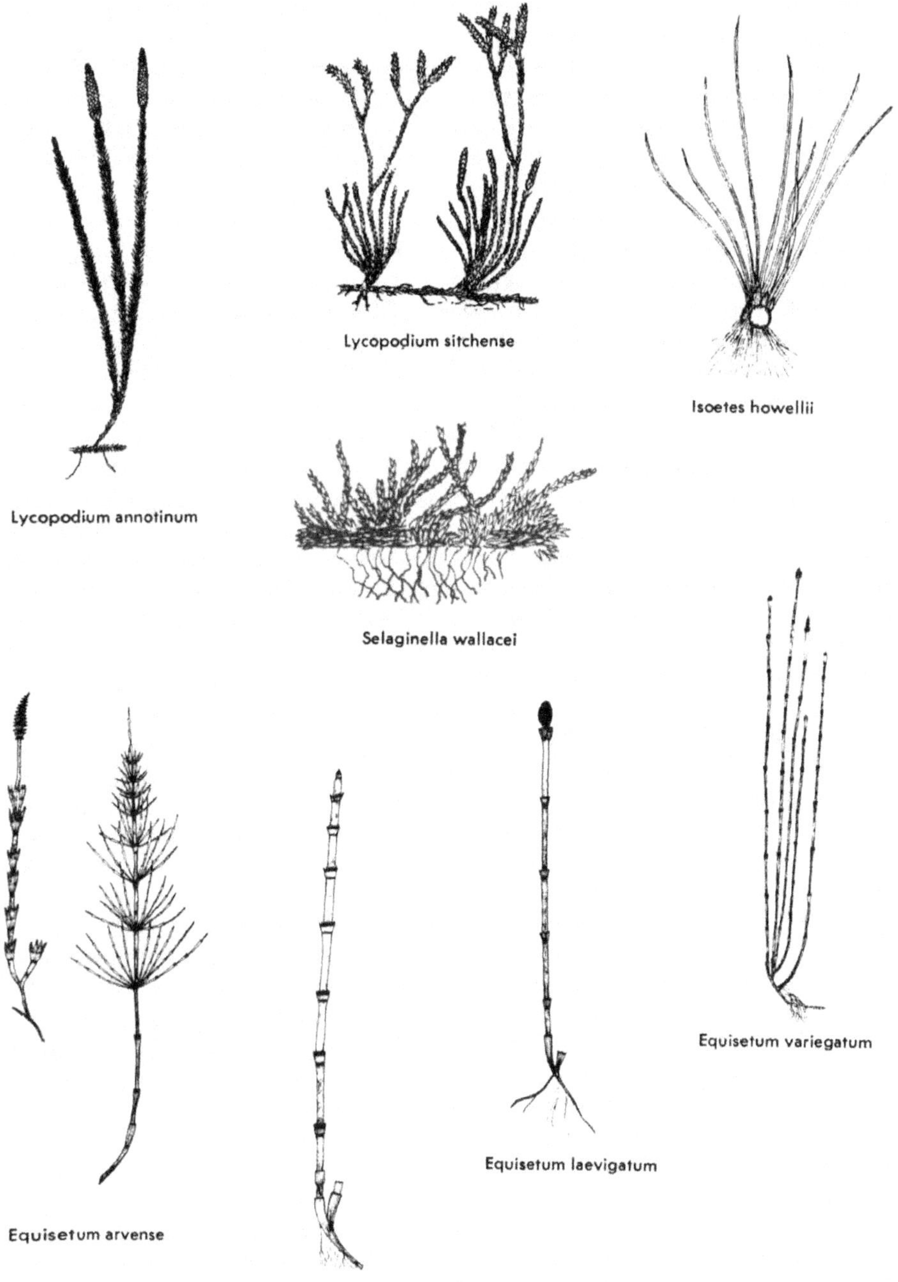

Lycopodium sitchense
Isoetes howellii
Lycopodium annotinum
Selaginella wallacei
Equisetum variegatum
Equisetum arvense
Equisetum hyemale var. affine
Equisetum laevigatum

Equisetum arvense L.   Common Horsetail
    Rhizome tuber-bearing, felted, somewhat angled; fertile stems annual, erect, 5-30 cm tall, flesh-colored, smooth, appearing and withering earlier than the green sterile ones; sterile stems erect or prostrate, green, angled and solid, 10-60 cm tall, the many branches in whorls along the stem; sheaths pale, loose, persistent with 8 to 12 large greenish or brownish teeth; fruiting cone blunt, 0.5-3 or 4 cm long.
Common in moist sandy places near water.

Equisetum hyemale L. var. **affine** (Engelm.) A. A. Eat.   Scouring Rush
    Aerial stems all alike, evergreen, 20-150 cm tall, persisting several seasons, with 2 rows of silica tubercles in the furrows between the 19 to 40 rough ridges; central cavity large; sheaths longer than broad, mostly flared above, with dark bands above and below the middle; teeth dark brown, prolonged into a white tip, eventually falling in small groups; fruiting cones 1-3 cm long, apiculate.
Moist shady places up to about 5000 feet.

Equisetum laevigatum A. Br.   Smooth Scouring Rush
    Aerial stems annual, all alike, usually simple, 20-100 cm tall, 2-8 mm thick, the 16 to 30 ridges smooth, with inconspicuous crossbands of silica; sheaths green, longer than wide, flared upward, banded at the top only, or sometimes also at the base, or throughout; the teeth thin, black-based and white-margined, early deciduous; the central cavity large, the walls thin, the stomata sunken in the furrows; fruiting cones blunt or sometimes apiculate, 1-2 cm long.
Wet shady banks and meadows at lower mountain elevations, about 5300 feet.

Equisetum variegatum Schleich.   Northern Scouring Rush
    Aerial stems slender, evergreen, 10-30 cm tall, usually from a branched, tufted, sometimes felted, base; stems 5- to 12-ridged, the stomata in 2 rows; sheaths flared, green with a black band at the tip; leaves 4-angled with a deep central groove extending above to the teeth and below to the stem ridges; teeth black with white or hyaline margins, prolonged into a deciduous bristle; the central cavity small when present; fruiting cone small, sessile, strongly apiculate.
Wet lake shores, bogs and stream banks, about 5000 to 8000 feet.

OPHIOGLOSSACEAE   Adder's-tongue Family

Herbaceous plants with a short underground stem and fleshy roots; leaf of 2 parts: the sterile portion leaf-like, the fertile portion a stalked, spore-bearing spike or panicle; bud enclosed by the usually underground base of the stalk; sporangia large, naked, opening by a transverse slit; spores many, yellowish.

Botrychium Sw.
    Fleshy perennial plants; roots coarse and fleshy; leaves 1 to 3, mostly compound; the common stalk entirely or partly underground, the aerial portion bearing the sterile leaf-like blade below the fertile terminal stalked spike or panicle; sporangia large and

round, in 2 rows on the pinnules; spores many, yellow. (Next year's bud borne at the base of the common stalk, sometimes concealed.)

1. Leaf-like portions of the plant attached to the stalk at or near ground level
   2. Plant robust; sterile leaf-like blades thick, leathery, large, 2 or 3 per stalk _________ *B. multifidum*
   2. Plant small and delicate; sterile leaf-like blades thin, mostly solitary, often long-petioled ____ *B. simplex*
1. Leaf-like portions of the plant attached to the stalk at or about the middle of the plant, not close to the ground
   3. Segments of the leaf-like portions rounded at the tips
      4. Segments of the leaf-like portions crescent-shaped, few _______________ ________ *B. lunaria*
      4. Segments of the leaf-like portions many, not crescent-shaped _____ _____________ *B. boreale*
   3. Segments of the leaf-like portions ending (or seeming to) in pointed tips, sharp rather than rounded
      5. Leaf-like blade 1-6 cm long, 1-8 cm broad ______ ________________________ *B. lanceolatum*
      5. Leaf-like blade 5-40 cm long, 10-30 cm broad ____ _________________________ *B. virginianum*

Botrychium boreale Milde   Northern Grape Fern
   B. pinnatum St. John

Plant 3-25 cm tall, yellowish-green; sterile blade oblong to triangular in outline, rounded at the tip, 2-7 cm long, 1-4 cm wide, bipinnate, attached near or above the middle of the stalk; pinnae 3 to 6 pairs, oblong, rounded or coarsely lobed; fertile spike a compound panicle, mostly 1.5-6 cm long.
Shady boggy coniferous woods, 4600 to 7200 feet.

Botrychium lanceolatum (S. G. Gmel.) Angstr.   Sharp-leaved Grape Fern

Plant 5-30 cm tall; sterile blade sessile, attached mostly above the middle of the plant, triangular in outline, 1-6 cm long, 1-8 cm broad, once or twice pinnately divided, the segments acute, mostly longer than wide; fertile portion stout, 1-3 cm long.
Moist open mixed and coniferous woods, 5000 to 7200 feet.

Botrychium lunaria (L.) Sw.   Moonwort
   B. minganense Victorin

Plant 3-28 cm tall; sterile blade nearly sessile, oblong in outline, 1-12 cm long, 1-5 cm broad, once pinnately divided, the segments broader than long, crowded and often overlapping, lunate or reniform; fertile portion about as long as the sterile blade; sporangia reddish-brown.
Occasional small colonies in moist shady mixed and coniferous woods, 5400 to about 8000 feet.

Botrychium multifidum (S. G. Gmel.) Trevis.   Leathery Grape Fern
   B. silaifolium Presl

Plant 20-60 cm tall with a short rhizome and several coarse fleshy roots; leaf-like sterile blades 1 to 3, evergreen, compound, 4-25 cm long, 5-20 cm wide, fleshy, triangular in outline, attached to the stalk close to the ground; the fertile spike large, branched, long-stalked, 3-20 cm long; bud hairy, only partly covered by the common stalk.
Occasional in boggy ground near streams in moist shady coniferous woods, 5200 to about 7500 feet.

Botrychium simplex Hitchc.   Little Grape Fern
Plant slender, 3-20 cm tall; common stalk very short above ground; sterile leaf-like

portion stalked, attached close to the ground, 1-5 cm long, 0.5-2.5 cm broad, simple to pinnately- or ternately-pinnately-divided, ovate to oblong in outline, rounded or boat-shaped at the tip; fertile portion lax, simple to compound, conspicuously long-stalked, the spike 1-4 cm long.

Boggy ground near streams and moist open meadows in the mountains, at 7200 feet.

Botrychium virginianum (L.) Swartz — Virginia Grape Fern

Plant 10-75 cm tall; common stalk slender, 7-25 cm long, half to ⅔ the height of the plant; sterile blade sessile, deltoid, 5-40 cm long and 10-30 cm wide, 2 to 4 times ternate-pinnately compound, attached at or above the middle of the plant; fertile stalk about 4-17 cm long, the spike branched, 2.5-15 cm long; bud hairy, not completely covered by the common stalk.

Near streams in moist shady coniferous woods, at about 5000 to 6500 feet.

POLYPODIACEAE   Fern Family

Leafy rhizomatous plants; fronds (leaves) coiled in the bud, the blades simple to much divided; sporangia small, borne on specialized fronds or usually in clusters (sori) on the underside of some or all of the fronds, naked or covered by a protective membrane (the indusium) or by the inrolled leaf-margins.

1. Leaves and leaflets thick, rather stiff, leathery, not much divided into small segments
  2. Leaf margins toothed .... *Polystichum*
  2. Leaf margins not toothed
    3. Leaves green; sori separate on the back .... *Polypodium*
    3. Leaves bluish-green; sori appearing to run together to form continuous lines
      on the margins of the leaflets, not separate .... *Pellaea*
1. Leaves and leaflets soft, thin, usually divided into many smaller segments, flexible (except *Pteridium*)
  4. Petioles (stipes) yellow to green or greenish
    5. Leaves mostly over 3 dm tall
      6. Petiole long; blade usually much broader than long .... *Pteridium*
      6. Petiole short; blade always longer than broad .... *Athyrium*
    5. Leaves seldom, if ever, as much as 3 dm tall
      7. Leaves of 2 kinds: the fertile taller and with narrower segments than
      the sterile ones .... *Cryptogramma*
      7. Leaves all alike, or at least appearing so
        8. Sori separate on the backs of the leaflets
          9. Leaves mostly fewer than 5; petioles short; plants common ...*Cystopteris*
          9. Leaves many, mostly over 15; plants usually associated
          with rocky slides and slopes .... *Athyrium*
        8. Sori not separate, continuous along the margins of the leaflets
        beneath .... *Cryptogramma*
  4. Petioles dark, brown to nearly black, but not green
    11. Leaf blades mostly broader than long; petioles much longer than the blades .... *Adiantum*
    11. Leaf blades definitely longer than broad; petioles shorter than the blades
      12. Leaves densely brownish-woolly beneath .... *Cheilanthes*
      12. Leaves not at all brownish-woolly beneath .... *Woodsia*

Adiantum L.

Fragile ferns of damp places, with creeping rhizomes; leaves decompound or 1 to 3 times pinnate; petioles black and shining, forked in some species; leaf segments broader than long (ours), the upper margins free and incised, the lower attached; sori under the marginal upper reflexed lobes of the pinnules.

Adiantum pedatum L.   Maidenhair Fern
Delicate graceful ferns; rhizomes short and thick; fronds few, nearly circular in outline, 25-100 cm tall, with 3 to 9 oblong divisions; petioles forked, dark and shiny; leaf segments spreading, their upper margins cleft or lobed; sori solitary, oblong, covered by the inrolled margins of the leaf segments.
Mossy shady streambanks, up to about 5000 feet.

Athyrium Roth
Ferns medium to large, with erect rhizomes; frond-bases of previous years persistent; leaves closely clustered at the base but spreading outward above, the blade 2 to 4 times pinnate; sori roundish, oblong or lunate; indusia shaped like the sori and attached along the same vein, or missing.

Leaf blades usually large, 30-200 cm long, flexible, broadly lance-shaped; sori few......*A. filix-femina*
Leaf blades usually 20-40 cm long, somewhat stiff, narrow; sori very numerous,
   roundish ....*A. distentifolium*

Athyrium distentifolium Tausch var. americanum (Butters) Cronq.
A. alpestre var. *americanum* Butters   Alpine Lady Fern
Rhizomes forming large tufts; fronds usually 20-40 cm long, mostly 3-pinnate, short-petioled; blades oblong-lanceolate with 8 to 17 pairs of segments, the larger pinnae 2.5-8 cm long; sori very numerous, small and roundish, without an indusium.
Usually among granite rocks and boulders or at the base of granitic cliffs and slides, 6000 to about 8000 feet.

Athyrium filix-femina (L.) Roth   Lady Fern
Large ferns with short rhizomes; leaf bases of previous years persisting; fronds soft and thin, broadly lanceolate, 2 to 3 times pinnate, 30-200 cm long, closely clustered at the base but spreading outward above; petiole short with brown or blackish scales near the base; sori roundish, minute, near the midvein; indusium short, straight or lunate, usually ciliate on the free edge.
Wet or marshy meadows, woods and streambanks, 5000 to 7500 feet.

Cheilanthes Sw.
Small, rock-loving ferns with scaly rhizomes; fronds evergreen, 2 to 4 times pinnate, woolly or scaly, the segments small, often bead-like; sori rounded, numerous, with a common indusium formed by the recurved margins of the pinnules.

Cheilanthes gracillima D. C. Eat.   Lace Fern
Rhizomes scaly; fronds many, 4-15 cm long, narrowly ovate-lanceolate, 2-pinnate, mostly dark green and glabrous above, brownish-woolly beneath; pinnules mostly longer than wide, their margins curved over the sporangia beneath.
Crevices of dry granitic rocks and cliffs, 4500 to about 9000 feet.

Cryptogramma R. Br.
Small rock-loving ferns with scaly rhizomes; leaves glabrous, evergreen, mostly 2 to

3 times pinnate, appearing all alike or the fertile ones noticeably taller than the sterile ones and with longer, much narrower pinnules; pinnule margins reflexed to form an indusium covering the marginal sori beneath.

Fertile leaves taller than the sterile ones, the segments noticeably narrower and longer than
   those of the sterile leaves .... *C. crispa*
Fertile leaves and the sterile (mostly missing or inconspicuous) all alike .... *C. densa*

Cryptogramma crispa (L.) R. Br.   Parsley Fern
C. acrostichoides R. Br.

Small rock-loving rhizomatous ferns; fronds many, densely tufted, 2-15 cm tall, 2 to 3 times pinnate, glabrous, of two kinds: the fertile fronds taller and with fewer and narrower segments than the shorter-stalked sterile ones; sori marginal; false indusium continuous, formed by the reflexed margins of the pinnules.
Crevices of mossy rocks, slides and cliffs, 4500 to about 8500 feet.

Cryptogramma densa (Brackenr.) Diels   Oregon Cliff Brake
Cheilanthes siliquosa Maxon

Rhizome short and branched; fronds evergreen, many, clustered, glabrous, ovate or deltoid, usually all alike, the sterile when present small and inconspicuous, the fertile 2.5-15 cm long, 3-pinnate, the stipes longer than the blades, the pinnules crowded, tapering to a sharp-pointed tip; pinnule margins reflexed to form an almost continuous indusium over the sporangia beneath.
Crevices of cliffs and moist rocky slopes, 5000 to about 7000 feet.

Cystopteris Bernh.

Small delicate glabrous ferns with scaly rhizomes; fronds solitary or few, 1 to 4 times pinnate; sori roundish, borne on the veins near but not on the leaf margins; indusium attached at one end, free and lacerate at the other, thus hood-like, disappearing and leaving the mature sori naked.

Cystopteris fragilis (L.) Bernh.   Bladder Brittle Fern
Small delicate glabrous ferns of moist shady rocky places; fronds erect, single or few together, mostly 5-20 cm tall, 1 to 3 times pinnate; sori separate, small, roundish, covered by a hood-like indusium attached at one end when young but pushed back and withered later so the sori appear naked.
Common in moist rocky shady woods, 4500 to about 8500 feet.

Pellaea Link.

Small rock-loving ferns, with stout brown-woolly scaly rhizomes; fronds evergreen, erect, glabrous, 1 to 4 times pinnate, the pinnae large; petioles shiny, wiry, dark, brittle, breaking off easily and leaving a persistent base; sori near the ends of the veins eventually confluent, sometimes naked; indusium membranous, continuous, formed by the reflexed leaf margins.

Leaf segments mostly 2-parted, mitten-shaped, the veins evident; petioles breaking easily
   near the rhizome; sporangia nearly hidden by the reflexed margins of the leaflets .... *P. breweri*
Leaf segments simple, oval to oblong, the veins not evident; petioles not breaking easily;
   sporangia conspicuous, not hidden by the margins .... *P. bridgesii*

Botrychium boreale

Botrychium lanceolatum

Botrychium lunaria

Botrychium virginianum

Botrychium simplex

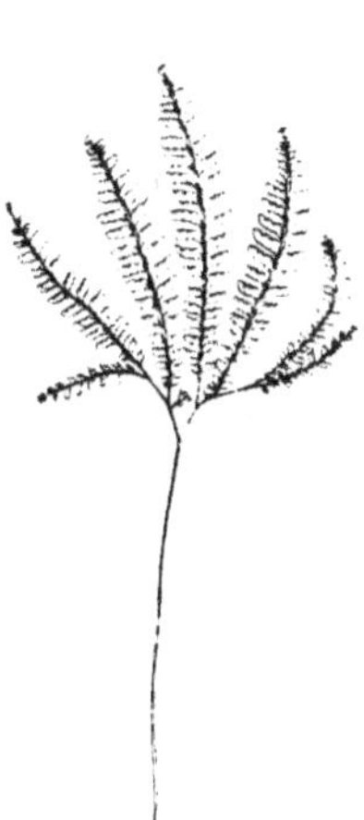

Cheilanthes gracillima

Adiantum pedatum

Cryptogramma crispa

Pellaea breweri D. C. Eaton   Brewer's Cliff-brake
Rhizome large and scaly, with persistent corrugated old petiole bases; fronds 4-15 cm long, crowded, glabrous, simply pinnate; petioles dark, shiny and brittle, corrugate near the base and breaking easily; pinnae, especially the lower ones, 2-parted (mitten-like) ; sporangia nearly concealed by the thin, whitish, reflexed pinnae margins.
Rock crevices and exposed cliffs of calcareous rock, 7800 to 8500 feet.

Pellaea bridgesii Hook.   Bridges' Cliff-brake
Rhizome short; fronds blue-green, many, glabrous, 8-25 cm tall; petioles coppery, persistent; frond blades simply pinnate, the pinnae mostly oval to cordate-oblong, opposite, nearly sessile, coriaceous, sometimes reflexed to form an indusium but the sori mostly not concealed.
In an open granite-boulder-strewn meadow, about 6000 feet.

Polypodium [Tourn.] L.

Ferns of shady locations; rhizomes creeping; leaves attached to knobs on the rhizomes, their blades simple, pinnate or pinnatifid; sori round to elliptical, mostly developed toward the upper portions of the blades; indusium usually missing.

Polypodium hesperium Maxon   Licorice Fern
Rhizome creeping, slender, with many knoblike swellings; leaves small, 5-27 cm long, usually jointed to the rhizome, the naked petiole nearly as long as the blade, the blade deltoid-oblong, 1 to 3 times pinnate or pinnatifid, the segments alternate, blunt; veins free; sori large, separate, round or oval, without an indusium.
Mossy cliffs and rocky slopes, about 4500 to 5000 feet.

Polystichum Roth

Coarse, often large, evergreen ferns of woods and forests with scaly woody rhizomes; fronds several in a crown; petiole short and scaly; blades simple to tri-pinnate or pinnatifid, scaly and thick, the segments reduced upward, their marginal teeth spiny; veins free; sori round, in rows; indusium peltate, sometimes missing.

Leaves 10-60 cm long; lower leaf segments mostly smaller than the middle ones; teeth of the leaf segments conspicuously spreading outward..*P. lonchitis*
Leaves mostly larger, 50-150 cm long; lower leaf segments not much smaller than the middle ones; teeth of the leaf segments closely curved inward...*P. munitum*

Polystichum lonchitis (L.) Roth   Holly Fern
Fronds evergreen, thick and glossy, 10-60 cm long; pinnae mostly 25 to 30 on each side of the rachis, the upper and the lower ones progressively smaller than the middle ones, the margins spiny-toothed, the teeth widely spreading-ascending or curved upward; sori large, round, usually in 2 rows; indusium peltate when present.
Rocky mountain slopes, often in shade, about 5500 to 9200 feet.

Polystichum munitum (Kaulf.) Presl   Christmas or Sword Fern
Plants large and coarse; leaves 50-150 cm long; pinnae mostly 35 to 70 on each side of the rachis, the lower ones not much reduced, the margins serrate with closely appressed or ascending incurved teeth; sori in 2 rows; indusium prominent.
Moist coniferous woods, reported up to about 7200 feet.

Pteridium Scop.

Coarse ferns with woody rhizomes; fronds large, pinnately decompound, deciduous; sori marginal, covered by the inrolled margin.

Pteridium aqualinum (L.) Kuhn var. pubescens Underw.   Bracken; Brake Fern

Large coarse ferns; rhizome woody; leaves deciduous, solitary, large, mostly 50-200 cm tall, much dissected, the petioles shining, the blades hairy or tomentose at least beneath; sori linear, marginal, continuous; indusium narrow and villous.
Rocky shaded mountain slopes, 5000 to about 7000 feet.

Woodsia R. Br.

Small tufted rock-loving ferns; rhizome scaly and short-creeping; fronds few to many, jointed to the rhizome, once to twice pinnate; sori round and flat; indusium inferior, disc-like with spreading unequal segments.

Leaf blades and petioles covered with flat jointed whitish hairs..*W. scopulina*
Leaf blades and petioles without hairs though sometimes glandular..*W. oregana*

Woodsia oregana D. C. Eaton   Oregon Woodsia

Rhizomes short and scaly; fronds few, linear to lance-oblong, glabrous, sometimes glandular, mostly 7-25 cm long, once to twice pinnate, the dead petiole-bases persistent, the lobes of the segments often reflexed and covering the sori; indusium of several white bead-like unequal strands radiating from beneath the sori.
Crevices of rather dry cliffs and slopes, up to about 5000 feet.

Woodsia scopulina D. C. Eaton   Rocky Mountain Woodsia

Rhizome short and scaly; fronds numerous, 8-35 cm long, oblong-lanceolate, chaffy at the base, the blades glandular-puberulent and with flattened, jointed, whitish hairs, at least beneath; indusium deeply divided into unequal, spreading, variously cleft segments.
Dry rock slides, crevices, and mossy cliffs in open woods, 4600 to about 6000 feet.

CUPRESSACEAE   Cypress Family

Trees or shrubs with opposite or whorled scale-like leaves; staminate cones small; ovulate cones woody or fleshy; scales 2 to 12, opposite or grown together, 1-2.5 cm long; ovules 1 or 2 per scale.

Juniperus [Tourn.] L.

Evergreen trees or shrubs with shredded bark; leaves opposite or in whorls of 3, scale-like; staminate cones 3-5 mm long, the stamens opposite or in 3's; ovulate cones small, of 3 to 8 fused fleshy scales each with a single basal ovule, the cones pulpy and berry-like at maturity, 1- to several-seeded, bluish-black or purple.

Plants low spreading shrubs; leaves in whorls of 3, stiff, needle-like with a very sharp
  point..*J. communis* var. *montana*
Plants erect shrubs or small trees; leaves opposite, in 2's, scale-like, not so
  sharp-pointed..*J. scopulorum*

Juniperus communis L. var. montana Ait.   Dwarf or Prostrate Juniper
   J. sibirica Burgsd.; *J. c.* var. *saxatilis* Pallas
Aromatic low spreading or prostrate shrub, 1-3 m tall, forming large patches on the

ground; leaves 7-12 mm long, in whorls of 3, dark green, stiff and sharp-pointed; staminate cones with 12 to 20 stamens; ovulate cones berry-like, blue-purplish with a white bloom, 1- to 3-seeded.

Occasional on open conifer-covered slopes and mountainsides, 4650 to 9800 feet in our mountains.

Juniperus scopulorum Sarg.   Rocky Mountain Juniper; Red Cedar

Tree to about 15 m tall and 1 m in diameter, or branched at the base, sprawling and much shorter; leaves in 2's, scale-like or needle-like, dark green or glaucous, with an inconspicuous gland on the back; staminate cones usually with only 6 stamens; ovulate cones berry-like, blue and glaucous, with a sweet resinous pulp and 1 or 2 seeds.

Fairly common on dry sunny hillsides and in open mixed woods, 4600 to about 6500 feet.

PINACEAE   Pine Family

Resinous, mostly evergreen trees or shrubs, commonly monoecious; leaves linear, needle-like or scale-like, arranged in spirals, single on the branches or in clusters or whorls, deciduous or persistent; stamens and ovules borne in cones, the staminate cones small, the ovulate larger and woody; cone scales separate, woody, spirally arranged, each with one or more ovules at the base and subtended by a bract; seeds winged.

1. Leaves (needles) in clusters up to 5, or in dense whorls of 10 to 40
   2. Leaves evergreen, 2 to 5 in a cluster with a papery sheath at the base ....*Pinus*
   2. Leaves deciduous, 10 to 40 in a cluster, on short spur-shoots, without a basal papery sheath...*Larix*
1. Leaves (needles) single on the branches
   3. Leaves 4-sided, the mature ones stiffly prickly-pointed; cones hanging from the branches...*Picea*
   3. Leaves flat, flexible, blunt or pointed but not prickly; cones either erect on the branches or hanging
      4. Cones standing erect on the branches, usually near the top of the tree ....*Abies*
      4. Cones hanging downward
         5. Cones up to 4 cm long, their bracts hidden by the scales............................*Tsuga*
         5. Cones 4 to 10 cm long, their bracts conspicuously longer than the scales, the tips curved outward and away from the top of the cone ....*Pseudotsuga*

Abies [Tourn.] Mill

Resinous, pyramidal, evergreen trees with whorled branched; leaves linear, sessile, spreading from all sides of the branchlets or sometimes twisted and appearing 2-ranked, flat or 4-sided with stomates on both sides or only beneath; staminate cones suspended; ovulate cones erect, usually at the top of the tree; scales tightly packed, falling at maturity with the short bracts and seeds intact, leaving the cone axis on the branches; seeds winged.

Tree of the lowlands, large, up to 90 m tall; leaves dark green and shining above, forming flat sprays at the ends of the branches, giving off an unpleasant odor when crushed ....*A. grandis*
Tree of upper elevations, smaller, spire-like, much narrowed at the top, mostly up to 40 meters tall; leaves pale gray-green, slightly grooved above, flat beneath, often twisted upward on the branches, fragrant when crushed ....*A. lasiocarpa*

Abies grandis (Dougl.) Lindl.   Grand Fir; Balsam Fir; White Fir

Large forest tree up to 90 meters tall; branches and leaves horizontally-spreading,

Cystopteris fragilis

Pellaea breweri

Polypodium hesperium

Polystichum lonchitis

Pteridium aqualinum var. pubescens

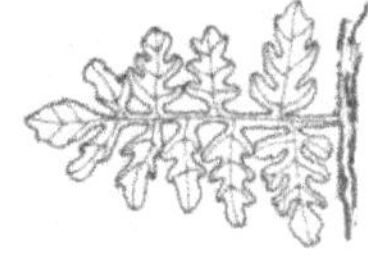

Woodsia oregana

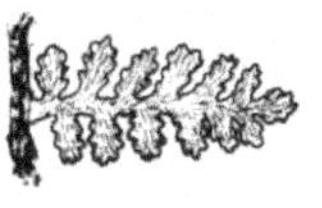

Woodsia scopulina

Juniperus communis var. montana

forming flat sprays; leaves flat, 2-4 cm long, dark green and shining above, silvery-white beneath, blunt or notched at the tip; staminate cones yellowish; ovulate cones green, oblong, 6-18 cm long; bracts shorter than the scales, toothed and short-pointed; seeds brownish. (Sometimes called "Stinking Fir" due to its strong unpleasant odor.) Common in coniferous forests up to about 5000 feet.

Abies lasiocarpa (Hook.) Nutt. Alpine Fir; White Balsam Fir
Narrow spire-like forest tree mostly up to about 40 meters tall; branches short and crowded; leaves twisted so as to curve upward, pale blue-green, rounded or notched at the tip, 2.5-3.5 cm long with white lines of stomates on both sides; staminate cones bluish; ovulate cones green or deep purple, 6-10 cm long; bracts shorter than the scales, toothed and short-pointed; seeds winged. (Leaves, branches and even long-dead wood retain a pleasant fragrance.)
Abundant on mountain slopes, usually between 6000 and about timberline (8000 feet in the Wallowa Mountains) but sometimes growing as low at 4600 feet and then broader and less spire-like.

Larix [Tourn.] Adans.
Tall pyramidal trees; leaves deciduous, soft, spirally arranged into clusters crowded on short spur-like twigs; staminate cones yellow; ovulate cones woody, on twigs of previous years, the scales roundish, shorter or longer than the bracts; seeds triangular, shorter than the wings.

Larix occidentalis Nutt. Mountain Larch or Tamarack
Deciduous tree up to 75 m tall, the bark dark with shallow grooves and often divided into large scaly patches at the base; branches slender; branchlets covered with spur-like lateral twigs; leaves flatly triangular, green, soft, deciduous, 2.5-5 cm long, thin and needle-like, 10 to 40 in a cluster; staminate cones pale yellow on naked shoots; ovulate cones 2.5-3.5 cm long, on leafy shoots, woody, short-stalked, the bracts much longer than the persistent scales; seeds winged.
Occasional in mountain valleys and on slopes between 4500 and 6000 feet.

Picea Link.
Tall forest trees with thin scaly bark; leaves spirally arranged on the branchlets, stiff, linear, often very sharp pointed, 4-sided with stomates on all sides or flattened with stomates on either the upper or the lower surface; ovulate cones maturing the first year, hanging, mostly on the upper portion of the tree; scales thin, flexible, persistent.

Picea engelmannii Parry Engelmann's Spruce
Tall forest tree up to 50 meters with thin scaly bark, whorled branches, and a narrow pyramidal crown; leaves spirally arranged on the branchlets, 2-3 cm long, linear, ill-scented, soft and glaucous, flexible when young but often stiffly very sharp-pointed when older, somewhat 4-sided with 2 to 5 rows of stomates on each side, leaving small knobs on the branchlets after falling; staminate cones pendulous, yellow to purple, 1-1.5 cm long; ovulate cones mostly on the upper part of the tree, pendulous, 4-7 cm long, light brown, deciduous with their thin shining scales attached after the winged seeds have fallen.

Common tree in our mountains, either scattered in open valleys or forming large dense stands, from about 5000 to 8000 feet.

Pinus [Tourn.] L.

Evergreen trees or sometimes shrubs; leaves of two kinds: the secondary green and needle-like in bundles of 2 to 5, the others membranous and scale-like forming a sheath surrounding the base of the bundle; staminate cones numerous; ovulate cones single or clustered, becoming woody, the scales numerous, with 2 ovules, the bracts small; seeds often winged.

1. Leaves mostly 5 in a cluster
    2. Cones purplish, 2.5-8 cm long, remaining closed on the branches for some years, finally dropping the core of the cone with only a few lower scales still attached......*P. albicaulis*
    2. Cones light brown, 6-25 cm long, opening at maturity and falling with all the scales attached..*P. flexilis*
1. Leaves 2 or 3 in a cluster
    3. Leaves 2 per cluster; cones 3-6 cm long...*P. contorta*
    3. Leaves mostly 3 (sometimes 2) per cluster; cones 7-20 cm long...............*P. ponderosa*

Pinus albicaulis Engelm.   White Bark Pine; Nut Pine

An alpine often dwarfed tree or shrub, 5-15 m tall, the trunk silvery gray or white-barked, erect or contorted or prostrate; leaves in clusters of 5, crowded at the ends of the gray nearly naked flexible branches; staminate cones red; ovulate cones red to purple, ovoid, 2.5-8 cm long, remaining closed after maturity, shedding seeds and scales individually, finally dropping the cone core with only a few basal scales remaining; seeds obovoid, 8-12 mm long, dark brown, wingless, edible.
The common subalpine to alpine tree on our mountain slopes and ridges, from about 7400 feet to about 9600 feet.

Pinus contorta Dougl. var. **latifolia** Engelm.   Black or Lodgepole Pine

Slender tree usually 20-25 meters tall but sometimes up to 50 meters, with a straight trunk and scaly, very thin, smooth bark; branches slender, forming a long narrow crown; leaves 3-6 cm long, yellowish to dark green, in 2's; staminate cones clustered; ovulate cones 3-6 cm long, often paired, ovoid and slightly oblique, some shedding seeds at maturity, others remaining closed and persistent on the branches for years; cone scales thin and narrow, purplish-brown, spiny-tipped; seeds winged.
In dense stands at lower elevations, becoming scattered on our mountain slopes and in the valleys, up to about 8000 feet.

Pinus flexilis James   Limber Pine

Tree usually 4-15 meters tall, ours with a stout, often twisted and much-contorted trunk, and long light-gray branches; leaves in 5's, stiff and sharp-pointed, 3-6 cm long; staminate cones red; ovulate cones ovoid, 5-15 cm long, short-stalked, light brown, falling entire at maturity; scales broad and thick, spreading apart at maturity; seeds dark brown, the wing remaining attached to the scale.
Sporadic; usually associated with limestone or shale in rather dry open places, from abont 5100 to about 8000 feet.

Pinus ponderosa Dougl. ex Loud.   Blackjack; Ponderosa Pine

Large forest tree up to 75 meters tall, capable of living up to 500 years; bark thick,

fissured, brown, at maturity shedding reddish plates or flakes near the base; branches turning upward at the ends; leaves 12-25 cm long, usually 3 to a cluster, yellowish-green, thickly bunched; staminate cones 2-3 cm long, in crowded clusters; ovulate cones ovate, 7-20 cm long, reddish-purple to brown; cone scales brown, thin, with a slender prickle at the tip; seeds reddish brown, winged.
Scattered forest trees of open places, mostly between 4500 and about 5000 feet in our area.

Pseudotsuga Carr.

Large trees with ascending or drooping branches and rough, furrowed bark; leaves flat, petioled, appearing 2-ranked; staminate cones axillary; ovulate cones oblong-ovoid; scales rigid, short and persistent, the linear bracts forked and awned, longer than the scales; seeds shorter than the wings.

Pseudotsuga menziesii (Mirb.) Franco Douglas or Red Fir
Large tree up to 80 or 90 m tall with rough, furrowed bark; the middle and upper branches spreading or ascending but the lower ones drooping; leaves appearing 2-ranked, flat, 2-3 cm long, petioled; staminate cones reddish; ovulate cones brownish, pendent, 4-10 cm long, oblong-ovoid; scales persistent, rigid and pubescent; bracts conspicuous, longer than the scales, 3-lobed at the tip, the middle lobe longer, mostly reflexed (in ours).
Common forest tree, 4500 to about 7000 feet.

Tsuga Carr.

Forest tree with lax nodding top and slender branches; leaves flat or angled, appearing 2-ranked with stomates only on the under surface, or 2-ranked, or spreading all around the branchlets and with stomates above and beneath or only beneath; ovulate cones usually pendulous, their scales persistent, much longer than the bracts.

Tsuga mertensiana (Bong.) Carr. Mountain Hemlock
Forest tree 25-50 m tall, frequently with a nodding leading shoot; leaves somewhat 4-sided, spreading all around the branchlets, 1.5-2 cm long, blunt- or round-pointed, yellow-green to light-blue-green with stomates on both surfaces; staminate cones bluish, very small; ovulate cones sessile, purplish-brown. cyclindric, ours 2.5-3.5 cm long, pendulous, their scales persistent, very thin, longer than the bracts; seeds dark brown, winged.
Occasional in small colonies on conifer-covered mountainsides, 6000 to about 7000 feet.

HYDROCHARITACEAE Frog's-bit Family

Submersed or floating perennial aquatic plants; leaves alternate, opposite or whorled, usually sessile; flowers regular, mostly unisexual, 1 or more surrounded by a spathe formed by fusion of bracts; sepals 3; petals 3, white, often reduced or missing; stamens 3 to 12; ovary 1- to 3-chambered, inferior; styles 3 to 6; fruit dry to berry-like, many-seeded, maturing under water.

Elodea Rich. in Michx.
Characters of the family.

Abies lasiocarpa

Larix occidentalis

Picea engelmannii

Pinus contorta var. latifolia

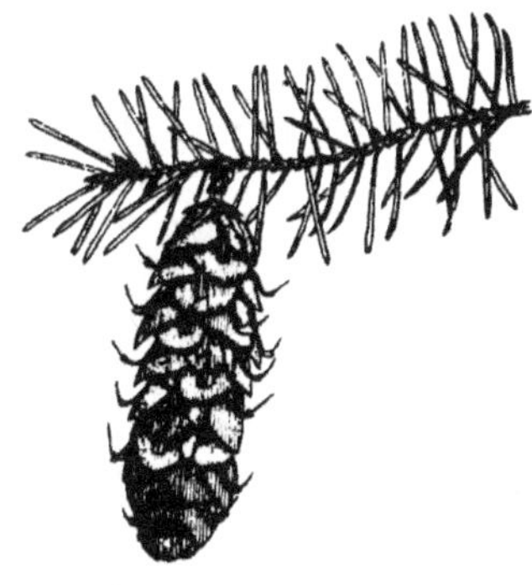

Pseudotsuga menziesii

Tsuga mertensiana

Elodea canadensis

Elodea canadensis Rich. in Michx.   Rocky Mountain Waterweed
    E. planchonii Casp.; *Anacharis canadensis* Planch.

Dioecious aquatic herbs; stems submerged, leafy, dichotomously-branched, up to 20 cm long; leaves mostly in 3's above, ovate-oblong, 6-15 mm long; flowers perfect or imperfect, from a 2-cleft spathe; staminate flowers 1 to 3, early dehiscent and floating on the water, sepals 3, petals 3 or none, stamens 9 in 2 series; pistillate flowers 2-3 mm long, solitary with a perianth tube 3-15 cm long, 3 sepals, 3 petals, stamens none or 3 and rudimentary; perfect flowers similar to the pistillate but with 3 to 9 stamens; capsule about 6 mm long.

Shady mountain lakes at about 7400 feet.

POTAMOGETONACEAE   Pondweed Family

Aquatic perennial herbs; stems flat or round; leaves floating or submersed, opposite, alternate or whorled, the stipules conspicuous, sometimes sheathing; flowers perfect, sessile in peduncled spikes or small axillary clusters; perianth segments 4; stamens 4, attached to the perianth segments; pistils 4, 1-carpellary; fruit an ovoid or obovoid keeled achene.

Potamogeton L.

Perennial aquatic herbs; leaves alternate or the upper ones sometimes opposite, often of two kinds, the floating petioled, their blades broader than the sessile or short-petioled narrower submerged ones; spikes mostly cylindric, axillary, long-peduncled, usually at or above the surface of the water; flowers small, perfect, protected in the bud by the sheathing stipules; perianth of 4 sepaloid segments; stamens 4; pistils 4; fruit a keeled achene.

1. Upper leaves usually floating, long-petioled, the blade usually broad, elliptic or ovate;
    lower leaves sometimes without blades
    2. Lower leaves underwater, folded, 2-5 cm wide with 25 to 60 veins .... *P. amplifolius*
    2. Lower leaves underwater, without blades, 1-2 mm wide with 19 to 35 nerves or veins ...*P. natans*
1. Upper leaves usually underwater, sessile or nearly so, the blade usually narrow
    3. Upper leaves with only 3 to 5 nerves or veins .... *P. praelongus*
    3. Upper leaves with 7 to 25 or more veins
        4. Stems reddish, up to 100 cm long .... *P. alpinus*
        4. Stems greenish, 30-60 cm long .... *P. richardsonii*

Potamogeton alpinus Balbis   Northern Pondweed

Whole plant usually reddish; stems up to 1 m long; floating leaves when present oblanceolate to lanceolate, petioled, 2.5-8 cm long, 1-2.5 cm wide with 7 to 15 nerves; submersed leaves sessile, lanceolate to linear, 2-20 cm long, 7-18 mm wide, mostly 7-nerved; stipules 1.2-3.5 cm long; spikes long-peduncled, 1.5-3.5 cm long; achene about 4 mm long, 3-keeled, smooth or pitted.

Frequently found in slow streams and quiet ponds and lakes, between 7000 and 7500 feet.

Potamogeton amplifolius Tuckerman   Large-leaved Pondweed

Stems 30-120 cm long; floating leaves oval to oblong-elliptic, leathery, 5-10 cm long, 2-5 cm wide, long-petioled, 25- to 45-veined; stipules free, usually persistent, many-nerved, 4-10 cm long; submersed leaves usually short-petioled, 8-20 cm long, 2-6 cm wide, the upper elliptic or oval, folded and arched with 25 to 45 nerves, the lower sometimes crisped and narrower; spikes dense, 2.5-8 cm long; peduncles 5-18 cm long, thick; achenes keeled, 4-5 mm long.

Not common to the Wallowa Mts.; in deep water of lakes and streams. Ours from an elevation of 5600 feet.

Potamogeton natans L.   Common Floating Pondweed

Stems 60-150 cm long; floating leaves long-petioled, 4-12 cm long, 2.5-5 cm wide, ovate to elliptic, thick, 19- to 35-nerved; submersed leaves bladeless, leathery, soon disappearing; stipules fibrous, 4-10 cm long; spikes dense, long-peduncled, 3-5 cm long; achenes 3-5 mm long.

Collected from shallow water of Duck Lake, Wallowa Mountains.

Potamogeton praelongus Wulf   White-stemmed Pondweed

Stems white, zig-zag, branched, up to 3 meters long; leaves all submersed, sessile or short-petioled and clasping, ovate to oblong-lanceolate, 5-36 cm long and 1-3 cm wide, bright green, shining, translucent, with 3 to 5 conspicuous nerves; stipules free, white, 3-10 cm long, rather persistent; spikes dense, long-peduncled, 1-5 cm long; achenes obovoid, mostly 1-keeled, smooth, short-beaked, 4-5 mm long.

Apparently not collected since August 21, 1900 when collected "in shallow water of Wallowa Lake, at elevation 4000 feet, in the Wallowa Mountains" by William C. Cusick.

Potamogeton richardsonii (Bennett) Rydb.   Richardson's Pondweed

Stems greenish, 30-60 cm long, the internodes short and straight; leaves all submersed, sessile and clasping, ovate to lanceolate, usually under 10 cm long and 2 cm wide, crisp-margined, with 13 to 25 or more conspicuous nerves; stipules free, whitish, 1-2 cm long; spikes 1.5-4 cm long; achenes obovate, about 3 mm long, faintly keeled or rounded on the back.

Shallow slow or standing water, at about 5600 feet.

JUNCACEAE   Rush Family

Annual or perennial grass-like herbs; flowering stems round or flattened; leaves with open or closed sheaths and flat, gladiate, terete or channeled blades, or the blades undeveloped; inflorescence usually many-flowered, open or compact; flowers small, greenish to brown, composed of 6 distinct, scarious segments, in 2 sets; stamens mostly 3 or 6 but sometimes 1, 2, 4, or 5; pistil 3-carpellary; style 1; ovary superior; fruit a 3- to many-seeded capsule.

Leaves often hairy at least when young, flat or channeled and grass-like; sheaths closed;
   capsule 3-seeded..*Luzula*
Leaves glabrous, often seeming rounded, seldom flat and grass-like; sheaths open; capsule
   many-seeded ....*Juncus*

Juncus |Tourn.| L.

Annual or perennial grass-like herbs; stems usually pithy; leaves with open sheaths and terete to sometimes flat blades; flowers few, small, greenish to purplish-brown, in open or dense clusters; perianth small and inconspicuously colored, the 6 segments in

2 sets, usually similar but the inner set often shorter; stamens 3 or 6; fruit a many-seeded 1- to 3-celled capsule.

1. Inflorescence terminal on the flowering stem
    2. Plants small annuals
        3. Plants only 2-3 cm tall; flowers single, terminal on each peduncle............ *J. hemiendytus*
        3. Plants 4-20 cm tall; flowers usually lateral as well as terminal
            4. Perianth segments 2.5-4 mm long; plants rare in our area, usually 5-20
               cm tall...*J. sphaerocarpus*
            4. Perianth segments 4-7 mm long; plants common, usually 5-40 cm tall .... *J. bufonius*
    2. Plants larger, perennial; flowers in heads
        5. Heads mostly solitary, sometimes 3 or 2
            6. Perianth segments dark brown, 3-4 mm long...............................*J. mertensianus*
            6. Perianth segments chestnut to brown with a greenish center area, 4-6
               mm long... *J. regelii*
        5. Heads usually 3 to many; anthers mostly longer than the filaments
            7. Perianth segments all alike in length and width
                8. Perianth segments 3-4.5 mm long, about equaling the capsule
                    9. Leaves flattened
                        10. Stamens 3...*J. ensifolius*
                        10. Stamens 6
                            11. Heads 2 to 12; perianth segments dark
                              brown...*J. saximontanus*
                            11. Heads 25 to 100; perianth segments straw-
                              colored...*J. xiphioides*
                    9. Leaves mostly terete, narrow...*J. nevadensis*
                8. Perianth segments 5-6.5 mm long, mostly longer than the capsule
                    12. Perianth segments with broad silvery-hyaline margins........*J. longistylis*
                  12. Perianth segments not broadly silvery-hyaline margined........*J. howellii*
             7. Perianth segments not all alike, one set longer or broader than the other
                13. Perianth segments with broad silvery margins; auricles at the
                   tips of the sheaths well developed, truncate or rounded................*J. longistylis*
                13. Perianth segments without silvery margins; auricles
                 inconspicuous or linear and acute if developed............................ *J. orthophyllus*
1. Inflorescence appearing to arise below the tip of the flowering stem, therefore not
  terminal
    14. Leaf blades little or not at all developed
        15. Flowers 1 to 4 per stem; anthers longer than the filaments .... *J. drummondii*
        15. Flowers more than 4 per stem
            16. Anthers shorter than the filaments.......................................*J. filiformis*
            16. Anthers longer than the filaments ....*J. balticus*
    14. Leaf blades well developed
        17. Perianth segments brownish
            18. Perianth segments 3.5-4 mm long with a greenish mid-stripe.................*J. confusus*
            18. Perianth segments 6-7 mm long..*J. parryi*
        17. Perianth segments greenish
            19. Capsule 1-celled...*J. tenuis*
            19. Capsule 3-celled...*J. brachyphyllus*

Juncus balticus Willd.
Baltic Rush

Perennials with creeping rhizomes; stems 1.5-8 cm tall, wiry, often twisted; leaf-sheaths loose, the basal bladeless, the upper sometimes ending in a sharp point; panicle seemingly lateral, dense or spreading, up to 15 cm long; perianth segments 4-5 mm long, green or purplish-brown with a greenish midstripe, the outer 3 segments somewhat longer and narrower than the wider-margined inner ones; stamens 6, the anthers much

longer than the filaments; capsule ovoid, brown, sharp-pointed, about equaling the perianth; seeds striate.
Gravel bars and swampy streambanks, about 5000 to 6000 feet.

Juncus brachyphyllus Wieg.   Short-leaved Rush

Tufted perennial; stems 30-50 cm tall, stiff and striate-grooved; leaves basal, shorter than the stem, flat, about 2 mm wide, the auricles at the tips of the sheaths well-developed; panicle 3-6 cm long, appearing lateral, densely many-flowered; perianth 4-5 mm long, pale green or brown, the inner segments scarious to the tip, the outer rigidly acute and somewhat longer than the inner; stamens 6, the anthers equaling or shorter than the filaments; capsule 3-celled, about equaling the perianth; seeds pointed at each end.
Moist open grassy places, about 5000 feet.

Juncus bufonius L.   Toad Rush

Fibrous-rooted annual; stems branching from the base, 5-40 cm tall; leaves short and narrow; flowers solitary at the nodes or in one-sided groups; perianth 3-7 mm long, pale brown, scarious-margined, the outer segments usually longer; stamens usually 6, rarely 3, the anthers shorter than the filaments; capsule 3-celled, shorter than the perianth segments; seeds reticulate.
Moist wooded stream borders and pools, about 5500 to 5600 feet.

Juncus confusus Cov.   Colorado Rush

Tufted perennial; stems slender 30-50 cm tall; leaves very narrow, basal, the blades almost filiform, the sheaths tight, prolonged into conspicuous auricles at the tip; auricles whitish; inflorescence few-flowered, 1-2 cm long; perianth about 4 mm long, the segments acute, greenish with a brown stripe on either side and broad scarious margins; stamens 6, the anthers much shorter than the filaments; capsule 3-celled, oblong; seeds ridged, pointed at both ends.
Dry sand bar at 5800 feet.

Juncus drummondii E. Meyer   Drummond's Rush
   J. subtriflorus E. Mey.

Tufted mat-forming perennial; stems terete, 15-40 cm tall; basal leaf-sheaths bladeless or nearly so; flowers 1 to 3, rarely 4 or 5, each subtended by 2 brownish bractlets; perianth 5-7 mm long, the segments about equal, acutish, green with broad brown margins; stamens 6, the anthers longer than the filaments; capsule oblong; seeds striate, appendaged at both ends.
Moist ridges and slopes, meadows and lake shores, 7200 to 8500 feet.

Juncus ensifolius Wiks.   Three-stamened Rush; Dagger-leaved Rush

Perennial with creeping rhizomes; stems 2-edged, 20-60 cm tall; leaves flattened laterally, 2 to 5 mm wide, auricles not developed; inflorescence of 2 to 7 large many-flowered heads or of many small few-flowered heads; perianth dark brown or black to greenish, about 3 mm long, the segments equal, acuminate; stamens 3, the anthers shorter than the filaments; capsule oblong, dark brown; seeds reticulate.
Wet woods, about 4500 to 5600 feet.

Juncus filiformis L.   Thread Rush

Tufted perennial with creeping rhizomes; stems slender, terete, grooved, 4-60 cm tall; sheaths short and tight, usually bristle-like at the tip; inflorescence appearing to originate below the tip of the flowering stem, the involucral bract very long; panicle mostly 7- to 15-flowered; perianth 2.5-4 mm long, the segments green with white margins, the inner set somewhat shorter than the outer; stamens 6, the anthers a little shorter than the filaments or sometimes a little longer; capsule shorter than the perianth; seeds wrinkled, pointed at the ends.

Moist mountain meadows and muddy borders of lakes and streams, about 7200 feet.

Juncus hemiendytus F. J. Hermann

Small annual; leaves all basal, about half as long as the peduncles; flowers mostly 2-merous on peduncles about 2 cm tall; involucral bracts usually 2, unequal, the upper about 1 mm long, the lower sometimes reduced or even missing; perianth segments 2-3 mm long, narrowly lanceolate, stamens 2 or 3; capsules usually longer than the perianth; seeds smooth or reticulate.

Moist to wet meadows at about 5800 to 6000 feet.

Juncus howellii F. J. Herm.   Howell's Rush

Perennial with long rhizomes; stems clustered, flattened, 20-60 cm tall; leaves very narrow and grass-like; sheaths open at the top, the auricles erect; inflorescence terminal, 2-9 cm long, of 4 to 10 heads or of many smaller 3- to 10-flowered heads; involucral bract very short; perianth 5-6 mm long, dark brown with green stripe, the 3 outer segments rough near the tips, shorter and broader than the inner ones; stamens 6, the anthers much longer than the filaments; capsule ovoid or obovoid, shorter than the perianth; seeds appendaged and reticulate.

Moist ground at about 5500 feet.

Juncus longistylis Torr.   Long-styled Rush

Perennial sedge; stems clustered, stiff, 20-60 cm tall; sheaths with truncate or rounded auricles; stem leaves 1 to 3, flattened, grass-like, 1.5-4 mm wide; inflorescence terminal; heads usually 2 to 8, rarely solitary and large, mostly 3- to 8-flowered; perianth 5-6 mm long, brown with a broad greenish middle area and mostly broad silvery-white margins; stamens 6, anthers longer than the filaments; capsule oblong-ovoid, brown, mucronate, shorter than the perianth; seeds striate, white-tipped.

Moist to wet shady woods and bogs, about 5300 feet.

Juncus mertensianus Bong.   Mertens' Rush

Perennial sedge with short rhizomes; stems weak, clustered and somewhat flattened, 10-25 or up to 45 cm tall; leaves 1 to 4 on the stem, blades 1-3 mm wide; sheaths ending with rounded or acute auricles; inflorescence terminal, heads usually solitary, dark brown, many-flowered; perianth 3-4 mm long, the segments about equal; stamens 6, the anthers much shorter than the filaments; capsule obovoid to oval, dark brown, about as long as the perianth; seeds reticulate.

Moist to wet or mossy lake borders, streambanks and meadows, 7000 to 9200 feet.

Juncus nevadensis Wats.   Sierra Rush

Perennial with creeping rhizomes; stems single or tufted, 15-60 cm tall; sheaths

Potamogeton alpinus

Potamogeton amplifolius

Potamogeton natans

Potamogeton praelongus

Juncus bufonius

Juncus filiformis

Juncus hemiendytus

auricled; leaves 1 to 3 on the stem, about 1 mm wide; inflorescence terminal, 2-12 cm long; heads either 1 or 2 and large, or up to 30 and smaller, crowded together or somewhat separate from each other; perianth brown or purplish-brown, 3.5-4.5 mm long, the segments about equal, acuminate; stamens 6, the anthers longer than the filaments; capsule oblong with a short beak; seeds minute.
Mountain meadows, lakes and streams at about 5000 feet.

Juncus orthophyllus Cov.   Straight-leaved Rush
Perennial with creeping rhizomes; stems ·pale green, thick, flat, 20-40 cm tall; leaves mainly basal (sometimes 1 or 2 above the middle of the stem), grass-like, about equaling the stem or shorter, 1.5-6 mm wide, many-nerved; sheaths with inconspicuous linear, acute auricles; inflorescence terminal; heads 2 to 12, 5- to 10-flowered; perianth 6 mm long, dull brown with green midrib and scarious margins, rough on the back, the inner 3 longer and broader than the sharp-pointed outer ones; stamens 6, the anthers much longer than the filaments; capsule oblong-ovoid, nearly equaling the perianth; seeds reticulate.
Moist boggy meadows, 4500 to about 7000 feet.

Juncus parryi Engelm.   Parry's Rush
Matted perennial; stems clustered, slender, 10-30 cm tall; upper leaf blades 1-4 cm long, the basal sheaths bladeless or with scarcely-developed bristle-like blades; inflorescence seeming to originate below the top of the flowering stem; flowers 1 to 3, each subtended by 2 brownish bractlets; involucral bract 1-8 cm long; perianth 5-7 mm long, brownish, the inner set a little shorter than the outer, broadly scarious-margined; stamens 6, the anthers much longer than the filaments; capsule equaling or longer than the perianth; seeds finely striate, long appendaged at both ends.
Open slopes, meadows and borders of lakes and streams, 7000 to about 8500 feet.

Juncus regelii Buch.   Regel's Rush
Perennial with creeping rhizomes; stems single or closely clustered, 10-50 cm tall; leaves 1-4 mm wide, grass-like, 1 to 3 to a stem; auricles either not developed or rudimentary; inflorescence terminal; heads mostly 1 to 3 or 4, many-flowered; perianth segments 4-6 mm long, roughened above, dark brown with greenish center area, scarious-margined, the inner set shorter and somewhat broader; stamens 6, the anthers and filaments about equal; capsule brown, nearly equaling the perianth; seeds white-appendaged at each end.
Wet ground, about 5000 to 5600 feet.

Juncus saximontanus A. Nels.   Rocky Mountain Rush
Perennial with creeping rhizomes; stems 2-edged, 30-50 cm tall; leaves 2-4 mm wide, flattened laterally, gladiate, usually auricled; inflorescence terminal, somewhat loose; heads 2 to 15, each 3- to 10-flowered; perianth dark brown, about 3 mm long, the inner segments a little shorter than the outer; stamens 6, the anthers shorter than the filaments or sometimes longer; capsule dark brown, about equaling the perianth; seeds reticulate.
Boggy ground, sand and gravel bars, about 5000 to 5600 feet.

Juncus sphaerocarpus Nees   Round-fruited Toad Rush
Branching annual, 5-20 cm tall; stems many; leaves up to 5 cm long, basal, very

narrow; flowers single on the branches; perianth 3-4 mm long, pale green, spreading in fruit; stamens 6, the anthers shorter than the filaments; capsule 3-celled, green; seeds oblong.
Moist places, 5600 to 5800 feet.

Juncus tenuis Willd.   Slender Rush

Perennial; stems bright green, striate, usually spreading, 15-60 cm tall; leaves short, flat, very narrow; sheaths short and often expanded; auricles small and inconspicuous or large and scarious; inflorescence appearing to originate below the top of the flowering stem; panicle often pale green, 1-7 cm long, open or compact; involucral bracts 2 or 3; perianth segments spreading, green with white margins; stamens 6, the anthers shorter than the filaments; capsule 1-celled, about equaling the perianth; seeds reticulate.
Boggy woods about 5600 feet.

Juncus xiphioides E. Mey.   Iris-leaved Rush

Perennial with thick creeping rhizomes; stems flattened and 2-edged, 40-90 cm tall; leaves 3-10 mm wide, flattened laterally and gladiate; sheaths without auricles; inflorescence a large open compound panicle of numerous straw-colored or brownish heads each 3- to 20-flowered; perianth brownish, about 3 mm long; stamens 6, the anthers shorter or about equaling the filaments; capsule beaked, slightly longer than the perianth; seeds reticulate.
Bogs and wet places at about 5000 feet.

Luzula DC.

Grass-like perennial herbs; stems leafy, hollow; leaves long and flat, often with a fringe of hairs; sheaths closed; flowers in heads, panicles or spike-like clusters; perianth green to brownish; stamens 6; capsule 1-celled; seeds 3, usually smooth and shining.

1. Inflorescence loose and open; flowers 1 or 2 at the ends of the many slender mostly drooping branchlets
    2. Flowers dark brown, about 3 mm long; anthers longer than the filaments ....*L. glabrata*
    2. Flowers greenish to purplish-brown, about 1.5-2 mm long; anthers longer or shorter than the filaments
        3. Bracts and bractlets of the inflorescence deeply fringed; anthers about equaling the filaments; cauline leaves 2 or 3 and under 3 mm broad.........*L. wahlenbergii*
        3. Bracts and bractlets mostly entire to shallowly toothed; anthers shorter than the filaments; cauline leaves usually more than 3 and over 3 mm broad ....*L. parviflora*
1. Inflorescence not loose and open; flowers in dense head-like or spike-like clusters
    4. Spike solitary, dense, sometimes nodding; anthers slightly shorter than the filaments
        5. Bract under the inflorescence conspicuously longer than the flower clusters; spike erect, not nodding.................................*L. orestera*
        5. Bract subtending the inflorescence short and inconspicuous; spike nodding....*L. spicata*
    4. Spikes usually more than 1, mostly stiffly erect
        6. Flowers pale green to chestnut, 2-4.5 mm long; anthers longer than the filaments ....*L. campestris*
        6. Flowers 1.5 mm long, dark brown; anthers shorter than, to nearly as long as, the filaments.........................*L. subcongesta*

Luzula campestris (L.) DC.   Common Woodrush
L. multiflora (Retz.) Lej. and *L. comosa* E. Mey.
Tufted perennial; stems 10-60 cm tall; leaves 2-7 mm wide, tapering to a blunt point,

often long-hairy; flowers 8-15 in small clusters on branches of unequal lengths, the clusters crowded or set apart, globose to short-cylindric; bractlets fimbriate at the tips; perianth 2-4.5 mm long, pale green to chestnut brown; stamens 6, the anthers mostly longer than the filaments; capsule ovoid, about equaling the perianth; seeds reddish-brown.

Wet meadows and open grassy woodlands, 4500 to about 8000 feet.

Flowers 3-4.5 mm long; anthers about twice as long as the filaments..var. **congesta** (Thuill.) E. Mey.

Flowers 2-3 mm long; anthers about equaling the filaments..var. **multiflora** (Ehrh.) Celak.

Luzula glabrata (Hoppe) Desv.   Smooth Woodrush
   Perennial with long rhizomes; stems 15-50 cm tall; leaves grabrous except at the base, 3-12 mm wide, shining above; panicle loose and open, 3-10 cm long, usually nodding, the bracts brownish with ciliate margins; flowers usually single, the pedicels spreading; perianth about 3 mm long, dark purplish-brown; anthers much longer than the filaments; capsule almost black, about equaling the perianth; seeds dark brown.
Meadows, slopes and open coniferous woods, 7000 to 7500 feet.

Luzula orestera C. W. Shars.
   Densely tufted perennial 5 to about 20 cm tall; culms and inflorescence purplish; leaves mostly basal, thickish, 3-8 cm long, often ciliate; inflorescence a dense pyramidal cluster of 2 to 4 heads subtended by 1 or 2 longer bracts; bractlets entire or ciliate; perianth segments purplish-brown with hyaline margins, 2-3 mm long; anthers slightly shorter than the filaments; capsules purplish-brown, 2-3 mm long, shorter than the perianth; seeds dark brown.
Open boggy alpine meadows from about 7000 to 8000 feet.

Luzula parviflora (Ehrh.) Desv.   Small-flowered Woodrush
   Perennial; stems clustered, often decumbent, 10-80 cm tall; leaves glabrous, 3-10 mm wide, sharp or blunt at the tip, thin and shining, 2 to 5 on the stem; inflorescence open, nodding; flowers minute, single or sometimes 2 or 3 together on slender pedicels; perianth 1-2 mm long, green to brownish; anthers usually shorter than the filaments; capsule about as long as the perianth, greenish to purplish-brown; seeds brown.
Moist often boggy woods and meadows to alpine slopes and peaks, 6000 to about 8500 feet.

Plant taller than the species; perianth sometimes deep chestnut; capsule deep chestnut to almost black...var. **melanocarpa** (Michx.) Buch.

Luzula spicata (L.) DC.   Spiked Woodrush
   Perennial; stems 10-40 cm tall, usually nodding; leaves thick, stiffly erect, 1-4 mm broad, hairy toward the base; inflorescence spike-like, often interrupted, 1-3 cm long, usually nodding; bractlets hairy-fringed; perianth segments 2-3 mm long, brown with hyaline margins and sharp-pointed tips; anthers slightly shorter than the filaments; capsule shorter than the perianth; seeds ovoid to obovoid.
Open slopes, 7000 to 9595 feet.

Luzula subcongesta (Wats.) Jeps.   Donner Woodrush

Perennial; stems 20-50 cm tall with 3 to 5 leaves; basal leaves soft and green, mostly glabrous, 4-10 mm wide; inflorescence erect, of few to several head-like clusters; bracts small, fringed; perianth-segments 1.5 mm long, dark brown, hyaline at the tip; stamens half as long as the perianth, the anthers about equaling the filaments; capsules ovoid, light brown, about equaling the perianth; seeds brown, darker at the tip.
Wet grounds, about 7500 feet.

Luzula wahlenbergii Rupr.   Wahlenberg's Woodrush

Densely tufted perennial 15-40 cm tall; leaves thickish, dull green, often hairy on the margins, the basal 6-12 cm long and 3-8 mm broad, the cauline only 2 or 3 and reduced; inflorescence open, drooping, the flowers single on the branches; bracts deeply fringed into many fine divisions; flowers dark purplish-brown, the segments about 2 mm long, ovate-lanceolate; anthers about 5 mm long, the filaments equal or slightly longer; capsules ovoid, nearly black, longer than the perianth; seeds light yellowish-brown.
Open dry to moist meadows and slopes in the mountains, about 7000 to 9600 feet.

CYPERACEAE   Sedge Family

Annual or perennial grass-like herbs, fibrous-rooted or rhizomatous; stems (culms) slender, mostly solid and triangular but sometimes quadrangular, rounded or flattened; leaves usually 3-ranked, narrow with closed sheaths and parallel-veined blades, or the blades reduced or not developed at all; flowers small, perfect or imperfect, arranged in spikelets, 1 (rarely 2) in the axil of a bract or scale, the spikelets 1- to many-flowered; scales persistent or deciduous; perianth none or of 1 or more bristles or scales; stamens usually 3, rarely 1 or 2; ovary superior, 1-celled, 1-ovuled; style commonly 2- or 3-cleft, rarely 4; fruit a cylindrical, lenticular or 3-sided achene.

1. Flowers either with stamens but no pistil, or with a pistil but no stamens (unisexual, imperfect)
    2. Achene completely surrounded by the perigynium..*Carex*
    2. Achene not completely surrounded by the perigynium...*Kobresia*
1. Flowers with both stamens and pistil (bisexual, perfect), or at least one perfect flower in each spikelet
    3. Base of the style swollen into a persistent knob-like tubercle at the top of the achene; spikelet solitary...*Eleocharis*
    3. Base of the style not at all swollen, the achenes without a differentiated tubercle at the tip
        4. Culms hollow, jointed..*Dulichium*
        4. Culms solid, not jointed
            5. Perianth bristles 6 or more, very long in fruit...*Eriophorum*
            5. Perianth bristles 1 to 8 when present, short in fruit ....*Scirpus*

Carex L.

Perennial bisexual or sometimes unisexual herbs; stems solid, triangular or terete; leaves 3-ranked, grass-like, with closed sheaths; spikes one to many, clustered together or in a loose raceme, sessile or peduncled, the individual spikes wholly pistillate, wholly staminate, or bisexual and then either androgynous (the staminate flowers above the pistillate) or gynaecandrous (the pistillate flowers above the staminate); flowers unisexual, without a perianth, each subtended by a small bract or scale; staminate flowers mostly with 3 stamens; pistillate flowers surrounded by the perigynium and consisting of 1 carpel, 1 ovule, and a style with 2 or 3 stigmas (rarely 4); fruit an achene, lenticular, 3-angled or 4-angled.

1. Spikes either solitary on the culm or crowded together so as to seem to be one spike only
  2. Spike truly solitary on the culm; plants mostly small and delicate
    3. Leaves narrow, wiry, terete or appearing so, without an apparent blade; old leaves often remaining at the plant base; spikes mostly small
      4. Plants of higher elevations, between about 7400 and 10,000 feet
        5. Perigynia pubescent; stigmas 3..*C. filifolia*
        5. Perigynia glabrous; stigmas 2 or 3
          6. Stigmas 2..*C. pyrenaica*
          6. Stigmas 3..*C. subnigricans*
      4. Plants usually at elevations below 7000 feet
        7. Plants of shady bog situations, about 5300 feet; stigmas 2; spikes either unisexual or with both staminate and pistillate flowers in the same spike..*C. dioica*
        7. Plants of drier open places at about 6000 to 7000 feet; stigmas 3; spikes bisexual..*C. nardina*
    3. Leaves flat, more grass-like, with a noticeable though narrow blade; old leaves sometimes persisting at the base but not thickly intertwined; spikes small
      8. Perigynia and spike pale, light yellowish; spike with only 1 to 3 perigynia at the bottom..*C. geyeri*
      8. Perigynia and spike light to dark brown; perigynia more than 3 in a spike
        9. Spike dark, about 1 cm long; stigmas 2..*C. nigricans*
        9. Spike brownish, usually over 1 cm long; stigmas 3
          10. Pistillate scales longer than the perigynia and mostly concealing them; perigynia pubescent..*C. pseudoscirpoidea*
          10. Pistillate scales shorter than the perigynia and not concealing them; perigynia glabrous near the base..*C. scirpoidea*
  2. Spike not truly solitary though appearing so at first glance; spike truly composed of several very small spikes clustered together into a head
    11. Head about as broad as long, roundish to somewhat triangular and broader at the base than the top
      12. Head rounded rather than triangular; dark sedge of timberline elevations..*C. foetida*
      12. Head broader at the base than at the top
        13. Head greenish or yellowish to light or medium brown
          14. Head subtended by a well-developed, conspicuously long bract; perigynia pale green to tan, 3-4.5 mm long..*C. athrostachya*
          14. Head subtended by a very short and inconspicuous bract, or the bract missing; perigynia various
            15. Perigynia 3-4 mm long, shining, brownish..*C. jonesii*
            15. Perigynia 4-6 mm long, green to yellowish or brownish
              16. Perigynia yellowish, narrowly winged, about 4 mm long..*C. abrupta*
              16. Perigynia green to straw-colored to brownish, 4.5-6 mm long..*C. multicostata*
        13. Head darker, brown to almost black
          17. Perigynia under 3 mm long, shining, spreading, greenish-brownish..*C. illota*
          17. Perigynia 4-6 mm long, greenish to almost black
            18. Perigynia almost black, 5-6 mm long, strongly winged   *C. haydeniana*
            18. Perigynia not blackish, under 5 mm long

19. Perigynia greenish to tan or brownish with a brown-
tipped beak, about 4 mm long, narrowly winged..........*C. microptera*
19. Perigynia yellow or yellowish-green, 4-5 mm long,
broadly winged.................*C. festivella*
11. Head mostly longer than broad, the several spikes sometimes separated from
each other, but the head appearing cylindric rather than round or triangular
20. Head 3-10 cm long; plants coarse; perigynia spreading, 4-5 mm long.........*C. stipata*
20. Head mostly under 3 cm long; plants not coarse; perigynia various
21. Perigynia glabrous; stigmas 2
22. Scales dark, medium brown to greenish black; perigynia
greenish to tan or brown
23. Perigynia under 3 mm long, brown to blackish; plants of
middle elevations.................*C. limnophila*
23. Perigynia 4-6 mm long, straw-colored to brownish; plants
of high mountain elevations.................*C. phaeocephala*
22. Scales lighter, light or medium brown, mostly papery, often with
a green midrib
24. Perigynia broadly green-margined, 3-6 mm long, the beak
dark-tipped
25. Plants 30-80 cm tall; beak 2-toothed.................*C. hoodii*
25. Plants under 30 cm tall
26. Perigynia deep green or yellowish-brown, 3-4 mm
long.................*C. preslii*
26. Perigynia straw-colored to dark brownish, 4-6 mm
long.................*C. phaeocephala*
24. Perigynia narrowly or scarcely margined at all
27. Leaf-sheaths corrugated on the one side; perigynia
shining, mostly under 3.5 mm long, not greenish-
margined.................*C. neurophora*
27. Leaf-sheaths not corrugated; perigynia 3.4-5 mm long,
very narrowly margined, boat shaped; plants of high
elevations.................*C. leporinella*
21. Perigynia hairy; stigmas 3 or 4
28. Stigmas 3; plants mostly under 15 cm tall.................*C. concinna*
28. Stigmas 4; plants mostly 15-35 cm tall.................*C. concinnoides*
1. Spikes more than one, separated from each other, not in a close cluster
29. Spikes all sessile, that is, without stalks
30. Perigynia above the stamens in the spike; perigynia 3 to 40 in a spike
31. Spikes greenish-brown; perigynia usually 3 to 10 in a spike
32. Perigynia 2-2.5 mm long; sedge of high mountain elevations; rare in
our area.................*C. brunnescens*
32. Perigynia 2.5-4 mm long; sedge of middle mountain elevations;
infrequent, in moist shady woods near water.................*C. laeviculmis*
31. Spikes silvery-brown to pale green, grayish or straw-colored, with 10 to 30
perigynia in a spike; sedge of wet places.................*C. canescens*
30. Perigynia not above the stamens, the spike either with the perigynia below the
stamens or the spike entirely of stamens or entirely of perigynia; perigynia 1
to 3 in the bisexual spikes.................*C. disperma*
29. Spikes not all sessile, 1 or more stalked, sometimes very shortly so
33. Lowest bract mostly shorter than the inflorescence or about as long, sometimes
missing
34. Perigynia hairy; stigmas 3
35. Uppermost spike 2-5 cm long, staminate; perigynia densely pubescent,
the beak conspicuously 2-toothed.................*C. lanuginosa*
35. Uppermost spike only 1-2 cm long, staminate or sometimes with a few
perigynia at its base; perigynia sparsely pubescent to nearly glabrous,
the beak poorly developed.................*C. luzulina*

34. Perigynia without hairs; stigmas 2 or 3
   36. Scales light to medium brown; stigmas 3
      37. Uppermost spike 4-10 mm long; most if not all spikes nodding on flexible thin peduncles .... *C. capillaris*
      37. Uppermost spike 10-20 cm long; spikes mostly erect, either short-peduncled or sessile .... *C. luzulina*
   36. Scales dark brown to almost black; stigmas 2 or 3
      38. Perigynia flat; nerveless or nearly so
         39. Lower leaf sheaths purplish; culm leaves few; perigynia often with purple spots, stigmas 3 .... *C. spectabilis*
         39. Lower leaf sheaths brownish, not purple; culm leaves many; perigynia not purple-spotted, stigmas 3 .... *C. paysonis*
      38. Perigynia inflated or turgid at least above the achene, not flat
         40. Stigmas 2; base of plant with persistent old leaves through which culms are visible
            41. Perigynia curved, at least at the tip, and spreading outward .... *C. campylocarpa*
            41. Perigynia not curved or spreading, usually closely stretching upward, often grainy-textured or spotted ...... *C. scopulorum*
         40. Stigmas 3; perigynia often green
            42. Perigynia 2-3 mm long, usually swollen by the achene, yellow or green or purple .... *C. norvegica*
            42. Perigynia 3.3-4.5 mm long, not much swollen, usually green .... *C. raynoldsii*
33. Lowest bract longer than the inflorescence, or about equaling it at the top
   43. Scales dark, brown to nearly black; stigmas 2
      44. Perigynia conspicuously veined, flat, light bluish-greenish, early deciduous, about 3 mm long .... *C. kelloggii*
      44. Perigynia inconspicuously veined, if at all, yellowish to brownish, persistent
         45. Plant ashy-green; perigynia yellow-green to straw-colored, under 3 mm long, not veined .... *C. aquatilis*
         45. Plant not ashy-green; perigynia brownish to yellow-purplish, about 3 mm long, finely veined .... *C. eurycarpa*
   43. Scales light brown or chestnut to green; stigmas 2 or 3
      46. Spikes mostly less than 2 cm long; perigynia 1.5-4.5 mm long; plants 3-40 cm tall
         47. Perigynia hairy, narrowed to a long beak; spikes sometimes nearly basal .... *C. rossii*
         47. Perigynia without hairs or a beak; spikes not basal .... *C. aurea*
      46. Spikes mostly 2-10 cm long; perigynia 4-11 mm long; plants 30-120 cm tall
         48. Perigynia light brownish, curved and spreading outward at maturity, 4-7 mm long .... *C. rostrata*
         48. Perigynia pale greenish to light brown, not curved outward, 5-11 mm long .... *C. vesicaria*

Carex abrupta Mack.   Abruptly-beaked Sedge

Culms clustered, 20-70 cm tall; leaves 2-4 mm wide; spikes gynaecandrous, 5-8 mm long, densely clustered; bracts short or undeveloped; scales ovate, obtuse, chestnut brown with pale midrib, narrower and shorter than the perigynia; perigynia 4-5 mm long, strongly-nerved, thickish, yellowish-brown, wing-margined, serrulate above, the beak brown, half as long as the body; achenes lenticular, jointed with the style; stigmas 2. Sphagnum bog, about 7000 feet.

Juncus mertensianus

Juncus parryi

Juncus xiphioides

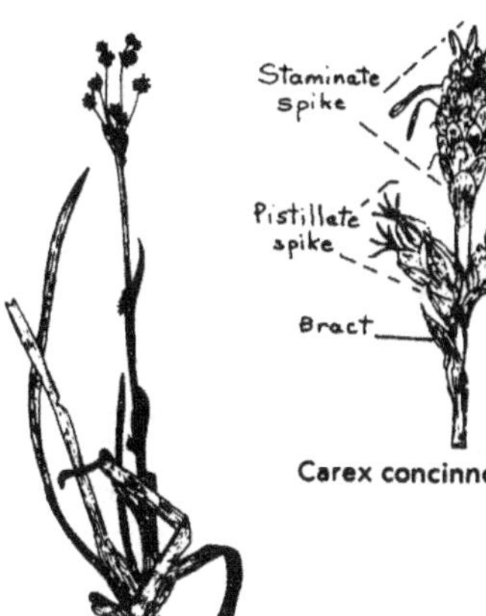

Carex concinnoides

Luzula wahlenbergii

Luzula subcongesta

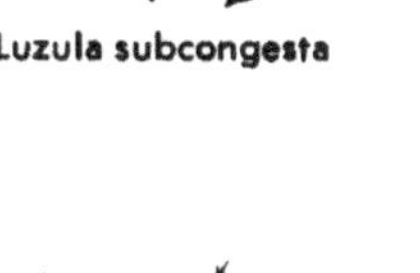

Carex aurea

Carex capillaris

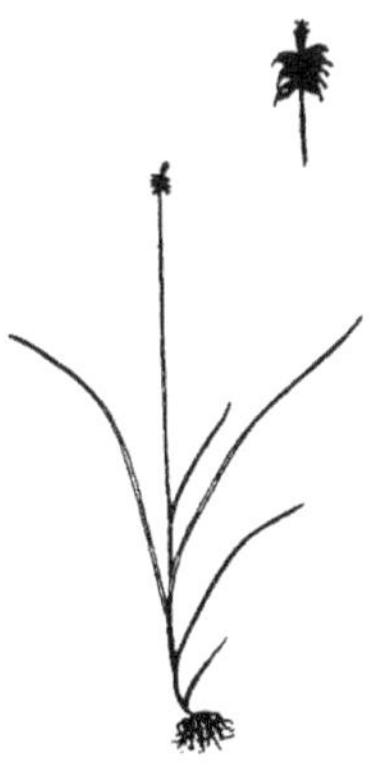

Carex dioica var. gynocrates

Carex aquatilis Wahl.   Water Sedge

Stems triangular, 30-100 cm tall, from long creeping rhizomes; leaves long, 2-8 mm wide; spikes several, cylindric, dense, 1.5-6 cm long, not closely crowded, mostly sessile, the upper 1 or 2 staminate, the others pistillate; bracts equaling or longer than the inflorescence; pistillate scales reddish-brown to nearly black with a lighter center, shorter or longer than the perigynia; perigynia flat, nerveless, 2.5-3.5 mm long, elliptic to obovate, brownish, reddish or pale green, red-spotted, the beak short and entire; achene lenticular; stigmas 2.

Shallow water and swampy ground, about 7000 feet.

Carex athrostachya Olney   Slender-beaked Sedge

Densely tufted plants; culms mostly smooth, slender, triangular, 10-100 cm tall; leaves flat, 1.5-4 mm wide, mostly shorter than the culms; spikes gynaecandrous, 5 mm long, crowded into a dense, greenish-brown head 1-2 cm long; pistillate scales mostly ovate, slightly shorter than the perigynia, green or light brown, 3-4.5 mm long, somewhat nerved and flattened, wing-margined; beak serrulate, half the length of the body, nearly round, the tip entire; stigmas 2; achene lenticular, jointed with the style.

Moist meadows and forest openings, 5700 to 7550 feet.

Carex aurea Nutt.   Golden-fruited Sedge

Incl. *C. hassei* Bailey

Culms 3-45 cm tall, triangular, weak, from slender whitish rootstocks; leaves short, rough, light green, blades 2-4 mm wide; uppermost spike 3-10 mm long, usually staminate but sometimes with some pistillate flowers, the other 3 to 5 spikes pistillate, peduncled, 4-20 mm long; bracts longer than the culms; pistillate scales ovate, shorter than the perigynia or equaling them, brownish, often hyaline-margined; perigynia obovoid, turgid, yellowish-brown, several-nerved, 2-3 mm long, beakless, whitish-papillate-granulose at the base or to the tip; stigmas mostly 2, sometimes 3; achene lenticular or 3-angled, jointed with the style.

Bogs, mossy gravel bars and creek bottoms, 5300 to 6150 feet.

Carex brunnescens (Pers.) Poir.   Brownish Sedge

Cespitose; culms 20-60 cm tall, slender, angled, rough above; leaf blades dark green, flat, narrow, shorter than the culms; bracts inconspicuous; spikes 4 to 9, aggregated or scattered, pale or brownish, gynaecandrous, 4-10 mm long, 4- to 10-flowered; pistillate scales ovate, thin, shorter than the perigynia, brownish with hyaline margins and green center; perigynia elliptic, 2-3 mm long, glabrous, green or brownish, white-puncticulate, fine-veined; beak minute; achenes lenticular, jointed with the style; stigmas 2.

Open woods and streambanks, about 5500 feet.

Carex campylocarpa Holm   Crater Lake Sedge

Plants forming tufts; culms triangular 40-60 cm tall; basal leaf sheaths reddish-purple below, without blades, spotted above; leaf blades flat and soft, 2-4 mm wide; spikes usually 3, the uppermost staminate, 6-8 mm long, the 2 (sometimes 3) others pistillate, 7-10 mm long; lowest bract short and black at the base; pistillate scales ovate, shorter and narrower than the perigynia, purplish-black; perigynia ovoid, nerveless, turgid, 3-4 mm long, at least the middle ones curving outward, greenish below, purplish-mottled,

granular and serrulate above; beak short, black, entire; stigmas 2; achenes lenticular, jointed with the style.
Sphagnum bogs, moist meadows and streambanks, 6000 to about 7600 feet.

Carex canescens L.   Hoary Sedge; Silvery Sedge
   Plants forming large clumps; culms slender, 25-80 cm tall, sharp-angled; leaves soft, glaucous, as long as the culms or shorter, 1-4 mm wide; bracts inconspicuous; spikes 3 to 9, gynaecandrous, 2-12 mm long, clustered or separated from each other, silvery-greenish, pale grayish or straw-colored; scales ovate, acute, hyaline, pale brown with green midrib, about equaling or shorter than the perigynia; perigynia 5 to 30 in a spike, grayish, pale green or straw colored, 2-2.5 cm long, narrowly ovate, lightly-nerved, white-puncticulate; beak short, serrulate; stigmas 2; achene lenticular, jointed with the style.
Swampy meadows at about 7200 feet.

Carex capillaris L.   Hair-like Sedge
   Plant clustered; culms slender, weak, 10-60 cm long; leaves mainly basal, narrow, shorter than the culms; spikes 1 to 5, the uppermost one staminate, the others pistillate, 5-15 mm long, 5- to 25-flowered, on slender drooping peduncles; pistillate scales obovate, greenish or light reddish-brown with broad white margins, shorter and often wider than the perigynia; perigynia elliptic, 2.5-3 mm long, narrow, green or chestnut brown, somewhat angled; beak narrow, white or yellowish, about one-fourth the length of the body; stigmas 3; achene triangular, jointed with the style.
Wet bogs, meadows and woods and mossy streambanks, 5000 to 5500 feet.

Carex concinna R. Br.   Low Northern Sedge
   Plants tufted, rhizomes black-scaly; culms lax and very slender, 5-20 cm tall; leaves basal, shorter than or equaling the culms, stiff, 1-2.5 mm wide; spikes 2 to 4, 3-8 mm long, the uppermost one staminate, the others pistillate, 2- to 12-flowered; lowest bract short, awn-tipped, sheathing; pistillate scales ovate, puberulent, dark brown, hyaline-margined, shorter than the perigynia; perigynia 2-3.5 mm long, turgid and puberulent, 2-ribbed; beak very short, 2-toothed; stigmas 3; achene triangular, jointed with the style.
Moist boggy woods and shady streambanks, about 5500 feet.

Carex concinnoides Mack.   Northwestern Sedge
   Plants with creeping rhizomes; culms smooth, slender, 15-40 cm tall; leaf blades stiff, light green, 5-20 cm long, 2-5 mm wide; spikes 1 to 4, somewhat clustered, the uppermost one staminate, 8-20 mm long, the others pistillate, 5-10 mm long, 5- to 12-flowered; bracts purplish; pistillate scales purplish or reddish-brown, ovate, narrower and either shorter or longer than the perigynia, with broad white ciliate margins; perigynia pubescent, 2.5-3 mm long, usually 3- or 4-sided, nearly nerveless; the beak short, narrow, 2-toothed; stigmas usually 4, sometimes 3 or 5; achene 3- or 4-angled, jointed with the style.
Dry woods, 4000 to 5000 feet.

Carex dioica L. var. **gynocrates** (Wormskj.) Ostenf.   Yellowish Bog Sedge
   C. gynocrates Wormskj.
   Delicate stoloniferous plants; culms very slender, stiff, smooth, not angled, 5-20 cm tall; leaves basal, very narrow and somewhat lax; spike solitary, 5-15 mm long, androgy-

nous, or sometimes entirely staminate or entirely pistillate; pistillate scales light-brown, ovate, acute, a little shorter and broader than the perigynia, the midrib conspicuous; perigynia crowded, lanceolate, 2-3.5 mm long, widely spreading and curved at maturity, nerved, chestnut brown and shining; beak short; stigmas 2; achene lenticular.
Collected only from one mossy bog along Hurricane Creek, at 5300 feet.

Carex disperma Dewey   Soft-leaved Sedge
     Lax, slender, rhizomatous plants; culms angled, weak, 15-60 cm tall; leaves about as long as the culms, the blades flat, narrow, deep green; spikes very small, each with 1 or 2 staminate flowers above the 1 to 5 perigynia below; bracts inconspicuous, or leaf-like and about 2 cm long; scales shorter than the perigynia or equaling them, ovate, straw-colored, hyaline with green midrib; perigynia 2 mm long, flattened, nerved, light green; beak minute, smooth; stigmas 2; achene lenticular, jointed with the style.
Shady boggy woods and mossy streambanks, 5300 to 6500 feet.

Carex eurycarpa Holm   Broad-fruited Sedge
     Tufted plants with long rhizomes; culms 40-90 cm tall, sharply-angled; leaves deep green, 2-5 mm wide, rough-margined, several to a culm; lower bract sheathless, leaf-like with a dark purple spot at each side of the base; spikes 2.5-4 or sometimes up to 8 cm long, the terminal one or 2 staminate, the other 2 to 5 cylindric, mostly pistillate, sometimes androgynous; scales shorter than the perigynia, purplish-brown or nearly black with green midrib; perigynia obovate to suborbicular, greenish to straw- or brownish-colored, nerved, granulose, about 3 mm long; beak very short, entire; stigmas 2; achene lenticular.
Wet meadows, about 5600 feet.

Carex festivella Mack.   Mountain Meadow Sedge
     Tufted plants; culms slender, 30 to 100 cm tall, sharply triangular and rough; leaves 2-6 mm wide; spikes gynaecandrous, 6 to 20 in an ovoid head, 1-2.5 cm long; bracts inconspicuous; scales ovate, shorter than the perigynia, brownish to black with light midrib; perigynia yellowish-green, thin and flat, appressed, 4-5 mm long, ovate, broadly wing-margined and serrulate below; beak smooth, terete, toothed, half as long as the body; stigmas 2; achene lenticular, jointed with the style.
Mountain meadows and ridges, 7000 to 9500 feet.

Carex filifolia Nutt.   Thread-leaved Sedge
     Densely tufted plants without rhizomes; culms wiry, 4-30 cm tall, triangular, smooth; leaves mostly basal, the blades very narrow, stiff, tightly folded, the outer sheaths persistent; spike solitary, 1-2 cm long, the upper part staminate and well developed, the lower with 5 to 15 perigynia; pistillate scales broad, obovate, obtuse or mucronate, concealing the perigynia, brownish with conspicuous shining white margins; perigynia 5 to 15, puberulent, 2-4.5 mm long, obovoid or ellipsoid, dull brownish; beak stout but short, toothed; stigmas 3; achenes triangular.
Dry ridges, 8000 to 9500 feet.

Carex foetida Allioni var. **vernacula** (Bailey) Kukenth.   Native Sedge
     C. vernacula Bailey
     Plants somewhat tufted; culms triangular, from creeping rhizomes, 2-25 cm tall;

leaves mostly basal, flat, thickish and stiff, 2-4 mm wide; bracts not developed; spikes numerous, small, androgynous, few-flowered, closely crowded into an almost globose head 8-16 mm long; pistillate scales brown, ovate, sharp-pointed, about equaling the perigynia; perigynia spreading, dark brown above, lighter below, often with greenish or pale margins, thin-walled, 3.5-4.5 mm long, the beak smooth, one-third the length of the body; stigmas 2; achene lenticular.
Stony slopes above Blue Lake, about 8500 feet.

Carex geyeri Boott   Geyer's Sedge
Culms from long branching rhizomes, slender, clustered, sharp-angled, 10-45 cm tall; leaves stiff, blades thick, flat, 1.5-3.5 mm wide, rough-margined; spike solitary, androgynous, the upper portion light brown, compact, 1-2.5 cm long, with straw-colored scales, the lower part with 1 to 3 perigynia; pistillate scales brownish or chestnut with light midrib and broad hyaline margins, sometimes awned, the upper ones shorter than the perigynia, the lower ones longer; perigynia obovoid, 6 mm long, smooth and shining, greenish or straw-colored, 2-keeled but nerveless, stipitate at the base; beak minute, entire; stigmas 3; achene triangular.
Dry open woods and meadows, 4500 to 6500 feet.

Carex haydeniana Olney   Cloud Sedge
C. nubicola Mack.
Tufted plants; culms 10-35 cm tall, erect or decumbent; leaves short and narrow; spikes 4 to 8, gynaecandrous, crowded into a head 12-18 mm long and 9-18 mm wide; bracts inconspicuous; pistillate scales ovate, acute, narrower and shorter than the perigynia, medium to dark brown with lighter center and hyaline margins; perigynia 15 to 35 per spike, ovate to elliptic or rotund, flat, serrulate and wing-margined, 4.5-6 mm long, dark brown or black, the beak dark and spreading, one-third to half as long as the body, serrulate and often 2-toothed; achenes lenticular, jointed with the style; stigmas 2.
Mountain slopes and lake borders, 8000 to nearly 10,000 feet.

Carex hoodii W. Boott   Hood's Sedge
Densely clustered; culms 30-80 cm tall, stiff and slender; leaves short, soft and flat, 1.5-3.5 mm wide; bracts mostly undeveloped or inconspicuous; spikes 5 to 10, androgynous, closely crowded into a head 8-20 mm long; pistillate scales about equaling the perigynia, ovate, sharp-pointed, brown with green midrib and broad hyaline margins; perigynia 5 to 10 per spike, often spreading, 3-5 mm long, narrowly ovate, green or chestnut-brownish with broad green margins, faintly nerved, serrulate above, smooth and shining, the beak flat, about half as long as the perigynia, sharply toothed; stigmas 2; achenes lenticular, jointed to the style.
Meadows, mountainsides and among rocky debris at the base of cliffs, between 4500 and 9000 feet.

Carex illota Bailey   Small-headed Sedge
Tufted plants; culms 10-35 cm tall, stiff, slender, smooth or rough above; leaves short, mostly basal, flat and stiff, 1.5-3 mm wide; bracts undeveloped; spikes 3 to 5, gynaecandrous, crowded into a small dense brownish-black head about as broad as long; pistillate scales broadly ovate, shorter and narrower than the perigynia, papery, dark brown to

greenish-black with light midrib; perigynia about 3 mm long, faintly nerved, smooth and shining, often spreading, yellowish or greenish to brownish-black, the beak dark, not serrulate; stigmas 2; achenes lenticular.
Bogs, wet meadows, seepy places near lakes, 7000 to about 8500 feet.

Carex jonesii Bailey   Jones's Sedge
Plants cespitose; culms slender, triangular, 15-50 cm tall; leaves short, mainly basal, very narrow; bracts not developed; spikes 5 to 10, androgynous, closely crowded into an ovoid head 1-2 cm long; pistillate scales ovate, longer or shorter than the perigynia, dark brown; perigynia 5 to 10, ascending, chestnut-colored with green margins, ovate-lanceolate, 3-4 mm long, clearly nerved, the beak shallowly toothed, dark brown; stigmas 2, short; achene lenticular, jointed to the style.
Bogs and wet meadows, 5500 to 5800 feet.

Carex kelloggii W. Boott   Kellogg's Sedge
   C. lenticularis Michx.
Plants densely tufted; culms slender, 20-90 cm tall, erect or drooping, usually shorter than the leaves; leaves somewhat glaucous, flat, 1.5-5 mm wide; lowest bract longer than the culm, the others short; spikes 3 to 6, the uppermost one staminate, 1-3.5 cm long, the others pistillate, cylindric, erect, close together or separated below, all nearly sessile, 1.5-6 cm long; pistillate scales narrowly ovate, dark-purplish brown or nearly black with green centers and margins, shorter than the perigynia; perigynia ovate, stipitate, appressed, pale green, 2-3 mm long, nerved and granular, the beak square-cut, dark-tipped, short; stigmas 2; achenes lenticular.
Bogs, wet meadows and lake borders, 4500 to 8200 feet.

Carex laeviculmis Meinsh.   Smooth-stemmed Sedge
Slender plants with short rhizomes; culms weak, 20-80 cm tall; leaves light green, flat and soft, about 2 mm wide; lowest bract evident, the others not; spikes 3 to 8, small and few-flowered, mostly gynaecandrous; pistillate scales keeled, shorter than the perigynia, brownish with green central area; perigynia 3 to 10 to a spike, appressed, ascending or spreading, green or brownish-green, 2.5-4 mm long, evidently nerved, the beak entire or 2-toothed; stigmas 2; achene lenticular.
Bogs in shady woods, 4500 to about 5600 feet.

Carex lanuginosa Michx.   Woolly Sedge
Plants with long creeping rhizomes; culms 30-100 cm tall, angled and rough above, reddish at the base; leaves 2-5 mm wide, rough, reddish and somewhat shredded below; the 1 or 2 lower bracts leaf-like; upper 1 to 3 spikes staminate, 1-6 cm long, the other 2 to 4 spikes pistillate or sometimes androgynous, 1-5 cm long, closely flowered; pistillate scales sharp-pointed or short-awned, brownish or chestnut with green central area, narrower and equaling to longer or shorter than the perigynia; perigynia 25 to 50 to a spike, 2.5-5 mm long, ovoid, densely pubescent, distinctly nerved, dark purplish-brown or chestnut; beak short, the 2 teeth rigid and spreading; stigmas 3; achene 3-angled, jointed with the style.
Bogs and wet meadows, about 5600 feet.

Carex leporinella Mack.   Sierra Hare Sedge

Plants densely clustered; culms smooth, angled, 10-30 cm tall; leaves slender, short, mostly near the base, 1-2 mm wide; spikes 3 to 6, gynaecandrous, in a head 1.5-3 cm long; lowest bract about equaling the inflorescence; pistillate scales ovate, covering the perigynia, acute, reddish brown with hyaline margins and sometimes with green midrib; perigynia 8 to 20, appressed, 3.5-5 mm long narrowly boat-shaped, serrulate and narrowly ciliate-wing-margined, stipitate, greenish to yellow to brownish; beak terete, smooth, entire; stigmas 2; achene lenticular, jointed with the style.
Muddy lake border, 7450 feet.

Carex limnophila Herm.   Water-loving Sedge

Tufted plants; culms 15-45 cm tall; leaves flat and narrow, near the base of the culms; spikes several, gynaecandrous, closely crowded into a head 7-13 mm long; pistillate scales about covering the perigynia, mostly hyaline, brownish to greenish-black; perigynia lanceolate, appressed-ascending, brownish or greenish, 2.5-3 mm long, serrulate above and wing-margined, distinctly nerved and often with 1 or 2 ventral transverse folds below the middle, the beak entire; stigmas 2; achene lenticular.
Wet or moist clearings in woods and along streams at 5600 to 5800 feet.

Carex luzulina Olney

Culms slender, sometimes drooping, 25-75 cm tall; leaves short, mostly basal, blades flat, pale, 3-7 mm wide; lowest bract shorter than the inflorescence; spikes 3 to 7, cylindrical, clustered and short-peduncled, or sessile above, separated and long-peduncled below, 8-24 mm long, the upper one mostly staminate, the others oblong, mostly pistillate or sometimes staminate at the tip of the spike; pistillate scales ovate, shorter than the perigynia, reddish-brown with light or green midrib extending to or near the apex, and hyaline, sometimes erose, margins; perigynia sessile, lanceolate, greenish to purplish-black, faintly nerved, 3.5-5 mm long, tapering to the 2-toothed short rough-margined beak; stigmas 3; achenes 3-angled, jointed with the style.
Bogs and mountain meadows, 5700 to 7000 feet.

Perigynia short-stipitate; beak poorly developed; pistillate scales dark reddish-purple or brownish-black with light center area, the midrib not extending to the apex..var. **ablata** (Bailey) F. J. Herm.

Carex microptera Mack.   Small-winged Sedge

Plants densely tufted, with short rhizomes; culms soft and smooth, not angled, 40-100 cm tall; leaves short, flat, flaccid, 2-5.5 mm wide; spikes gynaecandrous, 5 to 15 in a dense ovoid head; bracts scarcely developed; pistillate scales acute, shorter than the perigynia, brown with lighter midrib; perigynia ascending, 3.5-5 mm long, lanceolate, greenish-yellow to brownish, lightly nerved, serrulate and narrowly winged, beak brown-tipped, serrulate, half the length of the perigynia; stigmas 2; achene lenticular, jointed with the style.
Open woods and meadows, 5600 to 5800 feet.

Carex multicostata Mack.   Thick-fruited Sedge; Many-ribbed Sedge

Plants in loose clumps; culms slender above, triangular, 15-90 cm tall, rough above; leaves mostly basal, flat, short, 2.5-6 mm wide; bracts inconspicuous; spikes gynaecandrous, 3 to 10 in a head 1-3.5 cm long; pistillate scales narrower and shorter than the perigynia, ovate, reddish-brown or chestnut with lighter midrib and broad hyaline margins; perigynia 20 to 30 to a spike, appressed, ovate, thick, 3.5-6 mm long, green or straw-colored to brownish, serrulate and ciliate-wing-margined, conspicuously nerved; beak long, somewhat flattened, obliquely cleft at the tip; stigmas 2; achene lenticular. Mountain meadows and streambanks, about 5800 feet.

Carex nardina Fries var. **hepburnii** (Boott) Kuekenth.   Hepburn's Sedge
   Plants dwarf and densely cespitose; culms slender and wiry, 2-15 cm tall; leaves stiff and very slender, mostly basal; spike solitary, 5-12 mm long, androgynous; pistillate scales ovate, acute, dark with conspicuous midrib; perigynia 1 to 15 per spike, elliptic to obovate, 3-4.5 mm long, flat and glabrous, serrulate above, faintly nerved at maturity and stipitate, the beak 2-toothed, hyaline at the tip; stigmas 3, sometimes 2; achene lenticular or 3-angled.
Dry slopes at about 6000 to 7000 feet.

Carex neurophora Mack.   Alpine nerved Sedge
   Plants loosely clustered; culms 30-70 cm tall; leaves 1.5-4 mm wide, the lower ones nearly bladeless; spikes androgynous, crowded into a dense head 10-25 mm long, the staminate flowers inconspicuous, the pistillate with spreading perigynia; bracts little developed; pistillate scales ovate, brownish with lighter midrib, short; perigynia lanceolate-ovate, shining, 3-4 mm long, several-nerved, sharp-edged above, the beak serrulate, half the length of the perigynia; stigmas 2; achene lenticular, jointed to the style.
Meadows and streambanks, about 5000 to 6000 feet.

Carex nigricans C. A. Meyer   Blackish Sedge
   Plants with stout creeping rhizomes; culms 10-40 cm tall, stiff and smooth; leaves short, 4 to 9 to a culm, the blades 1.5-3 mm wide, not developed on the lower leaves; spike solitary, 8-20 mm long, the upper half staminate, the lower with 10 to 25 perigynia but sometimes the spike entirely staminate or entirely pistillate; bracts not developed; staminate scales persistent; pistillate scales short, dark brown or blackish with lighter margins, deciduous at maturity; perigynia 10 to 50, appressed at first but later spreading or reflexed, about 4 mm long, elliptic-ovate, stipitate, nerveless except for the marginal nerves, deep brown or blackish above, paler or greenish-yellow below, smooth and shining, the beak short, obliquely cleft at the tip; stigmas usually 3; achene 3-angled, jointed to the style.
Moist meadows, streambanks, lake borders and moist slopes, 7200 to about 8500 feet.

Carex norvegica Retz.   Norway Sedge
   C. media R. Br.; *C. vahlii* Schk.
   Culms tufted, slender, flexible, 10-70 cm tall; leaves few, glabrous, soft, up to about 3 mm wide, light green; spikes 2 to 5, sessile or nearly so, the terminal gynaecandrous, 0.6-1.4 cm long, the others pistillate, up to 1 cm long; lowest bract of the inflorescence about as long as the inflorescence; pistillate scales purplish- or brownish-black, whitish-margined, equaling or shorter than the perigynia and about as wide; perigynia elliptic to obovate, 2-3 mm long, yellowish-green to brownish to dark purple, swollen, glabrous; beak short, black; stigmas 3.
Shady streambanks and bogs, about 5300 feet.

Carex paysonis Clokey   Short-stalked Sedge
C. podocarpa Boott; *C. tolmiei* Boott
Plants tufted, with creeping rhizomes; culms 20-50 cm tall, leafy at the base, nearly smooth; leaves fairly stiff, 2.5-4 mm wide; bracts nearly sheathless; spikes 3 to 6, close together or the lowest more distant, the uppermost one staminate, 6-20 mm long; pistillate spikes 2 to 8, closely 20- to 40-flowered, oblong, 8-15 mm long; scales of both staminate and pistillate spikes deep purplish brown or nearly black, the pistillate shorter than the perigynia, ovate to lanceolate, acute; perigynia oblong-ovate, about 4 mm long, thin and flattened, nerveless except the ribs, purplish-brown-mottled above, yellowish below; beak short, cylindric, entire, purplish-black; stigmas 3, sometimes 4; achene triangular, jointed with the style.
Mountain meadows and rocky wooded slopes, 7000 to about 9500 feet.

Carex phaeocephala Piper   Mountain Hare Sedge
C. eastwoodiana Stacey
Plants forming large dense clumps; culms stiff, 5-30 cm tall, rough above; leaves short and stiff, clustered near the base, 1-2 mm wide; bracts short, when developed; spikes 6-12 mm long, gynaecandrous, 2 to 5 in a head 1-3 cm long; pistillate scales lanceolate to ovate, acute, covering the perigynia, dark brown with lighter midrib and hyaline margins, about 4 mm long, broadly-winged, serrulate and ciliate above; beak flat, short, 2-toothed; stigmas 2; achene lenticular.
Open mountain summits and other rocky places, 6700 to 9500 feet.

Carex preslii Steud.   Presl's Sedge
C. pachystachya Cham.
Plants densely tufted; culms slender, rough above, 15-70 cm tall, leaves flat, short, 1-3 mm wide; bracts little developed; spikes gynaecandrous, 2 to 8 in a head 6-20 mm long; pistillate scales equaling or shorter than the perigynia, ovate, acute, reddish brown with lighter center and margins; perigynia ovate, spreading, about 4 mm long, green or yellowish-brown, narrowly winged, serrulate, faintly nerved or nerveless, the beak yellowish-brown, one-third to half the length of the perigynia; stigmas 2; achene lenticular, jointed with the style.
Among boulders, broken rocks and other rocky places, 4500 to 9000 feet.

Carex pseudoscirpoidea Rydb.   Western Single-spiked Sedge
Culms in small tufts, 10-40 cm tall, rough above, reddened at the base; leaves short and stiff, 5 to 10 to a culm, 2-3 mm wide; spike usually solitary, dense, cylindric, staminate in some plants pistillate in others, 1-4 cm long, often with an inconspicuous bract somewhat below the head; scales broad, covering the perigynia, sometimes hairy on the back, brownish-black with hyaline, fringed-ciliate margins; perigynia appressed, ascending, 2-4.5 mm long, obovoid, triangular, pubescent, the beak very short, black, obliquely cleft, stigmas 3; achene triangular.
Moist meadows, lake borders and woods, about 8000 feet.

Carex pyrenaica Wahl.   Pyrenaean Sedge
Plants densely tufted; culms 2-30 cm tall, slender and wiry, smooth, somewhat angled, brownish at the base; leaves equaling or shorter than the culms, very narrow, 2 to 4 to a

culm, the lowest without blades; spike solitary, oblong, dense, 5-20 mm long, staminate flowers few, above the many pistillate ones; bracts not developed; pistillate scales ovate, chestnut to dark brown or blackish with lighter center and margins, shorter than the perigynia, eventually deciduous; perigynia spreading or deflexed at maturity, lanceolate, 3-4 mm long, thin, nerveless, brownish or blackish, stipitate; beak short, 2-toothed; stigmas 3; achene 3-angled, jointed with the style.
Among broken boulders, above 9000 feet.

Carex raynoldsii Dewey   Raynold's Sedge
Plants tufted; rhizomes creeping, short and stout; culms 20-70 cm tall, equaling or longer than the leaves, angled, smooth, purplish at the base, surrounded by last year's leaves; leaves flat, deep green, 3-8 mm wide; spikes 1 to 6, many-flowered, the uppermost one staminate, the others pistillate; bracts short, nearly sheathless; pistillate scales ovate, sharp-pointed, shorter and mostly narrower than the perigynia, dark reddish-brown to blackish or purplish-black with lighter center; perigynia rounded, elliptic or obovate, 3-4.5 mm long, several-nerved, light greenish-brown, the beak very short; stigmas 3; achene 3-angled; style deciduous.
Moist to dry meadows, forest clearings and open woods, 5000 to 7200 feet.

Carex rossii Boott   Ross' Sedge
C. brevipes Boott
Plants densely clustered; culms 5-30 cm tall, wiry, very slender, shorter or longer than the leaves; leaves 1-3 mm wide, the basal sheaths dark red; spikes close together or often with one or more near or at the base of the plant, all 2- to 20-flowered, 3-15 mm long, the uppermost solitary, staminate, the other 2 to 5 pistillate; bracts leaf-like, purplish-brown; pistillate scales ovate, sharp-pointed, purplish-red or chestnut with pale margins, mostly wider and shorter than the perigynia; perigynia 3-4 mm long, 3-sided or nearly globose, pubescent, 2-keeled, greenish, stipitate, the beak narrow, about one-third the length of the perigynium; stigmas 3, long; achene 3-angled, jointed with the style.
Open coniferous woods and meadows, 5000 to 6500 feet.

Carex rostrata Stokes   Beaked Sedge
C. utriculata Boott
Plants with creeping stolons; culms 3-angled, stout, 30-120 cm tall, rough above, mostly shorter than the leaves; leaves flat, nodulose, 2-12 mm wide; bracts long and leaf-like; spikes scattered, many-flowered, the upper 2 or 3 staminate, straw-colored, 1-7 cm long, the others pistillate or androgynous, 2-15 cm long; pistillate scales narrow, lanceolate, shorter or longer than the perigynia, acute or awned, yellowish to brownish; perigynia ovoid, rounded, 4-7 mm long, nerved, shining, greenish, straw-colored or brownish, spreading at maturity, the beak short, 2-toothed; stigmas 3; achene 3-cornered; style persistent.
Bogs and swampy borders of lakes and streams, 5200 to 7200 feet.

Carex scirpoidea Michx.   Canadian Single-spiked Sedge
Rhizomes creeping; culms 10-40 cm tall, reddish at the base; leaves flat, very narrow, brownish and somewhat puberulent; spikes unisexual, mostly solitary, dense, cylindric, 1.5-4 cm long; scales shorter than the perigynia, brown or blackish with whitish margins,

sometimes hairy and ciliate-margined; perigynia hairy, 2-3 mm long, the beak short; stigmas 3; achene 3-angled.
Bogs and streambanks, about 5300 feet.

Carex scopulorum Holm   Holm's Rocky Mountain Sedge
  C. miserabilis Mack.; *C. scopulorum* var. *bracteosa* (Bailey) F. J. Herm.
  Plants stoloniferous; culms 10-90 cm tall, stiff, triangular; leaves 2-7 mm wide, usually shorter than the culms; spikes 1-2.5 cm long, the uppermost spike usually entirely staminate, the lower 2 or 3 pistillate or with some staminate flowers at the tips; bracts evident, non-sheathing, blackish at the base; pistillate scales ovate, narrower and shorter than the perigynia, black, purplish or reddish-brown; perigynia spreading, 2-3 mm long, elliptic or obovate, papillose, turgid, pale greenish or yellowish to brownish-purple, nerveless except the 2 marginal ribs, the beak short and purplish-brown-tinged; stigmas 2; achene lenticular, sometimes 3-angled.
Bogs and swampy meadows, 5000 to about 8200 feet.

Carex spectabilis Dewey   Showy Sedge
  Plants in close tufts from fibrillose rhizomes; culms 20-110 cm tall, slender, purplish at the base; leaves flat, equaling or shorter than the culms, almost bladeless near the base, 2-7 mm wide; bracts shorter than the inflorescence; spikes cylindric, often nodding, 1-3 cm long, densely-flowered, the uppermost one staminate, the other 2 to 4 pistillate or sometimes with some staminate flowers at the tips; pistillate scales shorter than the perigynia, reddish-brown to purplish-black, usually with a white midrib, acute or awn-pointed; perigynia pale greenish or dark, elliptic to ovate, 3-5 mm long, flat, often purple-mottled; beak minute, 2-toothed; stigmas 3; achene 3-angled, jointed with the style.
Mountain meadows, usually above 8000 feet.

Carex stipata Muhl.   Awl-fruited Sedge
  Plants densely clustered, pale green; culms 30-100 cm tall, triangular, scabrous; leaves 4-10 mm wide, soft and flat; spikes numerous, few flowered, androgynous, in a compact head 3-10 cm long; bracts short and inconspicuous or well-developed; scales about equaling the perigynia, light brownish usually with greenish midrib, often awn-tipped; perigynia spreading, 4-5 mm long, stipitate, nerved, somewhat margined, yellowish-green or brownish, the beak flat and serrulate; stigmas 2; achene lenticular, jointed to the style.
Wet streambanks and mossy meadows, about 5500 to 6000 feet.

Carex subnigricans Stacey   Dark Mountain Sedge
  Plants with long creeping rhizomes; culms stiff, 2-20 cm tall; leaves very narrow, mostly basal, pale and stiff; spike solitary, androgynous, cylindric, 1-2 cm long; bracts not developed; pistillate scales light to dark or reddish brown with broad whitish margins, about as long as the perigynia; perigynia 10 to 40, ascending, elliptic to ovate, reddish-brown, nerveless and stipitate, 3.5-4 mm long, the beak short; stigmas 3; achene 3-cornered.
Meadows above 8000 feet.

Carex vesicaria L.   Inflated Sedge
  Plants tufted; culms 30-100 cm tall, angled, purplish at the base, mostly shorter than

the leaves; leaves 2-8 mm wide, flat, nodulose; some bracts developed; upper 2 to 4 spikes staminate or androgynous, 2-7 cm long, narrow, with long, white-tipped scales; the lower 1 to 3 spikes closely-flowered, pistillate, 1-7 cm long and up to 2 cm wide; scales shorter and narrower than the perigynia, acute to short-awned, yellowish to reddish-brown with light center and whitish margins; perigynia lanceolate to ovoid, smooth and shining, inflated, 5-8 mm long, greenish to yellowish or brownish, nerved, the beak 2-toothed; stigmas 3; achene 3-angled, continuous with the persistent style.
Wet meadows, swamps and shallow water, 7000 to 9000 feet.

Dulichium Pers.

Tall perennials with round or triangular hollow, jointed culms and short grass-like leaves, the lower ones without blades; spikes short, axillary, peduncled; spikelets 2-ranked, flat, many-flowered; scales of the spikelet 2-ranked, decurrent on the rachis; flowers perfect; perianth of 6 to 9 downward-barbed bristles; stamens 3; style 2-cleft, persistent; achene narrowly oblong.

Dulichium arundinaceum (L.) Britt.

Culms 30-100 cm tall; leaves flat, 2-15 cm long, 2.5-8 mm wide, the lower sheaths bladeless, brown near the tips; spikes peduncled, 4-25 mm long; spikelets 7 to 10 to a spike, narrow, spreading, 6- to 12-flowered, 1-2.5 cm long; scales 5-8 mm long, acuminate, strongly-nerved, brownish; perianth bristles brownish, longer than the achene; style persistent as a beak on the achene.
Collected by W. C. Cusick in a peat bog at Duck Lake in the Wallowa Mountains.

Eleocharis R. Br.

Annual or perennial small herbs; culms clustered, angled, terete, flat or grooved; leaves mostly basal bladeless sheaths or scales; spikelets solitary and terminal, bractless; scales hyaline, spirally attached, the lowest usually empty; flowers perfect; perianth of 1 to 12 barbed bristles, or none; stamens 2 or 3; style 2- or 3-cleft, the base expanded in some species and remaining as a tubercle at the top of the achene; achene lenticular, plano-convex or 3-angled.

1. Stigmas 3; achene mostly triangular
    2. Tubercle ¼ as long as the achene ....*E. acicularis*
    2. Tubercle not apparent on the achene ....*E. pauciflora*
1. Stigmas 2; achene not triangular ....*E. palustris*

Eleocharis acicularis (L.) R. & S.   Needle Spike-rush

Small tufted perennials with creeping rhizomes; culms densely clustered, slender, weak, 4-angled and grooved, 1-20 cm tall; basal sheaths truncate, reddish or purplish; spikelet 2-7 mm long, 2- to 17-flowered; scales oblong, thin, deciduous, pale with a green midrib and a brown stripe on either side, and pale margins; bristles 3 or 4 and minute, or none; stigmas 3; achenes about 1 mm long, pale, rounded to 3-angled, ribbed and cross-ridged as well; tubercle well developed and conspicuous, triangular-conic.
Shallow water and muddy borders of lakes, about 7000 to 7500 feet.

Eleocharis palustris (L.) R. & S.   Pale or Creeping Spike-rush
    E. mamillata Lindl.
Perennial with creeping rhizomes; culms 5-100 cm tall, clustered or scattered, slender

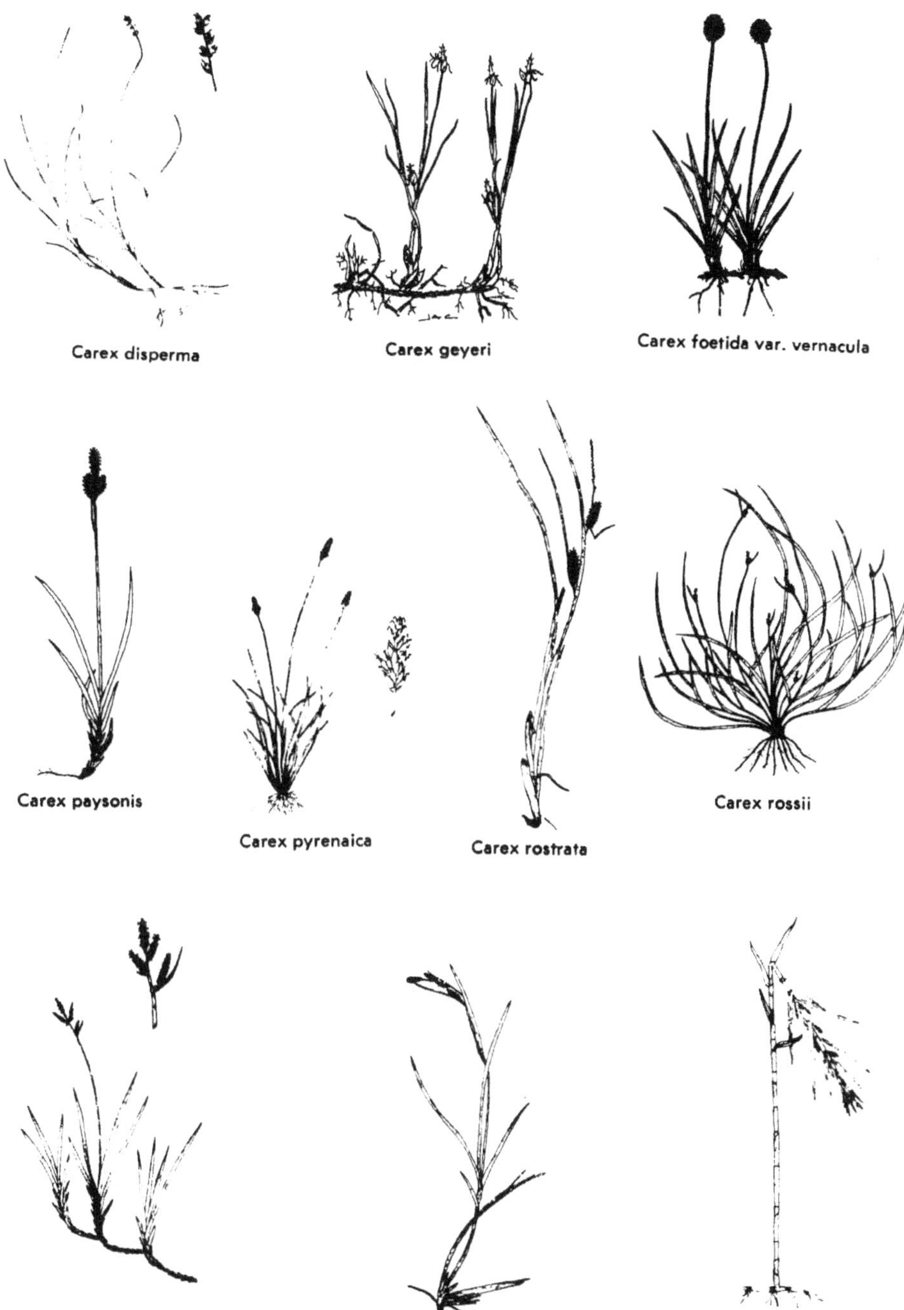

Carex disperma
Carex geyeri
Carex foetida var. vernacula
Carex paysonis
Carex pyrenaica
Carex rostrata
Carex rossii
Carex scopulorum
Carex spectabilis
Dulichium arundinaceum

to stout; sheaths often dark or reddish below, truncate above; spikelet 5-25 mm long, lanceolate to lanceolate-ovate, dense, brownish; scales pale green or dark purplish with green midrib and hyaline margins; perianth bristles sometimes none, usually 4, sometimes 5 or 6, barbed, longer than the achene; stigmas usually 2; achenes smooth to roughened, lenticular, yellow to brown, the tubercle developed, conic-triangular, constricted at the base.
Shallow muddy water and boggy moist lake banks from about 5700 to about 8000 feet.

Eleocharis pauciflora (Lightf.) Link   Few-Flowered Spike-rush
Scirpus pauciflorus Lightf.

Perennial herbs with slender reddish rhizomes bearing small tubers or buds; culms slender, 5-40 cm tall, clustered or scattered; sheaths truncate; spikelets 4-8 mm long, 2- to 10-flowered; scales lanceolate or ovate, all flower-bearing, dark brown with lighter midrib and margins, the 2 lower longer than the others; bristles 2 to 6, or none, barbed, shorter or longer than the achene; stigmas 3; achene 3-angled, finely reticulate, obovoid, 2-3 mm long, light grayish-brown, the beak pale, continuous with the achene.
Swamps and boggy borders of mountain lakes, about 7000 to 8000 feet.

Eriophorum L.

Perennial bog herbs with spreading rhizomes; culms erect, terete or triangular, mostly solid; leaves few, the basal grass-like, the upper sometimes reduced to sheaths; spikelet solitary and capitate, or several in an umbel, the inflorescence subtended by 1 or more bracts, or sometimes bractless; flowers usually perfect; perianth of 6 or more soft, very long, thin, white or brown bristles persisting in fruit; stamens 1 to 3; style 3-cleft; achene 3-angled, obovoid or ellipsoid, often appearing beaked at the tip.

Eriophorum gracile Koch   Slender Cotton-grass

Slender perennial bog plants; culms triangular to terete, 20-60 cm long; leaves narrow, 3 cm long or less, channeled, the upper shorter than the sheath, the tips blunt, the basal missing at flowering time; involucral bracts about 1 cm long; spikelets 7-16 mm long, usually 2 to 4 but sometimes 1 or up to 6, mostly nodding on slender pedicels; scales ovate, green or gray to nearly black with pale margins and prominent midrib; perianth bristles white, numerous, 1-2 cm long; achenes yellowish to light brown, about 3 mm long.
Shallow water, boggy meadows and swampy borders of lakes, about 5000 to 7000 feet.

Kobresia Willd.

Grass-like perennial sedges of mountainous places; culms solid, angled, leafy below; leaves narrow with closed sheaths; inflorescence a simple or compound spike of few-flowered spikelets; spikelets 1-flowered, the lower usually pistillate and the upper staminate; flowers without a perianth, subtended by scarious bracts or scales, the pistillate scale surrounding the achene but with open margins; stamens 3; stigmas 2 or 3, linear; achene sessile, 3-angled.

Spike solitary..*K. bellardii*
Spikes more than one, usually 3 to 12..*K. simpliciuscula*

Kobresia bellardii (All.) Degland
Densely tufted plants; culms slender, 2-50 cm tall; leaves equaling or shorter than the

culms, very narrow and revolute-margined, old brown sheaths of previous years persistent at the base but bladeless; spike solitary, 3 cm long; spikelets 8 to 20, mostly androgynous; scales ovate, scarious with brown center, 3-4 mm long; achene about 1.5 mm long, shorter than its scale.
Rarely collected in our mountains; alpine ridges.

Kobresia simpliciuscula (Wahl.) Mack.

Robust perennial; culms stiff, slender, 10-50 cm tall, striate, sharp-angled and rough above; leaves mostly near the base and about half the length of the culms, channeled, stiff, very narrow, the older persistent basal sheaths often with blades; inflorescence 1-4 cm long; spikes usually 3 to 12, 5-15 mm long; spikelets in each spike few, few-flowered, the upper staminate, the others androgynous or pistillate; bracts ovate, obtuse to acutish or mucronate, cinnamon brown; the pistillate scale (or incomplete perigynium) about 3 mm long, brown and shining, open nearly to the base; achene terete, a little longer than its scale; stigmas elongated, dark brown.
Reported by Morton E. Peck: "Banks of Hurricane Creek." (Based on collection of William C. Cusick?)

Scirpus [Tourn.] L.

Annual or perennial herbs; culms solid, angled or terete; leaves with closed sheaths, the blades developed or sometimes reduced or missing; spikelets in capitate heads, in simple or compound umbels, or solitary, terete or flattened, with or without bracts; flowers perfect, each subtended by a scale; scales spirally arranged in the spikelet, sometimes awn-tipped; perianth of 1 to 6 slender barbed bristles, or sometimes none in some species; stamens 2 or 3; style deciduous, 2- or 3-cleft, not expanded at the base; fruit a lenticular or 3-angled achene.

Scirpus microcarpus Presl   Small-fruited Bulrush

Perennial with scaly creeping rhizomes; culms stout, 60-150 cm tall; leaves grasslike, rough-margined, some of them often longer than the inflorescence, the sheaths loose, reddish-purple; involucral bracts several, sheathless, equaling or longer than the inflorescence; spikelets small, numerous at the ends of the spreading rays of large loose compound umbels; scales thin, dark brown or blackish with a green midrib which may be awn-pointed at the tip; bristles 4 to 6, barbed downwardly; achene lenticular, nearly white to pale brownish, slightly beaked.
Moist to wet streambanks, about 4500 to 5500 feet.

GRAMINEAE   Grass Family

Annual or perennial herbs, or rarely woody plants; stems (culms) usually hollow, swollen at the nodes; leaves 2-ranked, usually parallel-veined, composed of three parts: a sheath which encloses the culm by the overlapping of its margins, a blade which is usually flat and conspicuous, and an often inconspicuous colorless or hairy appendage (the ligule) just above the juncture of the sheath and the blade; flowers usually aggregated into spikelets of 2 to many 2-ranked flowers subtended by bracts or scales, the 2 lowermost bracts (the glumes) usually empty, rarely one or both glumes obsolete; flowers small, mostly perfect, without a perianth, usually enclosed by 2 scales (the

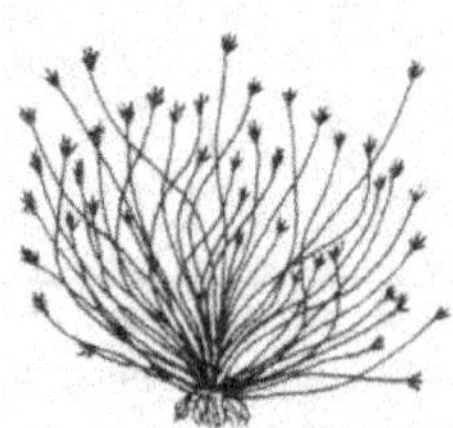

Eleocharis acicularis

Eriophorum gracile

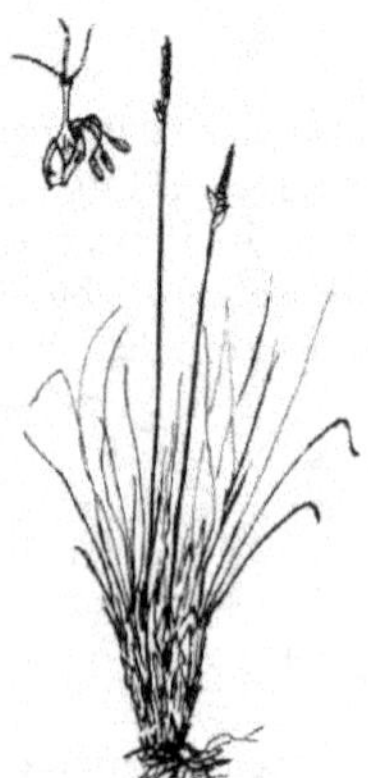

Kobresia bellardii

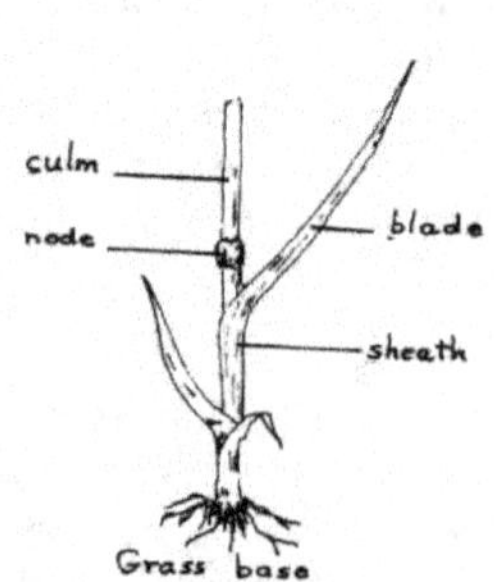

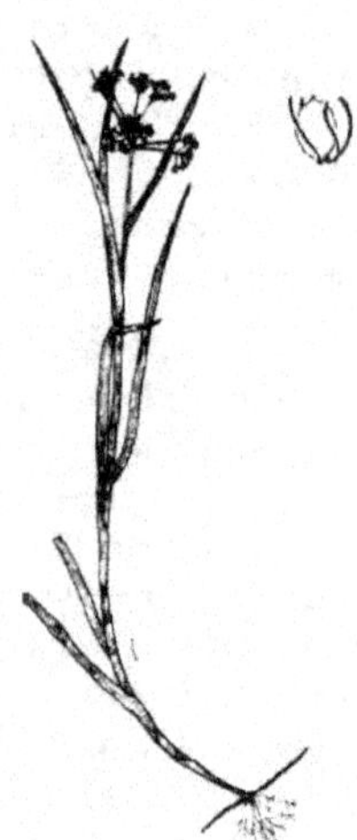

Scirpus microcarpus

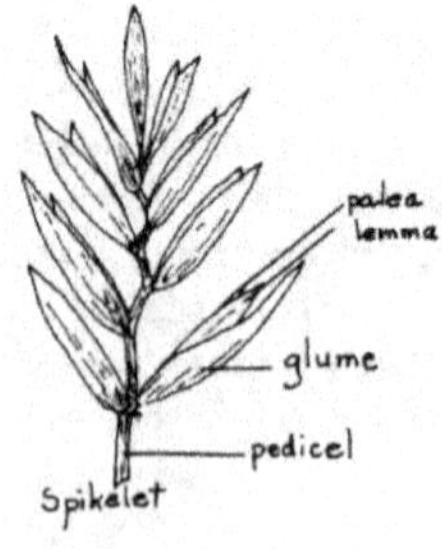

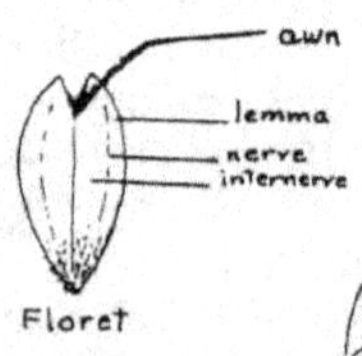

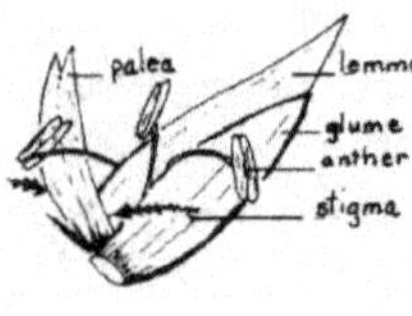

lemmas) which envelop the inner 2-nerved bract (the palea) ; stamens 1 to 6, usually 3; pistil 1, ovary 1-celled, 1-ovuled; styles usually 2, stigmas plumose; fruit a caryopsis or grain.

1. Spikelets with a pedicel (or stalk), in open or contracted, sometimes spike-like panicles
  2. Spikelets 1-flowered (Agrostideae)
    3. Spikelets breaking up below the glumes (which fall off with the spikelets) ; glumes without awns
      4. Panicle dense, compact, narrow, spike-like............*Alopecurus*
      4. Panicle open, the branches flexible, spreading or drooping............*Cinna*
    3. Spikelets breaking up above the glumes
      5. Lemmas hardened at maturity, rounded and awned; callus hairs conspicuous
        6. Awn long, persistent, twisted, bent more than once............*Stipa*
        6. Awn short or missing, not twisted, bent only once when present ......*Oryzopsis*
      5. Lemmas not hardened at maturity
        7. Glumes longer than the lemma, or at least equaling it
          8. Glumes ciliate on the keel............*Phleum*
          8. Glumes not ciliate on the keel
            9. Florets with hairs at the base half as long as the lemmas; palea present............*Calamagrostis*
            9. Florets naked at the base or with short hairs; palea small when present, or missing............*Agrostis*
        7. Glumes slightly shorter than the lemma (including the awn) ; lemma awned from the tip or the back or awn-pointed; plants small and wiry............*Muhlenbergia*
  2. Spikelets with 2 or more flowers
    10. Glumes as long as, or slightly longer than, the lemmas (or at least longer than the lowest lemma excluding the awn); lemmas usually with an awn on the back (Aveneae)
      11. Lemmas 2-cleft at the tip, with a flat bent or twisted awn arising from between the teeth............*Danthonia*
      11. Lemmas toothed but not as above
        12. Glumes 2-3 cm long; spikelets 2-flowered (sometimes with a rudimentary third floret), nodding; lemmas shallow-toothed; annual plants............*Avena*
        12. Glumes mostly less than 1 cm long; spikelets not nodding, mostly 2-flowered
          13. Lemma rounded on the back, awned from the middle or just below, abruptly narrowed and with 2 to 4 teeth at the tip............*Deschampsia*
          13. Lemma keeled on the back, the awn when present from above the middle, the tip mostly inconspicuously 2-toothed
            14. Rachilla joints very short, hairless or minutely hairy; lemma awnless or with a straight awn from between the minute apical teeth............*Koeleria*
            14. Rachilla joints slender, long-hairy; lemma with a bent awn on the back, from below the tip (sometimes missing or minute in *T. wolfii*) ....*Trisetum*
    10. Glumes shorter than the lowest lemma; lemmas without an awn, or the awn from the tip but not from the back below the tip (Festuceae)
      15. Lemmas keeled on the back
        16. Spikelets conspicuously compressed, in crowded one-sided clusters at the tips of the stiff panicle branches............*Dactylis*
        16. Spikelets not so conspicuously compressed, not usually one-sided
          17. Lemmas awned from a 2-cleft tip (except *B. brizaeformis* which is awnless) ; spikelets large............*Bromus*

17. Lemmas without awns; spikelets small..*Poa*

15. Lemmas rounded on the back (*Festuca* with a short slight keel at the tip)

18. Glumes papery; upper florets unlike the others, sterile or rudimentary; spikelets brownish or purplish, not green....................... *Melica*

18. Glumes not papery; florets all alike

19. Nerves of the lemma not coming together at the tip (or only very slightly so), remaining parallel; lemma without awns, mostly blunt at the tip...*Glyceria*

19. Nerves of the lemma coming together at the tip; lemma awned or awn-pointed

20. Tip of the lemma deeply 2-cleft; lemma awned or awn-tipped (except in *B. brizaeformis*)..................................... *Bromus*

20. Tip of the lemma not cleft; lemmas awned from the tip, or awn-pointed ....*Festuca*

1. Spikelets without pedicels (stalks) or nearly so, arranged on opposite sides of a single terminal rachis, aggregated into spikes or spike-like racemes (Hordeae)

21. Spikelets solitary at each joint of the rachis (rarely 2 in *Agropyron*), placed flatwise to the rachis; plants perennials; spikelets 2- to several-flowered....................*Agropyron*

21. Spikelets in 2's or 3's at each joint of the rachis, 1- to 6-flowered

22. Spikelets 1-flowered, in 3's at the nodes, not all alike, the lateral pair pedicellate and usually staminate..*Hordeum*

22. Spikelets 2- to 6-flowered, usually in 2's at the nodes, all alike; spikes dense

23. Rachis of the spike continuous, not breaking apart at maturity (though the rachilla breaks apart above the glumes and between the florets); glumes not elongating..*Elymus*

23. Rachis of the spike breaking up at the joints (below the glumes) at maturity; glumes usually awl-shaped, bristle-like and long, the spike appearing bristly..*Sitanion*

Agropyron Gaertn.

Coarse, mostly perennial grasses, often with creeping rhizomes; spikes large, green or purplish; spikelets sessile, usually solitary at each joint of the rachis, 3- to 12-flowered, breaking apart above the glumes and between the florets; glumes about equal, stiff, usually several-nerved and shorter than the first lemma, blunt, rounded or acute, awnless to short-awned; lemmas rounded on the back, firm, 5- to 7-nerved, usually acute, awnless or awned; palea about as long as the lemma.

1. Plants with creeping rhizomes; lemmas hairy; stems and leaves usually bluish-green...*A. dasystachyum*

1. Plants without creeping rhizomes, or the rhizome short; lemmas essentially without hairs; plants not usually bluish

2. Anthers about 5 mm long; spikelets about as long as the internodes of the rachis....*A. spicatum*

2. Anthers not over 2.5 mm long; spikelets crowded, up to 2 or 3 times as long as the internodes; glumes 4- to 7-nerved...*A. caninum*

Agropyron caninum (L.) Beauv.   Wheat-grass

Perennial essentially without rhizomes; leaf blades scabrous to long-hairy, usually flat, 2-5 mm broad; culms mostly 50-100 cm tall; spikes compact, about 4-15 cm long, the rachis slow to break apart; spikelets usually overlapping, 2 to 3 times as long as the internodes, 12-17 mm long, 4- to 5-flowered; glumes oblong-elliptic, hyaline-margined, 4- to 7-nerved, acute to awned; lemmas glabrous, ciliate-margined to scabrous or soft-hairy, awned to awnless, the awn mostly 5-25 mm long, straight or bent; anthers mostly 1-1.6 mm long.

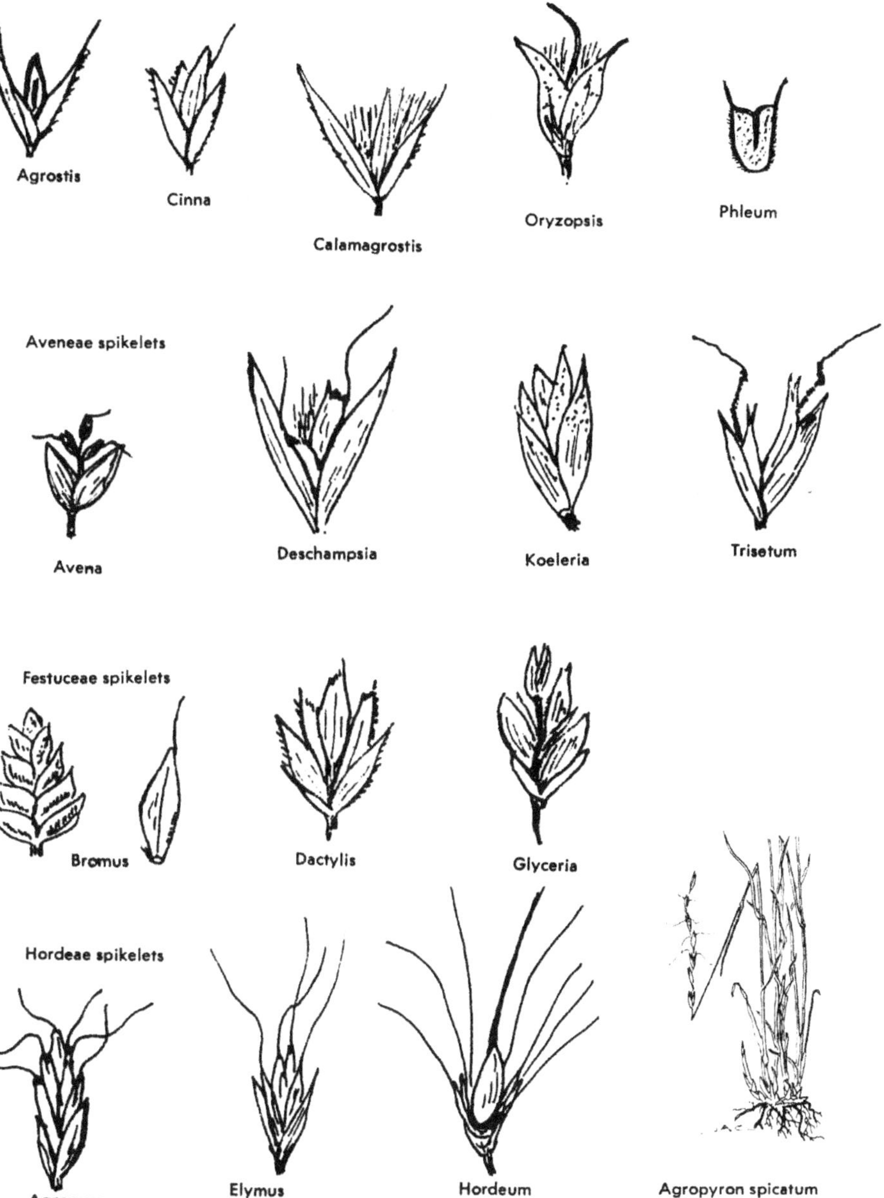

Agrostideae spikelets
Agrostis
Cinna
Calamagrostis
Oryzopsis
Phleum
Aveneae spikelets
Avena
Deschampsia
Koeleria
Trisetum
Festuceae spikelets
Bromus
Dactylis
Glyceria
Hordeae spikelets
Agropyron
Elymus
Hordeum
Agropyron spicatum

Streambanks at low elevations to dry rocky slopes and ridges at high elevations, 4500 to about 9600 feet.

1. Spike broad, compact, usually 4-8 cm long; lemmas and awns usually purplish
    2. Lemmas awnless or the awns up to 6 mm long; plants of upper elevations..........
      var. **latiglume** (Scribn. & Smith) C. L. Hitchc. (*A. trachycaulum* (Link) Malte)
    2. Lemmas with awns mostly 8-20 mm long; plants of low elevations......................
      var. **andinum** (Scribn. & Smith) C. L. Hitchc. (*A. violaceum* (Hornem.) Lange
            var. *andinum* Scribn. & Smith; *A. subsecundum* (Link) Hitchc.)
1. Spike slender, mostly 8-20 cm long; lemmas and awns rarely
  purplish..var. **majus** Scribn. (*A. tenerum* Vasey)

Agropyron dasystachyum (Hook.) Scribn.   Downy Wheat-grass
Perennial, usually glaucous; culms 40-100 cm tall, with creeping wiry rhizomes; blades shorter than the culms, stiff, scabrous, 1-4 mm wide; spike 5-20 cm long, not breaking apart; spikelets 4- to 11-flowered, 1-2.5 cm long; glumes 3- to 7-nerved, acute or awn-tipped, 6-12 mm long, usually hairy; lemmas obtuse, acute or awn-pointed, densely to slightly hairy, about 1 cm long.
Open grasslands and woods, 4500 to about 6000 feet.

Agropyron spicatum (Pursh) Scribn. & Smith   Wheat Bunch-grass
Green or glaucous, without rhizomes; culms slender, 40-120 cm tall, often in large dense clumps; leaf blades 1-3.5 mm wide, pubescent on one or both sides; spike slender, loose and open, 8-20 cm long; spikelets narrow, 6- to 8-flowered, 1-2 cm long; glumes narrow, 4- to 5-nerved, obtuse to acute or short-awned, 8-10 mm long; lemmas 1-1.5 cm long, awnless or the awn widely spreading, 1-2 cm long.
Dry meadows, open woods and rocky slopes and ridges, 4500 to about 9400 feet.

Agrostis L.

Delicate annual or usually perennial grasses; culms slender; leaf blades soft and scabrous; panicle spike-like or open; spikelets small, 1-flowered, breaking up above the glumes; glumes nearly equal, 1-nerved, acute to awn-pointed, keeled and usually scabrous; lemma thin, usually shorter than the glumes, 3-nerved, awnless or with a short dorsal awn, often hairy on the callus; palea when present usually shorter than the lemma.

1. Palea present, 2-nerved, at least half as long as the lemma
  2. Rachilla continued behind the palea as a minute bristle; small plants of mountain
    bogs and wet places
    3. Spikelets 2 mm long; leaves 2 mm wide .... *A. thurberiana*
    3. Spikelets 3-4.5 mm long; leaves about 1 mm wide .... *A. aequivalvis*
  2. Rachilla not evident as a bristle
    4. Plants alpine dwarfs without stolons, mostly up to 15 cm tall; panicle open..... *A. humilis*
    4. Plants of lower elevations, 20-50 cm tall, the culms stolon-like, creeping and
      rooting, only the upper part ascending; panicle not open.................*A. alba* var. *palustris*
1. Palea obsolete, or a very small nerveless scale (0.5 mm or so in *A. exarata*)
      5. Panicle narrow, compact, some of the lower branches bearing spikelets
        from the base
        6. Culms slender, densely tufted, 10-25 cm tall; lemma awnless, the
          midnerve reaching the tip; glumes scabrous on the keel only near
          the tip...*A. variabilis*

6. Culms stout, not in tufts although with dense basal foliage, 20-120 cm tall; lemma awned or not; glumes scabrous on the keel all the way..*A. exarata*
5. Panicle open, the capillary branches slender, wavy, scabrous, upright, spreading or drooping, without basal spikelet-bearing branches................*A. scabra*

Agrostis aequivalvis (Trin.) Trin.   Northern Bent-grass

Culms clustered, 20-80 cm tall; blades slightly scabrous, 1-3 mm wide; panicle open, 5-20 cm long; spikelets usually purplish, 3-4.5 mm long; glumes about equal, sharp-pointed; lemma equaling the glumes; palea slightly shorter than the lemma; rachilla minutely hairy.
Collected by William C. Cusick: "subalpine streambanks of Eagle Creek." No date. Apparently not collected since.

Agrostis alba L. var. **palustris** (Huds.) Pers.   Creeping Bent-grass

A. depressa Vasey

Culms 30-100 cm long; stems creeping and rooting, stolon-like, only the upper part erect; leaf blades short, narrow, stiff; panicle 5-30 cm long, usually compressed but sometimes loose, the lower branches in whorls; glumes acute, 2-3 mm long, the keel scabrous; lemmas shorter than the glumes; palea ½ to ⅔ the length of the lemma.
Boggy or moist shady woods, 4500 to about 5300 feet.

Agrostis exarata Trin.   Western Bent-grass

Perennial, mostly tufted; culms 20-120 cm tall, sometimes lying close to the ground and rooting at the nodes; leaf blades 1-10 mm wide, usually flat and scabrous; panicle narrow, open or closed and spike-like, 1-30 cm long, green or purplish; glumes about equal, 2.5-4 mm long, acute to awn-tipped, scabrous on the keel and sometimes also on the back; lemma 1.5-2.5 mm long, awnless or awned from the middle of the back; callus slightly hairy; palea very small.
Moist meadows and open coniferous forest, 4800 to about 7500 feet.

Agrostis humilis Vasey   Mountain Bent-grass

Culms very slender, tufted, 2-30 cm tall; leaves mostly basal, 2-10 cm long, about 1 mm wide; panicle narrow, 1-8 cm long, deep purple, somewhat spreading or more compact; spikelets about 2 mm long; glumes and lemmas awnless, about 1.5-2 mm long; palea a little shorter than the lemma.
Moist to wet meadows at about timberline, 7500 to about 7800 feet.

Agrostis scabra Willd.   Rough Bent-grass

A. hiemalis of some authors.

Culms 20-80 cm tall in small dense tufts; leaves mostly basal, scabrous, 1-3 mm wide; panicle open, 10-30 cm long, the many branches ascending to widely spreading or drooping; spikelets 2-3 mm long, usually at the ends of the delicate branchlets; glumes unequal, 1.5-2.5 mm long, acuminate, usually purplish; lemma shorter than the glumes, awnless or with a tiny awn.
Grassy mountain meadows, moist open woods and exposed rocky slopes, 4500 to about 9600 feet.

Agrostis thurberiana Hitchc.   Thurber's Bent-grass
Culms slender, in small tufts, 15-40 cm tall; leaves basal, crowded, 1-3 mm wide; panicle narrow, drooping, 5-10 cm long; spikelets green or deep purple, 2 mm long; glumes 2 mm long; lemma awnless, slightly shorter than the glumes, blunt and toothed at the tip; palea shorter than the lemma.
Moist or swampy meadows, mostly around lakes, 7000 to about 8000 feet.

Agrostis variabilis Rydb.   Variable Bent-grass
Densely tufted perennial; culms slender, 10-25 cm tall; leaves mostly basal, the blades 1-2 mm wide, blunt at the tip; panicle narrow, compact, 2-6 cm long; spikelets 2 mm long; glumes 2-2.5 mm long, scabrous, often purplish; lemma shorter than the glumes, usually awnless but rarely with a short awn from just below the middle.
Rocky creek bed on a steep exposed slope, at 9550 feet.

Alopecurus L.

Annual or perennial grasses; culms branched; leaf blades flat; panicles dense and spike-like; spikelets flattened, 1-flowered, small, breaking up below the glumes; glumes about equal, usually united at the base, ciliate on the keel, the tips rounded, blunt or acute; lemma 3- to 5-nerved, about equaling the glumes, the infolded margins united at the base, the awn straight, twisted or bent, from below the middle of the back; palea missing.

Alopecurus aequalis Sobol.   Little Meadow Fox-tail
Culms erect, spreading or lying near the ground, often rooting at the nodes when in standing water, 15-70 cm tall; leaf blades 1-5 mm wide; panicle narrow-cylindric, pale green, 2-8 cm long, about 4 mm wide; spikelets about 2.5 mm long; glumes about 2 mm long, united near the base, long-hairy or silky over the back; lemma glabrous, about equaling the glumes, the margins united about halfway, the awn straight, from about the middle of the back.
In shallow water, wet mud or low grassy open places, often near lakes, 5000 to about 7600 feet.

Avena L.

Annual or perennial grasses; panicles open, usually few-flowered; spikelets large, breaking above the glumes and between the florets; glumes about equal, thin, longer than the upper floret, 7- to 9-nerved; lemmas rigid, 5- to 9-nerved, rounded on the back, 2-toothed, the dorsal awn bent, twisted, straight or sometimes missing.

Avena sativa L.   Oats
Coarse annual; culms 30-80 cm tall; leaves numerous, the blades flat, scabrous, 4-8 mm wide; panicle loose and open; spikelets mostly 2-flowered, the florets not separating easily from the glumes; glumes 2-2.5 cm long, usually longer than the florets; lemmas rigid, thick and veiny, the awn straight, slightly twisted or curved, often missing from the second floret but usually present on the first.
Escaped from cultivation. Campground, open mixed woods, 5100 feet.

Bromus L.

Annual or perennial grasses; leaf sheaths mostly closed; leaf blades soft and flat;

panicles compact and dense or very open and lax; spikelets large, several- to many-flowered, breaking up above the glumes and between the florets; glumes unequal, acute, the first 1- to 3-nerved, the second usually 3- to 5-nerved; lemmas longer than the glumes, keeled or rounded on the back, 5- to 9-nerved, 2-cleft, the awn missing or usually protruding from between the teeth; palea usually shorter than the lemma, ciliate on the keels.

1. Plants annuals, fibrous-rooted
    2. Panicle mostly loose, open, ascending, spreading or drooping; pedicels mostly longer than the spikelets
        3. Awn missing or no more than 1 mm long; spikelets thick, swollen________*B. brizaeformis*
        3. Awn present, 4-12 mm long; spikelets not much swollen
            4. Spikelets 13-20 mm long, flattened; awns 4-10 mm long, straight______*B. commutatus*
            4. Spikelets 20-25 mm long, not flattened; awns 8-12 mm long, often bent or twisted________*B. japonicus*
    2. Panicle mostly narrow and close, though sometimes the lower branches drooping; pedicels often quite short
        5. Awns 4-10 mm long; pedicels short
            6. Spikelets flattened; panicle open, loose________*B. commutatus*
            6. Spikelets not flattened; panicle narrow, crowded, erect________*B. mollis*
        5. Awns 10-15 mm long, the pedicels long or short; plant often reddish, the spikelets slender________*B. tectorum*
1. Plants perennials
    7. Panicles mostly open, loose, spreading, often drooping, 7-18 cm long; pedicels longer than the spikelets
        8. Anthers 1.5-2 mm long; spikelets 15-23 mm long; awns mostly 3-4 mm long____*B. ciliatus*
        8. Anthers 3-5 mm long; spikelets 20-28 mm long; awns mostly 3-8 mm long______*B. vulgaris*
    7. Panicles erect or ascending, mostly narrow, 10-32 cm long; pedicels long or short
        9. Pedicels longer than the spikelets; spikelets 18-32 long
            10. Spikelets flattened; lemmas keeled on the back________*B. carinatus*
            10. Spikelets not flattened; lemmas rounded on the back________*B. orcuttianus*
        9. Pedicels shorter than the spikelets; spikelets 20-30 mm long
            11. Panicle closely erect, 8-12 cm long; awns not over 4 mm long; spikelets not flattened________*B. suksdorfii*
            11. Panicle more open, often spreading, 10-25 cm long; awns 3-15 mm long; spikelets flattened________*B. carinatus*

Bromus brizaeformis Fisch. & Mey.   Rattlesnake grass

Clustered annual; culms 20-60 cm tall; leaf blades hairy, 2-5 mm wide; panicle 1-sided, 4-15 cm long; spikelets few, flattened or swollen, drooping on slender branches, 8- to 18-flowered, 1.5-3 cm long; glumes obtuse, the second broader and twice as long as the first; lemmas inflated, about 1 cm long, broadly ovate, pale and smooth, awnless or nearly so.
Dry rocky open ground, 4500 to about 5000 feet.

Bromus carinatus H. & A.   California Brome-grass
    B. marginatus Nees

Erect perennial grass; culms 30-100 cm tall; leaf blades scabrous or pilose, 3-12 mm wide; panicle narrow and lax, 10-25 cm long, the lower branches spreading or drooping; spikelets 5- to 10-flowered, 2-3 cm long; glumes keeled, 7-11 mm long, acuminate; lemmas keeled, 10-20 mm long, fine- or short-hairy to nearly hairless, the awn straight, 3-15 mm long.
Wet meadows and woods, and streambanks, 4500 to about 8000 feet.

Leaves and stems often hairy; leaves mostly over 5 mm wide;
panicle not dense.............................var. **carinatus** (*B. marginatus* var. *seminudus* Shear)
With the species.

Bromus ciliatus L.   Fringed Brome-grass
B. richardsonii Link var. *pallidus* (Hook.) Shear
Plant pale green; culms slender, 50-120 cm tall, hairy only at the nodes; leaf blades
soft and lax, hairless or long-hairy, 4-10 mm wide; panicle loose and open, 7-25 cm long,
the branches drooping; spikelets 2-3 cm long, 7- to 9-flowered; glumes 1- or 3-nerved;
lemmas 8-15 mm long, hairless on the back to the tip, to densely silky-hairy near the
outer nerves and lower margins; awn straight, 3-5 mm long.
Swampy meadows, about 5000 to 6000 feet.

Bromus commutatus Schrad.   Hairy Chess
Annual; culms 20-100 cm tall; leaf blades long-hairy, 3-5 mm wide; panicle loose and
narrow, 7-15 cm long; spikelets flattened and nodding, 12-20 mm long, 5- to 9-flowered;
glumes obtuse, 3- to 9-nerved; lemmas hairless, about 1 cm long, angled just above the
middle, the margins inrolled; awn 4-10 mm long, straight or bent.
Dry open grassland on the moraines, 4500 to about 5000 feet.

Lemmas pubescent; with the species...................................var. **apricorum** Simonkai

Bromus japonicus Thunb.   Japanese Chess
Annual; culms erect or bent at the base, slender, 20-70 cm tall; leaf blades long-hairy,
2-4 mm wide; panicle loose and open, 7-20 cm long, the branches flexible, the lower ones
drooping; spikelets 1-2.5 cm long, 7- to 12-flowered; glumes broad, 3-8 mm long; lemmas
broad, blunt, smooth, 7-9 mm long, angled above the middle, 2-toothed at the apex; awn
8-12 mm long, twisted, bent and spreading, the lower ones in the spikelet shorter than
the upper ones; palea shorter than the lemma.
Dry grassy slopes of the moraines, about 5200 feet.

Bromus mollis L.   Soft Cheat
Annual; culms 20-90 cm tall; sheaths and leaf blades hairy, the blades 1.5-4 mm wide;
panicle erect, narrow, dense, mostly 3-10 cm long or reduced to a few spikelets; spikelets 1-2 cm long, 5- to 7-flowered; glumes broad, pubescent, 4-7 mm long; lemmas broad,
long-hairy, 2-toothed at the apex, 8-9 mm long, the awn straight, 6-10 mm long.
Introduced. Wallowa Lake, 4500 feet.

Bromus orcuttianus Vasey   Orcutt's Brome-grass
Tufted, light green, perennial grass; culms 40-120 cm tall, hairy below and at the
nodes; sheaths long-hairy; leaves mostly basal, the blades long-hairy or hairless, 5-9
mm wide; panicle 5-25 cm long, loosely 5- to 8-flowered, the pedicels short; glumes
narrow, smooth or scabrous, blunt or awn-tipped; lemmas narrow, 10-14 mm long,
scabrous or finely hairy over the rounded back; awn 5-8 mm long.
Dry hillsides and thickets, 5500 to about 6000 feet.

Bromus suksdorfii Vasey   Suksdorf's Brome-grass
Culms 50-100 cm tall; leaf blades hairless, 3-8 mm wide; panicle 7-12 cm long, dense
and narrow with short erect branches; spikelets little compressed, 2-2.5 cm long, mostly

5-flowered; glumes broad, 8-12 mm long, nearly without hairs; lemmas 12-14 mm long, hairy near the margin and on the lower part of the mid-nerve, often rough-hairy above; awn 2-4 mm long.
Dry rocky wooded slopes and thickets, between 6000 and 7000 feet.

Bromus tectorum L.   Downy Chess
Annual; culms slender, 20-60 cm tall; blades narrow, both long- and short-hairy; panicle open, 5-15 cm long, often purplish, the branches very thin and drooping; spikelets usually nodding, 1.2-3.5 cm long, 5- to 10-flowered; glumes narrow, scarious-margined, short-hairy as well as long-hairy; lemmas narrow, long-soft-hairy, 1-2 cm long, 2-toothed; awn rough, 1.2-3 cm long, straight or slightly bent.
Dry roadsides and on the moraines, 4500 to about 5200 feet.
Glumes and lemmas hairless.......................var. **glabratus** Spen. (*B. tectorum* var. *nudus*
With the species.   Klett. & Richter)

Bromus vulgaris (Hook.) Shear   Narrow-flowered Brome-grass
Perennial; culms 70-120 cm tall, usually hairy at the nodes; leaf sheaths hairless or soft-hairy; blades often glaucous, 7-12 mm wide, soft, hairy or hairless; panicle pale green, open, often drooping, 10-18 cm long; spikelets narrow, 5- to 8-flowered, 2-3 cm long; glumes narrow, hairy; lemmas narrow, slightly hairy over the back, hairy or ciliate near the margins or nearly without hairs or cilia, 8-13 mm long, the awn 3-8 mm long.
Shady open woods to moist mountain meadows, 4500 to about 6000 feet.
Sheaths long-soft-hairy; first glume 1-nerved; awns over 7 mm long;
range of the species...var. **vulgaris**
Sheaths hairless; first glume 3-nerved; lemmas nearly hairless; awns
4-6 mm long.................var. **eximius** Shear   TYPE LOCALITY: Wallowa Lake

Calamagrostis Adans.

Perennial grasses, usually with creeping rhizomes; panicles open or usually dense, narrow and spike-like; spikelets small, usually 1-flowered, breaking up above the glumes, the rachilla continued behind the palea as a hairy bristle; glumes about equal, 1- to 3-nerved, keeled, acute or tapering to a point; lemma equal to or shorter than the glumes, 5-nerved, the awn usually attached at or below the middle, the tip 4-toothed, the callus at the base with a tuft of hairs; palea shorter than the lemma.

1. Awn straight (see also *C. rubescens* with hairy sheath collar)
    2. Leaf blades 1.5-4 mm wide, often inrolled; panicle firm, dense, pale green to purplish; awn thick..*C. inexpansa*
    2. Leaf blades 4-8 mm wide, usually flat; panicle loose, open, nodding; awn slender..*C. canadensis*
1. Awn bent; panicle green to purplish or reddish
    3. Awn extended upward, about 1.5 mm beyond the glumes; panicle compact; plants of lower elevations..*C. purpurascens*
    3. Awn included in the glumes, or slightly longer, mostly protruding sidewards; plants of lower elevations
        4. Sheaths hairless on the collar; awn attached near the base of the lemma ...*C. koelerioides*
        4. Sheaths hairy on the collar; awn strongly bent and protruding sidewards, sometimes straight up...*C. rubescens*

Calamagrostis canadensis (Michx.) Beauv. Bluejoint
   Tufted perennial; culms 60-150 cm tall, from creeping rootstocks; leaf blades long and lax, scabrous, 4-8 mm wide; panicle nodding, narrow and dense or open with loose branches, 8-25 cm long; glumes green, straw-colored or usually purplish, 2-6 mm long, smooth or usually rough at least on the keel, acute to acuminate; lemma smooth, shorter than the glumes, the awn delicate, straight, usually attached just below the middle and about equaling the tip of the lemma, the callus hairs abundant, about as long as the lemma except for a few outer ones.
Swampy meadows around lakes in coniferous forest, 5000 feet to about 7400 feet.

Calamagrostis inexpansa Gray Northern Reedgrass
   C. hyperborea Lange var. *americana* Kearney
   Tufted perennial; culms 40-120 cm tall, with stout rootstocks; blades firm and stiff, scabrous, 2-4 mm wide; panicle narrow, dense and spike-like, 5-15 cm long, pale green or purplish; glumes 3-4 mm long, scaberulous; lemma as long as the glumes, scabrous, the awn attached just below the middle, straight or nearly so, about as long as the lemma, the callus hairs $\frac{1}{2}$ to $\frac{3}{4}$ the length of the lemma.
Bogs and wet meadows along streams in coniferous forest, 5200 to about 7100 feet.

Calamagrostis koelerioides Vasey Tufted Pine grass
   Tufted perennial with short thick rootstocks; culms clustered, slender, 40-80 cm tall; leaf blades short, erect, scabrous, 2-4 mm wide; panicle narrow, dense and spike-like, 6-12 mm long, green or usually purplish; glumes 5 mm long, hairless except the keel; lemma 5 mm long, the tip toothed, the awn from just above the base, sharply bent and slightly exserted at one side, callus hairs few, about 1 mm long.
Dry hills and stony slopes, 4500 to about 6000 feet.

Calamagrostis purpurascens R. Br. Purple Reed grass
   Culms slender, tufted, mostly 20-60 cm tall, with short horizontal rootstocks; leaf blades 2-6 mm wide, stiff, thick and scabrous; panicle 5-12 cm long, dense and spike-like, pale green, straw-colored, reddish or purplish; glumes 6-8 mm long, the keel scabrous; lemma 4-7 mm long, 4-toothed at the tip, the awn attached near the base, 7-8 mm long, bent or twisted near its tip, hairs of the callus and the rachilla about $\frac{1}{3}$ as long as the lemma.
Dry ledges, slopes and ridges above treeline, 9000 to about 9800 feet.

Calamagrostis rubescens Buckl. Pine grass
   Tufted perennial with creeping rhizomes; culms slender, 50-100 cm tall; leaf blades rough, 2-6 mm wide; panicle 7-20 cm long, spike-like, or loose, or interrupted, pale greenish-white or purplish; glumes 4-5 mm long, sharp-tipped; lemma pale and thin, shorter than the glumes, the awn twisted and bent, from near the base, extended out from the side or the top of the glumes, the hairs of the callus short.
Open pine woods, grassy slopes and along creeks, 4500 to about 6000 feet.

Cinna L.
   Tall perennial grasses usually in wet places; leaf blades broad and flat; panicles large, open or condensed; spikelets 1-flowered, flattened, breaking up below the glumes, the

Agrostis exarata

Alopecurus aequalis

Avena sativa

Bromus brizaeformis

Bromus tectorum

Calamagrostis canadensis

Cinna latifolia

Dactylis glomerata

Danthonia intermedia var. cusickii

rachilla remaining as a bristle beyond the palea; glumes equal, keeled, 1- to 3-nerved; lemma flat, about as long as the glumes, 3-nerved, mostly with a short straight dorsal awn from just below the tip; palea keeled.

Cinna latifolia (Trevir.) Griseb.   Drooping Woodreed
Culms solitary or few in a tuft, slender, 60-100 cm tall, often somewhat bulbous at the base; leaf blades 5-15 mm wide, deep green, soft, scabrous, narrowed at the base; panicle 15-30 cm long, very loose, the branches spreading or drooping; spikelets about 4 mm long; glumes about equal, scabrous or fine-hairy; lemma flattened, equaling the shorter glume, awnless or mostly with a very short awn at the tip; palea keeled.
Meadows, moist streambanks and coniferous woods, 4500 to about 7000 feet.

Dactylis L.
Perennial grasses; leaves flat; panicle branching; spikelets compressed, breaking up above the glumes, 3- to 5-flowered, in 1-sided clusters at the ends of the few stiff branches; glumes 2, narrow, unequal, acute, the keel hispid-ciliate, the tip short and awn-like; lemmas awn-tipped, 5-nerved, ciliate on the keel.

Dactylis glomerata L.   Orchard Grass
Culms 60-120 cm tall; blades scabrous, 2-11 mm wide; panicles 3-20 cm long, the branches few, stiffly spreading at flowering time but becoming erect later; spikelets 2- to 4-flowered, nearly sessile, crowded in 1-sided clusters at the ends of the branches; upper glume and the lemmas similar, scabrous, short-awned or sharp-pointed, bristly-ciliate on the keel.
Meadows and open woods, 4500 to about 5000 feet.

Danthonia Lam. and DC.
Tufted perennial grasses; panicles open or dense and spike-like, or the spikelet solitary; spikelets usually large, several-flowered, breaking above the glumes and between the florets; glumes about equal, large and broad, usually longer than the florets; lemmas rounded on the back, 2-toothed at the tip, the teeth usually extending into awns, and also with a rather stout, flat, twisted or bent awn arising from between the teeth and just below them.

Danthonia intermedia Vasey   Mountain Wild Oat-grass
Clustered perennial, 10-50 cm tall; blades hairy to nearly hairless, narrow, stiff and scabrous; panicle dense and narrow, 2-6 cm long; spikelet solitary, purplish, few-flowered; glumes mostly longer than the lemmas; lemmas 7-8 mm long, nearly hairless on the back, long-hairy along the margin below and on the callus, the teeth acute or awn-pointed, the dorsal awn up to 10 mm long, flat and twisted, especially below.
Dry ridges, moist shade, wet mountain meadows and boggy ground along streams and lakes, 4500 to about 9800 feet.
Culms taller, up to 160 cm; leaf blades without hair; spikelets long; swamps and along streams at about 7000 feet..var. **cusickii** Will.

Deschampsia Beauv.
Annual or perennial grasses; panicles narrow or open; spikelets silvery or purplish,

small, 2-flowered, breaking apart above the glumes; glumes nearly equal, usually longer than the upper floret; lemmas thin, abruptly narrowed, 2- to 4-toothed at the tip, bearded at the base with a straight, bent or twisted awn arising from below the middle of the back.

1. Plant slender, annual; leaves very few, narrow, rolled; glumes 5-8 mm long; panicle open ____*D. danthonioides*
1. Plant perennial; leaves more abundant, mostly basal
    2. Panicle very narrow, the branches close, pale green to purplish; leaves narrow; glumes 3-5.5 mm long____ *D. elongata*
    2. Panicle mostly open, the branches more spreading; spikelets purplish; leaves not so narrow, the blades 1.5-6 mm wide
        3. Glumes about 5 mm long, longer than the upper floret; lemmas awned from about the middle of the back_____________________________________*D. atropurpurea*
        3. Glumes as long as, or shorter than, the upper floret, 2.5-5 mm long; lemmas awned from the base, the awn deciduous__________________________*D. caespitosa*

Deschampsia atropurpurea (Wahl.) Scheele   Mountain Hairgrass

Perennial; culms tufted, slender, purplish at the base, 15-80 cm tall; blades flat, soft, deep green, 2-6 mm wide; panicle mostly loose and open, 5-10 cm long, the branches few, capillary, spreading or drooping; spikelets purplish, 4-5 mm long, sometimes 3-flowered; glumes broad, shining longer than the upper floret, nearly equal; lemmas 2- to 4-toothed, the callus hairs up to midlength, the awn from about the middle, twisted and bent but sometimes straight on the lower floret.
Wet meadows, streambanks, rock slides and lake shores, 6000 to about 9000 feet.

Deschampsia caespitosa (L.) Beauv.   Tufted Hair-grass

Perennial; culms densely tufted, 20-120 cm tall; leaves matted at the base, the blades stiff, mostly folded, 1.5-4 mm wide; panicle 8-40 cm long, open, loose and nodding, with slender branches, or the panicle narrow, contracted and dense at higher elevations; spikelets pale or purplish, sometimes 3-flowered; glumes narrow, smooth and shining, about as long as the florets; lemmas smooth, 4-toothed at the tip, the callus hairs short, the awn deciduous, from near the base of the back of the lemma, straight and included or somewhat bent and exserted and twice as long as the spikelet.
Bogs, moist or mostly wet meadows, streambanks and lake borders, 4500 to about 8000 feet.

Deschampsia danthonioides (Trin.) Munro   Annual Hair-grass

Slender annual, 5-50 cm tall; blades few, short and narrow; panicle open, 7-25 cm long; spikelets few, narrow, 5-7 mm long; glumes usually slightly longer than the upper floret; lemmas smooth and shining, often purplish, 2-3 mm long, the tip several-toothed and somewhat ciliate as well, the callus short-hairy, the awns bent, about 5 mm long, well exserted, arising from below the middle of the back of the lemma.
Grassland, open woods and moist meadows, 4500 to about 5500 feet.

Deschampsia elongata (Hook.) Munro ex Benth.   Slender Hair-grass

Perennial; culms densely tufted, slender, 20-120 cm tall; leaves mostly basal, blades short, soft and very narrow; panicle very narrow and close, pale greenish to purple, 5-30 cm long; spikelets narrow, 3-5 mm long; glumes narrow, acute, equaling or slightly longer than the upper floret; lemmas 2-3 mm long, smooth and shining, several-toothed

at the tip, callus hairs half as long as the lemma, the awn from just below the middle of the lemma, nearly straight, 3-4 mm long.
Moist woods and dry gravelly open ground, about lakes and along streams, 4500 to about 7600 feet.

Elymus L.

Usually tall perennial grasses; leaf blades stiff and inrolled along the margin, or broad and flat; spikes dense, sometimes compound; spikelets large, 2- to 6-flowered, usually sessile and in pairs at each node of the rachis, breaking apart above the glumes and between the florets; glumes about equal, rigid, 1- to 5- or 6-nerved, acute to awn-tipped; lemmas rounded on the back, awnless or often awned from the tip.

1. Glumes awned, the awn 1 or 2 times as long as the glume-body
    2. Awn of the lemma straight, 1-2 cm long .... *E. macounii*
    2. Awn of the lemma spreading when dry, 2-3 cm long .... *E. canadensis*
1. Glumes awnless or with a short straight awn; lemmas varying from awn-pointed to an
   awn up to 3 times the length of the glume-body, straight or spreading .... *E. glaucus*

Elymus canadensis L.   Canada Rye-grass

Green or often glaucous; culms thick, 1-1.5 meters tall; leaves mostly on the stem, the blades flat, 0.5-2 cm wide, rather rough; spike thick, bristly, nodding or drooping, 10-30 cm long; glumes 2- to 4-nerved, scabrous, the awn spreading, 1 or 2 times the length of the body of the glume; lemmas rough-hairy, 1-1.5 cm long, strongly nerved, the awn 2-3 cm long, spreading or bent when dry.
Dry hillsides, about 4500 feet.

Elymus glaucus Buckl.   Western Rye-grass

Culms 50-150 cm tall; blades thin, flat, lax, 5-15 mm wide, usually rough; spike usually dense, 5-20 cm long, erect or nodding; spikelets overlapping or separate, glumes 1-2 cm long, 2- to 5-nerved, acute or short-awned; lemmas about 1 cm long, awn-pointed or short awned, or the awn up to 3 times as long as the glume-body, straight or spreading.
Swamps, dry hillsides and shady open woods, 4650 to about 7000 feet.

Elymus macounii Vasey   Macoun's Wild-Rye

Culms 50-100 cm tall, slender, densely clustered; blades erect, usually scabrous, 10-20 cm long, 2-5 mm wide; spike slender, erect or nodding, 4-12 cm long, the rachis finally breaking apart; spikelets mostly 2-flowered, about 1 cm long excluding the awns; glumes very narrow, scabrous, about 1 cm long, short-awned; lemmas rounded, rough toward the tip, the awn straight, 1-2 cm long.
Dry subalpine ridges. (This species is said to be a hybrid between *Agropyron trachycaulum* and a species of *Hordeum*).

Festuca L.

Annual or perennial grasses; panicles narrow or open; spikelets few- to several-flowered, the rachilla breaking up above the glumes and between the florets; glumes awnless, unequal, shorter than the lemmas, narrow and acute; lemmas rounded on the back, 5-nerved, mostly acute, awned from the tip or from between the 2 apical teeth, or sometimes awnless; paleas usually about equaling the lemmas.

1. Awn of the lemma 6-20 mm long; leaf blades lax and flat .... *F. subulata*

1. Awn of the lemma shorter, minute to 5 mm long; leaf blades mostly stiff and folded or inrolled
    2. Panicle narrow, almost spike-like; awn missing, or up to 3 mm long
        3. Culms 40-100 cm tall, often bent and reddish at the base; awn usually present; basal sheaths reddish to brown, shredding into fibers with age _____*F. rubra*
        3. Culms 5-35 cm tall, erect, not curved or reddish at the base; awn of the lemma present or missing_____*F. ovina*
    2. Panicle loose and more open; awn obsolete, minute, or up to 5 mm long
        4. Awn 2-5 mm long; culms 10-100 cm tall; basal sheaths greenish, not shredding into fibers _____ *F. idahoensis*
        4. Awn obsolete or minute; culms 40-100 cm tall_____*F. viridula*

Festuca idahoensis Elmer   Idaho Fescue
    F. ovina var. *ingrata* Hack. ex Beal

Culms 20-100 cm tall, in large dense bunches; leaves abundant, mostly basal, stiff, very narrow, scabrous; panicle narrow, 5-20 cm long, the branches scabrous, appressed, ascending or somewhat spreading; spikelets few, mostly 5- to 7-flowered; glumes acute, very unequal; lemmas nearly round, about 4.5-7.5 mm long, the awn stout, usually 2-5 mm long.
Grasslands and open rocky slopes, 4800 to about 8600 feet.

Festuca ovina L. var. brevifolia (R. Br.) Wats.   Sheep Fescue
    F. supina Schur; *F. brachyphylla* Schult.

Densely tufted perennials; culms mostly 5-20 cm tall; leaves mostly basal, very narrow, short, soft; panicle very narrow, 2-7 cm long; spikelets 3- to 4-flowered; glumes and lemmas broad, not hardened; awn of the lemma 1-3 mm long, but sometimes missing.
Open rocky slopes, 8800 to about 9800 feet and probably higher.

Festuca rubra L.   Red Fescue
Perennials forming large loose clumps; culms bent or curved at the base, reddish or purplish, 20-100 cm tall; blades smooth, soft, very narrow; panicle 3-20 cm long, usually contracted and narrow; spikelets 4- to 7-flowered, pale green or bluish-green, often reddish-purplish; glumes very unequal; lemmas smooth or slightly rough near the tip, 5-8 mm long, the awn scabrous, 1-3 mm long.
Swampy meadows and streambanks, 4500 to about 5000 feet.

Festuca subulata Trin.   Nodding Bunchgrass
Culms leafy, erect, clustered, 40-120 cm tall; leaves scabrous, thin and lax, 3-10 mm wide; panicle loose, open, drooping, 10-40 cm long, the branches in 2's or 3's, spreading or reflexed; spikelets loosely 3- to 5-flowered; glumes thin; lemmas 3-nerved, somewhat keeled, nearly hairless, narrowed into a rough awn 6-20 mm long.
Shady banks and moist thickets, 4500 to about 5000 feet.

Festuca viridula Vasey   Mountain Bunchgrass
Perennial; culms 40-100 cm tall; blades soft, flat, 1-2 mm wide; panicle loose and open, 7-15 cm long, the branches in 2's, ascending or spreading; spikelets 9-12 mm long, 3- to 6-flowered; glumes nearly equal, broad, 3-7 mm long; lemmas keeled, thin and glabrous, scarious toward the tip, 6-8 mm long, acute and awnless or rarely minutely awned or sharp-pointed.

Dry slopes and bench lands, moist bottoms and wet or moist mountain meadows, 4500 to about 8000 feet.

Glyceria R. Br.

Aquatic or marsh perennials with creeping bases or rhizomes; culms simple; leaf blades flat; panicles open or compact; spikelets 5- to 15-flowered, linear to ovate, breaking above the glumes and between the florets; glumes short, unequal, usually 1-nerved and scarious; lemmas strongly 5- to 9-nerved, broad, rounded on the back, scarious at the blunt to acute tip.

1. Lemma nerves 5; second glume 3-nerved; leaf sheaths open at least below; spikelets often purplish..*G. pauciflora*
1. Lemma nerves 7; second glume 1-nerved; leaf sheaths closed; spikelets flattened
    2. Leaf blades 1-4 mm wide; culms slender..*G. striata*
    2. Leaf blades 6-9 mm wide; culms stout..*G. elata*

Glyceria elata (Nash) M. E. Jones   Tall Mannagrass
Panicularia elata Nash

Plants dark green; culms stout, 1-2 meters tall, from thick rhizomes; leaf blades flat, thin and lax, scabrous, 4-12 mm wide; panicle open and loose, especially below, 15-30 cm long; spikelets 3-5 mm long, ovate, 4- to 8-flowered; glumes short and nerveless, about 1 mm long; lemmas 7-nerved, firm, about 2 mm long, scarious at the tip.
Wet or swampy meadows, mossy streambanks and moist woods, 4500 to about 5000 feet.

Glyceria pauciflora Presl   Few-flowered Mannagrass
G. otisii A. S. Hitchc.; *Puccinellia pauciflora* (Presl) Munz

Culms thick from a creeping base, mostly 1 meter tall; blades lax, flat, scabrous above, 4-15 mm wide; panicle open or dense, nodding, 5-25 cm long, with flexible branches; spikelets 3- to 10-flowered, often purplish; glumes broad, 1-1.5 mm long, fringed, scarious-margined; lemmas oblong, scabrous, 2-2.5 mm long, 5-nerved (sometimes faintly 7-nerved), the tip erose-ciliate, blunt, usually with a band of dark purple.
Bogs and wet or moist meadows, lake borders and streamsides, 4500 to about 8000 feet.

Glyceria striata (Lam.) A. S. Hitchc.   Fowl Mannagrass
Panicularia striata A. S. Hitchc.

Plants pale green; culms slender, erect, 30-100 cm tall; blades flat or folded, firm, usually 1-6 mm wide; panicle open and loose, 5-20 cm long; spikelets ovate or oblong, 3- to 7-flowered, often purplish; glumes ovate, 0.5-1 mm long; lemmas 7-nerved, broad and firm, about 2 mm long.
Bogs, wet meadows and muddy streambanks, 4500 to about 5500 feet.

Hordeum L.

Perennial grasses (ours), mostly rather low and weedy; leaf blades flat; spikes dense and bristly; spikelets breaking apart above the glumes, usually 1-flowered, in 3's at the joints of the rachis, the middle spikelet usually sessile, the others usually pedicellate, the rachilla extending above the floret in the middle spikelet; lateral spikelets staminate, sometimes reduced to bristles; glumes narrow, often awned or awn-like; lemmas rounded, 5-nerved, usually long-awned.

Glumes 7-12 mm long; spikes much longer than thick...*H. brachyantherum*
Glumes 20-60 mm long; spikes about as broad as long......................................*H. jubatum*

Hordeum brachyantherum Nevski   Meadow Barley

Culms 20-100 cm tall, erect or spreading; blades 2-6 mm wide, scabrous or hairy; spike erect or nodding, 2-10 cm long, sometimes purplish; lateral spikelets small, short-pedicellate, scabrous, the glumes slender, unequal, awnlike, 7-12 mm long; middle spikelet glabrous, sessile, the awn about 1 cm long.
Dryish subalpine meadows and grassy slopes, about 6000 to 7000 feet.

Hordeum jubatum L.   Foxtail Barley

Culms erect or prostrate, 30-60 cm tall; blades 2-5 mm wide, scabrous; spike nodding, 5-10 cm long; lateral spikelets reduced to 1 to 3 spreading awns; middle spikelet sessile, the glumes slender, awnlike, 2-6 cm long, spreading; lemma 6-8 mm long, the awn 2.5-6 cm long.
Dry open mixed woods at about 5000 feet. (Campground).

Koeleria Pers.

Slender annuals or perennials; leaf blades narrow; panicles shining, dense and spike-like; spikelets small, 2- to 4-flowered, breaking apart above the glumes; glumes keeled, about equal in length but different from each other, the lower narrow, sometimes shorter, 1-nerved, the upper wider, broad above the middle, 3- to 5-nerved; lemmas keeled, scarious, shining, the lowest longer than the glume, 5-nerved, acute or short-awned from just below the 2-toothed tip.

Koeleria cristata (L.) Pers.   June Grass

Tufted perennial; culms usually clustered, 20-60 cm tall; leaves variable, soft or stiff, mostly basal, the blades 1-3 mm wide, hairless, scabrous or gray-hairy; panicle silvery-shining, spike-like, pointed, dense and crowded at first, loose and open later, often interrupted below, 4-15 cm long; spikelets 4-6 mm long, mostly 2-flowered; glumes and lemmas scabrous, about equal, awnless or awn-tipped.
Dry open grassland and meadows to rocky slopes in coniferous forest, 4500 to about 8000 feet.

Melica L.

Perennial grasses; culms often swollen at the base; leaf sheaths closed; leaf blades usually flat; panicle unbranched, narrow or sometimes open; spikelets 2- to several-flowered, the rachilla breaking up above the glumes, terminating in 2 or 3 empty lemmas rolled about each other; glumes unequal, thin, rounded on the back, scarious margined, strongly-nerved; lemmas thin or firm, rounded on the back, scarious-margined, awnless or sometimes awned from between the 2 teeth at the tip.

1. Panicle usually open and loose, the lower branches spreading or nodding; lemmas hairless; glumes broad and papery; plants mostly 15-40 cm tall; joints of the rachilla often swollen, wrinkled or spongy..*M. jugax*
1. Panicle narrow and dense, the branches close, mostly erect
    2. Lemmas hairy-ciliate near the base, 9-13 mm long; glumes narrow; plants mostly 30-180 cm tall; rachilla joints slender......................................*M. subulata*
    2. Lemmas not hairy-ciliate near the base, often less than 10 mm long; panicle sometimes open
        3. Culms densely clustered; lemmas 6-12 mm long; anthers usually over 2.5 mm long..*M. bulbosa*
        3. Culms not clustered, arising separately from the rhizome; lemmas about 7 mm long; anthers 2-2.5 mm long......................................*M. spectabilis*

Melica bulbosa Geyer   Onion-grass
   M. bella Piper
   Culms 30-120 cm tall, densely clustered, the base bulbous and usually curved; leaf blades 2-4 mm wide, glabrous, hairy or scabrous; panicle 6-20 cm long, narrow, dense, brownish or purplish, the branches short, appressed, stiff and overlapping; spikelets papery in age, 7-15 mm long, 3- to 6-flowered; glumes papery; lemmas 6-12 mm long, broad, thin, awnless, 5- to 7-nerved, rough or fine-hairy.
Rocky woods and open hillsides, 5000 to about 8000 feet.

Melica fugax Boland.   Little Onion-grass
   Culms slender, clustered, 15-60 cm tall, scabrous or fine-hairy, bulbous at the base; leaf blades 1.5-3 mm wide, fine-hairy or scabrous; panicle 8-15 cm long, usually open, the lower branches 2-5 cm long, stiffly spreading or reflexed at maturity; spikelets few, 5-15 mm long, usually purplish, mostly 2- or 3-flowered; glumes broad and papery, nearly equal; lemmas broad, 4-7 mm long, awnless.
Dry hills and moist open woods, 4500 to about 7000 feet.

Melica spectabilis Scribn.   Purple Onion-grass
   Culms 30-100 cm tall, usually not clustered, bulbous at the base; leaf blades hairy or not, 2-4 mm wide; panicle 7-15 cm long, narrow, the branches appressed; spikelets 1-1.5 cm long, purplish, loosely 3- to 8-flowered, the pedicels slender, curved or loosely flexible; glumes brown, broad and papery; lemmas blunt, about 7 mm long, scarious-margined, awnless.
Moist to wet meadows and open woods, 4500 to about 5000 feet.

Melica subulata (Griseb.) Scribn.   Alaska Onion-grass
   Culms 30-130 cm tall, solitary or clustered, strongly bulbous at the base; leaf blades scabrous or fine-hairy, usually 2-8 mm wide; panicle usually narrow, 8-20 cm long, the branches close or spreading; spikelets narrow, 12-24 mm long, loosely 2- to 5-flowered; glumes acute; lemmas 8-12 mm long, awnless but tapering to an acuminate point, scabrous or thinly hairy-ciliate on the keel and nerves.
Rocky open woods and slopes, about 4500 feet.

Muhlenbergia Schreb.

   Annual or mostly perennial grasses, tufted or rhizomatous; culms often branching; leaves narrow; panicle narrow and compact or open; spikelets small, mostly 1-flowered, breaking up above the glumes; glumes sometimes awned, usually shorter than the lemma, sometimes as long, obtuse to acuminate or awned, keeled or rounded on the back, the first sometimes small or even obsolete; lemma mostly 3- to 5-nerved, longer than the glumes, acute or 2-toothed, awned or short-pointed, callus hairs very short.

Plants small annuals, mostly 5-15 cm tall; roots usually fibrous .... *M. filiformis*
Plants larger perennials, 50-100 cm tall; rootstocks tough, scaly, creeping .... *M. andina*

Muhlenbergia andina (Nutt.) Hitchc.   Foxtail Muhlenbergia
   M. comata Thurb.
   Perennial; culms erect or spreading, wiry, 40-100 cm tall, from tough, scaly, creeping rhizomes; leaf blades 2-6 mm wide, scabrous; panicle narrow, spike-like, usually interrupted, 7-15 cm long, silky, often purplish; spikelets densely crowded on the branches;

glumes narrow, 3-4 mm long, sharp-pointed to awn-tipped, ciliate-scabrous on the keel; lemma scarcely equaling the glumes, the tip narrowed into a capillary awn 4-8 mm long, the basal hairs abundant, nearly as long as the lemma.
Gravel bars and wet meadows, about 5000 to 6000 feet.

Muhlenbergia filiformis (Thurb.) Rydb.   Slender Muhly

Fibrous-rooted annual or sometimes with perennial creeping rootstocks; culms very slender, branching below, erect or on the ground and rooting at the nodes, mostly 5-15 cm tall, sometimes up to 35 cm; leaf blades scabrous, flat, 1-2.5 mm long and about 1 mm wide; panicle very narrow, 1.5-8 cm long; spikelets few; glumes ovate, about 1 mm long; lemma minutely hairy, 2-2.5 mm long, sharp-pointed at the tip.
Open woods and wet mountain meadows near lakes, 4500 to about 8200 feet.

Oryzopsis Michx.

Slender clustered perennial grasses; leaf blades flat or inrolled; panicle narrow and spike-like or open; spikelets 1-flowered, breaking apart above the glumes; glumes nearly equal, blunt to sharp-pointed, 3- to 5-nerved; lemma hardened, about equaling the glumes, nearly round, usually hairy, the callus short and blunt, the awn short and deciduous, straight, bent or twisted; palea surrounded by the lemma.

Panicle 3-8 cm long, narrow and compact, spike-like; awn bent, sometimes twisted as well;
    spikelets short-pedicellate..*O. exigua*
Panicle 7-20 cm long, open and spreading, the branches weak and flexuous, paired; awn
    straight when present; spikelets long-pedicellate..*O. hymenoides*

Oryzopsis exigua Thurb.   Little Mountain Rice-grass

Culms densely tufted, stiff, scabrous, 15-30 cm tall; blades filiform, about 1 mm wide, stiffly erect, scabrous, 5-10 cm long, the 2 culm blades shorter; panicle narrow, 3-8 cm long; spikelets few, short-pedicellate; glumes broad, acute, about 3-6 mm long, lemma silky-hairy, about as long as the glumes, the awn stout, bent and sometimes twisted as well, about 5 mm long, from the 2-toothed tip of the lemma.
Sunny cliffs and ledges and dry open coniferous mountainsides, 6400 to about 9000 feet.

Oryzopsis hymenoides (Roem. & Schult.) Ricker   Indian Mountain Rice-grass

Densely tufted perennial; culms wiry, 30-60 cm tall; leaf blades slender, narrow, nearly as long as the culms; panicle open, 7-20 cm long, the branches weak, flexuous, paired, the branchlets paired, capillary, spreading; glumes 5-9 mm long, papery, 3- to 5-nerved, abruptly pointed; lemma turgid, about 3 mm long, blackish at maturity, densely long-white-hairy, the awn 4-6 mm long, thick, straight, early deciduous.
Dry open sandy slope near a creek (Slick Rock Creek on the Hurricane Creek Trail), about 5800 feet.

Phleum L.

Annual or perennial grasses; leaves flat; panicle narrow, dense and spike-like; spikelets 1-flowered, very small, breaking up above the glumes; glumes equal, keeled, sharp-pointed or awned; lemma colorless, usually hairy, shorter than the glumes, blunt or abruptly narrowed; palea narrow, nearly as long as the lemma.

Panicle long-cylindric, several times longer than wide; glumes 3-4 mm long; plants of
    roadsides and waste places at low elevations..*P. pratense*

Panicle short-cylindric or broadened at the base, 1½ to 2 times as long as wide; glumes
5-7 mm long; plants of middle to high mountain elevations .... *P. alpinum*

Phleum alpinum L. Mountain Timothy

Culms 15-60 cm tall, often lying on the ground, from a densely tufted base; leaf blades
mostly 3-6 mm wide; panicle appearing bristly, nearly rounded to short-cylindric, 2-5
cm long, 8-9 mm thick; glumes 5-7 mm long, long-ciliate on the keel and hairy on the
body, the awns thick, 1.5-2.5 mm long.
Mountain meadows, bogs, and moist open mixed or coniferous woods, 4650 to about
8500 feet.

Phleum pratense L. Timothy; Herd's Grass

Culms 50-150 cm tall from a swollen base, forming large clumps; leaf blades mostly
5-8 mm wide, scabrous above; panicle long-cylindric, mostly 5-10 cm long, 6-7 mm thick;
spikelets crowded; glumes about 3-4 mm long, abruptly narrowed, the thick curved awn
1-1.5 mm long; lemma hairy, the nerve bristle-like.
Moraines, dry roadsides, open fields and slopes, 4500 to about 5800 feet.

Poa L.

Annual or usually perennial grasses; culms often with one short leaf at about the
middle; leaves narrow, flat, folded or rolled, ending in a boat-shaped tip; panicles open
or narrow and contracted; spikelets 2- to 10-flowered, usually small, compressed, breaking up above the glumes and between the florets, the top floret rudimentary; glumes
acute, keeled, unequal to nearly equal, the first usually 1-nerved, the second usually
3-nerved; lemmas awnless, strongly keeled but sometimes rounded on the back, pointed
or blunt, usually 5-nerved, scabrous or hairy on keel and nerves, often scarious at the tip
and sometimes cotton-hairy or webbed at the base.

1. Plants annual
    2. Lemmas blunt, hairy on the nerves and lower keel, not webbed at the base;
       spikelets 3- to 6-flowered .... *P. annua*
    2. Lemmas pointed, not hairy (except scabrous on the keel), webbed at the base;
       spikelets 2- to 3-flowered.. *P. bolanderi*
1. Plants perennial
    3. Spikelets definitely flattened; lemmas keeled
       4. Plants with creeping rootstocks
          5. Lemmas hairless to fine-short-hairy on the back or nerves
             6. Lemmas webbed at the base.. *P. pratensis*
             6. Lemmas never webbed at the base.. *P. nervosa*
          5. Lemmas long-hairy on the back or on the nerves, often webbed at the
           base... *P. arctica*
       4. Plants without creeping rootstocks
          7. Lemmas webbed at the base; keel and nerves long-hairy .... *P. leptocoma*
          7. Lemmas without webby hairs at the base
             8. Lemmas definitely hairy on the keel or on the nerves or on both,
              and sometimes between the nerves as well
                9. Panicle about as broad as long; leaf blades 2-5 mm wide;
                  plant usually pale green .... *P. alpina*
                9. Panicle longer than broad; leaf blades not over 1 mm wide;
                  spikelets purplish, lemmas silky-hairy .... *P. rupicola*
             8. Lemmas mostly without hairs on the keel, nerves or between
              nerves, but sometimes rough-ish (scabrous) on the keel

```
10. Panicle mostly open
    11. Leaf blades narrow, scabrous; panicle narrow, 3-10 cm
        long; lemmas 4.5-6 mm long ....................................................... P. cusickii
    11. Leaf blades not scabrous; panicle spreading, 2-4 cm
        long; lemmas 3 mm long ...................................................... P. vaseyochloa
10. Panicle compact, narrow, sometimes spike-like
    12. Culm blades flat, usually 1.5-3.5 mm broad, the others
        folded or rolled ......................................................................... P. epilis
    12. Culm blades folded or rolled like the others; spikelets
        purplish
        13. Lemmas 3-4.5 mm long; plants 5-30 cm tall;
            panicle often loose ................................................... P. leibergii
        13. Lemmas 4.5 mm long; plants mostly over 30 cm
            tall; panicle narrow ............................................... P. suksdorfii
3. Spikelets not much flattened, narrow; keel and nerves of the lemma faint
    14. Panicle open, 5-12 cm long; culms usually curved at the base ........... P. gracillima
    14. Panicle contracted, loosely spike-like
        15. Spikelets 5-7 mm long; lower leaves often curled; culms slender ..... P. sandbergii
        15. Spikelets 7-10 mm long; lower leaves not curled; culms thick ....... P. scabrella
```

Poa alpina L.   Alpine Bluegrass

Clustered perennial; culms stout, 10-30 cm tall; leaves basal, the blades short, flat, glabrous, 2-5 mm wide; panicle ovoid, compact, 1-8 cm long, purplish, the lower branches often spreading or reflexed; spikelets flattened, broad, 5-6 mm long, 3- to 6-flowered; glumes somewhat unequal, abruptly acute, scabrous above, 3-4 mm long; lemmas 3-4 mm long, soft-hairy on the keel and near the base, hairy between the nerves but not webbed at the base.

Gravel bars and creek beds at low elevations, mostly at higher elevations in wet or mossy meadows and streambanks, 5200 to about 9600 feet.

Poa annua L.   Annual Bluegrass

Tufted green and glossy annual, sometimes rooting at the nodes and forming mats; culms flat, 5-30 cm long; leaf blades hairless, soft and loose, 1-3 mm wide; panicle ovoid, dense to open, 2-8 cm long; spikelets crowded, flattened, about 4 mm long, 3- to 6-flowered; glumes keeled, unequal, 1.5-2.5 mm long; lemmas obtuse, hairy on the lower part of the keel and the marginal nerves but not webbed at the base.

Moist open mixed woods, 4500 to about 5000 feet.

Poa arctica R. Br.   Arctic Bluegrass

? P. grayana Vasey

Perennial; culms clustered, erect or close to the ground, 10-30 cm tall; leaves nearly all basal, blades 2-3 mm wide, flat or folded, glabrous; panicle open, pyramidal, 5-10 cm long, the branches few, slender, spreading or reflexed, with a few spikelets toward the tip; spikelets 3- to 4-flowered, quite flattened, 5-8 mm long; lemmas often webbed at the base, densely soft-hairy on the keel and outer nerves and hairy between the nerves below.

Wet meadows, about 8000 feet.

Poa bolanderi Vasey   Bolander's Bluegrass

Annual; culms erect, 15-60 cm tall; leaf blades narrow, glabrous, 2-5 cm long, abruptly narrowed at the tip and appearing prow-like; panicle about half the length of the culm,

contracted at first, opening later, the branches unequal, remote, few, stiff, spreading or reflexed or sometimes all closely appressed; spikelets flattened, 2- to 3-flowered; glumes keeled, 2-3 mm long; lemmas smooth, acute, slightly webbed at the base, hairless except for the scabrous keel.
Moist open woods, 6000 to about 7000 feet.

Poa cusickii Vasey   Cusick's Bluegrass
Closely clustered perennials; culms slender, 20-60 cm tall; leaves abundant, mostly basal, the blades very narrow, rolled inward, scabrous, erect; panicle narrow, 3-10 cm long, pale brownish or purplish, rather open, the branches scabrous and ascending; spikelets 3- to 5-flowered, the florets usually pistillate: glumes 3-4 mm long; lemmas keeled, 4.5-6 mm long, smooth or scabrous.
Dry grassy or open rocky slopes in coniferous forest, 5000 to about 8000 feet.

Poa epilis Scribn.   Skyline Bluegrass
Culms solitary or in small clusters, 20-40 cm tall; basal leaf blades firm, narrow, folded or rolled, the 3 culm leaves shorter, flat, 2-3 mm wide; panicle ovoid, dense, 2-6 cm long, usually purple, the branches not spreading; spikelets 6-8 mm long, flattened, 3- to 6-flowered; glumes 4-5 mm long; lemmas thin, less than 6 mm long, nearly hairless.
Exposed ledges and ridges, rocky slopes and mountain meadows, 6000 to about 9400 feet.

Poa gracillima Vasey   Pacific Bluegrass
Perennial grasses; culms loosely tufted, usually curved at the base, 15-60 cm tall, often bluish-green; leaves mostly basal, the blades soft, flat or folded, very narrow, prow-like at the tips; panicle usually loose and pyramidal, open, 5-15 cm long, the branches in whorls, spreading or reflexed; spikelets narrow, 3- to 5-flowered, 4-9 mm long; glumes 3-6 mm long; lemmas about 5 mm long, rounded, scabrous, slightly keeled, curly-short-hairy at the base, not webbed.
Gravel bars and creek beds at lower elevations but mostly on exposed ridges and slopes at high elevations, 5100 to about 9600 feet.

Poa leibergii Scribn.   Leiberg's Bluegrass
Perennial grasses, usually clustered; culms erect, slender, 10-30 cm tall; leaves mostly basal, the blades short, firm and rolled inward; panicle narrow, 2-5 cm long, with only 3 or 4 spikelets, or open and up to 8 cm long, widely spreading, usually purple, the branches short, close, erect; spikelets few, loosely 2- to 8-flowered, mostly pistillate, 4-6 mm long; glumes 2-4 mm long; lemmas 3-4 mm long, smooth or sometimes scabrous near the base, not webbed.
High dry talus slopes, about 9600 feet.

Poa leptocoma Trin.   Bog Bluegrass
Perennial; culms solitary or few, slender, scabrous, often close to the ground, 10-50 cm tall; blades flat, short and lax, 2-4 mm wide; panicle 4-15 cm long, delicate, nodding, few-flowered, loose, the branches capillary, in pairs, ascending, spreading or reflexed; spikelets narrow, 4-5 mm long, often purplish, 2- to 4-flowered; glumes scabrous, acute, unequal; lemmas 3.5-4.5 mm long, webbed at the base, hairless or long-hairy on the keel and marginal nerves.
Granitic swampy meadows and streambanks, 4500 to about 8000 feet.

Deschampsia caespitosa

Elymus glaucus

Festuca viridula

Glyceria striata

Hordeum jubatum

Koeleria cristata

Melica bulbosa

Muhlenbergia filiformis

Oryzopsis exigua

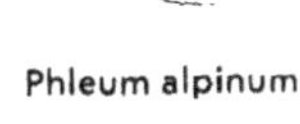

Phleum alpinum

Poa arctica

Poa gracillima

Poa nervosa (Hook.) Vasey   Creeping Bluegrass
  P. wheeleri Vasey; *P. olneyae* Piper; *P. vaseyana* Scribn.
  Culms erect, from slender creeping rootstocks, 30-80 cm tall; leaf blades long, soft.
pale beneath, 2-8 mm wide; panicle loose and open to rather compact, 5-15 cm long,
nodding, the capillary branches up to 8 cm long, in whorls of 2, 3, or 4; spikelets loosely
4- to 7-flowered, pale green, 6-9 mm long; glumes about 3 mm long; lemmas 4-5 mm
long, strongly nerved, scabrous or pubescent on the keel and lower part of the marginal
nerves, or hairless, not webbed at the base.
Moist exposed ridges, cliffs, talus slopes and open coniferous forest, as well as wet mountain meadows, 6000 to nearly 10,000 feet.

Poa pratensis L.   Kentucky Bluegrass
  Culms erect, tufted, from slender creeping rootstocks, 20-100 cm tall; leaf blades soft,
2-6 mm wide; panicle open, pyramidal, 3-10 cm long, loose, the branches in whorls of 3
to 5, ascending or spreading; spikelets flattened, crowded, 3-6 mm long, 3- to 7-flowered;
glumes scabrous; lemmas strongly keeled, silky-hairy on the keel and marginal nerves
below, otherwise hairless, webbed at the base.
Sunny grassy moraines to rocky meadows in coniferous woods, 5000 to about 7000 feet.

Poa rupicola Nash   Timberline Bluegrass
  Culms densely clustered, stiffly erect, rather bluish, 10-20 cm tall; leaf blades short
and stiff, 1-3 mm wide, usually folded; panicle narrow and compact, 2-7 cm long; spikelets about 4 mm long, purplish, 3- to 5-flowered; glumes nearly equal, scabrous on the
keel, acute, 2-3.5 mm long; lemmas silky-hairy on the lower keel and marginal nerves,
sometimes also hairy on the other nerves below, not webbed at the base.
Exposed ridges and slopes, about 9000 feet.

Poa sandbergii Vasey   Mountain Bluegrass
  P. secunda Presl
  Purplish clustered perennials; culms erect, 50-100 cm tall; leaves mostly basal, soft,
usually inrolled, often curled, up to 2 mm wide; panicle narrow, dense or open, 2-12 cm
long, the branches short, erect, ascending or rather spreading; spikelets 3- to 5-flowered,
5-7 mm long; glumes scabrous, about 4 mm long; lemmas curly-fine-hairy below, especially the keel and margins, not webbed at the base.
From boggy meadows and open woods at low elevations to dry exposed ridges and slopes
at high elevations, 6000 to nearly 10,000 feet.

Poa scabrella (Thurb.) Benth.   Hillside Bluegrass
  P. canbyi (Scribn.) Piper
  Green or bluish perennials; culms closely clustered, 50-120 cm tall; leaves basal,
abundant, blades flat, scabrous, very narrow; panicle narrow, 10-15 cm long, erect or
nodding, the branches short and appressed; spikelets 3- to 6-flowered, pale green or
purplish, 7-10 mm long; glumes acute, 4-5 mm long; lemmas rounded on the back, hairy
below.
Forest openings and on the moraines, 4500 to about 5000 feet.

Poa suksdorfii Vasey   Suksdorf's Bluegrass
  P. pringlei Scribn.
  Densely tufted perennials mostly 10-50 cm tall; leaves mostly basal, the blades folded, stiff, very narrow; panicle compact, spike-like, 2-5 cm long; spikelets 2- to 5-flowered, purplish, 6-8 mm long, the florets perfect or pistillate only; glumes thin, broad, 3-nerved, 4-5 mm long; lemmas about 4.5 mm long, keeled, scabrous or hairless, not webbed at the base.
Exposed peaks and ridges, 8400 to about 9500 feet or so.

Poa vaseyochloa Scribn.   Vasey's Bluegrass
  ? P. leibergii Scribn.
  In small, dense, soft tufts; culms erect, 10-20 cm tall; leaves mostly basal, folded or rolled, short and very narrow; panicle ovate, 2-4 cm long, open, the few capillary branches spreading; spikelets large, 1 or 2 per branch, flattened, 3- to 6-flowered, purplish, 5-7 mm long; glumes broad; lemmas 3 mm long, hairless or scabrous on the keel, not webbed at the base.
Wet rocks and moist rocky slopes, 4500 to about 7000 feet.

Sitanion Raf.

  Green or bluish tufted perennials; leaves narrow; spikes bristly; spikelets 2- to 6- or 8-flowered, without a pedicel, usually 2 at each node of the rachis, or up to 4, breaking apart easily and leaving each portion with a pair of spikelets attached at its upper end; glumes often bristle-like, the 1 to 3 nerves extending into 1 to 9 often very unequal awns; lemmas nearly round, faintly 5-nerved, 1-toothed at the tip, with 1 or more nerves extending into short awns from the tip.

Glumes 2-toothed at the tip, or undivided .... *S. hystrix*
Glumes cleft into at least 3 fine divisions, and sometimes up to 7 .... *S. jubatum*

Sitanion hystrix J. G. Sm.   Bottle-brush Squirrel-tail
  Culms stiff, erect to spreading or prostrate, 10-50 cm tall; blades hairless or fine-hairy, sometimes densely soft-white-hairy, 1-5 mm wide; spike 2-15 cm long, breaking apart easily; spikelets usually 2 at each node, 1- to 6- or 8-flowered; glumes very narrow, the tip undivided or 2-cleft, the 1 to 2 nerves extending into scabrous spreading awns 2-10 cm long; lemmas smooth or scabrous, sometimes bluish and hairy, the nerves extending into awns.
Dry gravelly open woods, dry rocky slopes and other usually exposed places, 4900 to about 9000 feet.

Sitanion jubatum J. G. Sm.   Big Squirrel-tail
  Densely clustered, 20-60 cm tall; foliage hairless or scabrous to white-hairy or even velvety; leaf blades rarely over 3 mm wide; spike dense, 3-13 cm long, breaking up easily; spikelets usually 2 at each node, 2- to 4-flowered; glumes split into 3 or more spreading awns 3-10 cm long; lemmas glabrous or short-hairy, the 1 to 3 awns spreading, 3-10 cm long.
Dry sandy ridge at 7200 feet.

Stipa L.

  Tufted perennial grasses; leaf blades usually rolled; panicle open or narrow; spikelets

1-flowered, breaking up obliquely above the glumes leaving a sharp-pointed callus; glumes thin and papery, narrow, acute or tapering to a point; lemma narrow, round, hard, usually with a long, persistent twisted and bent awn; palea enclosed by the lemma.

Awn conspicuously long-hairy to the second bend or throughout, up to 5 cm long............*S. occidentalis*
Awn slender, short-hairy to nearly hairless, 1-2 cm long..*S. lettermanii*

Stipa lettermanii Vasey   Porcupine Grass

Culms in dense close tufts, 30-60 cm tall; leaf blades short, crowded, narrow; panicle very narrow, loosely-flowered, 6-20 cm long; glumes 3-nerved, acuminate, 6-8 mm long; lemma slender and short-hairy on the body, longer at the tip, 4-6 mm long, the awn scabrous or fine-hairy, 1-2 cm long, twice bent, the callus short, not sharp; palea hairy, long and slender.
Dry open woods, about 5000 feet.

Stipa occidentalis Thurb.   Western Needle-grass

Culms clustered, 25-120 cm tall; leaf blades 1-5 mm wide, usually inrolled; panicle narrow, loose, 10-25 cm long; glumes 8-12 mm long, tapering to a point, the tips colorless; lemma pale brown, usually hairy and sometimes with longer hairs at the tip, 6-7 mm long, the awn 1.5-5 cm long, twice bent, long-hairy to the tip or the hairs shorter on the third portion, the callus sharp, about 1 cm long.
Open woods but always at the head of or along streams, 4500 to about 7500 feet.

Awn feathery-hairy over the first portion and usually also over the second...var. **occidentalis** (*S. oregonensis* Scribn).
Awn hairless to scabrous but not at all feathery-hairy, mostly under 3 cm long; callus blunt........var. **minor** (Vasey) C. L. Hitchc. (*S. columbiana* Macoun; *S. minor* Scribn.;
With the species.   *S. occidentalis* var. *idahoensis* Maze)

Trisetum Pers.

Clustered perennials; leaf blades soft and flat; panicles shining, open or narrow and dense; spikelets medium-sized, usually 2-flowered but sometimes 3- to 5-flowered; glumes usually unequal, the first shorter than the second; lemmas 5-nerved, keeled, 2-toothed at the tip, the awn curved or bent, arising from just below the teeth, (or the lemmas awnless, very short-awned, or awn-tipped in *T. wolfii*).

1. Awn of the lemma well developed, 5-14 mm long, bent or curved, prolonged beyond the glumes
    2. Awn 5-7 mm long; spikelets 4-7 mm long; glumes about equal ....*T. spicatum*
    2. Awn 10-14 mm long; spikelets 7-8 mm long; glumes unequal.........................*T. canescens*
1. Awn of the lemma missing or up to 6 mm long, straight, included in the glumes ....*T. wolfii*

Trisetum canescens Buckl.   Tall Trisetum

Culms clustered, erect or decumbent, 50-120 cm tall; blades flat, scabrous, pilose or canescent, 2-10 mm wide; panicle loose, narrow, sometimes interrupted and spike-like, 8-25 cm long; spikelets 7-8 mm long, 2- to 3-flowered; glumes smooth, except the keel, 5-7 mm long, the first narrower and shorter than the second; lemmas firm, somewhat scabrous, the upper longer than the glumes, the teeth awned, the dorsal awn bent, spreading and twisted below, 10-14 mm long, attached ⅓ below the tip.
Shady hillside woods and streambanks, 5000 to about 8000 feet.

Trisetum spicatum (L.) Richt. — Downy Oat-grass

Culms tufted, 10-50 cm tall; blades usually scabrous and somewhat hairy, 2-5 mm wide; panicle 2-15 cm long, dense and spike-like or interrupted below, pale green, shining-silvery, or often dark purplish; spikelets 4-7 mm long, 2- or 3-flowered; glumes smooth and glabrous or sometimes scabrous or long-hairy, the second glume a little longer and wider than the first; lemmas slightly scabrous, the first longer than the glumes, the teeth sharp-pointed, the awn bent, 5-7 mm long.

Cliffs, rocky slopes and exposed ridges in dry sandy soils mostly, 7000 to about 9600 feet and probably higher.

Trisetum wolfii Vasey — Beardless Trisetum

T. muticum Scribn.; *Graphephorum muticum* Heller

Culms loosely tufted, 30-100 cm tall; leaf blades scabrous or hairy, flat, 2-6 mm wide; panicle narrow, usually spike-like, green or pale, sometimes purplish, 6-20 cm long; spikelets usually 2- or 3-flowered; glumes nearly equal, 5-6 mm long; lemmas somewhat scabrous, awnless or with a minute straight awn below the tip, the teeth sharp-pointed but not awned.

Wet or swampy mountain meadows in coniferous woods and along creeks and lakes, 5000 to about 8000 feet.

SPARGANIACEAE   Bur-reed Family

Monoecious marsh or aquatic perennial herbs; stems erect or floating; leaves narrow, alternate, 2-ranked, parallel-veined, sheathing at the base; flowers in dense globose heads scattered along the upper parts of the plant, the staminate heads above the pistillate; staminate flowers with 3 to 5 stamens and bracts, pistillate flowers minute with a perianth of a few chaffy scales; the ovary mostly one-celled; fruit a nut-like 1- or 2-seeded achene.

Sparganium [Tourn.] L.

Characters of the family.

Leaves much longer than the inflorescence; staminate heads 2 to several; fruiting heads
7-20 mm in diameter..*S. angustifolium*

Leaves about equaling the inflorescence; staminate head usually solitary, sometimes 2;
fruiting heads rarely as much as 12 mm in diameter ....*S. minimum*

Sparganium angustifolium Michx. — Narrow-leaved Bur-reed

Stems soft, 30-100 cm long, floating or erect; leaves 2-6 mm wide, usually much longer than the stem, the upper ones dilated and sheathing; inflorescence simple, the upper 1 to 5 heads staminate, the lower 2 to 4 pistillate; fruiting heads 7-20 mm in diameter; achenes brown, spindle-shaped, stipitate and long-beaked.

Rooted in mud under 6 to 8 inches of water; mountain lakes at about 7000 to 7500 feet elevation.

Sparganium minimum (Hartm.) Fries — Small Bur-reed

Stems slender, weak, floating on water or weakly erect, 10-100 cm long; leaves floating or erect, narrow, flat, dark green, mostly 3-6 mm wide; inflorescence simple, the pistillate heads 1 to 3, axillary, below the mostly solitary staminate head; fruiting heads about

5-10 mm in diameter; achenes ellipsoid, dull greenish-brown, short-beaked, constricted at the middle.
Meadowy sedge-bog at about 5600 feet.

TYPHACEAE   Cat-tail Family

Perennial marsh or aquatic plants with creeping roots; stems solid and terete; leaves long, parallel-veined and pithy; inflorescence a dense terminal cylindric spike of minute unisexual flowers, the staminate flowers with 2 to 5 stamens, the pistillate of one pistil, the ovary one-celled and one-ovuled; fruit a small achene.

Typha [Tourn.] L.

Characters of the family.

Typha latifolia L.   Common Cat-tail
Aquatic perennial herb; stem solid, 1.5-3 m tall; leaves grayish-green, long, soft, flat, 5-25 mm wide; spike deep brown, uninterrupted, long-peduncled, the upper portion 10-30 cm long, composed of staminate flowers with one stamen and several long fine bristles, the lower portion about equal in length, composed mostly of 1-carpellary stipitate pistillate flowers mingled with a few sterile ones; fruit a long-stalked 1-seeded achene.
Roadside ditches and small bogs or marshy ground at about 4600 feet.

LILIACEAE   Lily Family

Mostly perennial herbs from bulbs, corms or rhizomes; leaves parallel-veined, mostly alternate; flowers solitary or clustered, regular, mostly perfect; perianth in 2 sets of 3 segments, free or united into a tube; stamens mostly 6; pistil 1; ovary superior to inferior, ours mostly 3-celled; styles free or united, the stigmas entire or 3-lobed; fruit a capsule or a fleshy berry.

1. Flowers blue or purple
    2. Flowers large, 1 to 4 on a stem
       3. Flower solitary, showy...*Trillium*
       3. Flowers 1 to 4, dull, mottled with greenish-yellow.......................................*Fritillaria*
    2. Flowers smaller, many on a stem
       4. Flowers bell-shaped, crowded in a terminal cluster..*Brodiaea*
       4. Flowers not bell-shaped, the segments spreading apart separately; flowers in
         an open raceme (sometimes dense in one species)..*Camassia*
1. Flowers yellow, green, white, creamy to rose-colored but not blue or purple
    5. Flowers bright yellow or orange, mostly nodding
       6. Perianth segments 2-5 cm long; leaves broad..*Erythronium*
       6. Perianth segments 1.2-2.5 cm long; leaves narrow...*Fritillaria*
    5. Flowers white, cream, green to pink or rose but not bright yellow or orange
       7. Flowers mostly 1 to 3 on a stem
         8. Flowers bright white; leaves 2, the blades broad..*Clintonia*
         8. Flowers mostly pinkish, often with dark spots on the petals; leaves more
           than 2, the blades narrow...*Calochortus*
       7. Flowers usually more than 3 per stem
         9. Stems branched
           10. Flowers 1 to 3 at the ends of the branches...*Disporum*
           10. Flowers more than 3, scattered along the stem in the leaf axils,
             the pedicels bent or twisted..*Streptopus*

```
9. Stems unbranched
    11. Flowering stems leafy
        12. Plants stiffly erect, usually 1 meter tall or more; inflorescence
            about 40 cm long, clearly branched............................................Veratrum
        12. Plants more lax, usually much shorter; inflorescence rarely
            over 15 cm long................................................................Smilacina
    11. Flowering stems mostly without leaves
        13. Flowers in a close terminal cluster mostly appearing almost
            hemispheric; onion odor usually conspicuous............................Allium
        13. Flowers in a more elongated raceme not appearing
            hemispheric; onion odor missing................................Zigadenus
```

Allium [Tourn.] L.

Perennial herbs with the characteristic odor and taste of onion; flowering stems from bulbs formed annually; leaves 1 to several, mostly linear and basal or nearly so; flowers in a head or umbel, subtended by 1 to 4 papery bracts; perianth segments 6, free, erect or spreading, 1-nerved; stamens 6; ovary sessile, 3-lobed, often crested, 3-celled, usually with 2 ovules in each cell; style 1, stigma entire or 3-cleft; seeds black, up to 6 per capsule.

```
1. Flowers white or pale pink (See also A. acuminatum)
    2. Flowering stem usually under 15 cm tall; leaves equaling or longer than the
       flowering stem
        3. Leaves breaking easily at flowering time; flower cluster loose and open;
           floral segments with dark midrib...........................................A. tolmiei
        3. Leaves persistent; flower cluster dense and crowded; floral segments with
           green midrib............................................................A. fibrillum
    2. Flowering stem mostly over 15 cm tall; leaves equaling or shorter than the flowering
       stem
        4. Flower cluster nodding at flowering time, the style conspicuously longer than
           the floral segments; perianth segments 4-6 mm long.....................A. cernuum
        4. Flower cluster erect at flowering time, the style not conspicuously longer than
           the floral segments; perianth segments 6-10 mm long....................A. madidum
1. Flowers deep rose; leaves shorter than the flowering stem
    5. Leaves mostly 2, narrow, 2-3 mm wide, usually withering early, flowering stem
       10-30 cm tall; plants of low elevations in our mountains................A. acuminatum
    5. Leaves 3 to 6, wider, 4-15 mm wide, persistent at flowering time; flowering stem
       30-80 cm tall; plants at middle to upper elevations ....................A. validum
```

Allium acuminatum Hook.   Hooker's Onion

Bulb ovoid, about 1.5 cm long, the reticulations on the coat strongly cell-like, regular, quadrangular; scape 1-3 dm tall, terete; leaves 2 or more, very narrow, shorter than the scape, 2-3 mm wide, usually withering early; bracts 2; umbels open, 7- to 25-flowered; perianth pink or deep rose-purple to white, 1-1.5 cm long, the segments spreading or curved at the tips; stamens shorter than the perianth segments; ovary inconspicuously 3-crested; seeds dull black.
Dry stony open ground, about 5000 feet.

Allium cernuum Roth   Nodding Onion

Bulb long-necked, ovoid, 3-6 cm long, without reticulations, the cells in regular longitudinal rows in the bulb coat; leaves thick, equaling or shorter than the scape, 1-6 mm wide, green and persistent; bracts 2, short; scape 1-6 dm tall; umbel nodding, 1- to many-

flowered; perianth rose-color or white, the segments 4-6 mm long; stamens and style longer than the perianth; capsule 6-crested; seeds dull black.
Shady streambank in mixed woods; about 5200 feet.

Allium fibrillum M. E. Jones   Jones' Onion
   Bulb ovoid, 1-1.5 cm long, the reticulations on the coat narrow and much contorted; scape 3-20 cm tall; leaves flat, equaling or longer than the scape, 1-4 mm wide, green and persistent; bracts 2; umbel open or crowded, few- to many-flowered; perianth segments white with green midrib or pale rose, 5-8 mm long, becoming papery in fruit; stamens and style shorter than the perianth, the stamens yellowish or purplish; ovary obscurely 6-crested or the crests missing; seeds black.
Moist or dry rocky ground in heavy soils, 5000 to about 7200 feet.

Allium madidum S. Wats.   Swamp Onion
   Bulb ovoid, 1-1.5 cm long, without definite reticulations in the coat; scape 1-2.5 dm tall, angled or terete; leaves 2, thick and channeled, equaling or shorter than the scape, 1-6 mm wide, 7-12 cm long, green and persistent; bracts 2; umbel usually 25- to 35-flowered; perianth segments keeled, white with green ribs or pale rose, 6-10 mm long, becoming papery; stamens three-fourths as long as the perianth, the anthers dark purple or yellowish; style longer than the perianth; ovary obscurely 3- to 6-crested or the crests missing; seeds black.
Moist or wet places in woods, about 6000 feet.

Allium tolmiei Baker   Tolmie's Onion
   Bulb ovoid, large, with or without cellular reticulations; scape 5-15 cm tall, flattened and winged; leaves 2, flat, thick, curved, 1-12 mm wide, equaling or usually longer than the scape, breaking off at maturity; umbel 25- to 60-flowered; perianth light rose-purple to nearly white with dark stripes, the segments 6-12 mm long; stamens $\frac{2}{3}$ to $\frac{3}{4}$ as long as the segments, the anthers pinkish or purplish or yellowish; capsule with 6 low crests, these sometimes obscure.
Dry rocky open places, often in sandy or clayey soil at about 3500 to 5000 feet.

Allium validum Wats.   Tall Swamp Onion
   Bulb oblong-ovoid, sometimes finely-reticulate, 3-5 cm long, from horizontal root-stocks; scape angled, flattened, 3-8 dm tall; leaves 3 to 6, flat or ridged, nearly equaling or usually shorter than the scape, 4-15 mm wide, persistent at maturity; bracts 2 to 4; umbels 15- to 30-flowered; perianth segments 5-10 mm long, deep rose-colored to nearly white; stamens about equaling or usually much longer than the perianth, the anthers yellowish or purplish; capsule 5 mm long, not crested; seeds dull black.
Swampy meadows, 6900 to about 8000 feet.

Brodiaea Smith

Perennial scapose herbs with bulb-like scaly corms; leaves 1 to 5, narrow, nearly basal; flowers in an umbel subtended by scarious bracts; perianth parts united below, the segments erect or spreading; stamens 6, in 1 or 2 rows; ovary sessile; style 1, stigmas 3; capsule beaked, loculicdal.

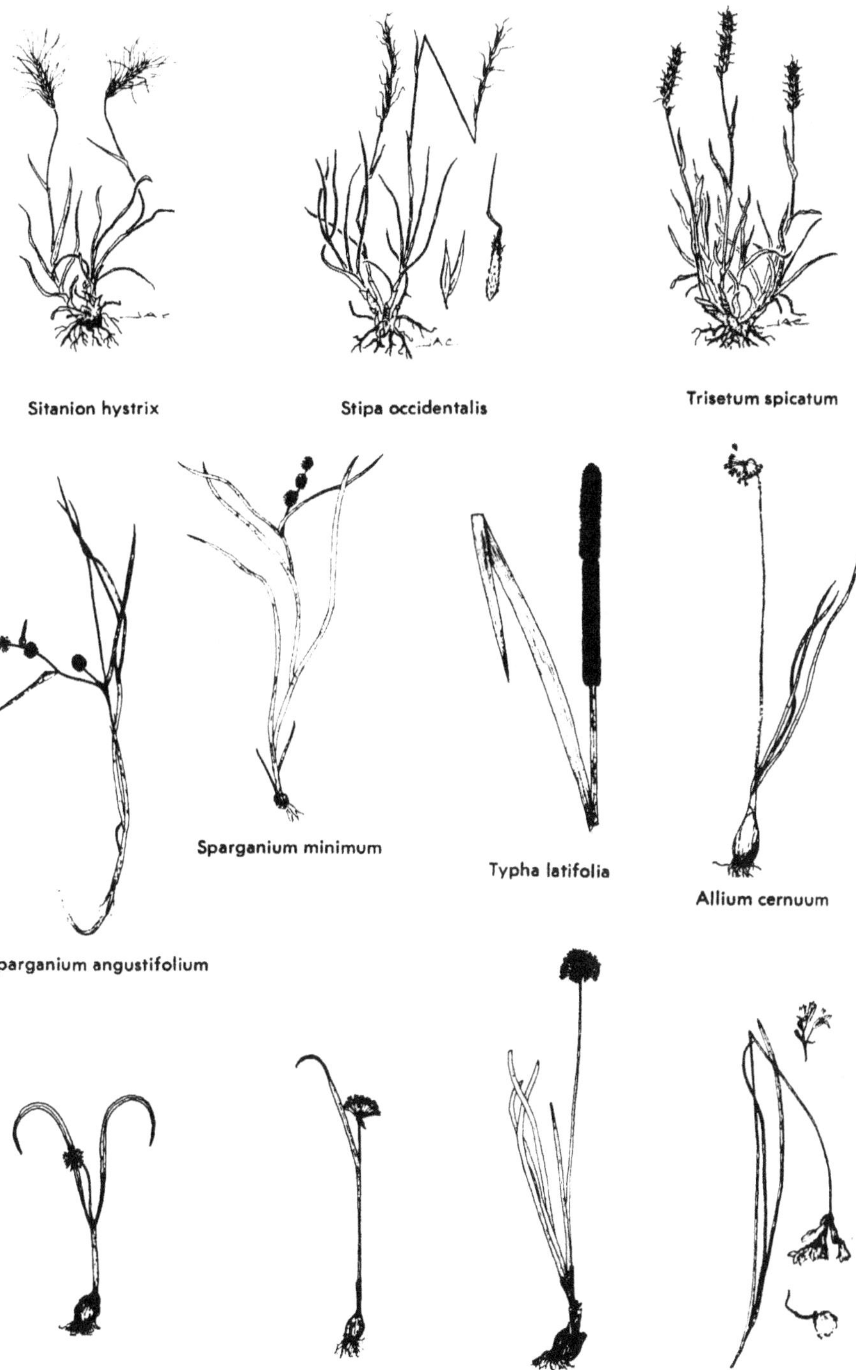

Sitanion hystrix

Stipa occidentalis

Trisetum spicatum

Sparganium minimum

Typha latifolia

Allium cernuum

Sparganium angustifolium

Allium fibrillum

Allium tolmiei

Allium validum

Brodiaea douglasii

Brodiaea douglasii Wats.   Large-flowered Brodiaea

Leaves linear, 1 or 2, 3-5 dm long, 5-10 mm wide, persistent; scape erect, 20-70 cm tall; umbel 6- to 20-flowered, the pedicels 2-3 cm long; perianth light to deep blue, 1.5-2.5 cm long, tubular, the lobes ruffled at the base, the tips spreading; stamens in 2 sets of 3, very unequally inserted on the perianth, the anthers pale blue; capsule stipitate, 6-7 mm long.

Meadows and grassy slopes, 4800 to 5400 feet.

Flowers usually larger; the filaments winged, the outer ones longer than the anthers, the inner very short..var. **howellii** (Wats.) Peck

Calochortus Pursh

Perennial herbs; stems from bulb-like coated corms; leaves few, alternate, clasping, linear-lanceolate; flowers few, showy; perianth of 6 segments, the 3 outer narrow and sepal-like, the 3 inner broad and petaloid, often hairy, usually with a glandular pit near the base; stamens 6; capsule elliptic to oblong, 3-angled, often winged, many-seeded.

Petals with a conspicuous rounded dark spot near the middle; flowers 1 to 4 in a cluster;
    capsule winged, 2-2.5 cm long...*C. eurycarpus*
Petals without a dark spot but with a green stripe down the middle; flowers usually 2;
    capsule narrowly winged, or wingless, 4.5-5.5 cm long...*C. macrocarpus*

Calochortus eurycarpus Wats.   Big-pod Mariposa Lily

Stem stiff, 10-45 cm tall; umbel 1- to 5-flowered; basal leaf flat, cauline leaf bract-like; sepals ovate-lanceolate, longer or shorter than the petals; petals white to lavender with a conspicuous dark spot in the middle, 2.5-4.5 cm long, the gland surrounded by long hairs and completely covered with short yellow hairs; capsule elliptic, 2-2.5 cm long, broadly 3-winged.

Sunny open wooded slopes and meadows, 4600 to 7600 feet.

Calochortus macrocarpus Dougl.   Green-banded Star Tulip

Stem stout, glaucous, 30-70 cm tall; leaves 3 to 5, shorter than the stem, linear, withering early; flowers usually 2; sepals lanceolate 3.5-5.5 cm long, purplish with broad scarious margins; petals obovate, 3-6 cm long, lilac or purple with yellow base and a longitudinal green stripe down the middle, sometimes also with a dark purplish band above the gland, the gland large, surrounded by fringed yellow hairs; anthers bluish; capsule lanceolate, 4.5-5.5 cm long, narrowly winged if at all.

Dry hillsides and open meadows, 4000 to 5600 feet.

Camassia L.

Bulbous perennials; stems scapose; leaves linear and basal; flowers large and showy, in racemes; perianth segments 6, all alike, free, 3- to 7-nerved; stamens 6, the filaments long and filiform; style 1, stigmas 3; capsule 3-angled.

Flowering stems usually more than 1, 40-80 cm tall, densely many-flowered; flowers pale
    blue; leaves 2-3.5 cm wide ....*C. cusickii*
Flowering stems usually solitary, 20-70 cm tall, the raceme open and few-flowered; flowers
    usually deep purplish blue; leaves 1-2 cm wide..*C. quamash*

Camassia cusickii Wats.   Cusick's Camas

Bulbs large, often clustered, malodorous; leaves numerous, 2-3.5 cm or more broad,

shorter than the scapes; scapes stout, clustered, 40-80 cm tall; raceme densely crowded, 25-40 cm long; perianth pale blue, the segments 1.5-3 cm long, 3- to 5-nerved, the lowest separate from the other 5, all withering separately; capsule oblong, 1.5-2 cm long.
Wooded mountainsides, about 4500 to 5000 feet, but not common.

Camassia quamash (Pursh) Greene   Common Camas
Bulb globose or ovoid, usually black-coated; leaves few, 8-20 mm wide, usually much shorter than the scape; scape 20-70 cm tall; raceme loosely few- to many-flowered, 10-25 cm long; perianth dark purplish-blue or sometimes light blue (or white), the segments 1-3.5 cm long, 3- to 9-nerved, the lowest separated from the others, all withering separately; bracts longer than the pedicels; anthers yellow to blue; capsule oblong-obovoid, 1-2.5 cm long.
Moist to wet meadows and open woods, about 5800 feet.

Clintonia Raf.

Perennial herbs; stems from elongated rhizomes; leaves 2 or 3 (ours), essentially basal, broad and flat; scape erect, simple; flowers terminal, solitary (ours) to umbellate, perfect, showy; perianth segments alike, distinct; stamens 6; ovary 2- to 3-celled; fruit a round, few-seeded, blue or black berry.

Clintonia uniflora (Schult.) Kunth.   Blue-bead
Stems mostly underground, from creeping rhizomes; leaves mostly 2, thin, oblanceolate to obovate, 8-15 cm long, 2-7 cm broad, pubescent, with ciliate margins; scapes shorter than the leaves, often with 1 or 2 small bracts; flowers usually solitary, white, 1.5-2 cm long; berry deep blue, round or pear-shaped, 6-10 mm long.
Moist shady coniferous woods and bogs, 4600 to 5600 feet.

Disporum Salisb.

Perennial herbs with slender horizontal rhizomes; stems branching, leafy; leaves alternate, sessile, broad and veiny, clasping; flowers 1 or few in small clusters; perianth segments 6, similar, distinct; stamens 6; ovary 3-celled; stigma entire or 3-cleft; fruit an ovoid red or yellow few-seeded berry.

Disporum trachycarpum (Wats.) B. & H.   Fairy Bells
Stem usually branched and pubescent, 3-6 dm tall; leaves ovate to oblong-lanceolate, 4-12 cm long, oblique at the base, sometimes ciliate-margined, 5- to 11-nerved; flowers solitary or in 2's or 3's, creamy-white, 8-14 mm long, narrowly bell-shaped; stamens equaling or slightly longer than the perianth; style 3-lobed; berry broadly obovoid to globose, fleshy-papillose, 7-10 mm broad, 4- to 18-seeded.
Shady coniferous woods, often near streams, 4000 to 6000 feet.

Erythronium L.

Low perennial herbs from deep-seated corms; stem simple; leaves usually 2, sometimes 3, often mottled, large and unequal, appearing basal; flowers large and showy, nodding, 1 or more in a loose raceme; perianth segments similar, free; stamens 6; ovary 3-celled; style 3-lobed or entire; capsule 3-angled, loculicidal.

Erythronium grandiflorum Pursh   Yellow Fawn Lily
Leaves 7-20 cm long, oblong-lanceolate, not mottled; scape 8-35 cm tall, bearing a
solitary flower or a raceme of 2 to 6 flowers; perianth segments lanceolate, bright yellow,
rarely pink, 2-5 cm long; filaments dilated at the base, the anthers reddish-purple; style
long and slender; capsule 3-6 cm long, narrowed to a short stipe.
Moist woods and open grassy slopes, 4000 to 5500 feet.

Fritillaria [Tourn.] L.

Perennial herbs with small scaly bulbs encircled by many smaller rice-like bulblets;
stems erect and unbranched; leaves scattered, alternate or whorled, linear to lanceolate;
flowers solitary or few, bell-shaped, usually nodding; perianth segments 6, similar and
free with a gland pit near the base; stamens 6, short; ovary sessile; capsule 6-angled,
sometimes winged, many-seeded, loculicidally dehiscent; seeds flat.

Flowers yellow or orange, sometimes tinged with red or purple..*F. pudica*
Flowers brownish-purple, mottled with greenish yellow..*F. atropurpurea*

Fritillaria atropurpurea Nutt.   Checker Lily; Purple Fritillary
Bulb with a few large scales; stem 12-60 cm tall; leaves 6 to 20, linear, scattered or
whorled, 3-12 cm long; flowers bell-shaped, mostly 1 to 4 or 6, dull brownish-purplish,
mottled with greenish yellow or white, the segments 8-20 mm long; styles free nearly to
the base; capsule obovoid, 1-1.5 cm long, angled.
Dry gravelly slopes at low elevations.

Fritillaria pudica (Pursh) Spreng.   Yellow-bells
Bulb with a few large fleshy scales and many smaller ones; stems 8-30 cm tall; leaves
mostly 2 and nearly opposite, or more than 2 and alternate or somewhat whorled, linear-
lanceolate, 3-16 cm long; flowers nodding, bell-shaped, usually 1 but sometimes 2 or 3,
yellow or orange, or sometimes tinged with red or purple with age, the segments 12-26
mm long; styles united; capsule obovoid, 1.5-3 cm long.
Open grasslands and in woods, 4000 to 6600 feet.

Smilacina Desf.

Perennial herbs with horizontal rhizomes and unbranched leafy flowering stems;
leaves alternate, sessile or short-petioled, ovate to lanceolate, strongly nerved; flowers
small in a terminal raceme or panicle; perianth parts 6, not united; stamens 6; style 1;
ovary 3-celled; fruit a round, greenish to red berry; seeds 1 or 2.

Flowers minute, very many in a dense cluster..*S. racemosa*
Flowers larger, only 5 to 10 in an open raceme ....*S. stellata*

Smilacina racemosa (L.) Desf.   Western False Solomon's Seal
    S. amplexicaulis Nutt.
Stems from narrow, fleshy rhizomes, 3-12 dm tall, somewhat angled; leaves finely
pubescent, ovate to broadly lanceolate, 8-20 cm long, sessile or short-petioled and clasping; panicle densely-flowered, 3-15 cm long; flowers creamy-white, 1.5-2.5 mm long;
berries bright red, purplish-spotted, 4-7 mm long; seed usually solitary, sometimes 2 or 3.
Moist wooded slopes, 4000 to 5000 feet.

Calochortus eurycarpus

Calochortus macrocarpus

Camassia quamash

Clintonia uniflora

Disporum trachycarpum

Erythronium grandiflorum

Fritillaria atropurpurea

Fritillaria pudica

Smilacina racemosa

Smilacina stellata

Smilacina stellata (L.) Desf.   Starry False Solomon's Seal
S. liliacea (Greene) Wynd.; *S. sessilifolia* (Baker) Nutt.
Flowering stems from rhizomes, 2-6 dm tall; leaves sessile, flat or folded, elliptic, 4-17 cm long, heavily veined; flowers creamy-white, 3-7 mm long, 5 to 10 in a terminal raceme; berry greenish-yellow, turning blackish, 5-10 mm long.
Moist shady woods, streambanks and open places at low elevations.

Streptopus Michx.

Branching leafy perennial herbs with creeping rhizomes; leaves ovate, alternate, sessile or clasping, many-nerved; flowers small, 1 or 2 together, drooping, bell-shaped; pedicels axillary, bent or twisted at the middle; perianth segments 6, all alike, free, the outer ones flat, the inner keeled; stamens 6, the filaments short and flat; ovary 3-celled; fruit an oval or roundish many-seeded greenish to red berry.

Streptopus amplexifolius (L.) DC.   Large Twisted Stalk
Stem from a short fibrous-rooted creeping rhizome, 3-12 dm tall, usually branching below the middle; leaves ovate to lanceolate, 5-15 cm long, 2.5-5 cm wide; peduncles 1- or 2-flowered, sharply bent and jointed, twisted at the joint, usually 1.5-3 cm long; flowers 8-15 mm long, greenish- or yellowish-white, spreading or recurved; stamens unequal; berries oval or elliptic, many-seeded, 10-18 mm long, green to yellow or red.
Moist shady coniferous woods, streambanks and thickets, 4000 to 7000 feet.

Trillium L.

Low perennial herbs with short rhizomes and stout fleshy stems; leaves 3, whorled, broadly ovate and veiny, closely subtending the solitary terminal flower; perianth parts unlike, the outer set of 3 green and persistent segments, the inner 3 mostly white to pink-purplish, deciduous or withering; stamens 6, the filaments short; ovary 3-celled, 3- to 6-angled or lobed; fruit a fleshy many-seeded berrylike capsule.

Trillium petiolatum Pursh   Round-leaved Wake Robin
Flowering stems mostly underground, usually only 2-3 cm above ground; leaves long-petioled, round-ovate, not mottled, 6-12 cm long, 5-10 cm broad; flowers sessile in the axils of the leaves; sepals green, oblong-elliptic, 1.5-6 cm long; petals oblanceolate, 2.5-4.5 cm long, purplish or brownish to maroon; anthers purple, 1-3 cm long.
Damp woods and meadows at about 5000 feet.

Veratrum L.

Large leafy-stemmed perennial herbs with short rhizomes; leaves broad, clasping, strongly veined; flowers numerous in a terminal panicle or raceme; perianth white or green, bell- or saucer-shaped, the 6 segments all alike; stamens 6, free from the perianth segments and opposite them; fruit a 3-lobed, 3-celled capsule.

Flowers white with greenish veins; branches of the inflorescence erect or spreading....*V. californicum*
Flowers greenish; branches of the inflorescence drooping ....*V. viride*

Veratrum californicum Durand   California False Hellebore
Stems 1-2 meters tall, tomentose above; leaves numerous, sheathing, 20-30 cm, 10-20 cm wide, broadly oval to ovate; inflorescence dense, 20-60 cm long, tomentose, the lower

branches ascending or spreading; perianth segments white or greenish-white, clawed, elliptic to obovate, 7-15 mm long, with 2 green glands at the base forming a "V"; capsule 2.5-3.5 cm long, the seeds numerous, broadly winged, 1-1.5 cm long.
Wet meadows, streambanks and moist woods, about 4500 feet.

Veratrum viride Ait. Green False Hellebore

Stems 5-20 dm tall, very leafy; leaves 15-30 cm long, 7-15 cm wide, sheathing, oblong-elliptic, reduced upwards; panicle 2-7 dm long, narrow, open and loose, the lower branches spreading and usually drooping; perianth parts oblong-elliptic, yellowish-green to deep green, 6-10 mm long, woolly on the outside; stamens short; capsule 2-2.5 cm long, many-seeded.
Swamps and thickets to moist woods and meadows, 5000 to about 8000 feet.

Zigadenus Michx.

Perennial herbs with narrow coated bulbs; stems leafy; leaves mostly basal, grasslike, reduced above; flowers in terminal racemes or panicles, white or creamy, the perianth bell-or saucer-shaped, the segments ovate to lanceolate, alike, the outer ones usually with a yellowish or greenish glandular spot near the base; stamens 6, free from the perianth, equaling or longer than the perianth segments; styles 3; fruit a 3-celled, many-seeded capsule.

1. Perianth segments 8-11 mm long; plants of boggy meadows; inflorescence open, loosely-flowered .... *Z. elegans*
1. Perianth segments under 7 mm long; plants of drier open places; inflorescence closely many-flowered
    2. Stamens distinctly longer than the perianth; leaves mostly shorter than the stem; lower branches of the inflorescence on longer stems than those above.......... ....*Z. paniculatus*
    2. Stamens about as long as the perianth; leaves nearly as long as the stem; lower branches of the inflorescence not elongated... *Z. venenosus*

Zigadenus elegans Pursh Glaucous Zigadene

Bulbs long-ovoid, membranous-coated, solitary or clustered; stems 15-100 cm tall, nearly leafless; leaves mostly basal, glaucous, 10-40 cm long, 2-15 mm wide, flat or folded, reduced upward; raceme open, loosely flowered, 6-15 cm long; perianth segments greenish- or yellowish-white, spreading, ovate to obovate, 8-11 mm long, not clawed, each with a dark obcordate gland at the base; styles free; capsule oblong, 1.5-2.5 cm long; seeds abundant.
Bogs, moist meadows, grassy slopes and lake borders, 5300 to 8000 feet.

Zigadenus paniculatus (Nutt.) Wats. Panicled Zigadene

Bulb ovoid, 3-4 cm long; stem stout, 30-70 cm tall; leaves 10-50 cm long, mostly basal, sheathing, the cauline reduced upward; inflorescence a panicle, 10-30 cm long, the lower branches elongated, the others shorter and closely-flowered; perianth segments acute to acutish, unequal, mostly ovate, 3-5 mm long, yellowish-white, the outer ones sessile, the inner ones clawed; basal glands greenish, distinct, about as broad as long; stamens longer than the perianth; capsules 1-1.8 cm long.
Open moraines and dry slopes, to about 5000 feet.

Zigadenus venenosus Wats. Poison, Death or Deadly Camas

Bulb ovoid, 2-3 cm long; stem slender, 20-70 cm tall; leaves nearly as long as the stem,

4-8 mm wide, mostly basal, the 1 or 2 cauline reduced upward, keeled and scabrous-margined; inflorescence 10-20 cm long, usually racemose; pedicels about 2 cm long, ascending or erect in fruit; perianth white to cream-colored, bell-shaped, the segments clawed, obtuse, ovate, unequal, 4-8 mm long, each with a thick yellowish-green basal gland usually broader than long; stamens about equaling the perianth or slightly longer; capsules cylindric, 1-1.5 cm long.

Wet meadows and open rocky or grassy slopes, 5000 to 8600 feet.

Upper stem leaves all sheathing; perianth parts 4-5 mm long, scarcely clawed, the gland thin and ill-defined; capsules oblong or oblong-elliptic, 1-1.5 cm long; meadows..var. **gramineus** (Rydb.) Walsh

IRIDACEAE   Iris Family

Perennial herbs with bulbs or rhizomes; leaves 2-ranked, parallel-veined, equitant; flowers often showy, perfect, in umbels, racemes or panicles; perianth in 2 series of 3 segments each; stamens 3; ovary inferior; style 3-cleft; fruit a 3-celled, loculicidal capsule.

Perianth segments not all alike; styles petal-like .... *Iris*
Perianth segments all alike; styles not petal-like.. *Sisyrinchium*

Iris [Tourn.] L.

Perennials (ours); stems erect; leaves linear, equitant, mostly basal; flowers 1 or more, often large and showy, the perianth of 3 broad outer segments (sepals) spreading and usually reflexed, the 3 inner ones narrow and erect, all joined at the base to form a short somewhat flared tube; style branches 3, often petal-like; stamens 3; capsules 3- to 6-angled with numerous seeds.

Iris missouriensis Nutt.   Western Blue Flag

Stems terete, essentially leafless, 20-60 cm tall; leaves few, mostly basal, 5-10 mm wide, about equaling the stem or shorter; flowers closely subtended by the involucral leaves, 1 to 4, usually 2, pale blue, purple-lined, the perianth tube flared above, 5-12 mm long; sepals 5-6 cm long, the petals a little shorter; stigmas broad, notched; capsule oblong, 3-5 cm long, 6-angled.

Meadows and streambanks, about 4000 to 5000 feet.

Sisyrinchium L.

Delicate tufted perennial herbs sometimes with short rhizomes; stems flattened, somewhat winged to roundish; leaves equitant, sheathing, narrow and grasslike; flowers 1 to few in umbels subtended by 2 involucral leaves; perianth segments all alike, spreading, blue or pink to rose purple, sometimes white; filaments united; style branches linear; fruit a leathery round or obovoid loculicidal capsule.

Flowers light to dark blue, yellow-eyed at the base, the segments 5-15 mm long .... *S. idahoense*
Flowers rose- to reddish-purple, occasionally white, the segments 15-20 mm long .... *S. douglasii*

Sisyrinchium douglasii Dietr.   Grass Widows

Stems solitary or clustered, 15-30 cm tall, somewhat flattened but not winged; leaves stiff and narrow, the 1 to 4 cauline ones sheathing, the blades 2-15 mm broad, the basal

leaves bract-like with reduced blades; spathe solitary and terminal, the outer bract often much longer than the flower; flowers mostly 2, the perianth 1.5-2 cm long, deep reddish-purplish, occasionally white, the segments 5-nerved, the tips notched or with a short bristle; filaments united only about half-way; capsule 5-9 mm long, often tinged with purple; seeds brown.
Moist or dry, open grassy places, 4500 to 5000 feet.

Sisyrinchium idahoense Bick.   Idaho Blue-eyed Grass
Stems usually simple, flattened and winged and essentially leafless, 10-45 cm tall; leaves about half as long as the stems, 1-3.5 mm wide; spathe usually sessile and terminal, the inner bract broader than the outer and much shorter than the flowers; flowers usually 1 to 3, the perianth 5-15 mm long, light blue to purplish blue, yellow at the base; filaments united almost to the tip; ovary glandular-pubescent; capsule round to obovoid, 3-6 mm long; seeds blackish.
Moist grassy boggy meadows and streambanks, 5000 to 5500 feet.

ORCHIDACEAE   Orchid Family

Perennial herbs (ours) with corms, bulbs, rhizomes or tubers; leaves parallel-veined, linear to oval or sometimes the leaves reduced to scales; flowers usually perfect, irregular and showy, in racemes, panicles, spikes, or solitary; perianth in 2 sets, all alike or the outer ones greenish, one of the inner series, the lip, usually larger, often spurred or pouched at the base; stamens 1 or 2, united with the style to form the column; stigmas 3; ovary inferior; fruit a 1-celled, 3-valved, many-seeded capsule.

1. Plants with green leaves, at the base or on the stem
     2. Flowers 1 to 4, usually large, showy and pouched
         3. Flower rose- or flesh-colored; leaf one, at the base..*Calypso*
         3. Flowers 1 to 4, white or greenish; leaves 2 or more, on the stem......................*Cypripedium*
     2. Flowers more than 4, often many, small, in a terminal spike
         4. Leaves several, scattered along the stem
             5. Leaves 2, opposite; stems mostly up to 20 cm tall...*Listera*
             5. Leaves mostly more than 2, not opposite
                 6. Lip with a spur as long as the lip, or shorter, or longer; spike
                     usually over 15 cm long...*Habenaria*
                 6. Lip without a spur; spike (ours) mostly about 3 cm long.............*Spiranthes*
         4. Leaves 1 to few, all basal or nearly so
             7. Leaves whitish-marbled, in a basal rosette...*Goodyera*
             7. Leaves not as above
                 8. Flowers with a spur; spike over 5 cm long or the plant with only
                     1 broad basal leaf..*Habenaria*
                 8. Flowers without a spur; spike only about 3 cm long...................*Spiranthes*
1. Plants without green leaves
     9. Plants completely white; rare in our mountains...*Eburophyton*
     9. Plants yellowish, purplish or reddish-brown; fairly common.............................*Corallorhiza*

Calypso Salisb.

Low herb with a corm; stem scapose; leaf solitary, basal; flower solitary, terminal, the lip conspicuously swollen, horned at the tip and bearded within, the other 5 segments different from the lip but like each other.

Calypso bulbosa (L.) Oakes   Fairy Slipper

Scape 7-15 (or rarely up to 30) cm tall from a corm; leaf solitary, basal, ovate, 3-6 cm long; flower rose-colored to magenta, sometimes whitish or flesh-colored, 1.5-2 cm long, the 3 sepals and 2 petals alike, the lip pouched, white-hairy within, lined, mottled and streaked with maroon or purple; capsule about 1 cm long.
Rich moist shady woods, 4500 to 5600 feet.

Corallorhiza Chat.

Yellowish or reddish plants with underground coral-like branching rhizomes; flowering stems with sheathing bracts or scales but without green leaves; flowers yellow to reddish-brown or purple, in racemes, the 2 lower sepals sometimes forming a spur united with the ovary; the lip simple or lobed; the column slightly curved above the lip; capsules pendulous.

1. Lip white or whitish; spur inconspicuous or missing
    2. Lip conspicuously covered with dark red spots; stems light yellow to brownish-purple; spur yellowish..*C. maculata*
    2. Lip usually not red-spotted; stems yellowish; spur if present small, attached to the top of the ovary...*C. trifida*
1. Lip mostly reddish-purple
    3. Flowers dull purple or pinkish, the spur prominent ....*C. mertensiana*
    3. Flowers mostly flesh-colored with reddish-brown to purplish longitudinal stripes, the spur missing...*C. striata*

Corallorhiza maculata Raf.   Spotted Coral-root

Stems brownish-purple (sometimes light yellow), 20-50 cm tall, with 2 to 4 sheathing scales; sepals and petals 3-nerved, dull reddish or brownish-purple, 6-13 mm long, the lip white, usually spotted and lined with dark red, 3-lobed, 2-toothed near the base, the central lobe large and wavy-margined; spur yellowish; column thick; capsules drooping, 1-2 cm long.
Dry coniferous woods, 4500 to about 5000 feet.

Corallorhiza mertensiana Bong.   Western Coral-root

Scapes reddish, 15-50 cm tall, usually with 3 sheathing bracts; sepals and petals spreading or erect, dull purple or pinkish, 6-10 mm long, 3-nerved, the 2 lateral sepals joined below the lip to form the prominent spur which is joined to the ovary half-way; lip broadly oblong, reddish-purple without spots, entire- or wavy-margined and sometimes with a small tooth on each side at the base; column slender and curved; capsules 1.5-2.5 cm long.
Coniferous forest, 4500 to 5200 feet.

Corallorhiza striata Lindl.   Striped Coral-root

Scape dull pinkish or purplish, 15-50 cm tall; perianth parts, except the lip, 7-17 mm long, flesh-color with 3 (sometimes 4 or 5) reddish-brown to purplish longitudinal stripes; lip 8-15 mm long, dark reddish-purple-striped, mostly entire, about equaling the petals, the margins thickened; spur none; column purple-spotted near the base; capsules drooping, 12-25 mm long.
Shady woods, about 4800 feet.

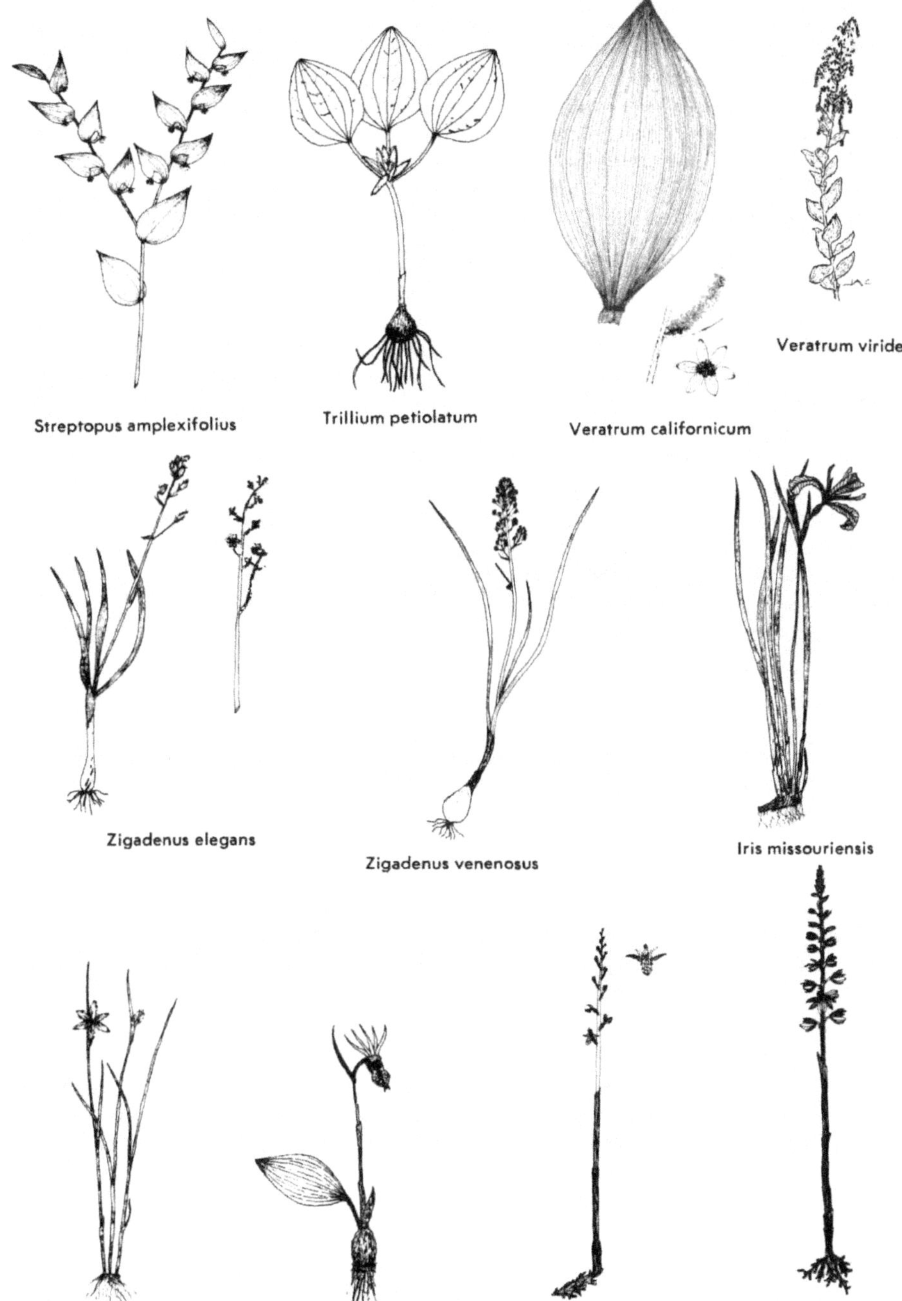

Streptopus amplexifolius

Trillium petiolatum

Veratrum californicum

Veratrum viride

Zigadenus elegans

Zigadenus venenosus

Iris missouriensis

Sisyrinchium douglasii

Calypso bulbosa

Corallorhiza maculata

Corallorhiza striata

Corallorhiza trifida Chat.   Pale or Yellow Coral-root

Plants yellowish; scapes slender, 10-30 cm tall with 2 to 5 sheathing scales; perianth parts yellow or greenish-yellow to nearly white, sometimes dull purple, 1-nerved; sepals about 5 mm long; lip shorter than the petals, 3.5-4.5 mm long, whitish, sometimes red-spotted, 2-lobed near the base, 3-nerved, the margins upturned; spur, if any, small, adnate to the top of the ovary; column broad; capsules oblong, about 1 cm long.
Bogs in dense coniferous forest, 4500 to 6000 feet.

Cypripedium L.

Glandular-pubescent herbs with leafy stems and large sheathing leaves; flowers 1 or more, showy; sepals distinct, spreading, the lateral pair united under the lip; petals long and narrow; lip inflated, sac-like, with incurved margins; column curved; fertile anthers 2, one on each side of the short column, the third sterile, enlarged, often petal-like; stigma terminal, 3-lobed.

Stem leaves 2, opposite; flowers 1 to 4 in a cluster..*C. fasciculatum*
Stem leaves more than 2, alternate; flowers 1 to 3 but not clustered together..................*C. montanum*

Cypripedium fasciculatum Kell.   Clustered Lady's Slipper

Stem 5-40 cm tall, hairy near the base, glandular above; leaves 2, cauline, elliptic, opposite; flowers 1 to 4, clustered, greenish with brownish-purple veining, 15-25 mm long; lip 8-10 mm long, greenish-yellow with purplish-brown margins.
Open coniferous woods, about 5000 feet.

Cypripedium montanum Dougl.   Mountain Lady's Slipper

Stem thick and leafy, 20-70 cm tall; leaves broadly ovate-elliptic, glandular-pubescent, 5-15 cm long, usually sessile and sheathing; flowers usually 2, sometimes 1 or 3, in the axils of leaflike bracts; sepals and petals brownish-purple, often twisted and curled, 4-6 cm long; lip obovoid, 1.5-3 cm long, conspicuously pouched, white- or pinkish-purplish-tinged and veined with purple; sterile anther yellowish-white, usually purplish-spotted.
Moist shady coniferous woods, about 5000 to 5500 feet.

Eburophyton Heller

Whole plant white; stems from creeping rhizomes; leaves reduced to scarious sheaths; flowers several, with scarious bracts, in a terminal spike-like raceme; lateral sepals keeled, spreading, the upper sepal and petals erect, the lip free, sac-like at the base, constricted in the middle, the margins broad and wing-like; column arched over the lip; pollinia 4, linear.

Eburophyton austiniae (Gray) Heller   Phantom Orchid

Cephalanthera austinae Gray

Plant white, turning brown with age, 20-50 cm tall; leaves 2 to 5, reduced to sheathing bracts; spike loosely 5- to 20-flowered; sepals and petals nearly equal, white or creamy, 1-2 cm long; lip slightly shorter, the sac-like base broadly yellow wing-margined, the nerves wavy-crested.
Rare in our mountains; moist deep woods.

Goodyera R. Br.

Scapose glandular-pubescent herbs with alternate to basal leaves; flowers small in a terminal raceme; spur missing; lip entire, pouched at the base, pointed and curved at the tip; anther 1, attached to the base of the short straight column; capsule erect.

Goodyera oblongifolia Raf.   Rattlesnake Plantain

Scape glandular-pubescent, 10-40 cm tall; leaves 5-20 mm long, in a basal rosette, the blades elliptic-lanceolate, dark green blotched with white; raceme 5-15 cm long, somewhat one-sided, often spiral; flowers greenish-white, the sepals and petals about 8 mm long, 1 sepal and 2 petals united to form the hood over the lip, the lip with a swollen base and recurved or spreading pointed tip; capsule about 1 cm long.
Coniferous woods, 4000 to 6400 feet.

Habenaria Willd.

Perennial herbs with fleshy or tuberous roots; stems with one to several cauline or basal leaves; flowers small in a terminal spike or raceme, white to yellowish or green; sepals and petals erect, spreading or reflexed, 3- to 7-nerved; column short, the 2 pollen sacs separate; lip reflexed, extended at the base into a well-developed pouched, or cylindric and tapering, spur.

1. Leaf solitary at the base..*H. obtusata*
1. Leaves 2 or more, basal or on the stem
    2. Leaves only 2 or 3, at or near the base of the plant
        3. Spur as long as the lip or only slightly longer; plant with an unpleasant odor..*H. unalascensis*
        3. Spur much longer than the lip; plant fragrant ....*H. elegans*
    2. Leaves scattered on the stem, not strictly basal
        4. Spur pouched, much shorter than the lip ....*H. saccata*
        4. Spur cylindric, equaling or longer than the lip, or slightly shorter
            5. Flowers white
                6. Spur shorter than or about equaling the lip.......................................*H. dilatata*
                6. Spur distinctly longer than the lip ....*H. leucostachys*
            5. Flowers greenish
                7. Spike densely flowered; spur usually shorter than the lip..........*H. hyperborea*
                7. Spike loosely fewer-flowered; spur equaling or longer than the lip..*H. sparsiflora*

Habenaria dilatata (Pursh) Hook.   Boreal Bog Orchid

Stems leafy, 15-100 cm tall, from swollen roots; leaves sheathing, reduced upward, 4-10 cm long; spike lax to dense; flowers white, fragrant, 10-14 mm long, the upper sepal and 2 petals close, somewhat hooded, the other segments spreading; lip obtuse, rhombic-dilated at the base, 5-8 mm long; spur equaling or shorter than the lip, cylindric or curved.
Bogs, wet meadows and springy streambanks, 5500 to 7200 feet.

Habenaria elegans (Lindl.) Boland.   Elegant Rein Orchid

Plants with 1 to 3 fleshy tubers; stems 40-70 cm tall; leaves 1 to 3, basal, sheathing, oblanceolate, withering early, 1-20 cm long and up to 3.5 cm wide; spike loosely to densely flowered, 15-30 cm long; flowers faintly fragrant, greenish-white, the upper sepal curved downward, the others spreading; lip broadly lanceolate, fleshy, wider at the base, joined with the column, the spur filiform, 8-18 mm long, straight or curved, tapering to the pointed tip; pollen sacs touching.
Dry open mountainside in coniferous woods, about 5000 feet.

Habenaria hyperborea (L.) R. Br.   Green-flowered Bog Orchid
Stem stout, 10-100 cm tall; leaves reduced upward, lanceolate, 5-20 cm long, 1-3 cm wide; spike short and dense or longer and loosely-flowered; flowers fragrant, light to deep green, sometimes purplish-tinged, 10-12 mm long, the upper sepal and 2 lateral petals united into a hood, the other segments spreading; lip lanceolate, 4-7 mm long; spur slender, cylindric, straight or curved, shorter or mostly longer or equaling the lip. Shady bogs, 5300 to 5500 feet.

Habenaria leucostachys (Lindl.) Wats.   White-flowered Bog Orchid
Stem stout, 20-100 cm tall, from thick tubers; leaves sheathing, reduced upward, 4-10 cm long; flowers white, 15-20 mm long; lip lanceolate, rhombic at the base, about 8 mm long; spur filiform, curved, 12 to 16 mm long, slightly to much longer than the lip. Bogs and springy streambanks in woods, 4700 to 7000 feet.

Habenaria obtusata (Banks) Richards.   Small Northern Bog Orchid
Stem slender, 4-25 cm tall; leaf solitary, basal, obovate, 4-12 cm long, the petiole winged; raceme loosely 3- to 15-flowered; flowers greenish to yellowish-green, the upper sepal erect, the others curved at the tip, the petals united with the upper sepal; lip white, 5-9 mm long, linear-lanceolate, narrowed and curved upward at the tip; column with erect, flap-like appendages; spur tapering to the tip, usually 5-8 mm long. Boggy mossy banks of Hurricane Creek in dense coniferous shade, about 5300 feet.

Habenaria saccata Greene   Slender Bog Orchid
Stem 30-100 cm tall, from swollen roots; leaves sheathing, oblong-elliptic to lanceolate, 3-10 cm long, reduced and bract-like above; spike open, loosely few-flowered, 10-30 cm long, the bracts conspicuous; flowers fragrant, greenish or purplish, 2-14 mm long, the upper sepal and 2 lateral petals forming a hood; lip obtuse, purple, 5-7 mm long; spur purplish or greenish-purple, pouched, about $\frac{1}{2}$ to $\frac{2}{3}$ the length of the lip. Boggy places in coniferous woods, 5000 to 8000 feet.

Habenaria sparsiflora Wats.   Sparsely-flowered Bog Orchid
Stem 30-80 cm tall; leaves reduced upward, lanceolate; spike few-flowered, elongated, 10-40 cm long; flowers greenish, 10-12 mm long; hood 6-8 mm long; lip linear, obtuse, 6-14 mm long; spur a little shorter to slightly longer than the lip, linear, somewhat curved, narrowed at the tip. Wet or boggy places, 5300 to 6800 feet.

Habenaria unalascensis (Spreng.) Wats.   Short-spurred Rein Orchid
Stem 20-60 cm tall; leaves 2 or 3 at or near the base, lanceolate to oblanceolate, 8-15 cm long, withering early; raceme 10-30 cm long, usually narrow and loosely-flowered; flowers greenish with an unpleasant odor, 8-10 mm long; sepals and petals about equal; lip oblong-ovatish, obtuse, 2.5-5 mm long; spur narrow, equaling or slightly longer than the lip. Shady moist or dry woods, 4500 to 6000 feet.

Listera R. Br.

Small herbs with rhizomes; stems short, slender; leaves 2, cauline, opposite, broad, sessile; flowers greenish, small and inconspicuous, spurless, in a terminal raceme; sepals and lateral petals similar, 1- to 3-nerved; lip longer than the sepals, pointed forward or angled downward, the tip notched or deeply lobed; anther jointed to the slender column.

1. Lip narrow, deeply cleft into 2 lobes
    2. Leaves mostly elliptic; lip finely hairy and with ciliate margins ....*L. borealis*
    2. Leaves broader, mostly ovate-cordate; lip without hairs................................*L. cordata*
1. Lip wedge-shaped or widened at the tip, rounded or slightly notched at the tip but not deeply cleft
    3. Ovary and capsule glandular-hairy; lip ciliate on the margin .... *L. convallarioides*
    3. Ovary and capsule not glandular-hairy; lip not ciliate on the margin ....*L. caurina*

Listera borealis Morong   Northern Twayblade

Plant 7-15 cm tall, somewhat puberulent-glandular above; leaves opposite or nearly so, above the middle of the stem, lanceolate to elliptic, 1.5-5 cm long; flowers 3 to 15, grayish to yellowish-green, in an open or congested raceme; sepals and petals 1-nerved, curved, mostly 4-6 mm long; lip oblong-obovate, finely puberulent and ciliate-margined, 7-11 mm long, the tip 2-lobed and somewhat broader than the middle and base, 3-nerved; anther and column arched over the lip.
Open to dense coniferous woods, mostly in deep forest soil, about 5600 feet.

Listera caurina Piper   Western Twayblade

Stem glandular-pubescent above, 10-30 cm tall; leaves broadly lanceolate to ovate, nearly opposite, 2.5-6 cm long; raceme 5- to 25-flowered, open, with conspicuous bracts and slender glandular-pubescent pedicels; flowers yellowish-green, the sepals and petals, except the lip, 1-nerved, 3-5 mm long; lip spatulate, 4.5-7.5 mm long, rounded or sometimes slightly notched at the tip with a tooth in the notch and with a pair of small teeth at the base; capsule glabrous.
Moist, often boggy, coniferous woods, 4500 to 6300 feet or sometimes higher.

Listera convallarioides (Sw.) Nutt.   Broad-lipped Twayblade

Stem glandular-pubescent above, 10-35 cm tall; leaves opposite, broadly ovate to orbicular, 3-8 cm long; flowers yellow-green, 5 to 25 in a raceme, the bracts and pedicels about 3-8 mm long; sepals and petals 1-nerved, about 5 mm long, reflexed and scarious in flower; lip wedge-shaped, 8-13 mm long, pointing outward, shallowly 2-lobed at the tip and often with a tooth in the notch and with a pair of teeth near the base, the margin finely ciliate; ovary and capsule usually glandular-pubescent.
Moist boggy places in coniferous woods, often near streams, 5300 to 5600 feet.

Listera cordata (L.) R. Br.   Heart-leaved Twayblade

Stem 6-20 cm tall, sometimes glandular-pubescent above the leaves, otherwise glabrous; leaves opposite at about the middle of the stem, broadly ovate-cordate to truncate or subcordate at base, 1-3.5 cm long with a short prickle; raceme mostly 6- to 16-flowered, the bracts and pedicels 1-3 mm long; sepals and petals pale green to greenish-purple, 2.5-4.5 mm long, spreading in anthesis; lip 4-11 mm long, narrow, deeply cleft into 2 linear lobes with a nearly erect tooth on each side at the base; column short and thick; capsule glabrous.
Moist coniferous woods, 5800 to 6800 feet.

Spiranthes L. C. Rich.

Plants with fleshy roots; stem leafy below, bracted above; flowers small, white, spurless, spirally arranged in a close terminal spike; sepals and lateral petals united below into a long hood enclosing the column and most of the lip; lip broad at base, dilated and spreading above; column very short; stigma ovate, covering the anther.

Spiranthes romanzoffiiana Cham. & Schl.   Hooded Ladies' Tresses
Stem 10-60 cm tall; leaves narrowly oblong, 8-20 cm long, 3 to 5 near the base, abruptly reduced to sheathing bracts above; spike dense, 3-15 cm long; flowers dull white to cream or greenish-white, 6-8 mm long, spirally arranged in 1 to 4 rows; floral bracts 1-2 cm long, whitish or pale green; hood mostly 7-12 mm long; lip oblong, about as long as the sepals, the tip rounded or flared or recurved; column short and beaked. Bogs, wet meadows and lake borders, 5600 to 8200 feet.

SALICACEAE   Willow Family

Dioecious shrubs or trees with simple, alternate, often stipulate leaves; flowers in catkins, without a perianth, each flower subtended by a scale and with either a cup-shaped glandular disk or enlarged basal glands; staminate flowers with 1, 2, or many stamens; pistillate flowers with one pistil of 2 to 4 carpels and stigmas, with or without a common style; fruit a 2- to 4-valved capsule with many minute seeds.

Plants mostly shrubs in our mountains but some trees; winter bud-scale only one; stamens
  usually 2 ....*Salix*
Plants trees, not shrubby; winter bud-scales several; stamens 6 to many, inserted on a
  concave disk .... *Populus*

Populus L.

Trees; bud scales sometimes resinous; leaves ovate, cordate or lanceolate, serrate; flowers in drooping catkins, each flower subtended by a cup-shaped oblique disk; catkin scales finely fringed or incised, early deciduous; stamens 6 to 60, rarely only 4; ovary sessile; stigmas 2 to 4, entire or 4-lobed; capsule 2- to 4-valved, maturing along with the development of the leaves; seeds with long conspicuous coma.

Leaves mostly longer than broad, noticeably resinous and fragrant (like the winter buds),
  shining above; petioles roundish .... *P. trichocarpa*
Leaves about as broad as long, not resinous or fragrant; petioles flattened ....*P. tremuloides*

Populus tremuloides Michx.   Quaking Aspen
Tree usually about 15-18 meters tall with smooth greenish-white bark becoming rough and dark on older trees; bud-scales shiny but not resinous; leaves 3-5 cm long, broadly cordate-ovate to nearly orbicular, dark green above, paler beneath, abruptly acuminate, the margins glandular-toothed, the petioles slender and flattened; catkins 2-10 cm long; catkin scales 3- to 5-lobed, fringed with long hairs; stamens 6 to 14; stigmas 2; capsule conical, glabrous.
Streambanks and mountain slopes, often in large groves, about 4900 to 6000 feet.

Populus trichocarpa T. & G.   Balm Cottonwood; Black Cottonwood
Tall rough-barked, ashy-gray tree up to about 65 meters or more; winter bud scales up to 2 cm long, very resinous, fragrant, long-pointed; leaves fragrant, very strongly resinous, 3-15 cm long, ovate to often oblong-lanceolate on young trees, acute at the apex, broadly deltoid to rounded or cordate at the base, glabrous at maturity, dark green and

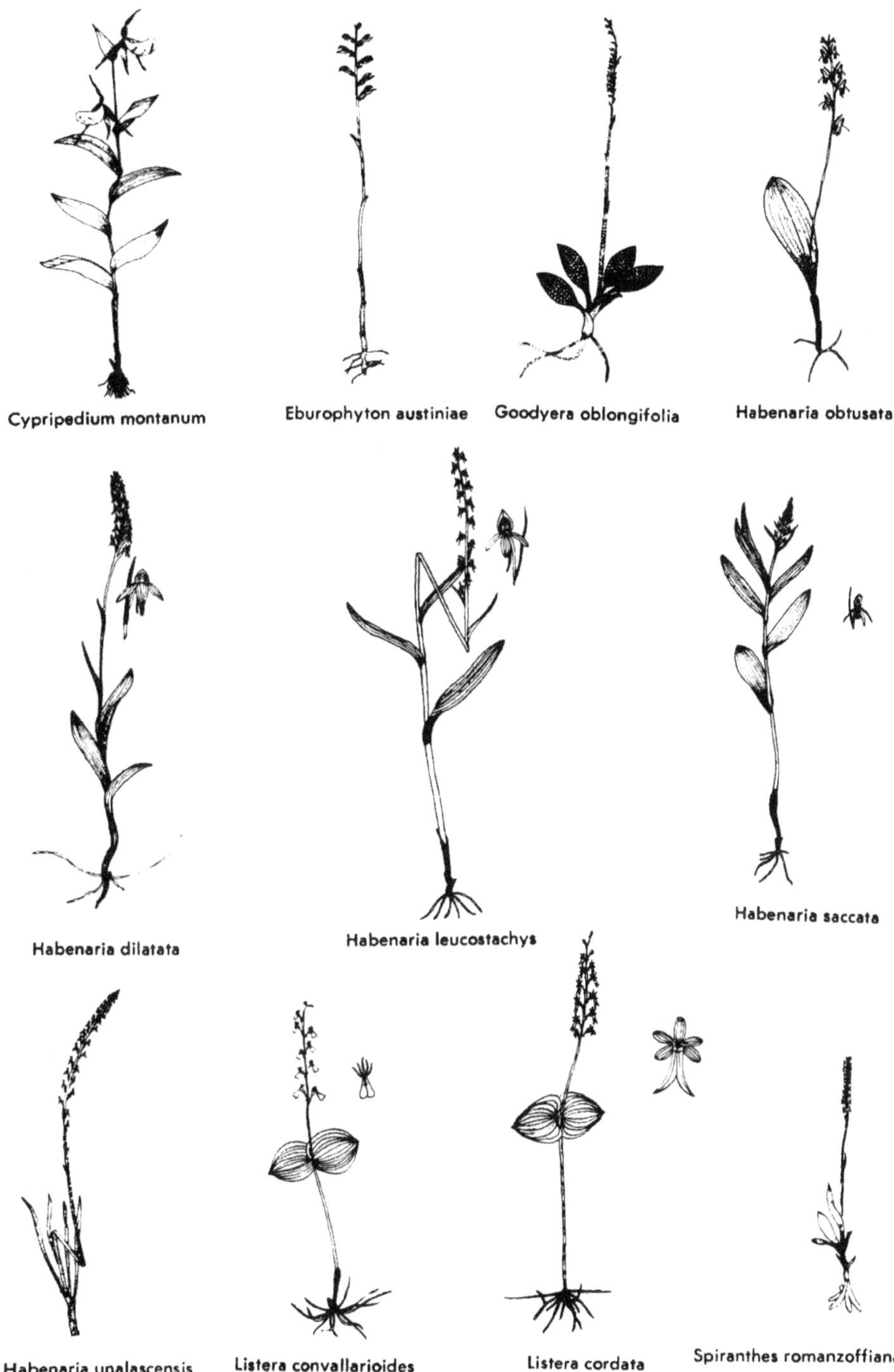

Cypripedium montanum
Eburophyton austiniae
Goodyera oblongifolia
Habenaria obtusata
Habenaria dilatata
Habenaria leucostachys
Habenaria saccata
Habenaria unalascensis
Listera convallarioides
Listera cordata
Spiranthes romanzoffiana

shining above, pale and usually glaucous beneath, the margins finely toothed; petioles terete; catkins 2-20 cm long, the scales deciduous at anthesis; stamens 30 to 60; ovary and capsules densely hairy to glabrous, subglobose to ovoid.
Mostly along streams below 5000 feet.

Salix L.

Trees or shrubs, erect to prostrate or mat-forming; winter bud scale solitary, not resinous; leaves narrow, short-petioled, with or without stipules; catkins sessile to pedunculate, appearing before, with or after the leaves; catkin scales entire or rarely toothed; flowers with 1 or 2 ventral glands but without a disk; stamens 1 to 10 but typically 2 or 5; ovary and capsule 2-valved, glabrous or hairy; style entire or bifid, sometimes obsolete; stigmas 2, entire to bifid.

1. Plants dwarf, prostrate or creeping, often forming mats; stems up to about 1 meter tall but mostly much shorter
  2. Mature leaves hairless or nearly so
    3. Scales dark, conspicuously long-hairy; style visible, 0.5-1.5 mm long
      4. Pistillate catkins mostly 12- to 25-flowered; leaves 8-15 mm long; stems only to about 5 cm above ground level .... *S. cascadensis*
      4. Pistillate catkins mostly 25- to 75-flowered; leaves 15-50 mm long
        5. Style under 1 mm long; stems sometimes up to 40 cm tall ... *S. arctica*
        5. Style 1-1.5 mm long; stems rising only 5-10 cm above ground .... *S. petrophila*
    3. Scales pale or yellowish, either hairless or inconspicuously short-hairy; style nearly obsolete
      6. Leaves mostly 1 cm long or less; pistillate catkins mostly 1 cm long with 3-6 fruits .... *S. nivalis*
      6. Leaves 1.5-3 cm long; pistillate catkins 1-2 cm long with up to 25 or more fruits .... *S. saximontana*
  2. Mature leaves hairy at least beneath and on the margins
    7. Leaf margins rolled under and glandular .... *S. vestita*
    7. Leaf margins not rolled under, not glandular .... *S. brachycarpa*
1. Plants taller, mostly over 1 meter tall, sometimes tall trees
  8. Mature leaves essentially hairless; capsules mostly hairless
    9. Pistillate catkin scales yellow or yellowish, often deciduous
      10. Young twigs reddish, chestnut or grayish; stamens 3-10 in the staminate catkins; style short but evident in the pistillate catkins
        11. Stipules leafy, glandular-toothed, about 1 cm long; leaves glaucous beneath .... *S. lasiandra*
        11. Stipules usually missing; leaves green above, paler but not glaucous beneath .... *S. caudata*
      10. Young twigs dark, brown or blackish; stamens 2; style obsolete or missing in pistillate catkins
        12. Capsule hairy, 5-9 mm long .... *S. bebbiana*
        12. Capsule hairless, 4-5 mm long .... *S. melanopsis*
    9. Pistillate catkin scales brownish to nearly black, mostly persistent
      13. Capsule hairy, 6-8 mm long .... *S. lemmonii*
      13. Capsule usually hairless, mostly under 6 mm long
        14. Pistillate catkins sessile or nearly so
          15. Leaves yellowish-green above, glaucous beneath; petioles 8-15 mm long; capsules 4-5 mm long .... *S. lutea*
          15. Leaves darker green above than beneath, not glaucous; petioles 5-10 mm long; capsules 4-8 mm long .... *S. pseudomonticola*
        14. Pistillate catkins peduncled, sometimes shortly so
          16. Capsules greenish

17. Leaves glaucous beneath; pedicel of the capsule long-
    hairy......*S. barclayi*
17. Leaves not glaucous beneath; pedicel either hairless or
    short-hairy......*S. pseudomyrsinites*
16. Capsules not greenish
    18. Shrubs mostly under 1 meter tall
        19. Leaf margins toothed......*S. commutata* var. *denudata*
        19. Leaf margins entire or nearly so, not toothed......*S. farriae*
    18. Shrubs mostly over 1 meter tall (to 7 or more meters
        sometimes)
        20. Capsules thinly short-hairy......*S. commutata* var. *puberula*
        20. Capsules hairless
            21. Leaf margins glandular-toothed; pistillate cat-
            kins up to 7 cm long
                22. Pedicels of capsules up to 1.5 mm
                long......*S. pseudomonticola*
                22. Pedicels 2.5-4 mm long......*S. mackenzieana*
            21. Leaf margins not glandular; pistillate catkins not
            over 4 cm long......*S. lutea*
8. Mature leaves hairy on one or both sides; capsules mostly hairy
    23. Pistillate scales dark brown to black
        24. Capsules about 8 mm long
            25. Capsules short-hairy; scales blackish......*S. scouleriana*
            25. Capsules not hairy, greenish; scales dark......*S. barclayi*
        24. Capsules mostly 3-6 mm long
            26. Leaves densely hairy on one side at least
                27. Hairs of the leaves short and velvety beneath, only thinly
                covering the upper surface
                    28. Young twigs thinly cobwebby-hairy; style mostly under
                    1 mm long......*S. sitchensis*
                    28. Young twigs hairless or glaucous and shining but not
                    hairy; style 1-1.5 mm long
                        29. Pistillate scales black, densely hairy; pistillate catkins
                        3-6 cm long......*S. bella*
                        29. Pistillate scales brown to black, thinly hairy; pistillate
                        catkins 1-4 cm long......*S. subcoerulea*
                27. Hairs of the leaves long and dense on both sides
                  30. Hairiness silky......*S. wolfii*
                  30. Hairiness cobwebby, not silky......*S. eastwoodiae*
             26. Leaves thinly hairy to nearly hairless
                31. Capsules thinly short-hairy to hairless
                  32. Leaf margins rolled inward......*S. lasiolepis*
                  32. Leaf margins not rolled inward......*S. commutata*
                31. Capsules densely grayish-hairy......*S. wolfii*
    23. Pistillate scales light brown to yellowish, sometimes falling early or missing;
    style very short or obsolete; capsules short-hairy
        33. Peduncles of the pistillate catkins up to 7 cm long, leafy; leaves narrow,
        pointed at both ends; pistillate catkins 3-10 cm long......*S. exigua*
        33. Peduncles of the pistillate catkins short, not leafy though sometimes
        with 1 or 2 small leaf-like bracts; leaves and catkins various
            34. Young twigs of the season hairy or tomentose, sometimes thinly so
                35. Pistillate catkins 1.5-2 cm long and almost as wide......*S. brachycarpa*
                35. Pistillate catkins 3-5 cm long......*S. bebbiana*
             34. Young twigs of the season not hairy, sometimes yellowish or bluish-
            glaucous; pistillate catkins 1-2.5 cm long......*S. geyeriana*

Salix arctica Pall.   Smooth Alpine Willow
   S. anglorum Cham.
   Stems creeping and rooting, 10-40 cm long, tending to form mats; leaves elliptic, entire, glabrous at maturity, 1-5 cm long, glaucous and veiny beneath, not persistent more than one season; catkins 1-4 cm long with 25 to 75 fruits at maturity, on short leafy peduncles of the lateral branches; scales brownish-black, persistent, long-hairy; stamens 2, united part or all the way; capsule nearly sessile, densely white-hairy, 3-7 mm long; style 0.75 mm long.
Dry to moist open places and slopes, 7600 to 9300 feet.

Salix barclayi Anderss.   Barclay's Willow
   Shrub 10 to about 80 cm tall with dark twigs; stipules small and inconspicuous to leaf-like and conspicuous; leaves obovate to elliptic, 3-8 cm long, 1.5-3.5 cm wide, crenate with glandular teeth or nearly entire, tomentose on both sides when young, the under side becoming glabrous, glaucous, veiny, the upper side green and glabrate except on the midrib and veins; petioles 5-10 mm long; catkins 1-7 cm long, on short leafy peduncles, developing with the leaves; catkin scales dark brown or blackish, long-hairy; stamens 2; capsule glabrous, greenish, 4-6 or 8 mm long; pedicel hairy; style 0.8-1.8 mm long; stigmas long.
Bogs and wet meadows near lakes, 7200 to 8200 feet.

Salix bebbiana Sarg.   Bebb's Willow
   Shrub or small tree, 1-5 meters tall, the young twigs short and brownish; stipules when present small and dentate; leaves narrowly elliptic to broadly oblanceolate, 2-8 cm long and 1.5-3 cm wide, nearly entire, dull or deep green above, glaucous or paler beneath with conspicuously raised veins, pubescent on both sides when young becoming glabrate with age; catkins appearing before or with the leaves, the staminate 1-2.5 cm long, sub-sessile, the pistillate 2.5-5 or 6 cm long on short peduncles; scales narrow, persistent, hairy, yellowish or light brown; capsule thinly pubescent, 5-9 mm long; style nearly obsolete; stigmas short, bifid.
Streambanks, 4700 to 4850 feet.

Salix bella Piper   Beautiful Willow
   Shrub 2-4 meters tall; twigs yellowish to purplish black, shining or pruinose, glabrate; leaves lanceolate to oblong-lanceolate or -oblanceolate, 4-8 cm long, 1.5-2.5 cm wide when mature, green and becoming glabrous above, densely opaque-silvery-tomentose beneath with glabrous, yellowish midribs, margins nearly entire; catkins developing before the leaves, the staminate 2-3 cm long, nearly sessile, the pistillate 3-6 cm long, short-peduncled; scales black, densely long-woolly-hairy; capsules 4-6 cm long, gray-silky; style 1-1.5 mm long; stigmas entire or bifid.
At about 3000 to 5000 feet in mountains.

Salix brachycarpa Nutt.   Short-fruited Willow
   Low shrub; stems prostrate or erect, creeping and rooting, up to about 1 meter long; twigs dark or reddish, hairy-tomentose; stipules inconspicuous and deciduous; leaves often crowded, white-hairy on both sides when young, later nearly glabrous above, glaucous beneath, mostly entire-margined, obovate to elliptic, 1-3 cm long and 0.5 to 1.5 mm

wide, larger on young shoots, with the upper 3 or 4 narrower and more "strap-shaped" than the lower ones on the shoot; catkins developing with the leaves on short, leafy-bracted peduncles; scales yellowish or light brown to blackish or greenish, short-hairy on both sides; staminate catkins 5-15 mm long; pistillate catkins 1-2 cm long and often nearly as wide; stamens 2; style 0.5-0.8 or sometimes up to 1.5 mm long; stigmas bilobed, very short, capsules densely tomentose, 3-5 mm long.
Mostly clambering over rocks in boggy meadows and lake borders, 5300 to 9000 feet.

Salix cascadensis Cockerell   Cascade Willow
Prostrate creeping shrub about 5 cm tall, forming dense mats; leaves thick, entire, narrowly elliptic, 8-15 mm long, green and shining above, pale beneath, arachnoid when young, becoming glabrate, midrib prominent, some older leaves usually persisting; catkins appearing with the leaves, the pistillate 5-20 mm long, 12- to 25-flowered, on short leafy lateral branches only; scales brownish, long-hairy; capsules usually villous-tomentose, 4-5 mm long; style 1-1.5 mm long.
Moist alpine meadows and rocky slopes, about 8000 feet.

Salix caudata (Nutt.) Heller   Caudate Willow
Shrub 2-5 m tall; twigs and branches shining, reddish-brown; leaves lanceolate, 6-13 cm long, short-petioled, green, glabrous, never glaucous, margins glandular-toothed; stipules usually missing; catkins on leafy peduncles, 2-5 cm long; scales yellow, toothed, glabrate outside; capsule glabrous, pale brownish, 5-7 mm long; style short.
Along mountain streams, about 5000 feet.
The less hairy form..var. **bryantiana** Ball & Bracelin

Salix commutata Bebb   Variable Willow
Shrub up to 3 m tall with dark twigs; stipules leaf-like, up to 1 cm long, glandular-serrate and deciduous; leaves elliptic to elliptic-obovate, entire or glandular-toothed, 2-8 cm long, loosely long-woolly-villous on both sides when young, becoming glabrate eventually; petioles short and thick; catkins appearing with or after the leaves, on short leafy peduncles, the staminate 1.5-3 cm long, the pistillate mostly 3-6 cm long at maturity; scales light to dark brownish, persistent, long-woolly; capsule glabrous or rarely sparsely hairy, 3-6 mm long; style 0.5-1.5 mm long; stigmas short.
Mostly in swampy lake meadows, 7400 to 8000 feet.   TYPE LOCALITY: Wallowa Mts.
Leaves glabrous, serrate-margined..var. **denudata** Bebb
Capsule thinly puberulous...var. **puberula** Bebb

Salix eastwoodiae Cockerell   Eastwood's Willow
    S. californica Bebb
Low spreading shrub 0.5-2 m tall; twigs dark brown, usually tomentose; leaves elliptic to obovate, 4-6 cm long, 1-2 cm wide, green and grayish-tomentose on both sides, entire or glandular-denticulate, especially the lower leaves; catkins developing with the leaves, leafy-pedunculate, the staminate 1-3 cm long, the pistillate 2-5 cm long; scales brownish, tomentose; capsules 5-6.5 mm long, grayish-tomentose; style 1-1.5 mm long.
Mountain bogs, 6000 to nearly 10,000 feet.

Salix exigua Nutt.   Slender Willow
A slender grayish shrub 2-4 m tall; twigs villous-tomentose; leaves linear to linear-

oblanceolate or elliptic, acute at both ends, 4-20 cm long, 2-15 mm wide, entire or glandular-toothed, silky- or silvery-hairy on one or both sides; catkins on leafy peduncles up to 7 cm long, appearing after the leaves, the staminate 2-4 cm long, the pistillate 3-6 cm long; scales conspicuous, villous to glabrate, yellow; capsules 4-6 mm long, glabrous or villous; style obsolete; stigmas sessile.
Along streams and other wet places, about 5000 feet.

Salix farriae Ball   Farr's Willow
Dwarf shrub 0.3 to about 1 m tall; young twigs shining, yellowish, older branchlets bright red to dull brown; stipules small when present; petioles short and twisted; leaves elliptic to oblanceolate, nearly entire, glabrous, mostly 3-5 cm long and 1-2 cm wide, glaucous beneath with slender raised veins; catkins appearing with or after the leaves on short leafy peduncles, the staminate 1-2 cm long, the pistillate 1.5-4 cm long at maturity; scales brown or blackish, persistent, long-hairy within, nearly glabrous outside; capsules glabrous, 4-6 mm long; style short; stigmas short.
Wet meadows, lake shores and streambanks, about 8000 feet.

Salix geyeriana Anderss.   Geyer's Willow
Shrub 1-5 m tall; twigs slender, dark and glaucous; stipules minute or none; leaves petioled, glaucous, narrowly linear-oblanceolate to elliptic, 2-8 cm long, 5-10 mm wide, the margin revolute, entire or denticulate; catkins nearly sessile or on short leafy peduncles, appearing with the leaves, the staminate about 1 cm long, the pistillate subglobose, numerous, 1-2.5 cm long at maturity; scales persistent, thinly long-hairy, brown, black or yellowish with red tips; capsules 3-7 mm long, thinly short-hairy; style stout and very short; stigmas cleft.
Wet meadows and streambanks, about 4000 feet.

Salix lasiandra Benth.   Red Willow
Tree up to 17 m tall; twigs shining, yellow or deep red; leaves lanceolate to oblanceolate, mostly 6-15 cm long and 1-3 cm wide, dark green and shining above, glaucous beneath, the margins glandular-crenate-serrulate; petioles stout and glandular; stipules leafy, glandular-toothed, up to 1 cm long; catkins peduncled, appearing with the leaves, the staminate stout, 2-7 cm long with 3 to 8 (usually 5) stamens, the pistillate 3-12 cm long at maturity; scales yellowish, usually dentate, sometimes glandular, hairy; capsules pale brownish, glabrous, 4-8 mm long; style 0.5-1.0 mm long.
Along streams, 4000 to 6000 feet.

Salix lasiolepis Benth.   Arroyo Willow
Shrub or small tree 1-3 m tall; twigs usually pubescent, yellowish-olive to reddish; stipules sometimes large and leaf-like on young shoots, later minute or missing; leaves oblanceolate to elliptic-oblong, 3-11 cm long, 0.5-2.5 cm wide, thick and firm, dark green and glabrate above, pale, glaucous and mostly puberulent beneath, the margins revolute, mostly entire; catkins appearing before the leaves, sessile or short-peduncled, the staminate 2.5-4.5 cm long, the pistillate 2.5-6 cm long; scales dark brown or blackish, persistent, densely long-woolly-villous; capsules glabrous, 3-5.5 mm long; style 0.3-0.8 mm long.
Rocky streambanks, about 5500 feet.

Salix lemmonii Bebb — Lemmon's Willow

Shrub 0.5-5 m tall; twigs silky, dark and shining, sometimes glaucous; stipules small or none; leaves lanceolate to oblanceolate, veiny, 4-10 cm long, 1-1.5 cm wide, nearly entire, silky when young, later glabrous, deep green and shining above, glaucous beneath; catkins appearing with the leaves, short-leafy-pedunculate, the staminate 1-3 cm long, the pistillate 2-5 cm long; scales silky-pilose, dark brown to black; capsules silky-tomentose, 6-8 mm long; style 0.5-0.8 mm long; stigmas cleft.
Moist rocky slopes and along streams, about 5800 feet.

Salix lutea Nutt. — Yellow Willow

A shrub 2-7 m tall; twigs shining, yellow or reddish-brown; stipules ovate to lunate, serrulate to entire; leaves lanceolate to oval or obovate, 4-10 cm long, glabrous, serrulate to entire, mostly yellowish-green, glaucous beneath; petioles 8-15 mm long; catkins nearly sessile, the peduncles with 2 or 3 small bracts, the staminate 2-3 cm long, the pistillate 2-4 cm long; scales brown or black, thinly long-pilose; capsules 4-5 mm long, glabrous; styles less than 0.5 mm long.
Along streams, up to 7000 feet.

Salix mackenzieana (Hook.) Barratt — Mackenzie's Willow

A shrub or small tree, 2-7 m tall; twigs shining, brown or yellowish, pilose at first or glabrous from the start; leaves lanceolate to oblong-ovate, glabrous on both sides, glandular-serrulate to nearly entire, 6-10 cm long, dark green above, glaucous beneath; stipules conspicuous in new growth, petioles 5-12 mm long; catkins appearing with the leaves on short-bracted peduncles, the staminate dense, 2-4 cm long, the pistillate lax, 2.5-6 cm long; pedicels glabrous, 2.5-4 mm long; scales brownish, tomentose; capsules glabrous, 4.5-6 mm long; style about 0.5 mm long.
Moist woods, up to 5000 feet.

Salix melanopsis Nutt. — Dusky Willow

Dark green shrub or small tree 3-6 m tall; twigs and branches shining, brown to blackish; leaves oblanceolate to elliptic or linear, 4-9 cm long, spinulose-denticulate to nearly entire, mostly glabrous, dark green above, pale and somewhat glaucous beneath, short-petioled, often with small dentate stipules; catkins appearing after the leaves on leafy branchlets, singly or in clusters, the staminate 3-5 cm long, the pistillate 4-9 cm long; scales yellowish, sometimes pilose, the pistillate often with 3 to 5 nerves; capsules glabrous, 4-5 mm long, sessile or nearly so; pedicel 5-9 mm long; style none.
Moist rocky streambanks and bars, and on rocky slopes, 4500 to 7000 feet.

Salix nivalis Hook. — Snow Willow

Creeping mat-forming shrub; stems mostly buried, only about 2 or 3 cm above the ground; twigs yellowish; stipules none or minute; leaves elliptic to obovate or suborbicular, sometimes notched at the tip, 7-12 mm long, 4-8 mm wide, glabrous, bright green above, glaucous and strongly net-veiny beneath, margins entire and revolute; petioles yellowish; catkins appearing after the leaves, 3- to 6-flowered, up to 1 cm long, globose or oblong, on short yellowish peduncles; scales nearly glabrous, yellowish or greenish; capsules tomentose, about 3 mm long; style very short.
Open rocky slopes, ledges and meadows, 8000 to 9800 feet.

Salix petrophila Rydb.   Alpine Willow

Dwarf matted shrub, creeping; branches rising only 5-10 cm above ground, brown or yellowish; leaves elliptic to oblanceolate, veiny, 1.5-5 cm long, about 1 cm wide, becoming glabrous and deep green above, pale and somewhat glaucous beneath, entire-margined; petioles yellow; catkins appearing with the leaves; scales brown to blackish, long-hairy, often fringed; staminate catkins 1-3 cm long; the pistillate lax, 2-4 cm long; capsules sessile, gray-tomentose, 4-6 mm long; styles 1-1.5 mm long.
Rocky summits above 8000 feet.

Salix pseudomonticola Ball   Mountain Willow
  S. monticola Bebb

Shrub 1-5 m tall; twigs shining, yellowish to brownish; stipules small and deciduous, larger and foliaceous on young shoots; petioles 5-10 mm long; leaves mostly elliptic or elliptic-obovate, 3.5-8 cm long, 1-3 cm wide, veiny, glabrous when fully developed, green above, glaucous beneath, the margin glandular-crenate-serrate to nearly entire; catkins appearing just before or with the leaves, subsessile on very short peduncles, often sub-tended by small leafy bracts, the staminate 2-3.5 cm long; stamens 2, the filaments glab-rous; pistillate catkins 2-7 cm long at maturity; scales oblanceolate, brown, long-hairy on both sides; capsules 4-8 mm long, glabrous; pedicel 1-1.5 mm long, glabrous; style 0.6-1.8 mm long.
Swampy streambanks, about 7000 feet.

Salix pseudomyrsinites Anderss.   Firm-leaf Willow

A bushy shrub 1-3 m tall; twigs glandular, lustrous, bright chestnut to dark brown; stipules when present glandular-margined; leaves lanceolate-oblong to elliptic-oblanceo-late, 3-7 cm long, 1-2 cm wide, mostly glabrous, green on both sides but darker above, conspicuously veiny beneath, the margins glandular-serrulate or nearly entire; catkins appearing with the leaves on leafy-bracted peduncles up to 1 cm long, the staminate 1-2 cm long with 2 stamens and free glabrous filaments, the pistillate 2-4 cm long at maturity; scales persistent, brown or blackish, thinly white-pilose; capsules greenish, 4-5 mm long, glabrous; pedicels 1-1.5 mm long, usually pubescent; styles 0.5-0.7 mm long.
Boggy lake borders at about 8000 feet.

Salix saximontana Rydb.   Rocky Mountain Willow

Dwarf glabrous shrub, 2-25 cm tall; leaves elliptic to obovate or suborbicular, 1.5-3.5 cm long, green above, glaucous and netted-veiny beneath, margins revolute and entire; catkins appearing after the leaves, 1-2 cm long, mostly up to 25- or more -flowered; scales yellowish, nearly glabrous; capsules sessile, 3-4 mm long, densely white-tomen-tose; style very short.
Mountain summits above 9000 feet.

Salix scouleriana Barratt   Scouler's Willow

A tall shrub or small tree 1-13 meters tall; twigs chestnut to yellowish-green; bark dull gray; stipules minute to large, leaf-like and denticulate; leaves variable, hairy when young usually becoming glabrous and dark green above and reddish-hairy beneath, but sometimes becoming glabrous on both sides, or puberulent above and glaucous, net-veined and densely rusty-villous beneath, oblanceolate or obovate to elliptic, thick, entire

or occasionally glandular-toothed, 3-12 cm long and 1-3.5 cm wide; catkins appearing before or with the leaves, densely-flowered, sessile or bracteate-short-peduncled; scales blackish, obovate, persistent, densely long-hairy; staminate catkins 2-4 cm long, stamens 2, filaments free; pistillate catkins 2-5 cm long; capsules long-beaked, short-hairy, about 8 mm long; pedicels pubescent, 1.5 mm long; style 0.3-0.5 mm long.
Our common willow along streams, in swamps and drier upland places, to about 6000 feet.

Salix sitchensis Sanson — Sitka Willow

A shrub or small tree 1-8 m tall; twig branchlets dark, dull or shining; bark smooth, gray; stipules small or well-developed and leaflike; leaves obovate, oblanceolate or eliptic, 4-9 cm long, 1.5-3.5 cm wide, green and usually glabrous and veiny above, densely gray-silvery or white-satiny short-pubescent beneath, margins entire or minutely toothed; catkins appearing before or with the leaves, densely-flowered, nearly sessile on short leafy-bracteate peduncles; scales light brown to blackish, long-hairy and persistent; staminate catkins 2.5-5 cm long, stamen 1, filaments glabrous, anthers violet; pistillate catkins 2 to 8 or more cm long at maturity; capsules nearly sessile, 3-6 mm long, silky-pubescent; style 0.3-0.8 mm long, sometimes up to 1.2 mm.
Streambanks, lake shores, moist meadows and woods, 4500 to 7550 feet.

Salix subcoerulea Piper — Bluish Willow

Shrub 1-7 m tall; twigs glabrous, bluish-lustrous, brown to blackish; leaves oblong-lanceolate to oblanceolate, 3-7 cm long, 0.8-2.5 cm wide, nearly entire, green and slightly pubescent above, densely silvery-tomentose beneath with yellowish midveins; petioles short; catkins appearing with or before the leaves, sessile to very short-pedunculate, densely flowered, 1-4 cm long; scales thinly long-hairy, brown to black; capsules nearly sessile, silvery-silky-pubescent, 3.5-5 mm long; style 1-1.5 mm long, yellowish or brown; stigmas entire or cleft.
Swampy prairie and wooded streambanks, 5000 to 5200 feet.

Salix vestita Pursh — Rock Willow

Dwarf shrub, prostrate or creeping or erect, 4 to 40 or more cm tall; twigs shining, angular, brown; stipules absent; leaves petioled, elliptic-ovate or -obovate to nearly orbicular, 2-6 cm long, 1-4 cm wide, veiny, thick and firm, dark green and glabrous above, glaucous and long-white-hairy beneath, the margins revolute and glandular; catkins appearing after the leaves on hairy leafless peduncles; scales brown, persistent, hairy all over or just at the tip; staminate catkins 1.5-3.5 cm long, stamens usually 2, sometimes 4, filaments hairy below; pistillate catkins 2-5 cm long at maturity; capsules sessile or nearly so, tomentose, about 4 mm long; style nearly obsolete.
Open moist rocky slopes, streambanks and meadows, 5500 to 9200 feet.

Salix wolfii Bebb var. idahoensis Ball — Idaho Willow

Low shrub 0.7-3 m tall; twigs and branches shiny, yellowish to chestnut; stipules when present small, leaf-like and often glandular-serrate; leaves short-petioled, mostly elliptic, 3-7 cm long and 1-2 cm wide, entire, dull green, grayish-tomentose or shiny-silky-hairy on both sides but more densely so beneath; catkins appearing with the leaves on short leafy-bracteate peduncles; scales dark brown or blackish, persistent, long-woolly-hairy;

staminate catkins 1-2 cm long, stamens 2, filaments glabrous; pistillate catkins densely flowered, 1.5-3 or 4 cm long at maturity; capsules 3.5-5 mm long, hairy; styles 1-1.5 mm long.
Streambanks and moist low ground, 5000 to about 8000 feet.

BETULACEAE   Birch Family

Shrubs or trees; leaves alternate, serrate, deciduous; flowers imperfect; staminate flowers 1 to 6 per bract in loose pendulous catkins, stamens 1 to 10, the calyx none or 2- to 4-parted; the pistillate flowers 2 to 3 per bract, in short catkins, heads or spikes, the perianth when present 3- to 4-parted, adnate to the ovary; ovary 3-carpellary, 1- or 2-celled with 1 or 2 ovules in each cell; style 2-cleft; fruit a winged or wingless nut.

Pistillate catkins usually 3 to 6 per branch, the scales woody and persistent; stamens 4 .... *Alnus*
Pistillate catkin solitary on the branch, the scales thin and deciduous; stamens 2 .... *Betula*

Alnus Hill

Trees or shrubs; leaves deciduous, simple, toothed or lobed; flowers in clusters of 2 to 5 catkins, appearing with or before the leaves; staminate flowers in long pendulous catkins, 3 to 6 per bract, stamens 1 to 4, the perianth 4-parted; pistillate flowers in short erect cone-like catkins, 2 per bract, perianth none; fruit a small nutlet.

Cones 1-2 cm long on slender peduncles longer than the cones; winter buds acute; leaves
  shiny..*A. sinuata*
Cones about 1 cm long on thick peduncles shorter than the cones or the cones sessile;
  winter buds blunt; leaves dull..*A. tenuifolia*

Alnus sinuata (Regel) Rydb.   Sitka Alder

Sweet-scented shrub or small tree 2 to 5 m tall; winter buds resinous, acute; leaves ovate, 3-15 cm long, acute at the tip, rounded or cuneate at the base, sinuate and doubly serrate-denticulate, pale and somewhat hairy beneath, glabrous and often glutinous above; petioles 1-3 cm long; catkins developing with the leaves on the season's growth; staminate catkins 5-10 cm long with ovate scales, the pistillate 3 to 6 per branch, ovoid-ellipsoid, 1-2 cm long, the scales truncate, thickened at the tip; fruit a winged nutlet.
Moist shady woods, streambanks and open mountain slopes, 4000 to 7000 feet.

Alnus tenuifolia Nutt.   Thin-leaved Alder

Shrub or small tree 1-10 m tall; winter buds slightly resinous, blunt; leaves elliptic to ovate-oblong, 5-10 cm long, rounded at the base, acute to rounded at the tip, deeply lobed and doubly toothed, usually glabrous, dull dark green above, yellow-green beneath; petioles short and stout; catkins developing before the leaves on the previous season's growth; staminate catkins 3-10 cm long; pistillate catkins sessile or short-peduncled, ovoid to oblong, 8-13 mm long, their scales truncate and 3-lobed at the thick apex; fruit a narrowly-bordered nearly orbicular nutlet.
Along mountain streams, 4500 to about 5500 feet.

Betula L.

Trees or shrubs, usually glandular; bark smooth, papery, aromatic, resinous, marked by long lenticels; leaves deciduous, alternate, usually toothed; catkins blooming with or before the leaves, the staminate pendulous, 1 to 4 in a cluster, the pistillate generally

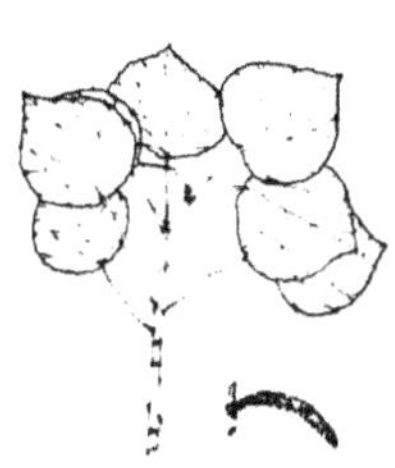

Populus tremuloides

Populus trichocarpa

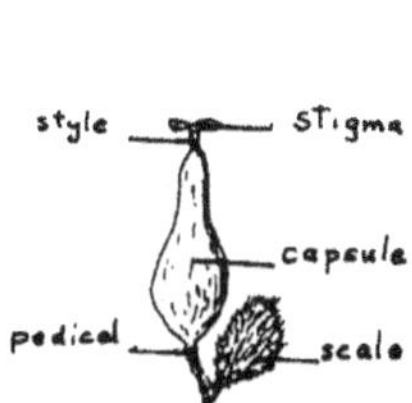

Salix capsule

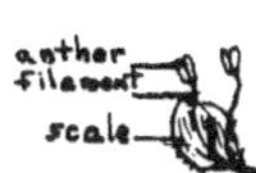

Salix

Salix barclayi

Salix lemmonii

Salix mackenzieana

Alnus sinuata

Betula glandulosa

erect, paired or solitary; flowers subtended by bracts, 1 to 3 per cluster, the staminate usually with 2 stamens, the pistillate with a 2- to 4-parted perianth and a sessile ovary with 2 spreading styles; fruit a winged nutlet, deciduous with the 3-lobed scale.

Leaves broadest at or near the base, pointed at the tip; leaf margins with sharply-pointed teeth..*B. occidentalis*
Leaves broadest at or about the middle, narrowed at the base, mostly rounded at the tip; teeth of the leaf margins rounded, not sharply pointed...*B. glandulosa*

Betula glandulosa Michx.   Glandular Birch
Shrub to 2 meters tall, the twigs conspicuously covered with crystalline resinous warty glands; leaves reticulate, obovate to orbicular, 1.2-3 cm long, rounded at the tip, thick and leathery, glandular, green and glabrous above, paler beneath, the margins crenate-toothed; mature pistillate catkins 1-2.5 cm long, mostly erect, sessile or nearly so, the scales 3-lobed; fruit a nutlet with a narrow wing.
Bogs and gravelly bars and banks along streams and lakes, 5300 to 7600 feet.

Betula occidentalis Hook.   Water Birch
B. fontinalis Sarg.
A shrub or small tree up to 11 meters tall; bark dark bronze and shining; twigs glandular; leaves broadly ovate, acute at the tip, 2-5 cm long, green above, pale and shining beneath with glandular dots, the margins sharply though unevenly and often double serrate; mature catkins 1.5-3 cm long; peduncles glandular; scales ciliate, 3-lobed, the middle lobe the longest; fruit a winged nutlet.
Bogs, along streams and in gravelly creek beds, 5000 to 5800 feet.

URTICACEAE   Nettle Family

Herbs with stinging hairs; leaves simple, alternate or opposite; flowers small, unisexual (ours), greenish, single or in catkin-like panicles, heads or racemes, the calyx deeply and unequally 2- to 4-parted, petals none; staminate flowers with 4 stamens; pistillate flowers with a 1-carpellary pistil and style; fruit an achene surrounded by the larger inner sepals.

Urtica [Tourn.] L.
Annual or perennial herbs with stinging hairs; leaves opposite, flowers axillary, unisexual (ours), in catkin-like inflorescences; calyx 2- to 4-parted; stamens 4; fruit a flattened achene.

Urtica dioica L. ssp. gracilis (Ait.) Selander   Northwest Nettle
Perennial herb 1-3 m tall with stinging hairs; leaves opposite, 6-20 cm long, mostly ovate-lanceolate, serrate, short-petioled; flowers in lax, drooping axillary catkin-like clusters, mostly unisexual, the calyx 2- or 4-parted, petals none; staminate flowers with 4 stamens; pistillate flowers with unequal sepals, the inner ones larger, surrounding the developing fruit; fruit an achene.
Low moist ground in shady woods, about 4500 to 7500 feet.

SANTALACEAE   Sandalwood Family

Herbs (ours) with horizontal rootstocks; leaves entire, opposite or alternate; flowers small, perfect or unisexual; petals none; calyx of 4 or 5 petaloid sepals adnate to the base of the ovary or to a disk; stamens 4 or 5, inserted on the fleshy disk; ovary inferior, 1-loculed, ovules 1 to 4; style 1; fruit a 1-seeded nut or drupe.

Comandra Nutt.

Glabrous perennial herbs with alternate leaves; flowers in cymes; calyx adnate with the hollow lobed receptacle; stamens 5; fruit nut-like.

Comandra umbellata (L.) Nutt.   Bastard Toad-flax

Glabrous perennial herbs parasitic on roots of other plants; stems leafy, 15-45 cm tall; leaves sessile, alternate, 1.5-3 cm long, narrowly lanceolate; flowers perfect, 3-7 mm long, cymose; petals none; calyx 5-lobed, greenish-white or purplish, about 4 mm long, the tube lined with a 5-lobed fleshy disk; fruit a globose drupe, blue, purplish or brown. Open woods about 6000 feet.

LORANTHACEAE   Mistletoe Family

Evergreen dioecious shrubs or herbs parasitic on trees; stems dichotomously branched, swollen at the joints; leaves opposite, either well-developed and thick or reduced to connate scales; flowers imperfect (ours), small, solitary or clustered, petals none, calyx 2- to 5-lobed, either greenish and inconspicuous or colored, showy and petaloid, the tube adnate to the ovary; stamens as many as the calyx lobes and inserted on them; ovary inferior, 1-celled, 1- to several-ovuled; style simple or none; fruit a berry.

Arceuthobium Marsch.-Bieb.

Small, yellowish or greenish-brown shrubs parasitic on coniferous tree branches; stems jointed, fragile, terete to angled, swollen at the nodes; leaves reduced to opposite connate scales; flowers 1 to several, axillary, the calyx inconspicuous, 2- to 5-parted, the stamens adnate to the sepals in the staminate flowers, the calyx adnate to the ovary in the pistillate flowers; stigma 1, entire or lobed; style none; ovary inferior, 1-loculed; fruit a small, ovoid, greenish or bluish berry.

1. Plants parasitic on Lodgepole pine; stems 1-6 cm long..*A. americanum*
1. Plants parasitic on Ponderosa pine, Douglas Fir and Larch
    2. Plants parasitic on Ponderosa pine; stems 2-15 cm long........................*A. campylopodum*
    2. Plants parasitic on Larch or Douglas Fir; stems 0.5-6 cm long
        3. Parasites on Larch; stems much branched, 2-6 cm long........................*A. laricis*
        3. Parasites on Douglas Fir; stems nearly unbranched, 0.5-3 cm long........*A. douglasii*

Arceuthobium americanum Nutt.   American Leafless Mistletoe

Plants greenish-yellow; branches dichotomous or whorled; staminate plants 2-6 or more cm long; pistillate 1.5-3 cm long; staminate flowers sessile on short lateral stems, usually 2 to several to a node, 2 mm broad, the calyx lobes rounded on the back; pistillate flowers smaller, short-pedicellate; fruit a bluish berry, 2-3 mm long. Parasitic on *Pinus contorta.*

Arceuthobium campylopodum Engelm.   Yellow Leafless Mistletoe

Plants orange-yellow to olive-green or brownish; stems 2-15 cm long; staminate spikes 5-20 mm long, the flowers 2 to a node, 1.5-3 mm broad, yellow or orange to green, the

calyx 4-parted or rarely 3- to 5-parted; pistillate flowers 1 or 2 to a node, sessile or pedicellate; fruit 3-5 mm long, bluish, drooping on curved pedicels.
Parasitic on *Pinus ponderosa.*

Arceuthobium douglasii Engelm.   Douglas Leafless Mistletoe
Stems very dwarf, 0.5-3 cm long, greenish-yellow or bluish-green, the branches few; staminate flowers greenish or yellow, mostly paired at the nodes, the calyx lobes rounded on the back, 2 mm long; pistillate flowers usually paired at the nodes, short-pedicellate; fruit a purplish berry, about 4 mm long.
Parasitic on *Pseudotsuga menziesii.*

Arceuthobium laricis (Piper) St. John   Larch Dwarf Mistletoe
Stems 3-6 cm long, greenish-yellow; scales acute; staminate spikes dense, 3- to 7-flowered, the calyx 3-lobed, the lobes ovate, acute, keeled, 2 mm long; fruit a berry about 4 mm long.
Parasitic on *Larix.*

POLYGONACEAE   Buckwheat Family

Annual or perennial herbs, shrubs, rarely trees or vines, with jointed stems and usually alternate sheathing-stipulate entire leaves; flowers generally perfect, small, usually cymose, often involucrate; perianth 2- to 6-parted or -cleft, the segments in 2 series, the inner set sometimes toothed and with a callosity in the center; stamens usually 3 to 9, inserted near the base of the calyx; pistil 1; ovary superior, 1-celled; ovule 1; styles 2 or 3, sometimes 4; fruit an angled achene, often winged.

1. Calyx 6-parted
    2. Flowers in small clusters, each cluster surrounded by a funnel-shaped, often toothed or lobed, collar (the involucre); leaves without sheaths at the base of the petiole; stamens 9..*Eriogonum*
    2. Flowers without an involucre; leaves with often papery sheathing membranes at the base of the petiole; stamens 8 or fewer.. *Rumex*
1. Calyx 4- or 5-parted but never 6-parted
    3. Sepals 4, the inner enlarging in fruit; leaves rounded or kidney-shaped; plants of high elevations ....*Oxyria*
    3. Sepals 5, equal and similar even in fruit; leaves variously shaped but not much rounded or kidney-shaped..*Polygonum*

Eriogonum Michx.

Annual or perennial herbs or shrubs, usually tomentose, with entire alternate to whorled, petiolate leaves without stipules; flowers mostly perfect, involucrate; involucres toothed or lobed, campanulate or cylindric, solitary or several in simple to compound umbels, cymes or heads, subtended by leaf-like to scale-like bracts; perianth segments 6, white to shades of yellow and purple, free or united, with or without a stalk-like stipitate base, glabrous to tomentose, the inner set of 3 often unlike the outer; flowers perfect to imperfect; stamens 9, long-hairy near the base; pistil 3-carpellary; ovary 1-celled, 1-ovuled; styles 3; stigmas capitate; achene 3-angled, rarely lenticular.

1. Leaves only at the base of the plant, not on the flowering stems
    2. Leaves conspicuously long-petioled; plants not densely matted at the base
        3. Leaf blades somewhat triangular, broadest at or near the base; leaves usually green on the upper side

Eriogonum caespitosum Nutt.   Cushion Eriogonum

A low cushion-forming perennial with spreading branches 5-20 cm long and persistent old leaves at the base; leaves obovate to linear-lanceolate, 5-20 mm long, white-tomentose on both sides, revolute-margined; flowering stems 2-10 cm long, leafless, without bracts; involucre single, the 6 to 10 lobes recurved; flowers numerous, exserted, yellow aging to rose or brownish-purple; perianth 5-6 mm long, tomentose, short-stipitate, the inner and outer sets unequal; filaments long-hairy; achene sparsely pubescent or glabrous.
Rocky or gravelly open ridges, 9000 feet and above.

Eriogonum chrysops Rydb.   Talus Eriogonum
E. kingii T. & G.

Grayish-woolly, prostrate, dwarf, much-branched shrub, forming mats up to almost a meter across; leaves tomentose on both sides, 1-4 cm long, spatulate to oblong-obovate, short-petioled; flowering stems 1-10 cm tall, glandular-pubescent to glabrous or floccose, leafless; inflorescence head-like with 3 to 7 sessile involucres subtended by 3 to 5 bracts; involucres loosely floccose to glandular-puberulent with 5 unequal, erect segments; perianth yellow, glabrous to glandular-puberulent, about 2.5 mm long, non-stipitate, the segments similar, partially united; flowers mostly imperfect; filaments long-hairy; achene glabrous.
Scree, talus slopes and on open rocky slopes and ridges, 9300 to 9800 feet.

Eriogonum compositum Dougl.   Heart-leaved Eriogonum
Perennial from a woody taproot and branching crown, usually covered with old leaf-

bases, erect to prostrate, forming mat-like clumps up to about 30 cm broad; leaves 3-25 cm long, lanceolate to deltoid or ovate, white-tomentose on both sides to glabrate and greenish above, long-petioled; flowering stems leafless and without bracts, 4-20 cm tall, glabrous or nearly so; inflorescence a compound umbel of 4 to 10 rays subtended by a whorl of linear to leaf-like bracts; involucres glabrate or glandular-puberulent to lanate, the segments usually reflexed; perianth creamy white to yellow, glabrous to glandular-puberulent, stipitate; filaments glabrous; achene pubescent on the upper angles.
Dry alpine slopes, about 9000 feet.

Eriogonum douglasii Benth.　　　　　　　　　　　　　　　　　Douglas' Eriogonum
Perennial with erect shrubby branches 5-40 cm tall; leaves whorled at the tips of the branches, narrowly oblanceolate, 1-3 cm long, grayish-lanate beneath, glabrate to lanate above, revolute-margined; flowering stems 5-10 cm tall; inflorescence of 2 to several umbellately arranged involucres subtended by a whorl of leaves; involucres usually tomentose with 6 to 10 spreading to reflexed lobes; flowers numerous, forming a globose head; perianth yellow or white, sometimes pinkish, strongly villous-tomentose to very rarely glabrous, stipitate; filaments villous on the lower half; styles usually coiled; achenes pubescent above.
Dry open rocky places at about 8000 to 8500 feet.

Eriogonum flavum Nutt.　　　　　　　　　　　　　　　　　　　Golden Eriogonum
E. piperi Greene
Cespitose grayish-tomentose perennial with a woody taproot and a branched crown, usually densely covered with crowded old leaf bases, forming mats up to about 30 cm broad; leaves sometimes green and nearly glabrous above, crowded, 3-10 cm long, linear to narrowly oblanceolate; flowering stems leafless, 5-30 cm tall; inflorescence umbellate, subtended by 4 to 6 usually leaf-like bracts; involucres long-hairy, to tomentose, 4-9 mm long, truncate, or with 4 or 5 short erect lobes; perianth 4-6 mm long, yellow, sometimes tinged with pink or red, long-hairy to silky or mealy-glandular, stipitate; filaments villous; achene pubescent above.
Dry open cliffs and meadows to alpine scree, slopes and ridges, 4500 to 9800 feet.

Eriogonum heracleoides Nutt.　　　　　　　　　　　　　　　　Creamy Eriogonum
Tomentose perennial from a branched woody base, forming large clumps; leaves linear to oblanceolate, 2-8 cm long, densely grayish-tomentose beneath, sometimes less so and greenish above; flowering stems 10-70 cm tall, usually with a whorl of leaf-like bracts about midlength (ours); inflorescence a simple to compound umbel subtended by leaf-like to reduced bracts; rays 2-5 cm long; involucres woolly, the lobes reflexed; perianth white to cream or ochroleucous, occasionally rose-tinged, glabrous, stipitate, 5-6 mm long; filaments villous below; achene pubescent above.
Dry rocky or gravelly slopes and ridges, 4500 to 7000 feet.

Eriogonum microthecum Nutt.　　　　　　　　　　　　　　　　Bushy Eriogonum
Branched low shrubby perennial 10-60 cm tall, the younger branches tomentose; leaves crowded, grayish-tomentose beneath, greenish and less tomentose above, 1-3 or 4 mm long, linear-elliptic to narrowly obovate, short-petioled, often revolute; flowering branches leafy below, 3-20 cm long, glabrous to tomentose or floccose; inflorescence an

open compound umbel, usually flat-topped with scale-like bracts; involucres single, about 2.5 mm long, tomentose to glabrous, the teeth usually ciliate; perianth glabrous, white or pink to yellow or greenish-yellow, not stipitate, the segments united about ⅓ the length, the inner narrower; filaments long-hairy near the base; achenes glabrous. Dry sandy or rocky soils, about 4500 feet.

Eriogonum ovalifolium Nutt.   Oval-leaved Eriogonum
Cespitose perennial forming broad mats; leaves crowded, white-lanate on both sides to greenish and less densely tomentose above, spatulate or elliptic to rhombic or oval, 1-20 mm long, usually short-petioled; flowering stems leafless, 2-20 cm tall, tomentose; inflorescence usually a congested head of several involucres, sometimes somewhat umbellate, subtended by 3 or more linear to foliaceous bracts; involucres 3-5 mm long, woolly-tomentose; perianth white, cream or ochroleucous to yellowish with green and pink veins, non-stipitate, 3-4 mm long, glabrous, the segments free almost to the base, the outer broader than the inner; filaments hairy below; ovary glabrous. Low woodlands to alpine ridges and talus slopes.

Alpine or subalpine dwarfed plants; leaves mostly under 1.5 cm long including the petiole, nearly white or silvery on both sides, the blade nearly round; flowering stems mostly 1-6 cm tall..var. **nivale** (Canby) M. E. Jones

Eriogonum sphaerocephalum Dougl.   Round-headed Eriogonum
Stems thick, shrubby, erect or lying close to the ground, much branched, up to 30 cm tall; leaves oblanceolate, densely white-cobwebby-hairy underneath, less densely so above, 1.5-3 cm long, crowded at the ends of the branches, the margins often rolled inward; flowering stems 4-10 cm tall, with a whorl of leaves at the middle or often branched at about the middle, with several rays; involucres long-hairy, about 5 mm high, the lobes curving outward; flower cluster roundish, dense; flowers hairy, whitish, creamy or light yellow, tapering to a false stipe, the 2 sets about similar. Dry open places; probably outside our range.

Eriogonum strictum Benth.   Blue Mountain Eriogonum
Mat-forming perennial with woody stems up to 10 cm long; leaves grayish-tomentose beneath, thinly so and grayish to green above, 5-25 mm long, elliptic to ovate or oval, often long-petioled; flowering stem leafless, 10-40 cm tall, usually tomentose; inflorescence open and branched with the involucres solitary, to umbellate and the involucres nearly capitate at the ends of the branches, the bracts mostly linear; involucres 3-5 mm long, tomentose or sometimes nearly glabrous, with 5 short ciliate teeth; perianth glabrous, white or cream to pinkish or yellow, non-stipitate, the outer segments twice as broad as the inner; filaments long-hairy; ovary glabrous. Dry rocky slopes and cliffs, 4500 to about 7200 feet.

Eriogonum thymoides Benth.   Thyme-leaved Eriogonum
Cespitose grayish-tomentose perennial with shredded bark, from a thick root; leaves many, matted, linear to linear-spatulate, 3-10 mm long, revolute, tomentose beneath, sericeous above; flowering stems 2-8 cm tall with a whorl of leaves at about the middle; involucres single, short-hairy; perianth 4-6 mm long, cream to yellow or white, often

turning deep rose, white-long-hairy, stipitate; flowers sometimes imperfect; filaments
and achenes pubescent.
Open places and ridges at low elevations.

Eriogonum umbellatum Torr.   Yellow Eriogonum
   Perennial from a branching crown above a strong taproot; branches prostrate and
forming broad mats or sometimes erect and 10-30 cm tall; leaves oblong or elliptic to
obovate, the blade 1-4 cm long, glabrous on either side to grayish-tomentose beneath and
green and lanate above; flowering stems erect, leafless, 10-25 cm tall, tomentose or glabrate; umbel of 2 to 10 unequal rays; involucres solitary, lanate to crisp-pubescent, many-
flowered, 5-8 mm high, the lobes usually reflexed; inflorescence a simple to compound
open umbel, subtended by a whorl of leaf-like bracts; perianth glabrous, usually cream
or yellow, sometimes greenish-yellow, often tinged with rose or purple, stipitate; filaments long-hairy below; achene pubescent above.
Rock crevices, talus slopes and ridges, 4500 to about 9000 feet.

Plants neither dwarfed nor prostrate, generally 10-40 cm tall; leaves greenish to white on
one or both sides, usually over 1 cm broad; flowering stems at least 10 cm tall, the umbel
usually open, compound; flowers yellow..............var. **croceum** (Small) Stokes ex Davis

Oxyria Hill

   Low glabrous perennial herbs with thick rootstocks, erect stems and acrid juice; leaves
mostly basal, long-petioled, the blade rounded to kidney-shaped, the stipules sheathing;
flowers perfect, in terminal panicles; perianth 4-parted nearly to the base; stamens 6,
the filaments short; ovary 1-celled; styles 2, short; stigmas fringed; achenes flattened,
broadly winged.

Oxyria digyna (L.) Hill   Mountain Sorrel
   Glabrous, often reddish-tinged, perennial from a taproot and a crown; leaves mostly
basal, long-petioled, the blade kidney-shaped to cordate, 1-5 cm broad; flowering stems
usually several, 1-25 cm tall with reddish or brownish membranous stipules; panicle
dense, 1-15 cm long; perianth about 1.5 mm long, one pair of segments keeled, narrow,
reflexed in fruit, the other pair erect, oblong-obovate, green or reddish; achene flat, oval,
broadly winged.
Among rocks and on slopes mostly above 7000 feet but sometimes as low as 5800 feet.

Polygonum L.

   Annual or perennial herbs, or sometimes shrubs, usually with swollen joints, sheathing
stipules and alternate, entire, petioled leaves; flowers mostly perfect, solitary or usually
clustered in 1 to several axillary, spike-like to paniculate racemes; perianth usually
5-parted, often petaloid, greenish, white or reddish, the outer segments sometimes large
and keeled; stamens 3 to 9, in 2 series; styles 2 to 4; stigmas small; achenes lenticular
or 3-angled.

1. Flowers and fruits clustered at or near the top of the stem
    2. Plants 25-70 cm tall; leaves up to 20 cm long, basal or on the stem
        3. Leaves numerous, all on the stem, large and short petioled; flower cluster
          not dense...*P. phytolaccaefolium*
        3. Leaves few, basal, long-petioled; flower cluster dense........................*P. bistortoides*

2. Plants mostly under 25 cm tall; flower clusters mostly spike-like, sometimes interrupted
    4. Flowering stems 10-25 cm tall; leaves basal..*P. viviparum*
    4. Flowering stems mostly under 10 cm tall; leaves not basal, short petioled and small
        5. Leaves of the flower clusters white-margined................................*P. polygaloides*
        5. Leaves of the flower clusters either not white-margined or the margin mostly not visible; stem leaves few, very narrow................................*P. kelloggii*
1. Flowers and fruits scattered along the main stems and the branches, the flowers solitary or in small clusters in the axils of the leaves
    6. Flowers or fruits, at least some of them, curved on their stalks so as to spread outward or curve downward
        7. Perianth usually 3-3.5 mm long................................*P. douglasii*
        7. Perianth mostly 4-5 mm long................................*P. majus*
    6. Flowers and fruits all growing upward, none curved downward
        8. Leaves usually over 10 mm long, narrowly elliptic, mostly well over twice as long as broad
            9. Fruits (achenes) black and shining; perianth parts united less than halfway; leaves reduced upward to bracts among the flowers............*P. sawatchense*
            9. Fruits brownish, dull or shiny; perianth parts united halfway; leaves bluish-green, only slightly reduced upward................................*P. aviculare*
        8. Leaves about 10 cm long, not narrowly elliptic, sometimes rounded at the tip, shorter, mostly about twice as long as broad
            10. Leaves many, crowded on the stem, often rounded at the tip; plant usually lying close to the ground................................*P. achoreum*
            10. Leaves few, not crowded, not rounded at the tip, oval in shape; plant usually erect, the stem often zig-zag................................*P. minimum*

Polygonum achoreum Blake   Prostrate Knotweed

Bluish-green annual, often prostrate; leaves numerous, closely crowded, often overlapping, oval to obovate, 1-2.5 cm long, rounded at the tip, narrowed to a short jointed petiole; stipules conspicuous, 5-11 mm long; flowers 1 to 4, axillary; pedicels 1-4 mm long; perianth about 3 mm long, greenish, the parts connate at least halfway, white-margined, the 3 outer broader and longer than the 2 inner ones; styles 3; achene 3-angled, yellowish-brown.
Dry rocky ground at about 5000 feet.

Polygonum aviculare L.   Common Knotweed

Glabrous prostrate or erect annual with terete, wiry, striate, branched stems 10-120 cm long; leaves bluish-green, narrowly oblong to oblanceolate, 6-30 mm long, on short jointed petioles; stipules lacerate; flowers in axillary clusters of 1 to 5, the pedicels erect; perianth about 2.5 mm long, the 5 lobes united about halfway, greenish with white, pink or red margins; stamens 8, rarely 5; styles 3; achene brownish, smooth or striate, dull or shining.
Common weed of dry gravelly ground.

Polygonum bistortoides Pursh   Smokeweed; Snakeweed

Perennial from thick fleshy rootstocks; stems 1 or more, 25-70 cm tall, glabrous; leaves chiefly basal, long-petioled, not jointed to the stem, the blade elliptic to oblong-oblanceolate, glaucous, up to 20 cm long; cauline leaves few, sessile, reduced upward; stipules brownish, not lacerate; racemes terminal, dense and spike-like, solitary, 2-4 cm long with

papery brownish bracts; perianth 5-lobed, white to pinkish; stamens 8; achenes 3-angled, brownish, smooth and shining.
Wet or moist boggy mountain meadows, 5500 to about 6000 feet.

Polygonum douglasii Greene   Douglas' Knotweed
   Pale somewhat glaucous annual with long ascending branches and wiry, erect, terete or ridged branching stems 10-80 cm tall; leaves linear to narrowly oblong, 1-5 cm long, sessile or nearly so, jointed at the base; stipules short-sheathing, lacerate; flowers 1 to 3 or 4 per node, in a long, loose raceme; pedicels 1-3 mm long, reflexed by maturity; perianth segments 5, about 3 mm long, greenish with white or reddish margins; achene 3-angled, black, smooth and shining.
Dry to moist rocky or sandy soils in meadows and on open slopes, from 4500 to about 8500 feet.

Polygonum kelloggii Greene   Kellogg's Knotweed
   Glabrous annual with erect angled stems 2-8 cm tall; leaves few, linear, 5-25 mm long, jointed at the base; stipules 2- to 3-cleft or lacerate; flowers in crowded terminal clusters as well as in the leaf axils; bracts linear to lanceolate, green or with a very narrow white margin; pedicels less than 1 mm long; perianth about 2 mm long, the 5 segments united near the base, green-striped with white margins; stamens 8, only 3 with anthers; achenes 3-angled, light yellow to greenish-brown, smooth and shining but sometimes other achenes on the same plant dull, striate and dark brown.
Dry or moist gravelly or sandy slopes or meadows, 5000 to 6200 feet.

Polygonum majus (Meisn.) Piper   Wiry Knotweed
   Erect annual 10-35 cm tall, simple or branched; stem angled, wiry; leaves linear to oblong, 2-5 cm long, reduced upward, sessile, jointed at the base; stipules lacerate; flowers in 2's or 3's, early reflexed, in long racemes with short linear or subulate bracts; perianth 4-4.5 mm long, white with a green or red midvein; achenes reflexed, 3-angled, black and shining, smooth to granulose.
Dry gravelly or heavy soils in pine woods, 5000 to 6000 feet.

Polygonum minimum Wats.   Zigzag Knotweed
   Leafy annual, mostly branched from the base, 5-15 cm tall, the branches often zigzag, angled or terete, somewhat scurfy; leaves oblong-elliptic to ovate or obovate, 5-15 mm long, jointed at the base, sessile or nearly so; stipules lacerate; flowers mostly in 2's or 3's in the axils of most of the leaves; perianth about 2 mm long, the lobes greenish with narrow white or pinkish margins; stamens 5 to 8; achenes 3-angled, greenish-black, smooth and shining.
Moist meadows and dry rocky slopes, 5000 to 7300 feet.

Polygonum phytolaccaefolium Meisn.   Alpine Knotweed
   Glabrous to pubescent perennial 50-200 cm tall, from a large crown and thick root; stems usually several, thick, branched and channeled; leaves all cauline, broadly lanceolate, 3-15 cm long, short-petioled, somewhat crowded above, the margins often crisped and undulate; stipules not lacerate; flowers in loose, leafless to leafy-bracteate terminal and axillary panicles; perianth white to greenish-white, 2.5-3 mm long, the segments

Urtica dioica ssp. gracilis

Comandra umbellata

Arceuthobium americanum

Eriogonum caespitosum

Eriogonum flavum

Eriogonum heracleoides

Oxyria digyna

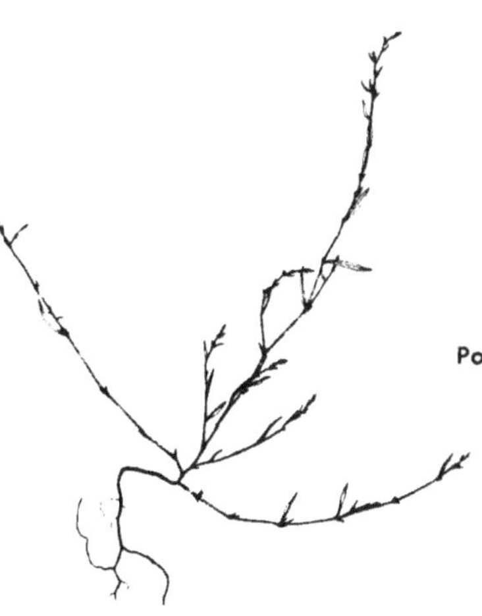

Polygonum majus

Polygonum aviculare

Polygonum bistortoides

united only at the base; stamens 8; styles free; achenes 3-angled, yellowish-brown, smooth and shiny.
Moist to dry meadows, streambanks, rock slides, talus and open slopes, 6000 to 8200 feet.

Polygonum polygaloides Meisn.   White-margined Knotweed
Glabrous, usually branched annual, 5-20 cm tall with angled stems and narrowly linear leaves 1-3 cm long, jointed at the base; stipules lacerate; flowers 1 to 4 in the axils of crowded, broad, white-margined floral bracts, the inflorescence short and dense; perianth 2-3 mm long, the segments united at the base, pinkish with a green or rose-red mid-rib and white to pinkish margins; stamens usually 8; style 3-parted to about the middle; achenes 3-angled, dark brownish to nearly black, dull and striate.
Moist to dry rocky woods, often with Ponderosa pine, about 5500 to 6000 feet.

Polygonum sawatchense Small   Sawatch Knotweed
Annual, 5-25 cm tall with angled, dull green, scaberulous branches; leaves oblong to elliptic-oblanceolate below, reduced upward to short linear bracts, 5-25 mm long, jointed at the base, the midvein prominent and often keeled; stipules lacerate; flowers 1 to 4 in the axils of nearly all the leaves on the stems, not becoming reflexed; perianth green with white margins, 2-3 mm long, the segments united near the base; stamens 6 to 8; style cleft to the base, very short; achenes 3-angled, smooth, black and shiny.
Dry rocky or sandy hillsides or slopes, 5000 to 7000 feet.

Polygonum viviparum L.   Bog Knotweed
Perennial with thick rootstocks and slender erect stems 10-25 cm tall; leaves chiefly basal, long-petioled, not jointed to the stems, 3-10 cm long, the blade oblong to lanceo-late; cauline leaves 2 to 4, much narrower, reduced upward and becoming sessile; stipules brown, sheathing, not lacerate; inflorescence a single terminal bracteate raceme 3-10 cm long with small reddish to purplish bulblets instead of flowers in the axils of the lower floral bracts; perianth greenish, pale rose or white, 3-3.5 mm long; stamens 8 and exserted when developed but rudimentary and short in the pistillate flowers; styles 3, nearly free; achenes when developed, 3-angled, smooth or granular, dull or shining.
Moist to wet bogs, streambanks and meadows in shady woods, 5300 to 8200 feet.

Rumex L.
Annual or perennial herbs, often reddish-tinged, with grooved stems; leaves entire or undulate, flat or crisped, often large; stipules scarious and sheathing; flowers usually perfect, in large panicles often; perianth segments 6, rarely 4, the inner 3 enlarging and enclosing the fruit, becoming papery and often winged, one or more with a grainlike callosity on the back; stamens 6; styles 3; achene 3-angled, usually smooth, brownish to nearly black.

Leaves 2.5-8 cm long, the lower ones broader at the base than at the tip; perianth about
1 mm long .... *R. acetosella*
Leaves 5-15 cm long, the lower ones tapered and narrowed to the petiole; perianth about
3 mm long .... *R. salicifolius*

Rumex acetosella L.   Red or Sheep Sorrel
Dioecious glabrous perennial with spreading rootstocks and 1 to several stems 10-60

cm tall; leaves linear to ovate, the lower ones hastate, 2.5-8 cm long, petioled below, nearly sessile and lanceolate above; flowers imperfect, yellowish or reddish, in large but narrow leafless panicles; pedicels jointed under the flowers; perianth about 1 mm long, without callosities; achenes smooth.
Weed of grassy slopes, woods and meadows, 4600 to 6100 feet.

Rumex salicifolius Weinm.   Willow Dock

Glabrous perennial from a stout taproot, usually with leafy, prostrate, grooved stems 30-70 cm tall; leaves flat and entire, bright green, petioled below, the upper nearly sessile, 5-15 cm long, narrowly lanceolate; racemes short and congested into a dense spikelike panicle, or sometimes more open; pedicels jointed near the base; perianth segments 3 mm long, with or without callosities on the back; achenes about 2-2.5 mm long, smooth and shining.
Low moist ground, mountain meadows and streambanks, 5800 to 7300 feet.

CHENOPODIACEAE   Goosefoot Family

Annual or perennial herbs or shrubs, glabrous to pubescent with mealy or fleshy herbage; leaves simple, mostly alternate, sometimes scale-like, without stipules; flowers inconspicuous, perfect or imperfect, one to many in axillary or terminal clusters, spikes, panicles or cymes with or without bracts, the perianth usually greenish, mostly 5-lobed but sometimes 2 to 4 or 6, or reduced to a single segment, or absent in the pistillate flowers; stamens free, usually as many as the perianth segments and opposite them; ovary superior, 1-celled, 1-ovuled; styles 1 to 3; fruit a utricle.

1. Mature leaves and bracts very spiny; stems often purplish..*Salsola*
1. Mature leaves not spiny; stems green or sometimes reddish
    2. Perianth segments and stamens usually 3 to 5; fruit surrounded by the perianth
      lobes...*Chenopodium*
    2. Perianth segment and stamen usually solitary, sometimes 3; fruit not surrounded
      by the perianth lobes ....*Monolepis*

Chenopodium L.

Annual or perennial glabrous, white-mealy or glandular, often strongly scented, herbs with alternate or opposite, entire, toothed or pinnatifid leaves, often turning reddish or purplish with maturity; flowers minute, perfect, sessile in small spike-like or paniculate clusters (glomerules); perianth 5-parted or rarely 4 or 3, the lobes enclosing the fruit; stamens 5 or fewer, opposite the perianth lobes; styles 2 or 3, or none; seed 1.

1. Flowers in dense head-like rounded clusters; calyx turning red and pulpy at maturity....*C. capitatum*
1. Flowers not in tight rounded clusters; calyx not turning red with age
    2. Mature leaves pale green, mealy underneath; calyx lobes keeled.........................*C. album*
    2. Mature leaves often becoming reddish, not at all mealy; calyx lobes not keeled ....*C. rubrum*

Chenopodium album L.   Pigweed; White Goosefoot

Branched annual 20-100 cm tall, usually glabrous below, somewhat mealy above, the stems grooved and angled; leaves pale green, rhombic-ovate to lanceolate, entire or irregularly toothed, 2-10 cm long, mealy beneath; flowers in glomerules in axillary and terminal spikes or panicles; perianth deeply cleft and keeled, usually completely enclosing the fruit; pericarp closely adherent to the black, shining, horizontal seed.
Boggy coniferous woods, about 5600 feet.

Chenopodium capitatum (L.) Asch.   Strawberry Blite

Bright green glabrous annual 20-100 cm tall, usually branched; leaves triangular near the base, hastate, entire to toothed or lobed, 4-10 cm long, long-petioled, the upper leaves shorter-petioled, reduced and often entire; inflorescence an interrupted spike of axillary glomerules about 5 mm in diameter; perianth segments 3 to 5, fleshy, becoming enlarged and reddish, shorter than the fruit; utricle flattened sidewise, reddish-brown, only partly covered by the perianth; seed erect.
Moist to dry ground at about 5000 to 6000 feet.

Chenopodium rubrum L.   Red Goosefoot

Glabrous, freely branched annual, 10-50 cm tall usually; leaves rhombic-ovate to deltoid, often hastate, green, often becoming reddish-tinged, fleshy, nearly entire to irregularly toothed or lobed, 1.5-15 cm long, gradually reduced upward, the petioles equaling or shorter than the blades; flowers glomerate in short simple axillary spikes as well as a longer terminal, compound, bracteate spike; perianth segments 3 to 5, reddish, about equaling the fruit; utricle green, strongly compressed, with a thin, dark brown pericarp; seeds mostly erect.
Shady woods about 5000 feet.

Monolepis Schrad.

Small annuals with alternate, entire to hastate, fleshy leaves; flowers small, in axillary clusters (glomerules), without bracts, polygamous to monoecious; perianth of a single persistent greenish segment; stamens 1 or 2, or none; stigmas 2; utricle flattened; seed vertical.

Monolepis nuttalliana (Schult.) Greene   Patata

Nearly glabrous freely branched prostrate to erect annual 1-40 cm tall; stems thick and fleshy; herbage mealy to glabrate; leaves lanceolate, short-petioled to sessile, 1-6 cm long, hastately lobed near the base, entire to sometimes toothed above; flowers in dense, sessile, axillary glomerules; perianth segment oblanceolate or spatulate; pericarp pitted, adherent to the dark brown seed.
Moist grassy woods and slopes, 4500 to about 5800 feet.

Salsola L.

Annual or perennial herbs or shrubs, glabrous to pubescent; leaves mostly alternate, linear, spinulose, succulent; flowers perfect, sessile, solitary or clustered in the axils of upper, often spiny, bracts, each with 2 small sharp-pointed bracteoles; perianth mostly 5-parted, sometimes 4, the segments not united, often with a broad horizontal wing in fruit; stamens 5, or sometimes fewer; styles 2 or 3; utricle flattened, closely encircled by the calyx; seed generally horizontal.

Salsola kali L. var. **tenuifolia** Tausch   Tumbleweed; Russian Thistle; Wind Witch

Glabrous to pubescent annual (ours), usually freely branched, the stems often purplish and striate, up to 3 feet long, becoming hard and round and shrubby and twisting off to become tumbleweeds; leaves nearly filiform, spinulose, green or glaucous, the lower 3-6 cm long, the upper shorter, broader and hardened with age; flowers solitary in the upper leaf axils, subtended by sharp-pointed bracteoles; perianth segments united near the base, the wings membranous and veined, usually reddish or purplish, the tips curved over the fruit and then erect; fruit cup-shaped; seed large, black and shining. Roadside weed at about 4500 feet.

AMARANTHACEAE   Amaranth Family

Mostly annual or perennial herbs with opposite or alternate, simple, usually entire leaves without stipules; flowers very small, without petals, perfect or imperfect, solitary or mostly closely crowded in dense racemes or spikes, subtended by 1 or more bracts; sepals 3 to 5, or 1, free or united at the base, usually papery; stamens usually the same number as the sepals, sometimes fewer or more numerous, the filaments free or united at the base; pistil 2- to 3-carpellary, sometimes 5; ovary superior, 1-celled; styles 2 to 5, or 1; fruit a 1-seeded capsule (ours) ; seeds erect or inverted.

Amaranthus L.

Glabrous to hairy annuals, monoecious to dioecious; leaves alternate, the margins entire, crisped or undulate; flowers inconspicuous in small glomerules in dense axillary and terminal spikes or panicles, subtended by scarious pungent bracts; sepals usually 5, sometimes fewer, free; ovary 1-celled; fruit (ours) a circumscissile 1-seeded capsule, sometimes an indehiscent utricle; seeds smooth.

Amaranthus retroflexus L.   Rough Pigweed

Dioecious annual 30-100 cm tall, simple, or well-branched, usually pubescent; leaves ovate or rhombic-ovate, somewhat pubescent, 2-8 cm long, dull green, the margins mostly entire; flowers crowded in simple to compound, axillary and terminal spikes 8-15 mm thick, 2-10 cm long; bracts rigid-spine-tipped; sepals spatulate to lanceolate, spiny-tipped; stamens mostly 3 or 5; styles 3; capsule smooth; seed compressed, black and shining.
Roadside weed at about 4500 feet.

AIZOACEAE   Carpet-weed Family

Annual or perennial herbs, often succulent, ours with prostrate stems; leaves opposite, whorled, without stipules; flowers perfect, solitary or in axillary or terminal clusters; calyx 4- or 5-lobed or -parted, sometimes up to 8, the segments free (ours) ; petals none; stamens 3 to many; styles 3 to 20; fruit various, either a dehiscent capsule or indehiscent and nutlike.

Mollugo L.

Branched prostrate annual herb; leaves alternate to whorled (ours) ; flowers small, without petals, axillary; sepals 5, free, persistent, papery; stamens 3 to 5, sometimes 2 or up to 10; pistil mostly 3-carpellary; styles 3 to 5; fruit a 3-to 5-celled loculicidal capsule; seeds many.

Mollugo verticillata L.   Carpet Weed

Glabrous prostrate annual with dichotomously-branched stems up to 30 cm long; leaves 4 to 6 in a whorl, obovate to oblanceolate, entire, 5-30 mm long; flowers greenish, single in the axils, on slender pedicels; sepals 3-nerved, white inside; stamens usually 3;

capsule slightly longer than the sepals; seeds minute, smooth and shining or slightly granular.

Dry places near old logging roads and creeks, about 5000 feet.

PORTULACACEAE   Purslane Family

Annual or perennial succulent herbs (ours) with simple opposite, alternate or basal leaves, the margins entire; flowers perfect and mostly regular; sepals generally 2, sometimes up to 5 or 8; petals 3 to 16, mostly 5, sometimes none, free or often united at the base; stamens 3 to 20, opposite the petals when of the same number and basally attached to them; ovary mostly superior, 1-celled; styles 2 to 8; fruit a capsule, circumscissile or dehiscent by 2 or 3 valves; seeds 1 to many.

1. Flowers in dense roundish clusters; petals 4; plants usually prostrate................................*Spraguea*
1. Flowers solitary to many, usually in open inflorescences; petals usually more than 5;
   plants mostly erect
    2. Stamens 5 to 50; leaves thick, fleshy, few, mostly narrow, basal.............................*Lewisia*
    2. Stamens 1 to 5; leaves mostly thin, green, numerous, narrow to broad, basal as well
      as on the stem
        3. Plants with thin, slender, fibrous roots; stamens 2 to 5; plants annuals................*Montia*
        3. Plants with deep-seated corms, fleshy roots or runners; stamens 5; plants
          mostly perennials...*Claytonia*

Claytonia L.

Glabrous succulent herbs, ours mostly perennial, from deep corms or fleshy roots or stolons; leaves opposite, alternate or basal; flowers mostly racemose, perfect, regular; sepals 2; petals 2 to 6, often unequal in length and width, mostly pinkish; stamens 5; styles 3; capsule 3-valved; seeds usually dark and shining.

1. Leaves opposite, more than 2, scattered on the stem in pairs, broadest at the tip,
   narrowing to the base...*C. chamissoi*
1. Leaves alternate or mostly basal (except for sometimes 2 opposite leaves on the flowering
   stem near the inflorescence)
    2. Leaves (except the pair on the flowering stem) broader than long
        3. Leaves heart-shaped at the base; flowers white; bracts missing in the
          inflorescence...*C. cordifolia*
        3. Leaves not heart-shaped at the base; flowers mostly pink, some at least
          subtended by bracts under them...*C. sibirica*
    2. Leaves throughout longer than broad
        4. Flowering stems with only one pair of opposite leaves
          5. Basal leaves numerous, thickish, in a rosette close to the ground; plants
            of high elevations...*C. megarhiza*
          5. Basal leaves missing (rarely 1); plants growing erect, usually at lower
            elevations...*C. lanceolata*
        4. Flowering stems not with one pair of opposite leaves; stems either with
          several alternate leaves or with a disk formed by partial or complete union
          of the stem leaves
          6. Flowering stem with 3 to 5 or more alternate leaves; basal leaves
            crowded, broader, thickish...*C. parvifolia*
          6. Flowering stem not with alternate leaves but with a circular disk under
            the inflorescence; basal leaves numerous, long and narrow; plants
            sometimes becoming reddish...*C. perfoliata*

Polygonum phytolaccaefolium

Polygonum viviparum

Rumex acetosella

Chenopodium album

Monolepis nuttalliana

Amaranthus retroflexus

Salsola kali var. tenuifolia

Mollugo verticillata

Claytonia chamissoi Ledeb.   Toad-lily
   Montia chamissoi (Ledeb.) Robins. & Fern.
   Perennial with widely spreading creeping and rooting stolons; leaves opposite, oblanceolate to narrowly obovate, 1.5-4 cm long, several pairs on the stem; flowering stems erect, simple or branched above, 5-20 cm tall; flowers 3 to 10 in terminal and axillary racemes, often replaced by bulbils; pedicels recurved in fruit; sepals nearly equal; petals 5, white or pinkish, 5-9 mm long; stamens usually 5; ovules 3; capsules 1-1.5 mm long; seeds 1 to 3, black.
Wet, muddy or boggy, coniferous woods, 5300 to about 5800 feet.

Claytonia cordifolia Wats.   Broad-leafed Claytonia
   Montia cordifolia (Wats.) Pax & Hoffm.
   Perennial 10-30 cm tall from slender horizontal rootstocks; basal leaves several, erect, long-petioled, the blades rounded-ovate to nearly orbicular, 2-7 cm broad and almost as long, usually cordate-based; stem leaves 2, sessile; raceme 3- to 10-flowered, without bracts, lengthening with age; pedicels 10-20 mm long, spreading or recurved in fruit; sepals 3-5 mm long; petals 5, white, obovate, 8-12 mm long, capsules equaling the calyx.
Wet to moist places, mostly along streams, 5000 to 8000 feet.

Claytonia lanceolata Pursh   Western Spring Beauty
   Perennial from a globose corm; basal leaves 1 to few or none, the cauline 2, opposite, lanceolate, not united; flowering stems including the underground portion up to 15-20 cm tall; inflorescence an open raceme of several to many long-pedicelled flowers; sepals ovate, about 4.5 mm long; petals mostly 5, pink or white with pink lines; stamens 5; styles 3; capsule ovoid; seeds 3 to 6, black and shining.
Usually near moist banks, springs and melting snows, between 5800 and about 7000 feet.

Claytonia megarhiza (Gray) Parry var. **bellidifolia** (Rydb.) R. J. Davis
   Perennial from a fleshy, much elongated and often branched, root and thick caudex; leaves basal, many, 3-7 cm long, fleshy, broadly spatulate, long-petioled; flowering stems many, about equaling the leaves; sepals 2, green to reddish, acute, broadly ovate; petals usually 5, white to pale pink; stamens as many as petals and adnate to their claws; style 1; stigmas 3; capsule ovoid, 3-valved; seeds 1 to 6, black and shiny.
Among rocks and pebbles on talus slopes, between 8100 and about 9400 feet.

Claytonia parvifolia Moc.   Streambank Spring Beauty
   Montia parvifolia (Moc.) Greene
   Perennial with slender rootstocks and spreading branches 3-8 cm long; leaves obovate to oblanceolate, crowded at the base, alternate on the stems and reduced upward, the petiole shorter or longer than the blade; flowers mostly solitary; sepals unequal, about 2.5 mm long; petals 5, 7-10 mm long, white or pinkish; stamens 5; capsule about equaling the calyx or longer; seeds 2, black and shining.
Mossy streambanks and moist woods, 4600 to about 7200 feet.

Claytonia perfoliata Donn var. **depressa** (Gray) Jeps.   Miner's Lettuce
   Montia perfoliata (Donn) Howell
   Reddish annual, erect or spreading, 4-10 cm tall; basal leaves many, long-petioled, broadly rhomboidal, mostly shorter than the flowering stems; cauline leaves 2, opposite,

either completely united into a disk below the inflorescence or open on one side; flowers several in a somewhat whorled, crowded, short raceme; sepals about 2.5 mm long; petals 5, white or pinkish, 2-4 mm long; stamens 5; capsule globose, about equaling the calyx; seeds 3, black and shining.
Moist shady woods and open sandy valleys, 4500 to about 6600 feet.

Claytonia sibirica L.   Candy flower
Montia sibirica (L.) Howell
Annual or perennial with slender taproot; basal leaves few, long-petioled, acute, broadly rhombic-ovate; cauline leaves 2, opposite, not united, rounded-ovate, subtending the inflorescence; racemes long, lax, bracteate, 1 or more on each stem, sometimes branched with a single leaf subtending the branch; pedicels long and spreading; sepals 3-5 mm long; petals 5, white with deep pink lines, 6-10 mm long; stamens 3 to 5, the capsule about equaling the calyx; seeds 1 to 3, black and shining.
Moist shady woods, about 5100 to 6800 feet.

Lewisia Pursh

Glabrous somewhat succulent perennial herbs from a globose corm or a fleshy root and caudex; leaves entire, basal or cauline, the cauline mostly bractlike; inflorescence bracteate, 1- to many-flowered; sepals 2, persistent, often glandular-serrulate; petals 5 to 9, white or pinkish to deep magenta-rose; stamens 4 to 12 or more; style 1 with 3 or more stigmas; capsule ovoid, circumscissile at the base and then splitting toward the apex; seeds 3 to many, dark and shining, nearly smooth.

1. Flowering stems 2 or 3 times longer than the basal leaves, 11-35 cm tall, several-flowered; root thick and fleshy..*L. columbiana*
1. Flowering stems about as long as the leaves, mostly under 10 cm tall; flowers 1 to 3 per stem; roots various
  2. Flowers usually solitary with a pair of bracts just below the middle of the stem; root thick, fleshy, sometimes branched
    3. Flowers pure white, 9-15 mm long; sepals not glandular on the teeth........ *L. nevadensis*
    3. Flowers mostly pink or sometimes reddish or white with pink lines, 6-10 mm long; sepals glandular at the tips of the teeth ....*L. pygmaea*
  2. Flowers mostly 2 to 25 on the stem, rarely only 1, most or all of them with a pair of calyx-like bracts close beneath; root a globose corm .... *L. triphylla*

Lewisia columbiana (Howell) Robins.   Columbia Lewisia
Succulent perennial from a large root and caudex; basal leaves numerous, 2-10 cm long, narrowly oblanceolate to oblong; stem leaves few; scapes 10-30 cm tall, the panicle simple, loosely several- to many-flowered, the bracts glandular-toothed; sepals 2, glandular-dentate; petals usually 7 to 9, whitish or pinkish to magenta-rose, 5-13 mm long; stamens 5 or 6; ovules mostly 5 to 7; capsules ovate, almost as long as the sepals; seeds black and shining.
Among rocks, 4600 to about 7000 feet.

Lewisia nevadensis (Gray) Robins.   Nevada Lewisia
Perennial with a fleshy root; basal leaves 2 to 5, linear-lanceolate, 4-8 cm long; scapes mostly 3-5 cm high with opposite bracts below the middle; flowers solitary, white; sepals 5-10 mm long, broadly ovate, abruptly acute, mostly entire, the vein not prominent;

petals 6 to 8, about equaling the sepals; stamens 6 to 12; stigmas 3 to 6; capsule ovoid; seeds many, black, smooth and shining.
Moist to dry coniferous woods, near streams or melting snows, 4600 to about 8400 feet.

Lewisia pygmaea (Gray) Robins.   Dwarf Lewisia
Small perennial from a simple or branched thick fleshy root, 0.5-6 cm long, sometimes forked; leaves basal, 1-5 cm long, few, linear with widened hyaline bases; scapes several, 1-3 cm tall with opposite bracts about the middle; flowers 1 to 3; sepals 5-7 mm long, mostly broadly rounded, heavily veined, glandular-toothed, sometimes entire; petals white or greenish-white to deep pink or rose, about equaling the sepals; stamens 4 to 12, stigmas 3 to 5; capsule 4-6 mm long; seeds 18 to 20, dark and shining.
Gravelly or rocky open slopes, about 8000 feet to about 9500 feet.

Lewisia triphylla (Wats.) Robins.   Three-leaved Lewisia
Perennial from a globose to ovoid corm with 1 or more filiform stems 3-7 cm tall; basal leaves up to 5 cm long, mostly missing at flowering time; cauline leaves 2 to 4, opposite or semi-whorled, linear, 2-4 cm long; inflorescence bracteate, sometimes branching; flowers mostly 1 to 3; sepals 2, 3 or 4 mm long but lengthening in fruit; petals mostly 5, pinkish, longer than the sepals; stamens 5; capsule ovoid, about equaling the calyx; seeds 10 or more, dark brown and shining.
Moist cliffs along streams, springy ground and near melting snows, from about 4600 to about 8000 feet.

Montia L.

Small succulent annual herbs (ours); leaves alternate to basal, few, mostly narrowly linear; flowers solitary to few in loose, sometimes one-sided, racemes; sepals 2, persistent; petals 5; stamens 3 or 5; style 3-cleft; capsules 3-valved.

Montia linearis (Dougl.) Greene   Narrow-leaved Montia
Claytonia linearis Dougl.
Erect annual to 10 cm tall, much branched from the base; cauline leaves alternate, linear; racemes several, loosely 5- to 10-flowered, often nodding and one-sided; sepals 2.5-4 mm long but up to 6 mm in fruit and strongly veined; petals 5, white, about as long as the calyx; stamens 3; capsule ovoid, about equaling the calyx; seeds 3, black and shining.
Moist mossy meadows, streambanks and springy woods, 4600 to about 6500 feet.

Spraguea Torr.

Taprooted perennials with leaves mostly clustered at the base; inflorescence of 1 or more close-flowered umbellate heads; flowers minute; sepals 2, papery-margined, persistent, much larger than the 4 unequal, quickly-withering petals; stamens 3; style filiform; stigma short-lobed; capsule 2-valved; seeds few, tesselate, black and shining.

Spraguea umbellata Torr.   Pussy-paws
Dwarfed perennial with long somewhat fleshy roots; leaves numerous, in clustered basal rosettes, 1-3 cm long, oblanceolate to obovate-spatulate, mostly with acute tips, broadly petiolate; scapes few, 2-6 cm tall, naked or with 1 or more reduced bract-like leaves, bearing at their tips densely flowered umbels; sepals scarious, white or pinkish

Claytonia chamissoi

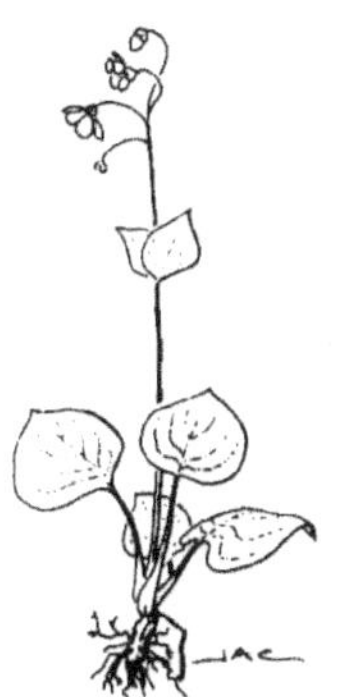

Claytonia cordifolia

Claytonia lanceolata

Claytonia megarhiza var. bellidifolia

Claytonia perfoliata var. depressa

Lewisia nevadensis

Lewisia triphylla

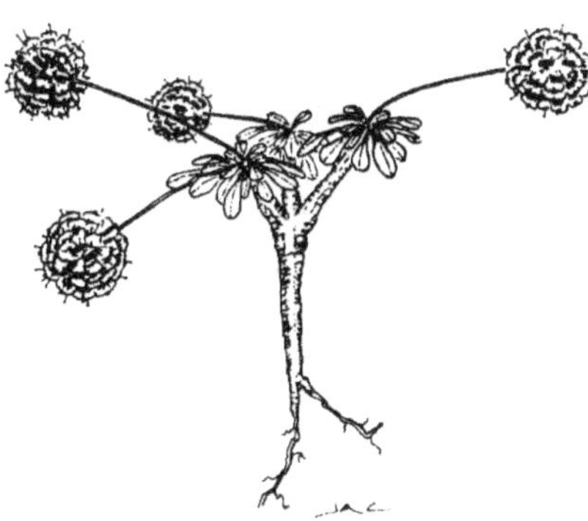

Spraguea umbellata var. caudicifera

Montia linearis

with greenish center; petals 4, white or pinkish, about equaling the sepals; seeds tesselate, about 1 mm long.

Often in dry sandy frequently disturbed places in meadows or on slopes, 7000 to about 9500 feet.

Leaves shorter, broader and more often spatulate; the
caudex branched..var. **caudicifera** Gray
With the species.

CARYOPHYLLACEAE   Pink Family

Annual or perennial herbs, sometimes shrubby, with swollen nodes and mostly opposite entire leaves with or without stipules; flowers regular, mostly perfect, solitary to cymose or umbellate; sepals usually 5, sometimes 4, free or united into a tube; petals as many as sepals or fewer or none, variously lobed, toothed, fringed or appendaged; stamens alternating with the petals and usually of the same number, sometimes fused with them at the base to form a short tube; styles 1 to 5, free or united below; ovary 1-celled, sometimes imperfectly 2- to 5-celled, often stalked; fruit a many-seeded capsule dehiscing by as many, or twice as many, valves or teeth as styles, or sometimes a 1-seeded utricle.

1. Flowers mostly white, sometimes tinged with pink
    2. Flowers showy; calyx 1.5-2 cm long, expanding in fruit; flowering stems mostly
        over 30 cm tall..*Lychnis*
    2. Flowers mostly small, not showy; calyx mostly under 1 cm long; flowering stems
        mostly well under 30 cm tall
            3. Calyx divided into 5 free green segments (sepals), sometimes slightly united
                only at the base
                    4. Petals when present with 2 or more lobes
                            5. Styles usually 3; capsules rounded to oblong; stems usually slender....*Stellaria*
                            5. Styles 5; capsules cylindric; stems thickish..................................*Cerastium*
                    4. Petals when present not at all lobed (sometimes with a shallow notch
                        at the top)
                            6. Styles 3, opposite the petals, fewer than the sepals.....................*Arenaria*
                            6. Styles 4 or 5, alternating with the petals, as many as the sepals.............*Sagina*
            3. Calyx tubular from the fusion of the segments, the top 5-lobed or -toothed;
                flowers sometimes pinkish-tinged .... *Silene*
1. Flowers pink to lavender, usually very small
    7. Plants forming dense thick cushions, mostly of high mountain elevations...........*Silene acaulis*
    7. Plants forming circular prostrate mats, mostly of dry locations at low elevations;
        leaves with papery stipules...*Spergularia*

Arenaria L.

Annual or perennial herbs with sessile opposite leaves and small flowers solitary or in heads or cymes; sepals 5, 1- to 3-nerved; petals 5 or none, white, shorter or longer than the sepals; stamens usually 10 on a disk; styles usually 3; capsule 1-celled, dehiscing from the tip by 3 entire or 2-toothed valves; seeds globose or kidney-shaped.

1. Flowering stems with 1 or 2 crowded little head-like clusters of flowers at the top; stem
    leaves very narrow..*A. congesta*
1. Flowering stems with flowers solitary or in open groups; leaves various
    2. Leaves "needle-thin," mostly at the base of the stems; plants perennials
        3. Plants forming prostrate roundish mats or cushions; flowering stems mostly
            under 10 cm tall

4. Stems brittle, breaking easily at the nodes; upper stem leaves closely
    crowding the flowers..*A. nuttallii*
4. Stems not brittle; flowers separated from the upper leaves
      5. Plant delicate; sepals 3-4 mm long, the tips pointed..................... *A. rubella*
      5. Plant rather coarse, not delicate; sepals 4-5 mm long, the tips
        incurved or hooded, usually purplish............................*A. obtusiloba*
3. Plants with leaves crowded at the base but not forming roundish mats or
  cushions; flowering stems mostly over 10 cm tall
      6. Basal leaves stiff, sharp to the touch, nearly as long as the 1 to 3 pairs
        of stem leaves..*A. aculeata*
      6. Basal leaves soft to the touch, twice as long as the 2 to 5 pairs of stem
        leaves..*A. capillaris*
2. Leaves not needle-thin, mostly over 2 mm broad, not mostly basal; plants annual or
  perennial
      7. Leaves 3-7 mm long; flowers mostly more than 5 or 6; plants mostly annual,
        sometimes becoming perennial..*A. serpyllifolia*
      7. Leaves 10-50 mm long; flowers usually 2 or 3 but sometimes 1 or up to 6;
      plants perennial
          8. Leaves and sepals rounded or blunt at the tip; petals about twice as long
           as the sepals..*A. lateriflora*
          8. Leaves and sepals pointed at the tip; petals slightly shorter or slightly
           longer than the sepals..*A. macrophylla*

Arenaria aculeata S. Wats.   Needle-pointed Sandwort

Cespitose glaucous perennial forming basal cushions; flowering stems 5-22 cm tall,
mostly glandular-pubescent above; leaves mostly basal, 1-2 cm long, linear, glaucous,
stiffly spreading, sharp-pointed; flowers few to many on long pedicels; sepals ovate, 2-4
mm long, somewhat pink-purplish at the tips, scarious-margined; petals often twice as
long as the sepals; capsule shorter or longer than the calyx.
Open rocky slopes, crevices and ridges, about 5700 to 9300 feet.

Arenaria capillaris Poir.   Slender Mountain Sandwort

A. formosa (Fisch.) Reg.
Cespitose glaucous perennial with many flowering stems 5-20 cm tall; basal leaves
many, linear, not rolled; cauline leaves at least half as long as the basal; flowers few;
sepals 3-4 mm long, ovate, often purplish-tinged; petals often twice as long as the sepals;
capsule ovoid, longer than the calyx.
Open rocky places, 7500 to 8000 feet.

Arenaria congesta Nutt.   Dense-flowered Sandwort

Cespitose glabrous perennial from a branched caudex; flowering stems 15-70 cm tall;
leaves linear, somewhat sharp-pointed, 0.5-12 cm long, the basal often forming mats;
flowers many in a head-like cluster; sepals scarious-margined, acute or acuminate, 3-6
mm long; petals longer than the sepals; capsule shorter or longer than the calyx.
Rocky slopes in open woods, often under Ponderosa pine, about 5000 to 6000 feet.

Arenaria lateriflora L.   Side-flowered Sandwort

Pubescent perennial 5-25 cm tall, from slender rhizomes, often rooting at the nodes,
producing sterile and flowering stems; leaves narrowly oval or oblong-lanceolate to
-oblanceolate, obtuse or rounded, 1-3 cm long, ciliate on the veins and margins, sessile
or very short petioled; flowers 1 to 6, axillary or terminal; pedicels to 3 cm long; sepals

2-3 mm long, obtuse or acute, white-margined; petals about twice the length of the sepals, obovate, nearly entire; styles 3; capsules globose to ovoid, shorter to twice the length of the calyx.
Open coniferous woods, about 5000 to 5600 feet.

Arenaria macrophylla Hook.   Large-leaved Sandwort
   Puberulent perennial from slender rhizomes, forming loose patches of both sterile and flowering stems; leaves mostly lanceolate, acute, 1-3 cm long, sometimes up to 7 cm; flowers 1 to 5 in a cyme, on long pedicels; sepals mostly 3-6 mm long, acute or acuminate; petals shorter or longer than the sepals, depending on whether the flowers are staminate or pistillate; capsule globose-ovoid, shorter than the calyx.
Open to shady, dry to moist woods and streambanks, 4900 to 6900 feet.

Arenaria nuttallii Pax   Brittle Sandwort
   Perennial with a taproot and many brittle, glandular-hairy, trailing to decumbent or matted stems; leaves subulate, 6-10 mm long, sharp-pointed, 3-nerved; flowers in small open cymes; pedicels 5-15 mm long; sepals 4-5 mm long, acute or acuminate to sharp-pointed, 1- to 3-nerved; petals shorter or longer than the calyx; capsule ovoid, shorter than the sepals.
Talus, open slopes and ridges, rock crevices, above 9000 feet.

Arenaria obtusiloba (Rydb.) Fern.   Blunt-lobed Sandwort
   Cespitose perennials; flowering stems glandular-pubescent, 1-6 cm tall, 1- or 2-flowered, with persistent old dried leaves at the base and mostly 1 or 2 pairs of cauline leaves; basal leaves 1-nerved, 4-8 mm long, linear, obtuse, rather rigid, often glabrous; flowers solitary or 2; sepals 4 mm long, obtuse, 3-nerved, glandular-pubescent; petals longer than the sepals; capsule ovoid-cylindric, longer than the calyx.
Steep rocky slopes, mostly over 9000 feet.

Arenaria rubella (Wahl.) J. E. Sm.   Variable Sandwort
   A. propinqua Richards.
   Prostrate cespitose perennial with a small taproot and branched crown, glandular-pubescent; flowering stems many, forming small cushions, simple or dichotomously branched, 1-10 cm tall; flower solitary, or sometimes few; leaves mostly basal, linear, 3-10 mm long, obtuse, 3-nerved; sepals 3-4 mm long, acute, scarious-margined, plainly 3-nerved; petals shorter or longer than the sepals; capsule narrowly ovoid, longer than the calyx.
Gravel bars at low elevations and dry granite slopes at upper elevations, 5100 to 9500 feet.

Arenaria serpyllifolia L.   Thyme-leaved Sandwort
   Branched puberulent annual with slender stems mostly 10 cm tall but sometimes up to 30 cm; leaves ovate, 3-7 mm long, acute, sessile or very short petioled; flowers in open cymes, long-pedicelled; sepals about 3 mm long, lanceolate-ovate, acuminate; petals about 2 mm long; capsule ovoid, about equaling the calyx.
Moist to dry sandy soils in grassy woodlands, about 4500 to 5000 feet.

Cerastium L.

Glandular-pubescent annual, biennial or perennial herbs often rooting at the nodes; leaves opposite; flowers white, in terminal dichotomous cymes; sepals 5, free to the base; petals 5 or none, always notched or 2-lobed; stamens 10, rarely fewer; styles usually 5, free, opposite the sepals; capsules cylindrical, 1-celled, usually curved, dehiscent by 10 apical teeth.

Petals equaling or shorter than the sepals; flower stalks (pedicels) mostly shorter than the calyx; plants tending to sprawl and root at the nodes ....*C. vulgatum*

Petals obviously longer than the sepals; pedicels longer than the calyx; plants with trailing stems but the flowering stems mostly erect ....*C. arvense*

Cerastium arvense L.   Meadow Chickweed

Cespitose perennial with trailing sterile, glabrous to glandular-pubescent stems often forming broad mats, the flowering stems erect, 5-50 cm tall; leaves linear to oblanceolate or oblong-ovate, 1-3 cm long, the cauline often with short sterile shoots or secondary leaves in the axils; flowers loosely cymose, solitary or few, the upper bracts scarious-margined; sepals 4-7 mm long, glandular-short- to -long-hairy; petals about twice as long as the calyx, deeply 2-lobed; capsule globose-ovoid to cylindric, as long as the calyx or longer.

Mossy bogs, gravelly bars and streambanks, and rocky dry slopes, 5100 to 9800 feet.

Cerastium vulgatum L.   Common Mouse-ear

Glandular-hairy biennial or perennial with simple or tufted, erect to prostrate stems tending to root at the nodes; flower stems erect, 20-40 cm tall; leaves deep green, mostly oblanceolate, 1-2.5 cm long, pubescent, somewhat crowded on the prostrate stems, those on the flowering stems more widely spaced, larger and sessile; bracts small, slightly if at all scarious-margined; flowers several in loose cymes; sepals hirsute, 4-7 mm long; petals 2-cleft, about equaling the sepals; capsule cylindric, about twice as long as the calyx.

Moist shady boggy woods, about 4500 to 6100 feet.

Lychnis L.

Annual to perennial herbs with opposite leaves; flowers perfect or imperfect, usually cymose, sometimes single and terminal; calyx tubular to inflated in fruit, mostly 10-nerved, 5-toothed; petals 5, white to deep red, the claw narrow and often auricled above, the blade notched to deeply 2- to 4-lobed and with 2 to 4 tubular basal appendages; stamens 10, connate; styles 5, rarely 4; capsule usually 1-celled, dehiscing by twice as many valves as styles.

Lychnis alba Mill.   White Campion

Stout dioecious perennial or biennial, glandular-pubescent throughout, with stems 10-100 cm tall; leaves lanceolate to oblanceolate, 3-10 cm long and 2 cm wide, the lower ones narrowed to a petiole, the upper sessile; flowers showy, in open cymes, fragrant, night-blooming; calyx 1.5-2 cm long and tubular at anthesis, 10-nerved in staminate flowers, 20-nerved and much inflated in fruit in the pistillate flowers; petals obovate, white, 2-3.5 cm long, the claw about as long as the calyx, broad and auriculate above, the

blades bilobed about halfway, with triangular fringed appendages at the base; styles 5; capsule 1-celled, ovoid, cylindric, dehiscing by 5 bifid valves.
Moist shady to dry sunny roadsides, campgrounds, moraines and waste places, to about 5500 feet.

Sagina L.

Low, often matted, annual or perennial herb with opposite leaves and small perfect flowers; sepals 4 or 5; petals 4 or 5 or none, white when present, entire to notched, usually shorter than the sepals and alternate with them; stamens usually as many as the sepals, sometimes fewer, or sometimes twice as many; styles as many as the sepals, sometimes fewer, or sometimes twice as many; styles as many as the sepals and alternate with them; capsule valves as many as the sepals and opposite them; seeds many.

Sagina saginoides (L.) Britt.   Arctic Pearlwort

Glabrous biennial or perennial, densely tufted, often matted, with basal rosettes of narrowly linear leaves 5-15 mm long; stems many, very slender, mostly 2-5 cm long, often bearing only 1 flower; cauline leaves mostly 3-6 mm long, scarious; pedicels 5-20 mm long, terminal or axillary, often curved; sepals 5 or 4, glabrous, about 2 mm long; petals a little shorter than the sepals when present; stamens usually 10; capsule as long as the sepals, or twice as long.
Moist to dry rocky or gravelly slopes, streambanks and bogs, 5300 to 9000 feet.

Silene L.

Glabrous to pubescent annual to perennial herbs, with opposite or whorled entire leaves; flowers solitary or usually in cymes, white, pink, red or purple, perfect or imperfect; calyx tube 5-lobed, 10- or more-nerved, often inflated in fruit, cylindric, ovoid or campanulate; petals 5, entire to often cleft or toothed or appendaged at the base, the long claws often auricled; stamens 10, fused with the petals; styles 3, rarely 4 or 5; ovary 1-celled or incompletely 3-, 4- or 5-celled; capsule dehiscent by 6 or rarely 3 or 8 to 10 apical teeth; seeds numerous.

1. Plants dwarf, forming mats or thick cushions, mostly alpine .... *S. acaulis*
1. Plants taller, not forming thick cushions, from low to upper elevations
    2. Stem leaves many, crowding the flowers, reduced upward, withering early near the base .... *S. menziesii*
    2. Stem leaves few; basal leaves numerous, persistent
        3. Petals 2-lobed; plant rarely glandular .... *S. douglasii*
        3. Petals deeply 4-lobed, the lobes often again lobed; plant usually viscid-glandular .... *S. oregana*

Silene acaulis L.   Moss Campion

Low cushion-forming perennial from a woody root; stems glabrous or pubescent, usually 3-6 cm tall; leaves crowded, linear, 4-15 mm long, glabrous to scabrous or ciliate near the base; flowers perfect to imperfect, solitary, sessile or pedunculate; calyx 3-10 mm long, glabrous, tubular-campanulate, frequently purple or pinkish; petals rose-pink, lavender, reddish-purple, or rarely white, entire or emarginate, 8-12 mm long; appendages usually 2, sometimes minute or even lacking; capsule 3-locular.
Mostly in moist rock crevices on steep unstable sandy slopes at upper elevations but also on gravel-bars, in bogs and along shady streams at lower elevations, 5500 to about 9800 feet.

Silene douglasii Hook.   Douglas' Campion

Cespitose perennial from branching rootstocks, finely and densely pubescent through-out and sometimes slightly glandular above; stems many, 10-60 cm tall; leaves 2-8 cm long, oblanceolate to linear-lanceolate, mostly petioled and matted at the base, the cauline 1 to 8 pairs becoming smaller and sessile; flowers in 1- to 7-flowered cymes; calyx cylindric, sometimes glabrous or glandular, 10-14 mm long, becoming inflated and papery in fruit, the teeth scarious-margined; corolla creamy-white or greenish, pink, or purplish-tinged; petals cleft into 2 entire lobes, the blade appendaged at the base, the claw sometimes auricled; styles 3, sometimes 4 or 5; capsule ovoid, 1-celled.
Dry rocky meadows and slopes in open coniferous woods, 5200 to 8400 feet.

Silene menziesii Hook.   Menzies' Campion

Glandular-pubescent to hirsute dioecious perennial, low and somewhat matted, with slender rootstocks and erect or decumbent, dichotomously-branched stems mostly 5-30 cm tall; leaves 2-6 cm long, numerous, acute, lanceolate to oblanceolate-obovate; flowers 1 to several in leafy, open cymes; calyx 6-8 mm long, tubular-campanulate, 10-nerved; petals white, 2-lobed, the lobes entire to erose, appendaged or not, with or without small lateral teeth, the claw glabrous, without auricles; styles 3, short in the staminate flowers, longer than the petals in the pistillate flowers; capsule stipitate, equaling the calyx.
Bogs, streambanks, moist meadows and wooded slopes, 4500 to 8000 feet.

Silene oregana Wats.   Oregon Catchfly

Perennial, finely short-pubescent throughout, glandular above, from branching root-stocks; stems 2 to several, erect, 25-50 cm tall; leaves lanceolate to oblanceolate, 3-8 cm long, the lower petioled, the cauline 3 to 6 pairs becoming reduced and sessile, puberu-lent or glabrous; calyx oblong-cylindric, 10-15 mm long, glandular, 10-nerved, the teeth scarious-margined; petals pinkish-white, the blade 3-5 mm long, deeply cleft into 4 lobes, the lobes sometimes again cleft; appendages 4, linear; claw longer than the calyx, some-what erose with narrow auricles; styles usually 3; capsule oblong, 6-8 mm long.
Dry or sometimes moist rocky slopes and talus on exposed ridges, 6900 to 9600 feet.

Spergularia Pers.

Low annual or perennial herbs, glabrous or pubescent, with fleshy subulate leaves and scarious stipules; flowers small, rose, pink or whitish, perfect, in leafy terminal cymes; sepals 5, free, the margins colored or scarious; petals entire, 5 or fewer, or none; stamens 2 to 10; styles 3, free; ovary 1-celled; fruit a capsule dehiscent to the base by 3 valves; seeds several.

Spergularia rubra (L.) Presl   Purple Sand Spurry

Glabrous to glandular-pubescent annual or perennial with many slender prostrate or decumbent stems mostly 4-30 cm long, forming dense mats; leaves usually fascicled, 6-15 mm long, minutely spine-tipped; stipules conspicuous, silvery; sepals oblong-lanceolate, glandular-pubescent; petals pinkish or reddish, about as long as the sepals; stamens 6 to 10; capsule about as long as the calyx.
Dry stony ground in open coniferous woods, 4500 to about 6200 feet.

Stellaria L.

Slender annuals or perennials with ovate, lanceolate or linear leaves and perfect solitary or cymose white flowers on long slender pedicels; sepals usually 5; petals usually 5, 2-cleft, sometimes missing; stamens 10, or 5, or fewer; styles usually 3, occasionally 4 or 5; capsule globose to oblong, dehiscing by twice as many valves as styles.

1. Petals much longer than the calyx, sometimes notched at the tip..*S. jamesiana*
1. Petals not longer than the calyx, either equaling or shorter, or missing
    2. Petals about equaling the calyx; leaves narrowly elliptic, mostly over 10 mm long
        3. Flowers 1 to few in the axils of the leaves, their stalks (pedicels) erect............*S. longipes*
        3. Flowers more numerous, their pedicels spreading or bent downward................*S. graminea*
    2. Petals definitely shorter than the calyx, or missing; leaves mostly ovate, under 10 mm long
        4. Flowers mostly solitary in the leaf axils all along the stem; petals usually missing; leaves numerous
            5. Sepals rounded at the tip; leaves ciliate at the base................................*S. obtusa*
            5. Sepals pointed at the tip; leaves not ciliate at the base, the margins ruffled..*S. crispa*
        4. Flowers more than one in axillary or terminal groups; petals present and short, or none; leaves few to many
            6. Stems with more than 1 or 2 pairs of leaves; petals equaling the calyx or missing; bracts leaf-like................................*S. calycantha*
            6. Stems with 2 or 3 pairs of leaves; petals minute or none; bracts small and not leaf-like................................*S. umbellata*

Stellaria calycantha Bong.   Bog Starwort

Essentially glabrous perennial with slender, prostrate to erect stems 10-40 cm long; leaves thin, sessile, ovate to lanceolate, ciliolate at the base, 7-25 mm long; flower solitary and axillary but also several in terminal leafy-bracteate cymes; pedicels 1-4 cm long; sepals usually 5, scarious-margined, 2-4.5 mm long; petals about equaling the sepals to rudimentary or even missing; capsule narrowly ovoid, usually about twice as long as the sepals.
Wet shady places in coniferous woods, about 4800 feet.

Stellaria crispa C. & S.   Ruffled Starwort

Low spreading perennial, glabrous throughout or ciliate on the leaves, with slender creeping rootstocks and weak, decumbent or prostrate stems 5-30 cm long; leaves lanceolate to ovate, nearly sessile, thin, 1-2 cm long, the margins often crisped; pedicels axillary, 6-20 mm long; flowers single in the axils all along the stem; sepals usually 5, 2.5-4 mm long, scarious-margined, 3-nerved; petals usually missing, when present shorter than the sepals and deeply cleft; capsules ovoid.
Moist shady banks and among rock boulders, 4500 to 8500 feet.

Stellaria graminea L.   Lesser Starwort

Essentially glabrous perennial from creeping rootstocks with 4-angled weak stems up to 100 cm long; leaves narrowly lanceolate, sessile, 1.5-3 cm long, usually long-ciliate at the base; flowers many in terminal cymes; pedicels spreading or reflexed, 1-4 cm long; sepals 3-nerved, acute, usually ciliolate, 3.5-5.5 mm long; petals longer, shorter, or about equaling the sepals; capsules about equaling the calyx.
Moist mixed woods near campground, about 5100 feet.

Arenaria aculeata

Arenaria congesta

Arenaria macrophylla

Arenaria rubella

Arenaria serpyllifolia

Cerastium arvense

Lychnis alba

Silene acaulis

Sagina saginoides

Silene oregana

Spergularia rubra

Stellaria jamesiana Torr.   Sticky Starwort

Perennial with fleshy thick roots and slender rootstocks, glandular-pubescent through-out or glabrate below; stems 4-angled, 10-40 cm tall, weakly erect or ascending; leaves narrowly lanceolate, sessile, 2-10 cm long, usually ciliate at the base and papillate-rough-margined; flowers many in leafy-bracted axillary and terminal cymes; sepals 4-6 mm long, broadly scarious-margined; petals deeply lobed, much longer than the sepals; capsule ovoid, shorter than the calyx.
Moist or dry open rock slopes and meadows, about 6000 feet.

Stellaria longipes Goldie   Long-stalked Starwort

Low perennial with slender rhizomes and slender, 4-angled, erect or ascending mostly glabrous stems 5-30 cm tall; leaves sessile, stiff and rigid, narrowly lanceolate, 1-3 cm long, sometimes ciliate at the base; flowers solitary to few in scarious-bracteate cymes, on erect pedicels up to 8 cm long; sepals glabrous or sometimes ciliolate, 3-nerved, scarious-margined, about 4 mm long; petals 2-cleft, mostly slightly longer than the sepals but sometimes slightly shorter; capsule green or purplish, slightly longer than the calyx.
Bogs, moist meadows and streambanks, 4700 to 7000 feet.

Stellaria obtusa Engelm.   Rocky Mountain Starwort

Glabrous low matted perennial with many prostrate stems 3-15 cm long; leaves ovate, 5-10 mm long, sessile or short-petiolate, long-ciliate at the base; flower single, axillary; pedicels 5-25 mm long; sepals 4 or 5, obtuse, 2-2.5 mm long; petals missing; stamens 8 to 10, capsule globose-ovoid, equaling or slightly longer than the calyx; styles 3 or 4.
Wet meadows and along streams, about 5500 feet.

Stellaria umbellata Turcz.   Umbellate Starwort

Perennial with slender rootstocks, glabrous throughout, sometimes the leaves ciliate; stems slender, numerous, creeping and rooting below, 5-20 cm long; leaves ovate or oblong to lanceolate, thin, 1-2.5 cm long, the margins smooth but often crisped; flowers several in terminal and axillary, scarious-bracteate, umbel-like cymes, on pedicels up to 3 cm long; sepals scarious-margined, 2-5 mm long; petals minute or none; capsule ovoid, 4-5 mm long.
From seepy rocky slopes to sandy dry talus, 6100 to 8500 feet.

NYMPHAEACEAE   Water Lily Family

Perennial acaulescent aquatic herbs with thick creeping rhizomes and long-petioled, peltate or cordate floating or emersed leaves; flower solitary, axillary, long-peduncled, usually showy, often odorous; sepals 3 to many, greenish to yellow or purplish, often petaloid; petals 3 to many, whitish to greenish-yellow, red or blue; stamens 3 to many; pistils 1 or 3; carpels 1 to several, free or united into a compound ovary; styles short or none; fruit leathery and follicular or a berry-like capsule.

Nuphar J. E. Smith

Aquatic perennial herbs with thick rhizomes and long-petioled, large, cordate, usually floating leaves; flowers showy, yellow; sepals 5 to 12, thick, yellow or reddish, the outer ones smaller than the others and greenish, petaloid; petals many, smaller than the sepals, stamen-like; stamens many, the filaments broad and flattened; pistil one, several-carpellary; stigma broad and flat, 7- to 24-rayed, almost sessile, with a scalloped margin; fruit a many-seeded indehiscent leathery berry-like capsule.

Nuphar polysepalum Engelm.   Wokas; Western Yellow Pond Lily
Aquatic perennial; leaves cordate, mostly floating, the blade leathery, 10-45 cm long, on terete petioles up to 2 meters long; sepals 6 to 12, yellow, often tinged with red, the outer greenish, 3-6 cm long; petals 12 to 18, lanceolate, thick, inconspicuous, greenish-yellow and somewhat purplish, 10-15 mm long; stamens numerous, reddish or purplish; stigma 2-2.5 cm broad, 15- to 25-rayed; fruit ovoid to cylindric, 5-9 cm long, constricted at the neck.
Shallow mountain lakes, 5600 to 7400 feet.

CERATOPHYLLACEAE   Hornwort Family

Aquatic herbs with dissected whorled leaves; flowers unisexual, very small, axillary; perianth (involucre) of 8 to 15 greenish segments; staminate flowers of 10 to 16 sessile anthers; pistillate flowers 1-carpellary, 1-ovuled; fruit an achene beaked by the persistent style.

Ceratophyllum L.
Characters of the family.

Ceratophyllum demersum L.   Hornwort
Stem delicate, 3-4 meters long, branched; leaves whorled, dissected into very narrow toothed segments, 5-25 mm long; achenes when present 4-6 mm long, flat, with a straight spine up to 12 mm long between 2 very short spreading basal spines.
Ponds and quiet waters, Duck Lake, 5600 feet.

PAEONIACEAE   Peony Family

Glabrous herbs or shrubby perennials; leaves large, ternate (ours), without stipules; flowers regular, showy; sepals 5, thick, persistent, usually unequal, greenish or colored; petals 5 to 10, purplish to red or white; stamens numerous, perigynous, based on a conspicuous disc; carpels usually 5, free; fruit a leathery dehiscent follicle; seeds many, often with an aril.

Paeonia L.
Characters of the family.

Paeonia brownii Dougl.   Western Peony
Glaucous perennial herb with thick roots; stems several, fleshy; leaves mostly basal, fleshy, compound; flowers solitary, large and showy; sepals leathery, greenish-purple, 10-18 mm long, unequal; petals 5, deciduous, brownish-red, equaling the sepals; stamens many; follicles 2 to 5, leathery, about 2 cm long.
Dry talus and open Ponderosa pine woods and slopes, about 5000 to 5700 feet.

RANUNCULACEAE   Buttercup Family

Annual or perennial herbs, sometimes woody; leaves mostly basal or alternate, but rarely opposite or whorled, mostly compound, without stipules; flowers perfect or imperfect, regular or irregular, showy to inconspicuous, single or paniculate; sepals 3 to 15, early deciduous, greenish to petaloid and showy; petals free, 4 to 10 or sometimes none, showy to minute and inconspicuous, sometimes spurred, often with a gland covered by a scale; stamens usually many, spirally arranged; pistils usually 2 to many, free, 1-celled with 1 to many ovules; fruit follicles, achenes or berries.

1. Plants rooted in the mud of shallow streams; petals white..*Ranunculus*
1. Plants not growing in streams; petals white to colored
    2. Flowers brightly colored: yellow, pink, red, blue or purple
        3. Flowers usually yellow, sometimes tinged with pink or red
            4. Flower with 5 spurs curving inward..*Aquilegia*
            4. Flower without spurs..*Ranunculus*
        3. Flowers not yellow, mostly blue, pink or purplish
            5. Flowers either with a helmet-like hood or a spur
                6. Flowers blue-purple, with a spur; petals 4..*Delphinium*
                6. Flowers blue or bluish-white, with a hood; petals 2 to 8..*Aconitum*
            5. Flowers regularly shaped, neither hooded nor spurred
                7. Flowers showy, large; petal-like sepals usually 4..*Clematis*
                7. Flowers not showy, smaller; petal-like sepals mostly 5 or more............*Anemone*
    2. Flowers white, greenish-white, or cream
        8. Flowers only 1 or 2 per stem
            9. Leaves lobed or divided or toothed, usually thin..*Anemone*
            9. Leaves not lobed or divided, sometimes ruffled, usually thickish or fleshy........*Caltha*
        8. Flowers usually more than 2 per stem and plant
            10. Leaflets numerous, mostly over 10 per leaf
                11. Flowers with 1 pistil; berries shining, white or red; leaves large............ *Actaea*
                11. Flowers with 2 or more pistils; fruit spindle-shaped achenes; leaves
                  smaller..*Thalictrum*
            10. Leaflets fewer, rarely over 10 per leaf
                12. Plant woody, usually climbing over other shrubs and trees; style
                feathery in fruit..*Clematis*
                12. Plant not woody; style not feathery..*Trautvetteria*

Aconitum [Tourn.] L.

Perennials with a tuberous root; stems erect or trailing; leaves alternate, palmately divided; flowers showy and irregular; sepals 5, petaloid, purple, the upper sepal forming a beaked hood, the lateral and lower sepals smaller; petals 2 to 8, the upper ones concealed by the hood, the others reduced or missing; stamens many; pistils 3 to 6, forming follicles in fruit.

Aconitum columbianum Nutt.   Columbia Monkshood

Stems from a short tuber, 30-200 cm tall, glandular-pubescent above; leaves 5-15 cm wide, mostly cauline, 5- to 7-lobed, incised, long-petioled below, becoming sessile above; raceme simple or branched; sepals deep purplish-blue or white with purplish margin, the hood 10-25 mm high and beaked, the lateral and lower sepals shorter; the 2 upper petals hidden by the hood; pistils 2 to 5, forming follicles in fruit.
Moist to wet meadows and streambanks, bogs and lake borders, 5500 to about 7800 feet.

Actaea L.

Tall perennial herbs with stout rootstocks and ternately compound leaves; flowers small, white, in terminal racemes; sepals 3 to 5, petaloid; petals 4 to 10; stamens many, the filaments long; pistil 1, ovary 1-celled, stigma bilobed; fruit a somewhat poisonous red or white shiny berry.

Actaea rubra (Ait.) Willd. Baneberry
  A. arguta Nutt.
Stems 40-100 cm tall, branched; leaved cauline, few, 2- to 3-ternate with pinnate toothed and lobed segments; flowers white, many, long-pedicelled, in elongating terminal racemes; sepals whitish; petals white; stamens longer than the petals; berry globose, shining, white or red.
Moist shady mixed woods to dry open slopes, 4500 to about 5000 feet.

Anemone L.

Perennial herbs; leaves compound or dissected, basal except for 2 or 3 cauline which form an involucre below the flower; flower usually solitary on long peduncles; sepals 5 to 9, showy, petaloid; petals none; stamens and pistils many; fruit a head of many pubescent or woolly achenes; styles short, glabrous or plumose.

1. Flowers large and showy, white, the petal-like sepals 2-3 cm long; plants conspicuously
    hairy; fruit with long feathery styles..*A. occidentalis*
1. Flowers smaller, white, pink, reddish or bluish-purple, the sepals always under 2 cm
    long; fruit sometimes woolly or hairy but the styles glabrous
    2. Flowering stems hairy, at least toward the base; fruit woolly or hairy
        3. Flowers mostly 1 per plant, usually white, sometimes tinged with blue on the
            back (drying yellowish or cream)
            4. Basal leaves mostly 1 to 3, sometimes missing, the lobes rounded at the
                tip, not all deeply cleft; plant delicate, the stem weak..................*A. parviflora*
            4. Basal leaves numerous, persistent, the lobes pointed at the tip, most of
                them deeply cleft; plant not delicate, the stems erect even in fruit......*A. drummondii*
        3. Flowers mostly more than 1 per plant, mostly reddish, pinkish-yellow, or
            bluish-purple; fruit densely hairy...*A. multifida*
    2. Flowering stems essentially hairless; basal leaf solitary, often missing; fruit silky-
        hairy..*A. quinquefolia*

Anemone drummondii Wats. Drummond's Anemone

Hairy perennial 20-30 cm tall with a branched caudex; basal leaves many, long-petioled, the blades 1-5.5 cm wide, 3 to 4 times ternately compound; involucral leaves similar to the basal; flowers usually single; peduncles in fruit up to 20 cm long; sepals 7 to 9, white tinged with lilac-blue, drying yellowish or cream, 9-10 mm long; achenes in a dense woolly globose cluster; style slender.
Moist rocky meadows and shady open woods, mostly near streams, about 5000 to 6000 feet.

Anemone multifida Poir. var. globosa Torr. & Gray Cliff Anemone

Perennial with 1 or 2 hairy stems 10-25 cm tall rising from a stout branched caudex; basal leaves many, long-petioled, 2-4 cm wide, ternate or quinate and cleft several times; involucral leaves similar but short-petioled; peduncles 1 to 3, about half the total plant height, bearing 1 or more flowers; sepals 5 to 8, yellowish to reddish or pinkish-purple, 6-12 mm long; achenes in a dense ovoid cluster; style reddish, 1-1.5 mm long, thickened at the base.
Cliffs, open talus slopes and rocky lake borders, about 6900 to about 9500 feet.

Anemone occidentalis Wats.   Mountain Pasque Flower

Rather coarse perennial with silky-hairy stems 10-30 cm tall from a stout caudex; stems 1-flowered; basal leaves long-petioled, ternate, twice pinnately-decompound; involucral leaves similar, nearly sessile; sepals white or faintly purplish, 2-3 cm long; achenes long-hairy; styles silky-plumose, 2-3 cm long.
Open rocky slopes and meadows in coniferous woods, flowering near melting snows usually, 6700 to about 8000 feet and probably higher.

Anemone parviflora Michx.   Northern Anemone

Perennial with slender rootstocks; stems 1 or 2, simple, rather weak, 1-flowered, 5-20 cm tall, sparsely long-hairy; basal leaves long-petioled with ternate, lobed blades, often missing; involucral leaves sessile, more deeply 3-lobed; sepals 5, white, purplish on the back, unequal; achenes long-hairy but not woolly; style straight, 1.5-2 mm long, glabrous.
Moist mossy banks of lakes and streams and boggy meadows of coniferous forest, 5300 to about 8000 feet.

Anemone quinquefolia var. **oregana** (Gray) Robins.   Windflower
A. oregana Gray; *A. piperi* Britt.
Essentially glabrous perennial with light or dark, horizontal or vertical slender rhizomes; basal leaf solitary, sometimes separated or missing, when present trifoliate, lobed and serrate; flowering stems delicate, mostly single, 1-flowered, 10-30 cm tall, sometimes curved at the base, nodding when in fruit; involucral leaves like the basal but mostly larger and shorter-petioled; sepals 5 to 8, mostly white, but often pink, rose, blue, purple or reddish, 8-16 mm long, often unequal; stamens 35-100; achenes 2-4 mm long, pubescent; style about 0.5 mm long, glabrous.
Moist shady woods and forests, 4500 to about 5000 feet.

Aquilegia L.

Perennial having mostly basal ternately compound leaves with lobed cuneate leaflets and 1 to few large showy erect or pendent yellow to red flowers; sepals 5, petaloid; petals 5, each extended at the base into a tube (the spur) mostly curving inwardly at the tip; stamens many, the inner ones reduced to staminodia; carpels 5, free, in fruit forming erect or spreading follicles.

Flowers yellow or the sepals occasionally pink; spur hooked at the tip .... *A. flavescens*
Flowers red or pink, or the base and blades of the spur yellowish; spur straight, not hooked
  at the tip...*A. formosa*

Aquilegia flavescens Wats.   Yellow Columbine

Perennial herbs, glandular-pubescent throughout, with a simple or branched caudex; stems 20-70 cm tall; leaves mostly basal on long petioles, the blades 3-cleft, thin, lobed, the cauline reduced upward; flowers 1 to several, nodding; sepals yellow to pinkish, 1.5-2.5 cm long; petals cream-yellow; spurs slender, 10-15 mm long, incurved; follicles usually 5, about 2 cm long.
Moist often rocky woods and meadows, 5000 to about 8000 feet.

Aquilegia formosa Fisch.   Crimson Columbine

Similar to *A. flavescens* but differs in being red and yellow instead of yellow; usually

Stellaria crispa

Stellaria longipes

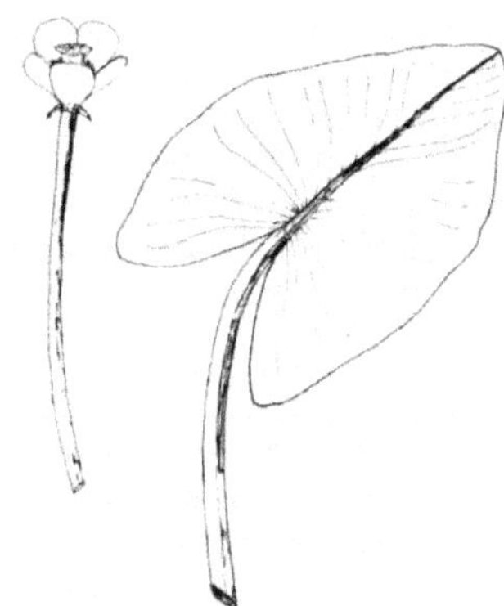

Nuphar polysepalum

Paeonia brownii

Ceratophyllum demersum

Aconitum columbianum

Actaea rubra

Anemone occidentalis

Anemone multifida var. globosa

found at lower elevations and averages taller, the stems 15-100 cm tall; sepals pale to deep red; spurs usually red and straight rather than incurved; blade of the petal 2-6 mm long.
Open wooded mountainside, about 4800 feet.

Caltha L.

Fleshy perennial with simple, crenate to dentate leaves and showy white or yellow flowers on a naked or leafy scapelike stem; sepals large, deciduous, petals none; stamens many; pistils 5 or more; fruit a follice with many seeds.

Caltha leptosepala DC. White Marsh Marigold

Succulent perennial with sometimes concealed scapes from which rise single-flowered peduncles 3-10 cm tall; leaves longer than broad, cordate at the base, coarsely crenate on the margins; sepals 6 to 12, white; petals none; fruit short-stipitate follicles about 12 mm long when ripe.
Wet gravelly streambanks and boggy places, 7200 to about 8600 feet and probably higher.

Clematis L.

Herbaceous dioecious or perfect-flowered erect perennial herbs or somewhat woody climbers; leaves opposite, pinnately compound, the leaflets entire to dissected; flowers mostly large, often showy, solitary or paniculate; sepals 4 or 5, petaloid, spreading or erect, white, blue or purplish; petals minute or none; stamens many; pistils clustered; fruit an achene with a long plumose style.

1. Flowers white or cream, the petal-like sepals 6-15 mm long; plant a woody climber over
   other vegetation; fruit long-hairy..*C. ligusticifolia*
1. Flowers not white, mostly blue to blue-brown-purple, single and showy; plants herbs or
   woody vines
    2. Petal-like sepals blue, thin, free at the base; plants often climbing, woody vines....*C. columbiana*
    2. Petal-like sepals blue-brown-purple, the tips curved outward, the flower urn-shaped,
       leathery, 2-3 cm long; plants not vines..*C. hirsutissima*

Clematis columbiana (Nutt.) T. & G. Purple Virgin's Bower

Somewhat woody perennial climber; leaves ternate; leaflets mostly ovate, thin, acuminate, entire or toothed, asymmetrically-cordate at the base, 3-15 cm long; flowers solitary, nodding, on long axillary peduncles; sepals 4, ovate to oblong-lanceolate, 2.5-4 cm long, blue or purple; achenes densely short-pubescent; styles 3-6 cm long, feathery.
Erect when young, crawling and creeping over other vegetation later, mostly in moist shady mixed woods near streams or lakes, 4500 to about 7000 feet.

Clematis hirsutissima Pursh Leather-flower; Sugar Bowls

Erect somewhat long-hairy perennial herbs with a woody caudex; stems solitary or clustered, 15-60 cm tall; leaves in several pairs, the upper ones 2 to 3 times pinnate with linear-lanceolate segments, the lower ones reduced becoming entire; flowers urn-shaped, large, solitary on long peduncles, nodding; calyx leathery, the 4 or 5 sepals brownish-purple, glabrous and deeply colored inside, densely long-hairy outside, 2-3 cm long, united at the base, the tips free and curved outward; achenes densely long-hairy; styles plumose 2-5.5 cm long.
Grassy mixed woods and often under Ponderosa pine, about 4500 to 6500 feet.

Clematis ligusticifolia Nutt.   Traveler's Joy; Pipestems

Dioecious woody climber; stems up to 10 m or more long; leaves compound, the 3 to 7 leaflets ovate-lanceolate, 3-6 cm long, acuminate, rounded at the base, toothed or lobed; flowers few, paniculate; sepals white, hairy, 6-12 mm long, spreading or reflexed; pistillate flowers with sterile stamens; achenes pubescent; styles 2.5-5 cm long. Clambering over bushes and trees along streams and in thickets and woods, about 5000 feet.

Delphinium L.

Annual or perennial herbs with erect stems, palmately lobed or divided leaves and showy, irregular, blue or purple (rarely white) flowers in terminal racemes; sepals 5, petal-like, the upper one prolonged into a straight or curved spur; petals 2 or 4, the upper pair with a spur hidden inside the calyx spur, the lower pair small, shallowly to deeply notched; stamens many; carpels usually 3; style persistent; fruit a many-seeded follicle; seeds angled or winged.

1. Stems several, mostly over 60 or 70 cm tall, sometimes up to 200 cm tall; fruit usually
    hairy...*D. occidentale*
1. Stems mostly single and under 60 cm tall; fruit various
        2. Flowers often crowded, usually many, in a spike-like raceme, the pedicels shorter
            than the flowers; leaves developed on the stem and at the base
                3. Petal-like sepals 7-9 mm long, the spur usually straight; plants 40-100 cm tall....*D. burkei*
                3. Petal-like sepals 9-12 mm long, the spur often curved at the tip; plants 10-60
                    cm tall..*D. depauperatum*
        2. Flowers few, not crowded in the raceme, the lower pedicels usually much longer
            than the flowers; sepals 13-20 mm long; leaves few, mostly basal, the segments
            narrow; plant 10-40 cm tall...*D. nuttallianum*

Delphinium burkei Greene   Tall Meadow Larkspur

D. simplex Dougl. not Salisb.; *D. distichum* Geyer

Perennial with a small cluster of somewhat fleshy fusiform roots; stems 40-100 cm tall, usually finely crisp-puberulent, sometimes also glandular above; leaves of two kinds, the basal often deciduous by anthesis, long-petioled, the blades fleshy, 3-6 cm wide, the segments broad and obtuse; leaves of the stem usually numerous, short-petioled, overlapping, the segments linear; raceme spike-like, finely crisp-puberulent to glandular-villous; the flowers crowded, small, 10 to many; pedicels ascending, short, glandular; sepals puberulent, cupped forward; spur slender, 11-17 mm long; lower petals blue, deeply lobed; upper petals nearly white; follicles puberulent, usually glandular as well. Moist granitic soil in gulches and meadows, 4500 to about 6000 feet.

Delphinium depauperatum Nutt.   Meadow Larkspur

D. cyanoreios Piper; *D. diversifolium* Greene

Slender perennial with short branching tuber-like fleshy roots; stem weak, usually single, 10-60 cm tall, often glabrous and glaucous below, mostly pubescent above with straight, spreading, yellow or white hairs; leaves few, 3- to 5-parted, the basal segments deeply cleft into obtuse oblong lobes, the cauline leaves linear-lobed and much reduced; inflorescence mostly glandular-pubescent with straight hairs, often compound, 5- to 20-flowered, the pedicels erect to spreading, usually no longer than the sepals, the flowers small, bright blue; sepals deep violet-purple or blue, usually glandular-villous, the spur slender, curved at the tip, about 12-14 mm long; petals bluish to nearly white; upper petals white or tinged with blue, dark-veined, notched; lower petals pale blue, long-villous; follicles 6-17 mm long, spreading pubescent or appressed viscid-puberulent to sometimes glabrous.

Mountain meadows and moist hillsides, often in poor soil, 4500 to about 8000 feet.

Delphinium nuttallianum Pritz. ex Walp.   Upland Larkspur
D. nelsonii Greene; *D. pauciflorum* Nutt. in T. & G. not D. Don

Perennial with roots fleshy or fibrous, single and globose, or clustered and fusiform; stem usually single, 10-40 cm tall; leaves few, thin, pubescent or nearly glabrous, mostly basal, dissected into numerous narrowly linear or oblong-lanceolate lobes 1-5 mm wide; racemes lax, 3- to 15-flowered, the pedicels spreading-ascending, glabrous to pubescent, the lower ones very long; sepals nearly equal, deep purplish to nearly white; lower petals deep blue or purplish to white, yellowish or brownish, usually purplish-tinged and heavily pencilled, deeply 2-cleft; upper petals bluish-tinged; follicles glabrous to pubescent 7-22 mm long.

Dry slopes and ridges, gravelly banks and wet meadows, 4500 to about 6000 feet.

Plant mostly crisp-puberulent and eglandular but sometimes glandular; lower petals brownish or yellowish-purple..var. **fulvum** C. L. Hitchc.
Occasional in the mountains.

Delphinium occidentale Wats.   Western Larkspur

Tall perennial from a vertical woody thickened root, often glaucous, darker near the base, crisp-puberulent throughout to glabrous below and crisp-puberulent to glandular-puberulent in the inflorescence; stems several, hollow, 60-200 cm tall, leafy; basal leaves often withered by flowering time, the 3 to 5 main lobes again cleft into sharply-toothed segments, the leaf blades pubescent on both sides, 5-15 cm broad; inflorescence up to 35 cm long, narrow, many-flowered, puberulent, often glandular and branched; flowers small; pedicels spreading, viscid-pubescent; sepals puberulent and sometimes glandular, bluish-purple to nearly white; spur straight or nearly so, 10-15 mm long; lower petals blue; upper petals nearly white to pale blue; follicles 10-16 mm long, straight, puberulent to viscid-pubescent.

Moist meadows and along streams, about 6000 to 6500 feet.

Ranunculus L.

Glabrous or hairy terrestrial or aquatic perennial herbs with fibrous roots; stems erect or prostrate and rooting at the nodes; leaves entire to lobed, parted or compound, sessile to petioled and dilated at the base; flowers minute to conspicuous; sepals 5, mostly deciduous, yellowish or purplish-tinged, spreading or reflexed; petals usually 5, yellow or white, clawed, with a nectary and scale at the base of the blade; stamens 10 to many; pistils 5 to many, developing into a cluster of achenes; achenes glabrous or hairy, tapering into a short or long, straight or curved to hooked beak.

1. Plant an aquatic; petals white; leaf segments very narrow...*R. aquatilis*
1. Plant growing on the dry ground; petals usually yellow and glossy
    2. Leaves lobed, divided or otherwise parted
        3. Plants hairy at least near the base, mostly over 20 cm tall; leaves thin, mostly hairy

Anemone parviflora

Anemone quinquefolia var. oregana

Aquilegia flavescens

Clematis columbiana

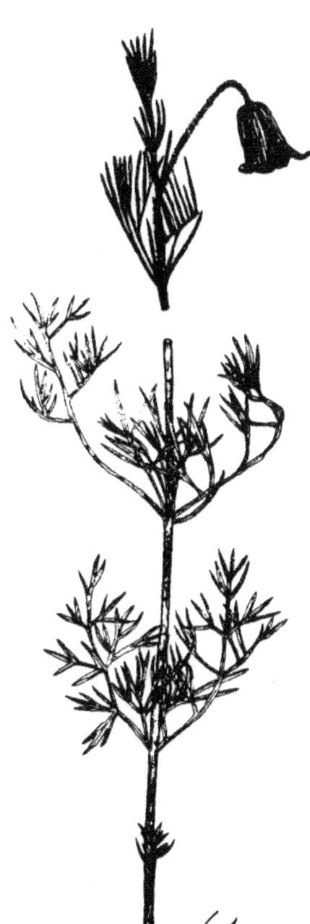

Clematis hirsutissima

Delphinium nuttallianum

Caltha leptosepala

Delphinium burkei

    4. Stem usually solitary; petals only 2-3 mm long; basal leaves only 2 or
       3; receptacle hairless..*R. uncinatus*
    4. Stem 1 to mostly several; petals larger, 8-18 mm long; basal leaves
       usually more than 2; receptacle hairy..*R. orthorhynchus*
  3. Plants not hairy, mostly under 20 cm tall; leaves thickish, fleshy, without
    hairs
      5. Basal leaves shallowly 3-lobed but not deeply cleft further into many
        smaller segments; cluster of achenes roundish; plants 5-15 mm tall ...*R. glaberrimus*
      5. Basal leaves deeply 3-lobed and most lobes again cleft several times
        into smaller segments; cluster of achenes cylindrical or broader at the
        base than above; plants 10-40 cm tall
        6. Middle lobe of the basal leaves not lobed further, or shallowly
          3-lobed; petals 5-10 mm long...*R. eschscholtzii*
        6. Middle lobe of the basal leaves deeply 3-parted, as are the other
          lobes also; petals 7-12 mm long...*R. suksdorfii*
  2. Leaves entire, sometimes the margins toothed or wavy but not divided into lobes
    7. Stems mostly prostrate or creeping and rooting at the nodes; petals 2-4 mm
      long...*R. flammula*
    7. Stems erect or nearly so, not rooting at the nodes; petals 4-10 mm long
      8. Basal leaves rounded to oval, mostly broader and heart-shaped at the
       base; petals 4-7 mm long..*R. populago*
      8. Basal leaves elliptical, tapering at both tip and base; petals 5-10 mm
       long...*R. alismaefolius*

Ranunculus alismaefolius Geyer ex Benth. var. **hartwegii** (Greene) Jepson

Water Plaintain Buttercup

Glabrous perennial with fibrous roots; stems several, 5-40 cm long; leaves entire, slightly sinuous, the blades 1-4 cm long, ovate to lanceolate and tapering to the petiole, becoming sessile upwards; flowers several; pedicels up to 15 cm long in fruit; sepals 5, 3-5 mm long; petals 5, yellow, 5-10 mm long; nectary scale broadly ovate; receptacle ovoid, glabrous; stamens 25 to 90; achenes 10 to 60, glabrous; beak straight, about 1 mm long.
Moist to wet boggy meadows and streambanks in coniferous woods, 6500 to 7300 feet.

Ranunculus aquatilis L. var. **capillaceus** (Thuill.) DC.   White Water Buttercup

Glabrous aquatic perennial with stems rooting at the nodes; leaves alternate, 2-4 cm long, submerged, finely dissected into many filiform segments; pedicels 1-3 cm long; sepals 5, deciduous; petals white, 5-10 mm long; stamens 5 or 10 to 25; achenes 10 to 15, in round clusters, glabrous or hairy; beak deciduous.
Rooted in shallow, running streams, about 6500 feet.

Ranunculus eschscholtzii Schlecht.   Timberline Buttercup

Glabrous perennial with caudex about 1 cm long; stems 1 to several, scapose, 10-40 cm tall; basal leaves petioled, the blades roundish to kidney-shaped, 1-3 cm long and about as broad, deeply 3-lobed, the middle lobe entire or again 3-lobed, the other lobes again shallowly lobed into 3 to 5 obtuse segments; cauline leaves if present alternate, 1 or 2, similar to the basal; flowers 1 to 3; pedicels 2 to 12 cm long; sepals 5, spreading, purplish-tinged, deciduous; petals 5, yellow, 5-10 mm long, obovate; scale small, triangular, pocket-like; receptacle glabrous, elongating in fruit to 15 mm long; stamens 40 to 125; achenes glabrous or finely pubescent, 20 to 80 in an ovoid to cylindrical cluster; beak 0.8-1.5 mm long, straight or curved.

Moist meadows and cliffs and wet rocks and creek borders, about 7000 to 8500 feet and possibly higher.

Ranunculus flammula L. Creeping Buttercup

Typically a low glabrous perennial with slender roots and stems erect, or prostrate or creeping and rooting at the nodes, 5-40 cm long; leaves simple, entire, the blade ovate to oblanceolate to linear, 1-4 mm wide, the basal petioled, the cauline becoming sessile; pedicels 1-2 cm long; sepals 5, 2-4 mm long; petals mostly 5, yellow, 2-4 mm long, the nectary scale glabrous, pocket-like; receptacle nearly ovoid, glabrous; achenes smooth, 5 to 25 in a subglobose cluster; beak thick, almost obsolete.
Moist marshy sandy ground bordering lakes, about 6000 to 7500 feet.

Leaves linear, up to 1 mm wide..var. **filiformis** (Hook.) Michx.

Leaves ovate-lanceolate, up to 4 mm wide..........................var. **ovalis** (Bigelow) Benson

Ranunculus glaberrimus Hook. Sagebrush Buttercup

Glabrous perennial with thick fleshy roots; stems several, erect to prostrate, 5-15 cm long; basal leaves long-petioled, the blades thick, mostly longer than broad to nearly round, entire to shallowly 3- to 5-lobed; cauline leaves similar or more deeply 3-parted, alternate, short-petioled to sessile; flowers 1 to few, long-pedicelled; sepals 5, purplish-tinged on the back, 5-8 mm long, deciduous; petals 5, yellow to almost white, 5-15 mm long; nectary scale forming a deep pocket, ciliate-margined; receptacle enlarged in fruit, globose; stamens 40 to 80; achenes round, 30 to 150 in a large globose head; beak straight, slightly winged.
Wet to moist stony slopes and rocky coniferous woods, 4500 to about 5600 feet.

Ranunculus orthorhynchus Hook. var. **platyphyllus** Gray Swamp Buttercup

Hairy perennial with tapered roots; stems erect, thick, spreading-hairy, usually branched, 20-100 cm tall; leaves 4-12 cm long, mostly basal, blades broadly ovate in outline, pinnate; leaflets 3 to 7, irregularly toothed and lobed into linear, acute segments; cauline leaves alternate, the segments linear; pedicels up to 15 cm long, sepals 6 to 9, often purplish, long-hairy, reflexed, deciduous; petals 5, yellow, sometimes reddish or purplish on the back, 8-18 mm long; nectary scale glabrous, flabellate; receptacle nearly round, hairy, up to 7 mm long; stamens 50 to 70; achenes about 3.5 mm long, 12 to 35 in an ovoid cluster, smooth and glabrous; beak straight, about 3 mm long.
Along ditches and streams and in other wet places in woods, 5000 to about 6100 feet.

Ranunculus populago Greene Blue Mountain Buttercup

Weak glabrous perennial with fleshy fibrous roots; stems 1 to few, 10-30 cm tall; leaves succulent, the basal long-petioled, 3-5 cm long and nearly as broad, roundish to reniform or ovate, truncate or cordate at the base, entire or denticulate; cauline leaves narrower, becoming sessile above; flowers 1 to 3 or 5, long-pedicelled; sepals spreading, 2.5-4 mm long, becoming reflexed; petals 5, yellow, 4-8 mm long; nectary scale glabrous, pocket-like; receptacle globose, hairy; stamens 15 to 30; achenes 7 to 25, glabrous or pubescent, smooth, about 2 mm long; beak straight, about 0.7 mm long.
Moist to wet mossy streambanks, lake borders and meadows, about 5500 to 7600 feet.

Ranunculus suksdorfii Gray   Suksdorf's Buttercup
   R. eschscholtzii var. *trisectus* (Eastw.) Benson
   Glabrous perennial with a usually branched caudex 1-2 cm long; basal leaves thin,
deeply 3-parted, the middle lobe and the others deeply cleft into 3 to 7 acute lobes;
scarious stipular leaf-bases 1.5-2.5 cm long; petals yellow, 7-12 mm long; achenes hispid
or glabrous.
Moist rocky ridges and slopes, often near melting snows, 6500 to about 9300 feet and
probably higher.

Ranunculus uncinatus D. Don var. **parviflorus** (Torr.) Benson   Little Buttercup
   A somewhat hairy perennial with coarse fibrous roots; stem solitary, 20-50 cm tall;
basal leaves with petioles up to 20 cm long, the blades 2-6 cm long, deeply 3-lobed, cor-
date-deltoid, the segments again lobed and toothed; cauline leaves few, alternate; pedicels up to 6 cm long; sepals 5, reflexed or spreading, deciduous; petals 5, yellow, 2-3 mm
long; nectary scale glabrous; receptacle globose, glabrous; stamens 10 to 20; achenes
10 to 30 in a globose cluster, smooth, slightly hairy; beak broad, 1-2 mm long, recurved
and hooked.
Moist to wet open woods, about 4500 to 5500 feet.

Thalictrum [Tourn.] L.

   Erect perennial herbs with an unpleasant odor and few 2 to 3 times ternately compound leaves with lobed and toothed leaflets; flowers perfect or imperfect, small,
apetalous, paniculate or racemose; sepals 4 or 5, greenish-white; stamens 8 to 30 or
more with filiform often elongate purplish filaments; pistils 4 to 9, the style short, the
stigma purplish, persistent, often elongating; fruit a turgid or compressed ribbed achene,
sessile or short-stipitate.

1. Flowers with both stamens and pistils present; anthers to 2 mm long; rare in our area
   2. Anthers 0.7 mm long, about half as long as the filaments _______________________ *T. sparsiflorum*
   2. Anthers about 2 mm long, as long as the filaments or longer________________________*T. alpinum*
1. Flowers imperfect, either the stamens or the pistils missing; common
   3. Anthers shorter than the filaments; achenes spreading, bending downward, or erect
     4. Achenes erect, 4-6 mm long, the stigmas not purplish ____________________*T. fendleri*
     4. Achenes spreading or bending downward, 6-8 mm long, the stigmas
     purplish____ *T. occidentale*
   3. Anthers longer than the filaments; achenes erect or ascending, 4-5 mm long ________*T. venulosum*

Thalictrum alpinum L.   Arctic or Dwarf Meadow-rue
   Stems 5-30 cm tall, solitary and sometimes with a small leaf near the base, glabrous
or sometimes glandular; leaves mainly basal, leathery, biternate, the leaflets nearly orbicular to cuneate, pale green especially beneath, slightly revolute-margined; flowers
perfect in a simple raceme; stamens 10, the anthers about equaling the filaments; achenes
sessile, about 3 mm long.
Reported to be in alpine meadows.

Thalictrum fendleri Engelm.   Fendler's Meadow-rue
   Stems 30-80 cm tall, often purplish, usually branched above; leaves 3 times ternate, the
leaflets 1-2 cm long, ovate to obovate, mostly 3-lobed with toothed margins, often glandular-puberulent beneath; inflorescence a large leafy panicle; flowers imperfect; sepals
greenish-white, about 3 mm long; stamens 18 to 25, the anthers shorter than the filiform

Delphinium occidentale

Ranunculus aquatilis

var. capillaceus

Ranunculus eschscholtzii

Ranunculus flammula

Ranunculus glaberrimus

Ranunculus populago

Ranunculus suksdorfii

Ranunculus uncinatus var. parviflorus

Thalictrum occidentale

Trautvetteria caroliniensis

purplish filaments; achenes obovate, 4-6 mm long, slightly puberulent and glandular, 6-nerved.

Moist places in coniferous woods at upper elevations in the mountains.

Thalictrum occidentale Gray   Western Meadow-rue

Dioecious perennial; stems mostly branched above, 20-100 cm tall; leaves cauline, thin, 3 to 5, pale beneath, 3 to 5 times ternate, usually 3-lobed, the lobes entire or 2- to 3-lobed or toothed and often oblique; flowers in open panicles; sepals 2-5 mm long, greenish-white or purplish; petals none; stamens many, the filaments 4-8 mm long, filiform and purplish, about twice the length of the anthers; achenes 6-8 mm long, spindle-shaped with 3 nerves on each side.

Moist to dry woods and meadows and streambanks, about 5000 to 7000 feet.

Thalictrum sparsiflorum Turcz.   Few-flowered Meadow-rue

Strong-scented leafy-stemmed glabrous perennial 30-100 cm tall; leaves 2- to 3-ternate, the leaflets 1-2 cm long, cordate-based, glandular beneath with sessile glands; inflorescence a leafy raceme or panicle; flowers perfect; sepals greenish-white, about 3 mm long; filaments about 4 times as long as the anthers; achenes 5 to 10, glandular-puberulent, strongly compressed, about 4 mm long with 6 to 10 nerves, the beak straight.

Reported by W. C. Cusick in 1908 from Catherine Creek, Union County, as "very rare."

Thalictrum venulosum Trel.   Veiny-leaved Meadow-rue

Mostly glabrous dioecious perennial; stems 20-70 cm tall; leaves cauline, 1 to 3, 2 to 4 times ternate, the leaflets 1-2 cm long, firm, veiny beneath, 3-lobed and the lobes 2- to 3-toothed; panicle narrow, compact and ascending; sepals 2-4 mm long, greenish-white; stamens 10 to 20, the anthers slightly shorter than the filiform filaments; achenes ovoid, about 4 mm long with 8 unbranched nerves.

Thickets and shady banks and woods, about 5000 to 7000 feet.

Trautvetteria Fisch. & Mey.

Rhizomatous herbs with mostly basal palmately lobed leaves; flowers small in terminal panicles; sepals small, greenish-white, early deciduous; petals none; stamens many, conspicuous, the filaments clavate; achenes many, angled, inflated, tipped by a short recurved style.

Trautvetteria caroliniensis (Walt.) Vail.   Westen False Bugbane

Glabrous rhizomatous herb with stout stems 20-100 cm tall; leaves mainly basal, long-petioled, palmately deeply 5- to 10-lobed, the lobes acute, irregularly lobed and toothed; cauline leaves 1 or 2, alternate, short-petioled; flowers in terminal panicles; sepals 3-5 mm long, whitish; petals none; stamens many, white; achenes about 4 mm long.

Moist to wet, mostly boggy, places in dense shady coniferous woods, 4500 to about 7500 feet.

BERBERIDACEAE   Barberry Family

Perennial herbs or shrubs with alternate or basal simple or compound deciduous to evergreen leaves, the petioles usually dilated at the base; flowers regular and perfect, solitary or in racemes, spikes or panicles; perianth usually of 4 or 5 series of free seg-

ments in 3's; sepals and petals apparently 6 each, unlike or alike, the inner series sometimes glandular and considered to be scales or nectaries; stamens mostly as many as
petals and opposite them, sometimes more or fewer, the anthers opening by 2 uplifting
valves; pistil 1, ovary 1-celled; style short or none; fruit a follicle, capsule or berry.

Berberis L.

Perennial shrubs, often with long rhizomes; leaves (ours) persistent with dentate-
spiny leaflets; flowers yellow, in axillary bracteate racemes, the perianth segments in
3's; sepals 6 to 9, in 2 or 3 series; petals 6, in 2 series, each with a pair of basal glands;
stamens 6, opposite the petals, closing around the pistil when touched; ovary 1-celled;
stigma peltate; fruit a 1- to few-seeded, glaucous, blue-black berry, sometimes red or
white.

Berberis repens Lindl.   Oregon Grape
Mahonia repens G. Don
Stems stoloniferous and creeping close to the ground, 10-20 cm tall; leaflets 3 to 7,
ovate to elliptic, 3-9 cm long, glossy or dull on the upper surface, dull and minutely
papillate beneath, the margins spinulose-toothed; racemes densely many-flowered;
berry bluish, globose to oblong, 7-8 mm long.
Dry rocky coniferous woods, 4650 to 6200 feet.

FUMARIACEAE   Fumitory Family

Annual or perennial herbs with alternate or basal glaucous dissected leaves; flowers
perfect, irregular, usually racemose or paniculate, rarely solitary; sepals 2, small and
bractlike; petals 4, slightly united into 2 unlike pairs, one or both of the outer pair
saccate or spurred at the base and spreading at the tips, the 2 inner petals smaller, not
spurred at the base, their tips thickened and united over the stigma; stamens 6, in 2
groups of 3; pistil 1, 2-carpellary; stigma usually 2-lobed; fruit either a several-seeded,
2-valved capsule or an indehiscent 1-seeded nut.

Flowers white, flesh-colored or pinkish, usually flattened and with 2 spurs at the base............*Dicentra*
Flowers yellow or creamy-white, not flattened, with 1 spur at the base ....*Corydalis*

Corydalis Medic.

Glabrous and usually glaucous annual or perennial herbs with several times decompound leaves; flowers in terminal and axillary racemes or panicles, yellow or white to
deep pink; sepals 2; corolla irregular, deciduous; petals 4, one of the outer pair spurred
at the base, the inner pair narrow, not spurred, keeled on the back, connate at the tip;
stamens 6, in 2 sets, opposite the outer petals; capsule 2-valved, linear or oblong, many-
seeded.

Plants 10-40 cm tall; flowers 12-18 mm long, yellow, in a few-flowered short inflorescence.......*C. aurea*
Plants 50-100 cm tall; flowers 20-25 cm long, cream or white, in a many-flowered
  inflorescence 10-30 cm long..... ....*C. cusickii*

Corydalis aurea Willd.   Golden Corydalis
Glabrous and glaucous winter annual or biennial, freely branched and leafy from the
base, often decumbent or sprawling, 10-40 cm tall; leaves pinnately parted and dis-

sected into many linear to oblong segments; racemes short, few-flowered; sepals short, erose, yellowish-white; corolla yellow, 12-18 mm long, the spur rounded at the tip, curved downward; capsule linear, torulose, 2-3 cm long, usually curved and pendulous; seeds black and shining.
Dry or moist soils in lightly-shaded woods, about 5000 feet.

Corydalis cusickii S. Wats.   Cusick's Corydalis
    C. caseana var. *cusickii* (Wats.) C. L. Hitchc.
    Greenish to glaucous perennial from thick, fleshy roots; stems 50-200 cm tall, stout and branched; leaves 3 to 6, cauline, 20-60 cm long or longer, tripinnate, the leaflets oblong-elliptic to lanceolate; racemes densely flowered, 10-30 cm long; flowers cream-white, sometimes violet or rose-purple-tinged, 2-2.5 cm long, the spur stout, straight or slightly curved upward, 15-18 mm long, much longer than the rest of the flower; capsules oblong, turgid, 12-15 mm long; seeds shiny black and smooth.
Wet streambanks, 4500 to 7000 feet.

Dicentra Bernh.

    Scapose perennial herbs with fleshy roots or rhizomes and long-petioled dissected leaves; flowers usually flattened and nodding, solitary or in racemes or panicles, white to pinkish or somewhat purplish or yellow; sepals 2; petals 4, the outer pair saccate or spurred at the base, the inner connate near the tip, sometimes crested on the back; stamens 6, in 2 sets; stigma 2-lobed; fruit an elongated 2-valved capsule; seeds several.

Flower solitary, shaped like a steer's head; stem about 5 cm tall; leaf solitary, close to the
    ground, often separated from the flowering stem ....*D. uniflora*
Flowers several in a terminal one-sided inflorescence, the petals spurred at the base; stems
    12-25 cm tall; leaves often more than 1 ....*D. cucullaria*

Dicentra cucullaria (L.) Bernh.   Dutchman's Breeches
    Scapose perennial from a short rootstock covered with small bulbous tubers; leaves basal, long-petioled, the blade several times ternately compounded into linear-oblong segments; scapes taller than the leaves; flowers pendulous, 3 to 10 in a loose terminal raceme; corolla 12-20 mm long, white or pinkish with yellow tips, the inner petals crested, the outer each with a basal, divergent, saccate spur, the tips spreading; capsules fusiform, about 12 mm long; seeds black and shiny.
Moist shady woods, cliffs and streambanks, 5000 to about 6700 feet.

Dicentra uniflora Kell.   Steer's Head
    A small delicate scapose perennial from a cluster of small fleshy roots to which the scape and leaves are attached separately underground; leaves few, long-petioled, glaucous, mostly about as long as the scapes, ternately once or twice divided into oblanceolate to oblong segments; scapes 4-8 cm tall, with 1 or 2 small bractlets near the solitary flower; flowers white to pinkish, 12-15 mm long, cordate at the base, the outer petals widely spreading, recurved nearly to the base, the inner petals connate, sagittate above the base, not crested, purple-tipped; capsule ovoid-ellipsoid, 10-13 mm long, on often prostrate scapes; seeds black and shining.
Gravelly moist places and often under logs in shady coniferous forest, 4900 to 6600 feet.

CRUCIFERAE   Mustard Family

Annual to perennial herbs, rarely shrubby, pubescent with simple, forked or branched to stellate hairs, or glabrous; leaves alternate; flowers usually in bractless racemes, rarely solitary; sepals 4, deciduous or persistent; petals 4, rarely 2 or none, the blade entire or lobed, usually clawed, yellow, white, pink, blue or purple; stamens unequal, 6, or rarely 2 or 4; pistil 1, of 2 united carpels; ovary superior; style persistent, or none; fruit a silique or a silicle, (a pod), stipitate to nonstipitate, 2-celled or rarely 1-celled, 2-valved or rarely indehiscent; seeds 1 to several in 1 or 2 rows per locule.

1. Petals yellow, yellowish-white or cream
  2. Flowers rather large and showy, fragrant; plant a strong perennial with several stem leaves and a rosette of basal leaves..*Erysimum*
  2. Flowers smaller and not showy; stem leaves fewer
    3. Leaves simple, not lobed or divided, sometimes the margins toothed or ruffled or wavy
      4. Pods flattened, mostly longer than broad; flowering stems often leafless or nearly so..*Draba*
      4. Pods not flat, mostly roundish; flowering stems usually with some leaves
        5. Plants mostly prostrate on the ground, the many branches spreading outward..*Lesquerella*
        5. Plants erect, branches none or few to many
          6. Plants commonly branching from the base, 10-30 cm tall..............*Alyssum*
          6. Plants usually unbranched; stems mostly 30-100 cm tall ....*Camelina*
    3. Leaves lobed or parted or cleft, at least near the base of the plant
      7. Pods with a portion at the tip not filled with seeds (the beak)
        8. Pods 3-15 mm long, rounded and also arched................................ *Rorippa*
        8. Pods 30-90 mm long; plants mostly over 20 cm tall
          9. Pod with a stalk (the stipe) 3-10 mm long at its base; petals sometimes white..*Chlorocrambe*
          9. Pod without a stipe above the pedicel; petals yellow....................*Brassica*
      7. Pods without a beak at the tip
        10. Hairs of stems and leaves simple, unbranched .... *Sisymbrium*
        10. Hairs branched or in star-like formations ....*Descurainia*
1. Petals white to pink or purplish, not yellow
  11. Leaves simple and entire, or sometimes irregularly, shallowly or inconspicuously toothed
    12. Stem leaves few or poorly developed or none
      13. Pods wedge-shaped, spreading; flowers purplish...................... *Phoenicaulis*
      13. Pods elliptic to oblong, short and flat; flowers white to pinkish or lavender........ *Draba*
    12. Stem leaves several, well-developed, sometimes near the base only
      14. Stem leaves thin, the base heart-shaped ....*Cardamine*
      14. Stem leaves thicker, not heart-shaped
        15. Pods longer than broad, 4-angled
          16. Plants hairless or the hairs when present not branched .... *Arabis*
          16. Plants with hairs branched or star-like .... *Halimolobos*
        15. Pods rounded, not longer than broad; plants grayish-hairy, 10-30 cm tall..*Alyssum*
  11. Leaves, at least the basal ones, lobed, parted or divided or deeply toothed
    17. Pods longer than broad, mostly 3 or more times longer
      18. Basal leaves conspicuously divided into many small leaflets; hairs of stem and leaves not branched ....*Cardamine*
      18. Basal leaves lobed or deeply toothed but not cleft into leaflets; hairs of the plant forked or star-like (radiating from a central point)........ *Arabis*
    17. Pods not much, if any, longer than broad, mostly roundish

19. Pods roundish
   20. Pods shallowly or deeply notched at the top ....*Thlaspi*
   20. Pods not notched at the top.................. ....*Lepidium*
19. Pods not roundish
   21. Pods heart-shaped, mostly notched at the top; plants not hairy above......*Capsella*
   21. Pods rather elliptic in shape; plants gray-hairy, of high elevations ....*Smelowskia*

Alyssum L.

Low branching stellate-pubescent annual or perennial herbs with simple leaves and small racemose flowers; sepals persistent to quickly deciduous; petals yellowish or cream fading to white; stamens 6, unequal; style very short; stigma nearly entire; fruit a silicle, ovate, oblong or orbicular, compressed, notched at the tip; valves nerveless, dehiscent; seeds wingless, 1 or 2 in each locule.

Alyssum alyssoides L.   Small Alyssum

Grayish-stellate-pubescent annual or biennial mostly 10-30 cm tall, usually branched from the base; leaves entire, narrowly oblanceolate, 5-25 mm long; racemes numerous, 5-15 cm long; sepals pilose as well as stellate, persistent, becoming reflexed; petals pale yellow, fading to cream or white, 2-4 mm long, bifid; silicles stellate, orbicular, notched at the apex, winged; seeds 2 in each locule.
Introduced; usually in dry sandy open places, 4600 to about 6000 feet.

Arabis L.

Annual or perennial herbs, sometimes shrubby, glabrous or pubescent with simple, forked or stellate hairs; leaves entire or toothed to lyrate pinnatifid, often in a basal rosette, the cauline with or without auricles, alternate and commonly clasping the stem; flowers white, pink or reddish-purplish, cream or yellowish; sepals greenish to purple, erect; stamens 6; siliques linear, compressed parallel to the partition or somewhat quadrangular; style missing or very short; stigma entire or 2-lobed; seeds in 1 or 2 rows in each locule, winged or wingless.

1. Flowers pink, rose or purple
  2. Pods erect or ascending
    3. Petals pale pink
      4. Plants mostly 10-20 cm tall; petals 5-8 mm long; seeds in 1 row in each
        locule; pods 2-6 cm long...*A. microphylla*
      4. Plants mostly 30-80 cm tall; petals 7-12 mm long; seeds in 2 rows in
        each locule; pods 3-9 cm long...*A. drummondii*
    3. Petals purple, 4-10 mm long; plants 10-25 cm tall; seeds in 1 row in each
      locule; pods 2-6 cm long.............................. ....*A. lyallii*
  2. Pods widely spreading or curving downward, not erect
    5. Plants mostly 10-20 cm tall
      6. Stems densely stellate-hairy near the base of the plant; petals rose-
        purple, 4.5-7 mm long; pods 2.5-4 cm long, to 2.5 mm wide, often
        1-sided; plants of higher elevations...*A. lemmonii*
      6. Stems glabrous or nearly so to the base, very slender; petals pale pinkish
        to purple, 5-8 mm long; pods 2-6 cm long, 1-2 mm wide; plants of lower
        elevations ....*A. microphylla*
    5. Plants mostly 30 cm tall or taller
      7. Pods spreading, 4-12 cm long, 1.5-2 mm wide; plants 40-80 cm tall;
        petals pink to purplish, 8-15 mm long..*A. sparsiflora*

    7. Pods strongly bending downward, 3-7 cm long, 1-2 mm wide; plants
       10-100 cm tall; petals white to pinkish-purple..*A. holboellii*
1. Flowers white, cream, or yellowish
    8. Pods mostly 1-2 cm long; stems numerous from a clustered base .... *A. nuttallii*
    8. Pods 3-10 cm long; stems solitary or few
       9. Petals mostly 3-6 mm long, mostly yellowish- or greenish-white
          10. Pods strongly flattened; seeds in 1 row in each locule; flowers greenish-
             white, cream or pinkish-tinged...*A. hirsuta*
          10. Pods not strongly flattened; seeds in 2 rows in each locule; flowers
             yellowish-white...*A. glabra*
       9. Petals 6-12 mm long, white to pale rose or pinkish
          11. Pods spreading or bent downward, 3-7 cm long; plants 10-100 cm tall....*A. holboellii*
          11. Pods erect, 3-9 cm long; plants mostly 30-80 cm tall .... *A. drummondii*

Arabis drummondii Gray   Drummond's Rock Cress

Biennial or short-lived perennial with somewhat glaucous glabrous or sparsely stellate-pubescent leaves; stems 1 or more, 30-80 cm tall; basal leaves petioled, oblanceolate-elliptic, 2-7 cm long, mostly entire, forming a rosette; cauline leaves many, overlapping, sessile and auricled, 1.5-3 cm long; racemes 5- to 50-flowered; sepals glabrous 3-4.5 mm long; petals white or pale rose, 7-12 mm long; pods erect, glabrous, 3-9 cm long, 2-3 mm wide, compressed; style obsolete or nearly so; seeds biseriate, winged on one side and at the tip.
Moist rocky meadows and slopes, 4600 to 6900 feet.

Arabis glabra Bernh.   Tower Mustard

Biennial or short-lived perennial with a simple crown; stems erect, mostly simple, 30-150 cm tall, glabrous and glaucous above, pubescent with simple hairs near the base; basal leaves wing-petioled, oblanceolate to oblong, entire or toothed to pinnately-parted, 3-7 cm long, greenish, pubescent with simple hairs; cauline leaves sessile, overlapping, lanceolate or ovate-lanceolate, all but the lowest glabrous, 5-15 cm long and up to 4 cm wide, conspicuously auricled; racemes many-flowered; sepals glabrous, about 3 mm long; petals cream or yellowish-white, 3-6 mm long; siliques erect, linear, glabrous, 4-10 cm long, 1.5-2 mm wide, slightly compressed; seeds in 2 rows at least in the lower part of the pod.
Dry gravelly bars and creek banks in lightly-shaded woods, 4500 to 5200 feet.

Arabis hirsuta (L.) Scop.   Hairy Rock Cress

Biennial or short-lived perennial with a crown, coarsely stellate-pubescent to the inflorescence; stems 1 to several, 15-100 cm tall, glabrous above but hairy with mostly simple hairs at the base; leaves entire to dentate or denticulate, the basal petioled, oblanceolate to obovate, 2-8 cm long, usually hirsute; cauline leaves mostly entire, sessile and auricled, ovate-lanceolate to narrowly elliptic, 2-12 cm long, up to 3 cm wide, the upper ones sometimes glabrous; racemes many-flowered; pedicels erect to appressed, 6-12 mm long; petals 4 or 5 mm long mostly, greenish-white or cream to pinkish; pods glabrous, linear, 3-8 cm long, 1-2 mm wide, erect or appressed; style very short; seeds in 1 row in each locule.
Cliffs and rocky creek banks, 4700 to 7000 feet.

Arabis holboellii Hornem.   Holboell's Rock Cress

Biennial or short-lived perennial with a simple caudex; stems 1 to several, simple or branched above, 10-100 cm tall, glabrous above but hairy with stellate or branched hairs below; basal leaves 1-5 cm long, oblanceolate, entire or toothed, stellate to branching-hairy, forming a rosette; cauline leaves lanceolate, usually overlapping, narrowly oblong to lanceolate, entire or toothed, sessile and auricled or clasping, stellate- pubescent or the upper ones glabrous; racemes 20- to 100-flowered; pedicels 5-15 mm long, reflexed to geniculate; sepals 2.5-5 mm long, glabrous or hairy; petals 5-10 mm long, usually pinkish-purple to nearly white; pods mostly glabrous, 3-7 cm long and 1-2 mm wide; style obsolete; seeds in 1 row in each locule, or irregular, but not in 2 rows. Open rocky slopes, meadows and light open woods, 4800 to 8000 feet.

Cauline leaves auricled, often revolute and clasping; pods pendulous-secund to -appressed...var. **retrofracta** (Grah.) Rydb.
Cauline leaves not auricled though sometimes clasping; pods not appressed...var. **pendulocarpa** (A. Nels.) Rollins

Arabis lemmonii Wats.   Lemmon's Rock Cress

Cespitose perennial with several stems 5-40 cm tall, glabrous or stellate-pubescent and glaucous above, densely hairy below with stellate to branched pubescence; basal leaves 1.5-2 cm long, forming a rosette, oblanceolate to obovate, entire or with a few shallow teeth, densely and finely grayish-pubescent to nearly glabrous; cauline leaves oblong-lanceolate, the upper ones glabrous or nearly so, sessile and auricled; sepals purple, 2.5-3.5 mm long; petals rose-colored, 4.5-7 mm long; pods glabrous, often one-sided, erect, spreading or reflexed, 2.5-4 cm long and 1.5-2.5 mm wide; style obsolete; seeds orbicular, narrowly winged, in 1 row in each locule. Talus slopes, rock slides, cliffs and rocky alpine meadows, 6500 to 9550 feet.

Plants nearly glabrous; the basal leaves not at all felty; pods usually not over 2 mm broad; stems usually several and not over 20 cm tall..................var. **paddoensis** Rollins Rocky places between 6500 and 7850 feet.

Arabis lyallii Wats.   Lyall's Rock Cress

Perennial with a caudex; stems several, slender, 10-25 cm tall, glabrous or hairy near the base; basal leaves 6-30 mm long, in a rosette, elliptic-oblanceolate, glabrous or ciliate to finely hairy; cauline leaves mostly auricled, narrowly oblong to lanceolate, usually glabrous; racemes 3- to 15-flowered; sepals glabrous or pilose, often purplish; petals purple or rose-colored, mostly 4-6 mm long; pods glabrous, 2-6 cm long; style short; seeds narrowly winged, in 1 row in each locule. Alpine ridges, slopes, rock slides and cliffs, and rocky woods and meadows at lower elevations, 4500 to 9400 feet.

Arabis microphylla Nutt.   Small-leaved Rock Cress

Cespitose perennial with several very slender stems 10-30 cm tall (rarely up to 70 cm), glabrous or somewhat pubescent at the base; leaves oblanceolate to oblong, 1-3 cm long, entire to slightly toothed, nearly glabrous or ciliate to minutely grayish-hairy, the basal in a rosette, the cauline auricled; racemes 3- to 25-flowered; sepals glabrous; petals pink to purplish, 5-8 mm long; pods ascending, spreading or slightly reflexed, glabrous, 2-6 cm long; style nearly obsolete; seeds slightly winged, in 1 row in each locule. Dry mountain slopes at lower elevations, about 4500 feet.

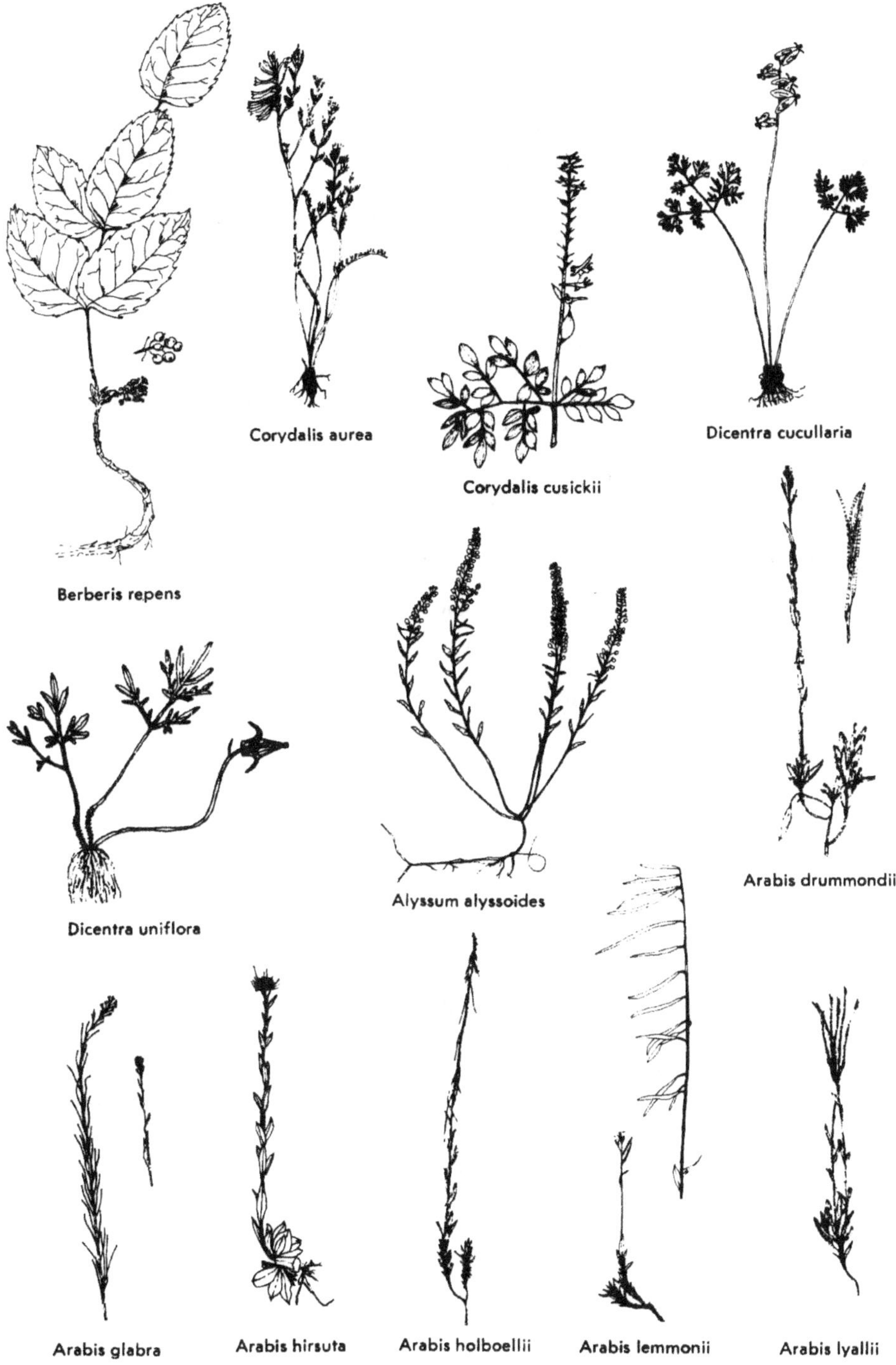

Corydalis aurea
Corydalis cusickii
Dicentra cucullaria
Berberis repens
Arabis drummondii
Dicentra uniflora
Alyssum alyssoides
Arabis glabra
Arabis hirsuta
Arabis holboellii
Arabis lemmonii
Arabis lyallii

Arabis nuttallii Robins.   Nuttall's Rock Cress
Stems many, clustered, slender, 8-35 cm tall; plant completely glabrous to sometimes long-hairy below; leaves numerous in a rosette, ciliate and thinly hairy beneath, glabrous above, oblanceolate to obovate-lanceolate, the lower petioled, 1-4 cm long, entire or sometimes toothed, the upper sessile, 0.5-2 cm long; pedicels 1-2 cm long; sepals 3 mm long; petals 6-8 mm long, white or pale lilac; siliques 1-4 cm long and 2 mm wide, erect-ascending, glabrous, compressed; seeds not winged, in 1 row in each locule.
Dry grassy almost treeless slope at about timberline, 8000 feet.

Arabis sparsiflora Nutt. var. **subvillosa** (Wats.) Rollins   Sickle-pod Rock Cress
Biennial or short-lived perennial; stem solitary, or few, 30-100 cm tall, hairy to sometimes glabrous above; leaves 2-9 cm long, entire to few-toothed, oblanceolate to linear-lanceolate, usually densely fine-hairy; basal leaves petioled and toothed, in a rosette; cauline leaves auricled, entire, becoming reduced and sessile upward; racemes many-flowered, elongating in fruit; sepals 3-6 mm long, usually stellate-hairy; petals 8-15 mm long, pink to purplish; pods 4-12 cm long, glabrous, arched, ascending to spreading-drooping on usually conspicuously-hairy pedicels; style obsolete; seeds slightly winged all around, in 1 row in each locule.
Dry rocky places, often with sagebrush and Ponderosa pine, about 5000 to 5800 feet.

Brassica L.

Annual to perennial glabrous to hairy large herbs with branching stems; leaves alternate, sessile, entire or toothed, the upper sometimes auriculate-clasping, the lower in a rosette and often pinnatifid; flowers yellow to white in long racemes; pods linear, rounded or quadrangular, beaked, usually torulose; valves 1- to 3-nerved; seeds globose, in 1 row in the locule.

Brassica campestris L.   Rutabaga; Common Mustard
Taprooted branching annual or biennial, glaucous and nearly glabrous, 20-100 cm tall; basal leaves petioled, lyrate-pinnatifid, the margins sinuate-dentate; cauline leaves oblong to ovate-lanceolate, becoming sessile upward, auriculate-clasping, the margins entire; petals yellow, 6-10 mm long; pods 3-7 cm long on ascending to spreading pedicels 7-25 mm long; beak nearly round, about 1 cm long.
Waste places and campgrounds, about 5600 feet.

Camelina Crantz

Erect annual hirsute to stellate herbs; leaves entire to toothed or wavy-margined; flowers small, pale yellowish, in terminal racemes; petals spatulate; stamens 6; pods obovate, slightly flattened, very narrowly wing-margined, the valves 1-nerved; seeds not winged, in 2 rows in each locule.

Camelina microcarpa Andrz.   Hairy False Flax
Annual 30-100 cm tall; stems simple or occasionally branched, hairy near the base, often glabrous above; leaves mostly cauline, 2-8 cm long, lanceolate or oblong, nearly entire, sessile to winged-petioled, pubescent, the upper ones sagittate-clasping; raceme elongated in fruit; sepals about 3 mm long; petals nearly white, 4-5 mm long; pods 4-7

mm long and about half as wide, strongly margined, on spreading-ascending pedicels 1-2 cm long; style 2-2.5 mm long.
Roadsides and campgrounds, about 5000 feet.

Capsella Medic.

Pubescent annual herbs with leaves mostly in a basal rosette; flowers small, white, racemose; stamens 6; pods triangular, compressed, shallowly notched, the valves keeled; style short; seeds many in each locule, not margined.

Capsella bursa-pastoris (L.) Medic.　　　　　　　　　　　　Shepherd's Purse

Glabrous to pubescent branching annual 10-50 cm tall; leaves lanceolate to oblong-oblanceolate, mostly 3-6 cm long, nearly entire to toothed, lobed or pinnatifid, the basal petioled, in a rosette, the cauline auricled, becoming sessile and clasping; racemes many-flowered, the pedicels spreading or ascending, 7-15 mm long; petals 1.5-4 mm long, white; pods triangular, flattened, 4-8 mm long, notched above; style short; seeds not margined.
Common weed, up to about 5000 feet.

Cardamine L.

Nearly glabrous annual to perennial herbs; leaves mostly at or near the base, entire, lobed or divided; flowers in a raceme, white to pink, rose or purple; stamens 6; pods linear, slightly compressed, dehiscing upward from the base; seeds wingless, in 1 row in the locule.

1. Leaves divided into many small leaflets; pods longer than wide; petals 2-7 mm long
　　2. Basal leaves in a well-developed, persistent rosette; leaflets throughout mostly
　　　about as broad as long..*C. oligosperma*
　　2. Basal rosette missing or poorly developed; leaflets mostly longer than broad....*C. pennsylvanica*
1. Leaves not divided into leaflets, nearly circular, often wavy-margined; petals mostly
　7-9 mm long..*C. cordifolia*

Cardamine cordifolia Gray var. lyallii (Wats.) Nels. & Macbr.　　Large Mountain Cress

Perennial with slender rhizomes; stems glabrous to pubescent near the base, 10-60 cm tall; leaves cordate to reniform, glabrous, entire, or shallowly sinuate or lobed, mostly cauline, 3-10 cm long, the basal often very long-petioled, the upper shorter-petioled; sepals 3-4 mm long; petals white, long-clawed, mostly 7-9 mm long; pods straight, 2-3.5 cm long, the pedicels short and spreading, the beak very short; seeds flattened but not winged.
Gravel bars and shady streambanks in mixed woods, 4500 to 6700 feet.

Cardamine oligosperma Nutt.　　　　　　　　　　　　Little Western Bitter Cress

Taprooted annual or biennial, sparsely hairy throughout to nearly glabrous, usually with several stems 10-40 cm tall; leaves pinnate, hirsute or ciliate to glabrous, the basal in a rosette; leaflets 5 to 11, ovate or obovate to linear-lanceolate, entire to toothed or lobed, the terminal one the largest, up to 3 cm long; racemes few-flowered; petals white, 2-4 mm long; stamens usually only 4; pedicels ascending, in fruit 3-15 mm long; pods erect, 2-3 cm long and 1-1.5 mm wide, glabrous to hirsute, the beak short; seeds 15 to about 20, oblong-oval, narrowly wing-margined.

Raceme mostly under 2 cm long; stems shortened........var. **kamtschatica** (Regel) Detl.
Gravel bars and moist banks in open mixed woods, 4500 to about 5500 feet.

Cardamine pennsylvanica Muhl.   Pennsylvania Bitter Cress

Much like *Cardamine oligosperma* but the leaflets of the cauline leaves narrower and
longer; pods narrower, mostly 0.7-1.5 mm wide; seeds about 24 to 40, without a wing
margin.
Gravel bar at about 4600 feet.

Chlorocrambe Rydb.

Glabrous perennial herbs with thick stems and thin petioled hastate leaves; flowers
greenish-white or yellowish in lax racemes; sepals alike and spreading; petals toothed
or somewhat fringed; stamens 6, the anthers tending to coil; pods nearly terete, linear,
slightly compressed, widely spreading, the valves 1-nerved; stigma entire; seeds in 1
row, plump, not margined.

Chlorocrambe hastata (Wats.) Rydb.   Spearhead

Glabrous perennial with simple or branched erect stems 60-150 cm tall; leaves 1-10 cm
long, deltoid to lanceolate, hastate, entire to irregularly lobed, the lower sometimes
lyrate, the upper reduced; pedicels 6-10 mm long, spreading to reflexed; sepals greenish-
white or yellowish, 4-6 mm long; petals white, emarginate, 6-8 mm long, irregularly
toothed near the base; filaments longer than the petals; pods nearly terete, stipitate, 4-9
cm long; style short.
Stony brushy hillsides and dry slopes, about 4500 to 5000 feet.

Descurainia Webb. & Berth.

Annual or biennial branched herbs pubescent with stellate or branched hairs often
mixed with glandular hairs, or nearly glabrous; leaves pinnatifid to finely dissected,
compound; flowers inconspicuous, racemose; petals clawed, yellow to cream; stamens
6; pods small, linear to clavate or fusiform, nearly terete or somewhat angled; style short
and thick; pedicels slender; seeds in 1 or 2 rows.

Style conspicuous; plants usually branched; pods mostly longer than their stalks .. ..*D. richardsonii*
Style obsolete; plants sometimes branched, sometimes not; pods about as long as their
   stalks.. *D. pinnata*

Descurainia pinnata (Walt.) Britt. ssp. **intermedia** (Rydb.) Detl.

Western Tansy Mustard

Nearly glabrous, non-glandular annual 10-70 cm tall, the stems simple or branched;
leaves mainly cauline, broadly lanceolate to oblanceolate, the lower petioled, 3-10 cm
long, commonly pinnate-pinnatifid into linear, toothed segments; upper leaves reduced,
less dissected; pedicels mostly 6-12 mm long, spreading to ascending, often S-shaped;
sepals short; petals in shades of yellow, 2-3 mm long; pods 4-12 mm long, clavate or
elliptic, slightly shorter to longer than the pedicels; seeds 1 to 20 per locule, in 2 rows,
about half the length of the pod.
Sandy soil in open places, about 5000 feet.

Descurainia richardsonii (Sw.) Schulz ssp. **viscosa** (Rydb.) Detl.

Mountain Tansy Mustard

Greenish annual herb, stipitate-glandular above, nearly glabrous to stellate-pubescent, 20-100 cm tall, usually branched; leaves thin, 5-10 cm long, ovate to oblanceolate or oblong, the lower pinnately compound with broad, parted or lobed oblong segments, the upper pinnate with toothed or cleft divisions; inflorescence racemose, glandular, densely-flowered; pedicels 4-9 mm long, spreading to ascending; sepals 1-2.5 mm long; petals pale to deep yellow, slightly longer than the sepals; pods straight or arched, 5 to 17 mm long, torulose, glabrous, ascending to widely spreading; seeds in 1 row.
Moist coniferous slopes, 4600 to 5800 feet.

Draba L.

Low tufted annual, biennial or perennial herbs mostly stellate-pubescent, with leafy or scapose stems; leaves simple, entire or denticulate; inflorescence racemose; flowers small, white or yellow to reddish or violet; pods flattened, linear to ovate, few- to many-seeded; style short, the stigma nearly entire.

1. Flowering stems with several alternate leaves
    2. Petals yellow or yellowish, sometimes fading to white but the veins yellowish
        3. Pods usually hairless, 8-15 mm long; stalks of the fruit (pedicels) about as long as the fruit ____*D. stenoloba*
        3. Pods hairy, 3-12 mm long; pedicels noticeably longer than the fruit, up to 3 cm long, spreading widely and sometimes curving downward; petals light yellow____*D. nemorosa*
    2. Petals white or cream, 2-lobed; pods pubescent
        4. Plants annuals; style very short or missing; petals sometimes yellow; pods not contorted or twisted____*D. praealta*
        4. Plants perennials; style present, often conspicuous; pods often contorted or twisted____*D. lanceolata*
1. Flowering stems leafless, rarely with a reduced leaf, often with a small cluster of leaves at the base
    5. Plants annuals, the stems often weak and bending; petals white, 2-lobed; pods glabrous, 3-10 mm long____*D. verna*
    5. Plants perennials, often matted or cushion-like at the base; leaves small and overlapping
        6. Pods about twice as long as wide, often twisted and contorted; leaves grayish-hairy____*D. lonchocarpa*
        6. Pods about as long as wide, mostly roundish to oval, sometimes twisted and contorted
            7. Pods hairless, 6-8 mm long, sometimes contorted; leaves 2-9 mm wide____*D. lemmonii*
            7. Pods hairy; leaves with simple, forked or branched hairs as well as hair-like cilia along the margins
                8. Cilia only on the lower quarter of the leaves; upper part of the leaf densely covered with short much-branched hairs, especially beneath____*D. oligosperma*
                8. Cilia all around the leaf margin; leaves densely to thinly hairy, the midrib conspicuous
                    9. Under surface of the leaves dense with long loose tangled hairs; flowering stems hairy____*D. paysonii*
                    9. Under surface of the leaves thinly covered with simple or branched hairs; flowering stems without hairs______________________*D. densifolia*

Draba densifolia Nutt.   Alpine Whitlow-grass
Cespitose matted branched scapose perennial; leaves linear, obtuse, mostly 5-8 mm long and up to 1 mm wide, glabrous, the midrib prominent, the margins ciliate; scapes mostly glabrous, 0.5-7 cm long, elongating in fruit, 3- to 12-flowered; petals pale yellowish to white, 2-4 mm long; pods ovate, 2-7 mm long, compressed, sparsely pubescent with simple to stellate hairs; style about 1 mm long; seeds wingless, about 2 mm long.
Dry rocky slopes and ridges, 9300 to 9400 feet, but possibly both below and above these elevations.

Draba lanceolata Royle   Lance-leaved Whitlow-grass
Grayish leafy perennial with 1 to several stems 5-25 cm tall; leaves pannose with stellate to much-branched hairs, the basal in a rosette, oblanceolate, 1-3 cm long, entire to denticulate, sometimes ciliate; cauline leaves several, lanceolate, dentate, pubescent with forked hairs; racemes 10- to 50-flowered, elongated in fruit, sometimes bracteate; petals white, 3-5 mm long, emarginate; silicles 4-12 mm long, 1.5-3 mm wide, soft-pubescent, often contorted; style 0.2-0.8 mm long; seeds 20 to 50.
Open dry "saddles" and in rock crevices of sandy ridges, about 7900 feet.

Draba lemmonii Wats. var. **cyclomorpha** (Pays.) O. E. Schulz
                                                             Lemmon's Whitlow-grass
Cespitose matted scapose perennial from a branched woody caudex; leaves fleshy, obovate to oblanceolate, 4-15 mm long, obtuse, ciliate, glabrous or sparingly hairy with simple and forked hairs; peduncles 2-12 cm long, hairy with simple and branched hairs; raceme short and closely 5- to 20-flowered; pedicels spreading, about equal to the pods; sepals pubescent or sparsely villous; petals yellow, about 5 mm long; pods ovate to elliptic, glabrous, contorted or twisted, 4-8 mm long and 2-5 mm wide; style about 1 mm long; seeds 4 to 16.
Exposed talus slopes and sandy ridges, 8500 to 9400 feet.

Draba lonchocarpa Rydb.   Twisted Whitlow-grass
Cespitose scapose perennial, somewhat grayish; basal leaves tufted, spatulate to obovate, 2-15 mm long and 1-5 mm wide, acutish, densely-gray-stellate, ciliate toward the base, the midrib prominent; stem leaves sometimes up to 4; scapes 1-8 cm long, glabrous or sparsely stellate-pubescent; raceme 3- to 15-flowered, elongating in fruit to half the length of the peduncle or longer; pedicels mostly shorter than the fruit; petals white, 2-4 mm long; pods linear, dark-colored, smooth and shiny, elliptic to oblong-oblanceolate, 3-10 mm long and 1-2 mm wide, often contorted, glabrous to stellate-pubescent; style to 0.5 mm long; seeds 8 to 30.
Dry exposed ridges at about 9000 feet, and probably higher as well.

Draba nemorosa L.   Wood Whitlow-grass
Annual 5-25 cm tall, stem loosely stellate-pubescent especially near the base; leaves 0.5-2 cm long, oblong-ovate or lanceolate, sessile, obtuse, dentate, on the lower third of the stem and reduced upward; petals yellow fading white, 1-4 mm long; racemes elongated in fruit up to ¾ the height of the plant; pedicels scattered, divergent, often as much as 1-2 cm long; pods elliptic, 5-10 mm long, pubescent or glabrous; style lacking; seeds 25 to 50.
Open woods, about 4500 to 5000 feet.

Arabis microphylla

Arabis nuttallii

Arabis sparsiflora var. subvillosa

Camelina microcarpa

Capsella bursa-pastoris

Brassica campestris

Cardamine cordifolia var. lyallii

Cardamine pennsylvanica

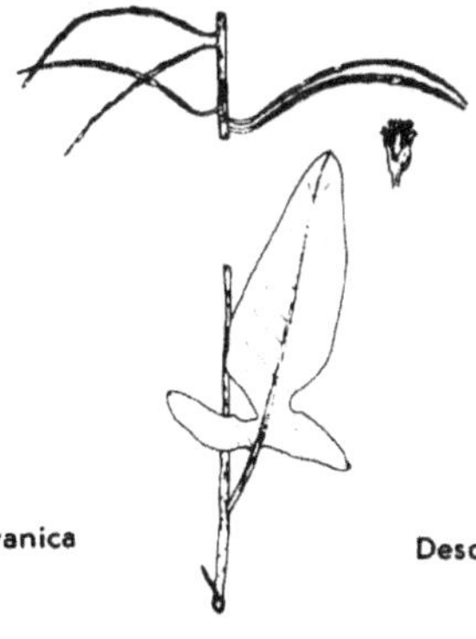

Chlorocrambe hastata

Descurainia richardsonii ssp. viscosa

Draba lemmonii var. cyclomorpha

Draba oligosperma Hook.   Few-seeded Whitlow-grass
Cespitose matted scapose canescent perennial with a much branched caudex; leaves very crowded, linear to linear-spatulate, obtuse, 3-6 mm long (ours), pubescent especially near the base, the midrib prominent; scape 1-10 cm long; flowers 3 to 15 on pedicels 3-10 mm long; petals 3-4 mm long, light yellow to off-white, fading in age; pods ovate, elliptic to oblong-obovate, 2.5-8 mm long and 2-4 mm wide, slightly inflated, glabrous to thickly (ours) pubescent with all kinds of hairs; style up to 1 mm long; seeds 2 to 10, about 1.5 mm long.
Treeless slopes, ledges, cliffs and ridges, 8000 to 9575 feet and probably higher.

Draba paysonii Macbr. var. **treleasii** (Schulz) C. L. Hitchc.   Payson's Whitlow-grass
Cespitose scapose matted perennial sometimes with many short dichotomous branches; old leaves long-persistent on the stems; leaves incurved, linear to linear-oblanceolate, long-ciliate, slightly crisped when dried, ours 3-5 mm long, the upper surface with simple and forked hairs, the lower surface with elongate, tangled branched hairs; scapes leafless, 0.5-6 cm long, long-hairy; raceme short, 3- to 10-flowered; pedicels usually shorter than the fruit, villous; sepals pubescent, 2 mm long; petals light yellow or white, 2-4 mm long; pods broadly elliptic to suborbicular to lanceolate-ovate, slightly inflated in ours, 2.5-4 mm long and about 3.5 mm broad, mostly pubescent but sometimes glabrous; seeds 3 to 10, not winged.
Exposed ridges and unstable sandy talus slopes, 9400 to about 9700 feet and probably higher.

Draba praealta Greene   Tall Whitlow-grass
Annual or short-lived perennial; stems 1 to several, erect, mostly branched from the base, 3-30 cm tall, pubescent with simple and stellate hairs, sparingly long-hairy near the base; leaves entire to few-toothed, mostly in basal rosettes, 3-30 mm long, oblanceolate, rather densely pubescent with simple and 2- to 7-rayed hairs; cauline leaves 1 to 6, lanceolate to ovate; petals mostly white, 1-3.5 mm long; raceme 3- to 15-flowered, elongated in fruit; pods narrow, lanceolate, 1-14 mm long, often twisted, up to 2.5 mm broad, soft-pubescent; pedicels spreading, shorter than the fruit; style very short; seeds 20 to 70.
Dry shady streambanks in open woods, 5500 to 5800 feet.

Draba stenoloba Ledeb.   Slender or Alaska Whitlow-grass
Winter annual, usually branched from the base, 5-30 cm tall; stem erect, slender, pubescent near the base with stellate and forked hairs, grooved and shining; leaves mostly in basal rosettes, oblanceolate, 1-4 cm long, nearly glabrous above, densely stellate beneath; stem leaves 1 to few, usually entire, oblanceolate or lanceolate; sepals about 2 mm long, hairy; petals yellowish, 2-3 mm long; racemes 5- to 30-flowered, elongating in fruit; fruiting pedicels ascending, 6-15 mm long, about equaling the length of the pods; silique linear-oblong, 8-12 mm long and 1-2 mm wide, erect, glabrous, straight or slightly curved; seeds 16 to 40.
Shady moist open woods near streams, 7200 feet.

Draba verna L.   Vernal Whitlow-grass
Annual with leafless stems 4-20 cm tall, pubescent near the base, glabrous above; leaves all in a basal rosette, 10-25 mm long, oblong or spatulate, nearly entire, pubescent

with stiff stellate hairs; petals white, about 2.5-4 mm long, deeply 2-lobed; pods elliptic-obovate, 4-8 mm long, glabrous; pedicels long, ascending, 15-25 mm long in fruit; seeds 30 to 60.
Moist shady woods, about 4500 feet.

Erysimum L.

Annual to perennial herbs pubescent with 2- to 4-forked hairs; leaves simple, alternate, entire to toothed or lobed; flowers yellow, showy, in crowded racemes; petals in shades of yellow, often orange or reddish to purple, long-clawed; stamens 6; pods linear, elongated, flattened to quadrangular or nearly terete; valves nerved, deciduous; style often beaklike with a 2-lobed stigma; seeds in 1 row in each cell, wingless to wing-margined.

Erysimum capitatum (Dougl.) Greene   Wallflower
Biennial or short-lived perennial, grayish to greenish, the stems mostly simple, 20-100 cm tall; basal leaves abundant, in a rosette, petioled, unequal in size, entire to dentate, 3-12 cm long; cauline leaves lanceolate to oblanceolate, sessile; petals yellow, deep orange or reddish, 15-25 mm long; pedicels ascending or spreading, 4-8 or 13 mm long; pods narrowly linear, slightly flattened, quadrangular, straight or curved, 3-10 cm long; style short and thick; seeds slightly or not at all winged.
Dry gravelly hillsides, streambanks, talus and rocky slopes, from about 5000 to 9200 feet.

Halimolobos Tausch

Biennial or perennial herbs with simple or forked to stellate hairs and simple, toothed, petiolate to sessile, sometimes auricled leaves; flowers in racemes; petals (ours) white, yellow or pinkish; stamens 6; pods linear, sessile, dehiscent, terete to flattened, often torulose; style prominent; seeds numerous, in 1 or 2 rows in the locule, not margined or winged.

Halimolobos virgata (Nutt.) Schulz
Biennial with 1 to several simple to branching stems 10 to over 300 cm tall, grayish-pubescent with long and short simple to branched hairs; basal leaves lanceolate to oblanceolate, 3-6 cm long, in a rosette, petiolate, denticulate to dentate; cauline leaves reduced, becoming sessile and auricled; racemes many-flowered; pedicels ascending, 7-11 mm long; sepals often purplish; petals white, usually pinkish-veined, about 4 mm long; pods erect, glabrous, 1.5-4 cm long, slightly flattened to terete-angular; seeds crowded, irregularly in 2 rows, not margined or winged.
Moist rocky slopes in shady mixed woods, about 4700 feet.

Lepidium L.

Annual to sometimes shrubby perennial herbs with little or no pubescence; leaves pinnatifid, lobed or entire, auricled or sagittate; flowers small, racemose; petals white to yellow, or missing; stamens 2 or 4 or 6; pods oblong, round, ovate or obovate, flattened, often wing-margined and notched; seeds 2, not winged.

Petals usually present and longer than the sepals; pods glabrous, their pedicels 4-5 mm
 long, spreading .... *L. virginicum*
Petals none, or rudimentary and much shorter than the sepals; pods pubescent on both
 sides; pedicels 3-4 mm long, ascending .... *L. densiflorum*

Lepidium densiflorum Schrad. var. pubicarpum (Nels.) Thell.

Common Pepper Grass

Branched annual 20-50 cm tall, pubescent to glabrate, pale dull green; leaves 3-10 cm long, lanceolate, pinnatifid or dentate, nearly entire above, not auricled; racemes numerous, glabrous; pedicels flattened, about equaling the fruit; petals none or vestigial, or white and about equaling the sepals; stamens 2 or 4; pods pubescent on both sides, about 3 mm long, notched and slightly winged at the tip.
Dry roadsides and campgrounds, about 5000 feet.

Lepidium virginicum L. var. pubescens (Greene) C. L. Hitchc.

Tall Western Pepper Grass

Sparsely to densely pubescent annual or biennial 15-60 cm tall, branching above; leaves 4-6 cm long, obovate to oblanceolate, the basal entire and toothed to pinnate, the cauline reduced upward and often entire, all early deciduous, racemes numerous, elongate, many-flowered; pedicels puberulent to hairy, usually longer than the fruit; petals white, 1-3 mm long, sometimes missing; pods glabrous, nearly orbicular, notched, 2.5-4 mm long.
Dry sandy ground, about 4500 feet.

Lesquerella S. Wats.

Stellate-pubescent annual or perennial herbs with simple, entire to toothed leaves and showy yellow racemose flowers; petals yellow to reddish or purplish-tinged; pedicels straight to sigmoid; stamens 6; pods ovate to oblong, inflated to flattened; style usually prominent; seeds in 2 rows, sometimes margined or slightly winged, flattened.

Pods plumb, slightly flattened, usually broader than long; stems prostrate; stalks of flowers
and fruit spreading or curved downward..*L. sherwoodii*
Pods less plump, also slightly flattened, usually longer than broad; stems ascending or
prostrate; stalks of flowers and fruit ascending, often S-shaped...................................*L. occidentalis*

Lesquerella occidentalis Wats. ssp. diversifolia (Greene) Maguire & Holm.

Wallowa Bladder-pod

Densely stellate-pubescent perennial with a large thickened caudex bearing persistent old leaf bases and usually with several prostrate to erect silvery-greenish flowering stems usually under 10 cm long; basal leaves 2-8 cm long, in a rosette, ovate, or elliptic to nearly orbicular, usually entire, often greenish, densely stellate; cauline leaves oblanceolate, usually entire; pedicels often sigmoid, 5-10 mm long; petals narrow, yellow, about 7 mm long; pods densely stellate-pubescent, about 5 mm long and not so broad, orbicular to oblong or obovate, moderately flattened, thinly margined near the tip; seeds usually 2 in each locule.
Exposed slopes and ridges of coniferous forest, 5500 to 9550 feet.

Lesquerella sherwoodii Peck

Sherwood's Bladder-pod

Stellate-pubescent freely-branched biennial or short-lived perennial with a number of ascending or prostrate stems 10-40 cm long from a short caudex; leaves canescent, entire or wavy-margined, the basal 1.5-3 cm long, orbicular to spatulate, long-petioled, the cauline more narrowly oblanceolate to spatulate; petals light yellow, about 7 mm long; fruiting racemes often lax and long; pedicels 6-15 mm long, spreading, recurved or sigmoid; pods densely stellate, turgid, slightly flattened, about 4 mm broad, usually broader than long; seeds 2 or 3 in each locule.

Rocky slopes, cliffs and talus at higher elevations and shady sandy rocky places near streams at lower elevations, 5000 to 8500 feet.

Phoenicaulis Nutt.

Cespitose canescent perennial with a leafy caudex and short bracteate flowering stems; flowers racemose; sepals slightly gibbous at the base; petals showy, long-clawed, pinkish or purple; stamens 6; pods non-stipitate, linear, flattened parallel to the partition, the valves 1-nerved; seeds in 1 or 2 rows, not wing-margined.

Phoenicaulis cheiranthoides Nutt.   Dagger-pod

Parrya menziesii Greene

Cespitose perennial from a thick taproot and branched caudex covered with dry old leaf bases of dead leaves; flowering stems 6-20 cm tall, nearly glabrous; leaves mostly in basal rosettes, grayish with a dense, fine, stellate pubescence on both sides, 2.5-15 cm long, oblanceolate, petioled, entire; cauline leaves sessile, auricled, narrowly lanceolate, up to 2 cm long, glabrous to ciliate or sparsely hairy; flowers numerous; sepals often pink or purplish; petals 8-15 mm long, usually reddish-purple, sometimes almost white; pedicels 10-15 mm long; pods widely spreading, glabrous, 2-8 cm long, tapering toward the tip, 2- to 6-seeded.

Dry sandy soil in passes and other open places, about 8000 feet or possibly higher as well.

Rorippa Scop.

Annual to perennial aquatic or marsh herbs with simple to pinnate leaves and small racemose flowers; sepals deciduous to persistent; petals white or purplish-tinged to yellow; stamens 6, or fewer; fruit a short pod, oval to linear, not stipitate, terete to slightly flattened; style prominent to almost lacking; seeds minute, in 2 rows in each cell, sometimes irregularly in 1 row.

Stems erect, single or in clusters; leaf segments usually oblong, pointed; style thick; pods curved, 6-15 mm long ....*R. curvisiliqua*

Stems spreading or prostrate; leaf segments rounded, blunt; style slender; pods straight, 3-8 mm long ....*R. obtusa*

Rorippa curvisiliqua (Hook.) Bessey   Western Yellow-cress

Annual or biennial 10-50 cm tall, glabrous to sparsely hairy; leaves 2-10 cm long, from nearly entire or toothed to pinnatifid with linear to ovate, entire to toothed segments; racemes numerous; pedicels 2-6 mm long; petals light yellow, 1-2 mm long; pods curved, 6-15 mm long, nearly terete.

Low moist or wet places, mostly in meadows, 5500 to 6500 feet.

Rorippa obtusa (Nutt.) Britt.   Blunt-leaved Yellow-cress

Glabrous annual with branched spreading or prostrate stems 10-30 cm tall; leaves 2-6 cm long, oblong-oblanceolate, pinnatifid with obovate or rounded segments usually sinuately-toothed but sometimes entire; pedicels mostly 2-4 mm long, spreading or ascending, usually shorter than the pods; sepals early deciduous; petals narrowly spatulate, very pale yellow, 1 or 2 mm long; pods oval to oblong-lanceolate, 3-8 mm long.

Wet lake border in coniferous forest, about 7300 feet.

Sisymbrium L.

Annual to perennial rather hairy herbs; leaves lobed to pinnatifid; flowers racemose, yellow or white; sepals spreading; petals clawed; stamens 6; fruit a dehiscent pod, narrowly linear, terete or nearly so, nonstipitate, the valves 1- to 3-nerved; stigma 2-lobed; seeds in 1 row, not winged.

Sisymbrium altissimum L.   Tumble Mustard

Erect, widely-branching annual, hairy near the base but glabrous above, 30-150 cm tall; lower leaves 8-20 cm long, petioled, lanceolate to oblanceolate, lobed to pinnatifid; upper leaves pinnatifid into linear segments; pedicels usually spreading, 4-10 cm long; sepals about 4 mm long; petals pale yellowish, about 7 mm long; pods linear, terete, rigid, spreading, 5-10 cm long; seeds in 1 row in each locule.
Common weed of roadsides and campgrounds, 4500 to 5200 feet.

Smelowskia C. A. Mey.

Low cespitose canescent perennial with a branching caudex and entire to pinnate or pinnatifid leaves; flowers racemose, small; petals white or creamy to purplish-tinged, spatulate; stamens 6; pods ovate to linear, glabrous to pubescent, nearly terete or slightly flattened, the valves keeled; seeds few to numerous.

Smelowskia calycina (Desv.) C. A. Mey. var. americana (Regel & Herd.) Drury & Roll.

Plant densely cespitose from a branched caudex covered with dried old leaf bases; flowering stems 5-20 cm tall, densely pubescent with a mixture of long and short simple to forked or branched hairs; leaves deeply pinnatifid, ovate to obovate, 1-10 cm long, densely gray-stellate; petioles ciliate near the base; pedicels erect to ascending, 6-10 mm long; sepals often pinkish- or purplish-tinged; petals white to purplish-tinged, 4-8 mm long; pods lanceolate, 5-11 mm long, pointed at both ends.
Exposed ridges and slopes, mostly above 9000 feet.

Thlaspi L.

Glabrous annual or perennial herbs with entire to toothed or lobed leaves, the basal forming a rosette, the cauline auricled and clasping the stem; flowers in racemes; sepals erect; petals white or purple; stamens 6; pods oblong-elliptic to cuneate or obcordate, acute to emarginate, flattened, often wing-margined; style conspicuous to obsolete; seeds 2 or more in 1 row in each locule.

Pod roundish with a broad margin and a deep notch at the top; plant a glabrous annual ....*T. arvense*
Pod shield-shaped with a narrow margin, either shallowly notched at the top or not at all;
   plant a glaucous perennial...*T. glaucum*

Thlaspi arvense L.   Field Penny Cress

Glabrous annual with erect branching stems 20-50 cm tall; basal leaves early deciduous, oblanceolate, petioled, 2-6 cm long; cauline leaves oblong to lanceolate, dentate to sinuately lobed, sessile below but becoming auricled and clasping above; pedicels spreading to upcurved, 7-15 mm long; sepals white-margined; petals white, 3-4 mm long; silicles nearly orbicular, narrowly notched, wing-margined all around, 8-17 mm long; style nearly obsolete.
Open sunny roadsides and meadows, 4500 to 6000 feet.

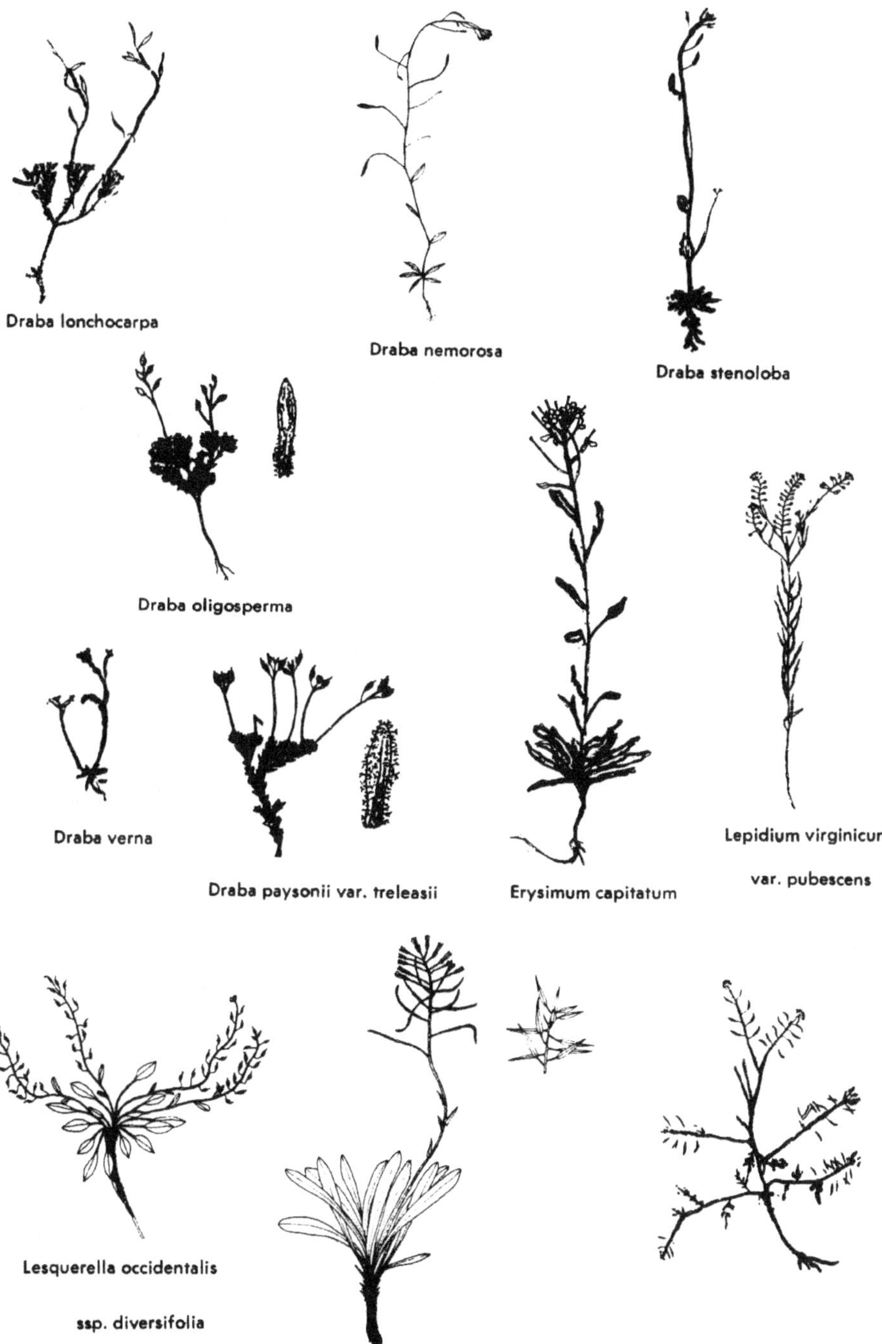

Draba lonchocarpa
Draba nemorosa
Draba stenoloba
Draba oligosperma
Draba verna
Draba paysonii var. treleasii
Erysimum capitatum
Lepidium virginicum
var. pubescens
Lesquerella occidentalis
ssp. diversifolia
Phoenicaulis cheiranthoides
Rorippa curvisiliqua

Thlaspi glaucum Nels.   Glaucous Penny Cress
   T. alpestre L.
   Bluish perennial with a branched woody base; stems 10-60 cm tall; basal leaves obovate, 1-2 cm long, dentate to entire, petioled; cauline leaves oblong, shorter than the
internodes, sessile, auricled and clasping the stem; pedicels spreading; petals about 5 mm
long; silicles shield-shaped, narrowly obovate, 4-10 mm long, the margins keeled and
slightly winged; style 1-3 mm long.
Dry sandy or rocky places, often in woods, 4500 to 7000 feet.

DROSERACEAE   Sundew Family

Annual, biennial or perennial herbs with leaves mostly in a basal rosette, often curled
in the bud, their surfaces covered with stalked glands that trap and digest small insects;
flowers in one-sided, terminal inflorescences; sepals mostly 5 or 4, persistent; petals as
many as the sepals; stamens 4 to 20; ovary free or adnate to the calyx, 1- to 5-loculed;
styles 1 to 5; fruit a 1-celled loculicidal capsule; seeds numerous.

Drosera L.

Small acaulescent biennial or perennial aquatic or bog plants with mostly basal gland-
ular-viscid leaves; flowers perfect, in terminal raceme-like cymes, ours on leafless scapes;
sepals, petals and stamens 4 to 8, often 5; styles 3 to 5, deeply cleft and seemingly twice
that number; capsules 1-celled, 3- to 5-valved; seeds numerous.

Drosera anglica Huds.   Long-leaved Sundew
   D. longifolia of many authors, but not L.
   Bog plant with erect leaves, the blades linear- to oblong-spatulate, 1-3 cm long, tapering to longish rather glandular-hairy petioles; scapes 6-18 cm tall, glabrous; racemes
one-sided, mostly 2- to 7-flowered; calyx segments united about $\frac{1}{3}$ of the length; petals
white, longer than the sepals; stamens short; seeds fusiform.
Swamps and quaking bogs, Duck Lake at about 5600 feet.

CRASSULACEAE   Stonecrop Family

Annual or perennial mostly fleshy or succulent herbs or rather shrubby plants; leaves
alternate, opposite or whorled, mostly entire, without stipules; flowers usually perfect
and regular, cymose to axillary, or rarely solitary, usually of 4 or 5 parts; calyx essentially free from the ovary; petals as many as the sepals, distinct or united at the base,
often colored; stamens as many as the petals or twice as many; pistils usually 4 or 5,
1-carpellary, distinct or united near the base, each subtended by a small scale-like nectary; styles short or long, often beak-like; fruit a dehiscent, 1-celled follicle; seeds
numerous.

Sedum L.

Annual, biennial or perennial herbs or semishrubs with alternate, opposite or whorled,
flat or terete, fleshy leaves; flowers mostly perfect, in terminal cymes, usually of 5 parts
but sometimes 3- to 7-parted; calyx segments free nearly to the base; petals free or
united about halfway, usually yellow but sometimes white, pink or purple, or reddish;

stamens usually twice as many as the petals; carpels free or united at the base; follicles few- to many-seeded, erect or widely spreading, tipped by the short, tapered styles.

1. Flowers mostly yellow; stem leaves often missing by flowering time; plants with creeping stems and sterile shoots, mostly in dry locations
    2. Lower leaves with a strong central ridge (keel), the leaf tip pointed; upper part of the stem usually with leafy bulbil-like clusters (propagules); plants of low to middle elevations..*S. stenopetalum*
    2. Lower leaves appearing swollen or rounded, not strongly keeled, the surface bumpy with little swellings (papillae); stems mostly without propagules; plants mostly at upper elevations..*S. lanceolatum*
1. Flowers purple, pinkish or reddish, less than 5 mm long; leaves thick, closely crowded on the stems, not falling off easily; plants of wet rocks and cliffs at upper elevations............ *S. roseum*

Sedum lanceolatum Torr.   Stonecrop

  S. stenopetalum of some authors

Glabrous perennial with sterile basal shoots and rosettes; flowering stems usually 5-20 cm tall; leaves alternate, linear or linear-lanceolate and terete or nearly so to ovate and slightly flattened, 5-20 mm long, smooth or mostly minutely papillate; flowers axillary in somewhat crowded cymes, 5-parted; sepals 2-3.5 mm long; petals yellow, often tinged with red, lanceolate, free, 6-7 mm long; follicles erect, united at the base, the styles erect or divergent.

Open dry exposed places, in rocky, gravelly or sandy soil, 5300 to 9595 feet or higher.

Sedum roseum (L.) Scop. ssp. integrifolium (Raf.) Hulten Roseroot or Rosewort

  Rhodiola integrifolia Raf.

Glabrous glaucous perennial with fleshy rootstocks; stems usually clustered, 3-15 cm tall; leaves cauline, obovate, flattened but fleshy, sessile, 7-20 mm long, entire to serrulate; flowers crowded in small head-like cymes, usually deep purple, rarely reddish, 4- to 5-parted, mostly polygamous; sepals 1-2 mm long; petals dark- or greenish-purple, distinct, 1-3 mm long; stamens 10, shorter or longer than the petals; carpels erect, distinct, the styles beak-like at the tip.

Moist to wet cliffs, wet rocks, springy places, ridges and rocky slopes, 7200 to 9550 feet.

Sedum stenopetalum Pursh   Narrow-petaled Stonecrop

  S. douglasii Hook. of some authors

Glabrous perennial with rootstocks and numerous sterile shoots; flowering stems up to 20 cm tall; leaves alternate, lanceolate, thin and scarious, keeled or nerved on the back, mostly 5-15 mm long, usually deciduous by anthesis, those of the sterile shoots crowded, the upper cauline usually with bulbil-like propagules (leafy buds) in the axils; flowers 5-parted, in a few-forked tight cyme, or sometimes solitary, some or all of them occasionally sterile, becoming propagules; sepals about 2 mm long; petals yellow, 6-12 mm long; follicles widely spreading, not glandular-papillate.

Open to shaded, grassy to rocky slopes, cliffs and crevices in coniferous woods, 5200 to 9595 feet.

SAXIFRAGACEAE Saxifrage Family

Annual or perennial herbs with alternate (rarely opposite) or basal simple to compound leaves mostly without stipules; flowers mostly perfect, regular or occasionally slightly irregular, perigynous to epigynous, usually small, several to many but sometimes few or solitary; calyx well developed, 5-lobed or -parted but rarely 4- or 6-parted or otherwise irregular, greenish or white, sometimes petaloid, usually at least partially adnate to the pistil, frequently with a free, connate, tubular to campanulate portion (the hypanthium); petals free, usually as many as the calyx lobes and alternating with them, or missing, usually inserted toward the top of the hypanthium when present; stamens usually 5 or 10 (only 3 or 2 in *Tolmiea*), borne on the calyx tube, the filaments not united; carpels usually 2 or 3 but sometimes 4, 5 or 6, united partially or completely, or rarely free; ovary superior to inferior, mostly 1- to 3-celled, rarely 4- or 5-celled; stigmas mostly capitate or discoid, sometimes more elongate; fruit a capsule, or rarely separate follicles; seeds 1 to numerous per carpel.

1. Leaves clustered at the base of the plant, sometimes 1 or 2 small bracts on the flowering
   stem; plants mostly over 10 cm tall
     2. Leaves thin, sometimes hairy; flowers with lobed petals; inflorescence narrow,
       strung-out, rather long.. *Mitella*
     2. Leaves thickish or succulent, sometimes hairy or lobed and toothed, sometimes not;
       flowers solitary to numerous on the stems
       3. Flowers mostly solitary, the stem sometimes with 1 or more small bracts;
         petals fringed; leaves mostly broader than long, not lobed or hairy................... *Parnassia*
       3. Flowers never solitary, mostly several to many; petals sometimes missing,
         not lobed when present; leaves nearly circular to longer than wide, lobed or
         toothed on the margin or the margin entire
         4. Leaves cordate (heart-shaped) at the base; inflorescence crowded,
           oblong, narrow; petals not lobed, often missing................................. *Heuchera*
         4. Leaves not cordate at the base; inflorescence not as above; petals
           usually present... *Saxifraga*
1. Leaves on the stem as well as at the base; plants sometimes under 10 cm tall
     5. Flowering stems mostly under 10 cm tall; leaves opposite or alternate...................... *Saxifraga*
     5. Flowering stems mostly over 10 cm tall; leaves alternate on the stem
       6. Leaves thin, hairy, 3- to 7-lobed, the teeth pointed; fruit segments 2, very
         unequal.. *Tiarella*
       6. Leaves fleshy or thickish; flowering stems mostly solitary; fruit segments
         equal
         7. Flowers few in an elongated narrow inflorescence, the petals lobed,
           white or sometimes pinkish or purplish, sometimes replaced by small
           bulblets.. *Lithophragma*
         7. Flowers several in a compact inflorescence broader than long, rather
           flat-topped, the petals not lobed, not usually pinkish or purplish.............. *Suksdorfia*

Heuchera L.

Herbaceous perennials with thick scaly rootstocks; stems leafy or naked; leaves mostly basal, long-petioled, lobed and crenate-dentate; flowers regular to irregular in open or spike-like panicles or racemes; calyx 5-lobed, greenish, yellowish, or reddish tinged, saucer-shaped to cylindric or tubular, adnate to the lower part of the ovary but the hypanthium free; petals usually 5, sometimes fewer or none, white to greenish-yellow; stamens 5; ovary inferior, 1-celled with two style-like dehiscent beaks tipped by the true styles when present; stigmas capitate; capsules many-seeded.

Petals none, or much shorter than the calyx when present... *H. cylindrica*
Petals usually present, equaling or much longer than the calyx.. *H. cusickii*

Heuchera cusickii Rosend., Butt. & Lak.   Cusick's Heuchera

Flowering stems 15-30 cm tall; leaves 1-2.5 cm broad, glabrous, round-reniform, with wide shallow sinuses, the petioles glabrous or glandular-puberulent; inflorescence short, dense and spike-like; petals equaling to much longer than the sepals.
Reported by S. Head: "3 miles up Kettle Creek."

Heuchera cylindrica Dougl.   Alpine Alumroot
H. ovalifolia Nutt.

Perennial with short thick rhizomes; flowering stems 10-30 cm tall, sometimes taller, finely glandular-pubescent to long-hairy, with one or more greenish to brownish, gland-ular-ciliate, scarious bracts; leaves basal, glandular-pubescent to long-hairy, the blades thick, mostly 1-2.5 cm broad and slightly longer, usually rounded to cordate, lobed or toothed, ovate or ovate-oblong to nearly reniform; inflorescence dense, spike-like, 1-6 cm long mostly, sometimes up to 20 cm; calyx 5-10 mm long, white or greenish-yellow, campanulate, sometimes longer on one side than the other, the 5 sepals longer than the hypanthium; petals sometimes 5, usually fewer, or obsolete; stamens short; ovary in-ferior, tapered above to empty style-like beaks tipped with very short true styles; stigmas capitate; capsules 6-10 mm long.

Leaves and lower stems finely glandular-pubescent; leaf blades thick, mostly 1-2.5 cm broad, the base slightly if at all cordate...var. **alpina** Wats.
Leaves and lower stems glabrous to slightly glandular-pubescent; leaf blades frequently over 2.5 cm broad, usually cordate at the base with a well-developed
sinus..var. **glabella** (T. & G.) Wheel.
Dry rocky slopes and cliffs in coniferous forest, 4792 to about 9400 feet.

Lithophragma Nutt.

Perennial herbs, usually glandular-pubescent, with simple stems and bulblet-bearing roots; leaves basal or cauline, palmately parted, lobed or crenate, the 1 or more cauline ones often with bulblets in the axils; flowers showy, sometimes replaced by small pur-plish bulblets in the few-flowered terminal racemes; calyx 5-lobed, partially adnate to the ovary, the hypanthium well-developed; petals 5, white or pinkish, clawed, lobed or entire, longer than the calyx; stamens 10, inserted on the hypanthium; pistil 3-carpel-lary; capsule 1-celled, 3-valved with many seeds.

Flowers mostly 2 to 5 on the stem, the petals usually with 5 lobes; reddish-purple bulblets
  sometimes in the axils of the leaves or replacing the flowers...*L. glabra*
Flowers usually 6 to 11 on the stem, the petals usually with 3 lobes; bulblets not developed
  on the plant ....*L. parviflora*

Lithophragma glabra Nutt.   Slender Fringe-cup; Rock Star
L. bulbifera Rydb.

A slender glandular-pubescent plant 5-30 cm tall, often reddish-purple; basal leaf blades deeply 3- to 5-cleft, mostly broadly reniform in outline, the petioles 1-5 cm long; cauline leaves 1 to 5, small, short-petioled to nearly sessile, sometimes with small red-dish-purple bulblets in their axils; flowers 2 to 5, sometimes replaced by bulblets, the inflorescence elongating with age; calyx 2-4 mm long; petals white to pinkish- or pur-plish-tinged, 3- to 5-cleft and these often again divided; ovary inconspicuously inferior. Grassy or rocky openings in coniferous woods, 4500 to about 6400 feet.

Lithophragma parviflora (Hook.) Nutt.   Small-flowered Fringe Cup; Star Flower
   Slender, glandular-puberulent plant 10-50 cm tall, often purplish above; basal leaf blades 1-5 cm broad, deeply 3- to 5-cleft, the divisions again cleft and lobed, the petioles 1-8 cm long; cauline leaves usually 2, the upper ones nearly sessile; raceme mostly 6- to 11-flowered, elongating to as much as 15 cm long; calyx 5-lobed, obconic, becoming clavate in fruit, up to 10 mm long; petals clawed, white to pinkish or purplish, 5-10 mm long, usually 3- to 5-cleft; ovary nearly completely inferior.
Sandy or rocky soil in dry or moist grassy open woods, 4500 to about 5500 feet.

Mitella L.

   Small perennials, glandular-puberulent and often hirsute; leaves mostly basal, the flowering stems leafless or with 1 to 3 leaves; flowers complete, regular, small, in simple racemes; calyx 5-lobed, saucer-shaped, adnate to the ovary more than half-way, the hypanthium gland-lined and flared; petals 5, white or pinkish- to purplish-tinged, 3-lobed or pinnatifid, rarely entire; stamens 10 or 5; pistil 2-carpellary, ovary 1-celled; fruit a capsule appearing almost circumscissile, many-seeded, often dehiscent before maturity.

1. Flowers 5 to 45, mostly appearing on only one side of the stem; petals white to purplish
   with 3 narrow segments
         2. Flowering stems with about 5 to 15 flowers; calyx 1.5-3.5 mm long.................................. *M. trifida*
         2. Flowering stems with about 15 to 45 flowers; calyx mostly 4-6 mm long .... *M. stauropetala*
1. Flowers 6 to 25, appearing on both sides of the stem; calyx greenish; petals greenish
   with 4 to 8 segments.. *M. pentandra*

Mitella pentandra Hook.   Bishop's Cap
   Perennial with short rootstocks and slender scapes 10-30 cm tall, minutely glandular-puberulent to glabrous, leafless or with 1 or 2 bracts or reduced leaves; leaves mostly basal, long-petioled, the blades orbicular to cordate, lobed or crenate-dentate, 2-6 cm broad, nearly glabrous or with scattered white hairs; flowers green, the raceme 6- to 25-flowered; calyx saucer- to cup-shaped, green; petals greenish, dissected into 8 filiform segments usually but sometimes 4 to 10; stamens 5, opposite the petals.
Moist or wet shady bogs, alpine meadows and woods, especially along streams, 4600 to 8000 feet.

Mitella stauropetala Piper   Side-flowered Mitrewort
   Hairy perennial with creeping rootstocks and 1 to 6 essentially leafless, glandular-puberulent scapes up to 50 cm tall; leaves reniform to cordate, sparsely hairy on both sides, glandular-ciliate, 2.5-7 cm broad, broadly crenate; racemes strongly one-sided, 15- to about 45-flowered; calyx turbinate, 4-6 mm long, greenish-white to purplish-tinged; petals white or purplish, cleft into 3 filiform segments usually but sometimes entire, twice as long as the sepals; stamens 5, opposite the sepals; ovary inferior.
Low and boggy places in moist shady woods and in meadows, 5000 to about 7000 feet.

Mitella trifida Graham   Three-toothed Mitrewort
   Slender hairy perennial with clustered, essentially leafless, glandular-hairy scapes 15- to about -40 cm tall; leaves cordate to cordate-ovate, 2-7 cm broad, lobed, crenate and minutely glandular-ciliate; racemes 5- to 20-flowered, often one-sided; calyx campanu-

Sisymbrium altissimum

Smelowskia calycina var. americana

Thlaspi glaucum

Thlaspi arvense

Drosera anglica

Sedum roseum ssp. integrifolium

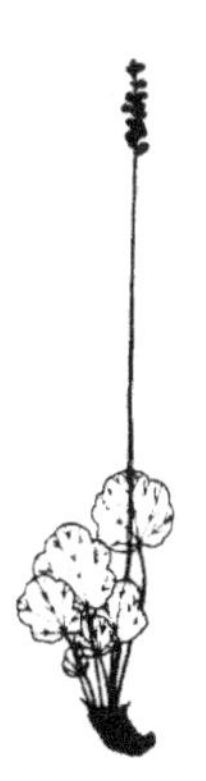

Sedum stenopetalum

Heuchera cylindrica

Lithophragma parviflora

late, whitish or purplish-tinged, 1.5-3.5 mm long; petals white to purplish-tinged, 3-cleft
or rarely entire; stamens 5, opposite the sepals; ovary inferior.
Shady moist mountain woods, about 6000 feet.

Parnassia L.

Glabrous essentially scapose herbs with short rootstocks and entire mostly basal
leaves; flowers large, solitary, white or yellow; calyx deeply 5-lobed, the short tube free
or adnate to the ovary; petals 5, entire to fringed near the base; fertile stamens 5, alternating with the petals; staminodia gland-tipped, clustered at the base of the petals, free
or united below to form a scale; pistil 4-carpellary; ovary 1-celled; styles short or none;
stigmas usually 4; fruit a loculicidal, ovoid, many-seeded capsule.

Parnassia fimbriata Konig   Fringed Grass of Parnassus

Plant with short rootstocks; flowering stem 1 to several, 15-30 cm tall with a single
cordate-clasping bract near the middle; leaves long-petioled, the blades reniform to
cordate, 2-4 cm wide, 7- to 9-nerved; sepals 4-7 mm long, entire or fringed; petals white,
about twice as long as the sepals, fringed below, erose to entire above; staminodia
thickened and scale-like, several-lobed or capitate-tipped; capsule ovoid, about 1 cm long.
Wet meadows, streambanks and mountain bogs, 5000 to about 9800 feet.

Saxifraga [Tourn.] L.

Perennial or occasionally annual herbs, usually glandular-hairy and often with bulbils
in the leaf axils or in the inflorescence; leaves simple, alternate or opposite or (mostly)
basal, entire, toothed or pinnatifid; flowers perfect, small, solitary or in cymose inflorescences; calyx adnate to the ovary at the base, 5-lobed, the hypanthium well- or weakly-
developed; petals 5, entire, usually white, sometimes marked with yellow or reddish,
greenish or purplish; stamens 10, sometimes petaloid; carpels usually 2, rarely 3 or 4
or 5, free or united, tapering into short beak-like extensions; stigmas capitate and enlarged or truncate; fruit a capsule or a pair of follicles dehiscing along or between the
beaks; seeds numerous.

1. Petals purple or lilac; leaves opposite, crowded and overlapping especially at the
   base..*S. oppositifolia*
1. Petals mostly white; leaves alternate on the stems or basal, sometimes crowded and
   matted at the base of the plant
      2. Plants mostly under 10 cm tall; flowering stems with more than one bract-like leaf
         3. Flowers mostly only 1 or 2 on delicate weak stems; leaves with 3 to 5 lobes ..... *S. debilis*
         3. Flowers mostly over 2 on stronger stems; leaves lobed or not
            4. Leaves lobed; plants glandular-pubescent
               5. Flowering stems several from a densely crowded base; leaves
                  usually 3-parted, sometimes not parted at all on the stem ....*S. caespitosa*
               5. Flowering stem usually solitary from a small basal rosette of
                  toothed leaves; leaf divisions often shallow................................ *S. adscendens*
            4. Leaves not lobed; plants essentially glabrous; stems matted and
               crowded at the base; petals with red spots................................*S. bronchialis*
      2. Plants mostly about 10-40 cm tall; flowering stems not leafy except sometimes for
       a small leaf-like bract; leaves all or nearly all at the base of the plant
         6. Leaf blades broad, circular in outline, the margins sharply-toothed
            7. Teeth of the leaf margin regular and even; leaf petioles not broadened
               at the base; anthers purple.............................. ....*S. odontoloma*

> 7. Teeth of the leaf margin again cleft evenly and regularly into 1 to 3
>   smaller teeth; petioles broader at the base; anthers pink..................*S. mertensiana*
> 6. Leaf blades not circular in outline, definitely longer than broad
>   8. Leaf margins ruffled, wavy or toothed; leaf blades narrowing into the
>   wide petiole; filaments often broader at the top than the bottom........*S. occidentalis*
>   8. Leaf margins entire, not wavy or toothed; leaf blades broader at the
>   base than the tip; anthers yellow, orange or green........................*S. integrifolia*

Saxifraga adscendens L. ssp. **oregonensis** (Raf.) Bacigalupi   Alpine Saxifrage
Densely tufted, glandular-pubescent short-lived perennial with a slender caudex and solitary leafy stems 2-10 cm tall; leaves obovate, 5-15 mm long, ciliate, entire or 3- to 5-toothed or shallowly lobed, the basal densely crowded; cauline leaves 3 to 15, often purplish; flowers few, cymose; calyx campanulate, adnate to the ovary all the way, purplish, 2.5-4 mm long; petals white with 3 greenish nerves, obovate, 3-5 mm long, deciduous; stigmas capitate; capsule 3.5-5 mm long.
Wet cliffs, rock crevices and gravelly meadows, about 9000 feet.

Saxifraga bronchialis L. var. **austromontana** (Wieg.) G. N. Jones   Matted Saxifrage
Matted perennial with leafy creeping horizontal rootstocks and flowering stems 6-15 cm tall; leaves crowded, narrowly lanceolate to obovate, 5-15 mm long, mostly entire, spinulose-ciliate, otherwise glabrous; inflorescence open, flat-topped, usually of 2 to 10 flowers, glabrate or somewhat glandular-puberulent; calyx 1.5-3 mm long, saucer-shaped, glabrous or ciliate, much longer than the hypanthium; petals 3.5-5 mm long, deciduous, white with maroon or orange veins and spots; filaments not dilated above; ovary with short stylar beaks; capsules usually purplish, 4-6 mm long.
Mostly on exposed cliffs and rocky slopes, rock slides and scree but sometimes on gravel bars and rocky streambanks where washed down from above, 5700 to 9600 feet and probably higher.

Saxifraga caespitosa L.   Tufted Saxifrage
Cespitose, often mat-forming, perennial with a woody rootstock and glandular-pubescent stems 3-15 cm tall; leaves mostly 5-10 mm long, glandular-pubescent and villous-ciliate with 3 to 7 obtuse lobes, or the cauline 1 to 5 leaves often entire; flowers 1 to 10 in an open inflorescence, glandular-pubescent, subtended by leafy bracts; calyx cleft about ⅔ of the way, 2.5-6 mm long, turbinate to campanulate, without a free hypanthium; petals white, 5-7 mm long, deciduous; filaments not clavate; capsules 5-7 mm long, adnate to the hypanthium less than halfway up, the carpels united nearly to the top.
Rocky slopes, cliffs and crevices in boulders, 4500 to about 9800 feet.

Saxifraga debilis Engelm.   Weak or Pygmy Saxifrage
Delicate loosely-tufted glabrous to glandular-pubescent perennial from a small root; stems usually several, leafy, 1-10 cm tall; leaves mostly basal, kidney-shaped, 5-15 mm broad with 3 to 7 rounded lobes, thin and glabrous; flowers 1 or 2 on a stem, long-pedicelled; calyx turbinate-campanulate, usually purplish, 3-4 mm long, without a free hypanthium, the sepals obtuse; petals deciduous, white with pinkish veins, 3 or 4 mm long, or up to 6 mm; capsules about 5 mm long, the carpels united halfway or more, the tips divergent.
Moist shady granite cliffs in coniferous forest, 8300 to 9500 feet.

Saxifraga integrifolia Hook.   Fleshy-leaved Saxifrage
Perennial, usually with brittle rhizomes and short corm-like propagules; flowering stems mostly single, leafless, 10-30 cm tall, hairy to nearly glabrous, usually reddish- or purplish-glandular above; leaves elliptic to lanceolate and either wing-petioled or nearly sessile, to ovate or deltoid and with slender petioles; leaf blades mostly 2-4 cm long and about half as wide, entire to sinuate or dentate, glabrous to ciliate or hairy; inflorescence mostly cymose-paniculate, the bracts sometimes rusty-hairy; calyx without a free hypanthium, the lobes 1-2 mm long, spreading or reflexed; petals when present ovate or obovate to oblanceolate, white to greenish or purplish, 1.5-3 cm long, deciduous, sometimes clawed at the base; stamens subulate, shorter than the calyx lobes; carpels distinct or nearly so, inferior, emerging at maturity as follicles 3.5-5 mm long.
Petals white; leaf blades deltoid to ovate or lanceolate, narrowed abruptly to slender petioles as long as the blades or longer, mostly glabrous..var. **claytoniaefolia** (Canby) Rosend.
Petals yellowish or greenish-white to pinkish-purplish; leaf blades mostly ovate, narrowed rather abruptly to slender petioles usually shorter than the blades..var. **columbiana** (Piper) C. L. Hitchc.
Wet or moist rocky streambanks, slopes and meadows, about 4500 to 9800 feet.

Saxifraga mertensiana Bong.   Wood Saxifrage
Succulent herb with bulbiferous rootstocks, tending to form large clumps; flowering stems usually with 1 to 3 leaves near the base, 15-40 cm tall, glabrous or usually soft-hairy and with purplish glands at least above; leaves orbicular, coarsely and doubly dentate, 2-10 cm broad, glabrous or sparsely pubescent, the petioles up to 4 times as long as the blades; stipules well-developed; bulblets usually present in the axils of the basal leaves; inflorescence a large open cyme, the flowers often reduced to pinkish bulbils; calyx parted nearly to the base, the sepals about 2 mm long, reflexed; petals white, obovate or elliptic, 3-5 mm long; filaments white, clavate, petaloid; anthers pink; ovary nearly superior; capsules about 5 mm long, the carpels united more than halfway.
Wet cliffs, rocky slopes and slides, and along streams, 4500 to about 8300 feet.

Saxifraga occidentalis Wats.   Western Mountain Saxifrage
Perennial with short thick rootstocks, usually forming large clumps; flowering stems leafless, curved, pubescent and usually reddish-glandular, 10-25 cm tall; leaves ovate to elliptic, up to 6 cm long, 1.5-3 cm broad, thick, green, toothed, sometimes reddish-tomentose beneath when young; inflorescence bracteate, circular, pyramidal or flat-topped, composed of 1 to several dense clusters; calyx deeply cleft, the tube broad, turbinate, the lobes 1-2.5 mm long; petals white, sometimes with 2 basal yellowish spots, elliptic, with or without a claw, deciduous, about 3 mm long; filaments white to reddish, often petaloid; carpels nearly free to the base with a broad glandular zone, greenish- to dark-reddish-purple, 2.5-6 mm long.
Moist rocky mountain slopes, 4700 feet.

Inflorescence small and compact, mostly less than 5 cm long at anthesis; petals not yellow-spotted; filaments not petaloid, though clavate.................var. **wallowensis** Peck
With the species.

Saxifraga odontoloma Piper   Mountain Meadow Saxifrage
    S. arguta D. Don

Perennial with horizontal rootstocks; stem single, leafless, 20-60 cm tall, glabrous near the base but pubescent with reddish, purplish or yellowish gland-tipped short hairs in the inflorescence; leaves orbicular to kidney-shaped, 2-8 cm broad, glabrous, coarsely crenate-dentate with gland-tipped teeth, the petioles 4-20 cm long; inflorescence an open panicle up to 30 cm long, often purplish; calyx pinkish or purplish, deeply cleft, without a free hypanthium; petals white with 2 or 3 greenish-yellow dots, deciduous, clawed, about 3 mm long; filaments dilated and petaloid above; anthers purple; ovary whitish below, dark purple above; capsules 4-8 mm long, the carpels united about halfway.
Boggy meadows and lake margins, and along streams, 5000 to about 8000 feet.

Saxifraga oppositifolia L.   Purple Saxifrage

Densely tufted and cushion-like caulescent perennial 2-5 cm tall, nearly glabrous, not glandular, often purplish-tinged throughout; leaves thick, pale green turning purple-brown, obovate to oblong, sessile, ciliate, 2.5-5 mm long, crowded, opposite and closely overlapping on the sterile shoots but fewer and often alternate and not overlapping on the flowering stems; flowers solitary at the branch-tips; calyx cup-shaped, deeply parted, 2.5-3.5 mm long, coarsely ciliate, without a hypanthium; petals persistent, obovate to oblong, clawed, purple or lilac, 5-9 mm long; stamens longer than the calyx, the filaments purple, short; styles purplish; stigmas capitate; capsules about 7 mm long, free from the calyx.
Rock crevices and scree above about 9000 feet, but also on a gravel bar at 5500 feet, undoubtedly washed down from above.

Suksdorfia Gray

Glandular pubescent perennials with fibrous roots from bulblet-bearing rootstocks; flowering stems leafy; basal leaves cordate to reniform, crenate to deeply divided, the cauline stipulate; inflorescence cymose; calyx lobes 5, erect, the tube adnate to the lower half of the ovary; petals 5, white or purplish-violet, clawed; stamens 5, opposite the calyx lobes, the filaments purplish; ovary 2-celled with axile placentation, prolonged into 2 style-like beaks; styles free; stigmas capitate; capsules many-seeded.

Suksdorfia ranunculifolia (Hook.) Engl.
    Hemieva ranunculifolia (Hook.) Raf.

Entire plant light to yellowish green; stem usually single from a cluster of bulblets, 10-40 cm tall, glandular-pubescent; lower leaves long-petioled, 1-4 cm broad, kidney-shaped, divided nearly to the base into 3 entire to crenately lobed segments, the 4 to 9 cauline leaves with shorter petioles which are dilated into foliaceous stipules, becoming sessile and without stipules at the inflorescence; inflorescence short, many-flowered; calyx campanulate, purplish, 4-6 mm high; petals white or purplish-tinged fading to yellowish, persistent, 3-6 mm long, not clawed; capsules about 4 mm long.

Tiarella L.

Slender erect rhizomatous herbs with leafy flowering stems; leaves mainly basal, long-petioled, simple or trifoliate; inflorescence a raceme or an elongate leafless panicle;

calyx campanulate, nearly or quite free of the ovary, the 5 lobes unequal; petals 5, clawed or clawless and linear-subulate; stamens 10, conspicuously exserted; ovary superior, 1-celled with 2 parietal placentae becoming nearly basal in fruit; styles 2; stigmas capitate; fruit a few-seeded, membranous capsule with 2 very unequal valves.

Tiarella unifoliata Hook.   Sugar-scoop
T. trifoliata L.

Flowering branches 10-50 cm tall, glabrous to white-hairy, viscid-puberulent to glandular-pubescent above; basal leaves cordate, hairy to glabrate in age, up to 4-12 cm broad, the 3 to 5 lobes unequal, crenate to crenate-dentate with mucronate teeth; cauline leaves 1 to 4, similar but smaller and shorter-petioled; inflorescence a narrow panicle; calyx white to pinkish, mostly 1.5-3 mm long, the upper lobe much longer than the hypanthium; petals white; stamens longer than the calyx; carpels oblong, the larger 9-12 mm long, the smaller 4-6 mm long.
Ravines in moist shady coniferous woods, about 5500 to 5600 feet.

GROSSULARIACEAE   Gooseberry Family

Deciduous shrubs (ours) or trees with simple, alternate, palmately-veined leaves mostly without stipules; flowers usually 2 to several in bracteate racemes, or solitary, perfect, rarely the plants dioecious; calyx at least partially adnate to the ovary and with a free hypanthium, usually persistent, 5-lobed or -parted; petals as many as sepals and usually much smaller; stamens as many as petals, alternate with them and inserted with them near or at the top of the hypanthium; pistil mostly 2-carpellary, the ovary inferior (ours), 1-celled with the styles free or united; fruit a berry (ours) or a capsule.

Ribes L.

Glabrous to pubescent and often glandular shrubs, the glands yellow, crystalline, sessile or stalked; stems sometimes with spines or bristles developed at or between the nodes; leaves alternate, variously lobed and toothed, usually rounded in outline, persistent or deciduous; flowers solitary or 2 to many in terminal or axillary racemes, perfect, mostly regular; calyx 5-lobed with a tubular to rotate often colored hypanthium; petals 5, smaller than the sepals, greenish-white, yellow, white, pink, red or purple; stamens 5, alternate with the petals; carpels 2, the ovary inferior, 1-celled; styles 2; stigmas usually capitate; fruit a many-seeded yellowish, reddish, bluish or black berry.

1. Stems with sharp spines or prickles; flowers mostly pinkish or purplish, 1 to 15 in drooping clusters; berries red to black
    2. Stems thickly covered with straight spines at the leaf nodes and also many shorter prickles in between the nodes; flowers pinkish, 7 to 15; berries glandular, dark black-purple ....*R. lacustre*
    2. Stems with 1 to 5 spines at the leaf nodes but few or no prickles in between the nodes; flowers mostly 1 to 7 in a cluster
        3. Flowers 3-5 mm long mostly; berries red to reddish-purple
            4. Leaves glandular-hairy, 1-2.5 cm broad; flowers 4 to 7 in a cluster; berries reddish ....*R. montigenum*
            4. Leaves 2-6 cm broad, not glandular-hairy; flowers 1 to 4 in a cluster; berries reddish-purple ....*R. inerme*
        3. Flowers 8-11 mm long; plants not glandular; leaves 1.5-3.5 cm broad; berries black ....*R. irriguum*

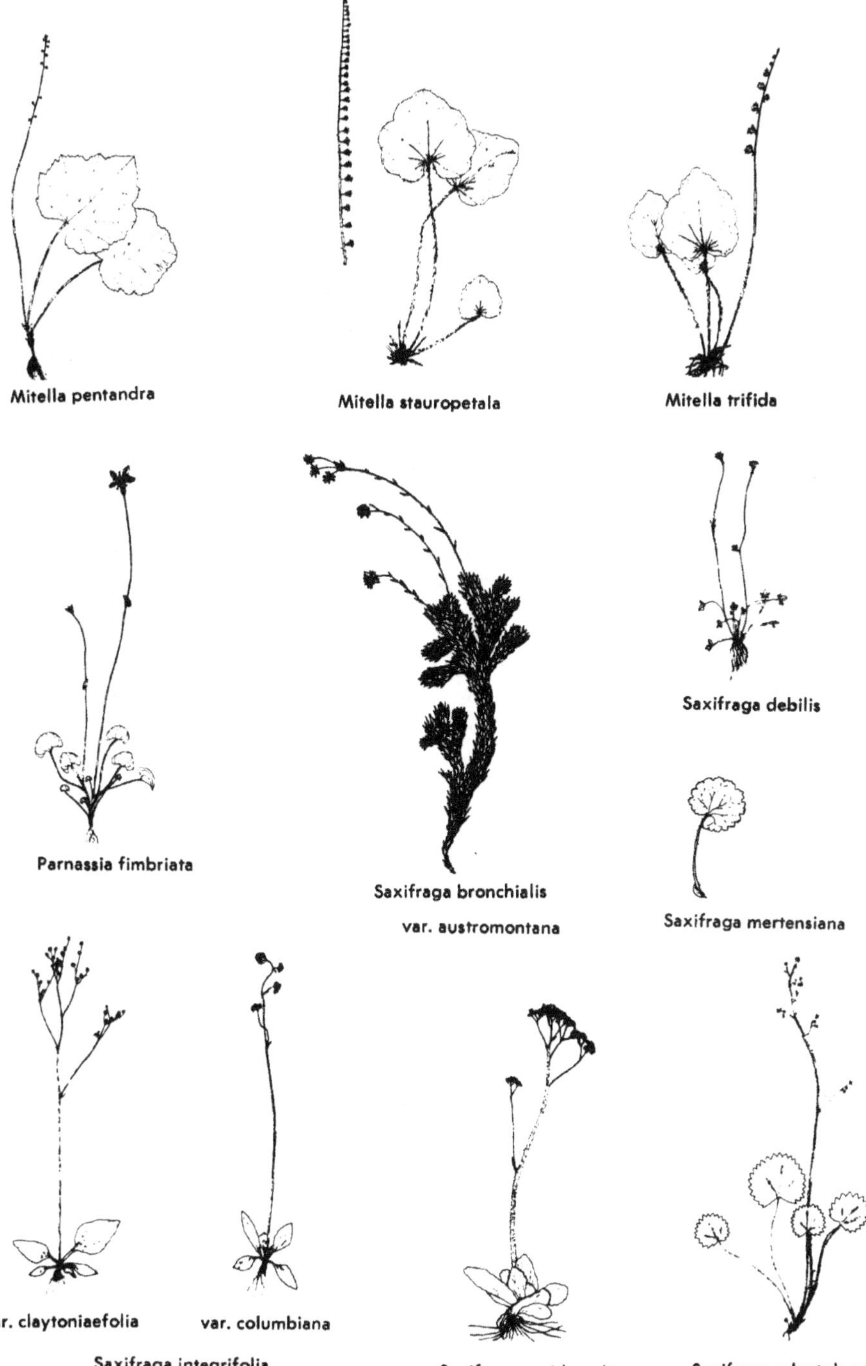

Mitella pentandra
Mitella stauropetala
Mitella trifida
Parnassia fimbriata
Saxifraga bronchialis
var. austromontana
Saxifraga debilis
Saxifraga mertensiana
var. claytoniaefolia
var. columbiana
Saxifraga integrifolia
Saxifraga occidentalis
Saxifraga odontoloma

1. Stems neither spiny nor prickly; flowers pure white to greenish-white and sometimes
    tinged with pink or red, few to over 15 in a cluster; berries red, bluish or black
      5. Flowers pinkish or reddish or creamy but not white or greenish-white
        6. Leaves 1-4 cm broad; flowers narrow, 1-2 mm broad near the base; berry red... *R. cereum*
        6. Leaves 5-8 cm broad; flowers about 5 mm broad near the base; berry deep
          bluish-black ....*R. viscosissimum*
      5. Flowers pure white or greenish-white, not pinkish or purplish; berries black;
        plants strong-scented
        7. Flowers pure white, mostly many more than 15 in an erect inflorescence up to
          17 cm long; leaves glandular on both sides; odor unpleasant ....*R. hudsonianum*
        7. Flowers creamy- or greenish-white, rarely over 10 in a cluster, the cluster
          usually drooping; leaves variously glandular
          8. Plant sticky-glandular with a pleasant odor; leaves glandular on both
            sides; calyx tube cylindric ....*R. viscosissimum*
          8. Plant not sticky-glandular; odor strong, resinous; leaves glandular
            only beneath; calyx tube bell-shaped ....*R. nigrum*

Ribes cereum Dougl.   White Squaw Currant

A much-branched spreading to erect shrub with light gray bark, 50-150 cm tall; leaves
1-4 cm broad, reniform-orbicular, puberulent and often glandular, or glabrate above,
3- to 5-lobed, toothed, pale gray-green; inflorescence pubescent and glandular with
short-stalked to nearly sessile glands; flowers few, crowded on short pendulous racemes;
pedicels jointed under the ovary, much shorter than the broad dentate bracts; calyx
8-10 mm long, white, greenish-white or pinkish, glabrous to pubescent and stipitate-
glandular, the hypanthium nearly cylindric, the lobes spreading-recurved; stamens
shorter than the petals, anthers tipped with a cup-shaped gland; berry dull to bright red.
Dry or moist rocky or gravelly open woods and meadows, 4500 to about 6000 feet.

Ribes hudsonianum Richards. var. **petiolare** Jancz.   Western Black Currant
    R. petiolare Dougl.

An erect shrub, 0.5-1.5 meters tall, glandular all over with sessile, yellow, crystalline
glands and with a strong, sweetish but unpleasant odor; leaves thin, long-petioled, 3.5-9
cm broad, glabrous to hairy, 3- to 5-lobed, toothed; racemes 5-17 cm long, densely
flowered; pedicels jointed below the flowers, much longer than the pointed bracts; calyx
white, saucer-shaped, 7-9 mm wide, gland-dotted, the sepals spreading; petals white,
short; stamens about equaling the petals; berry resinous-dotted, black, 7-12 mm long.
Moist shady coniferous woods, streambanks and thickets, 4500 to about 6000 feet.

Ribes inerme Rydb.   White-stemmed Gooseberry

Glabrous shrub 1-2 meters tall with flaky grayish bark; spines nodal when present,
4-10 mm long, few when present; leaves thin, mostly 2-6 cm broad, glabrous, broadly
ovate, rounded or cordate at the base, crenate-dentate, 3- to 5-lobed; petioles often longer
than the leaf blades; raceme 1- to 4-flowered, drooping, shorter than the leaves; pedicels
not jointed; hypanthium tubular-campanulate, about 3 mm long, greenish to red- or
purplish-tinged; petals white or pinkish, 1-1.5 mm long; stamens about equaling the
calyx lobes, glabrous; berry smooth, reddish-purple, edible.
Streambanks and thickets in meadows and on mountain slopes, about 4500 to 6000 feet.

Ribes irriguum Dougl.   Straggly Inland Black Gooseberry

An erect to widely spreading shrub, 1-3 meters tall with arched, puberulent, grayish

branches and with 1 to 3 straight spines up to 1 cm long at the nodes; leaves mostly 1.5-3.5 cm broad, ovate to cordate with 3 to 5 round-toothed lobes, puberulent on both sides, to glabrous above; racemes 1- to 5-flowered; pedicels short, not jointed; flowers 8-11 mm long; calyx glabrous, the hypanthium campanulate, the lobes twice as long as the tube, spreading, pale greenish or reddish- or purplish-tinged near the base; petals rounded, often fringed, 2-3 mm long, white or slightly pinkish; stamens about equaling the petals, shorter than the calyx lobes; styles slightly longer than the sepals, pilose below; berry globose, nearly black.
Streambanks and open coniferous woods, 4500 to 5500 feet.

Ribes lacustre (Pers.) Poir. Prickly Currant; Swamp Gooseberry
An erect, spreading or nearly prostrate shrub 1-1.5 meters tall with 1 to 3 large spines at the nodes and many weak prickles between the nodes, these sometimes missing; leaves cordate, 2-5 cm broad, the 5 to 7 lobes acute, sharply toothed, thin, glabrous or nearly so, never glandular; racemes 5- to 18-flowered, drooping, 3-4 cm long, usually glandular and puberulent; pedicels jointed just below the flowers; calyx saucer-shaped, pale yellowish-green to dull reddish-brown, the hypanthium lined with a pinkish or purplish disc, the sepals short and broad; petals pinkish, clawed, about half as long as the sepals; stamens shorter or longer than the petals; ovary glandular with reddish- to purplish-tipped hairs; berry dark black-purple, usually glandular.
Moist shady woods, streambanks and drier wooded rocky slopes, 5000 to about 7000 feet.

Ribes montigenum McClatchie Alpine Prickly Currant
Low, straggly, branched shrub 20-100 cm tall, densely short-pubescent and glandular, with slender or bristly internodal spines and 1 to 5 flattened nodal spines mostly 4-6 mm long but sometimes much longer; leaves 1.5-2.5 cm broad, deeply 5-lobed, the lobes deeply cleft and coarsely toothed; racemes short, axillary, 4- to 7-flowered; pedicels 1-5 mm long, jointed; hypanthium saucer-shaped, lined with a thin disc; sepals yellowish-green to pinkish; petals pinkish or purplish; stamens about equaling the petals; ovary glandular-bristly; berry reddish, glandular.
Talus slopes and open rocky places, 5000 to about 8000 feet.

Ribes nigrum L. European Black Currant
Stout shrub 1-2 meters tall with a strong odor; leaves glabrous, 5-10 cm broad, 3- to 5-lobed, glandular beneath, cordate and irregularly serrate; flowers greenish-white; racemes 4- to 10-flowered, pendulous, the bracts small; hypanthium campanulate, pubescent and glandular, the sepals longer than the hypanthium; petals about half as long as the sepals; berry nearly globular, black.
Escaped from cultivation; in moist shady woods near a stream, about 5000 feet.

Ribes viscosissimum Pursh Sticky Currant
Low erect to spreading often straggly shrub about 1 meter tall, soft-pubescent and usually glandular as well; leaves reniform-orbicular in outline, 5-8 cm broad, deeply cordate with 3 to 5 short, rounded, crenate-dentate lobes; petioles dilated at the base, densely glandular-pubescent; racemes 4- to 17-flowered, glandular-pubescent; pedicels jointed, about equaling the herbaceous bracts; ovary glabrous to glandular-pubescent; hypanthium cylindrical; calyx greenish to greenish-white or creamy-white, sometimes

pinkish- or purplish-tinged; petals white or cream, shorter than the calyx lobes; anthers tipped by a small cup-like gland; berry 10-12 mm long, deep bluish-black, glabrous to glandular-pubescent, sometimes glaucous.
Moist or dry, open or shady coniferous woods and along streams, 4500 to about 7000 feet.

HYDRANGEACEAE   Hydrangea Family

Trees, shrubs or vines with simple opposite leaves without stipules; flowers usually perfect and regular, corymbose, racemose or rarely solitary; calyx adnate to the ovary, usually without a free hypanthium, the lobes 4 to 6 or 10; petals 4 to 6, or 10, white, sometimes colored; stamens only 5, or twice as many as the petals, or many; pistil usually 3- to 5-carpellary, the ovary inferior, partially to completely; styles distinct to united; fruit a capsule, often woody; seeds numerous.

Philadelphus L.

Branching shrub with deciduous, entire or toothed, usually petioled leaves; flowers perfect, showy, often fragrant, borne solitary or in few-flowered false racemes or cymes or panicles; calyx adnate to the ovary up to the lobes, without a free hypanthium; sepals 4, rarely 5, persistent; petals white, 4 or 5, showy; stamens usually 20 to 40, rarely fewer than 10; pistil 4-carpellary (sometimes 3- or 5-); ovary inferior, 4-locular; styles united half their length; stigmas linear to capitate; fruit a woody capsule; seeds numerous.

Philadelphus lewisii Pursh   Western Syringa; Mock Orange
Branched deciduous shrub 1-2.5 meters tall; leaves elliptic to ovate, mostly 2-5 cm long, entire or denticulate, sometimes hairy on the veins, otherwise glabrous; flowers fragrant, in few-flowered racemes; calyx lobes 5-6 mm long; petals white, 10-20 mm long, obtuse or rounded and often notched at the tip; stamens 25 to 40, unequal; styles united halfway or more; ovary inferior; capsules ovoid-elliptic, 6-10 mm long.
Hillsides and canyons, up to about 4600 feet.

ROSACEAE   Rose Family

Herbs, shrubs or trees with alternate or basal, simple or compound, deciduous or evergreen leaves; flowers single to numerous, mostly regular; calyx usually free, often with bracteoles alternate with the lobes; sepals 5, or sometimes 4 to 10, seeming to be lobes of the hypanthium; petals 5, or sometimes 4 to 10 or reduced or missing, free, inserted on the rim of the hypanthium; stamens free, usually numerous but sometimes 10 or 5 or fewer; carpels 1 to many, usually free from each other and from the hypanthium; ovary inferior; styles free or united, the stigmas equaling the number of carpels; fruit achenes, follicles or fleshy drupes, drupelets or a single pome.

1. Plants woody, perennial shrubs or trees
   2. Plants mostly shrubs under 1 meter tall, sometimes quite small but woody at the base
      3. Plants thorny or spiny; leaves divided into leaflets
         4. Flowers white; leaves mostly with 3 leaflets; fruit soft and fleshy, often colored .... *Rubus*

4. Flowers pink to deep rose; leaves usually with 5 or more leaflets; fruit hard and dry..*Rosa*
3. Plants not thorny or spiny; leaves divided or not
    5. Leaves thickish, evergreen, toothed, often green above and whitish beneath; plants matted, only a few cm tall; flowers long-stalked, showy, white or yellow..*Dryas*
    5. Leaves not evergreen nor whitish beneath but sometimes toothed; plants taller, not matted; flowers variously colored, sometimes very small, sometimes showy
        6. Leaves and leaflets toothed almost all around except sometimes the very base; flowers white to pink
            7. Flowers 2 to 7 in a cluster, the petals white; leaves 6-15 cm long and a little wider..*Rubus*
            7. Flowers many more than 7 in a dense, conspicuous, flat-topped inflorescence; petals white, pink or red, 1-2 mm long; leaves 1-7 cm long and about half as wide, sometimes not toothed at the base..*Spiraea*
        6. Leaves either with 3 lobes or teeth only at the tips or the leaves not toothed at all; flowers mostly yellow
            8. Leaves not toothed at all, often silky-hairy at least underneath; shrub about 1 meter tall, rounded, with showy bright yellow flowers 1-2 cm in diameter..*Potentilla*
            8. Leaves with 3 lobes or teeth at their tips, often grayish-hairy beneath; shrub 1-2 meter tall, stiffly erect; flowers pale yellow, the petals 6-9 mm long..*Purshia*
2. Plants trees or tall shrubs, mostly over 1 meter tall
    9. Leaves divided into 5 to 11 toothed leaflets; flowers white; fruit orange or reddish; shrub 1-6 meters tall..*Sorbus*
    9. Leaves not divided into leaflets; flowers and fruit various
        10. Flowers very small, either in small inconspicuous clusters or in a large, conspicuous, often drooping inflorescence; leaves toothed or not
            11. Leaves thick, leathery, not at all toothed; plants straggly small trees 2-8 meters tall; flowers inconspicuous, on short shoots; fruit with conspicuous feathery styles..*Cercocarpus*
            11. Leaves toothed, thin; plants shrubs 1-5 meters tall; flowers in a large, branched, showy, often lacy and drooping inflorescence; fruit inconspicuous ....*Holodiscus*
        10. Flowers larger, mostly clustered on shoots; leaves toothed
            12. Plant a tree 2-8 meters tall with scattered sharp thorns 1-7 cm long; leaves sharply toothed; fruit red or black..*Crataegus*
            12. Plants not thorny; flowers white; fruit various
                13. Leaves cleft part-way into 3 to 5 lobes; leaves mostly 4-8 cm long and nearly as wide ....*Physocarpus*
                13. Leaves not cleft into lobes but toothed part or all the way around; plants tall shrubs or trees
                    14. Petals 4-7 mm long; stamens 20 to 25; fruit red, purple or black; leaves 3-10 cm long, toothed all around ....*Prunus*
                    14. Petals 10-20 mm long; stamens 12 to 20; fruit dark purplish; leaves 2-4 cm long, usually not toothed near the base of the leaf..*Amelanchier*
1. Plant not woody, usually smaller annual or perennial herbs
    15. Petals yellow
        16. Inflorescence a long-stalked dense head-like cluster of small flowers; leaves almost entirely basal, much divided; plants often prostrate except for the flowering stalk..*Ivesia*

16. Inflorescence not a dense head; leaves sometimes on the stems as well as at the plant base
    17. Plant a dwarf matted perennial mostly only a few cm tall; leaves and leaflets usually with 3 to 5 teeth only at the tips; flowers small, pale yellow; stamens 5..*Sibbaldia*
    17. Plants not matted, sometimes small perennials but mostly taller annuals or perennials; leaves and leaflets usually toothed all around; stamens 10 to many
        18. Style persistent and often conspicuous and feathery in fruit, not jointed to the ovary; basal leaves broad and well developed at the tip but conspicuously tapering toward the base with regularly smaller and smaller leaflets; plants often pinkish or purplish............................*Geum*
        18. Style deciduous, quite inconspicuous, jointed to the ovary, not feathery in fruit; basal leaves not as above; plants rarely reddish but mostly green..*Potentilla*
15. Petals and flowers not yellow
    19. Basal leaves divided into 3 to 7 leaflets; flowers white, cream, red or purple
      20. Basal leaves usually with only 3 leaflets; flowers white; plants often sending out long stolons which root at the nodes; fruit juicy............................*Fragaria*
      20. Basal leaves mostly divided into 7 leaflets; flowers usually purple or deep red, but sometimes white or cream; fruit dry............................*Potentilla*
    19. Basal leaves divided into more than 7 leaflets, sometimes up to 15, or the leaves all on the stems, not divided and not basal
      21. Flowers greenish, without petals; stamens 2 to 4............................*Sanguisorba*
      21. Flowers white, rose, pink or reddish; stamens more than 4
        22. Leaves divided into many smaller leaflets............................*Geum*
        22. Leaves not divided into leaflets at all............................*Spiraea*

Amelanchier Medic.

Shrubs or small trees with alternate deciduous leaves and small stipules; flowers white, in small racemes; calyx joined at the base to the ovary but with a free hypanthium lined with a glandular disc, the 5 lobes persistent; petals 5; stamens 10 to 20; styles 2 to 5, united; ovary 2- to 5-loculed, nearly or wholly inferior; fruit a 4- to 10-celled, reddish to purplish berry-like pome, dry to rather fleshy.

Amelanchier alnifolia Nutt. var. cusickii (Fern.) C. L. Hitchc.   Serviceberry

Shrubs or sometimes small trees, mostly 1-3 meters tall, eventually grayish-barked; leaves ovate to elliptic, usually 2-4 cm long, sharply serrate all around or only near the tips; raceme short, 3- to 20-flowered; hypanthium glabrous; calyx lobes glabrous on the outside; floccose or lanate inside; petals white, rarely pinkish, 1-2 cm long; styles usually 5; fruit globose, dark purplish, glabrous and glaucous.
Shady woods, mostly near streams or lakes, 4500 to 7450 feet.

Cercocarpus H. B. K.

Small trees or branched shrubs with simple alternate persistent leaves and small stipules; flowers small, apetalous, 1 to several at the tips of short branchlets; hypanthium tube long, persistent, the upper part and the stamens early deciduous; pistil 1; style long-plumose and persistent; fruit a hard achene included in the hypanthium tube.

Cercocarpus ledifolius Nutt.   Mountain Mahogany

A small sometimes straggly tree or shrub 2-8 meters tall, with grayish or reddish furrowed bark; leaves elliptic, thick, evergreen, 1-3 cm long, entire with revolute mar-

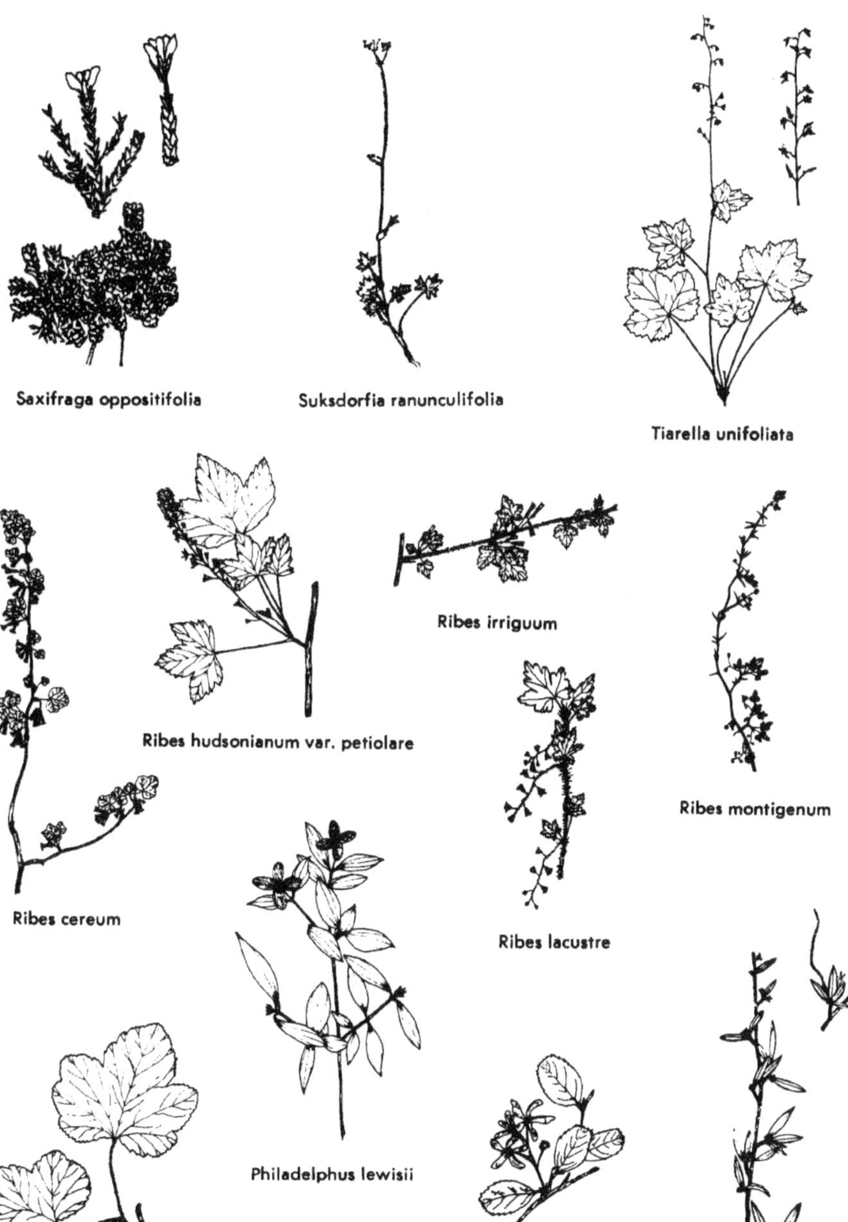

Saxifraga oppositifolia

Suksdorfia ranunculifolia

Tiarella unifoliata

Ribes hudsonianum var. petiolare

Ribes irriguum

Ribes montigenum

Ribes cereum

Ribes lacustre

Philadelphus lewisii

Ribes viscosissimum

Amelanchier alnifolia var. cusickii

Cercocarpus ledifolius

gins, glabrous, green and shining above, densely tomentose and resinous beneath; petioles very short; flowers sessile, 1 to 3 in the leaf axils; stamens numerous; calyx long-hairy; hypanthium 7-10 mm long, tomentose; achenes 5-7 mm long, the plumose tail 3-8 cm long.
Cliffs and open slopes in mixed woods, mostly near streams, 4500 to about 6500 feet.

Crataegus L.

Small thorny trees or shrubs with simple, alternate, petioled, toothed or lobed leaves and small deciduous stipules; flowers in axillary and terminal corymbs; hypanthium saucer-shaped, short, free above the ovary, disc-lined; sepals 5, reflexed; petals 5, white or pink, rounded at the tip; stamens 5 to 25; ovary 1- to 5-celled, inferior; styles 1 to 5, not united; fruit a small pome with 1 to 5 bony, 1-seeded nutlets.

Crataegus columbiana Howell · Thorn-apple; Hawthorn
C. piperi Britt.

Shrub or small branched tree 2-5 meters tall, the thorn usually 2-5 cm long, straight or recurved; leaves pubescent, ovate to obovate, 2-5 cm long, coarsely toothed or lobed, the divisions evenly and finely toothed and often gland-tipped; ovary and hypanthium crisp-pubescent to grayish-lanate; sepals pubescent, often glandular-serrate; petals white, 5-8 mm long; stamens 10; styles 2 to 4, sometimes 5; fruit purple or dark red, glabrous, 8-12 mm long.
Usually along streams at about 4500 feet.

Dryas L.

Low shrubs often forming large patches; leaves alternate, petioled, simple, entire to crenate-serrate; flowers showy, solitary on scape-like peduncles; calyx persistent, to-mentose, 8- to 10-lobed; petals 8 to 10, white or yellow; stamens numerous, borne on the calyx tube; pistils numerous, the styles persistent, elongated and plumose in fruit; fruit a 1-seeded indehiscent achene.

Petals yellow; flowering stem with 1 to 4 leaf-like tiny bracts..*D. drummondii*
Petals white or cream; flowering stem with only one bract, or none..*D. octopetala*

Dryas drummondii Richards. · Drummond's Mountain Avens
Dwarf prostrate shrub usually with freely rooting branches 5-20 cm long; leaves elliptic to obovate, thick, 1-3 cm long, up to 2 cm broad, crenate-serrate, dark green and nearly glabrous above, white-tomentose beneath; scapes 3-25 cm tall; calyx glandular, black-hairy; petals yellow, erect, often glandular and tomentose, 8-12 mm long; styles in fruit plumose, 2.5-4 cm long.
Exposed ridges and slopes at upper elevation but mostly among boulders, and on gravel bars in or near creeks at lower elevations, about 5000 to 9000 feet.

Dryas octopetala L. · White Alpine Mountain Avens
Dwarf prostrate shrub; leaves oblong to linear-lanceolate, 3-12 mm broad, 1-3 cm long, crenate, often strongly revolute-margined and glandular; scapes 3-20 cm tall, tomentose and glandular; calyx tomentose and glandular; petals white or cream-colored, glabrous, 10-12 mm long; achenes plumose-tailed.
Exposed ridges, slopes, ledges, cliffs and boulders, 8000 to 9750 feet and probably higher.

Fragaria L.

Perennial stoloniferous acaulescent herbs with basal, trifoliate, crenate-serrate leaves; flowers 1 or 2 to several on a scape; bractlets 5, alternating with the 5 calyx lobes; petals 5, white or rarely pink; stamens about 20; pistils numerous, borne on a hemispheric or conical receptacle which enlarges and becomes juicy and red in fruit; styles short and filiform; achenes small and nutlike.

Flowering stems mostly longer than the leaves; sepals 4 or 5 mm long..*F. vesca*
Flowering stems mostly shorter than the leaves; sepals 5-8 mm long..*F. virginiana*

Fragaria vesca L. var. **bracteata** (Heller) Davis   Western Strawberry

Rootstocks short and thick, up to 8 cm long; leaves very thin, the leaflets ovate, hairy above, silky beneath, 4-8 cm long; petioles and scapes slender, long-hairy; scapes often equaling or longer than the leaves; cyme loosely spreading, 3- to 15-flowered; calyx silky, sepals 4 or 5 mm long; petals white to pinkish, 8-11 mm long; fruit ovoid, succulent, up to 1 cm broad, the achenes either sunken in shallow pits in the receptacle or usually superficial and prominent.
Moist open woods and sandy mountain meadows, 4500 to 6000 feet.

Fragaria virginiana Duchesne var. **platypetala** (Rydb.) Hall

Broad-petaled Strawberry

Rootstocks thick and woody; leaves firm, the leaflets obovate, distinctly petioled, glabrous and glaucous above, silky beneath, 2-8 cm long; petioles and scapes rather thick, shaggy-hairy; scapes usually shorter than the leaves; cyme open, 2- to 15-flowered; calyx silky-long-hairy, sepals 5-8 mm long; petals white or pinkish, broadly obovate-orbicular, 5-12 mm long; fruit globose, 1-1.5 mm long, the achenes in shallow pits.
Moist woods, streambanks and mountain meadows, 4500 to 8000 feet.

Geum L.

Rhizomatous herbs with pinnately divided mostly basal leaves and few reduced cauline leaves; flowers solitary or in cymes, yellow, white, pinkish, red or purplish; calyx lobes 5, erect or reflexed alternating with the bracteoles; petals 5; stamens numerous, in several series, inserted on a disc at the base of the hypanthium; pistils numerous, the style straight or hooked or bent, often elongate and plumose in fruit.

1. Petals yellow; stem leaves alternate
   2. Fruiting heads roundish, the style hooked at the tip; flowering stems mostly over
     20 cm tall; calyx lobes reflexed
      3. Uppermost leaflet of the basal leaves much larger than the ones below it,
        nearly circular in outline..*G. macrophyllum*
      3. Uppermost leaflet of the basal leaves large but not circular, more nearly
        wedge-shaped as the ones below it, the teeth of the margin sharp and deep ...*G. aleppicum*
   2. Fruiting heads not roundish, the style straight; flowering stems mostly under 20
     cm tall; calyx lobes spreading ....*G. rossii*
1. Petals white or reddish to pinkish-purplish-tinged; stem leaves opposite; fruiting styles
  long and feathery...*G. triflorum*

Geum aleppicum Jaq. var. **strictum** (Ait.) Fern.   Yellow Avens

Perennial with short rhizomes; stems hairy, to 1 m tall; basal leaves several, oblong-obovate, to 15 cm long, lyrate-pinnatifid with 5 to 9 cuneate-obovate segments usually

doubly-toothed, the terminal lobe cuneate like the others, the margins of all deeply incised; cauline leaves several, reduced and becoming 3-lobed above; inflorescence cymose, unsymmetrical, leafy-bracted; hypanthium 3-4 mm long; sepals reflexed, 5-8 mm long; petals yellow, spreading, about equaling the sepals; stamens 60 to 100; receptacle densely short-pubescent; achenes flattened, 3-4 mm long; style of 2 distinct segments, the lower sometimes glabrous, the upper hirsute.
Wet meadows and boggy streambanks, 4500 to about 5500 feet.

Geum macrophyllum Willd.   Large-leaved Avens

Perennial 30-100 cm tall; stems prickly-hairy and often glandular; basal leaves lyrate-pinnatifid; leaflets 9 to 23, irregularly lobed and toothed, the terminal one the largest; cauline leaves few and reduced, with leaf-like stipules; flowers cymose; hypanthium saucer-shaped; sepals reflexed; petals yellow; achenes elliptic, the style in 2 sections, the lower persistent, reddish, hooked at the tip, the upper shorter, pubescent, yellowish, finally deciduous.
Moist woods, meadows and streambanks, 5000 to 6500 feet.

Geum rossii (R. Br.) Ser. in DC.   Slender-stemmed Avens
Sieversia gracilipes Greene

Perennial with thick rootstocks; basal leaves pinnatifid, silvery-sericeous on both sides, 1-15 cm long including the petiole; leaflets oblong in outline, entire or lobed and toothed; cauline leaves several, alternate, reduced; flowering stems 5-30 cm tall, hairy; flowers 1 to 4; calyx often purplish, the sepals 6-10 mm long; petals yellow, spreading, 6-12 mm long; stamens many, inserted near the tip of the hypanthium; pistils few to many; achenes hairy, 2.5-4 mm long; style straight, glabrous and persistent.
Mountain cliffs at high elevations. Reported by W. C. Cusick as "specimen or 2 seen in the Wallowa Mts."

Geum triflorum Pursh   Prairie Smoke; Grandfather's Beard
G. ciliatum Pursh

Perennial, soft-hairy throughout, 30-50 cm tall; basal leaves tufted, 10-20 cm long, pinnately divided, oblanceolate in outline, grayish-puberulent to long hairy; leaflets 9 to 20, lobed and toothed; flowering stems 1 to several in a cluster, with a pair of reduced opposite leaves at about the middle; flowers 1 to 9, mostly cymose; calyx reddish-purple to pink or nearly yellow with red veins, the bracteoles usually spreading, the sepals erect or converging, 8-12 mm long, petals white or yellow to pinkish or purplish-reddish tinged; achenes about 3 mm long, the lower style section plumose, purplish, 2.5-5 cm long, the upper section glabrous, 3-4 mm long.
Dry open slopes, meadows and cliffs, 4500 to 7200 feet.

Holodiscus Maxim.

Shrubs with alternate, simple, lobed or toothed leaves without stipules; flowers small, numerous, in loose pubescent panicles or racemes; calyx 5-lobed, the hypanthium saucer-shaped; petals 5, white, deciduous; stamens usually 20, inserted just above the disc lining the hypanthium; pistils 5; achenes hairy, 1-seeded, indehiscent.

Holodiscus discolor (Pursh) Maxim.   Ocean Spray
Erect shrub 1-5 meters tall; leaves petioled, ovate, 3-10 cm long, lobed to often double-

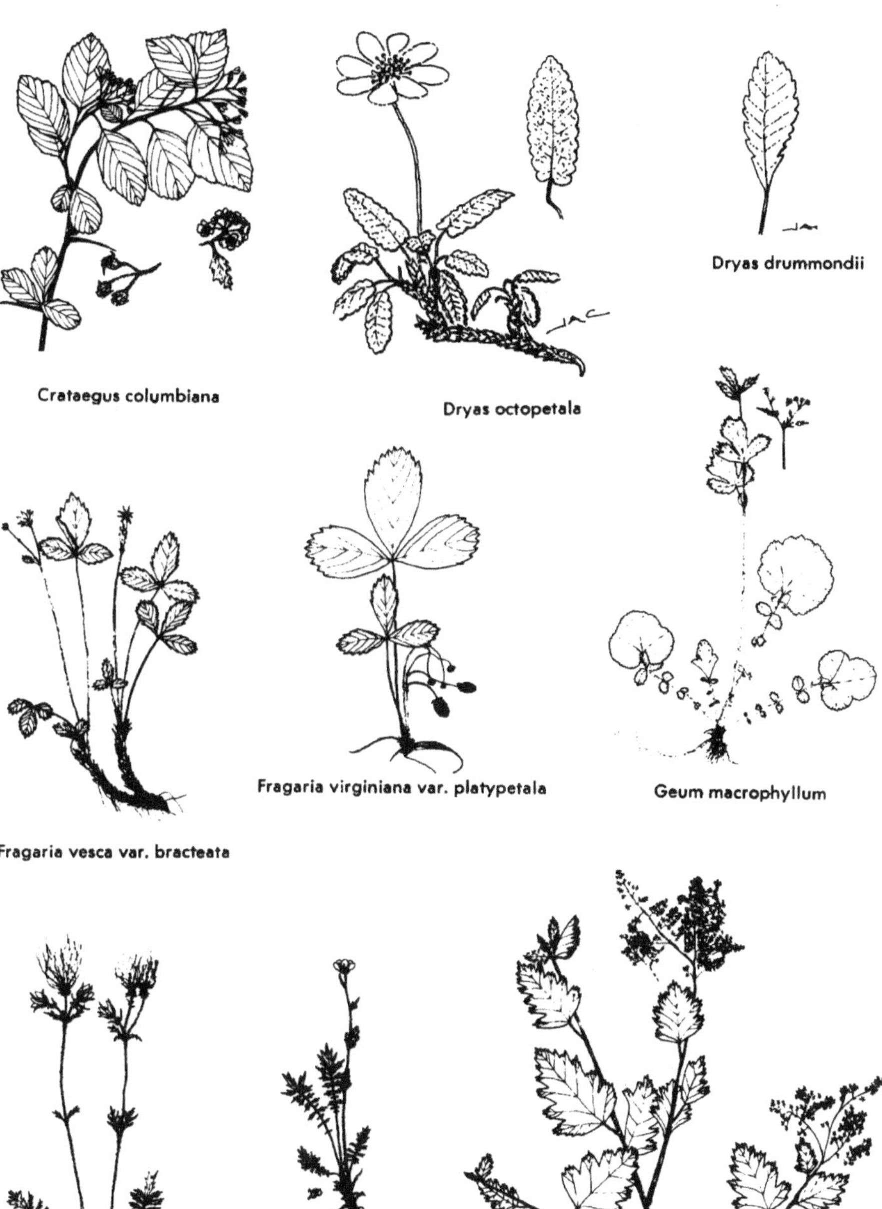

Dryas drummondii
Crataegus columbiana
Dryas octopetala
Fragaria virginiana var. platypetala
Geum macrophyllum
Fragaria vesca var. bracteata
Geum triflorum
Geum rossii
Holodiscus discolor

toothed, glabrous to pubescent above, long-hairy to tomentose beneath; inflorescence a large often nodding panicle, 7-20 cm long; sepals acutish, about 1.5 mm long; petals white, elliptic; achenes hairy, about 2 mm long.
Open woods, mostly near streams, 4600 to about 5000 feet.

Ivesia T. & G.

Perennial herbs, often glandular, with pinnately-divided mostly basal leaves and pentamerous flowers in open or dense cymes; hypanthium saucer-shaped to turbinate or campanulate; calyx lobes alternating with the bracteoles; petals deciduous, yellow (ours), white or purplish; stamens 5 (ours), sometimes more; pistils 1 to many, the style straight; fruit an achene.

Ivesia gordonii (Hook.) T. & G. Alpine Ivesia
Stems slender, 5-20 cm tall, minutely glandular; basal leaves numerous, puberulent and glandular, 4-16 cm long; leaflets usually in crowded pairs, deeply divided; cauline leaf usually solitary; cymes dense, hairy and glandular; calyx campanulate, yellowish; petals yellow, equaling or shorter than the calyx; stamens 5; pistils 1 to 6.
Mostly in sandy or gritty soil on exposed ridges and slopes, 8000 to 9600 feet or higher.

Physocarpus Maxim.

Shrubs with loose outer exfoliating bark and simple, petioled, palmately-lobed leaves; flowers in terminal corymbs; hypanthium campanulate, stellate-pubescent; petals 5, white; stamens 20 to 40, inserted at the edge of the disc; pistils 1 to 5; fruit 1 to 5 inflated dehiscent several-seeded follicles.

Physocarpus malvaceus (Greene) Kuntze Ninebark
Shrub 1-2 meters tall with grayish, shredding bark; leaves petioled, orbicular or ovate, 3- to 5-lobed, crenate-dentate, 3-6 cm long, glabrous to stellate-pubescent; calyx stellate-pubescent; petals equaling the calyx lobes; follicles usually 2, stellate-pubescent, united about half their length.
Rocky hillsides and moist open mixed woods, 4800 to about 5300 feet.

Potentilla L.

Herbs or shrubs with mostly compound, alternate, stipulate leaves; flowers solitary or in cymes; calyx with a saucer-shaped hypanthium, the 5 lobes alternating with the bracteoles; petals 5, usually yellow, sometimes white, reddish or purple; stamens 10 to 30, inserted on the disc near the base of the receptacle; pistils many, the style basal, lateral, or terminal or nearly so, deciduous, filiform to thickened at the middle; achenes smooth to reticulate.

1. Plant a yellow-flowered shrub, or the plant not a shrub and the flowers reddish or purplish
    2. Plant a well-rounded shrub nearly 1 meter tall with silky-hairy leaves and bright yellow flowers...*P. fruticosa*
    2. Plant not shrubby, usually in marshy places; leaves not silky-hairy; flowers reddish to purple...*P. palustris*
1. Plants yellow- to cream- to white-flowered, not shrubby
    3. Basal leaves oblong, the leaflets opposite each other on the petiole
        4. Flowering stems mostly 5-10 cm tall; petals 1-2 mm longer than the sepals

     5. Plants grayish-hairy; petiole of the basal leaves shorter than the leaf
blade..*P. ovina*
     5. Plants yellowish-green, glandular; petiole of the basal leaves 1 or 2
times longer than the blade...*P. brevifolia*
    4. Flowering stems mostly 15-100 cm tall; petals often pale and almost white,
slightly shorter or longer than the sepals; plant glandular at least in the
inflorescence
      6. Plants mostly under 40 cm tall; inflorescence often much branched,
spreading, open...*P. glandulosa*
      6. Plants mostly over 40 cm tall; inflorescence usually narrow and long,
the branches if any not spreading...*P. arguta*
  3. Basal leaves circular or semi-circular in outline but not oblong, the leaflets all
radiating from the same point of the leaf
    7. Basal leaves divided into 3 toothed leaflets
      8. Petals decidedly longer than the sepals; stem leaves only 1 or 2; all
leaflet margins shallowly cleft or toothed; plants nearly hairless, of high
elevations...*P. flabellifolia*
      8. Petals about half as long as the sepals; stem leaves many more than 2,
the margins toothed; plants much-branched usually, fine-hairy, of lower
elevations...*P. millegrana*
    7. Basal leaves divided into more than 3 leaflets, usually 5, the margins some-
times cleft or lobed almost to the midvein
      9. Leaves densely white-hairy beneath, green above, the lobe-like teeth
cleft more than halfway to the midvein; plants sometimes to 80 cm tall,
usually at low to middle elevations...*P. gracilis*
      9. Leaves green and inconspicuously hairy on both sides, the margins cleft
less than halfway to the midvein; plants mostly under 40 cm tall,
usually at high elevations...*P. diversifolia*

Potentilla arguta Pursh   Sharp-toothed Cinquefoil

Perennial herb, glandular-villous, 30-100 cm tall; basal leaves several, pinnate, 10-25
cm long; leaflets 7 to 9, the upper obovate, the lower smaller and more orbicular, coarsely
doubly serrate; inflorescence cymose, many-flowered, narrow, compact and strictly
erect; calyx glandular, the hypanthium saucer-shaped, the lobes 5-8 mm long and flared
at anthesis, but longer and erect in fruit; petals yellow, cream or white, obovate; styles
thickened at the middle and tapered at each end, inserted near the middle of the ovary.
Moist mountain meadow, 6400 feet.

Potentilla brevifolia Nutt.   Short-leaved Cinquefoil

Yellowish-green glandular-puberulent perennial herb 5-20 cm tall; basal leaves pinnate, long-petioled; leaflets 3 to 7, crowded, 6-10 mm long, orbicular to obovate, cleft
and crenate; cauline leaves few and reduced; hypanthium 4-5 mm broad, glandular-
puberulent; sepals ovate, glandular; petals yellow, obovate, spreading; stamens usually
20; pistils numerous, the style slender, attached above the middle of the ovary; achenes
smooth and greenish.
Exposed slopes, 8900 feet.

Potentilla diversifolia Lehm.   Mountain Meadow Cinquefoil

Perennial with slender clustered stems 10-45 cm tall, long-hairy, tomentose or nearly
glabrous with age; leaves mainly basal, palmate or pinnate; leaflets 5 to 7, oblanceolate
to obovate, mostly 1-3 cm long, toothed or lobed, pubescent with shaggy hairs; inflorescence open; sepals 4-5 mm long; petals bright yellow, obovate or obcordate, mostly 4-6

mm long; stamens usually 20, style slender, nearly terminal on the ovary.
Moist mountain meadows at lower elevations to alpine rocky slopes and ledges at higher elevations, 5700 to about 9600 feet.

Potentilla flabellifolia Hook.   Fringe-leaf Cinquefoil
 Perennial forming large clumps; stems minutely puberulent, slender, 15-30 cm tall; basal leaves long-petioled, ternate, short-pubescent to glabrate; leaflets 1-3 cm long, thin, cuneate-obovate to flabelliform, deeply crenate-dentate; cauline leaves 1 or 2 and reduced; flowers few; calyx saucer-shaped, long-hairy; petals yellow, obcordate, about 1 cm long; styles long and filiform, attached near the tip of the ovary; achenes smooth. Wet meadows and mossy lake banks, talus slopes and alpine ridges and cliffs, 5200 to about 8500 feet.

Potentilla fruticosa L.   Shrubby Cinquefoil
 Rounded, branching shrub 10-120 cm tall, the bark shredding; leaflets 3 to 7, crowded, 1-2 cm long, entire, grayish beneath, silky-hairy; flowers solitary or in small open clusters; calyx long-hairy, 7-8 mm long; hypanthium saucer-shaped; petals yellow, 5-15 mm long; achenes hairy.
Moist rocky meadows, mountain slopes, gravel bars and rock slides, 5000 to nearly 9900 feet.

Potentilla glandulosa Lindl.   Sticky Cinquefoil
 Glandular-hairy perennial; stems 15-50 cm tall, branching above; lower leaves pinnate, 10-30 cm long; leaflets 5 to 9, obovate, 1-3 cm long, thin, once or twice serrate; stem leaves reduced; inflorescence a leafy-bracted, several-flowered, open cyme; calyx about 7 mm long but up to 12 mm in fruit, the lobes triangular-ovate; petals deep yellow to cream or nearly white; style thickened at the middle and tapered at both ends, attached to the ovary below the middle.
Style filiform or nearly so to the base..............var. **glandulosa** (*P. rhomboidea* Rydb.)
Open woods, meadows and slopes, 5000 to about 7200 feet.

Potentilla gracilis Dougl.   Slender Cinquefoil
 Perennial 40-80 cm tall, commonly silky-hairy; leaves palmately-divided with 5 to 7 leaflets, long-petioled, oblanceolate, 2-8 cm long, nearly glabrous to hirsute, glandular, cleft halfway to the midrib or less, the teeth lanceolate, glabrous to pubescent above, densely white-tomentose underneath; cymes usually large and many-flowered; calyx often glandular and silky-pubescent, the lobes 6-7 mm long; petals yellow, longer than the sepals; style attached near the top of the ovary.
Plants taller; leaflets cleft over halfway to the midrib and more pubescent above, the lobes oblong-linear, about 1 cm long..var. **blaschkeana** Jepson
Plants taller than the species usually; leaflets deeply cleft, the lobes narrowly linear, revolute-margined, 1-2 cm long..var. **flabelliformis** Nutt.
Sunny mountain meadows, 5200 to about 7000 feet.

Potentilla millegrana Engelm.   Loose-flowered Cinquefoil
 Plant usually biennial; stems weak, sometimes decumbent, usually branched, very leafy, 15-80 cm tall, soft-pubescent or glabrate; leaves 3- to 5-foliate, pubescent; leaflets thin, 1-6 cm long, deeply serrate, oblanceolate to obovate; inflorescence leafy and open;

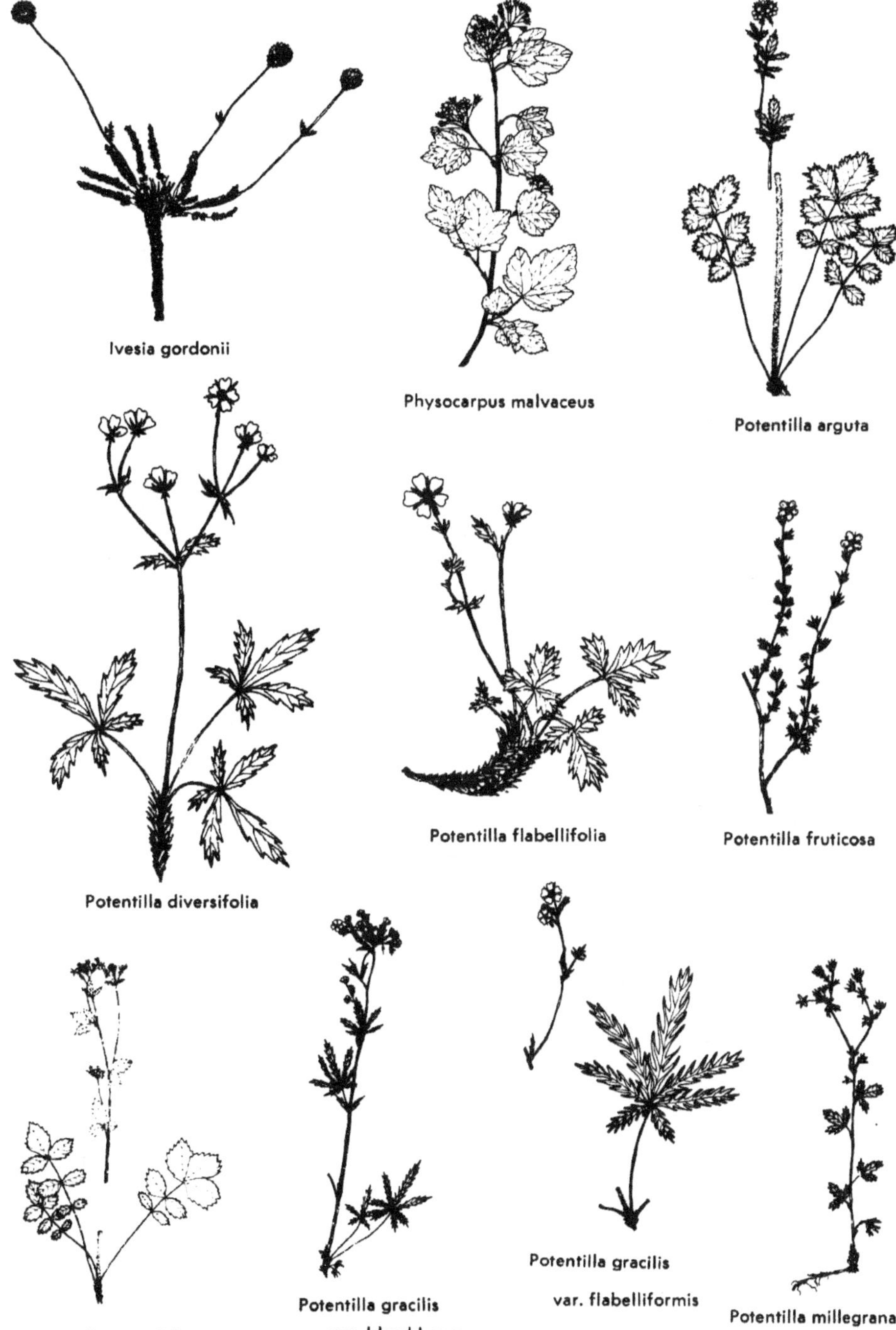

Ivesia gordonii

Physocarpus malvaceus

Potentilla arguta

Potentilla diversifolia

Potentilla flabellifolia

Potentilla fruticosa

Potentilla glandulosa

Potentilla gracilis
var. blaschkeana

Potentilla gracilis
var. flabelliformis

Potentilla millegrana

calyx soft-pubescent, often glandular, the lobes 4-5 mm long; petals pale yellow, shorter than the calyx lobes; achenes smooth, white or yellowish; style attached to the top of the ovary.
Moist ground in shady woods, 4650 feet.

Potentilla ovina Macoun

Perennial, mostly sericeous-hirsute and usually grayish; stems 2-15 cm tall; basal leaves tufted, pinnate, short-petiolate; leaflets 5-12 mm long, 9 to 21, deeply divided into 3 to 7 linear segments; cymes open, 3- to 7-flowered; calyx bowl-shaped, about 1 cm broad; petals yellow, obcordate, slightly longer than the sepals; style slender, attached near the top of the ovary.
Reported by William C. Cusick: "High ridges of the Wallowa Mts., 9000 feet alt. July 31, 1899." Apparently not collected since.

Potentilla palustris (L.) Scop.   Purple or Marsh Cinquefoil
Comarum palustre L.

Perennial with floating or prostrate usually reddish stems 20-60 cm long, often creeping and rooting at the nodes, pubescent and glandular above; leaves pinnate, the lower ones long-petioled; leaflets 5 to 7, oblong to oval, 2-6 cm long, sharply serrate; flowers several, wine-purple to red; calyx glandular and hirsute, 15 mm long, the sepals acuminate, greenish-purple; petals shorter than the sepals; style reddish, attached at about the middle of the ovary.
Bogs and swampy lake margins, Duck Lake, 5600 feet.

Prunus L.

Shrubs or trees with alternate serrate leaves; flowers in racemes, corymbs or umbels, or solitary on short shoots; calyx deciduous; petals white, pink or red; stamens 20 to 30, the filaments long; pistil 1; fruit usually a 1-seeded drupe with a hard bony endocarp surrounded by a fleshy, juicy mesocarp.

Flowers up to 10 in small, short, leafless clusters; fruit bright red to almost black, elliptic, very bitter..*P. emarginata*
Flowers many more than 10 in a longer, oblong inflorescence with 2 or more leaves at the base; fruit deep red, purple, or black, roundish, edible but puckery ....*P. virginiana*

Prunus emarginata (Dougl.) Walp.   Bitter Cherry

Shrub or small tree 1-15 meters tall; leaves elliptic to obovate, 2-8 cm long, glandular-serrate; flowers in few-flowered corymbose clusters; calyx lobes short, entire; petals obovate, 5-7 mm long, often pubescent; stamens about 20; fruit glabrous, bright red to almost black, 8-12 mm long, very bitter.
Moist woods, along streams and on dry open rocky slopes, 5000 to about 6000 feet.

Prunus virginiana L. var. melanocarpa (A. Nels.) Sarg.   Western Choke Cherry
P. demissa Walp. ssp. *melanocarpa* A. Nels.

Shrub or small tree 1-5 meters tall; leaves elliptic, oblong-ovate or oblong-obovate, serrate, 3-10 cm long; flowers in many-flowered terminal racemes; calyx lobes short, finely glandular-erose; petals orbicular, 5-6 mm broad; stamens about 25; drupe red to purple or black, 8-11 mm long, sweet and edible but astringent.
Wooded slopes, thickets and along streams, about 4500 to 5500 feet.

Purshia DC.

Shrubs with alternate, fascicled, deeply 3-cleft, usually glandular leaves; flowers solitary on short branches; sepals 5, spreading; petals 5, yellow; stamens about 25, inserted at the top of the persistent funnel-shaped hypanthium; pistils 1 or rarely 2, the style short; fruit a large beaked achene.

Purshia tridentata (Pursh) DC.   Antelope or Bitter Brush

A rigidly-branched shrub 1-3 meters tall; leaves wedge-shaped, 5-30 mm long, 3-toothed at the tip, pubescent to glabrate above and tomentose beneath, the margins usually revolute; flowers solitary, nearly sessile; calyx glandular and tomentose, 5-8 mm long; petals 5-9 mm long, yellow; achene thick in the middle and tapered at each end, pubescent and glandular, about 1 cm long.

Dry stony woods, mostly under Ponderosa pine, about 5800 feet.

Rosa L.

Prickly shrubs or vines with odd-pinnate leaves; stipules well developed; flowers large, solitary or in clusters; sepals 5; petals 5, pink to deep rose, yellow or white; stamens many, inserted on the silky disc lining the hypanthium; pistils many, free from each other and the hypanthium; fruit a bony achene enclosed in the reddish berry-like hypanthium (the hip).

1. Flowers mostly single, sometimes 2 or 3 together; petals 1-4 mm long
  2. Petals mostly 1-1.5 cm long, the calyx lobes without an expanded tip.................*R. gymnocarpa*
  2. Petals mostly 2.5-4 cm long, the calyx lobes with a long expanded tip......................*R. nutkana*
1. Flowers usually more than 2 or 3 together; petals 1.2-2.5 cm long.........................*R. woodsii*

Rosa gymnocarpa Nutt.   Little Wild Wood Rose

Slender shrub 30-150 cm tall, mostly with slender straight prickles; petioles and rachis very slender and usually glandular; leaflets 5 to 9, thin, 1-3 cm long, elliptic to oval, glabrous, mostly doubly serrate with gland-tipped teeth; flowers usually solitary; petals pink to deep rose, 1-1.5 cm long; hypanthium glabrous, ellipsoid, 1.5-3 mm thick at anthesis; pedicels stipitate-glandular; mature hips ovoid to ellipsoid, the free upper part of the hypanthium early deciduous.

Shady moist woods, about 4500 to 4600 feet.

Rosa nutkana Presl   Nootka Rose

Stems stout, 0.5-4 meters tall, usually with large paired prickles; stipules 1-2 cm long, glandular-toothed; petioles and rachis usually puberulent and often glandular; leaflets usually 7, elliptic or ovate, 1-7 cm long, usually doubly serrate with glandular teeth; flowers large, usually solitary; hypanthium 5-9 mm thick at anthesis, glabrous, sometimes with gland-tipped bristles on the back; sepals 1.5-4 cm long, often with leaf-like tips, glandular-toothed, usually glabrous; petals pink to deep rose, 2.5-4 cm long; hips purplish, globose, 1-2 cm long and thick in fruit.

Open woods in the foothills, 4500 to about 500 feet.

Stems more slender; leaflets and rachis sometimes glandular, sometimes not, otherwise glabrous or finely pubescent, coarsely toothed, the teeth usually not gland-tipped..................var. **hispida** Fern. (*R. spaldingii* Crepin). With the species.

Rosa woodsii Lindl. var. **ultramontana** (Wats.) Jeps.   Interior Rose

Shrubs 1-3 meters tall, the stems stout and with mostly straight prickles; leaflets about 7, elliptic to oval, coarsely serrate, the teeth not gland-tipped, 2-5 cm long, glabrous above, puberulent and often pruinose and minutely glandular beneath; flowers small, mostly in small corymbs; hypanthium glabrous, 3-5 mm thick at anthesis; sepals 1-2 cm long, usually expanded at the tip, glabrous or puberulent but not glandular; petals pink to deep rose, 1.5-2.5 cm long; hips globose to ellipsoid, 6-12 mm long and broad. Moist to dry open mixed woods, 4500 to about 5000 feet.

Rubus. L.

Perennial shrubs or trailing vines, often prickly, with alternate, simple to compound leaves; stipules well-developed; flowers perfect or imperfect, large, single to few, terminal or axillary, white, red or purple; hypanthium saucer-like, bractless; sepals 5; petals 5; stamens numerous; pistils several to many, borne on a conical, convex or flat receptacle; fruit composed of an aggregation of pulpy drupelets.

1. Stems prickly; leaves sometimes prickly on the back
    2. Prickles hooked or flattened, thickish; flowers mostly 2-7 together; fruit dark reddish blue to black..*R. leucodermis*
    2. Prickles straight, sometimes slightly flattened, not so thick; flowers 1 to 4 together; fruit yellowish to red..*R. idaeus*
1. Stems not prickly; leaf blades mostly over 5 cm broad; flowers 2 to 9 together..............*R. parviflorus*

Rubus idaeus L.   Western Red Raspberry

R. melanolasius Focke

Stems slender, 0.5-2 meters tall, bristly, the bark purple or yellow, often glaucous and flaking off; leaves with 3 to 5 leaflets; stipules 4-10 mm long; petioles, rachis and midveins usually bristly and glandular; leaflets 3-10 cm long, ovate to broadly lanceolate, sharply but irregularly toothed, usually nearly glabrous above and densely grayish-lanate beneath; inflorescence a short terminal or axillary raceme, glandular-hispid; calyx lobes about 4-8 mm long, reflexed; petals white, about 5 mm long; fruit light red, the drupelets tomentose.
Streambanks and open rocky slopes and meadows in moist woods, 4500 to about 6500 feet.

Rubus leucodermis Dougl.   White-stemmed Blackcap

Deciduous perennial with erect, glaucous, hooked-prickly stems 40-90 cm long; leaves with 3 to 5 leaflets; leaflets ovate, doubly serrate, sometimes lobed, 1.5-8 cm long, white-tomentose beneath; petioles, veins and peduncles prickly; stipules with stalked glands; flowers 2 to 7 in a corymb; calyx tomentose, often glandular, the lobes 8-10 mm long, reflexed; petals white, shorter than the sepals; fruit a reddish-purple to black finely tomentose raspberry 8-12 mm broad.
Open woods, about 4200 feet.

Rubus parviflorus Nutt.   Thimble Berry

Upright shrub 0.5-2.5 meters tall, puberulent and glandular but without prickles; leaves 5-15 cm broad, orbicular, pale and pubescent beneath, with 5 to 7 acute dentate lobes; petioles and peduncles glandular-hairy; flowers few, white, 2-4 cm broad, in

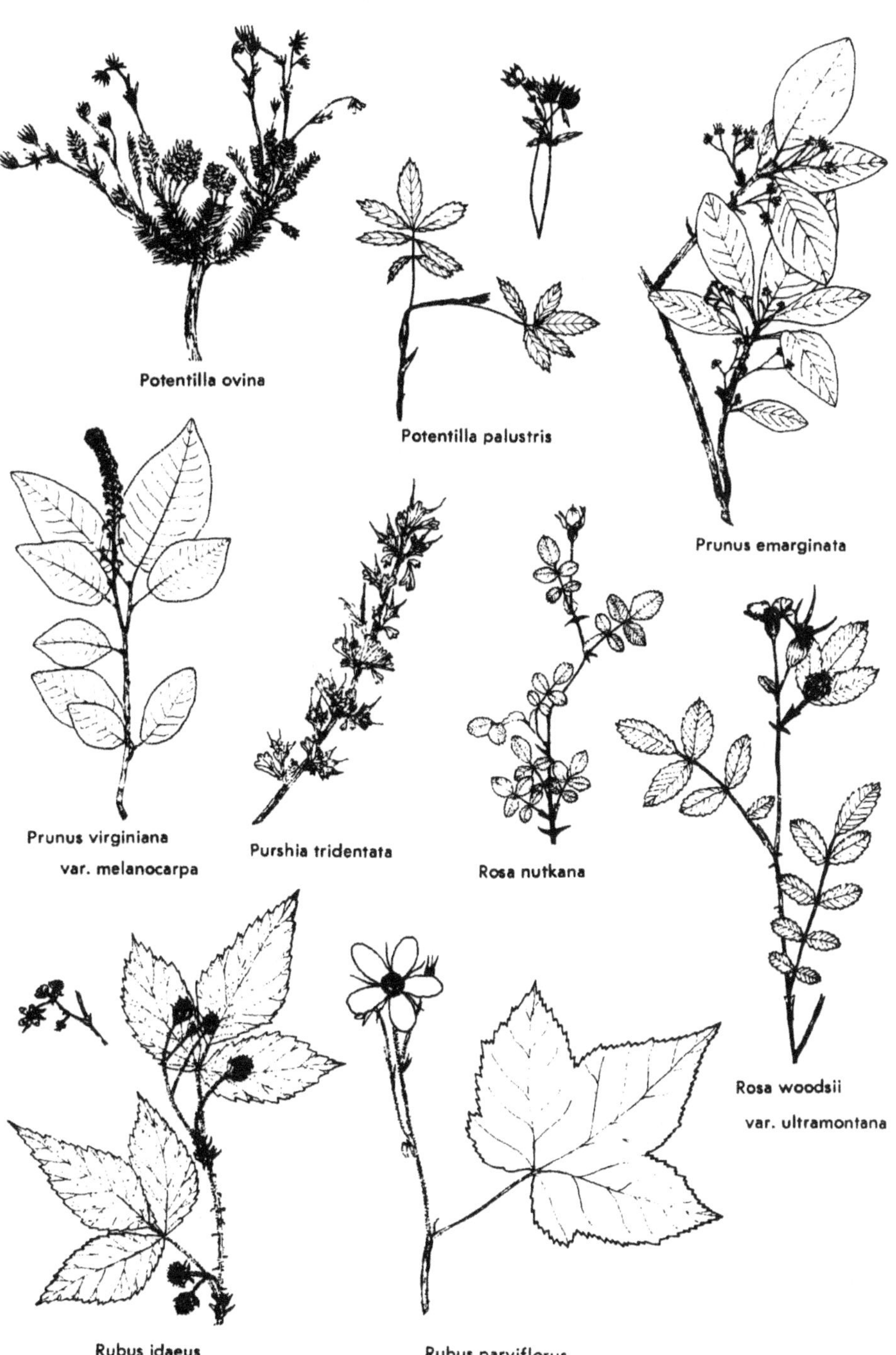

Potentilla ovina
Potentilla palustris
Prunus emarginata
Prunus virginiana
var. melanocarpa
Purshia tridentata
Rosa nutkana
Rosa woodsii
var. ultramontana
Rubus idaeus
Rubus parviflorus

terminal corymbs or flat-topped panicles; sepals long-appendaged, 1-1.5 cm long; fruit hemispheric, bright red, 1.5-2 cm broad.
Moist coniferous shady woods, usually near streams, 4500 to about 5800 feet.

Sanguisorba L.

Annual or perennial herbs with alternate, pinnately compound leaves and toothed or cleft leaflets; stipules free or united; flowers small, apetalous, perfect or imperfect, in dense terminal spikes or heads; hypanthium urn-shaped; sepals 4, petaloid, deciduous; stamens 2 or 4, or many; pistil 1, free from the hypanthium; fruit a one-seeded achene, enclosed in the quadrangular, winged hypanthium.

Sanguisorba occidentalis Nutt.   Western Great Burnet
Glabrous annual or biennial herb with branching leafy stems 10-60 cm tall; leaves pinnate-pinnatifid, 3-8 cm long; leaflets 11 to 17, deeply cleft or parted into linear segments; stipules simple to dissected like the leaflets; spikes cylindric, up to 3 cm long; flowers perfect, about 2-3 mm long; sepals 2 mm long, green with whitish margins; petals none; stamens usually 2; stigmas tufted, slender; fruiting hypanthium quadrangular, ellipsoid, about 3 mm long, narrowly winged.
Dry grassy woodlands (but moist in early spring), about 4500 to 6000 feet.

Sibbaldia L.

Dwarf perennial usually tufted herbs with trifoliate leaves and inconspicuous cymose flowers; hypanthium shallowly campanulate; sepals and bractlets 5; petals 5; stamens 5; pistils 5 to 20, the style lateral; fruit an achene.

Sibbaldia procumbens L.   Sibbaldia
Dwarf mat-forming perennial; leaves petioled, 3-foliolate; leaflets cuneate-obovate, 1-2 cm long with 3 to 5 apical teeth, slightly pubescent on both sides; stipules large, brown and scarious; peduncles nearly leafless, axillary, 4-8 cm tall; inflorescence few-flowered; calyx 4-5 mm long; petals yellow, shorter than the sepals; fruit a stipitate achene.
Moist rocky meadows, boggy lake borders and forest slopes and openings, mostly at higher elevations, 5800 to about 9200 feet and possibly higher.

Sorbus L.

Shrubs or trees with alternate, deciduous, pinnate to simple leaves with serrate leaflets and deciduous stipules; flowers perfect and regular, in large terminal compound corymbs; calyx united almost to the top of the ovary, with a short, disc-like, free hypanthium, the 5 lobes persistent; petals 5, white; stamens 15 to 20; ovary compound, inferior; styles 2 to 5, not united; fruit a fleshy, small, red to orange berry-like pome.

Leaflets oblong-elliptic, the tips tapering to a point at both ends, the marginal teeth small
  and fine; fruit orange to scarlet, not with a bluish tinge..*S. scopulina*
Leaflets wider, oval-oblong, the tips not tapered, rather broad and rounded or blunt, the
  marginal teeth larger and more pronounced; fruit red, with a bluish tinge....................*S. sitchensis*

Sorbus scopulina Greene var. **cascadensis** (G. N. Jones) C. L. Hitchc.   Rowan Tree
Shrub 1-6 meters tall; young growth grayish-hairy, stipules green, linear; leaflets

mostly 7 to 11, narrowly oblong-elliptic to oblong-lanceolate, 2-8 cm long, acute to acuminate at the tip, finely and sharply serrate almost to the base, glabrous and dark green above, pale beneath and sometimes long-hairy; inflorescence nearly flat-topped, pubescent, 70- to over 200-flowered; carpels 3 or 4; fruit orange to scarlet, about 1 cm long. Occasional in moist mixed woods, 4600 to about 6500 feet.

Sorbus sitchensis Roem.   Mountain Ash
S. occidentalis Greene

Shrub 1-4 meters tall; young growth reddish-brown-long-hairy; stipules brownish, reddish-pubescent; leaflets 7 to 11, oval-oblong to oblong-obovate, 2-7 cm long, rounded to semi-truncate at the tip, coarsely serrate to nearly entire, glabrous and dark green above, pale beneath and reddish-hairy on the midvein; inflorescence rounded, 15- to 80-flowered; carpels 4 or 5; fruit red, glaucous with a bluish cast, about 1 cm long. Occasional in moist mixed woods, 4600 to about 6500 feet.

Spiraea L.

Deciduous shrubs with simple toothed leaves; flowers small, perfect, in dense corymbs or panicles; calyx small and persistent; sepals 5; petals 4, white to pink, rose or purplish; stamens numerous, inserted under the margin of the disc; pistils 3 to 8, usually 5; fruit a small follicle.

Flowers white; inflorescence 5-15 cm broad .... *S. lucida*
Flowers deep rose; inflorescence 2-5 cm broad .... *S. densiflora*

Spiraea densiflora Nutt.   Mountain Meadow-sweet

A low shrub 20-100 cm tall, glabrous to puberulent; leaves ovate to elliptic, 1.5-4 cm long, finely serrate at least half their length, pale and veiny beneath; inflorescence 2-4 cm broad, flat-topped or rounded; flowers small; hypanthium glabrous outside, pubescent within; sepals about 1 mm long; petals rose-colored, 1.5-2 mm long; follicles 4 or 5, glabrous or ciliate, 2.5-3 mm long.
Moist woods, wet rocks, mossy banks and lake borders, 5600 to about 7600 feet.

Spiraea lucida Dougl.   White Meadow-sweet
S. betulifolia Hook. var. *lucida* (Dougl.) C. L. Hitchc.

A low shrub with creeping rootstocks and erect glabrous stems and branches, 20-100 cm tall; leaves obovate or oval, 2-7 cm long, glabrous, coarse and irregularly serrate and sometimes lobed, shining above, pale beneath; inflorescence flat-topped; hypanthium glabrous on the outside; petals white; follicles glabrous and shining.
Open rocky slopes and meadows and along mountain streams, 4500 to about 6000 feet.

LEGUMINOSAE   Pea Family

Annual to perennial herbs, shrubs or trees usually with alternate, compound, stipulate leaves; flowers usually irregular and perfect, in racemes, heads or spikes, or single; calyx of 4 or 5 divisions, sometimes partially united and unequal; petals usually 5, sometimes 3 or 1, the upper (standard or banner) the largest, enclosing in bud the 2 lateral petals (wings), and these enclosing the 2 lower united petals which form the keel; stamens usually 10, the filaments united in 1 group (monadelphous) or more often in 2 groups (diadelphous) of 9 and 1, occasionally all free, or only 5; pistil 1, simple; ovary superior, 1- to 2-celled; ovules 1 to many; fruit dehiscing by 2 longitudinal slits (a legume) or by transverse sutures (loment).

1. Leaflets 3, all radiating from the same spot; flowers yellow to yellowish, whitish, pinkish or red, sometimes slightly tinged with purple but not dark in appearance
  2. Flowers clear yellow
    3. Flowers in tight head-like small clusters; pods black..*Medicago*
    3. Flowers not in head-like clusters, the inflorescence usually several times longer than broad; pods yellowish..*Melilotus*
  2. Flowers not clear yellow, mostly white or whitish to sometimes yellowish, pinkish or reddish; pods inconspicuous; leaves often long-petioled..*Trifolium*
1. Leaflets usually over 3, mostly 5 to 25, sometimes all radiating from the same spot, sometimes opposite each other on a petiole-like rachis; flowers mostly bluish or purplish but sometimes whitish, yellowish or pinkish at least in part
  4. Leaflets 5 to 17, all radiating from the same spot
    5. Flowers blue or purplish, mostly in an elongated inflorescence up to about 20 cm long; plants erect or sometimes flat on the ground..*Lupinus*
    5. Flowers usually whitish or yellowish or tinged with pink, in heads 4-5 cm long and about as broad; stems erect..*Trifolium*
  4. Leaflets not radiating from the same spot, mostly opposite each other on a petiole-like rachis
    6. Topmost leaflet not developed but replaced by a thin, sometimes branched, thread-like curled tendril or by an unbranched spine-like bristle less than a cm long
      7. Tip of the style not hairy, but just below the tip the style flattened and hairy..*Lathyrus*
      7. Tip of the style hairy all around, not flattened or hairy below the tip................*Vicia*
    6. Topmost leaflet of the leaves usually developed and about the same as the other leaflets (rarely missing)
      8. Flowers yellow or yellowish
        9. Flowering stems with several leaves; plants mostly over 30 cm tall..*Astragalus*
        9. Flowering stems without leaves; plants usually under 30 cm tall......*Oxytropis*
      8. Flowers rose-purplish to blue or bluish-purple
        10. Calyx white-hairy like the leaves; flowers rose-pinkish, 11-22 mm long; pods with 1-8 obvious segments..*Hedysarum*
        10. Calyx mostly black-hairy but if white-hairy then the plant growing prostrate on the ground; flowers mostly bluish or purple, 5-13 mm long; pods not appearing segmented..*Astragalus*

Astragalus L.

Annual to perennial pubescent herbs with odd-pinnate leaves and persistent stipules; flowers in axillary racemes, rarely solitary, purple or reddish to white or yellowish; calyx tubular or campanulate; petals clawed, the banner usually reflexed, the wings usually longer than the keel; stamens 10, one separate from the 9 united ones; pods globose to linear, straight to coiled, thin-walled and inflated to thick-walled and flattened, 1-celled or becoming 2-celled by the inward development of one or both sutures; seeds small, few to many.

1. Flowers white, creamy or pale yellowish
  2. Leaflets 15-35 mm long, elliptic, pointed at both ends; flowers few to as many as 150; pods erect, 8-20 mm long, not flattened..*A. canadensis*
  2. Leaflets narrowly oblong, 5-20 mm long; flowers usually 15 to 40 in an inflorescence; pods hanging downward, 7-25 mm long, usually flattened..*A. collinus*

1. Flowers purplish, sometimes with some white or yellowish or pinkish areas
   3. Plants growing flat against the ground forming thick mats or tight rosettes; leaves whitish- or grayish-green
      4. Plants forming rather large mats or cushions; flowers mostly 1 or 2 together, 2-10 mm long; pods inconspicuous, 3-8 mm long..*A. kentrophyta*
      4. Plants usually forming tight rosettes; flowers mostly 3 to 10 in a cluster, 10-30 mm long; pods conspicuously woolly-long-hairy, 1-2.5 cm long ....*A. purshii*
   3. Plants mostly rising above the ground but if the stems on or near the ground then not forming mats or cushions or tight rosettes; leaves green or grayish
      5. Plants grayish-hairy, many-stemmed; leaves 1.5-5 cm long, the petiole short or missing; leaflets crowded, narrowly elliptic and pointed at both ends; flowers 8-13 mm long; pods spreading or hanging, 1.5-3 cm long....................*A. aboriginum*
      5. Plants green; leaves definitely petioled; leaflets not crowded, oval to oblong, the tips rounded or slightly notched; flowers 6-13 mm long, sometimes all on one side of the flowering stem; pods 8-25 mm long, black-hairy
         6. Flowering stems weak, slender, few, 5-25 cm tall; flowers 7-12 mm long, 8 to 16 in a cluster; pods usually hanging down, 8-14 mm long ....*A. alpinus*
         6. Flowering stems stronger, thick, many, 20-60 cm tall; flowers 6-10 mm long, 10 to 60 in a cluster; pods erect or spreading or hanging down, 8-25 mm long..*A. robbinsii*

Astragalus aboriginum Richards.
Milk Vetch

A. forwoodii var. *wallowensis* (Rydb.) Peck

Cespitose perennial, silky-hairy or tomentose to nearly glabrous, with a woody taproot and a much-branched crown; stems sometimes prostrate or spreading, 5-40 cm long; leaves 1.5-5 cm long, short-petioled to sessile, glabrous above; leaflets 7 to 15, oblong-lanceolate, mostly acute, 10-20 mm long; stipules large, oblong, united at the base; peduncles 3-15 cm long, longer than the subtending leaves; racemes 10- to 20-flowered, becoming elongate and lax in age; pedicels 1-2.5 mm long; flowers whitish or yellowish with a purple keel or completely purplish, 8-13 mm long; calyx 4-8 mm long, black-hairy, the tube campanulate, mostly longer than the teeth; banner erect, yellowish; wings purple-tinged, about 1 mm longer than the keel, 2-toothed at the tip; keel dark purple at the tip; pods horizontally spreading to pendulous, stipitate, membranous, arched or lunate, glabrous or crisp-hairy, 1.5-3 cm long, compressed, 1-celled, pointed at both ends. Rocky slopes and ridges, 8800 to about 9300 feet.

Astragalus alpinus L.
Alpine Rattleweed

Cespitose strigose to silky perennial with creeping rootstocks; stems slender, decumbent, 5-25 cm long; stipules united or nearly free; leaves 5-15 cm long; leaflets 13 to 23, ovate to oblong-elliptic; peduncles 7-14 cm long; racemes mostly 8- to 16-flowered, often one-sided in fruit; flowers 7-12 mm long, pale lilac to purplish, the keel tip darkest in color, the wings short; calyx campanulate, black-hairy, 3-5 mm long; pod usually pendulous, sometimes spreading, turgid, black-hairy, membranous or papery, ellipsoid, 8-14 mm long, short-stipitate.

Exposed rocky slopes and ridges at higher elevations but also in gravelly creeks at lower elevations, 5100 to about 9600 feet.

Astragalus canadensis L. var. mortonii (Nutt.) Wats.
Morton's Locoweed

A. mortonii Nutt.

Erect to decumbent perennial, glabrate and greenish; stems few to several, ascending,

30-80 cm tall; stipules free or some of them joined together, 6-15 mm long, triangular; leaves 10-20 cm long; leaflets 13 to 29, elliptic to oblong, 1.5-3.5 cm long, glabrous above; peduncles 5-20 cm long; racemes 3-15 cm long, up to 150-flowered; flowers ochroleucous to white, 10-18 mm long; calyx 6-9 mm long, asymmetrical at the base, pubescent with both white and black hairs, the teeth about equal; banner and wing petals slightly longer than the blunt usually purplish-tipped keel; pod erect, ellipsoid to oblong, 8-20 mm long, papery, glabrous or generally sparsely hairy, sessile or nearly so. Open woods, 4500 to about 6000 feet.

Astragalus collinus Dougl.   Hillside Milk Vetch

Finely crisp-puberulent to strigose taprooted perennial; stems several, erect to ascending, branching, 10-60 cm tall; leaves 3-8 cm long mostly; stipules not united; leaflets 11 to 25, linear-oblong to oblanceolate, 5-20 mm long, obtuse or notched, glabrous above; peduncles up to 15 cm long, longer than the leaves; racemes 15- to 40-flowered; flowers spreading to reflexed, creamy-white to yellowish or greenish-tinged, 10-15 mm long; the banner "stubby" and reflexed; wings longer than the banner and about equaling the blunt keel; calyx gibbous at the base, 7-10 mm long, crisply puberulent with white or blackish hairs; pods 7-25 mm long, pendulous, slightly compressed, linear-oblong, puberulent, stipitate, straight or slightly curved inward, the valves becoming leathery. Dry grassy hillsides, 4500 to about 5200 feet.

Astragalus kentrophyta Gray var. **implexus** (Canby) Barneby

Alpine Spiny Rattleweed

Grayish-green prostrate perennial forming low mats or cushions; stems and leaves hairy to nearly glabrous; leaflets 3 to 9, crowded, 1-9 mm long, spiny-tipped; flowers single or in 2's or 3's, 2-10 mm long; peduncles mostly 3-15 mm long; calyx campanulate, grayish- to blackish-hairy; corolla purplish, or sometimes white with pink or purplish keel-tip, 5 or 6 mm long; ovules 5 to 8 but seeds only 1 to 3; pod ellipsoid, compressed, 3-8 mm long, hairy.
Exposed cliffs, saddles and rocky places between 7900 and 9675 feet and probably higher, but sometimes also in gravelly creeks and bars as low as 5800 feet.

Astragalus purshii Dougl.   Pursh's Woolly Pod

Prostrate grayish-woolly perennial with stems seldom over 5 cm long; leaves crowded, 2-15 cm long; leaflets 9 to 13, acutish; stipules free at the base; racemes 3- to 10-flowered; flowers ochroleucous or yellowish to deep reddish-purple, 1-3 cm long; calyx tubular, the teeth short; pod sessile, densely long-hairy, 1-2.5 cm long, slightly flattened, straight to slightly arched.
Dry open slopes and rocky sandy meadows, about 5500 to about 8500 feet.

Astragalus robbinsii (Oakes) Gray var. **alpiniformis** (Rydb.) Barneby
A. occidentalis M. E. Jones
Greenish strigillose to glabrate perennial with creeping cespitose rootstocks and prostrate to erect stems 20-60 cm long; leaves glabrous 6-12 cm long; leaflets 7 to 19, 1-2.5 cm long, thin and succulent, paler beneath; racemes 10- to 60-flowered, rather one-sided; flowers 6-10 mm long, pale to deep purplish; calyx campanulate, usually black-hairy, the

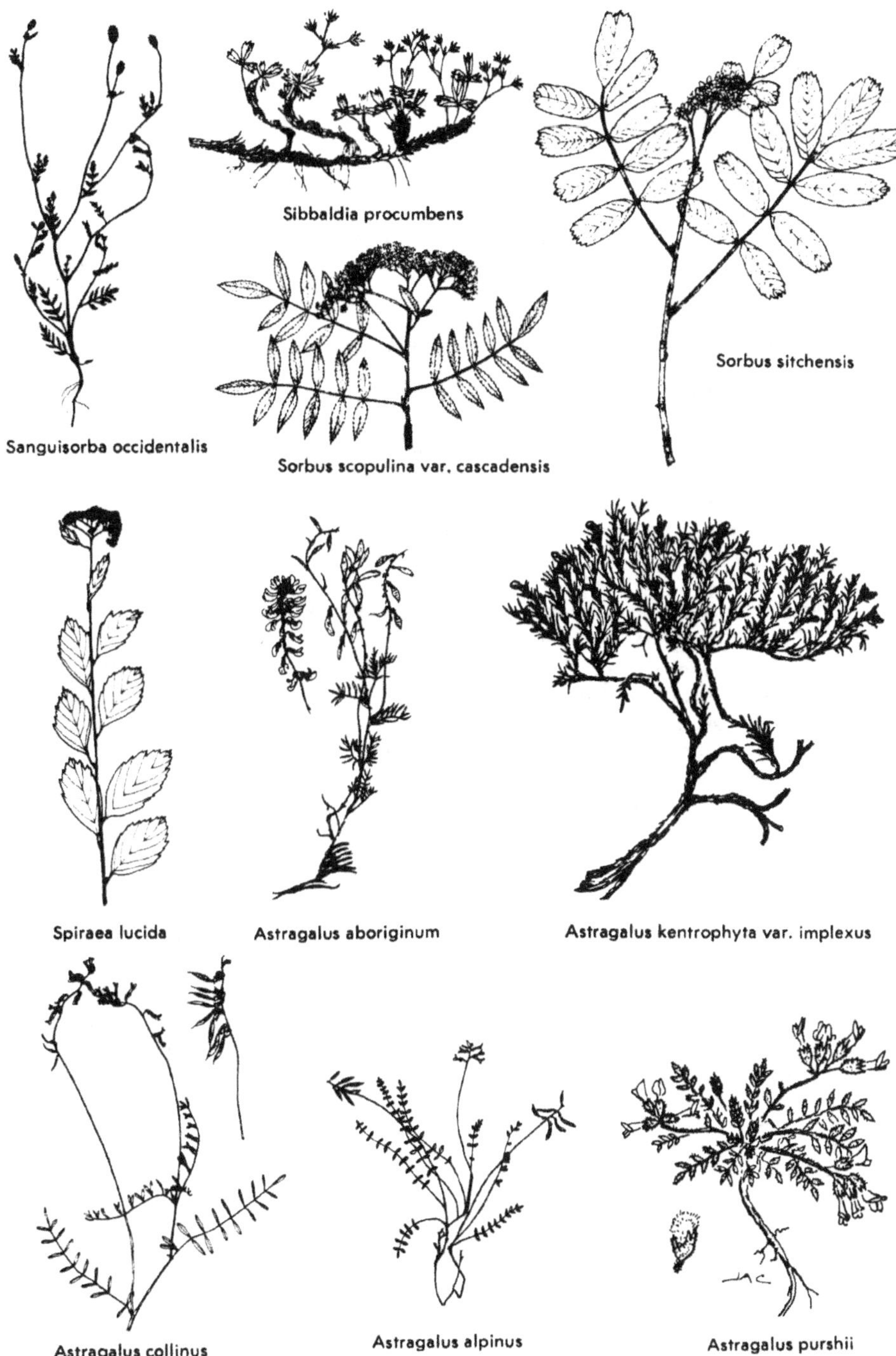

Sanguisorba occidentalis
Sibbaldia procumbens
Sorbus scopulina var. cascadensis
Sorbus sitchensis
Spiraea lucida
Astragalus aboriginum
Astragalus kentrophyta var. implexus
Astragalus collinus
Astragalus alpinus
Astragalus purshii

teeth about half as long as the tube; pods spreading to reflexed, membranous, black-hairy, 8-25 mm long, compressed, usually stipitate.
Gravelly streambanks, about 5000 feet.

Hedysarum L.

Herbaceous perennial herbs from woody taproots; stems clustered, hairy; leaves odd-pinnate, gland-dotted; stipules persistent; flowers showy in axillary, pedunculate, often one-sided racemes; calyx campanulate, bracteolate, the teeth about equal; corolla purplish or pink to yellowish-white, the keel obtuse, longer than the other petals; stamens 10, nine joined together the other free; style curved; fruit a loment, constricted into flat, oval to orbicular indehiscent segments breaking apart from each other easily.

Hedysarum boreale Nutt.   Northern Sweet-broom

Stems many from a heavy crown, grayish-strigose or nearly glabrous toward the base, 20-60 cm tall; stipules to 1 cm long, tan or brownish; leaves 5-15 cm long; leaflets 7 to 15, glabrous above and grayish-hairy beneath or hairy on both sides, elliptic-oblong, 10-25 mm long; peduncles 10-25 cm long; raceme 5- to 50-flowered, compact to elongated; flowers erect or spreading, pink, pinkish- to rose-purple or reddish-purple, 11 to 22 mm long; calyx teeth mostly longer than the tube; loment about 6 mm broad, the segments nearly round, mostly 2 to 8, narrow-margined.
Gravel bars, floodbanks, streamsides, rock slides and dry wooded slopes, usually among shrubs, 5000 to about 8000 feet.

Plants generally branched, greenish; leaves often glabrous above; racemes often up to 15 cm long with 12 to 20 carmine, magenta or purple flowers 11-17 mm long; pod usually with 2 to 5 or 6 segments...var. **boreale**
Plants generally unbranched, greenish; leaves glabrous to sparsely strigillose above; racemes shorter, 2-4 cm long, compact, usually with 5 to 15 purple flowers 18-20 mm long; pods mostly with 3 to 8 segments...............var. **mackenzii** (Richards) C. L. Hitchc.
With the species.

Lathyrus L.

Annual or perennial often rhizomatous herbs with stipulate leaves pinnately divided into 2 to 8 or 10 leaflets; tendrils usually well-developed but sometimes reduced to a short bristle; flowers axillary, 2 to many in a raceme, or sometimes solitary, pedunculate; calyx obliquely campanulate, the teeth nearly equal or the upper ones shorter; banner clawed, its blade usually reflexed; keel not at all beaked; stamens 10, in 2 groups; style curved, flattened, hairy down the inner face, persistent on the fruit; legume 1-celled, flat or sometimes terete, several-seeded.

1. Flowers white, sometimes with purple veins or tinged with blue or pink; leaves usually
   with a short bristle just above the uppermost pair of leaflets
      2. Leaves mostly with 2 pairs of leaflets; flowers often 2, 3 or 4 together, often
        spreading or curved downward...*L. nevadensis*
      2. Leaves mostly with 3 or more pairs of leaflets; flowers mostly 1 or 2 together, erect,
        seldom spreading or drooping.. ......*L. rigidus*
1. Flowers mostly pinkish to violet-purple; leaves with a conspicuous, green, thread-like,
   often branched and curled tendril above the uppermost pair of leaflets...................*L. pauciflorus*

Lathyrus nevadensis Wats. ssp. **cusickii** (Wats.) C. L. Hitchc.   Cusick's Sweet Pea
   Glabrous or sparsely pubescent perennial with slender erect stems 20-40 cm tall; leaves
3-6 cm long; leaflets 4 to 6, linear-lanceolate to linear, acute or spiny-tipped, 6-10 cm
long, strongly veined; stipules small and narrow; tendrils stout to vestigial or missing;
peduncles 1- to 4-flowered, about as long as the leaves; flowers about 2 cm long; calyx
teeth about equal; petals white, often purplish-veined, 2-2.5 cm long; pods 4-5 cm long.
Open coniferous woods and slopes, about 4500 feet.

Lathyrus pauciflorus Fernald   Brush Pea
   Glabrous taprooted perennial mostly 60-90 cm tall with thick, angled stems; stipules
dentate but mostly not lobed, about half as long as the leaflets; leaflets thick and fleshy,
mostly 6 to 13, linear to oblong-lanceolate or ovate-elliptic, 2-8 cm long, acute, veined;
tendrils well-developed, simple or branched; peduncles equaling or longer than the
leaves, 3- to 7-flowered, or up to 10; calyx glabrous or the teeth ciliate, 8-18 mm long,
the 2 upper teeth short, the lower about as long as the tube; corolla 13-27 mm long,
orchid or pinkish-lavender to violet-purple turning bluish; pods 3-5 cm long, narrow,
glabrous.
Leaflets narrowly oblong-elliptic, much longer than wide........................var. **pauciflorus**
Leaflets ovate to ovate-lanceolate, usually about twice as long as
wide...var. **utahensis** (M. E. Jones) Peck
Dry rocky hillsides and wooded slopes, 4500 to 6000 feet.

Lathyrus rigidus White   White Pea
   Glabrous perennial with a thick crown and a large taproot; stems many, angled, erect,
15-40 cm tall; stipules about as long as the leaflets, often toothed, the upper lobe the
longest; leaflets mostly 6 to 10, veiny, rather leathery, 1.5-3 cm long, oblong to oblanceolate, the tip sharply pointed; tendrils rudimentary, up to 5 mm long; peduncles equaling
or longer than the leaves; flowers 1 to 5, white to pinkish (rarely bluish), 2-2.5 cm long;
calyx about 8 mm long, the teeth ciliate, a little shorter than the tube; pod 3-5 cm long,
gradually narrowed to the base.
Pine woods, about 4500 feet.

Lupinus L.

   Annual or perennial herbs or shrubs with alternate palmately compound leaves of 5
to 17 leaflets; flowers in terminal racemes; calyx bilabiate, the tube often spurred on
the upper side, the lips entire or toothed; corolla showy; banner grooved, glabrous or
pubescent on the back, usually reflexed; wings usually glabrous, joined together and
enclosing the keel; keel glabrous or ciliate along the upper margins; stamens 10, in 1
series; pods flat, hairy, usually constricted between the seeds.

1. Calyx with a decided spur at its base on some if not all the flowers thus appearing mis-
    shaped or uneven; wings hairy near the upper tip; banner of the flowers hairy on the
    back or not ....*L. laxiflorus*

1. Calyx not spurred at the base; banner of the flowers hairy on the back or not; wings not
    hairy near the tip
        2. Banner conspicuously hairy on its back
            3. Flowers 6-8 mm long, closely crowded on the stem; flower stalks (pedicels)
                1-3 mm long; pods 1.5-2.5 cm long...*L. leucophyllus*

3. Flowers 8-12 mm long, further apart on the stem, sometimes scattered leaving
open spaces; pedicels 4-11 mm long; pods 2-3 cm long..*L. sericeus*
2. Banner not hairy on its back
   4. Leaves and leaflets hairy; leaflets 1-4 cm long and less than 1 cm broad;
flowers 6-13 mm long; pods 1-1.2 cm long..*L. lepidus*
   4. Leaves and leaflets not hairy; leaflets 4-9 cm long and up to 2 cm broad;
flowers 10-13 mm long; pods 2.5-3.5 cm long...*L. burkei*

Lupinus burkei Wats.   Large-leaved Lupine

L. polyphyllus Lindl. var. *burkei* (Wats.) C. L. Hitchc.

Perennial 30-80 cm tall becoming glabrous except in the inflorescence; leaves glabrous above, glabrate beneath; petioles 8-20 cm long, the lower ones the longer; leaflets 5 to 10, oblanceolate, bright above, pale beneath, 4-9 cm long; peduncles 5-10 cm long; racemes 8-16 cm long, many-flowered; pedicels 2-5 mm long, spreading-pubescent; flowers 10-13 mm long, not verticillate; calyx loosely pubescent, the lips mostly entire; petals blue, the banner with yellow center turning violet, glabrous; keel not ciliate; pods pubescent, 2.5-3.5 cm long.
Bogs, streambanks, meadows and among wet rocks, 5000 to about 7600 feet.

Lupinus laxiflorus Dougl.   Spurred Lupine

L. arbustus Dougl.

Perennial with a woody base; stems densely clustered, erect or ascending, appressed-silky, 30-80 cm tall; leaves cauline, long-petioled near the base; leaflets 7 to 11, oblanceolate, 3-5 cm long, glabrous above or pubescent on both sides; peduncles 3-8 cm long; racemes 8-18 cm long; pedicels 3-7 mm long; flowers numerous, 8-14 mm long; calyx spurred, the spur about 1-3 mm long, the upper calyx lip green and notched, the lower lip narrow, entire or 3-toothed; petals white or cream, or tinged with blue, purple, rose, or violet; banner pubescent on the back, not much reflexed; wings pubescent on the upper edge near the tips; keel ciliate most of its length; pods 2-3.5 cm long, silky-hairy.
Moist to dry open places, 4800 to about 8000 feet.

Plants 10-30 cm tall; racemes 3-4 cm long, compact; pedicels 2 mm long; flowers 8-10 mm long; calyx merely gibbous, not woolly; banner glabrous, suborbicular....................var. **laxiflorus** (*L. inyoensis* Heller var. *demissus* C. P. Smith)
Known from the Type Locality: Talus slope, Wallowa Mts., Baker Co., Oregon.

Lupinus lepidus Dougl.   Prairie Lupine

L. aridus Dougl.

Low spreading silky perennial 10-35 cm tall, the stems long and leafy or short and the leaves basal; leaves long-petioled, the leaflets 5 to 9, oblanceolate, hairy on both sides, 1-4 cm long; peduncles 2-15 cm long, shorter than the leaves; racemes densely flowered, 5-15 cm long, usually longer than the leaves; pedicels 1-5 mm long; calyx lips toothed to entire; flowers 6-13 mm long, verticillate, white to bluish; banner glabrous, sharply reflexed, the center yellow to purple; wings glabrous; keel strongly ciliate; pods silky, 10-12 mm long.

Plant prostrate and matted; leaflets usually less than 15 mm long; racemes under 5 cm long at anthesis...................................var. **lobbii** (Gray) C. L. Hitchc. (*L. lyallii* Gray)
Dry open places, 7000 to about 8000 feet.

Lupinus leucophyllus Dougl. var. **tenuispicus** (A. Nels.) C. P. Sm.   Woolly Lupine
Perennial with several erect often branched stems 30-80 cm tall; pubescence very short but spreading and tangled, grayish to rust-colored; leaves many, woolly on both sides, long-petioled; leaflets 7 to 10, oblanceolate to narrowly oblong, 3-5 cm long; peduncles 3-8 cm long; racemes very slender, many-flowered, 10-30 cm long; pedicels 1-3 mm long; flowers 6-8 mm long, white to lilac or purple; calyx densely villous, not spurred. the upper lip toothed, the lower entire; banner small, suborbicular, only slightly reflexed, densely pubescent over most of the back (very rarely glabrous) ; wings glabrous to sparsely hairy; keel ciliate on the upper margins; pods woolly, 1-2.5 cm long.
Plants with long spreading pubescence; leaflets more than 7 mm broad; racemes mostly longer than 20 cm; flowers 8-10 mm long.............var. **leucophyllus** (*L. erectus* Hend.)
Dry rocky open slopes, about 8000 feet.

Lupinus sericeus Pursh   Pursh's Silky Lupine
Perennial 20-50 cm tall with appressed silky hairs and villous with spreading hairs as well; leaves mostly cauline at flowering time; lower leaves long-petioled when present; leaflets 6 to 9, oblanceolate, 3-9 cm long, silky on both sides; peduncles 4-8 cm long; racemes mostly 12-15 cm long; pedicels 4-11 mm long, spreading-pubescent; flowers 8-12 mm long, verticillate or scattered; calyx not spurred, upper lip 2-toothed, lower entire; petals mostly lavender or blue, but sometimes yellowish or whitish; banner well reflexed, silky-hairy on the back, whitish or yellow at the center; wings usually glabrous; keel ciliate, its tip upturned; pods silky, 2-3 cm long.
Dry hillsides and grassy meadows, 4500 to about 7200 feet.
Spreading hairs missing below the inflorescence; pedicels spreading-pubescent; floral bracts often subpersistent...var. **flexuosus** (Lindl.) C. P. Smith
Grassy open places, 4500 to about 7200 feet.

Medicago L.
Annual or perennial herbs with trifoliate leaves, the leaflets usually toothed; flowers small, yellow or bluish-purple, in small umbels, or larger axillary racemes or heads; calyx teeth nearly equal, longer than the calyx tube; banner (standard) longer than the wings and the keel; stamens 10, one free and the other 9 united; pod curved or spirally coiled, reticulate or spiny, indehiscent, 1- to several-seeded.

Medicago lupulina L.   Black Medic
Pubescent to long-hairy annual with decumbent to erect stems 10-40 cm long; stipules entire to toothed; leaves petioled; leaflets 3, obovate-elliptic, 1-2 cm long, toothed near the tip; flowers 10 to 40, yellow, about 2 mm long, in short spike-like racemes; pod 1-seeded, glabrous to glandular-long-hairy, 2-3 mm long, reticulate, only the tip coiled, black when mature.
Moist woods as well as dry rocky places, 4650 to about 6000 feet.

Melilotus Juss.
Taprooted annual or biennial herbs with sweetly fragrant, glabrous or pubescent, trifoliate, petioled leaves; flowers small, white or yellow, in spike-like axillary racemes; calyx teeth nearly equal; corolla deciduous; stamens 10, 1 free, the other 9 united; pods straight, ovoid, reticulate, 1- to 4-seeded, usually dehiscent.

Melilotus officinalis (L.) Lam.   Yellow Sweet Clover
   Taprooted annual or biennial herb, glabrous to pubescent, 1-3 meters tall; leaflets 3, oblanceolate or obovate to narrowly oblong, serrulate; racemes 3-10 cm long; flowers yellow, about 5 mm long, the petals longer than the calyx; pods ovoid, pubescent, reticulate, about 3 mm long.
Meadows and open woods, 4500 to about 5300 feet.

Oxytropis DC.

   Cespitose perennial herbs with odd-pinnate mostly basal stipulate leaves; flowers white or cream to reddish or purple, racemose or spicate; calyx teeth nearly equal; petals clawed; banner (standard) erect; wings longer than the keel; keel tip pointed, toothed or beaked; stamens 10, 1 free and the other 9 united; pods leathery, often inflated, several-seeded.

Leaves with 7 to 17 silky-hairy non-glandular leaflets; flowers yellowish; pods 15-20 mm
   long .... *O. campestris*
Leaves with 15 to 57 long-hairy sticky-glandular leaflets; flowers cream or whitish,
   sometimes purplish-tinged; pods 10-15 mm long .... *O. viscida*

Oxytropis campestris (L.) DC. var. **cusickii** (Greenm.) Barneby   Cusick's Loco Weed
   Perennial with short stems clustered on a woody base;.stem and leaves densely silky-hairy but not glandular; leaflets mostly 7 to 17, oblong-lanceolate, 4-10 mm long; stipules membranous, long-ciliate, glabrous or glabrate; peduncles 5-12 cm long; racemes few-flowered, short and dense; flowers yellowish, 10-12 mm long; calyx grayish- to black-hairy, about 8 mm long; banner (standard) 10-12 mm long, deeply notched; pods cylindric, 15-20 mm long, sessile or nearly so, pubescent with white and black hairs, the beak about 5 mm long.
In cracks and crevices of exposed slopes and ridges and on ledges, 7900 to about 9900 feet.

Oxytropis viscida Nutt.   Sticky Loco Weed
   Acaulescent perennial with a branched woody caudex and short, clustered stems; herbage pilose-hirsute and viscid with wart-like glands; leaves 3-20 cm long; leaflets 15 to 57, linear-lanceolate to narrowly oblong, 5-25 mm long; stipules 6-12 mm long; peduncles equaling or longer than the leaves; racemes 2-7 cm long, spike-like, 7- to 30-flowered; flowers cream colored or reddish-purple to purplish-blue or violet, rarely white, 10-15 mm long; calyx grayish- to black-hairy, cylindric, 8-10 mm long; banner upturned; wings broadened; keel with a short straight beak; pods erect, 10-15 mm long, grayish- to black-hairy, the beak 3-6 mm long.
Moist open meadows, gravel bars and streambanks at lower elevations to crevices in drier exposed ridges and slopes at upper elevations, 5100 to about 9600 feet.

Trifolium L.

   Annual or perennial, taprooted or rhizomatous herbs with stipulate leaves; leaflets 3 to 9, usually toothed; flowers white, yellow, pink, red or purple, sessile or pedicelled, erect to spreading or reflexed, in usually pedunculate heads or short spike-like racemes: calyx 5-toothed, the teeth sometimes 2-toothed or 3- toothed; corolla persistent, the banner (standard) scarcely reflexed from the wings and the keel; stamens 10, 1 free

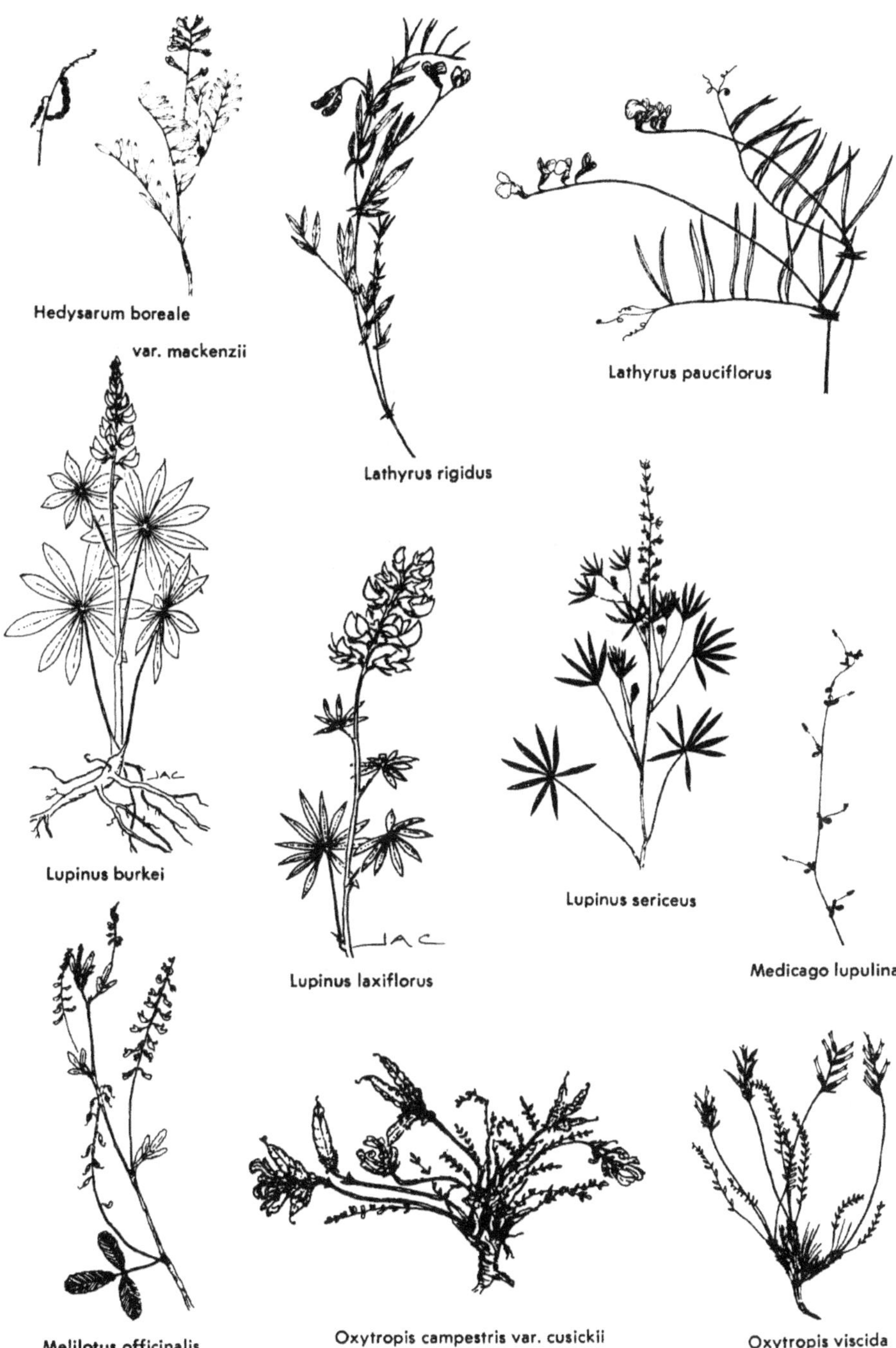

Hedysarum boreale
var. mackenzii
Lathyrus rigidus
Lathyrus pauciflorus
Lupinus burkei
Lupinus laxiflorus
Lupinus sericeus
Medicago lupulina
Melilotus officinalis
Oxytropis campestris var. cusickii
Oxytropis viscida

and the other 9 united; pods usually shorter than the calyx, 1- to several-seeded, dehiscent
or indehiscent.

1. Leaves divided into more than 3 leaflets; flowers clustered in a head 3-5 cm long and
   about as broad..*T. macrocephalum*
1. Leaves divided into 3 leaflets usually; flowers variously clustered
    2. Plants not hairy (sometimes with a few scattered hairs in *T. repens*)
        3. Flowers white or whitish
            4. Stems creeping along the ground and rooting; flowers white in heads
                1.5-2 cm broad; leaflets broadest at the top, usually notched .... *T. repens*
            4. Stems erect; flowers whitish or yellowish in a head 0.5-1.5 cm broad with
                a saucer-like toothed collar under it; plant a slender annual.............*T. cyathiferum*
        3. Flowers pink to purple
            5. Flowers pink or rose, 5-10 mm long, sometimes white; stems 30-80 cm
                tall...*T. hybridum*
            5. Flowers purplish, 11-18 mm long; stems 15-20 cm tall............................*T. productum*
    2. Plants hairy at least on the leaves and on the calyx teeth
        6. Flowers dark, mostly purplish to red
            7. Flowers red, 13-20 mm long, spreading or erect in a head nearly without
                a stalk..*T. pratense*
            7. Flowers purple or reddish-purplish
                 8. Heads loosely flowered; flowers light yellow to purple, 10-18 mm
                    long; leaflets about as broad as long...................................*T. latifolium*
               8. Heads more densely flowered; flowers dull reddish-purple, 12-19
                    mm long; leaflets longer than broad ....*T. longipes* ssp. *multipedunculatum*
        6. Flowers mostly lighter in color, yellowish- to pinkish-purplish
            9. Calyx teeth noticeably long-spreading-hairy; flowers pinkish to
                yellowish...*T. eriocephalum*
            9. Calyx teeth not so distinctly hairy, the hairs shorter, not spreading;
                flowers whitish to yellowish to pink-purplish..*T. longipes*

Trifolium cyathiferum Lindl.   Wide-collared Clover

    Glabrous annual, 10-30 cm tall; stipules ovate to lanceolate; leaflets 3, oblanceolate,
mostly obtuse, 1-2.5 cm long, spiny-toothed; heads axillary and terminal, 5-15 mm long
and about as broad; involucre flared to cup-shaped, nerved and dentate-bristly-mar-
gined; calyx glabrous, 2-5 mm long, the teeth setaceous, the lower ones 2- or 3-toothed;
corolla white, ochroleucous to pink or rose, about equaling the calyx; pod 2-seeded.
Moist rocky wooded hillsides, about 5300 to 5800 feet.

Trifolium eriocephalum Nutt.   Woolly-headed Clover

    Villous-pubescent taprooted perennial with 1 or more erect or decumbent stems 15-60
cm tall; stipules nearly entire, 2-5 cm long; leaflets 3, ovate or elliptic to almost linear,
2-7 cm long, entire to serrulate, long-petioled; heads axillary as well as terminal, 25- to
80-flowered, globose to ovoid, 2-3 cm broad, long-pedunculate; flowers pinkish or red
to yellowish, strongly reflexed, 12-17 mm long; pedicels 1 mm long; calyx plumose-
villous, 6-18 mm long, the teeth long and filiform; pod villous, 1- to 4-seeded.
Shady bogs, wet meadows and rocky slopes, 5400 to about 7400 feet.

Trifolium hybridum L.   Alsatian Clover

    Sparsely pubescent perennial with several stout, erect to ascending stems 30-80 cm
tall; stipules 5-20 mm long, ovate-lanceolate; leaflets 3, ovate to obovate, 1-3 cm long,
serrulate; heads globose, axillary, 1.5-2.5 cm broad; peduncles 5-10 cm long; flowers
white to pink, rose or reddish, reflexed, 5-10 mm long; pedicels 1-8 mm long; calyx

4-5 mm long, the teeth equaling or longer than the tube, sparsely hairy at the sinuses; pods 1- to 3-seeded.

Along roads and trails and in meadows, 4500 to about 6000 feet. Escaped from cultivation.

Trifolium latifolium (Hook.) Greene Broad-leaved Clover

Pubescent taprooted perennial with several stems 10-40 cm tall; stipules ovate to lanceolate, 5-15 mm long, erose-lacerate to entire; leaflets 3, ovate to obovate, 5-40 mm long, serrulate; heads axillary and terminal, short-peduncled, 2-3 cm broad; flowers yellow to purple, 10-18 mm long, erect to reflexed; pedicels 1-4 mm long; calyx finely pubescent, the teeth nearly equal; pod usually 1-seeded.

Pine forest and rocky slopes and ridges, 6000 to about 7000 feet.

Trifolium longipes Nutt. Long-stalked Clover

Glabrous to sparsely pubescent taprooted perennials or sometimes with long slender rhizomes; stems erect or trailing, 5-40 cm tall; stipules leaf-like, narrow, lacerate to entire, 2-2.5 cm long; leaflets 3, elliptic-lanceolate to obovate, 2-6 cm long, serrulate to nearly entire; heads terminal, subglobose, 1.5-3.5 cm broad, long-peduncled; calyx 7-9 mm long, glabrous to villous-pubescent; flowers white or ochroleucous to pink-purplish, 11-18 mm long, erect to reflexed; pods 1- to 4-seeded.

Moist mountain meadows and pine forests, 4500 to about 6000 feet.

Plant strongly rhizomatous; leaflets about 1 cm long, strongly-veined and mucronate; flowers 12-15 mm long, yellowish-white to pink or purple, strongly reflexed...var. **reflexum** A. Nels. (*T. oreganum* Howell)
With the species.

Trifolium longipes Nutt. ssp. **multipedunculatum** (Kenn.) J. M. Gillett

Taprooted pubescent perennial with stems often trailing and rhizome-like, rarely over 10 cm tall; stipules 5-20 mm long, lacerate; leaflets 3, lanceolate to obovate, thick and leathery, 5-15 mm long, setose-serrulate; heads subglobose, terminal, 2-3 cm broad; peduncles long; flowers red to purplish, 12-19 mm long, the lower ones reflexed; calyx pubescent, about half as long as the corolla, the teeth nearly equal, sometimes spreading and curling; banner, wings and keel acuminate; pods 2- to 4-seeded.

Mostly in wet meadows near streams in coniferous woods, about 7400 to 8600 feet.

Trifolium macrocephalum (Pursh) Poir. Large-headed Clover

Thick-rooted perennial, sparsely to densely pubescent; stems thick, erect, mostly 10-20 cm tall; stipules about 2 cm long, serrate; leaflets usually 5 to 9, sometimes 3 or 4, thick, 5-25 mm long, glabrous above; heads 3-5 cm broad and about as long, solitary and terminal on peduncles longer than the leaves; calyx villous-plumose, much shorter than the corolla; flowers 22-28 mm long, the banner yellowish, the wings and keel rose-pink to purplish; pods glabrous, 1- to 4-seeded.

Open wet rocky meadows, grassy coniferous slopes and springy places, about 4500 to 6000 feet.

Trifolium pratense L. Red Clover

Taprooted perennial, sparsely villous-pubescent, with decumbent or erect branching

stems 20-100 cm tall; stipules strongly veined, 1-3 cm long; leaflets 3, lanceolate to oblong-obovate, 2-6 cm long, often with a large dark spot near the middle; heads globose, 2.5-3.5 cm broad, terminal and sessile with 1 or 2 subtending leaves; flowers deep red, sessile, spreading to erect, 13-20 mm long; calyx 5-8 mm long, short villous-hirsute, the teeth pubescent with straight hairs, the 3 lower ones longer than the others; pods 2-seeded.
Rocky meadows and along trails in coniferous woods, 5000 to about 6150 feet.

Trifolium productum Greene   King's Clover
T. kingii Wats.

Glabrous taprooted perennial with slender ascending stems 10-40 cm tall; stipules entire to lacerate, 1-3 cm long; leaflets usually 3, ovate or elliptic to obovate, 1-5 cm long, spinulose-serrulate; peduncles longer than the leaves; heads 10-25 mm broad and about as long, axillary as well as terminal, the rachis prolonged above the head and usually branched; flowers 11-18 mm long, strongly reflexed, short-pedicelled; calyx glabrous, about ¼ as long as the corolla; corolla whitish, rose or purple-tipped, 10-12 mm long; pods 1-seeded.
Rocky places at about 6000 feet.

Trifolium repens L.   White Clover
Perennial, glabrous or with a few scattered hairs; stems creeping and rooting at the nodes, 10-60 cm long; stipules 3-10 mm long, acute; leaflets 3, obovate, emarginate or obcordate, denticulate, 1-2 cm long; heads globose, 1.5-2 cm broad, axillary, often long-peduncled; flowers 5-9 mm long, white or cream to pinkish, reflexed in age, the pedicels 1-5 mm long; calyx glabrous; corolla 2 or 3 times as long as the calyx.
Moist or dry meadows and shady woods, 5000 to about 6150 feet. Introduced.

Vicia L.

Annual or perennial herbs with trailing to climbing stems and pinnate stipuled tendril-bearing leaves; flowers axillary, solitary or in racemes, yellow or purple; calyx with 5 unequal teeth; banner emarginate; wings joined to the shorter oblong keel; stamens 10, the 1 free, the others united; style with a tuft of hairs just below the stigma; pods flat, 2- to several-seeded.

Vicia americana Muhl.   American Vetch
Glabrous to pubescent perennial with trailing or climbing stems 60-100 cm long; stipules deeply lacerate or toothed; leaflets 8 to 16, linear to oval, emarginate, some-times 3-toothed, apiculate, often low-serrate, 1-3 cm long; peduncles short; racemes short with 2 to 10 bluish-purple rather one-sided flowers 1-2.5 cm long; calyx 5-7 mm long, loosely pilose or woolly; pods glabrous, 2-4 cm long.
Open woods and grassy meadows and slopes, 4500 to about 5000 feet.

GERANIACEAE   Geranium Family

Annual or perennial herbs or shrubs with alternate or opposite, palmately lobed or pinnate leaves, usually with stipules; flowers regular or irregular, hypogynous, clustered; sepals 5 (or 4 to 8), usually persistent, not united; petals of the same number as the sepals; stamens 5, 10 or 15, often united at the base, often some without anthers; pistil of 3 to 5 (or 8) carpels, weakly united, each 1- or 2-ovuled; stigmas capitate or elongate; fruit a septicidal capsule, dehiscent into 3 to 5 (or 8) segments tipped with the persistent styles.

Flowers 10-15 mm broad; leaves divided into many narrow divisions, often in a basal
    rosette; beak of the fruit 2.5-5 cm long...*Erodium*
Flowers 25-35 mm broad; leaves divided into 3 to 7 divisions, not forming a basal
    rosette; beak of the fruit 1-1.5 cm long...*Geranium*

Erodium L'Her.

Annual herbs to sub-shrubs, our species with opposite leaves and small axillary umbellate, nearly regular flowers; sepals 5, persistent, petals rose-colored, pinkish or white, unequal; filaments 10, free, only the 5 longer ones with anthers, the others sterile; styles often twisted and spirally coiled at maturity; carpels narrowed at the base; seeds smooth.

Erodium cicutarium (L.) L'Her.   Red-stemmed Filaree or Stork's Bill

Pubescent glandular annual, acaulescent or the stems 10-50 cm tall, often reddish, with swollen nodes; leaves pinnate, mostly in a basal rosette, the many divisions narrow, deeply pinnatifid and toothed; stipules small; flowers 10-15 mm broad, 1 to 12 in an umbel; sepals with 1 or 2 terminal bristle-like hairs; petals pink or rose-purple, a little longer than the sepals; beak of the fruit 2.5-5 cm long.
Dry open ground, about 4500 feet.

Geranium [Tourn.] L.

Annual or perennial herbs (ours) with alternate or opposite mostly palmately-divided cleft or lobed leaves; flowers 2 or more in a cluster, showy, axillary, regular, rose-purple, pink or white; sepals and petals 5; stamens 10, usually all with anthers, 5 longer than the others; style persistent, becoming recurved; carpels often bursting open to shed their seeds.

Geranium viscosissimum Fisch. & Mey.   Sticky Geranium

Perennial, densely villous with usually viscid hairs interspersed with short glandular hairs especially in the inflorescence; stems thick, scape-like, 25-90 cm tall; leaves 5-12 cm broad, densely hoary, glandular, deeply 3- to 7-parted into sharply-toothed divisions, the petioles villous like the stems; flowering stems often scapose and shorter than the leaves, the pedicels glandular-hirsute; sepals generally 8-12 mm long, glandular-pubescent, awn-tipped; petals pinkish-lavender to purplish, 13-18 mm long; style column 2.5-3.5 cm long; fruit glandular-hirsute.
Meadows and grassy pine woods, about 5000 to 5200 feet.

LINACEAE   Flax Family

Annual or perennial herbs or shrubs with alternate or opposite entire leaves; stipules none, or if present small or gland-like; flowers perfect and regular, hypogynous, cymose or racemose; sepals 5, rarely 4 or 6, persistent; petals usually 5, sometimes 4, often showy, usually early deciduous; fertile stamens 5 (ours) to 10 or more, usually united at the base, often alternating with sterile ones; ovary usually with 5 (or 10) locules;

styles free or partly united; fruit a capsule (ours), usually with twice as many locules as styles; seeds 1 or 2 per locule.

Linum [Tourn.] L.

Mostly glabrous annual or perennial with alternate, opposite or whorled leaves; stipules none, or small and gland-like; flowers racemose to cymose; sepals 5; petals 5, blue, red, pinkish, yellow or white, deciduous; stamens 5, the filaments united at the base; styles 2 to 5, united or free; capsules septicidal, 2- to 5-loculed, the locules with incomplete false septa.

Linum perenne L.   Western Blue Flax
 L. lewisii Pursh

Glabrous perennial 10-60 cm tall, often branched at the base and prostrate; leaves alternate, linear, 1-3 cm long, sessile; pedicels 1-3 cm long; sepals ovate, 4-7 mm long; petals blue, rarely white, 10-23 mm long; styles 5, not united, longer than the stamens; capsules globose, 6-10 mm long; septa ciliate.

Mountain meadows and dry rocky slopes and ridges, 6000 to about 9400 feet.

EUPHORBIACEAE   Spurge Family

Monoecious or dioecious trees, shrubs or herbs with milky or acrid juice; leaves simple, alternate or opposite, entire, toothed or lobed; flowers usually apetalous; calyx often missing; stamens few to many, the filaments free or united; ovary 3- or 4-celled, or 1- to many-celled; styles as many or twice as many as cells in the ovary; fruit in ours usually a 3-lobed capsule separating into 1-seeded carpels.

Euphorbia L.

Herbs or shrubs with milky juice, glabrous to sparsely hairy; leaves simple, sometimes missing; stipules often present; flowers naked, in involucrate clusters; involucres perianth-like, solitary and axillary or in terminal cymes, usually with 4 glands (rarely a tooth-like 5th one also), alternating with tooth-like lobes, these sometimes appendaged; staminate flowers numerous, each represented by a single stamen; pistillate flower single, terminal, early exserted, 3-carpellary; styles 3; fruit a capsule usually separating into 3 one-seeded segments.

Euphorbia serpyllifolia Pers.   Thyme-leaved Spurge

Branched glabrous annual; stems 5-35 cm long, usually prostrate; leaves 3-15 mm long, ovate or narrowly oblong to obovate, usually serrulate near the tips; stipules free, linear; involucres about 1 mm long, campanulate; the 4 glands red, oblong, with white appendages, the 5th long, linear and entire; staminate flowers 5 to 18; capsules glabrous, about 2 mm long, sharply triangular; seeds white- to grayish-brown.

Roadsides and dry ground, 4500 to about 4900 feet.

CALLITRICHACEAE   Water Starwort Family

Small aquatic plants, submerged or emergent, rooting in mud; leaves opposite and 1-nerved or tufted at the ends of the branches and 3-nerved; flowers inconspicuous, axillary, perfect or imperfect, without a perianth, naked or enclosed by sac-like bracts, of 1 pistil or 1 stamen, or of both; styles 2; ovary 4-celled, separating into 4 one-seeded nutlet-like fruits.

Callitriche L.

Characters of the family.

Surface leaves, whether floating in water or growing on land, up to 4 mm broad; stems 5-20
    cm long; styles shorter than the narrow-wing-margined fruit..*C. verna*
Surface leaves up to 10 mm broad; stems 5-40 cm long; styles about twice as long as the
    wingless fruit...*C. heterophylla*

Callitriche heterophylla Pursh ex Darby   Varied-leaved Water Starwort
    C. bolanderi Hegelm.

Slender perennial growing in water or on muddy land; stems up to 40 cm long; submerged leaves linear, 0.5-2.5 cm long, 1-nerved; floating leaves broadly obovate, to 1 cm broad, 3-nerved; floral bracts present; fruit about as broad as long, sessile, obcordate; styles about twice as long as the fruit.
Boggy sedge meadows, pools and ponds, 7400 to about 8300 feet.

Callitriche verna L.   Vernal Water Starwort
    C. palustris L.

Slender perennial, submerged or floating in water or rooting in mud; stems 5-25 cm long; submerged leaves linear, 1-nerved, 5-22 mm long; floating and emergent leaves obovate, 3-nerved; floral bracts present; fruit sessile, about 1 mm long and slightly narrower, oblong-obovate, keeled on the back; styles 1-2.5 mm long.
Quiet cool water of ponds, vernal pools, lakes and slow streams, 5200 to about 7550 feet.

LIMNANTHACEAE   Meadow-foam Family

Delicate annuals, usually glabrous and juicy; leaves alternate, pinnate to pinnatifid; flowers regular and perfect on long axillary peduncles; perianth of 3 to 5 parts (sometimes 6); sepals nearly free; petals not united; stamens 6 to 10 or 12; pistil 2- to 5- or 6-carpellary; ovary deeply divided into globular segments; styles as many as the segments of the ovary, united at the base; fruit fleshy, nutlet-like, one-seeded.

Floerkea Willd.

Small delicate glabrous annuals with simple or branched stems and pinnate leaves; flowers tiny, solitary; petals much shorter than the sepals, both usually 3, sometimes 2 or 4; stamens 3 to 6; carpels usually 2 or 3; style 2- or 3-cleft above; fruits papillose-warty.

Floerkea proserpinacoides Willd.

Glabrous weak-stemmed annuals 10-25 cm tall; leaves few, long-petioled, 2-7 cm long, with 3 to 5 lanceolate to linear leaflets; flowers axillary, long-peduncled; sepals united at the base, 3-5 mm long; petals white or purplish, about half as long as the sepals; stamens 3 or 4, each attached to a scale-like gland, or sometimes 3 or more stamens without glands; fruiting carpels 1 to 3, nearly globular, separating at maturity.
Wet, often stony, springy, mossy places in partial shade, 5000 to about 6000 feet.

CELASTRACEAE   Staff-tree Family

Trees, shrubs or woody climbers, with opposite or alternate, deciduous or evergreen leaves with or without small stipules; flowers small, usually perfect, mostly axillary, greenish to reddish, single or in small clusters; sepals 4 or 5, persistent, united below; petals as many as sepals or rarely absent; stamens as many as sepals or twice as many, inserted on the broad flat or lobed disc; pistil mostly 3- to 5-carpellary; style 1, short; fruit in ours a 3- to 5-celled loculicidal capsule or follicle; seeds usually with a fleshy aril.

Pachistima Raf.

Glabrous evergreen shrubs with quadrangular stems, leathery opposite leaves and minute deciduous stipules; flowers small, inconspicuous, perfect, 4-parted, except the pistil, solitary or clustered in the leaf axils; stamens inserted at the edge of a flattened disc; ovary 2-celled, adherent to the disc; stigma 1; fruit a one- or two-seeded capsule; seeds with a white lobed aril.

Pachistima myrsinites (Pursh) Raf.   Mountain Lover; Oregon Boxwood
Low branched leafy glabrous shrub 20-100 cm tall, or sometimes almost prostrate; leaves leathery, oblong-lanceolate, 1-3 cm long, short-petioled, serrate, dark glossy green above, paler beneath; flowers 1 to 3, small, 4-parted, short-peduncled; petals reddish-brown or maroon or dark yellowish; capsules 3-5 mm long; seeds shining, black or dark brown, enclosed in a fringed whitish aril.
Coniferous shady forests, mostly near streams, 4500 to about 6000 feet.

ACERACEAE   Maple Family

Trees or shrubs, monoecious, dioecious, polygamous or perfect-flowered; leaves opposite, simple, palmately lobed to pinnately compound; flowers usually regular, perfect or imperfect, in corymbs or panicles; sepals 4 or 5; petals 4 or 5 or none; stamens 4 to 12, often 8, borne on the disc or hypogynous; disc lobed, thick, sometimes obsolete; pistil 1; styles 1 or 2; ovary superior, 2-celled; fruit of 2 long-winged samaras, united but separating at maturity.

Acer L.

Shrubs or trees with opposite leaves; inflorescence often drooping; flowers small; calyx 5- to 12-parted; petals none or the same number as the sepals; stamens 3 to 12; carpels 2 usually, each with 2 ovules; styles 2; carpels winged.

Acer glabrum Torr. ssp. douglasii (Hook.) Wesml.   Mountain Maple
Small tree 1-10 meters tall; stems glabrous with smooth grayish to reddish-purple bark; leaves 5-10 cm long, glabrous to sparsely glandular-puberulent, palmately 3- to 5-lobed, dentate; flowers in small, few-flowered clusters, polygamous, about 8 mm broad; sepals 5, or 4 or 6; petals the same number as sepals, or none; stamens usually twice the number of sepals, inserted at the outer edge of the disc; styles 2; samaras glabrous. the wings about 2 cm long.
Streambanks, edges of meadows and open slopes, 4500 to about 5500 feet.

Trifolium cyathiferum

Trifolium eriocephalum

Trifolium latifolium

Trifolium macrocephalum

Vicia americana

Erodium cicutarium

Geranium viscosissimum

Linum perenne

Euphorbia serpyllifolia

Callitriche verna

Floerkea proserpinacoides

Pachistima myrsinites

RHAMNACEAE   Buckthorn Family

Deciduous to evergreen shrubs, small trees or climbers; leaves simple, stipulate, alternate or opposite; flowers in axillary or terminal clusters, small, regular, perfect to imperfect; calyx 4- or 5-lobed; petals 4 or 5, rarely none; stamens as many as petals, opposite the petals, inserted at the edge of the disc; pistil 1; ovary superior or imbedded in the disc, 2- to 5-celled; ovules 1 or 2 to a cell; fruit a capsule, drupe or berry, or sometimes a samara; seeds 1 or 2 per locule.

Flowers solitary or in small clusters; leaves thin with one main vein; shrubs 0.5-3 meters tall ....*Rhamnus*

Flowers in large many-flowered clusters; leaves thick, shiny above, whitish beneath, with 3 prominent main veins; shrubs 2-5 m tall ....*Ceanothus*

Ceanothus L.

Prostrate to erect shrubs or small trees, sometimes spiny; leaves alternate to opposite, deciduous or evergreen; flowers in axillary or terminal cymes or panicles, very small, white or pinkish to deep blue or purple; calyx 5-lobed, the lobes petaloid and deciduous; petals 5, hooded and long-clawed; stamens 5, opposite the petals; ovary 3-lobed, imbedded in the disc and joined to it; disc joined to the calyx; style 1, 3-cleft; fruit a capsule, separating at maturity into 3 1-seeded carpels.

Ceanothus velutinus Dougl.   Greasewood; Sticky Laurel; Tobacco-brush

Shrub, 1-2 meters tall, evergreen, puberulent and strongly spice-scented; leaves alternate, ovate to elliptic, 2.5-10 cm long, finely and closely glandular-toothed, dark, smooth and varnished-shiny above, pale, velvety and prominently 3-nerved beneath; flowers white, in large dense panicles; capsules 4-5 mm long, 3-lobed, viscid-glandular.
Dry open mixed woods and mountain slopes, 4500 to about 5800 feet.

Rhamnus L.

Shrubs or small trees; leaves alternate, pinnately veined, deciduous or persistent; flowers small, perfect to imperfect, greenish-yellow, in axillary clusters; calyx 4- or 5-lobed, the hypanthium campanulate, the upper portion deciduous, the lower persistent at the base of the fruit; petals when present shorter than the sepals, slightly hooded; stamens short; ovary 2- to 4-celled, free from the disc; fruit 2 to 4 fleshy berries.

Rhamnus alnifolia L'Her.   Buckthorn; Alder-leaved Coffee Berry

Dioecious shrub, 0.5-3 meters tall, puberulent or glabrate; leaves deciduous, thin, oval to elliptic, 4-11 cm long, glandular-serrate; flowers 1 to 5 in axillary clusters, greenish, appearing with the leaves, of 4 or 5 parts, without petals; sepals mostly 5; berry bluish-black, 3-seeded.
Swamps, bogs and moist ground in woods, 4500 to about 6000 feet.

MALVACEAE   Mallow Family

Herbs, shrubs or trees with sticky juice; leaves alternate, stipulate, usually stellate-pubescent, entire to palmately lobed; flowers regular to slightly irregular, perfect or imperfect, often showy; sepals 5; petals 5, white, yellow, pink or lavender, usually fused at the base; stamens numerous, fused into a slender tube, the anthers freed separately or in small groups, dehiscing all the way around; pistil 1- to many-carpellary; ovary superior, the locules usually in a ring; fruit a loculicidal capsule or the carpels falling separately; seeds 1 to several in a locule.

Flowers rose-colored, the petals usually over 2 cm long; leaves 5-15 cm long; plants 1-2 meters tall..*Iliamna*
Flowers mostly pinkish to bluish-lavender to white, the petals 1-2 cm long; leaves mostly less than 5 cm long; plants mostly under 1 meter tall...*Sidalcea*

Iliamna Greene

Stellate-pubescent perennials with large stipulate deciduous lobed leaves; involucel bractlets 3, persistent; flowers large and showy, pinkish or lavender to rose-purple or rarely white, in axillary clusters; stamen-column hirsute, the filaments freed separately; stigmas capitate; fruit nearly globose; carpels hirsute as well as stellate-pubescent on the back, dehiscing their full length; seeds 2 to 4 per carpel.

Iliamna rivularis Greene   Wild Hollyhock; Streambank Globe Mallow
Branching perennial 1-2 meters tall, sparsely pubescent with simple as well as stellate hairs; leaves nearly orbicular, 3- to 7-lobed, 5-15 cm long, coarsely toothed with rounded teeth; flowers in loose raceme-like clusters; involucel bractlets linear, setaceous, 4-6 mm long; calyx finely stellate-puberulent, 6-8 mm long; petals deeply emarginate, rose or white, about 2 cm long; fruit 8-10 mm long, the carpels densely pubescent, 3- or 4-seeded. Mostly along streams, 4500 to about 4700 feet.

Sidalcea Gray

Annual or perennial (ours) herbs; leaves pubescent, alternate, palmately lobed or divided; flowers in terminal racemes or spikes, white to deep pink or pinkish-lavender, dimorphic; petals ciliate; staminal tube in 2 or 3 series of 10 to 20 or more stamens in each series; styles stigmatic their full length; carpels 5 to 10, indehiscent, 1-seeded, short-beaked or beakless.

Sidalcea oregana (Nutt.) Gray   Oregon Sidalcea
Erect perennial 20-150 cm tall, pubescent with simple or branched or stellate hairs, or a mixture of hairs, or glabrate; leaves orbicular, 5-10 cm broad, 3- to 7-lobed; inflorescence racemose, densely stellate-puberulent; calyx 3-9 mm long, finely-stellate to bristly; petals 1-2 cm long, light pinkish to deep rose-purple, the perfect flowers larger and lighter-colored than the pistillate ones; carpels about 3 mm long, the beak short or missing.
Meadows, along streams and in Ponderosa Pine woods, 5000 to about 6000 feet.

HYPERICACEAE   St. John's wort Family

Herbs, shrubs or small trees with opposite or whorled leaves; leaves (ours) gland-dotted; flowers regular and perfect; sepals and petals 4 or 5; stamens numerous, often in 3 or 5 groups; ovary 1- to 7-celled; fruit a many-seeded capsule or a berry.

Hypericum |Tourn.| L.

Annual or perennial herbs (ours) black-dotted throughout; leaves opposite; flowers yellow, usually in cymes; sepals and petals 5; stamens many, separate or in groups;

ovary 1-celled, or sometimes 3- to 6-celled; styles 3 to 6; fruit a capsule.

1. Plant a dwarf, the stems usually under 10 cm long, creeping along the ground and forming small mats; leaves yellowish, crowded and often overlapping; flowers about 5 or 6 mm broad, pale coppery-yellow..*H. anagalloides*
1. Plants mostly erect; stems up to 80 cm tall; leaves green, not yellowish; flowers bright yellow, 16-26 mm broad, the petals longer than the calyx
   2. Flowering stem mostly over 30 cm tall, mostly branched above, rising singly from a rosette of sterile short shoots at the base; plant a taprooted perennial................*H. perforatum*
   2. Flowering stems numerous, mostly under 30 cm tall; plant a perennial with slender spreading rhizomes ....*H. formosum*

Hypericum anagalloides C. & S.   Bog or Creeping St. John's wort

A low matted plant with creeping and rooting, as well as erect, stems 1-30 cm tall; leaves ovate, obovate or elliptic, obtuse, 2-15 mm long; flowers solitary or in few-flowered cymes; sepals unequal, slightly shorter than the petals; petals small, coppery-yellow; stamens 15 to 20, free from each other; styles 3, short, capsule 1-celled.
Wet bogs and moist meadows, 5700 to about 7500 feet.

Hypericum formosum H. B. K. var. nortoniae (M. E. Jones) C. L. Hitchc.

Western St. John's wort

Perennial plant with slender rhizomes and erect usually simple stems mostly under 30 cm tall; leaves 1-3 cm long, obovate to ovate-lanceolate, black-dotted; cymes few-flowered; sepals 3 or 4 mm long, black-dotted; petals yellow, black-dotted, longer than the sepals; stamens many, in 3 to 5 groups; styles slender; capsules 3-celled; seeds about 8 mm long.
Wet to moist meadows and slopes in the mountains, 7000 to about 8000 feet.

Hypericum perforatum L.   Common St. John's wort

Taprooted perennial; stems 30-80 cm tall, usually much-branched and with many sterile short shoots around the base; leaves sessile, 1-3 cm long, oblong or linear to obovate-lanceolate, obtuse at the tip, black-dotted along the margins; flowers in small clusters at the ends of the branches; sepals acute, black-dotted; petals twice as long as the sepals, bright yellow, black-dotted along the margins, 8-12 mm long; stamens united at their bases into 3 groups; styles 3, spreading; capsules acute, reddish, glandular, 3-celled.
Shady moist mixed woods, about 4500 feet. Weed poisonous to horses.

VIOLACEAE   Violet Family

Annual to perennial herbs (ours) with alternate or basal stipulate leaves; flowers perfect, mostly solitary on axillary peduncles, irregular (ours) ; sepals 5, persistent, not united, sometimes unequal; petals 5, hypogynous, the lowest the largest and often spurred; stamens 5, the filaments short or missing, the anthers closely joined around the style; ovary superior, 1-celled; style 1; fruit a capsule (ours) dehiscing by 3 valves, or a berry in some species; seeds large.

Viola [Tourn.] L.

Low annual or perennial caulescent or acaulescent herbs; leaves simple, stipulate; flowers ordinarily showy but often inconspicuous and cleistogamous later in the season, usually on long peduncles; petals 5, white, yellow, blue or violet, often with colored veins, the lowest petal spurred or saccate; stamens 5; style head bearded or glabrous.

1. Petals white to blue or bluish or purple
    2. Spur at the base of the flower conspicuous, longer than broad, sometimes hooked at the tip; flowers normally violet; style hairy at the top_______________________________*V. adunca*
    2. Spur short and often pouched; flowers white to bluish or violet-purple; plants of soggy meadows and banks
        3. Flowers definitely white, the petals with purple lines; petals 6-8 mm long; leaves kidney-shaped or nearly circular _______________________________*V. macloskeyi*
        3. Flowers bluish to violet-purple (rarely white); petals 10-15 mm long; leaves kidney-shaped
            4. Petals pale bluish; spur pouched; leaf blades 2.5-3.5 cm broad; flowers 10-13 mm long_______________________________*V. palustris*
            4. Petals violet or violet-purple; leaf blades 2.5-8 cm broad; flowers 10-20 mm long_______________________________*V. nephrophylla*
1. Petals yellow, sometimes tinged with blue or purple or white
    5. Leaf blades circular or nearly so; leaves mostly flat on the ground
        6. Leaves thick, leathery, dark green, usually hairy with brown dots on both sides, some at least lasting through the winter even under snow_______________*V. sempervirens*
        6. Leaves thinner, bright green, often hairy but without brown dots, usually withering in the fall_______________________________*V. orbiculata*
    5. Leaf blades either broader than long or longer than broad but not rounded or circular in outline
        7. Leaves thin, the blade heart-shaped at the base; flowering stems weak, up to 30 cm tall, leafy near the top but not near the base; flower stalk about as long as the leaf_______________________________*V. glabella*
        7. Leaves thicker, mostly tapering into the petiole; stems mostly underground, the plant rarely more than 15 cm above ground
            8. Leaf blades purplish, usually less than 4 cm long, conspicuously and heavily veined; some petals purple on the back_______________*V. purpurea*
            8. Leaf blades not usually purplish, often over 4 cm long, not conspicuously veined; petals sometimes purple on the back_______________*V. nuttallii*

Viola adunca J. E. Sm. Long-spurred Violet

Perennial with slender rootstocks, glabrous or pubescent, with several stems, short at first but elongating with age to as much as 10 cm tall; basal leaves broadly ovate, crenate, cordate at the base; petioles mostly much longer than the blades; stipules entire or lacerate; peduncles much longer than the leaves; flowers 5-15 mm long; petals light to deep blue or violet, white at the base, the spur narrow, usually half the petal length, often hooked at the tip; style head bearded.
Meadows, woods and open ground, 4500 to about 8000 feet and probably higher.

1. Flowers produced on short aerial stems

    2. Plants usually over 5 cm tall; flowers mostly blue throughout, the petals 10-15 mm long; leaves usually hairy_______________var. **adunca**

    2. Plants mostly dwarf, under 5 cm tall; petals 4-5 mm long, dark veined and with much white at the base; leaves not hairy_______________var. **bellidifolia** (Greene) Harrington

1. Flowers produced from a stemless base; petals lavender; leaves narrowly ovate_______________var. **cascadensis** (M. S. Baker) C. L. Hitchc.

With the species, up to about 9000 feet.

Viola glabella Nutt.   Woodland Violet
Perennial from thick scaly rootstocks; flowering stems erect, up to 30 cm tall, leafy above but not near the base; stipules entire; leaf blades reniform to ovate-cordate, acute, crenate-serrate; petioles of the basal leaves up to 20 cm long, the cauline very short; flowers 1 to 3 to a stem, 8-14 mm long; spur short; petals bright yellow with purple veins; style head bearded.
Moist woods, 4500 to 6700 feet.

Viola macloskeyi Lloyd   Sweet White Violet
Low acaulescent perennial from a slender rhizome and stolons; stipules membranous, glandular; petioles mostly 2-4 cm long; leaf blades ovate-cordate to orbicular, crenate; leaves and peduncles developing directly from the rhizome; petals white, 5-10 mm long, the spur short and purple-veined; style head glabrous.
Shady wet bogs, meadows and streambanks, 5100 to about 7300 feet.

Viola nephrophylla Greene   Northern Bog Violet
Glabrous acaulescent perennial; leaves cordate-orbicular or reniform, 2.5-8 cm broad, crenate; flowers violet to violet-purple, 10-20 mm long, the spur short, about as broad as long.
Moist shade and swampy meadows, about 5000 feet.

Viola nuttallii Pursh   Nuttall's Violet
Perennial from short erect rootstocks; stems mostly underground; leaves elliptic to ovate, lightly crenate-undulate to entire; peduncles about equaling the leaves; flowers 7-15 mm long; petals yellow, the lower with brownish-purple veins, the upper brownish-purple on the back; spur short; style head bearded.
Mostly in dry open places in mixed woods, 4500 to about 6000 feet.

Leaves shaggy-hairy, especially when young, the blades rather elliptic, tapering into the petiole, generally 4-8 cm long..var. **praemorsa** (Dougl.) Wats.
Leaves not hairy, the blades broadest at or near the base, generally less than 5 cm long..var. **vallicola** (A. Nels.) St. John
With the species.

Viola orbiculata Geyer   Round-leaved Violet
Perennial from scaly rootstocks; flowering stems very short; leaf blades almost orbicular, thin, crenate-serrate; flowers 10-15 mm long; spur short-saccate; petals whitish-yellow with purple veins.
Shady moist coniferous woods, about 4500 to about 7500 feet.

Viola palustris L.   Marsh Violet
Short-stemmed slender perennial 1-3 cm tall with slender creeping stolons; leaves glabrous to puberulent, round-cordate to reniform, crenate, 2-5 cm broad, the petioles 3-8 cm long; peduncles longer than the leaves or about as long; flowers white to pale violet, purple-veined, 1.5-2 cm long, the spur saccate, about half as long as its blade.
Boggy lake borders, streambanks and moist to wet mountain meadows, 4500·to about 8000 feet.

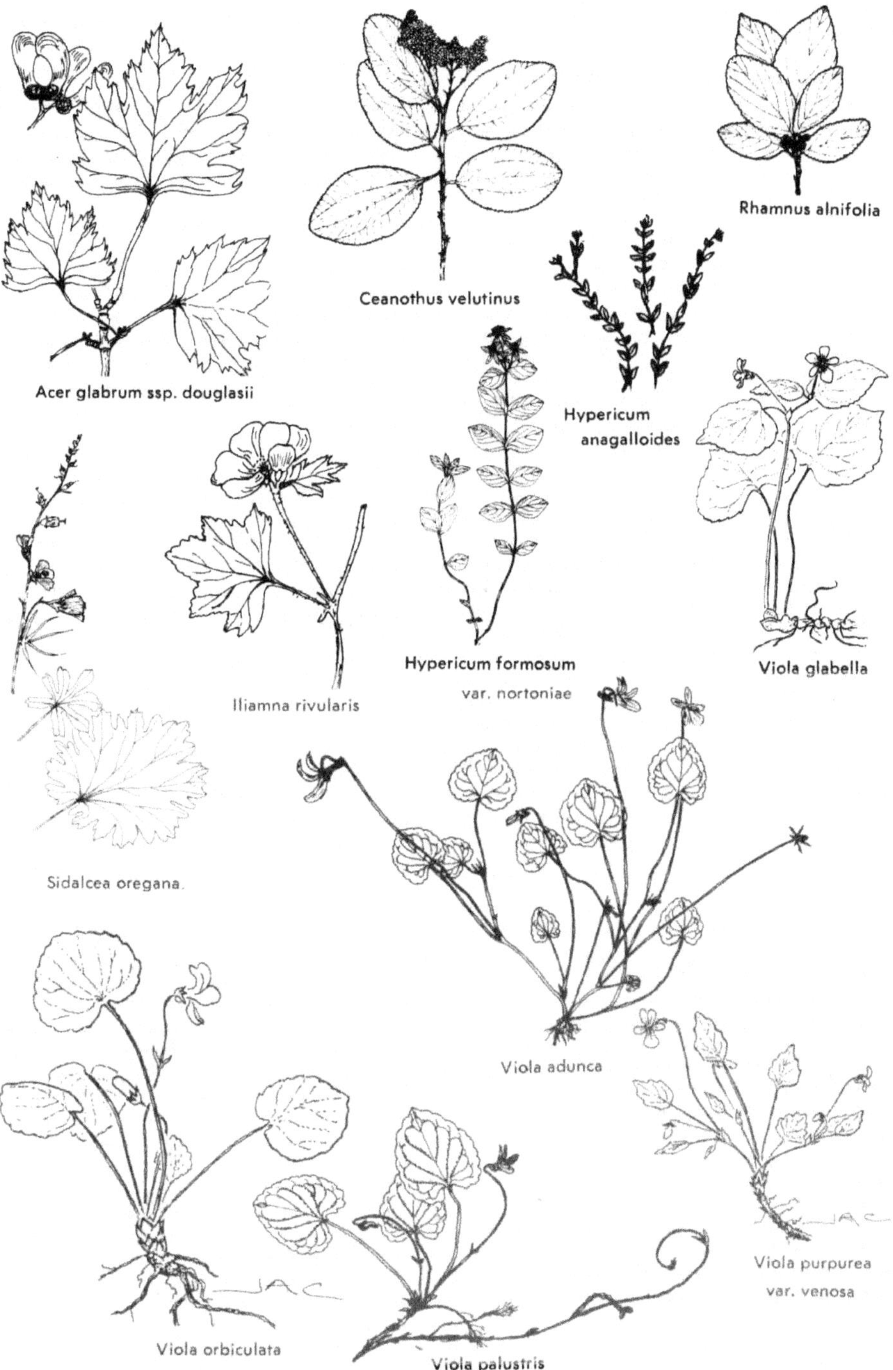

Rhamnus alnifolia
Ceanothus velutinus
Acer glabrum ssp. douglasii
Hypericum
anagalloides
Viola glabella
Iliamna rivularis
Hypericum formosum
var. nortoniae
Sidalcea oregana.
Viola adunca
Viola orbiculata
Viola palustris
Viola purpurea
var. venosa

Viola purpurea Kell. var. **venosa** (Wats.) Brain.   Mountain Violet
   Caulescent perennial 5-15 cm tall; herbage pubescent and purplish-tinged; stipules entire, lacerate or toothed; leaves long-petioled, thick, veiny, irregularly coarsely toothed, broadly ovate below, narrowed above; peduncles axillary; petals yellow with brown-purple veins, the upper ones purple or brown on the back, the spur very short; style head bearded.
Mountain woods, 4500 to about 7000 feet.

Viola sempervirens Greene   Evergreen Violet
   Perennial with slender stolon-like stems 5-30 cm long; leaves thickish, dark green, evergreen, usually strigose and brown-dotted beneath, 1-2.5 cm broad, round-cordate; stipules large and brownish; earliest flowers basal, the later ones few, cleistogamous; petals light yellow, 7-10 mm long; spur short, saccate.
Moist shady woods, 4500 to about 6000 feet.

LOASACEAE   Blazing-Star Family

   Annual or perennial herbs or shrubs, often with barbed, rough, viscid or stinging hairs; leaves opposite or alternate (ours) without stipules; flowers regular, solitary or in cymose clusters; calyx attached to the ovary, the lobes 5, sometimes 4, persistent; petals 4 to 10, united or free from each other; stamens petaloid, 5 to many in clusters opposite the petals, staminodia often alternating with the true petals; ovary 1- to 3-celled, inferior with 2 to 5 parietal placentae; fruit a capsule with 1 to many seeds.

Mentzelia [Plum.] L.

   Annual or perennial herbs with alternate barbed usually toothed or lobed viscid leaves; flowers solitary to clustered, subtended by bracts; free hypanthium short and flared; sepals 5; petals 5 to 10, yellowish to orange; stamens numerous, opposite the petals, the outer filaments petaloid; style 3-cleft; ovary inferior, 1-celled; capsule many-seeded.

Bracts at the base of the flower broader at the base than at the tip; seeds smooth between
   the angles .... *M. dispersa*
Bracts broadest at about the middle; seeds rough between the angles .... *M. albicaulis*

Mentzelia albicaulis Dougl.   White-stemmed Stick-leaf
   Annual 10-40 cm tall; stems often dichotomously branched, puberulent, shining-whitish; leaves 2-10 cm long, oblong to lanceolate, mostly sessile, entire to deeply lobed or toothed upward; flowers axillary in clusters of 1 to 3; calyx 1-2 cm long; petals obovate, 2-6 mm long, yellow; stamens 15 to 35, shorter than the petals; capsules 1-2.5 cm long, hispid; seeds tuberculate, irregularly angled.
Dry sandy soil, 4500 to about 6200 feet.

Mentzelia dispersa Wats.   Nada Stick-leaf
   Annual 10-60 cm tall, finely pubescent throughout; stems branching from the base; leaves oblong-lanceolate to ovate-lanceolate, entire to sinuate-dentate, 3-10 cm long, the lower alternate and short-petioled, the upper sessile and often opposite; flowers in the forks and in small leafy terminal clusters; calyx lobes 1.5-2.5 mm long; petals yellow,

2-6 mm long; stamens 15 to 35, shorter than the petals; capsules linear, 1-3 cm long, densely pubescent; seeds nearly smooth.
Dry sandy or gravelly soil, 4500 to about 5600 feet.

ELAEAGNACEAE   Oleaster Family

Deciduous (ours) or evergreen shrubs or trees; leaves opposite or alternate, silvery-scaly or stellate-pubescent; flowers small and inconspicuous, perfect or imperfect, solitary or clustered at the nodes; calyx tube enclosing the ovary and persistent in the pistillate or perfect flowers, the 4 calyx lobes deciduous, the staminate flowers with a 4-parted calyx; corolla missing; stamens 4 or 8; pistil 1-carpellary; style short; fruit a one-seeded achene or nutlet enclosed by the fleshy calyx tube and appearing to be a drupe.

Shepherdia Nutt.

Dioecious silvery shrubs with opposite entire leaves; flowers small, axillary, without petals; staminate flowers clustered at the nodes, with 4 spreading calyx lobes and 8 stamens; solitary pistillate flowers without stamens, the 4 calyx lobes short and erect, the 8-lobed hypanthium developing and becoming fleshy and enclosing the achene to form a drupe-like fruit.

Shepherdia canadensis (L.) Nutt.   Buffalo Berry; Soapberry

Erect branched shrub 0.5-2 meters tall, the young twigs brownish, the older branches silvery; leaves oval or oblong-ovate, 1-4.5 cm long, green above, densely silvery-stellate beneath with brownish scales; flowers brownish on the outside, greenish-yellow inside, 4 or 5 mm broad, without petals; fruit fleshy, 4-10 mm long, ellipsoid, red or yellowish.
Moist open woods, often near streams, 4500 to 9000 feet and probably higher.

ONAGRACEAE   Evening Primrose Family

Annual or perennial herbs or shrubs with opposite alternate or basal, simple to pinnatifid, glandular-stipitate leaves without stipules; flowers perfect, mostly regular, in leafy or bracteate terminal spikes or racemes, or solitary and axillary; calyx attached to the ovary and prolonged above as a free hypanthium; sepals and petals mostly 2 or 4 but sometimes 3 or 5 or missing, inserted at the top of the hypanthium; sepals separate or united, often turned to one side; petals white, yellow, pink, red, or lavender to purplish; stamens as many or twice as many as the petals, inserted at the top of the hypanthium; ovary inferior, usually 4-celled (sometimes 1-, 2- or 5-celled); style 1; stigma globose, discoid or 4-lobed; fruit a many-seeded capsule, rarely indehiscent, nut-like and only 1- or 2-seeded.

1. Leaves soft, thin, broad, opposite; flowers with 2 petals and 2 sepals, the petals about
   1 mm long ....*Circaea*
1. Leaves thicker, often narrower, either opposite or alternate; flowers with 4 petals and
   sepals usually over 1 mm long
        2. Petals white or yellow (sometimes turning pink or red with age)
            3. Flowers bright yellow; leaves sometimes in a basal rosette ....*Oenothera*
            3. Flowers white; leaves mostly on the stem
                4. Pods splitting early to reveal many seeds, each with a conspicuous tuft
                   of long hairs (the coma) at one end; leaves mostly opposite ....*Epilobium*

      4. Pods splitting later to reveal seeds but the coma missing; leaves mostly
          alternate ....*Gayophytum*
   2. Petals pink to purple, not white or yellow
      5. Seeds with a conspicuous tuft of hairs (coma) ....*Epilobium*
      5. Seeds without a coma
         6. Flowers without a stalk, closely crowded by the leaves, the inflorescence
           elongating with maturity; calyx lobes upright.....................................*Boisduvalia*
         6. Flowers with a stalk, not closely crowded on the stem; calyx lobes
           curved downward..*Clarkia*

Boisduvalia Spach

Hairy annuals with leafy stems; leaves simple, alternate, usually sessile; flowers small, diurnal, axillary or in leafy spikes; hypanthium short, funnelform; sepals 4, erect; petals 4, obovate, 2-lobed, purple to white; stamens 8, the set opposite the petals shorter than the other; stigma globose or with 4 short lobes; capsule 4-celled and 4-ribbed; seeds numerous, without a coma.

Boisduvalia densiflora (Lindl.) Wats.   Densely-flowered Boisduvalia

Simple to branched leafy annual 15-100 cm tall, canescent-pubescent or greenish, sometimes glandular; leaves many, crowded, entire to denticulate, the lower ones lanceolate, 1.5-5 cm long, the upper ones shorter and broader, becoming ovate and acuminate, 5-12 mm long; inflorescence of crowded terminal and lateral spikes which elongate in fruit; petals pale pink to rose-purple, 3-12 mm long, lobed nearly half their length; capsules straight, 6-10 mm long; seeds flat, brownish.
Dry rocky open ground, moist earlier in the season, about 5800 feet. Not common.

Circaea L.

Small perennial herbs with slender rootstocks and opposite, thin, broad leaves; flowers small, white, in terminal and axillary racemes; hypanthium very short, deciduous; sepals 2, reflexed; petals 2, white, notched; stamens 2, alternating with the petals; fruit indehiscent, nut-like, 1- or 2-seeded, usually covered with short hooked hairs.

Circaea alpina L.   Small Enchanter's Nightshade

Delicate perennial 10-60 cm tall, glabrous below, often puberulent above and in the inflorescence; leaves 2-6 cm long, cordate-ovate to ovate, nearly entire to slightly toothed, the petioles shorter than the blades; racemes often subtended by linear bracts; pedicels reflexed in fruit; sepals and petals 2, about 1 mm long; fruit obovoid, indehiscent, about 2 mm long, covered with hooked hairs.
Moist shady woods, 4600 to about 5600 feet.

Clarkia Pursh

Annual herbs with alternate or opposite simple leaves; flowers in leafy-bracted spikes or racemes, the buds erect, nodding or reflexed; hypanthium well-developed; calyx lobes separate or united, reflexed or spreading or all turned to one side; corolla regular to irregular; petals clawed, simple or lobed, cuneate to obovate; stamens 4 and alternate with the petals, or 8 (ours), the set borne on the petals shorter and sometimes not functional; stigma lobes 4, ovate to linear; capsules 4-celled, linear, roundish or 4-angled, often beaked; seeds crested, without a coma.

Flowers large, showy, conspicuous; petals lavender to rose-purple, deeply 3-lobed; calyx
lobes united and turned to one side; fertile stamens 4..*C. pulchella*
Flowers small, not showy; petals rose-purple, not conspicuously 3-lobed; calyx lobes green,
not united; fertile stamens 8 ....*C. rhomboidea*

Clarkia pulchella Pursh
Beautiful Clarkia

Finely-puberulent leafy annual 10-50 cm tall, simple to freely-branched; leaves linear-lanceolate to spatulate, 2-7 cm long; flowers slightly irregular, in short few-flowered racemes which elongate in fruit, the buds nodding; hypanthium lavender, short, the calyx lobes lavender, united and turned to one side; petals lavender to rose-purple, 3-lobed, 1.5-3 cm long, the claw with a tooth on each side; stamens 8, the set borne on the petals sterile and reduced, the anthers of the fertile ones coiling after shedding their pollen; stigmas oval-oblong, white, 1-3 mm long; capsules 1-2.5 cm long, straight or curved.
Dry to moist open sandy to rocky places, 4500 to about 5800 feet.

Clarkia rhomboidea Dougl.
Common Clarkia

Finely-pubescent annual 15-100 cm tall, simple or few-branched; leaves few, mostly about opposite, 2-7 cm long, lanceolate-ovate to elliptic; flowers few in loose racemes, the buds nodding; hypanthium hairy and white-scaly at the top; calyx lobes green, usually separate; corolla slightly irregular; petals 5-10 mm long, rose-purple, sometimes dotted, rhomboidal, the broad claw often toothed; fertile stamens 8, unequal; stigma lobes rounded, white to purple; capsules 1-3 cm long.
Dry to moist woods and rocky hillsides, about 4500 to 4600 feet.

Epilobium L.

Annual or perennial herbs mostly, sometimes shrubby, the perennials with stolons and rhizomes and sometimes wintering over by rosettes at their tips, or from bulblike turions; leaves opposite or alternate, sessile or short-petioled, entire to toothed; flowers perfect, usually in terminal racemes or panicles, occasionally axillary; hypanthium short or missing; sepals 4; petals 4, usually notched, rose-purple, pink, white or yellow; stamens 8, unequal; stigma oblong-clavate or 4-lobed; capsules linear to tapered at both ends, 4-celled; seeds with a tuft of silky hairs (a coma) at the tip.

1. Flowers large, showy, pink to purple; petals spreading, 10-20 mm long
    2. Stems mostly 10-30 cm tall; leaves 2-6 cm long; plants of moist to wet streambanks,
       gravel bars and creek beds..*E. latifolium*
    2. Stems mostly 50-100 cm tall, or more; leaves 5-15 cm long; plants of mostly dry
       rocky places..*E. angustifolium*
1. Flowers smaller and less showy, white to pink-purple; petals 2-12 mm long, not spreading
  usually
    3. Stems mostly over 30 cm tall, solitary, often branching at the top
        4. Leaves alternate, very narrow, 2-4 cm long, often with clusters of smaller leaves
          at the base of the petioles; plants glabrous annuals..*E. paniculatum*
        4. Leaves mostly opposite, broader, 1-7 cm long without clusters of smaller
          leaves; plants perennials
            5. Stems usually branching at the top; petals often pale to whitish; stems
              without over-wintering fleshy buds (turions) at the base..*E. adenocaulon*
            5. Stems not usually branched above; petals purplish or paler and pinkish;
              plants with well developed turions at the base..*E. brevistylum*
    3. Stems mostly under 30 cm tall (rarely to 40 cm), not usually branched above

   6. Plants many-stemmed, sometimes matted at the base
      7. Stems up to about 15 cm tall, often curved or bent or lying on or near
        the ground
        8. Leaves mostly in pairs near the stem base, alternate above, mostly
          broadly-rounded at the tip; stems sometimes hairy; capsules 2-5
          cm long
          9. Leaves without petioles, conspicuously crowded and over-
            lapping at the stem base..*E. oregonense*
          9. Leaves short-petioled, not crowded or overlapping at the
            stem base...*E. anagallidifolium*
        8. Leaves mostly not in pairs, alternate throughout, distinctly short-
          petioled, the tips round-pointed; stems often curved and bent
          and near the ground; capsules 2-2.5 cm long................*E. clavatum*
      7. Stems mostly over 15 cm tall; leaves and stems pale green, not hairy;
        capsules 4-7 cm long..*E. glaberrimum*
   6. Plants mostly with one (or few) stems
      10. Petals usually white, 2-5 mm long
        11. Petals 2-2.5 mm long; capsules glandular-hairy.................*E. pringleanum*
        11. Petals 2-5 mm long; capsules not glandular hairy.................*E. lactiflorum*
      10. Petals usually purplish, 2-8 mm long
        12. Petals 2-5 mm long..*E. halleanum*
        12. Petals 5-8 mm long..*E. hornemannii*

Epilobium adenocaulon Hausskn.   Northern Willow-herb

E. glandulosum Lehm. var. *adenocaulon* (Hausskn.) Fern.; *E. watsonii* Barbey var. *occidentale* (Trel.) C. L. Hitchc.

Perennial spreading by rootstocks that produce rosettes of leaves; stems freely branched above, glabrous below, 30-100 cm tall, glandular-pubescent in the inflorescence, the hairs incurved; leaves opposite, ovate to elliptic-lanceolate, 3-7 cm long, serrulate, the petioles winged and very short; inflorescence mostly compound, glandular-pubescent; sepals 2-5 mm long, often purplish; petals 3-10 mm long, notched, white or cream to deep purplish-red; capsules usually reddish, linear, 4-8 cm long, glandular-puberulent to glabrate; seeds papillate in lines; coma whitish.
Moist shady woods, about 6000 feet.

Epilobium anagallidifolium Lam.   Alpine Willow-herb

E. alpinum L. in part

Low matted perennials spreading by rhizomes and stolons, without turions; stems 5-15 cm tall, decumbent, generally crisp-puberulent in lines; leaves usually opposite and spreading, short-petioled, ovate, 1-2 cm long; flowers few, nodding to erect; pedicels 5-50 mm long; hypanthium short; sepals 1.5-6 mm long; petals 3-6 mm long, deep rose, pink, purplish or white, notched; stigma entire; capsule linear, mostly 2-4 cm long; seeds smooth; coma dingy.
Mostly on rocky slopes moistened by nearby melting snows, about 8000 to 9000 feet.

Epilobium angustifolium L.   Fire Weed

Perennial spreading by roots that form adventitious buds, glabrous except for fine puberulence in the inflorescence; stems few, erect, 0.5-2.5 meters tall; leaves alternate, lanceolate, nearly sessile and entire, 5-15 or 20 cm long; flowers many in long terminal racemes, subtended by small bracts; hypanthium scarcely developed; sepals 8-12 mm long, tinged lavender; petals rose to purple, or even white, clawed, 8-20 mm long; sta-

mens 8, shorter than the petals and often unequal, the filaments dilated below; style longer than the stamens, hairy at the base, the stigma 4-cleft; capsules 5-8 cm long, densely white-tomentose; seeds oblong; coma long and dingy.
Moist to dry rocky or open places, 5300 to 6300 feet.

Epilobium brevistylum Barbey   Slender Willow-herb
Perennial from slender rhizomes producing turions, dried scales of the previous year evident; stems erect, 5-90 cm tall, glabrous to pilose, often crisp-puberulent or glandular in the inflorescence; leaves opposite, linear- to ovate-lanceolate, mostly 1-4 cm long, sessile and clasping to short petioled, glabrous, entire to toothed; flowers rather few; fruiting pedicels 5-30 mm long; hypanthium 1.5-3 mm long; sepals 2-5 mm long; petals 3-6 mm long, purplish, pale or dark pink or white, notched; capsules glandular-pilose, about 4-6 cm long; seeds finely and densely papillate to nearly smooth; coma white to tawny.
Boggy streambanks and moist shady woods, 4650 to 5000 feet.

Plants glabrous; rare...var. **tenue** (Trel.) Jeps.
(*E. glandulosum* Lehm. var. *tenue* (Trel.) C. L. Hitchc.; *E. delicatum* var. *tenue* Trel.)
With the species.

Epilobium clavatum Trel.   Talus Willow-herb
E. alpinum var. *clavatum* (Trel.) C. L. Hitchc.
Low, densely-matted perennials spreading by stolons, without turions; stems purplish, 5-15 cm tall, decumbent, nearly glabrous to glandular-crisp-puberulent in lines; leaves broadly ovate, divergent, 1-2 cm long, almost entire, on short petioles, not reduced upward; flowers few, erect in bud; fruiting pedicels 1-2 cm long; sepals 3-4 mm long; petals 3-6 mm long, purplish to rose-colored or whitish; capsules purplish, subclavate, 1-2.5 cm long, 1.5-2 mm thick; seeds papillate; coma dingy.
Moist rocky slopes, slides and talus, 6000 to about 8500 feet.

Epilobium glaberrimum Barbey var. **fastigiatum** (Nutt.) Trel.   Smooth Willow-herb
Glaucous perennials from branching scaly rootstocks, without turions, often matted at the base; stems usually many, 10-30 cm tall, glabrous or slightly glandular-puberulent in the inflorescence, often purplish; leaves opposite, lanceolate to ovate, entire to denticulate, glabrous, pale, sessile and often clasping, numerous, usually crowded and overlapping, mostly 1-3 cm long; pedicels 5-20 mm long; flowers few; sepals 1-2 mm long, usually purplish-tinged; petals notched, deep-rose-purplish to pinkish-white, 4-8 mm long; capsules 4-7 cm long, slender, usually glabrous; seeds papillate; coma whitish.
Streambanks and moist woods, 6500 to about 7000 feet.

Epilobium halleanum Hausskn.   Hall's Willow-herb
E. glandulosum Lehm. var. *macounii* (Trel.) C. L. Hitchc.
Perennials with small turions; stems slender, 20-50 cm tall, glabrous below, glandular-puberulent above, finely pubescent in long lines from the lower leaf bases; leaves lance-linear to narrowly ovate, some with clasping base, 1.5-4 cm long, nearly sessile to usually petiolate, entire to serrulate; flowers small; calyx about 3 mm long; petals 2-5 mm long,

white to purplish; capsules 2-5 cm long, strigillose, not glandular; seeds smooth or papillate, hyaline-beaked.
Moist meadows and other wet places, often near melting snow, about 5700 feet.

Epilobium hornemannii Reich.   Hornemann's Willow-herb
Perennials with scaly rootstocks; stems slender, 10-30 or 40 cm tall, glabrous except for the crisp pubescence in lines below the leaf bases, slightly glandular above; leaves ovate to elliptic-ovate, 1.5-4 cm long, nearly entire or serrulate, on short petioles or nearly sessile; flowers few, erect; fruiting pedicels 1-2 cm long; sepals 3-5 mm long; petals 5-8 mm long, purplish or violet to white, notched; capsules linear, 2-5 cm long and less than 1 mm thick; seeds usually papillose; coma dingy.
Moist banks and meadows, talus slopes and rocky woods, 4900 to about 9200 feet.

Epilobium lactiflorum Hausskn.   White-flowered Willow-herb
E. alpinum of Am. authors, not L.; *E. alpinum* var. *lactiflorum* (Hausskn.) C. L. Hitchc.
Similar to *E. hornemannii* but less pubescent on the decurrent lines and in the inflorescence; stems usually decumbent; leaves 2-5 cm long, mostly short-petiolate, lanceolate to oblong-ovate, spreading, delicate, pale green, nearly entire or denticulate; flowers few; petals 2-5 mm long, white or cream-colored to rose-tipped; capsules linear, 4-5 cm long; seeds smooth, beaked; coma dingy.
Moist slopes, slides, bogs, banks and meadows, 4500 to about 8000 feet.

Epilobium latifolium L.   Broad-leaved Willow-herb
Perennial from a cespitose rootstock; stems 10-60 cm tall; leaves glaucous and glabrous or finely puberulent, mostly opposite, lanceolate to ovate, entire to denticulate, 2-6 cm long, nearly sessile; racemes 2- to 12-flowered, leafy-bracted; pedicels 3-40 mm long; hypanthium absent; sepals cleft to the ovary, lanceolate, purplish, 10-15 mm long; petals broadly ovate, deep to pale purple, or rarely white, 15-25 mm long; style shorter than the stamens; stigma deeply 4-cleft; capsules glabrous or canescent, 3-8 cm long; coma tawny.
Streambanks, gravel bars and creek beds, and wet meadows, 4500 to about 8000 feet.

Epilobium oregonense Hausskn.   Oregon Willow-herb
E. alpinum var. *gracillimum* (Trel.) C. L. Hitchc.
Stoloniferous perennials with erect stems 10-30 cm tall, glabrous or sparsely glandular above; leaves linear to oblong-lanceolate, mostly crowded on the lower part of the stem, reduced and remote above, sessile, glabrous, 1-2.5 cm long, entire to denticulate; flowers usually 1 to 3; fruiting pedicels 1-3.5 cm long; calyx 3.5-5 mm long, the lobes often purplish; petals pinkish, violet or purplish to cream-colored, 4-7 mm long, deeply notched; capsules slender, 2-5 cm long; seeds smooth; coma white.
Moist banks, meadows and bogs, 4500 to about 8000 feet.

Epilobium paniculatum Nutt.   Tall annual Willow-herb
Erect freely-branched annual with simple stem and shreddy bark below, 30-90 cm tall, glabrous except slightly glandular-puberulent in the inflorescence; leaves narrowly lanceolate to linear, usually alternate, petiolate, entire to denticulate, 2-4 cm long, early

deciduous and with fascicles of smaller leaves in the axils; racemes lax, few-flowered, terminal on the many branches of the panicle; bracts linear; pedicels 5-15 mm long, usually glandular-puberulent; hypanthium 2-3 mm long; petals obcordate, rose to pale pinkish or almost white, 3-6 mm long; capsules linear-clavate, usually slightly glandular-puberulent, 2-2.5 cm long; seeds flattened; coma tawny.
Moist or dry open ground, often in light woods, 4500 to 6000 feet.

Epilobium pringleanum Hausskn. var. tenue (Trel.) Munz   Glandular Willow-herb

Perennial with small loosely formed turions; stems 5-20 or 30 cm tall, very slender, glabrous below, pilose and glandular above, the hairs sometimes not in lines; leaves crowded above, ovate to oblong-linear, serrulate, 1-3 cm long, mostly shorter than the internodes, sessile or nearly so; flowers erect; hypanthium about 1 mm long; sepals 1-1.5 mm long; petals purple to white, 2-2.5 mm long, not spreading; capsules glandular-pubescent, mostly 3-4 mm long, glandular-pubescent; seeds with a dingy coma.
Moist meadows, bogs and rocky banks in shady woods, 5800 feet.

Gayophytum Juss.

Slender, usually widely-branching annuals; leaves small, entire, linear to lanceolate, alternate or the lower opposite, nearly sessile to short-petioled; flowers small in racemes or short spikes in the upper axils of the leaves; hypanthium essentially missing; sepals 4, usually reflexed, not united; petals 4, white, often drying pink or red; stamens 8 in 2 unequal sets; stigmas capitate; capsules linear to linear-clavate, 2-celled, 4-valved; seeds many, without a coma.

1. Petals not over 1 mm long
    2. Plants leafy, 5-15 cm tall; petals 1 mm long; capsules erect, without a stalk ....*G. humile*
    2. Plants 15-40 cm tall, not so leafy; petals 0.5 mm long; capsules with a stalk, usually
       curving downward ....*G. ramosissimum*
1. Petals 1-4 mm long
    3. Plants flowering from the base; petals 1-2.5 mm long; capsule slightly hairy ....*G. diffusum*
    3. Plants not flowering from the base; petals 2-4 mm long; capsules densely
       spreading-hairy.. *G. heterozygum*

Gayophytum diffusum T. & G. ssp. parviflorum Lewis & Szwey.

C. nuttallii of authors, not T. & G.   Spreading Gayophytum
Erect or usually branched plants 10-50 cm tall, appressed-puberulent to spreading-hairy above; leaves petioled, linear or linear-lanceolate, mostly 2-4 cm long, glabrous or strigose, reduced upward on the stem; sepals 2-3 mm long, reflexed; petals 1-2.5 mm long, white to pink; capsules 4-12 mm long, glabrous or pubescent, spreading or reflexed.
Dry rocky slopes and meadows, 5500 to about 8000 feet.

Gayophytum heterozygum Lewis & Szwey.   Zigzag Gayophytum

G. diffusum var. *villosum* Munz
Plants spreading-pubescent, strigulose or nearly glabrous, 15-50 cm tall, much-branched especially in the upper half, the central stem often zigzag; lower leaves to 6 or 7 cm long and 4-6 mm wide, the upper shorter and narrower; sepals 1.5-2.5 mm long; petals 2-4 mm long; capsules 5-10 mm long, the seeds evident within.
Dry sandy soil, rocky wooded places and gravel bars, 5800 to about 6600 feet.

Gayophytum humile Juss.   Dwarf Gayophytum
    G. pumilum Wats.
    Low very leafy annual 5-15 cm tall, diffusely-branched from the base, glabrous to grayish-pubescent; leaves linear to lance-linear, 0.5-3 cm long, entire, short-petioled; flowers sessile or nearly so, in crowded spikes; petals 1 mm long, white or pinkish; capsules flattened, linear, not torulose, 7-15 mm long.
Dry ground, 5000 to about 6000 feet.

Gayophytum ramosissimum T. & G.   Much-branched Gayophytum
    Diffusely branched annual 15-40 cm tall, essentially glabrous, the branches filiform; leaves lance-linear, 1-3.5 cm long, reduced upwards; pedicels filiform, 3-6 mm long, spreading to sharply reflexed; sepals and petals about 0.5 mm long; capsules torulose, 2-6 mm long on long reflexed pedicels; seeds glabrous.
Dry rocky slopes and ridges, 5500 to about 5800 feet.

Oenothera L.

    Caulescent or acaulescent annual, biennial or perennial herbs; leaves alternate or basal; flowers yellow or white turning reddish or purplish with age, sometimes fragrant, often nocturnal, in racemes or spikes; hypanthium evident, usually deciduous after anthesis; sepals 4, reflexed, mostly not united, sometimes united and turned to one side; petals 4; stamens 8, equal or unequal; stigma capitate, discoid or deeply lobed; capsules woody or membranous, straight, curved or coiled, 4-celled, dehiscent; seeds many.

1. Flowering stems leafy, 15-100 cm tall
    2. Plant a low delicate annual to 15 cm tall, branched from the base, often broader
       than tall..*O. andina*
    2. Plant a biennial or short-lived perennial, 30-100 cm tall, mostly taller than broad,
       branching above but not from the base..*O. biennis*
1. Flowering stems not leafy, the leaves all in a basal rosette; leaves equaling or longer
    than the flowers..*O. heterantha*

Oenothera andina Nutt.   Plateau Primrose
    Low much-branched annual, finely canescent-puberulent throughout to nearly glabrous, 2-15 cm tall and about as broad, or broader than tall; leaves alternate, linear to linear-oblanceolate, 5-15 mm long, the lower branches nearly leafless; flowers axillary and sessile, in crowded spikes; sepals reflexed; petals yellow, reddish in age, 1-5 mm long; stamens unequal; stigma capitate; capsules 5-6 mm long.
Dry granite sand, 7500 feet. Not common.

Oenothera biennis L.   Common Evening Primrose
    Simple or branched biennial or short-lived perennial 30-100 cm tall, usually grayish-strigose and with a mixture of longer, spreading hairs with reddish pustular bases; leaves lanceolate to oblanceolate or rhomboid, 3-20 cm long, 1-2.5 cm broad, entire to sinuate-denticulate; inflorescence a leafy-bracted spike elongating in fruit, the buds erect, the flowers opening in the evening or late in the day; free hypanthium 3-5 cm long; sepals 10-15 mm long, the free tips 2-4 mm long; petals 12-15 mm long, yellow; stigma lobes linear; capsules 2.5-4 cm long, rounded, linear-fusiform.
Moist open meadows near woods, 4500 to about 4600 feet.

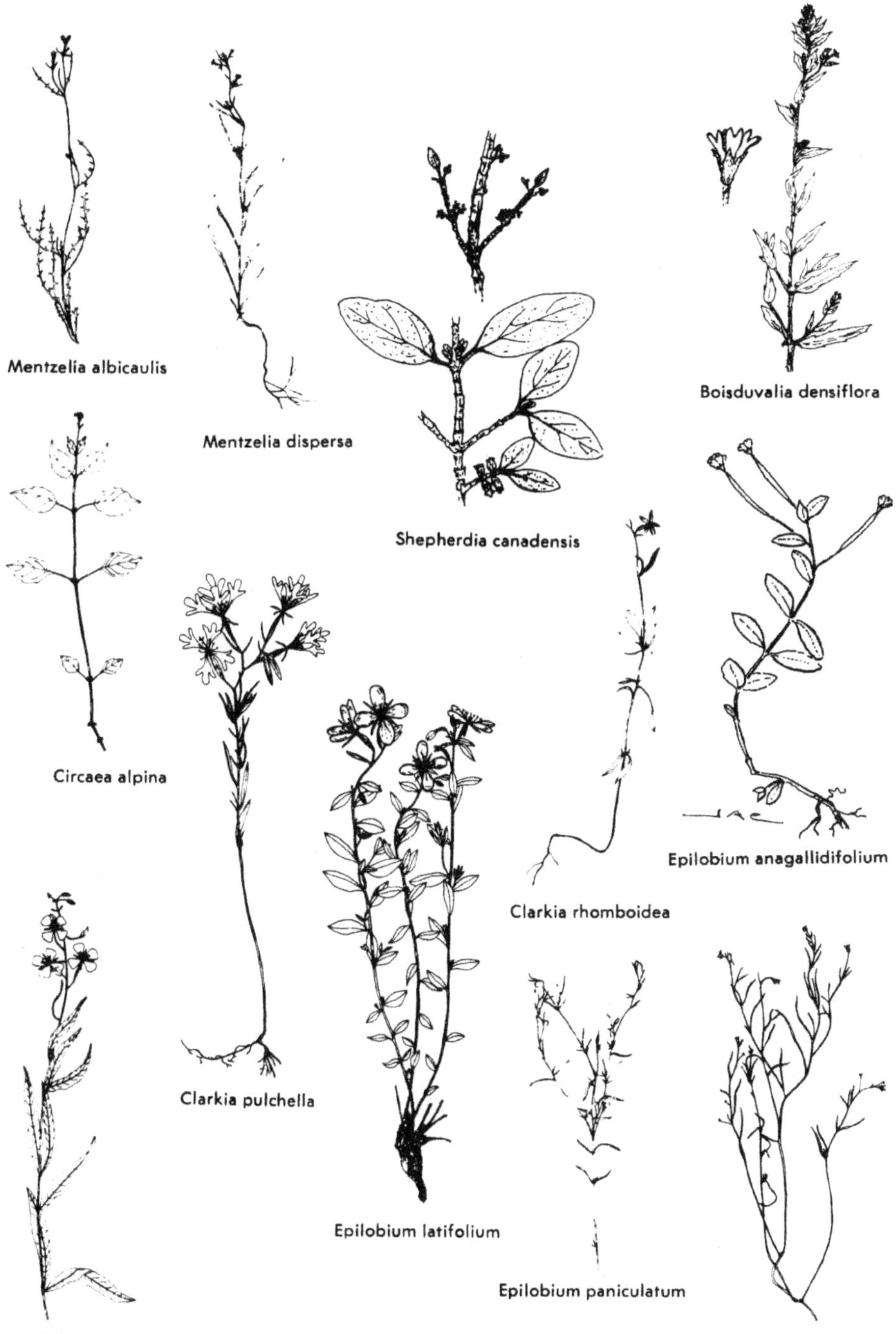

Mentzelia albicaulis
Mentzelia dispersa
Shepherdia canadensis
Boisduvalia densiflora
Circaea alpina
Clarkia pulchella
Epilobium latifolium
Clarkia rhomboidea
Epilobium anagallidifolium
Epilobium angustifolium
Epilobium paniculatum
Gayophytum ramosissimum

Oenothera heterantha Nutt. Northern Sun-cup

Acaulescent cespitose perennial with a long taproot, glabrous to sparingly pubescent; leaves 5-20 cm long, obovate to linear-elliptic, entire or denticulate to lobed or sinuate-pinatifid at the base, on winged petioles; flowers sessile; free hypanthium 3-9 cm long; sepals not united, 5-8 mm long; petals yellow, notched, 8-13 mm long; stamens unequal; stigma globose-discoid; capsules oblong-ovoid, 12-15 mm long, glabrous.
Bogs, meadows, streambanks and moist wooded slopes, 4800 to about 5800 feet.

HALORAGIDACEAE   Water Milfoil Family

Aquatic or terrestrial perennial herbs with alternate or verticillate leaves, variously dissected to nearly entire; flowers perfect or imperfect, axillary, solitary or clustered, or in interrupted spikes; calyx 2 or 4 sepals or reduced to a narrow ring on the rim of the adnate hypanthium; petals 2 or 4 or none, small and soon deciduous when present; stamens 1 to 8; ovary inferior, 1- to 4-celled; styles 1 to 4; stigmas often plumose; fruit nutlet-like or drupe-like with 2 to 4 one-seeded carpels.

Myriophyllum L.

Perennial aquatic herbs, ours with whorled leaves, the emersed leaves dissected to nearly entire and reduced, the submerged leaves pinnatifid into filiform segments; flowers usually imperfect, solitary, axillary or in leafy-bracted spikes, minute, usually the upper staminate and the lower pistillate; calyx lobes 4 and small or reduced to a ring, the tube joined to the ovary; petals 4, often missing; stamens 4 or 8; stigmas 4, plumose; fruit splitting into 4 indehiscent one-seeded nutlets.

Myriophyllum spicatum L. var. **exalbescens** (Fern.) Jeps.
Western Spiked Water Milfoil

Stems 30-100 cm long; leaves 3 to 5 at a node, 1-3 cm long, the submerged with filiform segments, the emersed bracteal leaves entire or nearly so, equaling or shorter than the fruit; spikes interrupted, 2-10 cm long; petals about 2.5 mm long, quickly deciduous; stamens 8; fruit nearly globose, about 3 mm long, rounded.
Ponds and quiet streams, about 5600 feet.

UMBELLIFERAE   Parsley Family

Annual or perennial herbs usually hollow-stemmed and aromatic; leaves alternate, sometimes opposite, or basal, usually compound, the petioles sheathing-dilated; inflorescence a compound or simple umbel subtended by involucral bracts or bractlets, or sometimes a compound head; flowers small, epigynous, perfect or often polygamous; hypanthium completely joined to the ovary; calyx teeth 5 or obsolete; petals 5, usually yellow or white, sometimes other colors; stamens 5, inserted on an epigynous disc, alternating with the petals; ovary 2-chambered with one pendulous ovule to a chamber; styles 2, distinct, usually borne on a swollen stylopodium; fruit a dry schizocarp, the 2 carpels (mericarps) attached to a carpophore along their ventral surfaces (commissure) flattened either at right angles to the commissure (laterally) or parallel with the commissure (dorsally) or terete, separating at maturity, each mericarp usually with one or more dark-colored oil tubes on the commissure and in the intervals; ribs 5, 1 median (dorsal) 2 marginal (lateral) and 2 between the dorsal and lateral (intermediate), some or all of them winged.

1. Plants mostly large, coarse, thick-stemmed; flowers white
    2. Leaves with 3 large leaflets 10-40 cm long and wide, sometimes toothed or lobed; petals of the outer flowers larger than those near the center; flower cluster (umbel) broad with 15 to 30 unequal rays up to 10 cm long .... *Heracleum*
    2. Leaves usually with more than 3 leaflets, the leaflets smaller; flowers all alike; umbels smaller
        3. Rays of the umbel 1-5 cm long, about equal in length; umbel usually solitary with 1 to 20 rays; leaflets lobed ....*Conioselinum*
        3. Rays of the umbel conspicuously unequal in length, sometimes up to 10 cm long; umbels often 2 or more with 4 to 45 rays
            4. Inflorescence whitish-hairy, the small clusters roundish and thick; plants pale green or yellowish...*Sphenosciadium*
            4. Inflorescence not whitish-hairy, the small clusters thin and delicate; plants deep to yellowish green...*Angelica*
1. Plants smaller, not so coarse; flowers white, yellow or purplish
    5. Flowers yellow
        6. Plants with many widely spreading branches; umbels numerous; fruit bristly..... *Sanicula*
        6. Plants more compact, if branched then only from near the base; umbels fewer; fruit not bristly
            7. Leaves dark green; calyx teeth green, well-developed; plants with a pleasant odor..*Pteryxia*
            7. Leaves pale to grayish or bright green; calyx teeth not developed; plants sometimes with an unpleasant odor............................... *Lomatium*
    5. Flowers usually white to purplish, sometimes fading to yellowish-white
        8. Plants mostly under 10 cm tall
            9. Plants with a taproot; mostly alpine plants............................ *Lomatium*
            9. Plants with a round tuber; mostly plants of lower elevations .... *Orogenia*
        8. Plants usually over 10 cm tall
            10. Leaflets usually small, narrow, numerous; plants taprooted
                11. Rays of the umbel usually conspicuously unequal in length and often widely spreading; small clusters of the umbel (the umbellets) usually with a collar of bractlets under them; flowers mostly yellow but sometimes fading to white............................... *Lomatium*
                11. Rays of the umbel about equal, mostly not spreading; umbellets without a subtending collar of bractlets; flowers white to greenish-white.. *Ligusticum*
            10. Leaflets larger or longer or wider than above and usually fewer; plants with thick fleshy roots
                12. Leaflets long and narrow, few, not toothed, almost withered by flowering time; fruit 2-5 mm long.. *Perideridia*
                12. Leaflets wider, more than a few, usually toothed and well-developed and persistent at flowering time; fruit 10-22 mm long .. ..*Osmorhiza*

Angelica L.

Large perennials from stout roots; leaves ternately or pinnately compound with broad toothed or lobed leaflets and sheathing petioles; inflorescence large, of one or more compound umbels, the flowers white, pink or purplish, or yellow, with or without an involucre or involucels; calyx teeth small or none; fruit elliptic to ovate, flattened dorsally, glabrous to scabrous or tomentose, the lateral and often also the dorsal ribs winged or all the ribs sometimes corky-thickened but not winged; oil tubes few to numerous.

Angelica arguta Nutt.   Shining Angelica

    A. lyallii S. Wats.

Plants stout, 60-200 cm tall, glabrous to scaberulous, especially in the inflorescence; leaves ternate-pinnately about twice compound, the leaflets ovate to lanceolate, 5-15 cm long, often oblique at the base, lobed or toothed, often mucronate, the upper leaves with inflated petioles; compound umbels 2 or more; rays of the umbel 18 to 45, unequal, 1-8 cm long, webbed; involucre none; involucels missing or few and filiform; fruiting pedicels up to 1 cm long, webbed; petals mostly white, glabrous; ovary glabrous; fruit elliptic to obovate, 4-8 mm long, the lateral ribs broadly winged, the dorsal narrowly so; oil tubes solitary in the intervals, several on the commissure.

Moist woods, streambanks and thickets, 4500 to about 5300 feet.

Conioselinum Hoffm.

Tall leafy-stemmed perennial with large decompound leaves and dissected or lobed leaflets; inflorescence sometimes puberulent, of one or more compound umbels; involucre few-bracted or missing; involucel of many small often scarious bractlets; flowers white; calyx teeth obsolete; stylopodium low-conic; fruit elliptic to oblong, dorsally flattened, glabrous, with broadly winged lateral ribs and sometimes narrowly winged dorsal ribs, or these low and corky; oil tubes 1 or 2 in the intervals, 2 to 4 on the commissure.

Conioselinum scopulorum (Gray) C. & R.

    Ligusticum scopulorum Gray

Rather slender perennial 30-100 cm tall; leaves lanceolate to ovate in general outline, the blades 10-20 cm long, 5-15 cm broad, once or twice pinnate or ternate pinnate, the leaflets ovate, 20-65 mm long, pinnately incised, the lobes mucronulate; petioles 10-25 cm long; cauline leaves with broadly dilated sheaths, pinnate to ternate-pinnate; involucre of 1 to several filiform bracts up to 1 cm long, or missing; involucel of several linear, acute, scarious-margined bractlets, often slightly connate at the base, 2-8 mm long, a little shorter than the flowers; rays 1 to 20, about equal, 15-50 mm long; pedicels 4-12 mm long; fruit oval, 4-6 mm long, slightly compressed dorsally, the dorsal ribs low, unwinged, the lateral narrowly corky-winged; seed much flattened dorsally in cross section.

Moist woods, about 4500 to 6700 feet.

Heracleum L.

Large stout pubescent biennial or perennial herbs; leaves very large, ternately or pinnately compound; leaflets broad, toothed or cleft; petioles sheathing and usually inflated; involucre usually none; involucel of many narrow bractlets, or missing; flowers white (yellow) or tinged with red or green, the petals of 2 sizes, the outer ones of the marginal flowers enlarged and often 2-lobed; calyx teeth minute or obsolete; stylopodium conic; fruit orbicular to obovate or elliptic, strongly flattened dorsally, usually pubescent, the lateral ribs broadly winged, the dorsal narrow; oil tubes large, 2 to 4 on the commissure, solitary in the intervals.

Heracleum lanatum Michx.   Cow parsnip

Single-stemmed tomentose to nearly glabrous perennial from a stout taproot or cluster

of fibrous roots, 1-3 meters tall; leaves 10-50 cm long and wide, ternately compound with broad, deeply-cleft and toothed cordate leaflets and inflated petioles; involucres and involucels of 5 to 10 deciduous bracts and bractlets up to 2 cm long; rays 15 to 30, unequal, 5-10 cm long; flowers white, the petals of 2 sizes; fruit broadly elliptic to obovate, 8-12 mm long, pubescent or glabrous.
Streambanks and moist shady woods, 4500 to about 5000 feet.

Ligusticum L.

Taprooted glabrous or pubescent perennial herbs with ternately or ternately-pinnate compound or dissected leaves; inflorescence of compound umbels without an involucre; involucels of linear bracts, or missing; flowers small, white or sometimes pinkish; sepals small or missing; stylopodium low-conic, the styles short; fruit oblong to ovoid, glabrous, sometimes slightly flattened laterally, the ribs prominent, sometimes slightly winged; oil tubes 1 to 6 in the intervals, 2 to 10 on the commissure.

1. Rays of the umbel 5 to about 15
    2. Plant usually with only 1 umbel (flower cluster) ; stems weak and slender, mostly
        leafless; plants mostly of upper mountain elevations_______________________________________*L. filicinum*
    2. Plant usually with 2 or 3 umbels; stems thick and strong, sometimes with 1 or 2
        much reduced leaves; plants of low to middle mountain elevations_______________*L. grayi*
1. Rays of the umbel 15 to 30 or so; stems usually quite thick and strong, 50-120 cm tall,
    with at least one well-developed leaf____*L. canbyi*

Ligusticum canbyi C. & R.   Canby's Lovage

Plants mostly 50-120 cm tall, glabrous or scaberulous, the inflorescence puberulent or glabrate; stems usually stout; leaves ternate-pinnate, the narrow leaflets lanceolate, 3-5 cm long, toothed or cleft into linear, acute divisions, at least one cauline leaf fairly well-developed, the others reduced; peduncles alternate or verticillate, the primary often 30-40 cm long; rays 15 to 30, 2.5-5 cm long; bractlets few, linear; fruit oval to oblong 4-5 mm long, the ribs narrowly winged; oil tubes 4 to 6 in the intervals, 6 to 8 on the commissure.
Moist to wet meadows, bogs and streambanks, sometimes in dry soil at the lower elevations, 4500 to about 7800 feet.

Ligusticum filicinum Wats. var. tenuifolium (Wats.) Math. & Const.

Fern-leaved Lovage

Slender glabrous plants with nearly scapose stems 10-60 cm tall; basal leaves thin, 5-20 cm long including the petiole, ternately-pinnately compound, dissected into many narrowly linear acute segments; umbel solitary or sometimes 2 or 3; rays mostly 5 to 13, 1.5-3 cm long; bractlets filiform when present; pedicels 3-8 mm long; fruit oblong, 3-6 mm long, the ribs narrowly winged; oil tubes 3 to 5 in the intervals, 6 to 8 on the commissure.
Moist to dry meadows, streambanks, bogs and fairly open coniferous mountain slopes, mostly 7400 to about 9200 feet, and probably higher.

Ligusticum grayi C. & R.   Gray's Lovage

Glabrous plants 20-60 cm tall; stems naked or with 1 or 2 much reduced leaves; basal leaves 10-30 cm long, ternately-pinnately compound, the leaflets 2-3 cm long, toothed or cleft into few lanceolate divisions; umbels 1 to 3; rays 5 to 14, 2-3.5 cm long; bractlets few, setaceous; fruiting pedicels 3-8 mm long; fruit elliptic-oblong, 4-6 mm long, the ribs narrowly winged.

Moist or sometimes dry mountain meadows, bogs and open wooded slopes, 5000 to about 7000 feet.

Lomatium Raf.

Short-stemmed or nearly acaulescent perennials with tuberous or slender roots; leaves ternately or pinnately compound; umbels compound; involucres little developed or none; involucels usually present, sometimes conspicuous; calyx teeth usually obsolete; flowers yellow, white or purple; fruit strongly flattened dorsally, the dorsal ribs filiform, the laterals winged; stylopodium none; oil tubes 1 to several in the intervals, 2 to 10 on the commissure.

1. Rays of the umbels 5 to 25, 1-10 cm long; plants mostly over 10 cm tall
    2. Leaflets few, narrow, up to 10 cm long; flowers yellow.. *L. triternatum*
    2. Leaflets numerous, mostly under 1 cm long
        3. Flowers white to purplish
            4. Plants densely and conspicuously hairy; flowering stems numerous, sometimes 10 or more..*L. macrocarpum*
            4. Plants nearly if not entirely without hairs; flowering stems few, mostly only 1 or 2..*L. cusickii*
        3. Flowers yellow, sometimes fading to whitish
            5. Leaves gray-green, very much dissected into hundreds of thread-thin segments; individual flowers or fruits noticeably stalked; plants mostly not hairy..*L. grayi*
            5. Leaves green, the segments fewer or wider or both; individual flowers not evidently stalked; plants 10-30 cm tall, sometimes reddish at the base; flowers pale..*L. montanum*
1. Rays of the umbels 1 to 4, under 0.5 mm long; plants 2-8 cm tall
    6. Plants hairy, 2.5-6 cm tall; flowers yellow to purplish..*L. oreganum*
    6. Plants not hairy, up to 8 cm tall; flowers white to purplish but not yellow; rare in our area..*L. greenmanii*

Lomatium cusickii (Wats.) C. & R.   Desert Parsley

Essentially glabrous short-stemmed plant 10-20 cm tall from a rather fleshy taproot; basal leaves ternately compound, the divisions few, linear, up to 7 cm long; umbels 1 or 2 to a stem, rays 5 to 12, unequal in fruit; involucels of several linear bractlets, scarious-margined, sometimes united; pedicels 1-6 mm long: flowers white, purplish or yellowish-white; fruit oblong, 7-13 mm long, glabrous, the wings narrower than the body; oil tubes 1 to 3 in the intervals, 5 on the commissure.

Dry sandy exposed ridges and saddles, 6000 to about 8500 feet.

Lomatium grayi C. & R.   Gray's Desert Parsley

Stemless to short-stemmed glabrous or minutely scabrous to granular perennial 20-60 cm tall, with an unpleasant odor; root long and thickened; leaves ternate-pinnately dissected into many acute, crowded, linear to filiform segments in several planes, the petiole bases dilated, shredded in age; involucre a reduced leaf or none; rays 7 to 22, spreading, up to 9 cm long, very unequal in fruit; involucel of several linear, acuminate, deciduous bractlets; pedicels 4-22 mm long: flowers yellow; fruit ovate to obovate-elliptic, 7-16 mm long, glabrous; wings thin, mostly narrow but sometimes as wide as

the body, the dorsal and intermediate ribs low and filiform; oil tubes 1 to 3 in the intervals, 2 to 6 on the commissure.
Rocky ledges, crevices and open slopes, 5000 to about 7200 feet.

Lomatium greenmanii Mathias   Greenman's Desert Parsley
   Dwarf caulescent glabrous perennial to 8 cm tall with a much branched caudex and a taproot; leaves once or twice pinnate, mostly basal and generally with a single reduced cauline leaf, the segments separate, up to 10 mm long, glabrous but with margins and midribs scaberulous; umbel with a few sessile sterile rays, the fruiting rays up to 2 mm long; bractlets few, scarious, filiform; flowers white; pedicels about 1 mm long; fruit ovate, glabrous, 3.5 mm long; wings much narrower than the body; oil tubes solitary in the intervals, 2 on the commissure.
Apparently not collected since the Type Collection: "Alpine ridge, Wallowa Mts., 9000′; 1900" William C. Cusick No. 2458. Another Cusick note: "May be a glabrous form of *Lomatium oreganum.*"

Lomatium macrocarpum (Nutt.) C. & R.   Large-fruited Lomatium
   Short-stemmed tomentose-puberulent to glabrate perennial 50 cm tall with a purplish base and a slender or thickened taproot; leaves small, clustered near the ground, ternate pinnate, pale or grayish; peduncles 10-25 cm long; rays 5 to 25, up to 8 cm long; involucel conspicuous, often longer than the flowers; pedicels 1-14 mm long; flowers white, purplish or yellowish; fruit narrowly oblong 9-20 mm long and 2-8 mm wide, glabrate or puberulent; wings narrow to wider than the body; oil tubes 1 to 3 in the interval, 2 to 6 on the commissure.
Open woods, 5400 to about 5800 feet.

Lomatium montanum C. & R.   Mountain Lomatium
   Acaulescent puberulent to glabrous plants, purplish at the base, 10-30 cm tall from a thickened, nearly globose tuberous root; leaves ternate, then 2 to 3 times pinnate into crowded oblong segments 2-10 mm long; rays 5 to 15, unequal, 1-6.5 cm long; bractlets obovate, purplish, separate or united at the base; pedicels 1-3 mm long; flowers yellow; fruit oblong-elliptic, 5-12 mm long, the dorsal and intermediate wings narrower than the body or about equaling it; oil tubes 2 to 4 in the intervals, 6 on the commissure.
Rocky wooded slopes, about 5800 feet.

Lomatium oreganum C. & R.   Blue Mountain Lomatium
   Cespitose alpine dwarf 2-8 cm tall with branching caudex and a taproot; leaves, peduncles, inflorescence and fruit hirtellous-puberulent; leaves all basal, ternate-pinnately dissected; flowers yellow; umbels simple, rays 1 to 4, very short; fruit oblong, about 5 mm long; wings much narrower than the body of the fruit; oil tubes 2 to 3 in the intervals, 4 on the commissure.
Shallow soil of exposed ridges and passes, 9400 to about 9800 feet and probably higher.

Lomatium triternatum (Pursh) C. & R.   Narrow-leaved Lomatium
   Puberulent to glabrate caulescent or nearly stemless plant 20-80 cm tall with a long slender taproot; leaves mostly basal, ternate or quinate, pinnately cleft into few, mostly linear, segments 1.5-12 cm long; rays 6 to 20, very unequal, up to 10 cm long; bractlets

filiform; pedicels 2-7 mm long; flowers yellow; fruit oblong-elliptic, glabrous, 9-13 mm long; wings narrow to very broad; oil tubes solitary in the intervals, 2 on the commissure. Open rocky woods and dry grassy meadows, 4600 to about 7000 feet.

Orogenia Wats.

Delicate low glabrous perennials with fleshy roots and stems mainly underground with bladeless sheathing bracts; leaves once to three times ternate with narrow entire segments; inflorescence a small compound umbel with few unequal rays, no involucre and few or no involucel bractlets; flowers white; calyx teeth obsolete; fruit oblong to oval with filiform dorsal ribs and corky-winged lateral ones, the commissure with a corky rib-like projection; stylopodium low or none; oil tubes several on the commissure and in the intervals.

Orogenia linearifolia Wats.   Great Basin Turkey Peas

Slender stems rising 5-15 cm from a deep-seated globose tuber; leaves 2 or 3, ovate with entire linear segments 1.5-7 cm long; inflorescence 1-2 cm long with 1 to 4 rays; fruit 3 or 4 mm long, oblong-oval with prominent dorsal ribs.
Moist shaded or open slopes and ridges, often near melting snowbanks, 4900 to about 6600 feet.

Osmorhiza Raf.

Caulescent pubescent to glabrate perennials with thick roots and petiolate pinnately compound leaves, the leaflets lanceolate to orbicular, toothed to pinnatifid; umbels terminal or axillary with few unequal rays; involucre and involucels when present of a few narrow foliaceous bracts or bractlets; flowers white, purple, greenish, yellow or pink; calyx teeth obsolete; stylopodium conic; fruit linear or clavate, obtuse or short-beaked, rounded or tapering toward the base, flattened laterally, glabrous to bristly hispid with filiform ribs, oil tubes obscure or none.

1. Flowers greenish; fruit shining, not hairy, rounded instead of tapering at the base; stems clustered..*O. occidentalis*
1. Flowers white to greenish-white; fruit bristly-hairy, tapered at the base
    2. Fruit beaked at the tip, mostly 12-22 mm long; stem leaves without a petiole or nearly so..*O. chilensis*
    2. Fruit not beaked at the tip, mostly 10-15 mm long; stem leaves mostly with a definite petiole..*O. depauperata*

Osmorhiza chilensis Hook. & Arn.   Mountain Sweet-Cicely
    O. nuda Torr.

Taprooted slender hispid to glabrous perennials with 1 to 3 stems 30-100 cm tall; leaves biternate, 5-15 cm long, orbicular, the basal long-petioled, the cauline 1 to 3 with shorter petioles; leaflets ovate-lanceolate, coarsely toothed, incised or lobed, mostly 2-7 cm long; umbels several, enlarging at maturity; rays 3 to 8, spreading-ascending, 2-12 cm long; involucre and involucels none or few; flowers greenish white (rarely pinkish); stylopodium conic; fruit 12-22 mm long, linear-oblong, tapering into a slender beak above, densely hispid and caudate at the base.
Moist woods, 4500 to about 6000 feet.

Osmorhiza depauperata Phil.   Blunt-fruited Sweet-Cicely

Slender hispid to glabrate perennials 15-65 cm tall; leaves orbicular, 4-11 cm long,

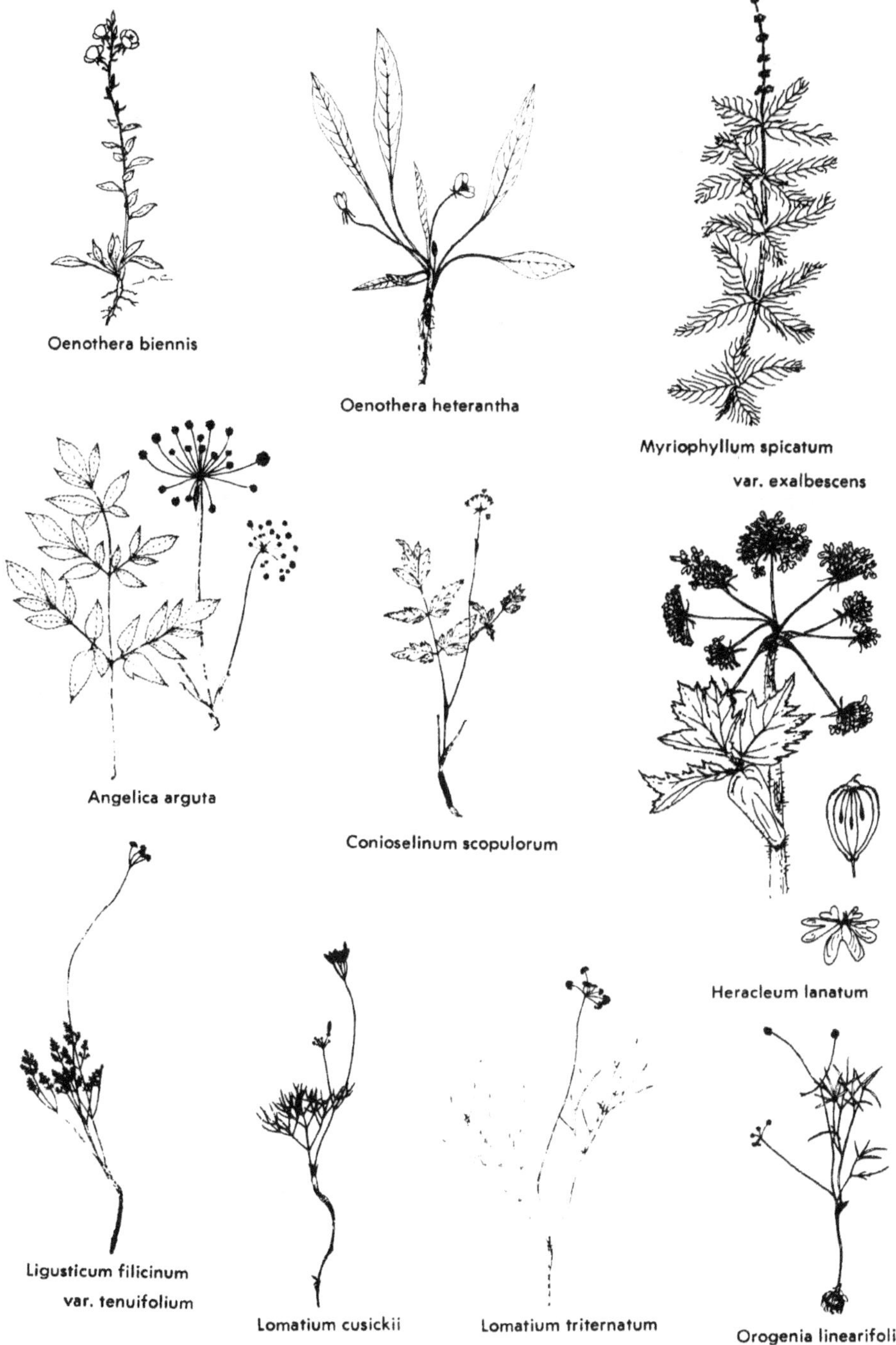

Oenothera biennis

Oenothera heterantha

Myriophyllum spicatum
var. exalbescens

Angelica arguta

Conioselinum scopulorum

Heracleum lanatum

Ligusticum filicinum
var. tenuifolium

Lomatium cusickii

Lomatium triternatum

Orogenia linearifolia

biternate or ternate-pinnate; leaflets ovate or lance-ovate, 1.5-5 cm long, coarsely serrate, incised or lobed; bractlets none; rays 2 to 5, widely and stiffly divergent, 2-7 cm long; flowers greenish-white; fruit 10-15 mm long, obtuse or rounded, not beak-like above, caudate and densely hispid at the base.
Moist shade of woods, often near streams, 4500 to about 7000 feet.

Osmorhiza occidentalis (Nutt.) Torr.   Western Sweet-Cicely
Stems stout, clustered, 30-120 cm tall from licorice-scented roots; herbage villous at the nodes and on the lower petioles, otherwise hirtellous or glabrous; leaves oblong to ovate, 10-20 cm long, 1 to 3 times ternate or ternate-pinnate; leaflets lanceolate to ovate, 2-10 cm long, serrate and usually incised or lobed and strongly veined; umbels with 5 to 16 rays in fruit, elongating to as much as 13 cm long; involucre and involucels usually lacking; flowers yellow; fruit glabrous and shining, 12-20 mm long, constricted below the tip but not beaked; obtuse at the base.
Mountain woods and meadows, thickets and open slopes, 5000 to about 7200 feet.

Perideridia Reichb.

Caulescent glabrous perennials with fleshy fascicled roots and slender stems; leaves pinnate or ternately-pinnately compound or dissected, with mostly narrow divisions; umbels compound; involucre of few to numerous entire narrow bracts; involucel of colored or scarious bractlets or obsolete; flowers white or pink; calyx teeth developed; stylopodium conic; fruit flattened laterally, glabrous, linear-oblong to orbicular, the ribs filiform; oil tubes 1 to 5 in the intervals, 2 to 8 on the commissure.

Petioles widened at the base; leaves much dissected, the divisions usually narrow, of 2
 kinds (some longer and wider than the others) ; fruit oblong 3-5 mm long..................*P. bolanderi*
Petiole not widened; leaves not much dissected, the divisions few and usually all alike;
 fruit roundish, 2-3 mm long...*P. gairdneri*

Perideridia bolanderi (Gray) Nels. & Macbr.   Mountain False Caraway
Stem slender, solitary, 20-80 cm tall, delicately attached to a cluster of fusiform roots; leaves 10-20 cm long, ternate-pinnately dissected into filiform divisions of 2 kinds: some longer and wider than the others, the terminal the longest, the lateral ones usually lobed and toothed; cauline leaves few and reduced, the petioles well-developed and inflated; umbels 1 to several; rays 10 to 20, 1-3.5 cm long at maturity; involucre of 1 to several narrow scarious bracts; involucels of narrow white-scarious bractlets; petals and sepals white; fruit oblong, 3-5 mm long; oil tubes 2 to 5 in the intervals, 6 on the commissure.
Moist or dry rocky slopes, hillsides or springy places, 4600 to about 5800 feet.

Perideridia gairdneri (H. & A.) Mathias   Western Yampah
Slender glabrous plants 30-120 cm tall; stem solitary, rising from fusiform tuberous roots; leaves 10-20 cm long, pinnate or sometimes bipinnate; leaf divisions few, linear or lanceolate, 2-15 cm long, entire or rarely lobed or toothed; cauline leaves several, well-developed; basal leaves withering before flowering time; petioles not much dilated; umbels 3 to 10 or more; rays 8 to 20, 1.5-6 cm long; involucre of a few subulate bracts; involucels of several linear, green or scarious setaceous bractlets, or none; petals white or pinkish; fruit suborbicular, 2-3 mm long; oil tubes solitary in the intervals, 2 on the commissure.
Dry rocky clayey soils in open woods, 4500 to about 6200 feet.

Pteryxia Nutt.

Low taprooted perennials with leaves ternately or pinnately dissected into small segments; bracts none; bractlets linear; flowers yellow or rarely white or purple; sepals prominent; stylopodium none; fruit narrowly oblong or ovoid, flattened dorsally, the lateral ribs and some or all of the dorsal ones thin-winged; oil tubes 1 to many in the intervals, 2 to many on the commissure.

Pteryxia terebinthina (Hook.) C. & R. — Wormwood Pteryxia
Cymopterus terebinthinus (Hook.) T. & G.

Plants short-stemmed, mildly aromatic, 10-60 cm tall, bearing at the base the shredded leaf bases from previous years; leaves numerous, 3-18 cm long, broadly ovate in outline, dark green, ternately-pinnately dissected into many small crowded somewhat confluent segments; peduncles stout, the stems leafless or with 1 or more leaves near the base; involucre usually none; umbel of 7 to 24 unequal rays up to 7 cm long at maturity; involucels of linear green bractlets 2-6 mm long; calyx teeth generally greenish; flowers yellow; fruit ovoid to ovoid-oblong, 5-11 mm long, the lateral wings thin, usually undulate-crisped, the dorsal the same; oil tubes 3 to 12 in the intervals, 6 to 20 on the commissure.

Dry open rocky slopes, 4500 to about 9300 feet.

Sanicula L.

Glabrous or pubescent biennial or perennial plants with nearly naked stems; leaves cleft or dissected, or rarely entire; umbels several or many, head-like, irregularly compound; rays few; flowers white, greenish-white, yellow, purple or blue, staminate and pedicellate or perfect and sessile or nearly so, each umbellet with both kinds or some entirely staminate; involucre foliaceous; involucels of several conspicuous bractlets; calyx-teeth persistent; stylopodium flat and disc-like, or none; fruit nearly round, densely covered with hooked prickles (ours) or tubercles.

Sanicula graveolens Poepp. — Sierra Snakeroot
S. nevadensis Wats.; *S. septentrionalis* Greene

Taprooted perennials 10-50 cm tall, the single stem obsolete to short and branched from the base, or elongated; leaves 2-5 cm long, alternate, ternate-pinnate, the segments usually oblong-ovate, the 3 to 5 lobes irregularly lobed or toothed; umbels with 2 to 9 rays; bracts foliaceous, pinnatifid; bractlets 6 to 10, confluent all around; flowers yellow, 10 to 15 in each umbellet, the staminate short-pedicellate, the perfect nearly sessile; fruit 3-5 mm long, covered with hooked prickles.

Dry sandy or gravelly soil in open or brushy mountain slopes and disturbed flats, 4800 to about 7200 feet.

Sphenosciadium Gray

Thick-rooted perennials with stout stems, scabrous to nearly glabrous but tomentose in the inflorescence; leaves 1- to 2-pinnately, or ternate-pinnately compound; leaflets irregularly toothed or cleft; petioles dilated; umbels compound; flowers scarious, white or purplish, sessile, in dense umbellate heads; involucre none; involucels of many tomentose deciduous setaceous bractlets; calyx teeth obsolete; stylopodium small, broadly conic; fruit tomentose, cuneate obovate, flattened dorsally, the ribs prominently winged above, the laterals widest; oil tubes solitary in the intervals, 2 on the commissure.

Sphenosciadium capitellatum Gray   Swamp White-Heads
Stout pale green plants 50-180 cm tall; leaves large, 10-40 cm long or more, scabrous to glabrate; leaflets linear-oblong to ovate-lanceolate, serrate to dentate, incised or pinnatifid; umbels 1 to several, densely tomentose; rays 4 to 18, mostly 1-5 cm long; umbellets well separated, roundish, 6-12 mm wide; involucre none; involucels of several scarious bractlets; flowers nearly sessile, pubescent, in dense roundish white or pinkish heads 7-12 mm wide; fruit 5-8 mm long, the wings widest at the top.
Moist or wet meadows, bogs or streambanks, at about 8000 feet.

CORNACEAE   Dogwood Family

Trees, shrubs or shrubby plants with entire opposite or rarely alternate or whorled leaves; flowers small, perfect or imperfect, sometimes with petaloid bracts; hypanthium joined to the ovary; sepals 4 or 5, very small; petals 4 or 5, or none; stamens usually as many as the petals, sometimes twice as many; pistil 1, the carpels 2 to 4; ovary inferior, 1- to 4-celled; ovules pendulous, 1 in each cell; style 1; fruit a drupe.

Cornus L.

Trees, shrubs or shrubby herbs usually with opposite, strongly-veined, petioled leaves; flowers in cymes or in heads subtended by 4 to 8 showy white or pinkish petaloid bracts; sepals 4, minute; petals 4, white to greenish, valvate; stamens 4; ovary 2-celled; fruit a small fleshy two-seeded drupe.

Cornus stolonifera Michx.   Red Osier Dogwood
Shrub 1-6 meters tall, glabrous to pubescent, the stems reddish to reddish-purple when young, becoming grayish, green or brown; leaves ovate or elliptic to obovate, 3-10 cm long, paler underneath than above; flowers in flat-topped cymes, 2.5-5 cm broad, without showy bracts; petals white, 2-4 mm long; styles 1-3 mm long; drupe bluish to white, roundish, 6-9 mm in diameter; stone smooth.
Moist soils along shady streams, often forming thickets, 4500 to about 5200 feet.

ERICACEAE   Heath Family

Trees, shrubs or perennial herbaceous plants usually with green foliage but also leafless fleshy white to brownish- or reddish-purple saprophytic plants; green leaves usually alternate, leathery, persistent or deciduous; flowers usually regular, white to pink, red or purplish; calyx lobes 4 or 5, often united at least at the base; corolla rotate to funnelform or urn-shaped, the 4 or 5 parts united or separated, rarely missing; stamens once or twice as many as the corolla lobes and free from them, the anthers often inverted, sometimes awned, opening by pores or longitudinal slits; ovary superior to inferior, 3- to 12-celled; style 1, straight or bent or curved; stigma entire to lobed; fruit a capsule surrounded by the fleshy calyx or a fleshy, drupe-like berry.

1. Plants without green leaves
    2. Plants pinkish or yellowish, mostly under 25 cm tall; short leaves or bracts present

    3. Flowering stem nearly naked except for a few small scale-like bracts near the
base; styles long, conspicuous in the flowers...*Pyrola*
    3. Flowering stem with several scale-like leaves 5-8 mm long; styles short,
usually hidden in the flowers... *Hypopitys*
  2. Plants reddish-brown, mostly much over 25 cm tall, glandular-hairy, the stem about
1 cm thick; leaves inconspicuous, near the base of the stem.................................*Pterospora*
1. Plants with well-developed green leaves
    4. Leaves needle-like, without an expanded obvious blade; flowers mostly bell-shaped;
low shrubby matted plants usually at upper mountain elevations
      5. Flowers pink to rose, the petals united, the calyx lobes dark red........................*Phyllodoce*
      5. Flowers white or cream
        6. Flowers densely glandular-hairy, cream-colored or yellowish-white, the
sepals green; leaves 5-12 mm long..*Phyllodoce*
        6. Flowers not glandular, clear white with reddish sepals; leaves 2-5 mm
long...*Cassiope*
    4. Leaves with a blade though sometimes quite narrow; flowers bell-shaped or not;
plants mostly at low to middle elevations in the mountains
      7. Leaves mostly at or near the plant base; flowers solitary or scattered on erect
stems, the style conspicuous, straight or turned to the side; plants not woody....... *Pyrola*
      7. Leaves often on the stems and branches as well as at the base; flowers mostly
more than 1, sometimes very small, the style not usually conspicuous
        8. Stems only a few cm tall, creeping along the ground and rooting or
forming mats; leaves thick and shining, evergreen; fruit red, berry-like
          9. Leaf blades nearly circular or broader at the base than at the tip;
flowers mostly solitary on stems about 3 cm tall..*Gaultheria*
          9. Leaf blades oblong or broader at the tip than at the base; flowers
usually several in a cluster, on stems 5-15 cm tall................................*Arctostaphylos*
        8. Stems mostly taller, not creeping and rooting or forming mats; leaves
deciduous or evergreen and persistent
          10. Leaves thin, deciduous; flowers solitary on the branchlets; plants
erect woody shrubs or semi-shrubs, often with angled stems.................*Vaccinium*
          10. Leaves thick, leathery, evergreen; flowers 1 to usually several in a
cluster; plants woody at the base at least
            11. Flowers deep pinkish-rose; leaves opposite, 1-4 cm long, the
margins rolled under..*Kalmia*
            11. Flowers white or sometimes faintly pinkish; leaves opposite
or not, 1-7 cm long
              12. Leaves opposite or whorled, 2-7 cm long, usually toothed;
plants woody at the base, 5-30 cm tall ....*Chimaphila*
              12. Leaves alternate, under 2 cm long usually, the margins
rolled under, not toothed; plants woody shrubs, over 30
cm tall, usually with fragrant flowers ....*Ledum*

Arctostaphylos Adans.

    Erect or creeping woody evergreen shrubs with alternate leathery leaves; flowers
perfect and regular in bracteate terminal racemes or panicles; calyx persistent, 5-lobed;
corolla white or pinkish, urn-shaped, 4- or 5-lobed; stamens 10, included; anthers with
2 reflexed awns, opening by pores; ovary superior, 4- to 10-celled; fruit globose, berry-
like, dry at maturity, with 4 to 10 (usually 5) stony 1-seeded nutlets.

Arctostaphylos uva-ursi (L.) Spreng.   Bearberry; Kinnikinnick
    Prostrate evergreen shrub often forming broad mats, the stems trailing and rooting,
the bark shredding, the erect branchlets pubescent, often 5-15 cm tall; leaves spatulate

to obovate, 1-2 cm long, glabrous, entire and short-petioled; flowers small, nodding, in few-flowered racemes; bracts persistent; corolla white or pink-tinged.
Dry to moist open to shady woods and meadows, 4500 to about 5500 feet.

Cassiope D. Don
Low shrubs with scale-like overlapping evergreen 4-ranked leaves; flowers solitary, nodding, white or rose-colored, terminal or axillary; calyx and corolla 4- to 5-lobed; stamens 8 or 10, included; filaments glabrous, anthers awned, opening by large pores; ovary superior; fruit a 4- or 5-celled loculicidal capsule.

Cassiope mertensiana (Bong.) G. Don   Western Mountain Heather
Low creeping alpine shrub, the stems slender, 5-30 or more cm tall, ascending or decumbent, forming large mats; leaves rounded or keeled on the back, 4-ranked, glabrous or ciliate; pedicels 6-20 mm long, minutely puberulent; flowers nodding, white or tinged with pink, nearly terminal; sepals usually reddish or pinkish; capsules ovoid.
Moist rocky slopes and banks, 7000 to 9595 feet.
Stems glabrous and more slender than the species; peduncles longer, glabrous and more slender than the species; leaves minutely ciliate with glandular or non-glandular hairs; pedicels glabrous...var. **gracilis** (Piper) C. L. Hitchc.
With the species. TYPE LOCALITY: Wallowa Mts.

Chimaphila Pursh
Woody low semi-shrubs, glabrous or nearly so, with creeping rootstocks and leathery, evergreen, opposite or whorled, short-petioled leaves; flowers solitary to usually several in few-flowered racemes, corymbs or umbels; sepals 5, persistent; petals 5, white or purplish; stamens 10, the filaments swollen and hairy below, the inverted anthers opening by pores on short tubes; ovary superior, 5-lobed; fruit a 5-celled capsule, loculicidally dehiscent from the top; seeds numerous, minute.
Flowers 1 to 3; leaves few, mostly elliptic or narrowly ovate...*C. menziesii*
Flowers 3 to 8; leaves many, broader at the tip than at the base, mostly whorled.................*C. umbellata*

Chimaphila menziesii (R. Br.) Spreng.   Little Prince's Pine or Pipsissewa
Stems 5-20 cm tall, glabrous and reddish; leaves lanceolate to narrowly ovate, opposite or whorled, glabrous, 2-6 cm long, serrate to entire, short-petioled and leathery; peduncles 2-5 cm long; flowers 1 to 3; pedicels elongating and becoming 2-4 cm long in fruit; sepals erose; petals spreading, white or pinkish, 5-6 mm long, concave; filaments hairy below; capsules 5-6 mm in diameter.
Shady moist coniferous woods, 4500 to about 5000 feet.

Chimaphila umbellata (L.) Bart. var. **occidentalis** (Rydb.) Blake
                 Western Pipsissewa
Stems 10-30 cm tall, usually branched, yellowish-green; leaves oblanceolate to obovate, in whorls of 3 to 8, glossy green, 2-7 cm long, serrate, short-petioled, glabrous; peduncles 5-10 cm long; pedicels usually puberulent and often glandular; flowers fragrant, 3 to 8 or more in a raceme or corymb; sepals denticulate-erose; petals tinged with pink or rose, ciliolate; swollen portion of the filaments ciliolate-margined but not hairy; capsules 6-7 mm wide.
Shady woods in coniferous forests, 4500 to about 6000 feet.

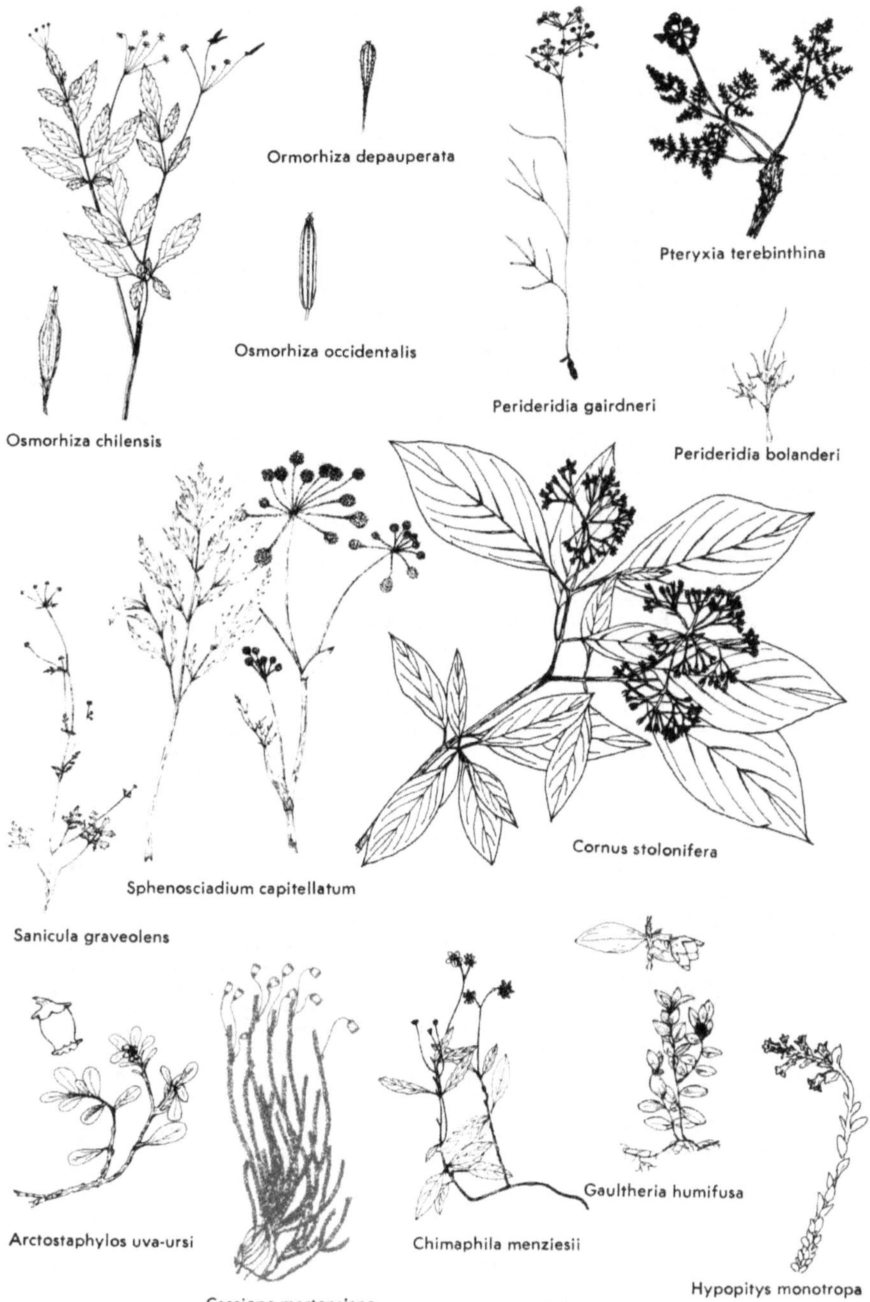

Ormorhiza depauperata
Osmorhiza occidentalis
Osmorhiza chilensis
Pteryxia terebinthina
Perideridia gairdneri
Perideridia bolanderi
Sphenosciadium capitellatum
Sanicula graveolens
Cornus stolonifera
Arctostaphylos uva-ursi
Cassiope mertensiana
Chimaphila menziesii
Gaultheria humifusa
Hypopitys monotropa

Gaultheria L.

Small erect to prostrate shrubs with shining evergreen leaves; flowers solitary or in racemes, axillary or terminal, white or pinkish; calyx and corolla 4- or 5-parted; stamens 8 or 10, included, anthers usually awned; ovary 4- or 5-celled; fruit a white or scarlet berry-like capsule surrounded by the persistent fleshy calyx.

Gaultheria humifusa (Grah.) Rydb.   Alpine Creeping Wintergreen

Low shrub with stems prostrate or ascending, mat-forming, the flowering branches 3-10 cm tall; leaves oval or ovate to nearly elliptic, 1-2 cm long, glabrous, entire or slightly toothed; flowers white or pinkish, solitary on short bracteate pedicels; corolla 5-lobed, slightly longer than the calyx; anthers without awns; fruit scarlet, berry-like. Moist or wet edges of meadows and moist mossy streambanks and woods, 6500 to about 9000 feet.

Hypopitys Hill

Fleshy white to yellowish or pinkish saprophytes with a dense mass of fleshy roots, unbranched stems and scale-like leaves without chlorophyll; flowers solitary or race-mose, nodding, but becoming erect in fruit; sepals and petals 5 or in later flowers 4 or 3; stamens 6 to 10, the filaments hairy, anthers opening by 2 unequal valves; ovary superior, 3- to 5-celled; fruit a loculicidal capsule.

Hypopitys monotropa Crantz   Pinesap

Plants 10-30 cm tall or more, finely pubescent, yellowish or pinkish, drying black; leaves scale-like, entire to fimbriate; racemes with few to many nodding flowers but becoming elongate with erect fruit at maturity; sepals ciliate and often erose-margined; petals about 1 cm long, often pubescent, ciliate-margined; filaments pubescent, not swollen; style pubescent; stigma lobed and bearded; capsules 4-8 mm long.
Deep forest soil in moist shady coniferous woods, about 5800 to 6000 feet.

Kalmia L.

Low evergreen shrubs with leathery evergreen alternate opposite or whorled leaves; flowers terminal, solitary or in small corymbs, long-pedicellate; calyx usually colored, 5-lobed; corolla saucer-shaped, the tube saccate with 10 keels extending to the lobes and sinuses; stamens 10, included, springing out of the corolla-sacs at flowering time; ovary superior, 5-celled; fruit a nearly globose septicidal capsule.

Kalmia polifolia Wang. var. microphylla (Hook.) Rehd.   Mountain Laurel

Ascending or erect branched glabrous plants usually 5-15 cm tall; leaves oblong-elliptic, 1-4 cm long, entire, revolute, opposite, dark glossy green above, pale and glandular-pubescent beneath; flowers deep pinkish-rose, 1-2 cm broad, in clusters of 3 to 10, on glabrous reddish pedicels 1-4 cm long; sepals sparsely ciliolate; filaments hairy just above the base; capsules nearly globose.
Moist boggy ground and wet mountain meadows, about 7000 to 8000 feet.

Ledum L.

Erect fragrant shrubs; leaves evergreen, alternate, often revolute-margined, glandular, petiolate and entire; flowers in terminal racemes or corymbs from large scaly buds;

calyx 5-lobed; petals 5, white, not united; stamens 5 to 10 with long slender filaments and short anthers opening by terminal pores; ovary 5-celled; fruit a nearly globose capsule dehiscing upward.

Ledum glandulosum Nutt.   Labrador Tea; Trapper's Tea

Shrub 0.5-2 meters tall, puberulent and glandular almost throughout; leaves oval or oblong to elliptic, petiolate, green above, pale resinous-glandular and puberulent beneath, sometimes revolute-margined; pedicels erect in anthesis, arched in fruit; flowers white, calyx ciliate; stamens 10, the filaments hairy near the base; capsules short-ovoid. Wet or moist shady mountain bogs, meadows and streambanks in open woods, about 6000 to about 8200 feet.

Phyllodoce Salisb.

Dwarf evergreen alpine shrubs; leaves crowded, evergreen, needle-like, alternate and revolute; flowers clustered at the tips of the branches on long glandular-pubescent pedicels; calyx usually 5-lobed; corolla 5-lobed, urn-shaped to campanulate; stamens 10, the anthers awnless, opening by pores; fruit a 5-valved nearly ovoid septicidal capsule.

Corolla pink to rose, bell shaped, not glandular-hairy; calyx lobes blunt at the tip, not
  glandular..*P. empetriformis*
Corolla yellowish to greenish-white, vase-shaped, glandular-hairy on the outside; calyx
  lobes pointed at the tip, glandular-short-hairy...*P. glanduliflora*

Phyllodoce empetriformis (Smith) D. Don   Pink or Rose Mountain Heather

Low matted branching shrub 10-50 cm tall; leaves linear-oblong, strongly revolute, glabrous or scabrous-margined, persistent; flowers fragrant, light to deep pinkish-rose; pedicels glandular pubescent; sepals dark red, ciliolate, otherwise glabrous; corolla campanulate, the tips of the lobes recurved; capsules globose.
Sunny alpine meadows and open coniferous forest, mostly between 7000 and 9000 feet.

Phyllodoce glanduliflora (Hook.) Coville   White or Yellow Mountain Heather

Low matted shrub 10-40 cm tall, glandular-pubescent nearly throughout; leaves crowded, linear, revolute; flowers yellowish to greenish-white, solitary or 3 to 8 in a cluster; sepal margins glandular-ciliate; corolla urn-shaped; filaments pubescent; anthers purple.
Alpine meadows and rocky open places in coniferous forest and above it, 7900 to nearly 9000 feet.

Pterospora Nutt.

Tall saprophytic herb with brownish or purplish glandular-pubescent herbage; leaves scale-like, mostly near the base; flowers many, nodding in a long narrow raceme; sepals 5; corolla urn-shaped with 5 short lobes; stamens 10, the anthers with 2 dorsal awns and dehiscing by longitudinal slits; ovary superior; fruit a 5-chambered loculicidal capsule.

Pterospora andromedea Nutt.   Pinedrops; Beechdrops

Stems unbranched from a thick ball-like mass of roots; stems 20-100 cm tall, reddish-brown, viscid-pubescent, fleshy at first but drying and remaining standing often for 1 or more years; leaves mostly near the base, 1.5-3.5 cm long; raceme erect, 10-50 cm long; flowers pendulous on recurved glandular-pubescent pedicels; calyx 5-parted, glandular-pubescent; corolla whitish, urn-shaped; capsules 8-12 mm broad, depressed-globose.

Moist shady coniferous and mixed woods, often under Ponderosa pine, 4500 to about 6000 feet.

Pyrola L.

Low glabrous perennial herbs with slender rhizomes and simple stems; leaves clustered at the base, sometimes missing, broad, veiny, evergreen; flowering stems leafless but with 1 to few bracts; flowers solitary or several in a single terminal raceme, short-pedicelled and mostly nodding; sepals 5; petals 5, white to greenish or pink-purple; stamens 10, filaments incurved, anthers inverted and dehiscent by 2 pores at the apparent tip; ovary superior; style straight, the stigma peltate with 5 marginal papillae, or the style bent to one side and the 5 stigmas encircled by a collar; fruit a 5-valved capsule.

1. Plants either with 1 flower and several leaves at the base of the plant or with several flowers and no true leaves at the base
    2. Flower solitary, pure white, nodding; leaves present at the base of the single stem... *P. uniflora*
    2. Flowers several on the stem, usually pinkish or cream but not white; small inconspicuous bract-like leaves at the base of the plant ....*P. aphylla*
1. Plants with 2 or more flowers on the stem and several well developed green leaves at the base
    3. Flowers white; style straight when visible
        4. Style 3-4 mm long, longer than the flower; flowers often all on 1 side of the stem..*P. secunda*
        4. Style only 1-2 mm long, shorter than the petals; flowers usually on both sides of the stem ....*P. minor*
    3. Flowers pinkish to yellowish or greenish-white; style curved or bent but not straight
        5. Petals mostly pinkish; leaves sometimes whitish along the main veins; flowers 5 to 25
            6. Leaves white-mottled; flowers sometimes yellowish to greenish-white.......... *P. picta*
            6. Leaves not mottled; flowers pink or rose or purplish-red ....*P. asarifolia*
        5. Petals white or greenish-white to cream
            7. Leaf petioles much longer than the blades; flowers mostly 2 to 8; leaves few, roundish..*P. virens*
            7. Leaf petioles about as long as the blades; flowers 10 to 20; leaves several, mostly longer than broad..*P. dentata*

Pyrola aphylla Smith   Leafless Wintergreen

Reddish-brown perennial with long slender rootstocks; small bracts and leaves usually developed on sterile branches but the flowering stems leafless, 5-20 cm tall, with several bracts; flowers 10 to 20; pedicels about 4 mm long; flowers about 7 mm long, greenish-white to pinkish with reddish calyx lobes; anthers with the pores on the side of very short tubes.

Mountainsides and coniferous woods.

This is not a true species. This name is given to the leafless forms of those plants of *P. asarifolia, P. dentata, P. picta* and *P. virens* which can be identified.

Pyrola asarifolia Michx.   Pink, Bog or Oregon Wintergreen

Perennial; leaves elliptic or orbicular, dark green and shining on the upper surface, obscurely crenulate or entire, the blades 3-7 cm long; petioles as long as the blades or

longer; scape 10-50 cm tall, 5- to 20-flowered, the pedicels reflexed, the few bracts pinkish; flowers pink or rose-purple; calyx lobes acute; anthers pinkish; style strongly declined and curved; stigmas at maturity longer than the collar.
Bogs, streambanks and moist woods, 4600 to about 7000 feet.

Pyrola dentata Smith   Toothed Wintergreen
Plant with slender rhizomes and short sterile branches with rosettes of leaves; leaves leathery, glaucous-green, lanceolate to spatulate to suborbicular, the blades 2-6 cm long, mostly not mottled, entire to serrulate or denticulate, the petiole about equaling the blade; flowering stems 1 to several, 10-25 cm tall, usually with some basal leaves but sometimes the leaves reduced or missing; raceme 5- to 20-flowered; flowers about 1 cm broad; petals greenish- or cream-colored, 4-8 mm long; style strongly curved, only slightly declined.
Woods, open forests and dry mountainsides at about 6800 to 7000 feet.

Pyrola minor L.   Common Wintergreen
Perennial herb with slender rhizomes; scapes single, 8-25 cm tall; leaves broadly elliptic to obovate, 1-3 cm long, crenulate, dark green and thin, rounded at the base; petioles about as long as the blade or longer; raceme 5- to 20-flowered; flowers nodding, white or pinkish; style straight, very short, without a collar; stigma wide and peltate, deeply 5-lobed.
Coniferous woods, 4700 to about 7400 feet.

Pyrola picta Smith   Shin-leaf; White-veined Wintergreen
Rhizomatous herb; leaves ovate to elliptic, mottled with white along the larger veins, leathery, denticulate to nearly entire, 2.5-7 cm long, entire or irregularly denticulate, sometimes pink-purplish beneath; flowering stems reddish-brown, 10-20 cm tall; racemes 10- to 25-flowered; flowers yellowish or greenish-white to purplish; style strongly declined, about 1 cm long.
Dry humus in shady coniferous forest, about 5000 to 6000 feet.

Pyrola secunda L.   One-sided Wintergreen
Perennial herbs with long creeping rhizomes; flowering stems 5-18 cm tall with 1 or 2 scarious bracts; leaves crenulate to serrate, oval to nearly orbicular, 1.5-7 cm long, rounded at the base; flowers crowded in a 1-sided raceme; petals white or pinkish; style straight or nearly so, exserted, longer than the fruit; stigma wide and peltate.
Moist shady woods and streambanks, 4600 to about 6700 feet.

Pyrola uniflora L.   Single-flowered Wintergreen
Moneses uniflora (L.) Gray
Glabrous perennial herbs with slender rootstocks; stem 1-3 cm tall; leaves crowded at the base of the stem, the blades orbicular to obovate, 1-2.5 cm long, crenate-serrate at least above the middle, the tip rounded or obtuse; scape 3-15 cm tall; flower solitary, white, nodding, fragrant; petals spreading; stamens 10; style straight, longer than the ovary; stigma peltate, 5-lobed.
Moist shady coniferous woods and mossy springy or boggy places, often on or near rotting wood, 4600 to about 6700 feet.

Pyrola virens Schweigg.   Greenish-flowered Wintergreen
    P. chlorantha Sw.
Perennial with slender rootstocks; leaves deeper green underneath than above; blades oval to obovate or orbicular, entire to shallowly crenate, rounded at both ends, 1-3 cm long, the petioles much longer; flowering stem 8-20 cm tall; racemes 2- to 10-flowered, calyx short; petals greenish-white, converging; style curved, little declined, with a collar below the lobed stigma.
Deep humus and moist or boggy places in coniferous forest, 4600 to about 5300 feet.

Vaccinium L.

Creeping to erect or vine-like shrubs with evergreen to deciduous (ours), thin (ours) to leathery, entire to serrulate leaves; flowers axillary or terminal, solitary or in small clusters; calyx lobes 4 or 5 or obsolete; corolla globose or urn-shaped, 4- or 5-lobed; stamens twice as many, or as many, as the corolla lobes, the anthers awned or awnless, prolonged into tubes; ovary inferior; fruit a many-seeded reddish to bluish berry.

1. Plants 50-200 cm tall; leaves 2-5 cm long, sharply long-pointed at both ends; berries purplish..*V. membranaceum*
1. Plants less than 50 cm tall; leaves mostly 1-3 cm long; berries red or bluish
    2. Branches rather stiffly erect, often crowded, thickly tangled and nearly leafless toward the plant base so the bare branches are exposed; plants mostly in shady coniferous woods, not forming mats..*V. scoparium*
    2. Branches not stiffly erect, usually spreading, less crowded, the leaves numerous, especially at the top of the plant and usually concealing the lower branches and plant base; plants of sunny mountain meadows, often forming mats....................*V. caespitosum*

Vaccinium caespitosum Michx.   Dwarf Huckleberry
Dwarf mat-forming shrub mostly 10-30 cm tall, spreading by rootstocks; twigs usually puberulent, terete or slightly angled; leaves usually oblanceolate, tapered to the base, 1-3 cm long, usually glabrous and glossy above, pale and somewhat glandular beneath, the margins glandular-serrulate especially above the middle; flowers nodding, single, axillary, whitish to pink; calyx lobes obscure; corolla urn-shaped, twice as long as thick; filaments longer than the awned anthers; berry blue-black with a bloom.
Wet meadows, sphagnum bogs and moist open slopes, about 7000 to 8400 feet.

Vaccinium membranaceum Dougl.   Mountain Huckleberry
Often large spreading glabrous shrub 50-200 cm tall; twigs slightly angled; leaves ovate to obovate or elliptic, sharply serrate, 2-5 cm long, acute, obtuse or rounded at the tip, sparsely glandular and paler beneath than above; flowers small, pale yellowish-pink or greenish-white, solitary; pedicels long, erect in fruit; calyx lobes obscure; corolla nearly globose or longer than broad; filaments shorter than the awned anthers; berries dark purplish-reddish-black without a bloom.
Coniferous mountain slopes, 4600 to about 7000 feet.

***Vaccinium scoparium** Leib.   Dwarf Grouse-berry
Low shrub, commonly glabrous or nearly so, 10-40 cm tall with many green broom-

---

* Plants which may be similar to *V. scoparium* but more consistently pubescent with fewer branches. somewhat larger leaves and flowers and a bluish or dark red berry may be *Vaccinium myrtillus* L.

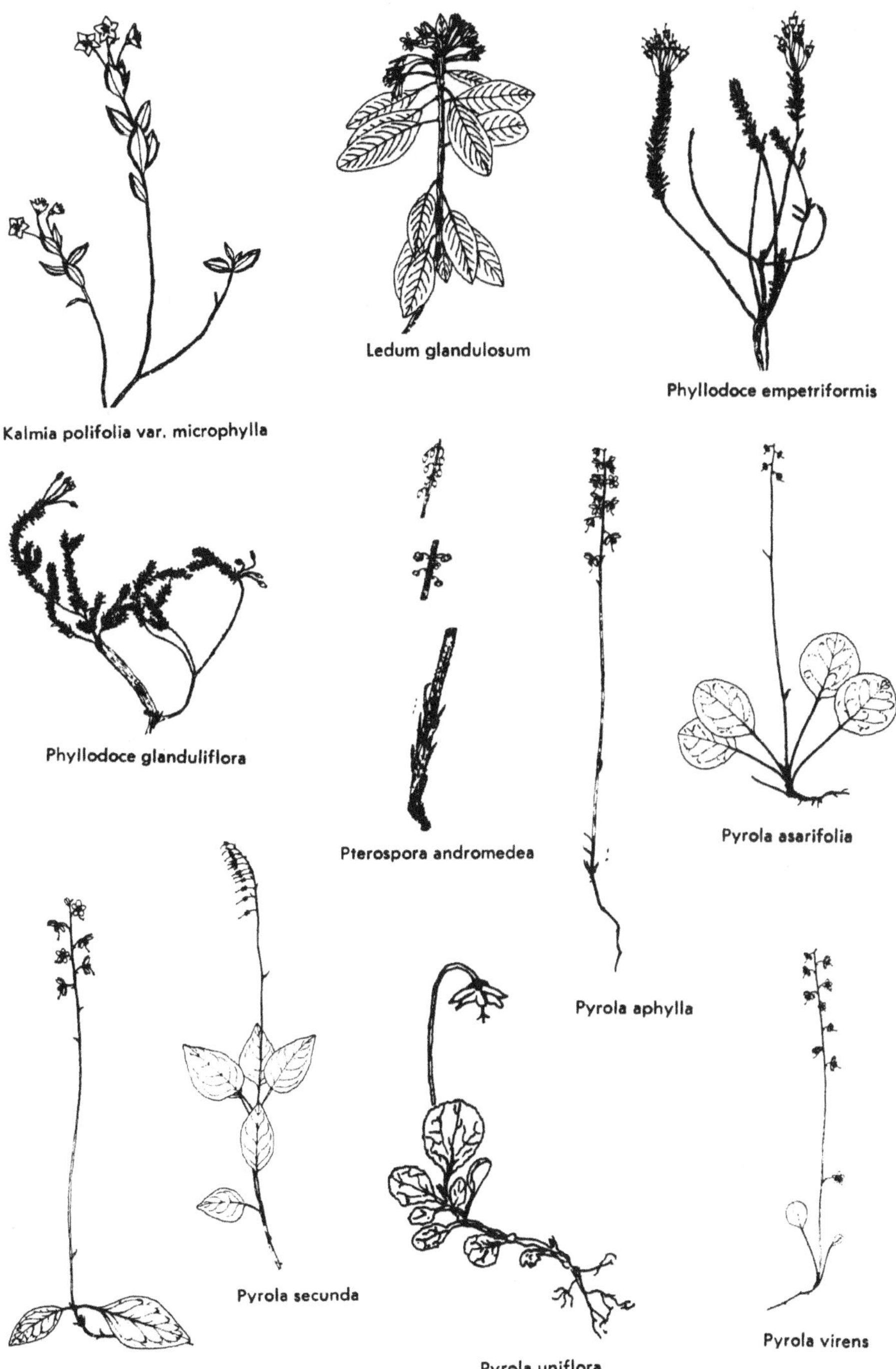

Kalmia polifolia var. microphylla
Ledum glandulosum
Phyllodoce empetriformis
Phyllodoce glanduliflora
Pterospora andromedea
Pyrola asarifolia
Pyrola aphylla
Pyrola picta
Pyrola secunda
Pyrola uniflora
Pyrola virens

like angled branches; leaves lanceolate to ovate, 8-16 mm long, acute, serrulate, shining above, conspicuously veiny and dull underneath; flowers pinkish, axillary, solitary; calyx scarcely lobed; corolla campanulate-urceolate; filaments glabrous, the anthers awned; berry bright red.
Moist shady banks and coniferous woods, about 5000 to 8000 feet and probably higher.

PRIMULACEAE   Primrose Family

Annual or perennial herbs with simple basal (ours) leaves; flowers regular, 5-parted (sometimes 4- to 9-), in terminal umbels (ours) on leafless scapes; calyx usually persistent, deeply lobed; corolla 4- to 9-parted, deeply or shallowly lobed, the lobes spreading or reflexed or sometimes missing; stamens inserted on the tube opposite the petals; ovary superior (ours), 1-celled with free-central placentation; style 1, simple; stigma usually capitate; fruit a 2- to 6-valved circumscissile or valvate capsule; seeds few to many.

1. Plants very small delicate annuals with inconspicuous white flowers ....*Androsace*
1. Plants larger perennials with larger showy flowers, mostly blue-purple but sometimes
     pink or white
    2. Corolla mostly blue-purple, the lobes about 1 cm long, spreading, slightly notched
          at the broad tips; stamens enclosed by the tube..*Primula*
    2. Corolla pinkish to purple or sometimes white, the lobes mostly much over 1 cm
          long, bent backward, their tips pointed; stamens exposed their entire length ....*Dodecatheon*

Androsace [Tourn.] L.

Small annual (ours) herbs with basal rosettes of simple leaves; flowering stems 1 or more, each with a terminal involucrate umbel of 2 to 25 small flowers; calyx 5-lobed; corolla tubular-campanulate with a short tube, constricted throat and spreading or reflexed lobes; stamens 5, included; filaments short, attached to the corolla tube; styles short; capsule globose; seeds many, brownish, pitted.

1. Flowering stems 1-4 cm tall; plants short-hairy with a taproot; corolla equaling or only
     slightly longer than the calyx, often pink, the lobes erect to spreading.....................*A. septentrionalis*
1. Flowering stems 3-10 cm tall; plants not hairy, the roots fibrous; corolla much longer
     than the calyx, the lobes mostly bent back...*A. filiformis*

Androsace filiformis Retz.   Slender Rock-jasmine
Glabrous annual with fibrous roots; leaves lanceolate, ovate or deltoid, in a basal rosette, often long petioled, the blades 4-17 mm long, entire or denticulate; flowering stems 1 or more, 3-10 cm tall, 3- to 20-flowered; pedicels 1-4 cm long; calyx thin, 2-3 mm long, the lobes flat; corolla white, much longer than the calyx, the lobes reflexed; capsules globose, twice as long as the calyx; seeds light brown.
Wet to marshy places in open woods, 5500 to about 6200 feet.

Androsace septentrionalis L.   Small Mountain Androsace
Taprooted puberulent to glandular annual; leaves, pedicels, calyx and petals sometimes pinkish; leaves in a basal rosette, oblanceolate, 1-2 or 3 cm long, sessile or on short winged petioles, the margins entire or denticulate; flowering stems 1-4 cm tall, glabrous or pubescent with simple or forked hairs or glandular-pubescent, 3- to 25-flowered; pedicels 1-3 cm long; calyx 2-5 mm long, the lobes acute; corolla 2.5-4 mm long, white or

pink, equaling or longer than the calyx, the lobes erect or spreading; capsules globose, slightly shorter than the calyx; seeds light to dark brown.

Moist open rocky slopes, mostly near melting snows, about 7900 to 8300 feet.

Dodecatheon L.

Glabrous or glandular-pubescent scapose perennial herbs from rhizomes or caudices, often with bulblets among the roots; leaves basal, entire to dentate, petioled; flowers showy, 4- to 5-parted in an umbel terminating the simple scape; calyx deeply 4- to 5-lobed, persistent; corolla showy, the 4 or 5 lobes long, white to purple, reflexed in flower; stamens 4 or 5; filaments short, separate or united into a tube; anthers attached at the base, the connective colored, smooth or wrinkled; fruit a 1-celled capsule, valvate to the tip or slightly below the operculate tip; seeds many.

1. Tube formed by the union of the filaments well developed between the anthers and the corolla, yellow, 1-3 mm long
    2. Leaves, stems and especially the calyx densely glandular; petioles mostly shorter than the leaf blades..*D. cusickii*
    2. Leaves, stems and calyx not glandular; petioles about as long as the leaf blades..*D. pauciflorum*
1. Tube uniting the filaments not over 0.5 mm long, if developed at all
    3. Leaves few, mostly only 2 or 3, the blade mostly over 1 cm broad, sometimes up to 2 cm; filaments not united into a tube; capsules 8-12 mm long, splitting just below the tip..*D. conjugens*
    3. Leaves several, usually more than 3 or 4, the blade usually less than 1 cm broad; filaments free or the tube less than 1 mm long; capsules 5-7 mm long, splitting to the tip..*D. alpinum*

Dodecatheon alpinum (Gray) Greene   Alpine Shooting Star
D. tetrandrum Suskd.

Plant glabrous, sometimes bulbiferous-rooted; leaves mostly 2-5 cm long, linear-oblanceolate, entire, somewhat crisped; scapes mostly 10-25 cm tall; flowers 1 to few, 4-parted; calyx purplish; sepals lanceolate, 4-7 mm long; corolla 10-18 mm long, the lobes rose-purple, whitish-yellowish below with a band of red-purple at the base; filaments separate or united into a tube less than 1 mm long; connectives deep purple, smooth or wrinkled; anthers purplish; capsule oblong-ovoid, 5-7 mm long, dehiscing by valves to the tip.

Wet meadows and banks of creeks and lakes, 4500 to about 8400 feet.

Dodecatheon conjugens Greene   Desert Shooting Star

Glabrous plant with short rootstocks; leaves 3-10 cm long, spatulate, obovate or oblong-oblanceolate, tapering to the petiole, 1-2 cm broad; scapes 10-25 cm tall; flowers 1 to 5, 4- or 5-parted; calyx purplish; corolla 0.5-4 cm long, the lobes white, rose-pink or purplish, pale at the base, sometimes with a narrow purple band; stamens purplish; anthers sessile, 4-8 mm long, dark purple to yellow; filaments free or in a short tube; connectives purplish and transversely wrinkled; capsules cylindric, 8-12 mm long, splitting into valves just below the tip; seeds brown.

Moist stony coniferous woods and shady banks, 4500 to about 6500 feet.

Dodecatheon cusickii Greene   Sticky Shooting Star

Finely glandular-puberulent plant with short rootstocks; leaves 3-10 cm long, oblance-

olate, obtuse, entire to inconspicuously toothed; scapes 5-30 cm tall, sometimes few-flowered; corolla rose-purple to lavender or sometimes white with a yellow area below and a purple line at the base; filament tube yellow, 1.5-3 mm long; anthers yellowish-purple; connectives purple, cross-wrinkled; capsules narrowly ovoid or sub-cylindric, 6-8 mm long.
Open grassy meadows and rocky slopes, about 4600 feet.

Dodecatheon pauciflorum (Durand) Greene   Few-flowered Shooting Star
Glabrous plant with short erect rootstocks; leaves 2-15 cm long, spatulate to oblance-olate, entire, obtuse, somewhat sinuous-margined, tapering to a winged petiole equaling or shorter than the blade; scape 15-45 cm tall; flowers 1 to 10 or more; calyx lobes purplish, 3-5 mm long; corolla 8-20 mm long, white to lilac, yellow at the base with a wavy purplish line; filaments united into a yellowish to purple tube 1.5-3 mm long; connectives purple, smooth; anthers yellowish to purple, 4-7 mm long; capsules nar-rowly ovoid, 5-15 mm long, glandular-hairy or glabrous.
Moist meadows and mixed woods, 4500 to about 5000 feet.

Plants dwarfed, usually only 2-5 cm tall with 1 or 2 flowers........var. **watsonii** (Tidestr.) C. L. Hitchc. (*D. radicatum* Greene ssp. *watsonii* (Tidestr.) Thompson)
Moist soils in open woods, 6000 to 8000 feet.

Dodecatheon dentatum Hook.   White Shooting Star
Although reported to have been collected in the Wallowa Mountains by two collectors it is possible they misidentified albinos of other species since authors claim it is not known from northeastern Oregon and only from one other Oregon collection from Multnomah County.

Primula L.
Fibrous-rooted perennial scapose herbs (ours) with basal leaves and showy flowers in involucrate umbels; calyx persistent, 5-lobed; corolla salverform, the lobes notched; stamens 5, included, the short filaments attached in the upper part of the corolla tube; ovary superior; style filiform, included; stigma capitate; capsule oblong to ovoid, valvate, many-seeded.

Primula cusickiana Gray   Wallowa Primrose
Glabrous perennial from fibrous roots; leaves 1.5-9 cm long, oblong to oblanceolate or spatulate, obtuse, sinuous or few-toothed or entire; scapes 3-20 cm tall; flowers 2 to 6 on pedicels 0.5-4 cm long; calyx 5-10 mm long, the acute lobes longer or shorter than the tube; corolla pale bluish-violet to purple, up to 15 mm long and as broad, the tube longer than the calyx, the lobes obovate, about 5 mm long; capsule ovoid, 2-7 mm long. Wet to moist stony slopes and springy places, always near or under Ponderosa pine, 5600 to about 6000 feet.

GENTIANACEAE   Gentian Family
Glabrous annual or perennial herbs with simple, opposite or whorled, entire, exstipu-late leaves; flowers usually showy, perfect, regular, gamopetalous, terminal and single or in several-flowered simple to compound cymes; calyx persistent, free from the ovary,

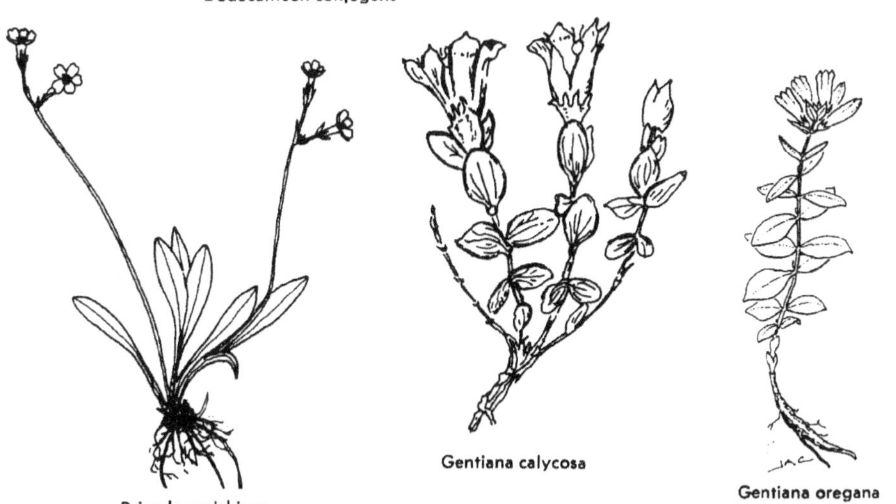

Vaccinium membranaceum
Vaccinium scoparium 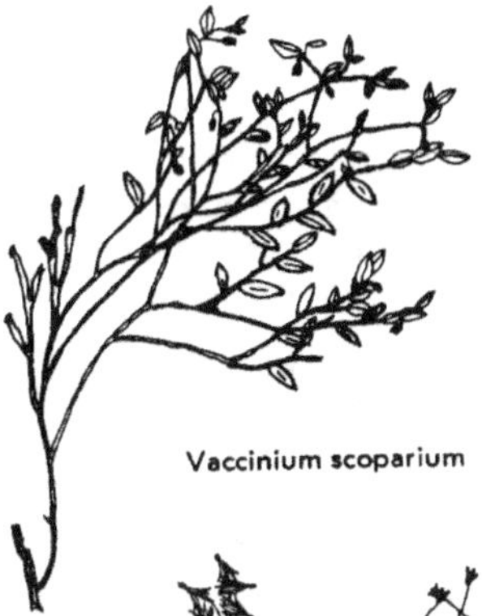
Androsace filiformis 
Dodecatheon alpinum
Dodecatheon cusickii 
Androsace septentrionalis
Dodecatheon pauciflorum
var. watsonii
Dodecatheon conjugens
Primula cusickiana
Gentiana calycosa
Gentiana oregana

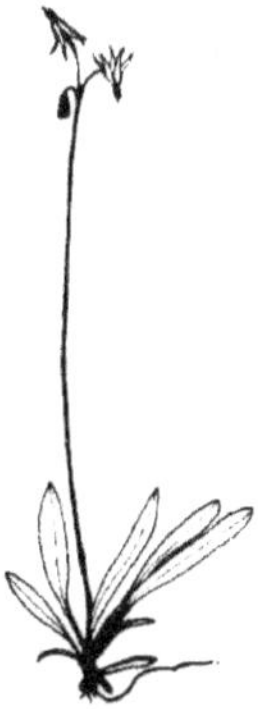

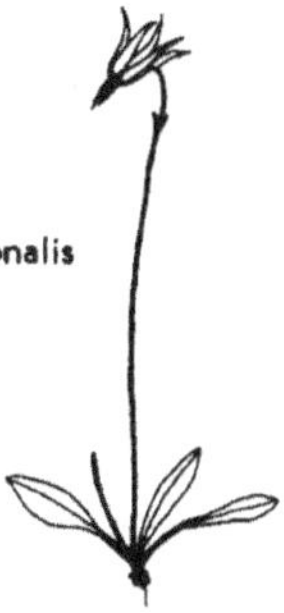

2- to 12-parted or -lobed, or the lobes missing; corolla funnelform to rotate, often marcescent, 4- to 12-parted; stamens inserted on the corolla tube, as many as the corolla lobes and alternate with them, the anthers 2-celled; ovary one-celled with 2 parietal placentae; style 1, simple or cleft and stigmatic near the tip; fruit a capsule, 2-valvate; seeds numerous, minute, striate or pitted, often winged.

1. Corolla funnel-shaped, the lobes shorter than the tube; flowers mostly blue or bluish-green
    2. Corolla usually over 2 cm long; plants usually large perennials..*Gentiana*
    2. Corolla mostly under 2 cm long; plants mostly small annuals..*Gentianella*
1. Corolla not funnel-shaped, the lobes scarcely if at all united into a tube; flowers purplish to blue or white..*Swertia*

Gentiana L.

Ours perennial glabrous herbs with rhizomes or fleshy roots; leaves opposite; flowers showy, solitary to many, 4- to 5-parted, yellowish to blue or purple, often tinged with green, terminal or axillary; calyx usually with 5 unequal lobes; corolla often closing quickly, tubular-funnelform, 4- or 5-lobed, often with plaits in the sinuses or with scales or glands at the base of the corolla lobes; stamens attached to the corolla tube; ovary sessile or striped; style short; capsule 2-valved, many-seeded.

1. Flowers mostly single on each stem; stems usually 10-20 cm tall, more than 1 or 2, often curved or weakly upright; leaves 1-3 cm long, nearly circular, thick and fleshy, crowded near the flower..*G. calycosa*
1. Flowers usually more than 1 on a stem; stems usually more than 20 cm tall; leaves 2-5 cm long, mostly longer than wide
    2. Calyx lobes very narrow, up to 8 mm long or obsolete; corolla lobes spreading............*G. affinis*
    2. Calyx lobes wider, 8-12 mm long, much longer than the tube; corolla lobes not spreading..*G. oregana*

Gentiana affinis Griseb. ex Hook.   Trapper's Gentian

Cespitose perennial from thick fleshy roots with several simple clustered stems 15-60 cm tall; leaves many, opposite, narrowly ovate, oblong or elliptic below to almost linear upwards, 2-5 cm long, obtuse; peduncles axillary, 1- to 3-flowered, 3-40 mm long; flowers in a raceme, each subtended by bracts; calyx lobes variable, unequal, obsolete or up to 8 mm long; corolla 2-4.5 cm long, funnelform, dark blue but tinged with green, the lobes short, the plaits of the sinuses cleft into 2 to 5 entire segments about half the length of the corolla lobes; stamens shorter than the corolla tube; stipe of the ovary 9-10 mm long; style short, cleft above; capsule 12-15 mm long.
Boggy ground in shady coniferous woods, 4500 to about 5300 feet.

Gentiana calycosa Griseb.   Mountain Bog Gentian

Cespitose perennial with thick fleshy roots and several erect, clustered, leafy stems 5-35 cm tall; leaves fleshy, roundish to ovate, 1-3 cm long; flowers mostly single and terminal or a few in the axils of the crowded upper leaves, sessile or pedunculate, subtended by a pair of bracts; calyx tube 4-10 mm long, the lobes unequal, longer or shorter than the tube, or obsolete; corolla funnelform, 3-3.5 cm long, deep blue, often greenish-tinged or rarely yellowish, the lobes rounded or pointed, the plaits of the sinuses usually cleft into 2 to 4 segments shorter or equaling the lobes; anthers 3 or 4 mm long; capsules 16 to 17 mm long, the stipe about 10 mm long; style short; seeds not winged.

Boggy to moist woods, open wet meadows and mossy streambanks, 7000 to about 9800 feet.

Gentiana oregana Engelm. ex Gray

Oregon Gentian

Perennial from a stout root; stems several, clustered, 20-55 cm tall, mostly simple; leaves ovate or oblong, obtuse, 2-4 cm long; flowers single or in 2's in the axils of the crowded upper leaves or a few lower down, subtended by a pair of bracts; calyx tube about 1 cm long, the lobes about equal; corolla broadly funnelform 2.5-6 cm long, blue, often greenish-tinged, the plaits of the sinuses lobed and laciniate-dentate, shorter than the lobes; capsules 25-35 mm long, the stipe about 15 mm long; seeds winged.
Moist open mixed woods and grassy slopes, 4500 to about 5800 feet.

Gentianella Moench.

Annuals (ours) with fleshy roots; stems simple or branched from the base; leaves opposite; flowers solitary to many, yellowish to blue; calyx lobes unequal; corolla without appendages (ours) between the lobes; stamens included in the corolla tube; ovary 1-celled; capsule sessile or stipitate.

1. Flower solitary on the unbranched stem; corolla 2-4 cm long; leaves 3 to 6 pairs..............*G. simplex*
1. Flowers 2 to many, the stems often branched and leafy; corolla mostly under 2 cm long
    2. Corolla tube fringed inside at the base of the lobes..*G. amarella*
    2. Corolla tube not fringed inside..*G. propinqua*

Gentianella amarella (L.) Borner ssp. acuta (Michx.) J. M. Gillett   Northern Gentian

Gentiana amarella L.

Annual or biennial 5-20 cm tall with simple or branched leafy angled stems; basal and lower stem leaves obovate, obtuse or rounded, the upper lanceolate, sessile, 1-4 cm long; flowers 1 to few but usually many, 1-2 cm long, 4- or 5-parted, in axillary cymes; pedicels unequal; calyx 5-10 mm long, the lobes unequal; corolla 8-12 mm long, dark to light blue or yellowish, the 4 or 5 lobes with a crown of long yellow hairs just above the base within; stamens included; ovary sessile; style missing; capsule slightly longer than the persistent corolla.
Boggy and moist mountain meadows, 4500 to about 8000 feet.

Gentianella propinqua (Richards.) Gillett

Meadow Gentian

Gentiana propinqua Richards.

Annual with angled stems, simple or much branched from the base; basal leaves oblanceolate, the cauline numerous, ovate-lanceolate; flowers 15-22 mm long, loosely cymose, becoming smaller near the base; calyx about half the corolla tube, the lobes unequal; corolla light purple, salverform when open, the sinuses not plicate, the lobes without a fringe of hairs within at the base; stamens included and equaling the corolla tube; anthers bluish-purple; ovary nearly sessile; capsule about equaling the corolla; seeds ovoid, pale yellow.
Moist shady woods and meadows, 4800 to about 5200 feet.

Gentianella simplex (Gray) Gillett

One-flowered Gentian

Gentiana simplex Gray

Simple-stemmed annual 5-25 cm tall; leaves 1-2 cm long, oblong, reduced downward; flower solitary, terminal, 4- or 3-parted, often long-peduncled; calyx 15-20 mm long,

lobed about halfway; corolla 20-35 mm long, dark blue, without appendages in the sinuses, the lobes half the length of the flower and with small oblong glands at the base of the stamens; stamens included; ovary long-stipitate; seeds striate.
Boggy creek banks and wet meadows, about 5200 feet.

Swertia L.

Glabrous perennial herbs (ours) with opposite or partly alternate or whorled entire leaves; flowering stems 1 or more; flowers 4- or 5-parted, cymose to thyrsoid; calyx 4- or 5-parted; corolla bluish-purple to white or greenish, rotate to campanulate, each lobe with 1 or 2 fringed glands at the base, the crown scale sometimes missing; stamens inserted on the base of the corolla tube; style very short; fruit a 1-celled capsule; seeds few.

1. Flowering stem single, 0.5-2 meters tall; plants many-flowered with whorled stem leaves; corolla greenish-white to yellowish..*S. radiata*
1. Flowering stems usually more than 1, 10-70 cm tall; plants with few to many flowers and opposite stem leaves; corolla purple to bluish or white
    2. Leaves mostly basal, white-margined; flowers light blue or white, 4-parted; plants sometimes short-hairy near the base..*S. albicaulis*
    2. Leaves on the stem and at the base, not white-margined; flowers few, bluish-purple with some green or white, 5-parted..*S. perennis*

Swertia albicaulis (Griseb.) Kuntze   Shining Swertia
Frasera albicaulis Dougl.
Mostly glabrous plants with a branched caudex and several flowering stems 20-50 cm tall; leaves 5-30 cm long, oblanceolate to spatulate, white-margined, mostly clustered in sterile basal shoots, the cauline paired, few and reduced upward; inflorescence interrupted, many-flowered; calyx lobes subulate, white-margined; corolla rotate, pale blue to occasionally white, the lobes 5-11 mm long, the fringed basal gland about half the length of each lobe or longer; filaments united by deeply lacerate crown scales; capsules about 10 mm long.
Open pine woods to exposed, nearly treeless, sandy ridges, 4500 to about 8400 feet.

Swertia perennis L.   Felwort
Plants with short rhizomes; stems single, 10-50 cm tall; basal leaves oblong-elliptic, 4-15 cm long, long-petioled; cauline leaves fewer, smaller, sessile; inflorescence a raceme of 4- or 5-parted pedicellate flowers; calyx lobes 4 or 5 mm long; corolla bluish-purple with some green or white; glands orbicular, fringed all around; capsules compressed, 7-12 mm long.
Boggy coniferous woods, 5300 to 5500 feet.

Swertia radiata (Kell.) Kuntze   Giant Swertia; Deer Tongue
Frasera speciosa Dougl. ex Griseb.
Glabrous to scabrous plant with a single stout flowering stem, 0.5-2 meters tall; basal leaves 25-50 cm long, oblanceolate; stem leaves in whorls of 3 to 5, much reduced; inflorescence 25-60 cm long, few-branched; calyx lobes lanceolate, 1.5-2.5 cm long; corolla rotate, yellowish- or whitish-green, purplish-mottled, each lobe with a pair of fringed glands at the base; crown scale wide with lacerate segments or missing; capsules 2-2.5 cm long.
Moist meadows and open wooded slopes, often near streams, 4500 to about 8000 feet.

MENYANTHACEAE   Buck Bean Family

Glabrous perennial aquatic or marsh herbs with thick rhizomes and alternate, long-petioled, simple to trifoliate leaves; flowers in simple to compound racemes or cymes on long naked peduncles, regular, gamopetalous; calyx 5-parted, free or attached to the ovary below; corolla salverform to rotate, the lobes fringed or bearded within; stamens 5, borne on the corolla tube; anthers sagittate, versatile; pistil 1, 2-carpellary; ovary 1-celled, partly inferior; styles dimorphic, short and thick or long and slender, or missing; fruit a capsule.

Menyanthes [Tourn.] L.

Glabrous perennial aquatic or subaquatic herb with shallow rhizomes and long-petioled trifoliate leaves; flowers white or purplish, racemose on long naked scapes, usually dimorphic, some with short styles and exserted stamens, others with exserted styles and short stamens; corolla funnelform, 5-parted, fimbriate or bearded within; ovary 1-celled, partially inferior; capsules elliptic, 1 cm long.

Menyanthes trifoliata L. Buck Bean

Plants with thick rhizomes covered with old leaf bases; leaves trifoliolate, the leaflets elliptic, 2-12 cm long, entire to undulate-margined; petioles 3-30 cm long; scapes erect, about equaling the leaves; raceme 5- to 30-flowered; pedicels 1-2 cm long; calyx 3-5 mm long, the lobes obtuse; corolla white, 8-10 mm long, the tube longer than the calyx, the lobes purplish-tinged, conspicuously bearded within; anthers purplish; ovary globose; capsules ovoid, about 8 mm long, many-seeded.
Shallow lake water near the boggy shore, about 5600 feet.

APOCYNACEAE   Dogbane Family

Trees, shrubs, vines or perennial herbs with milky juice and opposite, verticillate or sometimes alternate leaves; flowers solitary or in cymes, perfect, regular, 5-parted except the pistil; calyx persistent, free from the ovary; corolla convolute in the bud; stamens adnate to the corolla; ovary superior, the carpels distinct or united; fruit a pair of follicles or drupes; seeds often with a coma.

Apocynum L.

Perennial herbs with opposite entire leaves and small white or pink flowers in cymes; calyx 5-parted; corolla campanulate, 5-lobed, the tube with 5 appendages alternate with the stamens; anthers sagittate, surrounding the stigma, slightly joined at the tips; ovary of 2 carpels, the style short, the stigma shallow-lobed; fruit a pair of elongated terete follicles; seeds numerous with a conspicuous tuft of long silky hairs (coma).

Apocynum androsaemifolium L. Mountain Dogbane

Glabrous to tomentose plant, much branched, 10-50 cm tall; leaves spreading or drooping, opposite, petioled, ovate to lanceolate or oblong-elliptic, 1.5-9 cm long, usually mucronate; flowers pinkish, fragrant, usually in terminal cymes but often axillary as well; calyx lobes white or pink; corolla tubular or campanulate, mostly 5-8 mm long, the lobes erect, spreading or reflexed; follicles erect or pendulous, 5-15 cm long; coma pale tawny, 1-2 cm long.

Dry ground, often in open coniferous forest and on wooded mountainsides, 4500 to about 8000 feet.

Corolla tubular, 4-7 mm long; follicles usually erect...........................var. **pumilum** Gray
Corolla bell-shaped, broader at the mouth than at the base, 5-10 cm long; follicles usually hanging down...var. **androsaemifolium**
With the species.

POLEMONIACEAE   Phlox Family

Annual to perennial herbs or shrubs or vines; leaves opposite or alternate, simple or compound; flowers perfect, often showy, solitary or variously clustered in heads, panicles, cymes or glomerules; calyx 5-lobed; corolla 5-lobed, contorted in bud, the tube from nearly obsolete to several cm long; stamens 5, epipetalous; ovary superior, usually 3-loculed but sometimes 1, 2 or 4; fruit a capsule, usually loculicidal.

1. Leaves simple, not lobed or dissected, the margins mostly also undivided or toothed
   2. Leaves mostly opposite
      3. Plants erect annuals; leaves mostly opposite but the upper ones alternate..... *Microsteris*
      3. Plants low perennials, mostly forming cushion-like mats; upper leaves mostly
         opposite like the lower ones..*Phlox*
   2. Leaves mostly alternate, the margins sometimes lobed
      4. Flowers in rather crowded clusters at the top of the stem................*Collomia*
      4. Flowers on thin stalks in an open inflorescence ....*Gilia*
1. Leaves lobed or divided into leaflets
   5. Flowers mostly blue but often with some pink, white or yellow
      6. Leaves divided or cleft into many well-developed leaflets ....*Polemonium*
      6. Leaves lobed but not divided into leaflets; plants sprawling mat-forming
         alpines; stamens longer than the flowers..*Collomia*
   5. Flowers red or white or pink but not blue (except sometimes pale bluish-white in
     Linanthus)
      7. Leaves and calyx-teeth spiny-tipped; flowers in crowded head-like clusters;
         plants very small annuals, but not delicate... *Navarretia*
      7. Leaves and calyx-teeth not spiny-tipped; flowers in panicles or small clusters;
         plants annuals or perennials, sometimes small and delicate
         8. Flowers creamy or pale bluish-white, sometimes long-stalked; leaves
            opposite or appearing whorled, the many divisions very narrow............... *Linanthus*
         8. Flowers bright red, pink or rarely white; leaves alternate, the divisions
            not so narrow as above...*Gilia*

Collomia Nutt.

Annual or perennial herbs, mostly taprooted; leaves mostly alternate, entire to dissected; flowers in scattered head-like clusters or rarely solitary in the leaf axils; calyx herbaceous or chartaceous at least below; corolla trumpet- or funnel-shaped, bluish or pinkish to white or sometimes salmon or yellow; stamens equal or unequal in length and insertion; capsules ellipsoid to obovoid; seeds 1 to 3 per locule.

1. Stems many, sprawling over the ground often; plants alpine perennials; leaves often
  lobed or dissected; stamens and styles conspicuously longer than the flower.....................*C. debilis*
1. Stem solitary, erect; plants annuals of lower elevations; leaves not lobed or dissected
   2. Corolla 20-30 mm long, salmon or yellowish..*C. grandiflora*
   2. Corolla 5-15 mm long, pink, white or bluish...*C. linearis*

Collomia debilis (Wats.) Greene — Alpine Collomia

Perennial; stems many, 10-30 cm tall, sprawling or erect on the crown of a strong taproot; stems and leaves nearly glabrous to puberulent or glandular-pubescent; leaves obovate, entire to toothed or 3- to 5-lobed, 1-3 cm long; flowers clustered at the ends of the many, often matted, branches; calyx campanulate; corolla trumpet-shaped, mostly 1.5-3 cm long, blue or lavender to pink, white or cream, the tube much longer than the lobes; stamens equally inserted; filaments equal or unequal in length; style long-exserted; capsules obovoid, the locules one-seeded.
Loose shifting sand and gravel on exposed slopes, 8000 to 9400 feet and possibly higher.

Collomia grandiflora Dougl. — Large-flowered Collomia

Erect annual; stems simple or branched, 10-100 cm tall; leaves lanceolate, entire, sessile, 5-10 cm long, glabrous to puberulent, glandular or scabrous; flowers in congested heads subtended by foliaceous bracts; calyx glandular becoming chartaceous; corolla funnel-shaped, 2-3 cm long, mostly salmon or yellowish to nearly white; stamens unequally to nearly equally inserted; anthers blue, some exserted; capsules obovoid, the locules 1-seeded.
Dry rocky open places, 5300 feet.

Collomia linearis Nutt. — Narrow-leaved Collomia

Erect annual; stems 10-60 cm tall, pubescent and glandular above, less so to nearly glabrous below; leaves alternate, linear to lanceolate, 1-7 cm long, sessile or nearly so; flowers inconspicuous in a dense terminal leafy cluster; calyx campanulate, elongating in fruit; corolla pink or bluish to white, 8-15 mm long, the tube long and slender; stamens unequally inserted; capsules ellipsoid; locules 1-seeded.
Dry or moist open or shady woods, 4500 to about 6000 feet.

Gilia Ruiz & Pav.

Annual, biennial or perennial herbs with a taproot; leaves mostly alternate, entire or variously lobed and dissected, often in a basal cluster; flowers solitary or in various cymose inflorescences; calyx lobes equal and entire, often with a membrane forming a false tube which is ruptured by the developing capsule; corolla campanulate to funnel-shaped, blue, pink, red, yellow or white; stamens usually equal, sometimes unequal in length and point of insertion; capsule 3-celled; seeds 1 to many per locule.

1. Leaves mostly dissected into 3 or more segments; plants perennial or biennial; inflorescence several-flowered
    2. Flowers showy, trumpet-shaped, bright red, pink or yellow, 20-30 mm long in a long inflorescence; stems erect...*G. aggregata*
    2. Flowers white, not showy, 6-10 mm long, in congested heads; stems weak and often sprawling..*G. congesta*
1. Leaves usually not dissected at all; flowers usually small, single, numerous in the leaf axils or on the stem opposite a leaf; plants delicate annuals
    3. Corolla mostly under 3 mm long, whitish or faintly bluish or lavender; plants up to 20 cm tall...*G. tenerrima*
    3. Corolla 3.5-10 mm long, bright pink-lavender to pale bluish or nearly white; plants 2-30 cm tall...*G. capillaris*

Gilia aggregata (Pursh) Spreng. — Scarlet Gilia

Biennial or short-lived perennial, glandular-puberulent to glandless and pilose, or glabrate; stems 10-100 cm tall; leaves pinnately dissected into linear segments, the cauline reduced upward, the basal forming a rosette; flowers showy in a long narrow inflorescence; corolla trumpet-shaped, 2-5 cm long, scarlet or pink, rarely white or mottled; capsules ovoid.

Dry to moist open woods and rocky slopes and banks, usually associated with limestone, 4500 to 9800 feet and probably higher.

Gilia capillaris Kell.   Smooth-leaved Gilia

Annual 2-30 cm tall, often with blackish stipitate glands; leaves linear, 1-2 cm long; inflorescence an open panicle; calyx glandular-pubescent, much enlarged in fruit; corolla 5-10 mm long, pink or bluish to white, the tube longer than the lobes; filaments short, the anthers blue or white; capsule 3-4 mm long.

Dry or moist open woods and meadows, 5700 to about 6200 feet.

Gilia congesta Hook. var. viridis Cronq.   Frilly Gilia

Malodorous perennial with a short caudex, several stems mostly 10-20 cm tall and several short sterile shoots at the base; herbage grayish-arachnoid-tomentose, sometimes glabrous; leaves 1-2 cm long, 3- to 5-parted into linear segments, or entire; flowers in dense heads at the ends of the weak and often sprawling stems and branches; corolla white, the yellow tube about equaling the calyx; stamens and pistil slightly if at all exserted; capsule shorter than the calyx.

Dry to moist rocky open slopes at about timberline, 7000 to about 8400 feet.

Gilia tenerrima Gray   Delicate Gilia

Delicate annual up to 20 cm tall, glabrous or glandular-pubescent; leaves 1-2.5 cm long, simple, alternate, glandular; inflorescence an open panicle, the pedicels spreading and reflexed in fruit; corolla white, pinkish or bluish, 1-3 mm long; capsules glabrous; locules 1-seeded.

Dry sandy meadows and open wooded slopes, about 5800 feet.

Linanthus Benth.

Taprooted annual or perennial herbs with opposite leaves palmately parted into linear segments, rarely simple and undivided; inflorescence open and paniculate or in dense terminal clusters, the flowers sessile to long-pedicelled; calyx lobes deeply cleft, sometimes with a hyaline border, the pseudotube present or missing; corolla campanulate to almost salverform, the tube long and slender, glabrous or the pubescence scattered or in bands; stamens about equal in length and insertion; capsules 1- to several-seeded.

1. Flowers rather showy, yellowish-white, usually in crowded clusters at the tips of the many branches..*L. nuttallii*
1. Flowers very small on long thin spreading stalks, in an open inflorescence; plants delicate annuals branching near the top of the plant
  2. Corolla 2.5-5 mm long, about twice as long as the calyx or more, the tube hairy inside..*L. septentrionalis*
  2. Corolla 1.5-2.5 mm long, only slightly if at all longer than the calyx, the tube not hairy inside ....*L. harknessii*

Linanthus harknessii (Curran) Greene   Harkness' Linanthus

Slender annual 10-40 cm tall, puberulent to glabrate, simple below, freely branched

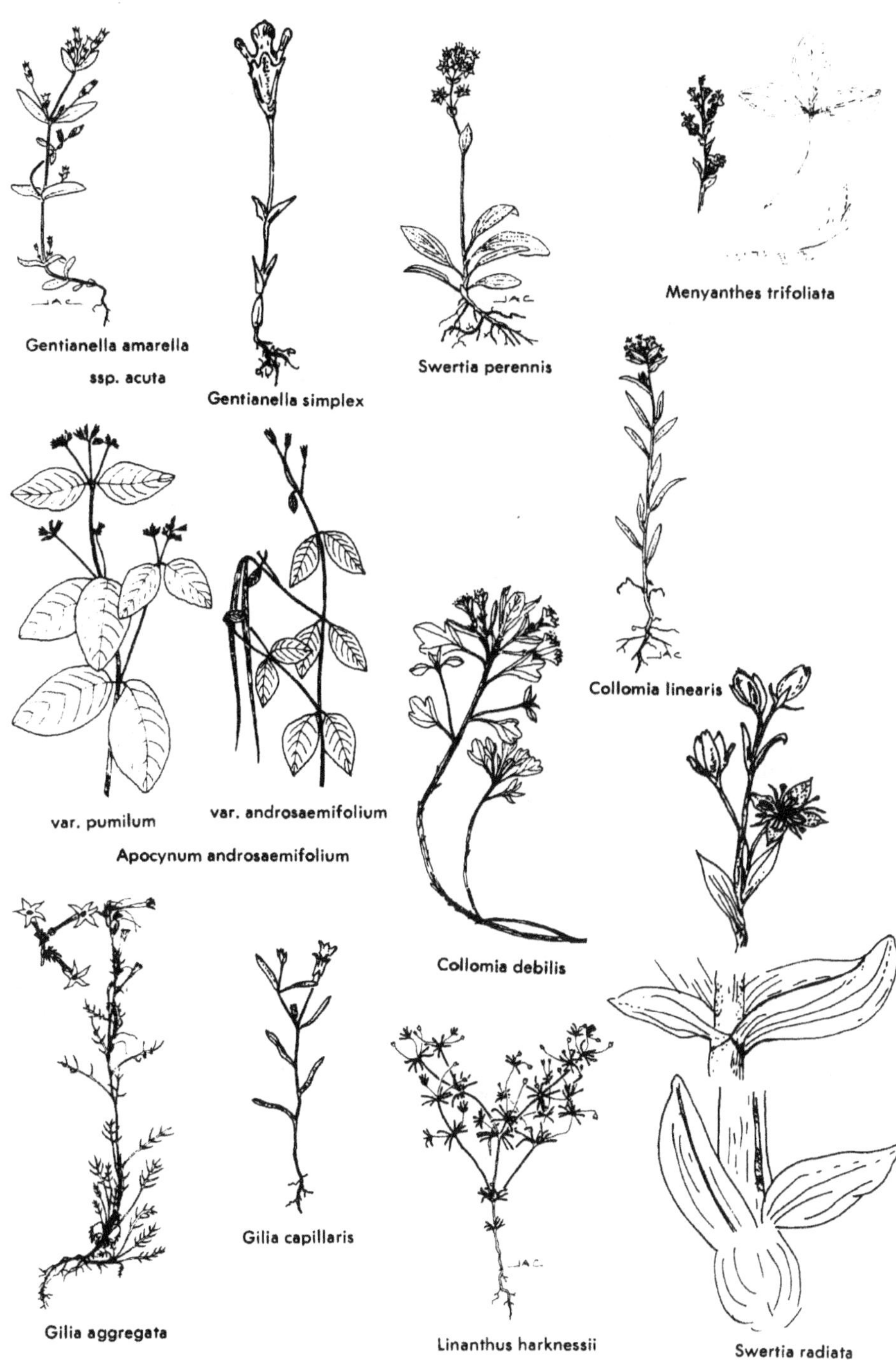

Gentianella amarella
ssp. acuta

Gentianella simplex

Swertia perennis

Menyanthes trifoliata

var. pumilum

var. androsaemifolium

Apocynum androsaemifolium

Collomia debilis

Collomia linearis

Gilia aggregata

Gilia capillaris

Linanthus harknessii

Swertia radiata

above; leaves 6-15 mm long, parted to the base into 3 to 6 or 7 linear divisions, rarely entire; flowers small, on long filiform pedicels which often spread at right angles; calyx campanulate; corolla white to pale blue, about equaling the calyx, glabrous within; stamens and stigma included; capsules 3-seeded, about equaling the calyx.
Moist shady woods, about 5500 feet to 7000 feet.

Linanthus nuttallii Greene   Nuttall's Linanthus
Linanthastrum nuttallii Ewan
    Taprooted aromatic perennial; stems branched from the woody base, up to 30 cm tall or more; herbage villous-hispid to glabrate; leaves fascicled, 5- to 9-parted into linear mucronate segments, 1-2 cm long; flowers nearly sessile in compact terminal clusters, closely subtended by the upper leaves; corolla white with yellowish throat, salverform, 12-15 mm long, the tube woolly-puberulent; capsules oblong, seeds 1 to 4 in each locule.
Dry rocky or sandy sunny slopes and open woods, 5300 to about 9200 feet.

Linanthus septentrionalis Mason   Northern Linanthus
    Slender annual 10-30 cm tall; stems simple or branched above; leaves opposite, 5- to 7-parted into linear segments; inflorescence open, the flowers solitary on long spreading pedicels; corolla 1-5 or 6 mm long, white to pale blue, definitely longer than the calyx, with a hairy ring within; stamens and style exserted; capsules with 2 to 8 seeds in each locule.
Forest clearings, dry or moist meadows and hillsides, 5000 to about 7000 feet.

Microsteris Greene

    Annual herbs with all but the upper leaves opposite; flowers small, terminal, solitary or paired; calyx membrane between segments ruptured by the developing capsule; corolla salverform, the tube short, the lobes spreading; stamens unequally inserted on the corolla tube; seeds few, large, one per locule.

Microsteris gracilis (Hook.) Greene   Pretty Little Phlox
Phlox gracilis Greene
    Low annual herbs up to 30 cm tall, simple or branched, puberulent or glandular-pubescent at least above; leaves entire, obtuse, up to 5 cm long, the upper lanceolate to linear, the lower elliptic to oblong or obovate; inflorescence an open cyme, glandular; flowers mostly in pairs: one pedicellate, the other nearly sessile; calyx ruptured early by the expanding capsule; corolla 5-15 mm long with white or yellowish tube and pink or purplish lobes.

Stem 5-25 cm tall, usually simple below and branched only above, the plant appearing taller than broad; corolla 8-15 mm long, the tube yellowish, the lobes pink or purplish..var. **gracilis**
Brushy open slopes, meadows and along streams, about 5000 feet.

Stem mostly 1-5 cm tall, usually much branched from the base, the plant thus seeming as broad as tall, or broader; corolla 5-8-10 mm long, the tube nearly white, the lobes purplish; pubescence abundant, coarse and glandular......var. **humilior** (Hook.) Cronq.
Dry brushy open slopes, 4500 to 6500 feet.

Navarretia Ruiz & Pav.

Annuals with alternate leaves, or the lower sometimes opposite, entire or divided into narrow, spine-tipped segments; herbage glandular-pubescent-villose, often reddish; flowers small, in dense terminal heads subtended by leafy bracts; calyx lobes unequal, spine-tipped, entire or cleft, the intervals hyaline below the developing capsule; corolla salverform to funnel-shaped, 5-parted or sometimes 4-parted; stamens included or exserted; stigma entire or 2- or 3-lobed; capsule ovoid or obovoid, 1- to 3-loculed, the partitions sometimes imperfect.

Corolla lobes only slightly, if at all, longer than wide, the mid-vein branched; leaves and bracts firm ....*N. intertexta*

Corolla lobes narrow, about twice as long as wide, the mid-vein not branched; leaves and bracts soft ....*N. minima*

Navarretia intertexta (Benth.) Hook. var. propinqua (Suksd.) Brand

Pin cusion plant

Simple or branched annual 6-20 cm tall, puberulent, becoming villous in the inflorescence; leaves 2-5 cm long, pinnately or binnately divided into filiform divisions, the rachis narrow; inflorescence capitate-congested; calyx white-hairy, the lobes unequal, 1 or 2 of them often trifid; corolla white or pale blue, 4-7 mm long, equaling or shorter than the calyx; stamens and style exserted; capsules thin-walled, 1- or 2-celled, indehiscent.

Grassy open coniferous woods, 4500 to about 6000 feet.

Navarretia minima Nutt.

Least Navarretia

Low branched annual up to 10 cm tall, with white or reddish pubescent stems and pale green leaves and bracts; leaves few, soft, 1-3.5 cm long, entire or (mostly) pinnate with the tips of the 1 to 3 pairs of lobes scarcely spiny; calyx 4-7 mm long, white-hairy, the sepals unequal, usually entire; corolla white, 4-6 mm long, equaling or shorter than the calyx, the lobes narrowly oblong; stamens and stigma exserted; capsules ovoid, indehiscent.

Moist open ridge in Ponderosa Pine woods, about 5800 feet.

Phlox L.

Perennial or rarely annual herbs, often shrubby below; leaves opposite or sometimes the upper ones alternate, entire, usually narrow; flowers often showy, in terminal cymes or sometimes solitary; calyx usually hyaline or scarious between the lobes; corolla salverform with slender tube and showy spreading lobes, white to pink, purple or blue; stamens short, irregular, inserted on the corolla tube; capsule 3-valved, rupturing the calyx tube eventually; seeds usually solitary or few in each chamber.

1. Plants low, compact and cushion-like with many short branches; leaves crowded, often
    stiff and sharp-pointed; flowers mostly solitary, sometimes 3 in a cluster
      2. Plants glandular; leaves 3-35 mm long, not very hairy, if at all
          3. Leaves mostly over 5 cm long, often crowding the flowers; flowers sometimes
            without stalks
               4. Leaves 5-13 mm long, bluish-green, the margins in-rolled; membrane
                  between the calyx lobes flat and smooth, the calyx ribs thick..............*P. caespitosa*
               4. Leaves 10-35 mm long, green, not much crowding the stalked flowers;
                  membrane between calyx lobes keeled or bulged ....*P. aculeata*

> 3. Leaves under 5 cm long, pale, grayish, the margins thickened; calyx 5-8 mm long .... *P. covillei*
>   2. Plants not glandular; leaves 5-20 mm long, rather woolly in appearance
>   5. Corolla tube 4-10 mm long; calyx woolly, the midrib thick, the membrane between the lobes flat and smooth .... *P. hoodii*
>   5. Corolla tube 9-17 mm long; calyx hairy, the membrane between lobes very slightly ridged .... *P. austromontana*
> 1. Plants not compact and cushion-like; leaves long, not stiff or sharp-pointed, the stem visible and long between leaves .... *P. longifolia*

Phlox aculeata A. Nels.   Needle-leaved Phlox

Stems 5-15 cm tall from a woody root crown and a taproot, glabrous and shiny near the base, glandular-pubescent above; leaves very narrow, 1.5-3 cm long, sometimes slightly hairy near the base; flowers short- to long-pedicellate; calyx about 1 cm long, glandular-pubescent, the tube about equaling the lobes or shorter, the scarious membrane keeled; corolla pink, white, lilac or bluish, the tube about 12 mm long, the limb 1-1.5 mm broad, the lobes blunt or emarginate.
Gravelly outwash, about 5700 feet.

Phlox austromontana Cov.   Western Mountain Phlox or Sweet William
P. douglasii var. *austromontana* Jeps. & Mason; *P. diffusa* ssp. *subcarinata* Wherry

Taprooted cespitose perennial forming loose to dense mats; stems numerous, tomentose or canescent to glabrate but not glandular, 5-30 cm tall; herbage pale grayish, leaves stiff and sharp-pointed, linear, often ciliate-margined, 5-20 mm long; flowers solitary; calyx tomentose, 6-10 mm long, sharp-toothed, the intercostal membranes with a low keel; corolla white to pinkish or purplish, the tube 9-17 mm long, the lobes 5-9 mm long; style 2-10 mm long.
Open slopes and hillsides, 4500 to about 5000 feet.

Phlox caespitosa Nutt.   Clustered Phlox
P. douglasii var. *caespitosa* Mason

Densely cespitose, taprooted shrubby perennial 5-15 cm tall, pubescent or glandular-pubescent at least above; leaves 3-ribbed, glaucous-green, linear, stiff and sharp-pointed, 5-13 mm long, the margins inrolled and often short-ciliate toward the base; flowers solitary, rarely 3; calyx 7-10 mm long, the intercostal membranes flat and narrow, the calyx ribs thick; corolla lilac to white, the tube 8-15 mm long, the lobes 7-10 mm long.
Dry exposed rocky slopes and ridges, mostly above treeline, 7600 to about 9900 feet.

Phlox covillei E. Nels.   Coville's Phlox
Cespitose, cushion-like tufted plants 5-10 cm across; leaves pale grayish, crowded on the short branches, stiff, narrow and sharp-pointed, 3-5 mm long, glandular-pubescent, ciliate on the very thick margins; flowers usually solitary and sessile; calyx glandular-pubescent, 5-8 mm long; corolla white to pale pink, the tube 8-10 mm long and hairy within, the lobes 4-8 mm long.
Talus and rocky slopes and ridges, 9500 to 9800 feet and probably higher.

Phlox hoodii Richards.   Gray Woolly Moss Phlox
P. douglasii var. *canescens* H. L. Mason; *P. hoodii* var. *canescens* (T. & G.) Peck

Taprooted cushion-forming plant, woolly-villous to almost glabrous or glandular;

leaves 5-11 mm long, awl-shaped, firm and pungent, rather woolly; flowers usually solitary; calyx woolly, 5-9 mm long; corolla bluish or pink to white, the tube 4-13 mm long; style 2-7 mm long.
Dry rocky places, about 5000 feet.

Phlox longifolia Nutt.   Long-leaved Phlox

Stems 10-40 cm long, often creeping below ground level, woolly at the base; herbage glabrous to glandular or hairy above; leaves narrowly linear-lanceolate, 1.5-10 cm long, not sharp-pointed, the internodes well developed; flowers fragrant, usually in small open cymes, pedicellate; calyx 10-12 mm long, inflated or keeled toward the base; corolla white to lilac or pink, the tube 10-18 mm long, the lobes 7-15 mm long; style 6-15 mm long.
Dry rocky meadows and open slopes, 5000 to 6000 feet.

Polemonium [Tourn.] L.

Annual or mostly perennial herbs, often glandular; leaves alternate, pinnately compound, the leaflets entire to palmately 2- to 5-parted; flowers solitary or variously clustered; calyx cup-shaped, enlarging with the capsule; corolla funnelform to nearly rotate, mostly blue or white but sometimes yellow, pink or purple; stamens equally inserted on the tube; capsules ovoid, seeds spindle-shaped, often black.

1. Corolla tube longer than the calyx
    2. Leaflets 3- to 5-toothed; corolla 18-30 mm long; calyx 8-16 mm long................*P. viscosum*
    2. Leaflets not toothed; corolla 12-15 mm long; calyx 5-8 mm long ....*P. elegans*
1. Corolla tube about equaling the calyx
    3. Plants with only 1 stem, 30-100 cm tall, mostly in or near water; styles
       conspicuously longer than the corolla..*P. occidentale*
    3. Plants with several flowering stems, 10-30 cm tall, often on dry land; styles about
       as long as the corolla..*P. pulcherrimum*

Polemonium elegans Greene   Elegant Polemonium

Glandular-pubescent perennial with a stout taproot and branching caudex; stems 5-12 cm tall; leaves chiefly basal, few on the flowering stems, 6-12 cm long; leaflets entire, opposite or offset, crowded; petioles short, expanded at the base; inflorescence a capitate cyme; calyx campanulate, densely glandular-pubescent, 5-8 mm long; corolla funnelform, 12-15 mm long, the lobes blue or violet, shorter than the yellow tube; stamens, ovary and style shorter than the corolla.
High dry slopes, 9000 to about 9700 feet and probably higher.

Polemonium occidentale Greene   Western Polemonium

Stem leafy, solitary, 30-100 cm tall, from a horizontal root, glandular-puberulent above; leaves glabrous, 6-12 cm long; leaflets 15 to 27, the upper 3 often confluent; inflorescence a cyme, viscid-puberulent; calyx glandular-puberulent, 4-10 mm long; corolla rotate-campanulate, blue, rarely white; stamens included, the filaments pubescent at the base; style conspicuously longer than the corolla.
Moist or wet boggy places, about 4500 to 5500 feet.

Polemonium pulcherrimum Hook.   Jacob's Ladder

P. columbianum Eastw.; *P. pulchellum* Bunge
Perennial from a branched caudex and a taproot; stems 10-30 cm tall; stems, leaves

and inflorescence glandular or glandular-villous or -tomentose to nearly glabrous; leaves 3-10 cm long, the cauline ones reduced; leaflets 11 to 25, entire, obtuse, opposite or offset, oval to orbicular; flowers in small cymes; calyx campanulate; corolla rotate-campanulate, blue with light yellow or white throat and yellowish tube; stamens about equaling the corolla, the filaments woolly at the base; ovary and style nearly as long as the corolla.

Moist rocky coniferous woods, about 5000 to 9000 feet, or higher.

Small compact plants, regularly taprooted, mostly under 25 cm tall; plants of high elevations..............................var. **pulcherrimum** (*P. viscosum* var. *pilosum* Greenm.)

Larger, more open, stouter plants, often 30-50 cm tall, the taproot poorly developed if at all; plants of low to medium elevations in the mountains......var. **calycinum** (Eastw.) Brand (*P. californicum* Eastw.; *P. humile* Willd.)

Polemonium viscosum Nutt. Skunkweed

 P. confertum Gray

 Viscid-pubescent ill-scented perennial with a stout taproot and branching caudex; stems 10-50 cm tall; leaves chiefly basal, few on the flowering stems, 8-18 cm long; leaflets mostly 3- to 5-parted, crowded, glandular-ciliate on the margins to glabrous; petioles expanded at the base; inflorescence almost funnelform, 18-30 mm long, bright blue or violet, occasionally white, the lobes shorter than the tube; stamens equaling or shorter than the corolla.

Exposed rocky slopes, 8600 to about 9550 feet.

HYDROPHYLLACEAE Waterleaf Family

Annual to perennial herbs or low shrubs; leaves alternate or opposite, entire to divided or pinnatifid; flowers solitary or cymose, regular and perfect; calyx 5-parted, free from the ovary; corolla 5-lobed with a pair of scales at the base of each stamen; stamens usually 5, inserted on the corolla tube near the base; pistil 2-carpellary; style entire to deeply 2-parted, deciduous; ovary superior, 1- or 2-loculed; fruit a loculicidal capsule, sometimes also septicidal, or irregularly dehiscent.

1. Flowers usually solitary, sometimes 2 or 3; plants annuals or perennials
  2. Plants stemless; leaves not toothed or lobed, usually forming a basal rosette.......*Hesperochiron*
  2. Plants with 1 or more stems; leaves toothed or lobed or divided, mostly on the stems...*Nemophila*
1. Flowers usually in several-flowered heads or inflorescences, never solitary; plants mostly perennials; stamens longer than the flowers
  3. Flowers usually in roundish head-like clusters; leaves and stems mostly thin and flexible; plants fibrous-rooted perennials...*Hydrophyllum*
  3. Flowers in more open spike-like, often coiled, clusters, usually elongating in fruit; leaves and stems usually thick and densely hairy, often bristly to the touch; plants mostly with very thick taproots and many thick branches at about ground level.........*Phacelia*

Hesperochiron S. Wats.

Dwarf acaulescent scapose perennials with a short root; leaves in a basal rosette, few, entire, ovate to oblong, petiolate; flowers single on basal peduncles; calyx cleft nearly to the base; corolla deciduous, white, often blue or purplish-tinged, funnelform or **rotate**;

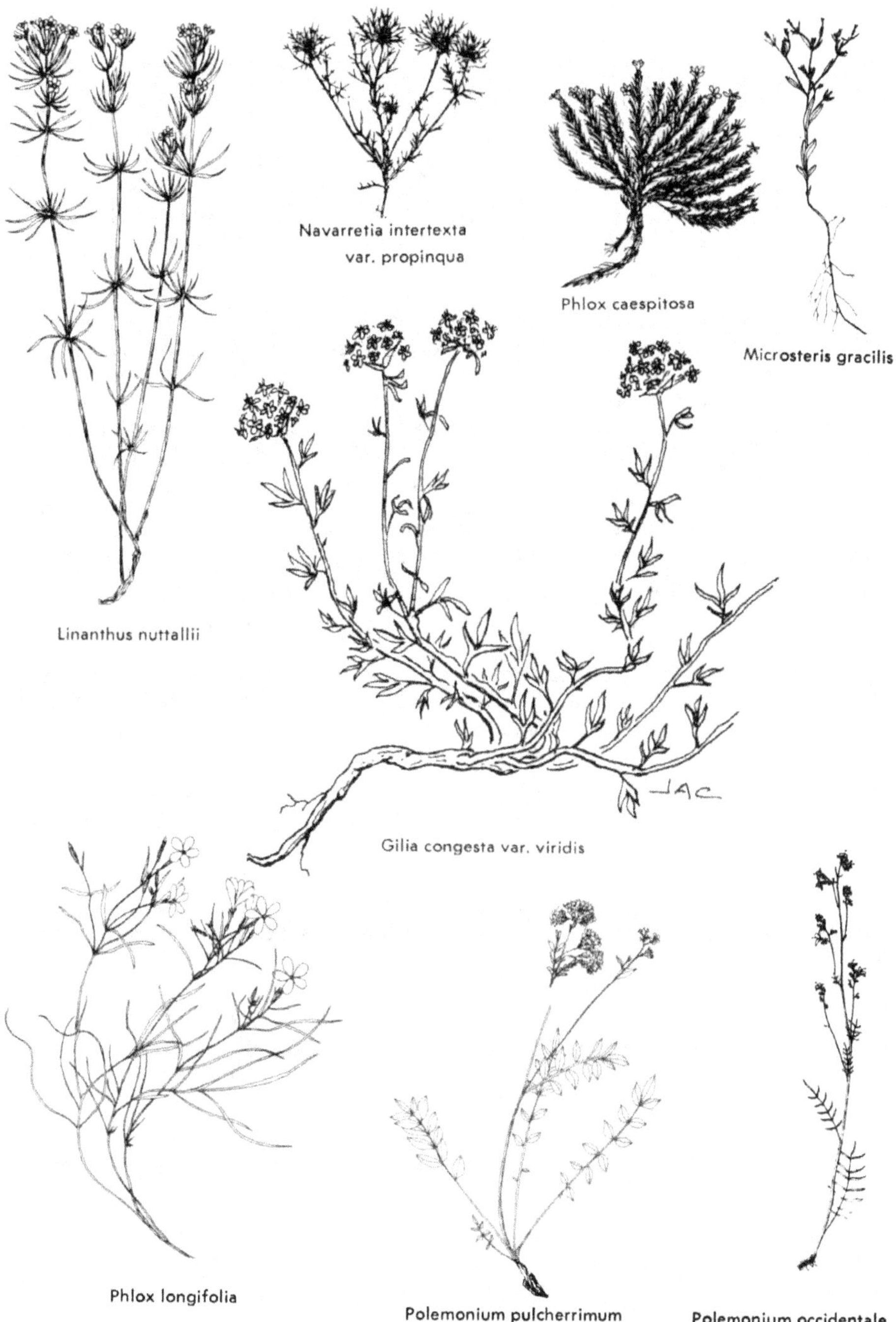

Linanthus nuttallii
Navarretia intertexta
var. propinqua
Phlox caespitosa
Microsteris gracilis
Gilia congesta var. viridis
JAC
Phlox longifolia
Polemonium pulcherrimum
Polemonium occidentale

stamens included, often unequal; filaments dilated at the base; style included, shortly 2-cleft; capsules loculicidal; seeds numerous.

Hesperochiron pumilus (Griseb.) Porter   Dwarf Hesperochiron
Taprooted plants producing slender rhizomes, sparsely short-villous to glabrate; leaves entire, tapering into the petiole, oblong to oblanceolate, 1.5-5.5 mm long; peduncles solitary or few, spreading or erect; calyx 3-9 mm long; corolla white to bluish with darker blue or purplish lines, rotate, hairy, 1-3 cm broad.
Moist to wet mountain slopes and meadows, 4800 to about 6400 feet.

Hydrophyllum L.
Perennial herbs with horizontal rootstocks and fleshy-fibrous or -tuberous roots; leaves basal and alternate, variously cleft or pinnatifid; flowers in open to dense clusters; calyx lobes unequal, united near the base; corolla campanulate, greenish-white to purple; filaments exserted, each flanked at the base by a pair of linear corolla appendages; style 2-cleft, exserted; capsules 1-locular, dehiscent by 2 valves; seeds 1 to 3.

Flowers in dense usually roundish clusters, the stalk, if present, shorter than the leaves;
leaflets with 2 or 3 teeth at their tips____*H. capitatum*
Flowers not always in globose clusters, the inflorescence sometimes open, equaling or longer
than the leaves; leaflets evidently toothed all along their margins_________________*H. fendleri*

Hydrophyllum capitatum Dougl.   Waterleaf; Woollen-breeches
Plants 10-45 cm tall with a short rhizome and a fascicle of fleshy-tuberous roots; stems short, pubescent; leaves few and large, mostly basal, 5-12 cm long, ovate, long-petioled, pinnatifid into 7 to 11 sessile leaflets, these sometimes cleft or toothed, pubescent; inflorescence globose, the peduncles much shorter than the leaves; calyx lobes ciliate and hairy on the back; corolla purplish blue to white, 5-9 mm long; style exserted.
Moist coniferous woods and wet meadows, 4800 to about 7400 feet.

Hydrophyllum fendleri (Gray) Heller   Fendler's Waterleaf
H. occidentale var. *fendleri* Gray
Perennial 25-90 cm tall with a rhizome and thickened fibrous roots; stems solitary, retrorse-hairy; leaves 6-30 cm long, 5-20 cm broad, pinnatified; leaflets sharply toothed, hairy on both sides; inflorescence open, of 1 to several cymes; calyx short-hairy, the lobes long-ciliate; corolla white to lavender to purplish, 6-8 mm long, campanulate; filaments hairy.
Moist meadows and grassy woods, 4500 to about 5000 feet.

Stems, peduncles, petioles and pedicels soft whitish-hairy; leaves paler beneath than above with soft short hairs; inflorescence usually shorter than the leaves; corolla 7-10 mm long; moist places, 4500 to 6000 feet_____________var. **albifrons** (Heller) Macbr.

Stems, peduncles, petioles and pedicels usually sparsely harsh-pubescent; leaves not whitish-hairy beneath; inflorescence usually about equaling the leaves but sometimes shorter or longer; corolla mostly 6-8 mm long; open meadows at about 5000 feet....var. **fendleri**

Nemophila Nutt.
Delicate, small, hispid or glabrous taprooted annual herbs; leaves all opposite, or all alternate, or opposite below and alternate above, petioled, variously toothed, lobed or

pinnately divided; flowers solitary and axillary or clustered in few-flowered terminal cymes; calyx deeply divided and usually with reflexed sepaloid auricles in the sinuses, or the auricles obsolete; corolla blue, purple, white or mottled; stamens included, each with a pair of scales at its base; style short, 2-cleft; capsules 1-locular, loculicidally dehiscent; seeds 1 to 20 with a deciduous or persistent, complete or partial outer covering, the cucullus.

1. Corolla 7-12 mm broad, violet with white center; capsule shorter than the fruiting calyx..*N. kirtleyi*
1. Corolla 1-4 mm broad, white or bluish, equaling or shorter than the calyx
   2. Leaves opposite or sometimes some of the upper ones not opposite; corolla a little longer than the calyx..*N. parviflora*
   2. Leaves alternate, none of them opposite; corolla shorter than the bristly-ciliate calyx..*N. breviflora*

Nemophila breviflora Gray   Great Basin Nemophila

Plants with weak, angled, reflexed-prickly stems, nearly prostrate to loosely erect, 10-30 cm tall, branching from the base; leaves mostly alternate, thin, sparsely but coarsely strigose, 1-3 cm long, pinnately parted into 3 to 6 acute lobes; flowers small, on very short pedicels; calyx 3-5 mm long with reflexed auricles; corolla white to pale purplish, shorter than the calyx; filaments and style short; seeds usually solitary, the outer covering, the cucullus, reduced and persistent.
Moist shady coniferous woods, 4500 to about 6100 feet.

Nemophila kirtleyi Hend.   Snake Canyon Nemophila

Branching plants, sparsely hispid; stems weakly erect, 10-30 cm tall; leaves all opposite or sometimes the upper ones alternate, oblong to ovate, 1.5-5 cm long, pinnately parted into 3 to 7 entire or few-toothed lobes, hispid; flowers axillary; calyx 4-6 mm long, the auricles reflexed; corolla bluish-violet with white center, broadly campanulate, 7-12 mm broad, the scales broad and fringed; style shortly cleft; seeds mostly 2 to 4, the cucullus small and deciduous.
Rocky shady streambanks and dry rocky slopes, about 5000 feet.

Nemophila parviflora Dougl. var. austiniae (Eastw.) Brand
                                   Small-flowered Nemophila

Plants with weak, brittle stems 5-50 cm long, branched from the base, erect or nearly prostrate; leaves all opposite, appressed-hispid, thin, ovate, 1-4 cm long, firm, small and not deeply pinnatifid, the 5 to 7 lobes entire to toothed or lobed, broad and obtuse, seldom narrowed at the base, the sinuses rounded; flowers on short pedicels; calyx 1-3 mm long with reflexed auricles; corolla campanulate, very small, bluish to white; capsules usually 4-seeded, the cucullus deciduous.
Shady moist to dry slopes in open coniferous woods, 4900 to about 6000 feet.

Phacelia Juss.

Taprooted annual or perennial herbs, pubescent and often glandular; leaves entire to pinnately dissected, all alternate or a few opposite; flowers often in dense terminal scorpioid cymes (sometimes lax and scarcely scorpioid); calyx deeply 5-cleft, often enlarged in fruit; corolla white, purple or blue, usually deciduous; filaments equal or often unequal, often flanked by a pair of scales at their base, or the scales obsolete or absent; style 2-cleft; capsules 1-loculed or sometimes imperfectly 2-locular, loculicidal, 2- to many-seeded.

1. Leaves, all of them, lobed or dissected into many smaller segments
    2. Plants glandular; leaves mostly on the stems rather than at the base; stems weak and brittle, often prostrate or weakly upright..*P. ramosissima*
    2. Plants not glandular; leaves mostly at the base of the plant though some also on the stems; stems stiffly erect, seldom prostrate..*P. sericea*
1. Leaves mostly not lobed or dissected though sometimes 1 or 2 pairs of small leaflets present below a larger leaf
    3. Leaves nearly all on the stems; flowers bluish-purple to nearly white; plants annuals..*P. linearis*
    3. Leaves several at the base as well as on the stems; flowers whitish to purplish; plants biennials or perennials
        4. Taproot thick with several woody branches at about ground level; stems usually several, erect or lying on the ground, rarely up to 50 cm tall; leaves thick, mostly silvery-hairy, not much lobed...*P. hastata*
        4. Taproot not so thick, not usually branched at ground level; stem usually single, erect, but sometimes with one central one and several shorter ones surrounding it; leaves thinner, not silvery-hairy, often with paired leaflets below the main blade..*P. heterophylla*

Phacelia hastata Dougl.   Mountain Scorpion Weed
    P. frigida Greene

Perennials up to 50 cm tall with a branched caudex above a taproot; stems several, mostly similar, erect or prostrate; herbage silvery to greenish-gray or white, the pubescence fine and close but with some bristly hairs also; leaves elliptic to ovate, conspicuously veined, all entire or sometimes some with a pair of small lobes, the basal petioled, elliptic, persistent, the cauline ones reduced upwards, becoming sessile; flowers usually in dense cymes, sometimes the inflorescence long and narrow; calyx often stiffly-long-bristly; corolla white to lavender or dull purple, 4-7 mm long; filaments exserted, usually hairy near the middle; mature seeds 1 or 2.

Dry sandy open places to moist rocky coniferous woods, 4500 to about 9800 feet and probably higher.

1. Flowers whitish; stems erect, mostly over 15 cm tall
    2. Leaves and stems appearing silvery-hairy; leaves usually without smaller leaflets................var. **leucophylla** (Torr.) Cronq. (*P. leucophylla* Torr.)
    2. Leaves and stems whitish or green, not appearing silvery-hairy; leaves elliptic, the larger ones with a pair of lobes or leaflets below the larger segment or leaf................................var. **leptosepala** (Rydb.) Cronq. (*P. leptosepala* Rydb.)
1. Flowers purplish or lavender; stems usually on or close to the ground only the tips rising up to 15 or 20 cm tall; leaves usually all without paired leaflets................................var. **alpina** (Rydb.) Cronq. (*P. alpina* Rydb.)

Phacelia heterophylla Pursh   Varied-leaved Scorpion Weed
    P. mutabilis Greene

Biennial or sometimes weak perennial with a rather slender taproot; stem single or sometimes surrounded by several shorter ascending curved ones, 10-120 cm tall; herbage grayish-green and bristly, the stems often glandular-pubescent; leaves thin, ordinarily

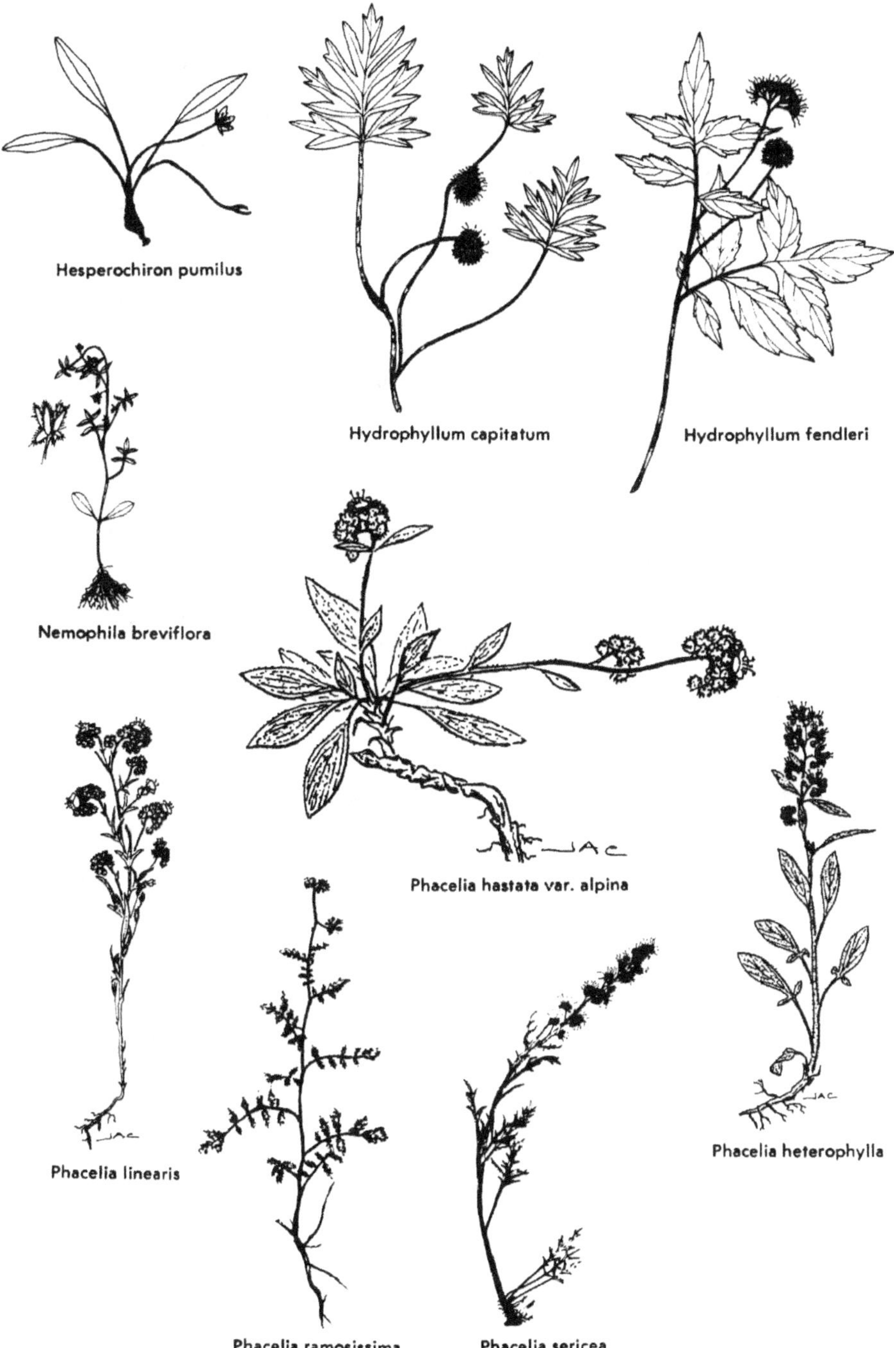

Hesperochiron pumilus
Hydrophyllum capitatum
Hydrophyllum fendleri
Nemophila breviflora
Phacelia hastata var. alpina
Phacelia linearis
Phacelia ramosissima
Phacelia sericea
Phacelia heterophylla

with 1 or 2 pairs of small lobes or leaflets and a terminal segment always much larger
(rarely all entire), sometimes prominently veined, the lower ones with slender petioles
usually longer than the blades; inflorescence short-hairy and very bristly, usually long
and narrow but sometimes open and branched or shorter and wider; calyx yellowish-
pilose and hirsute-ciliate, often purplish; corolla yellowish or greenish-white to purplish,
3-6 mm long; filaments long-exserted, hairy near the middle; style pubescent; mature
seeds 1 or 2.
Rocky slopes and open places, 4500 to about 7000 feet.

Phacelia linearis (Pursh) Holz.   Narrow-leaved Phacelia
Erect annual 10-50 cm tall; stem puberulent; leaves often more strigose, narrow,
1.5-11 cm long, alternate, entire or lobed, mostly cauline; flowers many in paniculate
cymes 10-30 cm long; calyx bristly-ciliate, 4-6 mm long; corolla rotate, bluish-purple
to nearly white; filaments sparsely hairy and minutely glandular, not exserted; seeds
usually 6 to 15.
Usually on dry rocky open ground, 4500 to about 5000 feet.

Phacelia ramosissima Dougl.   Branching Phacelia
Taprooted perennial 50-150 cm tall, odoriferous and strongly glandular-hairy; stems
several, nearly prostrate or weak, straggling and decumbent, simple or branched; leaves
8-20 cm long, pinnate, the lobes toothed, incised or pinnatifid; racemes short, dense,
helicoid, 2-8 cm long; calyx 4-6 mm long, little enlarged in fruit; corolla dull white to
pale bluish or lavender, 5-8 mm long; stamens and style exserted; filaments glabrous;
seeds 2 to 4.
Basaltic soil near Main Eagle Creek, about 5000 feet. Rare in our mountains.

Phacelia sericea (Graham) Gray   Gray or Silky Phacelia
Taprooted perennial 15-45 cm tall, densely silvery and appressed-silky throughout, or
the foliage greenish and nearly glabrous, not glandular; stems several, simple, erect or
ascending; leaves mostly at or near the base, pinnatifid with entire or sometimes cleft
segments; inflorescence a dense elongate raceme of many very short cymes; calyx 3 to
4 mm long; corolla purple or dark blue to white, 5-6 mm long, hairy; stamens long-
exserted, hairy at the base; seeds 8 to 18.
Open rocky places, 7200 to about 8600 feet.

Phacelia minutissima Hend.   Dwarf Phacelia
This dwarf Phacelia is believed to be in the Wallowa Mountains but there seems to
be no record of its collection since the original one. It is a taprooted annual 2-6 cm tall,
glandular and spreading-hairy, with erect stems and a few narrowly oblanceolate leaves
1-3 cm long, alternate above the base; flowers 1-4 cm long, racemose; calyx lobes often
foliaceous, becoming unequal; corolla lavender or pale blue, 3 or 4 mm long; filaments
glabrous, included; seeds 8 to 12.
Wet gravelly soil at moderate elevations.

BORAGINACEAE   Borage Family

Mostly herbs with alternate, sometimes opposite, simple entire leaves; flowers perfect,
usually in 1-sided scorpioid spikes, racemes or cymes tending to elongate and straighten

with age; calyx usually 5-lobed or 5-parted; corolla gamopetalous, regular or rarely irregular, 5-lobed, sometimes with appendages or crests in the throat; stamens as many as corolla lobes, borne on the corolla tube and usually included; ovary superior; carpels 2, deeply 2-lobed or -parted; fruit mostly of 4 one-seeded nutlets attached to the gynobase; style simple or 2- to 4-lobed.

1. Flowers yellow, orange or white (sometimes faintly bluish-white)
    2. Flowers yellow or orange
        3. Plants rough-hairy; flowers deep yellow or orange, usually in long narrow inflorescences..*Amsinckia*
        3. Plants smooth, never rough-hairy; flowers pale yellow, clustered in the axils of the leaves at the top of the stem; fruit shiny-smooth ....*Lithospermum*
    2. Flowers white or sometimes faintly bluish-white
        4. Plants prostrate, the several stems mostly spreading on the ground, 10-30 cm long...*Plagiobothrys*
        4. Plants usually erect, not prostrate on the ground
            5. Plants stiff-bristly and rough-hairy; flowers white, in spikes...................*Cryptantha*
            5. Plants not stiff-bristly or rough-hairy; flowers bluish-white, crowded in the axils of the upper leaves...*Lithospermum*
1. Flowers red, pinkish or blue
    6. Flowers red or maroon; nutlets easily sticking to passers-by...................*Cynoglossum*
    6. Flowers blue
        7. Flowers dark blue, scattered on long prickly-hairy stems sprawling over the ground; calyx enlarging in fruit and becoming veiny; annuals...................*Asperugo*
        7. Flowers light blue, sometimes pinkish in bud; stems not sprawling or prickly; calyx not enlarging in fruit
            8. Plants mostly under 30 cm tall
                9. Plants cushion-like, densely white-hairy; flowers very small, few, at the tops of the several stems mostly only a few cm tall; plants of high mountains..*Eritrichium*
                9. Plants not cushion-like or white-hairy; flowers various; plants of low to middle elevations in the mountains
                    10. Corolla up to 4 mm long; flowers produced from the base of the stems upward, the inflorescence many-flowered, often becoming long and narrow.....................................*Myosotis*
                    10. Corolla 1-2.5 cm long; flowers mostly at the top of the stems, not from the base, the inflorescence nodding, few-flowered, not elongating..*Mertensia*
            8. Plants mostly over 30 cm tall
                11. Flowers with long stalks (pedicels); corollas with a tube longer than the calyx...*Mertensia*
                11. Flower stalks short; corolla tube not conspicuous
                    12. Bracts present in the inflorescences; flower stalks erect or upright, especially when in fruit; plants mostly annuals ....*Lappula*
                    12. Bracts missing from the inflorescence; flower stalks curved or bent downward in fruit; plants biennials or perennials...............*Hackelia*

Amsinckia Lehm.

Taprooted coarse bristly annual herbs with alternate narrow leaves; inflorescence spike-like, elongating with age; calyx 5-parted or some of the segments fused together; corolla yellow or orange, funnel-shaped, the throat open or obstructed by appendages; nutlets keeled, mostly rough, triangular.

Stem slender; corolla orange-yellow, the throat open and hairless; stamens inserted irregularly above the middle of the corolla tube ....*A. intermedia*

Stem stout; corolla deep yellow, the throat constricted and nearly closed by hairy
appendages; stamens inserted evenly on the corolla tube below the middle..................*A. lycopsoides*

Amsinckia intermedia Fisch. & Mey.   American Fiddleneck
Stems erect, simple or branched, 20-90 cm tall, bristly-hairy and sometimes finely
pubescent; leaves linear to lanceolate, thinly hairy on both sides, up to 15 cm long and
2 cm wide; racemes up to 40 cm long; sepals often unequal, densely white-hirsute on the
margins, elongating to 6-12 mm in fruit; corolla orange-yellow, 8-10 mm long; nutlets
keeled down the back, ridged and sometimes papillate or roughened (muricate), greenish
or gray to black, 2.5-4 mm long.
Weed at roadsides, about 4500 feet.

Amsinckia lycopsoides Lehm.   Bugloss Fiddleneck
Stems erect to procumbent, 30-100 cm long, spreading-hispid and also with shorter
softer hairs; leaves bristly-hirsute, linear to lanceolate or narrowly ovate, 6-15 cm long,
1.5 cm wide, often crowded at the base; spikes bracteate below, not greatly elongating;
sepals not very unequal, 6-10 mm long, the margins densely long-ciliate; corolla deep
yellow, 7-10 mm long, the throat nearly closed by hairy sac-like intrusions; nutlets
triangular-ovate, 2.5-3 mm long, scarcely keeled or ridged but closely muricate.
Old logging road, about 5000 feet.

Asperugo L.

Procumbent annual with weak rough-hispid stems and entire, opposite to alternate
leaves; flowers solitary or 2 to 3 together in the upper leaf axils or forks of the branches;
calyx unequally 5-cleft, the lobes toothed and prickly-hispid, folding together in fruit;
corolla small, blue, campanulate, 5-lobed; nutlets 4, attached to the gynobase above the
middle.

Asperugo procumbens L.   Catchweed
Stems slender, procumbent or ascending, mostly 20-50 cm long, short-hispid; leaves
usually 3-6 cm long, scabrous, the lower oblanceolate and petioled, the upper reduced,
elliptic, becoming nearly sessile; flowers blue, short-pedicelled, 2-3 mm long and wide;
calyx in fruit 8-15 mm broad, dry and veiny; nutlets obliquely ovoid, granular-tubercu-
late, 2.5-4 mm long, enveloped by the calyx.
Weed of cultivated fields mostly, but invading campground and access roads.

Cryptantha Lehm.

Annual or perennial herbs with narrow leaves and harsh pubescence; inflorescence
naked or bracteate, scorpioid, spike-like; calyx 5-parted nearly or all the way to the
base; corolla white, small, the throat nearly closed by 5 well-developed appendages;
nutlets 1 to 4, smooth or rough, the scar narrow and elongate.

1. Plants annuals without a conspicuous basal tuft of leaves; corolla mostly 1-2 mm wide
at the widest place; inflorescence without bracts; spikes usually in 2's or 3's, mostly
above the leaves; style shorter than the nutlets
2. Calyx hairs conspicuously spreading widely outward or downward but not upward,
especially in the fruiting state; surface of the nutlets rough or granular..................*C. simulans*
2. Calyx hairs pointing or spreading outward and upward, sometimes inconspicuously;
nutlets smooth

3. Scar on the nutlet to the left or the right of the center of the inner (ventral)
 face..*C. affinis*
 3. Scar on the nutlet at the center of the inner face..*C. torreyana*
1. Plants biennials or perennials, rather coarse, usually with a well-developed tuft of basal
 leaves; corolla mostly 4-12 mm wide at the widest place; inflorescence sometimes
 elongating, usually bracteate
  4. Corolla 4-8 mm wide at the widest place; style equaling or slightly longer than the
  nutlets; nutlets smooth or rough..*C. nubigena*
  4. Corolla 8-12 mm wide at the widest place; style clearly longer than the nutlets;
  nutlets roughened or wrinkled, not smooth..*C. celosioides*

Cryptantha affinis (Gray) Greene   Slender Cryptantha

Slender annual, 5-40 cm tall, simple or branched, harshly pubescent throughout;
leaves 3-6 mm broad, narrowly oblong, scattered; spikes loosely-flowered, solitary or
paired, usually with a few leaf-like bracts below; calyx 2.5-4 mm long at maturity,
pubescent as well as bristly; corolla 1-2 mm wide; nutlets 4, smooth and shining, ovate,
often mottled, the scar near one margin, closed below; style to well beyond the middle
of the nutlets.
Dry or sometimes moist sunny canyons or open rocky wooded slopes, 4500 to about 5600
feet.

Cryptantha celosioides (Eastw.) Pays.   Northern Cryptantha

Biennial or short-lived perennial from a short woody root; stems 1 to several, 10-50
cm tall, tomentose and bristly; leaves tomentose as well as bristly, the basal ones crowded,
conspicuous, 2-8 cm long, spatulate to oblanceolate; cauline leaves reduced; spikes
aggregated into a terminal, often elongate, inflorescence; calyx densely bristly; corolla
white, broad and showy; nutlets ovate or lance-ovate, 3-5 mm long, rough and tuberculate
on both sides, the scar essentially closed; style longer than the nutlets.
Dry rocky mountain slopes and cliffs, 5100 to about 6900 feet.

Cryptantha nubigena (Greene) Pays.   Sierra and Wallowa Cryptantha

C. subretusa Johnst.

Slender dwarf perennial, 6-15 cm tall, with a taproot and branched caudex; stems
numerous; herbage sericeous-strigose and pustulate-bristly; basal leaves tufted, oblanceolate, up to 3.5 cm long; cauline leaves few and reduced; inflorescence narrow, the bracts
yellowish-hispid, terminal cluster not becoming elongate; corolla white, the tube about
equaling the calyx, the limb 3-8 mm wide; nutlets lanceolate or lanceolate-ovate, rough
on the back, smooth on the inner surface, the scar closed or nearly so; style equaling
or longer than the nutlets.
Dry open rocky or sandy places, about 8000 to 9000 feet.

Cryptantha simulans Greene   Pine Woods Cryptantha

Stems 15-50 cm tall with few erect branches, pale beneath the whitish, strigose hairs;
leaves linear or linear-oblong, scattered, 1-3 cm long, strigose on both sides; spikes solitary or in 2's or 3's, slender, sparsely-flowered, short or elongating in fruit; fruiting calyx
4-7 mm long, strigose-hirsute and short-bristly; corolla 1-2 mm wide; nutlets 4, ovate,
coarsely granular and with scattered, low tubercles, the scar closed; style a little shorter
than the nutlets.
In open Ponderosa pine woods, about 5000 feet.

Cryptantha torreyana (Gray) Greene   Torrey's Cryptantha
Annual, 10-40 cm tall, the stems erect, simple or branched, strigose and spreading-hairy; leaves linear to oblanceolate, hirsute, 2-5 cm long; spikes usually paired, without bracts, remaining clustered or becoming elongate; fruiting calyx 4-8 mm long, the mid-ribs bristly-hispid, the lobes joined above with usually spreading tips; corolla incon-spicuous, about 1 mm wide; nutlets 4, ovate, mostly 1.5-2.3 mm long, usually smooth and shining, the scar closed; style slightly shorter than the nutlets.
Rocky sunny hillsides and open mountain slopes, 4500 to about 6200 feet.

Cynoglossum L.

Taprooted annual, biennial or perennial herbs, often very large; leaves entire, usually long-petioled; flowers purplish, red, blue or white in false racemes or mixed panicles; calyx deeply cleft; corolla funnel-shaped or salverform, the tube short, the throat closed by 5 well-developed appendages; nutlets 4, divergent at maturity, covered with short barbed prickles, the scar broad from about the middle to the top.

Cynoglossum officinale L.   Hound's Tongue
Coarse biennial, villous or villous-hirsute throughout; stems 30-50 cm tall, or more; leaves oblanceolate or elliptic to more oblong and lanceolate, numerous, 15-30 cm long, the basal petioled, the others becoming sessile, clasping and reduced upward; racemes numerous, elongated in fruit; calyx lobes broad, 5-8 mm long in fruit; corolla dull red-dish-purple, the limb 6-8 mm broad; nutlets ovate, spiny, remaining attached to the style at maturity, the scar conspicuous.
Common weed of campgrounds and other disturbed locations, 4500 to about 5000 feet.

Eritrichium Schrad.

Dwarf cushion-like perennials with short stems and small silky-hairy leaves; flowers few, in small racemes; calyx cleft to the base; corolla blue, often with a yellow eye, the tube short, the limb with 5 spreading lobes; nutlets 1 to 4, smooth, margined, obliquely attached to the gynobase.

Eritrichium nanum (Vill.) Schrad.   Pale Alpine Forget-me-not
    E. elongatum (Rydb.) Wight
Cespitose perennial forming cushion-like mats; stems up to 6 cm long with scattered, narrow, loosely long-white-hairy leaves; flowers bright blue, 4-8 mm wide, in a short terminal cluster; nutlets 1 to 4, smooth.
Exposed rocky places, 7600 to nearly 9900 feet.

Hackelia Opiz

Mostly taprooted leafy perennials, or sometimes biennials; inflorescence paniculate, the pedicels becoming reflexed in fruit; calyx 5-parted, spreading or reflexed in fruit; corolla blue, pinkish or white, salverform, the throat conspicuously crested; nutlets glochidiate-prickly, longer than the style, attached to the gynobase by a large ovate scar.

Stem single from unbranched roots; inflorescence narrow, the branches tending upward
    rather than spreading widely outward..*H. floribunda*
Stems few to many from branched roots; inflorescence open, the branches spreading widely
    outward...*H. jessicae*

Hackelia floribunda (Lehm.) I. M. Johnston   Many-flowered Stickseed
Stout biennial or short-lived perennial, 30-120 cm tall; stems few or solitary, 2-8 mm thick toward the base; herbage rough-pubescent, appressed or spreading; leaves 4-20 cm long, the basal petiolate and oblanceolate when present, the cauline numerous, becoming lanceolate, sessile and reduced upward; inflorescence long and narrow with many ascending, densely-flowered branches; corolla blue with a yellow eye, the limb 4-7 mm wide; nutlets ovate, keeled and muricate on the back, the margined prickles broad, free nearly or all the way to the base, shorter prickles essentially missing.
Streambanks, gravelly bottoms, brushy sunny slopes and rocks, and moist cliffs in mixed woods, 5000 to about 8300 feet.

Hackelia jessicae (McGregor) Brand   Jessica's Tickweed or Stickseed
Taprooted robust perennial 30-100 cm tall; stems several, 3-8 mm thick toward the base; herbage crisp-hairy to soft-pubescent; leaves 8-15 cm long, petiolate and oblanceolate below, becoming reduced, sessile and lance-elliptic to oblong upward; inflorescence shorter, broader and looser than *Hackelia floribunda*; corolla small, pale blue, 3.5-5 mm wide; nutlets ovate, puberulent and muricate on the back with 1 or 2 short barbed prickles near the center, the marginal prickles broad at the base, free, with 1 or 2, or more, much shorter prickles in between.
Dry or moist meadows, open rocky slopes and cliffs, and along streams, 4500 to about 9000 feet.

Lappula Gilib.

Taprooted annual herbs with linear or oblong leaves; flowers in elongating leafy-bracted racemes, the short pedicels erect or ascending in fruit; corolla salverform, blue or white, small and inconspicuous, the short tube closed within; stamens included; nutlets 4, narrowly attached to the gynobase, with 1 or more rows of marginal glochidiate prickles.

Corolla 1.5-2.5 mm wide; nutlets 2-2.5 mm long; marginal spines of the nutlets in a single
  row, often swollen and connected to each other toward the base so as to form a border on
  the nutlet...*L. redowskii*
Corolla up to 4 mm wide; nutlets about 4 mm long; marginal spines of the nutlets in 2 rows,
  slender, not connected to each other at the base; our common species...............................*L. echinata*

Lappula echinata Gilib.   European Stickseed; Bristly-fruited Tickweed
Stem simple or freely-branched, 15-60 cm tall; herbage villous-hirsute; leaves narrowly oblanceolate to linear, sessile, 2.5-5 cm long; pedicels 1-3 mm long; calyx lobes linear, spreading in fruit; corolla blue, the limb up to 4 mm wide; nutlets about 4 mm long, muricate-prickly on the back, the marginal prickles in 2 rows, sometimes 3, not connected at the base, those of the outer row usually shorter than the inner ones.
Weed of dry creek beds and rocky streambanks, roadsides and other disturbed places, 4500 to about 5100 feet.

Lappula redowskii (Hornem.) Greene   Western Stickseed or Tickweed
Annual or occasionally biennial, simple or branched, 5-40 cm tall, or more, puberulent or short-hirsute throughout; leaves narrowly oblanceolate to linear, 1-3 cm long usually; flowers in the axils of leaf-like bracts, forming open lengthening racemes; pedicels 1-2 mm long; calyx lobes erect or only slightly spreading in fruit; corolla inconspicuous,

blue or white, the limb mostly 1.5-2.5 mm wide; nutlets 2-2.5 mm long, tuberculate on the back, the marginal prickles in one row, barbed, slender or swollen, separate or united at the base.
Weed of dry sunny hillsides, campgrounds and other disturbed places in woods, 4500 to about 5000 feet.

Lithospermum L.

Annual or perennial plants with alternate leaves and flowers axillary and solitary or in leafy-bracted spikes or racemes; calyx deeply cleft; corolla yellow or yellowish to white or bluish-white, funnel-shaped or salverform, the throat naked, pubescent or crested; nutlets 4 or fewer, hard and stony, smooth, pitted or wrinkled, basally attached to the receptacle, the scar large, often with a sharp rim.

Corolla white or bluish-white, 5-8 mm long, 2-4 mm wide at the top; flowers without a stalk
 (pedicel), scattered along the branches..*L. arvense*
Corolla yellow or yellowish, 8-12 mm long, 7-20 mm wide at the top; flowers pedicellate,
 clustered..*L. ruderale*

Lithospermum arvense L.   Corn Gromwell

Annual 10-70 cm tall, strigose, the 1 to several stems usually branched; leaves mostly 1.5-6 cm long, the lower ones oblanceolate and soon deciduous, the others lanceolate to oblong, sessile and narrow; flowers crowded in the axils of the upper leaves at first, becoming scattered at maturity; corolla white or bluish-white, funnel-shaped; nutlets gray-brown, wrinkled, pitted and coarsely tuberculate, keeled on the inner side.
Grassy slopes and open hillsides, 4500 to about 5000 feet.

Lithospermum ruderale Dougl.   Western Gromwell; Columbia Puccoon

Perennial 20-60 cm tall, strigose to somewhat spreading-hirsute with several stout stems clustered on a woody taproot; leaves numerous, pubescent, linear to lanceolate, 3-10 cm long, usually crowded above, the lower ones reduced; flowers in small clusters in the axils of the upper leaves, pedicellate; corolla light yellowish, 8-13 mm long; nutlets gray, smooth and shining, keeled on the inner side.
Dry rocky slopes and hillsides, 4500 to about 5000 feet.

Mertensia Roth

Perennial herbs, glabrous or pubescent; leaves alternate, soft and broad; flowers mostly in small terminal inflorescences, blue, pink or white; calyx cleft to the middle or to the base; corolla trumpet-shaped or tubular-funnel-shaped, shallowly lobed, crested or naked in the throat; nutlets wrinkled, attached to the gynobase near the middle.

1. Plants mostly less than 30 cm tall; corolla tube longer than the lobes; leaf blades usually
 broad at the tip, narrowed at the base
  2. Style protruding beyond the corolla; corolla tube 1.5-2 times as long as the
   lobes...*M. oblongifolia*
  2. Style as long as the corolla or shorter, not evident beyond the corolla; corolla tube
   2 to 3 times as long as the lobes ....*M. longiflora*
1. Plants mostly over 30 or 40 cm tall; corolla tube mostly about equaling the lobes, or
 shorter; leaf blades narrowed and pointed at the tip
  3. Tube of the corolla shorter than the corolla lobes; calyx 2-6 mm long...............*M. paniculata*
  3. Tube of the corolla equaling the corolla lobes; calyx 1-3 mm long ....*M. ciliata*

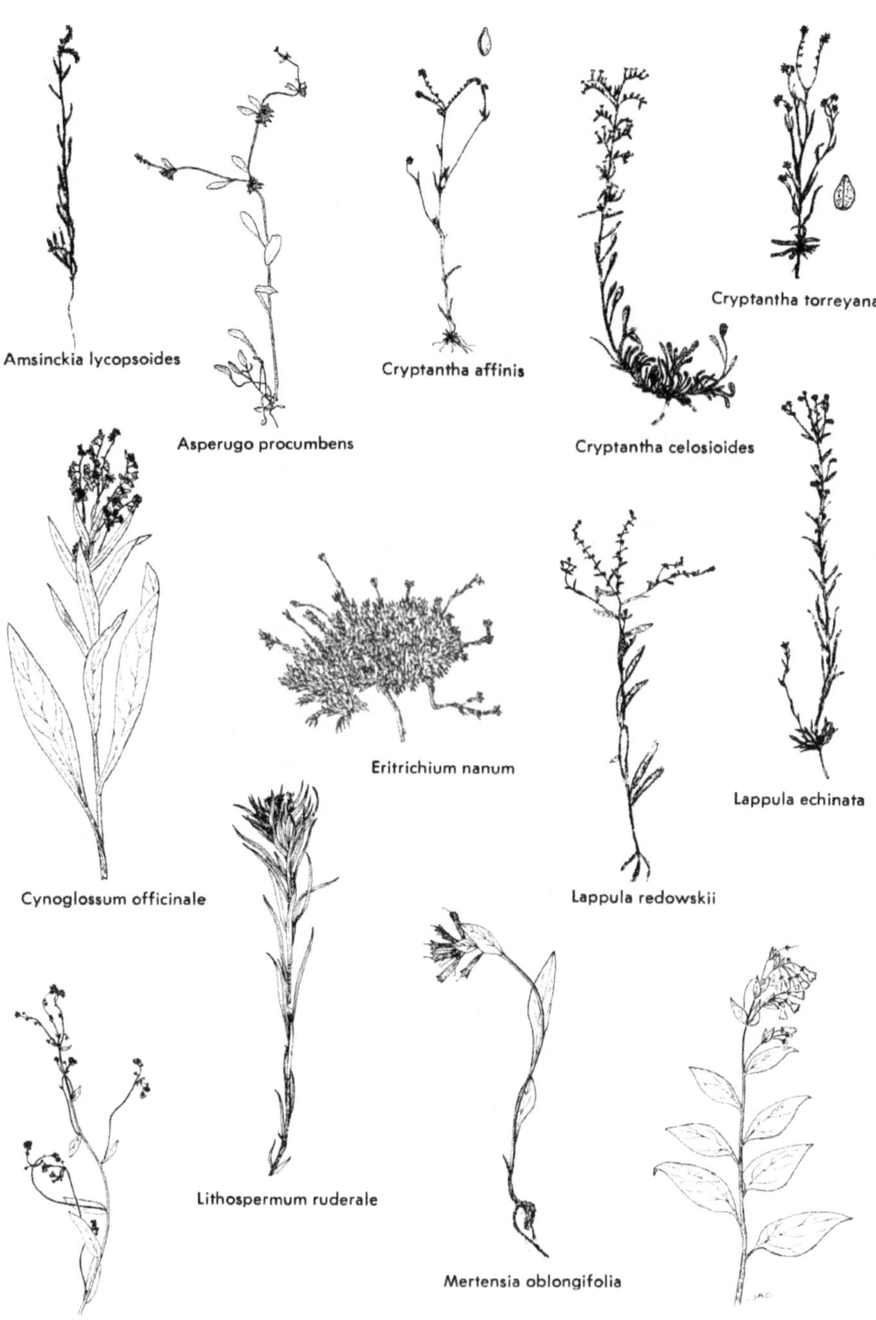

Amsinckia lycopsoides

Asperugo procumbens

Cryptantha affinis

Cryptantha torreyana

Cryptantha celosioides

Cynoglossum officinale

Eritrichium nanum

Lappula redowskii

Lappula echinata

Hackelia floribunda

Lithospermum ruderale

Mertensia oblongifolia

Mertensia paniculata var. borealis

Mertensia ciliata (Torr.) G. Don   Broad-leaved Lungwort
Stems several from branched woody roots, 15-150 cm tall; leaves mostly glabrous except sometimes the lower ones, veiny, the cauline ones elliptic to narrowly ovate, reduced upward, 3-15 cm long, tapering at the base, the lower ones, when present, elliptic to lance-ovate, long-petiolate; inflorescence open and well-branched; calyx 1-3 mm long, the lobes rounded or acute; corolla 10-17 mm long, the tube sometimes with a ring of hairs within; anthers about 1.2-2 mm long.
Streambanks, wet meadows and cliffs in coniferous woods, 4500 to about 6500 feet.

Mertensia longiflora Greene   Bluebells; Long-flowered Lungwort
Stems solitary or rarely 2 to 5 from shallow tuberous roots, 10-25 cm tall; basal leaves not devleloped; cauline leaves well-developed, few, sessile, obovate to oblong or oval, 2-6 cm long; inflorescence congested, the pedicels 1-6 mm long; calyx 3-5 mm long, glabrous, ciliate-margined; corolla 1.5-2 cm long, the tube about 1 to 3 times as long as the lobes, the style little exserted; nutlets 3 or 4 mm long.
Moist lightly shaded forest openings and mountainsides, 4500 to about 6500 feet.

Mertensia oblongifolia (Nutt.) G. Don   Leafy Bluebells
Glabrous perennial with several to many stems clustered on a stout, elongated root, 10-40 cm tall; basal leaves 2-15 cm long and up to 6 cm wide, elliptic to oblanceolate, petiolate, the lower cauline similar, the upper numerous, narrower and sessile; inflorescence congested at first, becoming loose and open in age; calyx 3-7 mm long, glabrous, ciliate-margined; corolla 1-2 cm long, the tube 1.3 to 2 times as long as the lobes; style included or slightly protruding beyond the corolla; nutlets wrinkled.
Moist slopes and sunny open mountain meadows, 4500 to about 6600 feet.

Mertensia paniculata (Ait.) G. Don var. **borealis** (Macbr.) L. O. Williams
      M. leptophylla Piper
Stems 1 to several from a stout root, 10-70 cm tall or more, glabrous or hairy; basal leaves when present long-petioled, veiny, 2.5-10 cm wide, cordate at the base; cauline leaves numerous, short-petioled to sessile, lanceolate to ovate, rounded at the base, gradually reduced upward; inflorescence lengthening with maturity; calyx 2-6 mm long, corolla 9-16 mm long.
Moist woods, cliffs and wet meadows, 5000 to about 8000 feet.

Myosotis L.

Low slender annual or perennial herbs, usually soft-pubescent; leaves alternate and entire; flowers small in slightly 1-sided many-flowered racemes lengthening with maturity; pedicels erect or spreading in fruit; calyx 5-cleft; corolla salverform, blue, pink or white, the throat crested; nutlets 4, smooth, glabrous or pubescent, the scar basal, small and flat.

Myosotis micrantha Pall.   Blue Scorpion Grass
      M. stricta Link
Annual or biennial 10-20 cm tall, simple or often branched from the base, hirsute-puberulent throughout; leaves oblanceolate to oblong or elliptic, up to 2 cm long; flowers scattered nearly to the base of the plant; fruiting pedicels ascending or spreading; calyx

3-5 mm long, the tube with spreading hooked hairs, the lobes appressed-hairy; corolla blue; nutlets brown or black; style short.
Moist or dry open places, mostly near water, 4500 to about 4800 feet.

Plagiobothrys Fisch. & Mey.

Small glabrate or soft-pubescent annual or perennial herbs with narrow leaves alternate above, opposite or forming a rosette below; flowers in scorpioid elongating racemes; calyx cleft nearly to the base; corolla white, salverform, small; stamens included; nutlets 4, ovoid to cruciform, keeled, smooth or rough, attached to the gynobase near the base, the scar small.

Plagiobothrys scouleri (H. & A.) Johnston var. penicillatus (Greene) Cronq.

P. cusickii (Greene) Johnston

Annuals with several prostrate to ascending stems 10-30 cm long; herbage strigose; leaves linear, mostly cauline, up to 5 cm long; racemes simple, loosely-flowered, elongating with maturity; fruiting calyx 2-4 mm long; corolla small, 1-4 mm wide at the top; nutlets 4, rough, tuberculate, sometimes also bristly; scar small.
Moist poorly drained soils, 4500 to about 6000 feet.

MENTHACEAE; LABIATAE   Mint Family

Herbs or shrubs or rarely trees or vines, mostly aromatic, with square stems and opposite leaves; flowers in axillary clusters or in terminal spike-like inflorescences, perfect, mostly irregular; calyx regular or irregular, often 2-lipped, mostly 5-toothed or 5-lobed; corolla usually 2-lipped and 5-lobed; stamens 4 in two groups or 2 by abortion of one pair, inserted on the petals; ovary superior, deeply cleft; style 2-lobed; fruit 4 one-seeded hard nutlets attached only at the base.

1. Flowers usually in dense spikes or heads at the top of the stem; flowers white, pinkish-purplish to blue-violet
      2. Leaves toothed or shallow-lobed on the margins; inflorescence 3-15 cm long
            3. Stamens extending beyond the corollas and bent so the 2 pairs cross over each other, the anther sacs parallel; flowers mostly pale pinkish-purple or rose........*Agastache*
            3. Stamens not usually extending beyond the corollas, the anther sacs spreading; flowers usually white, sometimes pale purple..*Nepeta*
      2. Leaves not toothed or lobed on the margins
            4. Plants aromatic; corolla pink-purplish; stamens extending beyond the corollas; stems numerous, erect, woody at the base...*Monardella*
            4. Plants not aromatic; corolla mostly deep blue-violet; stamens not usually extended beyond the corolla; stem usually single, weak and often bent or lying on the ground, not woody...*Prunella*
1. Flowers in small compact clusters in the axils of the leaves, scattered along the stems; flowers white or pink-purplish
      5. Leaves thick, veiny, white-woolly, the margins round-toothed; flower clusters sometimes to 1.5 cm broad, or more; flowers whitish ....*Marrubium*
      5. Leaves thin, soft, green, the margins with pointed teeth; flowers white or pinkish, in small axillary clusters..*Lycopus*

Agastache Clayton

Perennial herbs with mostly broad toothed leaves and small flowers in dense verticillate clusters forming terminal spikes; calyx campanulate, 15-nerved, the teeth often whitish, pinkish or blue, the 5 teeth separate or the 3 upper ones united; corolla 2-lipped, pink to violet or white, the lobes short, the 2 upper ones erect, the 3 lower spreading; stamens 4, usually exserted, the upper pair longer than the lower; anther sacs parallel or nearly so.

Agastache urticifolia (Benth.) Kuntze   Nettle-leaved Horsemint or Giant-hyssop
    Fibrous-rooted perennial 40-150 cm tall; stems numerous, simple or branched, finely puberulent to glabrous; leaves coarsely crenate or serrate, ovate to deltoid or subcordate, glabrous to scaberulous, 4-10 cm long, paler beneath, petiolate; inflorescence compact, 3-15 cm long; calyx often glandular, 8-10 mm long, the teeth pinkish-tinged; corolla whitish to pale violet or rose, 10-14 mm long; stamens conspicuously exserted.
Moist or dry rocky meadows and open slopes, about 5000 to 7000 feet.

Lycopus L.

Rhizomatous herbs with toothed cauline leaves and sessile, verticillate, axillary flowers; calyx campanulate, regular, 4- or 5-toothed; corolla small, funnel-shaped, the upper lip entire or notched, the lower 3-lobed; stamens 2, slightly exserted, the anther sacs parallel; nutlets smooth.

Lycopus uniflorus Michx.   Northern Bugle-weed
    Plants tuberous at the base and producing stolons from the lower leaf axils; stems slender, puberulent, 10-40 cm tall; leaves 2-8 cm long, short-petioled, coarsely serrate; calyx 2 mm long, scarcely if at all nerved; corolla white or pinkish, longer than the calyx; staminodes minute or obsolete; nutlets about equaling the calyx.
Bogs, marshy streambanks and lake borders, about 5600 feet. (Duck Lake)

Marrubium [Tourn.] L.

Perennial, mostly woolly, herbs with toothed, wrinkled petiolate leaves; flowers small, white or purple, in dense axillary clusters; calyx cylindric, 5- to 10-nerved with 5 to 10 spreading or recurved spiny teeth; corolla 2-lipped, the upper lip erect, entire or notched, the lower 3-cleft and spreading; stamens 4, included, the lower pair longer than the upper.

Marrubium vulgare L.   Common Hoarhound
    Perennial herb with stout, erect to prostrate, white-woolly stems 30-100 cm long; leaves oval to broadly elliptic, 2.5-5 cm long, canescent above, woolly beneath, crenate-dentate, rugose, petiolate; flowers in compact axillary clusters, white or purplish; calyx teeth usually 10, spiny and usually recurved; corolla deeply 2-lipped.
Dry gravelly roadside, 4600 feet.

Monardella Benth.

Aromatic annual or perennial herbs with small entire or serrate leaves; flowers borne in dense terminal heads subtended by several broad colored bracts; calyx tubular, 10- to 15-nerved with 5 short nearly equal teeth; corolla pink-purplish, scarcely 2-lipped, with 5 slender lobes; stamens 4, exserted; nutlets oblong, smooth.

Monardella odoratissima Benth.   Western Mountain Balm
    Stems numerous, clustered from a taproot and caudex, 10-50 cm tall, often decumbent

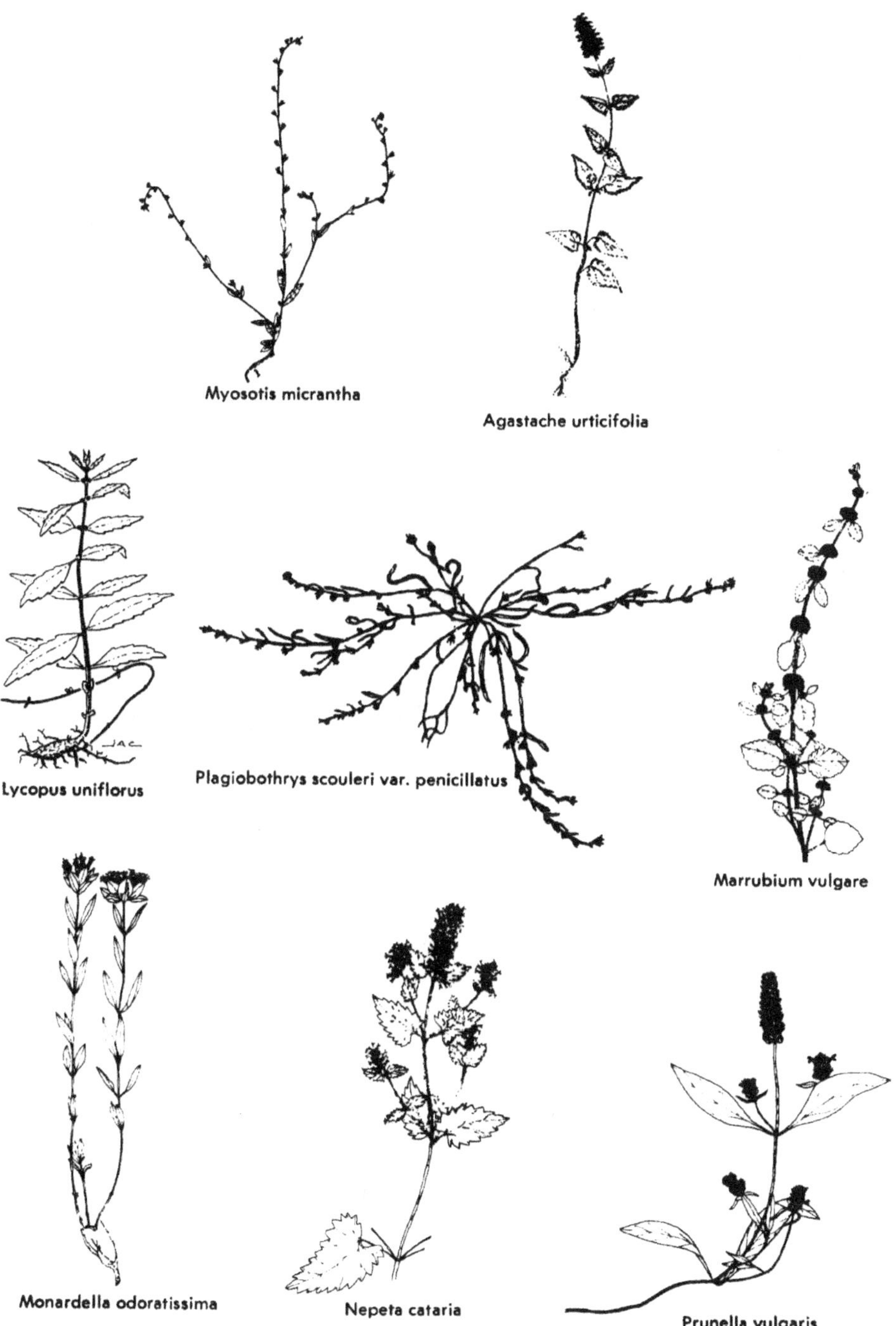

Myosotis micrantha
Agastache urticifolia
Lycopus uniflorus
Plagiobothrys scouleri var. penicillatus
Marrubium vulgare
Monardella odoratissima
Nepeta cataria
Prunella vulgaris

and woody at the base, puberulent and glandular at least above; leaves lanceolate, 1-3.5 cm long, entire, puberulent and glandular; bracts conspicuously subtending the head, 7-15 mm long, dry, purplish-tinged, pubescent on the veins and ciliate on the margins; calyx 6-8 mm long, 13-nerved; corolla pink-purplish, 1-2 cm long, the tube well exserted beyond the calyx, the lobes slender.
Open rocky slopes, meadows, creek beds and rock slides, 5000 to 9600 feet and probably higher.

Nepeta [Rivin.] L.

Annual or perennial herbs with broad toothed leaves; flowers in dense verticillate terminal spikes or axillary and cymose; calyx tubular, 15-nerved, the teeth unequal; corolla white or blue or rarely yellow, 2-lipped, the upper lip erect, 2-lobed or notched, the lower lip spreading, 3-lobed; stamens 4, in pairs; nutlets ovoid, smooth.

Nepeta cataria L.   Catnip

Taprooted canescent perennial 30-100 cm tall; stems erect and branched; leaves ovate to oblong, petiolate, coarsely crenate-serrate, 2.5-7 cm long and 1.5-5 cm wide; flowers in short dense spike-like clusters at the ends of the branches; calyx about 6 mm long; corolla whitish to pale purple, 10-12 mm long, 2-lipped, the broad middle lobe of the lower lip red-mottled and crenulate.
Dry sunny roadsides and slopes of the moraines, 4500 to about 5200 feet.

Prunella L.

Perennial herbs with entire to pinnatifid leaves; flowers verticillate in dense bracted terminal or axillary spikes or heads; calyx 2-lipped, 10-nerved, the upper lip broad and 3-toothed, the lower deeply 2-cleft; corolla strongly 2-lipped, the upper lip arched, the lower spreading and 3-lobed; stamens 4, in pairs; filaments 2-toothed at the tip, one tooth bearing the anther, the other sterile; nutlets ovoid, smooth.

Prunella vulgaris L.   Self-heal; Heal-all

Fibrous-rooted perennial with stems erect to decumbent or prostrate, 10-50 cm long, glabrous to sparingly pubescent; leaves ovate to lanceolate, 2-9 cm long, petiolate, entire or irregularly toothed; spikes 2-6 cm long, terminal, dense, composed of 3-flowered clusters, each subtended by a conspicuous green or purplish ciliate bract; calyx 10-12 mm long, strongly nerved, the tube short, the teeth spinulose-tipped; corolla blue-violet or rarely pink or white, 1-2 cm long.
Moist shady woods and streambanks, 4500 to about 5600 feet.

SCROPHULARIACEAE   Figwort Family

Herbs, or occasionally shrubs or vines, with simple to dissected, opposite or alternate leaves without stipules; flowers perfect, usually irregular; calyx of 4 or 5 free or united sepals, sometimes apparently fewer; corolla 4- or 5-lobed, usually tubular and 2-lipped, sometimes campanulate or rotate and nearly regular; stamens usually 4, sometimes 2 or 5, epipetalous; ovary superior, 2-carpellate; style solitary, the stigmas united or free; fruit a capsule; seeds many to few, the endosperm well developed.

1. Corolla galeate, that is, the upper lip forming a hood or beak enclosing the anthers; leaves alternate
    2. Leaves basal as well as on the stems, toothed or dissected or lobed ...._Pedicularis_
    2. Leaves usually all on the stems, cleft or entire, rarely toothed or dissected; calyx lobes 2 to 4
        3. Galea definitely longer than the lower lip; plants perennial...................._Castilleja_
        3. Galea only slightly if at all longer than the lower lip; plants annual
            4. Calyx cleft to the base into 2 segments; inflorescence few-flowered; rare in our mountains...................._Cordylanthus_
            4. Calyx not cleft to the base, the 4 calyx lobes about equal, sometimes seemingly only 2 by union of one pair; inflorescence many-flowered; common at lower elevations ...._Orthocarpus_
1. Corolla not galeate; leaves opposite or alternate
    5. Leaves mostly opposite on the stems, or at the base of the plant; anthers 2 or 4
        6. Leaves basal; anthers 2
            7. Corolla blue, not 2-lipped; sepals free...................._Synthyris_
            7. Corolla missing or vestigial; sepals united toward the base...................._Besseya_
        6. Leaves on the stems as well as sometimes at the base; anthers various
            8. Anthers 2; corolla slightly irregular, blue to white, 4-lobed...................._Veronica_
            8. Anthers 4; corollas variously colored
                9. Flowers blue or bluish, rarely white
                    10. Corolla rather showy; plants perennials ...._Penstemon_
                    10. Corolla very small, not showy; plants annuals, usually small......_Collinsia_
                9. Flowers yellow to purple or red but not blue or white
                    11. Plants large, 50-150 cm tall; leaves all on the stems; flowers yellowish-green with a maroon overcast, not showy...................._Scrophularia_
                    11. Plants smaller; leaves basal as well as on the stem; flowers yellow to rose or purple, the calyx strongly 5-angled...................._Mimulus_
    5. Leaves mostly alternate, basal as well as on the stem; stamens 4 or 5
        12. Plants mostly very tall, often coarse; flowers with spreading petals; stamens 5...................._Verbascum_
        12. Plants usually to about 40 cm tall, slender; flowers 2-lipped, the lower lip prolonged into a straight spur; stamens 4...................._Linaria_

Besseya Rydb.

Perennial fibrous-rooted herbs with petiolate basal leaves and erect flowering stems with alternate leaf-like bracts; inflorescence narrow and spike-like; calyx of 2 to 4 united segments; corolla none or vestigial or unequally 2-lipped when developed; stamens 2; stigma capitate; capsule flattened, loculicidal; seeds flattened, numerous.

Besseya rubra (Dougl.) Rydb.   Red Besseya

Perennial, loosely hairy throughout when young, becoming nearly glabrous later; stems solitary or few, 20-60 cm tall; leaves ovate, essentially basal, 4-12 cm long, petiolate, truncate or cordate at the base, the blades crenate-dentate; flowering stems with about 10 small bract-like leaves and a dense terminal spike-like raceme up to 20 cm long in fruit; calyx 3- or 4-lobed, often unequally so; corolla none or vestigial; filaments dark red; capsule glabrous or hairy, about as long as wide.
Open woods and rocky meadows, 4500 to about 5000 feet.

Castilleja Mutis

Annual or perennial herbs with alternate entire to cleft leaves, somewhat parasitic on the roots of other plants; flowers mostly in terminal spikes, subtended by yellow, purple or red bracts; calyx 4-cleft, often unequally so, the lobes either again lobed, notched or toothed, or the calyx appearing 2-cleft by fusion of the lobes, all usually colored like the bracts; corolla greenish (in ours) with a narrow tube and 2-lipped limb, the petals of the upper lip, the galea, united and enclosing the anthers, the lower lip usually 3-lobed, sac-like or reduced and rudimentary, usually much shorter than the galea; stamens 4, attached near or above the middle of the corolla tube, the anther-cells unequally placed; stigma capitate; capsule loculicidal, many-seeded.

1. Lower lip of the corolla noticeable, usually half or more the length of the upper lip (the galea), usually yellowish to green but sometimes red or purplish; leaf-like bracts below the flowers usually yellow or yellowish, rarely purplish or reddish
  2. Back of the galea hairy and also covered with gland-tipped hairs; flowers purplish or reddish
    3. Calyx equally cleft into 4 lobes pointed at the tip; plants mostly under 10 cm tall..*C. rubida*
    3. Calyx not equally cleft into 4 lobes, the lobes rounded at the tip; plants 5-15 cm tall..*C. ownbeyana*
  2. Back of the galea not glandular though often hairy; flowers yellow or yellowish
    4. Lobes of the lower lip, the sepals and the bracts usually yellow or yellowish; corolla usually longer than the calyx
      5. Calyx cleft into 4 equal pointed lobes; flowering stems sometimes branched above..*C. longispica*
      5. Calyx unequally cleft into 4 blunt or rounded lobes; flowering stems not usually branched
        6. Calyx tips deeply cleft and definitely rounded; bracts usually with 1 or 2 pairs of short lateral spreading lobes..*C. cusickii*
        6. Calyx tips shallowly cleft above; bracts broader than the leaves, usually with a pair of lateral lobes pointing upward rather than outward..*C. chrysantha*
    4. Lobes of the lower lip green or yellowish-green, nearly as long as the galea; corolla about as long as the calyx
      7. Calyx tips 1-5 mm long; corolla a little shorter than the calyx..............*C. pallescens*
      7. Calyx tips 5-10 mm long; corolla equaling the calyx or sometimes shorter, sometimes longer..*C. oresbia*
1. Lower lip of the corolla usually reduced, dark green and thick, mostly only about ⅛ the length of the galea or less but sometimes up to ⅓; leaf-like bracts showy, red or purple, rarely yellowish or whitish
  8. Leaves, especially the upper, and the leaf-like bracts ordinarily deeply cleft into 3 to 7 lobes (rarely none lobed); calyx cleft about equally or more deeply cleft above than below
    9. Plants with soft shaggy, often slender and entangled, hairs
      10. Stems and leaves glandular-sticky; plants sometimes thinly hairy to nearly hairless
        11. Leaf-like bracts scarlet (rarely yellow), deeply cleft into long rather blunt lobes; corolla 25-35 mm long, the galea nearly as long as the corolla tube..*C. applegatei*
        11. Leaf-like bracts yellow or yellowish, cleft into shorter more pointed lobes; corolla 15-25 mm long, the galea shorter than the corolla tube..*C. glandulifera*
      10. Stems and leaves scarcely, if at all, glandular-sticky; plants hairy
        12. Stem solitary from the root; bracts yellow below the red tips..........*C. suksdorfii*
        12. Stems usually more than one from the root; bracts greenish, yellowish or reddish
          13. Stems often sprawling, rarely branched; bracts, calyces, galea margins and the lobes of the lower lip red; rare..............*C. fraterna*

> 13. Stems erect, sometimes branched above, densely greyish-hairy
>   like the leaves; bracts usually yellow, sometimes red or reddish,
>   but the galea margins and lobes of the lower lip not red................*C. rustica*
>   9. Plants with stiff or bristly hairs; middle lobe of the leaves rounded at the tip,
>   the other lobes much narrower and sometimes pointed at the tip..................*C. hispida*
> 8. Leaves ordinarily not toothed or lobed; bracts mostly red or purple, usually not
>   lobed but if lobed not deeply divided
>   14. Flowering stems mostly over 30 cm tall, often branched above; corollas mostly
>   30-40 mm long; bracts mostly scarlet; plants of low to middle elevations in our
>   mountains..*C. miniata*
>   14. Flowering stems mostly 10-30 cm tall, seldom branched; corollas 20-30 cm
>   long; bracts crimson to rose-purple; plants of higher mountain elevations........*C. rhexifolia*

Castilleja applegatei Fern.   Wavy-leaved Indian Paintbrush

Perennial; stems clustered, glandular-hairy, 15-60 cm tall, simple to much-branched from a woody base; leaves 2.5-5 cm long, pubescent and glandular, linear-lanceolate to lanceolate, wavy-margined, the lower ones entire, the upper broader and usually 3-lobed with the middle lobe wider than the others, or rarely all the leaves entire or all divided and the segments acute; inflorescence conspicuous, bright red, scarlet or occasionally yellow; bracts deeply 3- to 5-parted, as long as or longer than the flowers, glandular-hairy, the lobes linear, acute, the middle one the widest; calyx 12-22 mm long, deeply and about equally cleft above and below, the 2 primary lobes again divided into 2 linear teeth 3-8 mm long; corolla 20-36 mm long, the galea pubescent or puberulent, 12-15 mm long with wide red thin margins, 5 or more times the length of the dark green, thickened, rudimentary lower lip.

Sandy gravelly soil and talus, about 8200 to 8300 feet.

Castilleja chrysantha Greenm.   Yellow Paint Brush

Common perennial; stems clustered, usually 10-30 cm tall, soft-hairy; leaves lanceolate, viscid-villous, entire or the upper ones sometimes lobed; bracts broader than the leaves, viscid-villous, pale yellow or rarely purplish, ovate and acute, entire or with short lateral lobes, mostly not concealing the flowers; inflorescence narrow, elongating with maturity; calyx 12-20 mm long, equally cleft a little less than halfway, the 2 primary lobes shallowly notched into 2 rounded segments; corolla 18-20 mm long, its galea 7-8 mm long with wide pale margins, the lower lip not greenish and thickened, 4-5 mm long; capsule 9 mm long.

Meadows, lake borders and streambanks, mostly in the open, 5500 to about 8500 feet. TYPE LOCALITY: Head of West Eagle Creek, Wallowa Mts., Oregon.

Castilleja cusickii Greenm.   Cusick's Paint Brush

Hirsute-pubescent perennial with several to many clumped unbranched stems; leaves many, lanceolate, with 1 to 3 pairs of slender spreading lateral lobes; bracts and calyces yellow or yellowish, the bracts rounded more often than the leaves, not so often lobed; calyx 22-30 mm long, cleft deeply and about equally, the primary lobes broadly rounded at the tips; corolla about as long as the calyx, the galea about 4 mm long, densely glandular-pubescent on the back, the lower lip 3 mm long, pubescent, the lobes whitish.

Moist granitic meadows, between 5000 and 6000 feet.

Castilleja fraterna Greenm.   Limestone Castilleja

Rare perennial; stems spreading or decumbent from a short branching caudex, 10-20 cm tall, glandular, finely pubescent below the more hairy inflorescence; leaves linear to oblong-lanceolate, entire, the upper ones broader and sometimes with a pair of short lobes; bracts shorter and broader than the leaves, acute, with a pair of short lateral lobes, greenish or the upper ones red-tipped; spike rather loosely flowered; calyx bright red, 20-25 mm long cleft nearly half its length into 2 primary lobes, these again divided into 2 rounded or acute segments 1-3 mm long; corolla 20-33 mm long, its galea short, puberulent, half the length of the tube, 7-11 mm long, with wide red margins, the lower lip thick, red, rudimentary, 2-4 mm long; capsule 10 mm long.

Moist or dry sandy soil at the base of limestone or sandstone cliffs and peaks, about 7000 to 8000 feet.

TYPE LOCALITY: Wallowa Mts., Oregon.

Castilleja glandulifera Pennell   Sticky Paintbrush

  ? *C. viscidula* Gray

Glandular-pubescent perennial; stems angular, 10-40 cm tall, clustered on a woody base; leaves linear-lanceolate, entire or usually with a pair of slender lobes, 1.5-4 cm long; bracts deeply cleft, glandular-hairy, 3- to 5-parted, shorter than the flowers, sometimes tipped with dull red or yellow; inflorescence inconspicuous; calyx 14-20 mm long, cleft ¼ to ½ its length, the primary lobes again divided into 2 acute segments 2-6 mm long; corolla 15-25 mm long, its galea 7-10 mm long, about ⅔ as long as the tube, greenish-yellow with yellowish or purplish margins, puberulent, the lower lip 1-2 mm long, dark green, thickened, rudimentary; capsule about 11 mm long.

Sandy granitic slopes, 6500 to about 9000 feet or higher.

Castilleja hispida Benth.   Harsh Castilleja

  C. angustifolia var. *hispida* Fern.

Perennial; stems clustered from a woody base, 20-60 cm tall; herbage finely hairy, sometimes harshly so on the leaves; leaves lanceolate to ovate, soft-hairy and occasionally viscid, the deeply cleft upper ones with 2 or 3 pairs of slender lobes, the lower (and sometimes all) entire, 2.5-5 cm long; inflorescence conspicuous, shaggy-hairy, bright red or scarlet, sometimes yellow or orange, the spike dense at first but elongating at maturity; bracts broad, 3- to 5-lobed, long and short hairy; calyx 1.5-3 cm long, red-tipped, cleft about ⅓ to ½ its length, the primary lobes again divided into acute or rounded segments 4-7 mm long; corolla 20-40 mm long, its galea 12-15 mm long, about equaling the tube, the margins thin and reddish, short-hairy, 5 or more times the length of the dark green, thickened, rudimentary lower lip; capsule at least 11 mm long.

Meadows and grassy slopes, about 5000 to 9000 feet.

Pubescence more villous than hispid; calyx lobes obtuse and rounded; meadows and open slopes, about 5000 feet...var. **hispida**

Pubescence usually strongly hispid-villous; calyx lobes acute; plants robust with thicker leaves more often entire or with only 1 pair of lobes...............var. **acuta** (Penn.) Ownbey

TYPE LOCALITY of *Castilleja hispida* ssp. *acuta* Pennell: Adams Creek, Wallowa Mts. Dry sandy soil on open or wooded slopes, 5000 to about 9000 feet.

Castilleja longispica A. Nels.   Parrot's Head Indian Paintbrush
Shaggy-hairy perennial with purplish clustered stems 10-35 cm tall; leaves 4-6 cm long, densely short-pubescent, linear or linear-lanceolate, the lower entire, the upper with 1 or 2 pairs of slender lobes; bracts yellowish with whitish spreading tips, shorter and broader than the leaves, 3- to 9-parted, usually shorter than the flowers; calyx yellow or yellowish 10-20 mm long, twice cleft about halfway into 4 linear segments; corolla 15-21 mm long, exserted beyond the calyx, its galea finely pubescent, 4-6 mm long, pale yellowish-green with thin pale margins, its lower lip slightly shorter, white or purplish, forming a 3-lobed prominent and puberulent pouch; capsule 7-8 mm long.
Dry sandy slopes, usually with sagebrush, about 6000 to 8000 feet.

Castilleja miniata Dougl. ex Hook.   Common Red Paintbrush
Perennial; glabrous, pubescent or sometimes viscid-hairy; stems few to many, often branched above, 20-80 cm tall; leaves commonly glabrous, linear or lanceolate, acute, entire or sometimes a few upper ones with a pair of short lobes; inflorescence conspicuous, bright red, scarlet or crimson or rarely yellow; bracts broader than the leaves, shorter than the flowers, the lower entire, the upper ones toothed or cleft into acute segments, puberulent and long-soft-hairy, often viscid; calyx 15-30 mm long, cleft nearly halfway into 2 lobes each with 2 linear-lanceolate teeth 3-9 mm long; corolla 20-40 mm long, its galea pubescent with thin red margins, a little shorter or about as long as the tube, 5 or more times the length of the dark green, thickened lower lip; capsule 10-12 mm long.
Bogs, meadows, streambanks, sandy or rocky openings in coniferous woods, 4500 to about 8500 feet. Our common *Castilleja* at lower and middle elevations.

Castilleja oresbia Greenm.   Pale Wallowa Paintbrush
Perennial, densely hairy with fine crisped hairs below the long-hairy inflorescence; stems 15-30 cm tall, simple or branched, clustered on a woody base, erect to decumbent; leaves linear-lanceolate, 2-3.5 cm long, entire near the base, 3-lobed above; bracts pale dull yellow, shorter but broader than the leaves, lanceolate or oblong with narrow lobes; calyx about 1 cm long, cleft ½ to ⅖ its length, about equaling the bracts, yellow-tipped; corolla pinkish with pale thin margins, about 1.5 cm long, the galea puberulent, narrow, short, lower lip green, about ½ the length of the galea with straight acute lobes; capsules 8 mm long.
Open ridges at about 7000 to 8000 feet. TYPE LOCALITY: Kettle Creek, Oregon.

Castilleja ownbeyana Pennell   Ownbey's Castilleja
Perennial, softly viscid-villous; stems densely clustered, unbranched, 10-15 cm tall, mostly decumbent or flexuous, the hairs not glandular; leaves linear-lanceolate, attenuate, entire or the upper ones with a pair of short lobes; bracts yellowish or dull red to purplish, broadly ovate, broader than the leaves with a pair of short lobes; flowers not hidden by the bracts; calyx yellowish or purplish, 12-18 mm long, cleft about halfway, the 2 broad lobes again divided into 2 short rounded lobes 0.5-1 mm long; corolla about equaling the calyx, 16-17 mm long, its galea puberulent, 6-7 mm long with wide thin red or purple margins, its lower lip about ⅔ the length of the galea, its lobes red or purple like the galea margins, not pouched; capsule 7-8 mm long.

Moist sandy soil, meadows and mountain slopes, 7700 to about 9600 feet.
TYPE LOCALITY: "Near the lake, Wallowa Mts." W. C. Cusick (? Ice Lake)

Castilleja pallescens (Gray) Greenm.   Pale Indian Paintbrush

Minutely pubescent perennial; stems clustered, 10-20 cm tall, usually purplish; leaves densely puberulent, 2-3 cm long, narrowly linear, entire or with a pair of lobes; bracts yellowish or purplish, broader than the leaves, mostly with a pair of lobes, ciliate; calyx 12-15 mm long, cleft about ⅓ to ½ way, the lobes notched into 2 obtuse segments 0.5-1 mm long; corolla about equaling the calyx, its galea 5-7 mm long, puberulent, with narrow pale thin margins, its lower lip about as long as the galea, greenish with pale lobes, pouched and pubescent; capsule 8 mm long.
Damp meadows at 7000 to about 8000 feet.

Castilleja rhexifolia Rydb.   Alpine Paintbrush

C. oreopola var. *subintegra* Fern.; *C. oregonensis* Gand.
Perennial; stems clustered from a woody base, 10-30 or more cm tall, usually unbranched, villous, viscid-villous or glabrate; leaves usually linear-lanceolate and all entire but sometimes the upper lobed, glabrate, pubescent or viscid-villous like the stems; inflorescence conspicuous, generally crimson but varying to scarlet or even yellow, often elongating in fruit; bracts usually rounded, oblong-ovate, entire or with 1 or 2 pairs of short lobes, villous-puberulent; calyx 15-25 mm long, cleft about halfway, the 2 primary lobes again divided into 2 usually blunt segments 3-6 mm long; corolla 20-35 mm long, its galea puberulent, usually much shorter than the tube and 4 or 5 times as long as the dark green, thickened lower lip.
Bogs, meadows, talus and moist slopes, mostly from about 7200 to 9300 feet or higher.

Castilleja rubida Piper   Little purplish Alpine Paintbrush

Perennial, crisp-puberulent and minutely glandular, villous in the inflorescence; stems clustered, often decumbent, reddish-purplish, 2-15 cm tall; leaves 1.5-2.5 cm long, linear or linear-lanceolate, entire or the upper ones with 1 or 2 pairs of slender lobes; bracts broader than the leaves, violet-purple to red-purple, with 1 to 3 pairs of linear lobes; inflorescence short and dense but the flowers usually not hidden by the bracts; calyx violet-purple to purple-red, in anthesis 10-12 mm long, twice cleft about ⅘ of its length into 4 nearly equal lobes; corolla 12-14 mm long, its galea glandular-pubescent, 4 mm long, ⅓ as long as the tube, purple, with thin, narrow, violet-purple margins, its lower lip slightly shorter, pouched, greenish or red-purple with red- or violet-purple lobes.
Sandy cliffs and open slopes mostly above timberline, usually if not always associated with limestone, 8000 to 9800 feet or higher.
TYPE LOCALITY: Keystone Basin, Wallowa Mts., 9000 feet. Cusick 2094.

Castilleja rustica Piper   Rusty Paintbrush

Perennial; finely pubescent below the hairy inflorescence; stems clustered, many 20-40 cm tall, often purplish, soft-hairy and often slightly glandular; leaves linear-lanceolate, entire or with a pair of lobes, thick, strongly nerved, densely puberulent; bracts yellow, greenish-yellow, or occasionally reddish, shorter and broader than the leaves with a pair of slender lobes, puberulent or villous, about equaling the flowers; calyx 10-15 or more mm long, yellow, cleft about ⅓ its length, each of the 2 lobes again divided into 2 acute

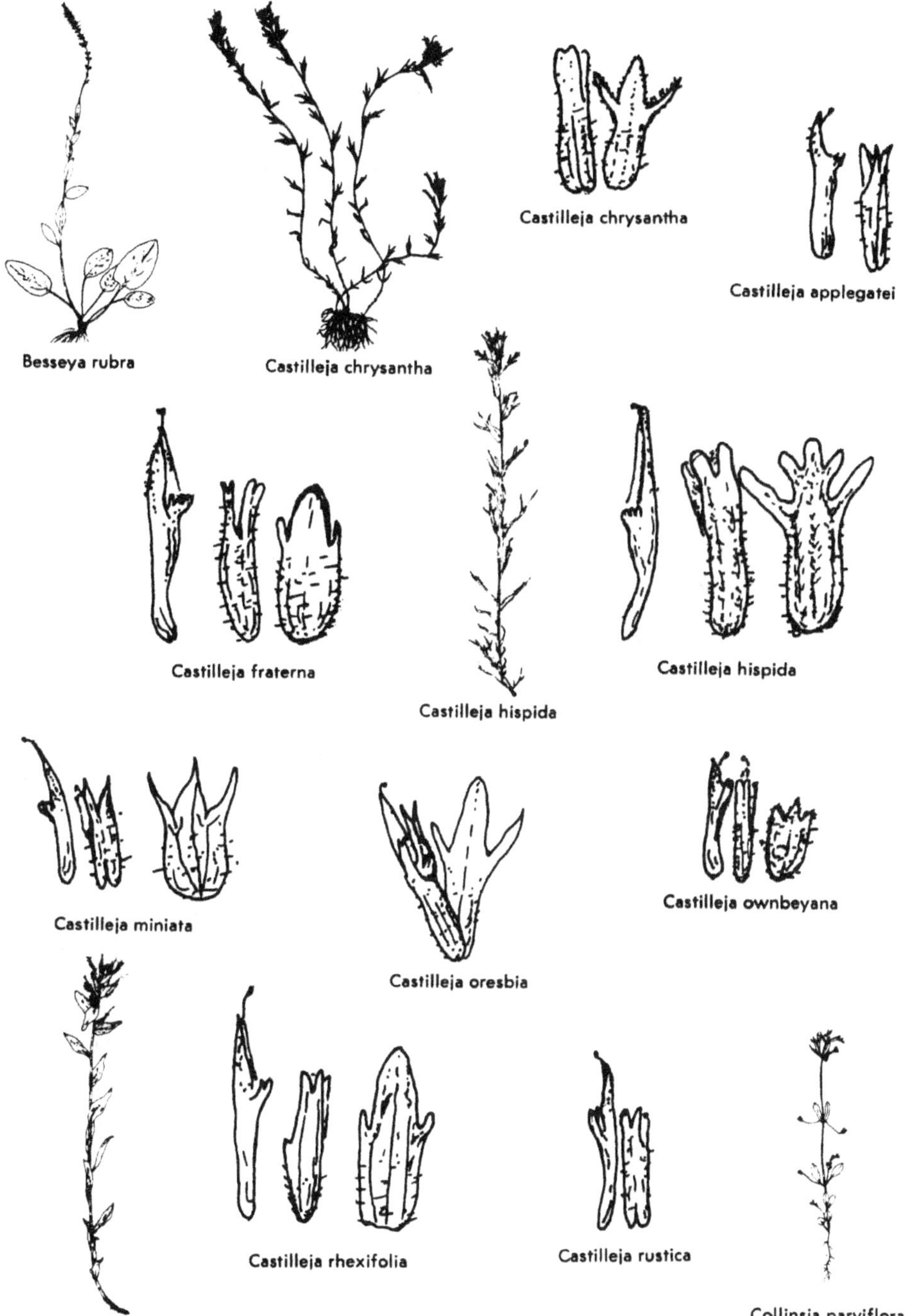

Besseya rubra

Castilleja chrysantha

Castilleja chrysantha

Castilleja applegatei

Castilleja fraterna

Castilleja hispida

Castilleja hispida

Castilleja miniata

Castilleja oresbia

Castilleja ownbeyana

Castilleja rhexifolia

Castilleja rhexifolia

Castilleja rustica

Collinsia parviflora

segments 1-2 mm long; corolla 15-25 mm long, its galea 7 mm long, about ⅓ as long as the tube, usually longer than the calyx, acutish, puberulent with narrow reddish thin margins, its lower lip rudimentary, 3 mm long, dark green, thickened, with straight acute lobes; capsule 1 cm long.

Dry cliffs and ridges near coniferous woods, about 5000 to 7700 feet.

TYPE LOCALITY: Granite cliffs of Wallowa River, 7500 feet. W. C. Cusick 2474: "only flower seen pale yellow, Aug. 14, 1900."

Castilleja suksdorfii Gray   Suksdorf's Castilleja

Stem usually solitary, 30-50 cm tall from a creeping base; stems and leaves hispid or villous to glabrate; leaves lanceolate, all entire or usually with 1 or 2 pairs of narrow lateral lobes; inflorescence elongating with maturity; bracts with long and short hairs, mostly 5-parted, shorter than the flowers, red at the tip, yellow below; calyx 20-30 mm long, the equal primary lobes again divided into 2 linear acute segments; corolla 30-50 mm long, the galea hairy on the back, about as long as the corolla tube, the lower lip very short, dark green and thickened.

Wet meadows or forest openings, especially near springs, about 7000 feet.

Castilleja wallowensis Pennell   Wallowa Castilleja

This species is believed to be a hybrid between *C. chrysantha* and *C. rhexifolia*, both of which are common to the area. TYPE LOCALITY: Alpine turf over granite, 82-8300', Mt. south of Ice Lake, head of Adams Creek, Wallowa Mts., July 28, 1937. Pennell 21109

Perennial; finely pubescent below the hairy inflorescence; stems clustered, 15 cm tall, angled, unbranched; leaves lanceolate, entire, 2-2.5 cm long; bracts dull purple, the upper with a pair of lobes, ovate or oval; calyx dull purple, about 13 mm long in anthesis, cleft about ⅓ its length, the 2 lobes again divided into 2 oblong rounded segments 1.5 mm long; corolla 15-18 mm long, its galea 5-7 mm long, yellowish-green with thin purple margins, finely glandular-puberulent or nearly glabrous, the lower lip 2-3 mm long, dark green with thin whitish free lobes.

Moist granitic soil, about 8000 to 8300 feet.

Collinsia Nutt.

Annual herbs with opposite leaves; flowers 1 to several in the axils of the upper leaves; calyx campanulate, the 5 lobes united near the base; corolla tube gibbous, strongly 2-lipped, the upper lip 2-lobed, the lower 3-lobed, pouched, enclosing the 4 stamens, the rudimentary stamen and the style; capsule loculicidal; seeds large.

Collinsia parviflora Lindl.   Blue-eyed Mary

Annual, minutely pubescent or rarely glabrous, sometimes glandular in the inflorescence; stems slender, weak, 5-40 cm tall; leaves petioled, oblong-lanceolate, entire to few-toothed, glabrous or short-hairy, 2.5-3.5 cm long, the upper ones often whorled, becoming sessile linear bracts; flowers on long pubescent pedicels, clustered above, solitary near the base; calyx 3-7 mm long; corolla 4-10 mm long, gibbous on the upper side, with white upper lip and violet-blue lower lip; capsule ellipsoid, shorter than the calyx.

Common in moist woods and open meadows, 4500 to nearly 7000 feet.

Cordylanthus Nutt.

Annuals, usually branched, with alternate entire or dissected leaves; flowers axillary or in small dense heads or spikes; calyx cleft to the base into 2 segments, sometimes one segment obsolete; corolla 2-lipped, tubular, the lips about equal, the upper sometimes with curved tip, the lower 3-lobed or obsolete; stamens 4 or 2; capsule loculicidal.

Cordylanthus capitatus Nutt.   Clustered Bird's beak

Usually branched glandular annuals 10-60 cm tall, with fine spreading pubescence; leaves 1-5 cm long, linear, entire or 3-parted; flowers 2 to 5 at the ends of the branches; bracts leaf-like; calyx 12-15 mm long, dull purplish, scarious between the nerves, curved at the tip; corolla 1-1.5 cm long, purplish, red or purplish above; stamens 2; capsule about 7-8 mm long, loculicidal.

Dry open places, 4500 to about 6000 feet.

Linaria Mill.

Annual or perennial herbs; leaves usually alternate, glabrous; inflorescence racemose, terminal; calyx 5-parted; corolla yellow, white or blue, 2-lipped, with a palate and a long-spurred tube; stamens 4; capsules dehiscent near the top of each cell.

Linaria vulgaris Hill   Butter-and-Eggs

Tufted perennial 30-100 cm tall from creeping roots, glabrous and usually glaucous; leaves linear, mostly 2-6 cm long; inflorescence at first a short dense raceme but elongating with age; flowers clear light yellow, 2-3.5 cm long, the palate bearded, orange, well-developed, the spur yellow, straight; capsules broadly cylindric, 1 cm tall; seeds flattened, winged.

Roadsides where probably introduced, about 5000 feet.

Mimulus L.

Annual or perennial herbs, sometimes shrubby, with opposite entire or toothed leaves; flowers solitary or several, axillary or in terminal racemes, often large and showy; calyx of 5 united sepals, their mid-veins prominent and often raised, the tube usually inflated; corolla 2-lipped, yellow, purple or violet, to red; stamens 4, the 2 pairs of different lengths; stigmas separate or united; capsule cylindric, loculicidal; seeds many.

1. Flowers yellow, 1 to many; corollas conspicuously 2-lipped, or sometimes not
    2. Corollas large, conspicuously 2-lipped, 1-4 cm long; one tooth of the calyx noticeably larger than the others; plants mostly perennials
        3. Plants with definitely creeping roots as well as stolons; flowers mostly 1 to 5 per plant; plants of high mountain elevations, usually less than 20 cm tall........*M. tilingii*
        3. Plants with stolons or fibrous roots, but not usually with creeping roots; flowers over 5, mostly many; plants of low to middle mountain elevations, often over 20 cm tall..*M. guttatus*
    2. Corollas smaller, 0.5-3 cm long, not so clearly 2-lipped; calyx teeth all about equal; plants annual or perennial, mostly smaller than above
        4. Plants annuals; corollas 0.5-1.5 mm long; calyx 4-8 mm long
            5. Leaf blades elliptic, the base tapered; pedicels (flower stalks) less than 1 cm long at flowering time; corollas 4-8 mm long................*M. breviflorus*
            5. Leaf blades nearly triangular, the base broadest, not tapered; pedicels usually much longer than the calyx at flowering time; plants usually densely hairy-glandular..*M. floribundus*

4. Plants perennials; corollas 1-3 cm long; calyx 4-13 mm long
    6. Leaves crowded at or near the plant base; flower mostly solitary, long-pedicellate; plants stoloniferous, often forming large dense mats......*M. primuloides*
    6. Leaves scattered along the flowering stems, pale, thin, hairy, tending to be slimy; flowers few, pedicellate; plants weak-stemmed, sometimes with a musk odor.................*M. moschatus*
1. Flowers red, purple or pink-purple
  7. Plants small, usually under 20 cm tall; corollas mostly under 30 mm long
    8. Flowers small and slender, 5-10 mm long, light purple to nearly red; corolla tube about as long as the calyx; annual plants 3-18 cm tall.................*M. breweri*
    8. Flowers 10-35 mm long, magenta to purplish; corolla tube longer than the calyx; plants 1-20 cm tall
      9. Corollas rich magenta; pedicels only 1-3 mm long; plants of dry places......*M. nanus*
      9. Corollas purplish-lobed but the tube yellow and the throat dotted; pedicels mostly longer, becoming 3-10 mm long after flowering; plants of moist places.................*M. clivicola*
  7. Plants large, usually 30-90 cm tall; corollas 30-55 mm long, pink-purple, longer than the calyx, the flowers pedicellate; plants perennials.................*M. lewisii*

Mimulus breviflorus Piper   Short-flowered Monkey Flower

Slender glandular-puberulent annual 3-20 cm tall, often much branched; leaves elliptic, denticulate or entire, 3- to 5-nerved, short-petiolate, 0.5-2 cm long; pedicels becoming 5-13 mm long after flowering; calyx angled, glandular-puberulent, 3.5-8 mm long, the teeth short and acute, enlarged and inflated in fruit; corolla pale yellow, 4-7 mm long, slightly 2-lipped with rounded lobes, pubescent at the throat; anthers glabrous; capsules 4-5 mm long.
Moist open places, about 5000 to 6000 feet.

Mimulus breweri (Greene) Rydb.   Brewer's Monkey Flower

Slender glandular-pubescent annual 3-18 cm tall, often reddish; leaves narrowly elliptic to oblanceolate, entire or toothed, obscurely veined, 0.5-3 cm long, nearly sessile; pedicels becoming 3-12 mm long; calyx 3-7 mm long, angled, the short teeth acute; corolla 5-10 mm long, light purple to nearly red, or the tube white and magenta at the base, the lobes rounded or notched, persisting some time after flowering; anthers glabrous; stigmas very unequal; capsules about 5 mm long.
Moist to drying sandy soil, gravel bars, creek beds, meadows and forest clearings and slopes, 4500 to about 7000 feet.

Mimulus clivicola Greene   Hill Monkey Flower

Slender glandular-pubescent annual 5-20 cm tall; leaves 3-nerved, narrowly oblanceolate or elliptic, entire or with a few scattered teeth, 0.5-2.5 cm long; pedicels becoming 3-10 mm long after flowering, shorter than the leaves; calyx angled, becoming 7-10 mm long, glandular-pubescent, the teeth sharp; corolla lobes purple, the tube yellow, the throat pink or yellow with red spots, 1.5-2 cm long, pubescent, bilabiate, persisting after flowering; anthers glabrous; stigmas equal; capsules 8 or 9 mm long.
Moist places in the foothills, about 5000 to 6000 feet.

Mimulus floribundus Dougl.   Free-flowered Monkey Flower

Slender annual, erect to nearly prostrate, white-villous, viscid-pubescent and glandular, sometimes slimy, 5-50 cm tall; leaves ovate, dentate, thin and pale, 1-3.5 cm long,

petioled; calyx 4-8 mm long, viscid-pubescent, ridged, the teeth acute and ciliolate; corolla yellow, often with red streaks or dots, 7-15 mm long, the tube slender; anthers glabrous; capsules 5 mm long.
Moist seepy cliffs and open places, 5000 to 5500 feet or so.

Mimulus guttatus DC.   Common Monkey Flower
Annual and fibrous-rooted, or perennial and stoloniferous or with rhizomes; glabrous below the finely glandular-pubescent inflorescence; stems 10-100 cm tall; leaves ovate to oval, dentate, 3- to 7-veined, 1.5-9 cm long, petiolate near the base, sessile above, sometimes united or clasping the stem; pedicels becoming 2-6 cm long; calyx becoming about 2 cm long, angled, the lobes acute, the upper longest, the others curving inward; corolla 1-4 cm long, strongly 2-lipped, yellow, the palate pubescent, often with red spots; anthers glabrous; capsules 10-12 mm long.
Wet banks and streamsides, about 5000 to 7000 feet or so.

Mimulus lewisii Pursh   Lewis's Monkey Flower
Glandular-pubescent perennial herb 30-90 cm tall; leaves sessile, strongly nerved, elliptic to ovate, dentate to entire, the larger blades 3-7 cm long, sometimes clasping the stem; pedicels 3-7 or 10 cm long; calyx 2-3 cm long, angled, the teeth about equal; corolla 3-5 cm long, showy, pink-purple, the throat yellow with purple-red spots; anthers ciliate; capsule about 1.5 cm long.
In bogs and wet meadows and streams and their banks, 5000 to about 8000 feet and probably higher.

Mimulus moschatus Dougl.
Perennial with slender rootstocks, viscid-villous with shining white hairs, often with a musky odor, tending to be slimy; stems weak, often prostrate and rooting below, 5-40 cm or more long; leaves thin and soft, ovate to elliptic ovate, dentate, 1-5 cm long, short-petioled or sessile; pedicels becoming 1-4 cm long; calyx 7-13 mm long, angled, the upper tooth a little larger than the others; corolla 15-30 mm long, yellow, often with dark lines or spots; capsules 6 mm long.
Wet soil, moist places and along streams, 4500 to about 7000 feet.

Mimulus nanus H. & A.   Dwarf Monkey Flower
Dwarf glandular-puberulent annual 1-12 cm tall; leaves elliptic to oblanceolate, entire, obscurely nerved, 1-3.5 cm long; flowers crowded, nearly sessile; calyx 5-9 mm long, the lobes about equal; corolla 1-2.5 cm long, rich magenta, the throat villous, striped with yellow and deeper red; capsules 7-11 mm long.

Mimulus primuloides Benth.   Primrose Monkey Flower
Perennial with slender stolons and bulblet-bearing rootstocks, forming dense mats, villous with white slimy hairs or glabrous; leaves crowded at or near the base, 4-25 mm long, elliptic-oblanceolate, sessile, dentate or entire; pedicels 1-10 cm long, rarely shorter in alpine plants; calyx 4-8 mm long, the teeth ciliate, acute, about equal; corolla 5-20 mm long, yellow, often with maroon dots, the lobes spreading and notched; anthers villous and ciliate; capsules 6-7 mm long.
Wet to moist, mossy boggy banks and meadows, 5500 to about 8400 feet.

Mimulus tilingii Regel   Tiling's Monkey Flower
    ? M. implexus Greene
    Perennial herb with creeping yellowish rhizomes and sometimes also stoloniferous, glabrous or nearly so; stems sometimes branched, 5-30 cm tall; leaves ovate, rhombic or broadly elliptic, dentate, under 1 cm to 3 cm long, the upper sessile; flowers solitary or few, long-pedicelled; calyx becoming 1.5-2 cm long, the upper tooth longer than the others; corolla 2-4 cm long, yellow, the throat with 2 hairy red- or brown-spotted ridges, the palate pubescent; anthers glabrous; capsules stipitate, 7-8 mm long.
Along and in rocky, gravelly or mossy cold streams, lakes and meadows, 7000 to about 8500 feet and probably higher.

Orthocarpus Nutt.

Slender annual herbs with alternate, entire or dissected narrow leaves; flowers in bracteate terminal spikes or racemes; calyx equally or unequally 4-cleft or -divided; corolla strongly 2-lipped, the upper lip (galea) narrow and pointed, its lobes united and enclosing the anthers, the lower lip slightly shorter, saccate-inflated, 3-toothed; stamens 4, the pollen sacs unequally placed; capsules loculicidal; seeds few to numerous.

Lower lip of the corolla 3-lobed; bracts green throughout; our common one.............................*O. hispidus*
Lower lip of the corolla sac-like, not appearing lobed; upper bracts pink-purplish, petal-
    like, with sharp-pointed tips; not common in our area..*O. tenuifolius*

Orthocarpus hispidus Benth.   Hairy Orthocarpus
    Slender plants 10-40 cm tall; herbage spreading-hairy, the hairs shorter and often glandular above; leaves 1-4 cm long, the upper cleft into 3 to 5 slender segments, the lower linear and entire; bracts ovate, green or slightly purplish, not showy, deeply cleft, shorter than the flowers; calyx 8-13 mm long, 2-cleft, with bifid segments; corolla white or light yellow, 12-20 mm long, pubescent, the lower lip inflated and trisaccate, the galea straight, slightly longer than the lower lip.
Moist open meadows, 4500 to about 6000 feet.

Orthocarpus tenuifolius (Pursh) Benth.   Thin-leaved Orthocarpus
    Plants 10-30 cm tall, puberulent; leaves very narrow, 1-5 cm long, the upper with 1 or 2 pairs of slender lobes, the lower entire; bracts 1-2 cm long, broader than the leaves, nearly covering the flowers, entire or with a pair of lobes, the upper petaloid with purple tips; calyx 2-cleft with bifid segments; corolla yellow or tipped with purple, 14-20 mm long, the lower lip saccate, slightly shorter than the sharply hooked galea.
Open slopes and hillsides, 4500 to about 6000 feet.

Pedicularis L.

Erect perennial herbs with alternate leaves and a usually spike-like raceme; calyx regular or irregular, cleft into 5, 4, or apparently 2 lobes; corolla yellow, white, purple or red, 2-lipped, the upper lip (galea) hooded, enclosing the anthers, often long-beaked, the lower lip usually shorter, 3-lobed; stamens 4; capsules loculicidal, flattened, glabrous; seeds several, turgid.

1. Upper lip of the corolla forming a long curved or contorted beak; leaves basal, dissected
    into narrow segments

    2. Corollas pale, creamy or white, the beak coiled and downcurved, its tip rather
inconspicuous..*P. contorta*
    2. Corollas purplish-red or pink, the beak arched, curving outward, the tip
conspicuous, finally turned upward..*P. groenlandica*
1. Upper lip not forming a beak as above; leaves scattered on the stems and branches,
sometimes dissected, sometimes merely toothed
       3. Flowers greenish-yellow, crowded into a single spike-like inflorescences; leaves
dissected, large...*P. bracteosa*
       3. Flowers rose-color, in several to many small clusters at the tips of the stems and
branches of the plant; leaves doubly-toothed on the margins, but not dissected
otherwise..*P. racemosa*

Pedicularis bracteosa Benth.   Lousewort

Perennial with coarse fibrous roots or often some of the roots tuberous-thickened;
herbage glabrous below the hairy inflorescence; stems 40-100 cm tall, leafy; leaves up
to 15 cm long, commonly cauline and basal, sessile or nearly so, pinnatifid, the segments
distinct, sharply dentate; calyx 12 mm long, the lobes filiform, glandular-pubescent, the
upper one much shorter than the others; corolla 13-21 mm long, yellow or purple to red,
the galea beakless or nearly so; capsule 12 mm long.
Roots tending to be tuberous-thickened; inflorescence hairy; calyx lobes little or not at
all glandular; corolla yellow or yellowish......................var. **pachyrhiza** (Penn.) Cronq.
Meadows and moist rocky openings in coniferous forest, 4500 to about 8000 feet.

Pedicularis contorta Benth.   White Coiled Lousewort

Plant glabrous throughout; stems clustered, 15-60 cm tall; leaves basal or nearly so,
5-18 cm long with 10 to 15 pairs of pinnules, each linear and serrate; inflorescence elongate, the bracts narrow, shorter than or equaling the flowers, cleft into linear divisions;
calyx 6-9 mm long, 5-lobed, the upper lobe the shortest; corolla 15-22 mm long, greenish-
yellow or yellowish-white, the galea purple-spotted ending in a long downcurved coiled
beak; capsules 9-10 mm long.
Bogs, meadows and drier open or wooded slopes, 5000 to about 9500 feet or so.

Pedicularis groenlandica Retz.   Elephant's Head

Plant glabrous throughout; stems solitary or few together, 15-70 cm tall; leaves basal
and cauline, 10-15 cm long with 12 to 15 pairs of serrate pinnules, the basal long-petioled,
the cauline becoming sessile upward; inflorescence elongate; bracts shorter than the
flowers with a few pairs of slender lobes; calyx 4-5 mm long with 5 entire equal ciliolate
lobes; corolla 1-2.5 cm long, pink- to red-purple, the galea arched, curved downward,
the tip then conspicuously turned upward, the lower lip small and spreading; capsules
6-8 mm long.
Wet meadows, bogs and mossy banks, 5300 to about 8400 feet and probably higher.

Pedicularis racemosa Dougl.   Leafy Lousewort

Fibrous-rooted perennial, glabrous or obscurely hairy above, 15-50 cm tall; leaves
chiefly cauline, nearly sessile, elliptic, 4-10 cm long, doubly serrate; inflorescence lax
and elongate, the flowers or flower clusters axillary or racemose, the bracts leaf-like;
calyx 5-8 mm long, unequally cleft into 2 segments each with a conspicuous tip; corolla
10-16 mm long, white or yellowish to rose, the galea arched and tapering into a downward incurved beak, the lower lip with broad lateral lobes; capsules 10-12 mm long.
Dry open slopes and coniferous woods, 4500 to about 8000 feet.

Penstemon Mitch.

Perennial herbs or shrubs; leaves opposite, rarely alternate, entire, toothed or pinnatifid, the lower usually petiolate, the upper sessile; flowers showy, in clusters or in open panicles, racemes or cymes; corolla tubular, 2-lipped, the upper lip 2-lobed, the lower lip 3-cleft, blue or purple to red, yellow or white; fertile stamens 4, paired, the sterile 5th a long filament often bearded; anthers 2-celled, the pollen sacs joined only near the tip; capsules septicidal; seeds numerous.

1. Flowers white or whitish; plants shrubby at the base..*P. deustus*
1. Flowers mostly blue or bluish, scarcely shrubby at the base (except *P. fruticosus*)
    2. Leaves toothed on the margins (sometimes not, in *P. fruticosus*)
        3. Anthers long-woolly with tangled hairs..*P. fruticosus*
        3. Anthers either without hairs or with inconspicuous, short, straight hairs
            4. Corollas 13-25 mm long; plants glandular-hairy in the inflorescence;
               clusters few-flowered..*P. wilcoxii*
            4. Corollas 22-32 mm long; plants not glandular-hairy in the
               inflorescence..*P. venustus*
    2. Leaves not toothed on the margins
        5. Leaves grayish-short-hairy; corollas 10-17 mm long, glandular-hairy, 3-6 mm
          wide at the mouth..*P. humilis*
        5. Leaves mostly hairless; corollas various
            6. Inflorescence glandular
               7. Stems 10-25 cm tall; leaves mostly rounded at the tip; corollas
                  10-13 mm long, with lines inside..*P. spatulatus*
               7. Stems 30-90 cm tall; leaves pointed; corollas 12-20 mm long,
                  without lines..*P. attenuatus*
             6. Inflorescence not glandular
               8. Corollas 18-38 mm long and about 10 mm wide at the mouth;
                 capsules 7-13 mm long; palate hairless
                   9. Corollas 18-28 mm long; pollen sacs 1.1-1.9 mm long.......*P. payettensis*
                   9. Corollas 25-38 mm long; pollen sacs 1.8-3.0 mm long; leaves
                     often bluish-glaucous..*P. speciosus*
               8. Corollas mostly under 18 mm long; capsules 3-7 mm long; palate
               bearded
                  10. Pollen sacs opening all the way from base to tip
                     11. Corollas 6-11 mm long, 2-3 mm wide at the mouth of the
                       tube; flower tube often slanting downward................................*P. procerus*
                     11. Corollas 11-15 mm long, 3-5 mm wide at the mouth of
                       the tube; flower tube not slanting downward................................*P. rydbergii*
                  10. Pollen sacs not opening all the way, remaining pouched;
                     corollas 15-20 mm long, the tube 4-7 mm wide at its mouth.......*P. globosus*

Penstemon attenuatus Dougl.   Taper-leaved Penstemon

Plants 10-70 cm tall, from a woody rhizome, glabrous below the inflorescence or finely puberulent on the stems, the basal rosette of leaves well developed; leaves deep green, entire or nearly so, lanceolate to oval, 4-10 cm long or more, reduced upward; inflorescence of 1 to several whorled clusters, glandular-hairy; calyx 4-7 mm long, the segments scarious-margined; corolla glandular-pubescent, pale yellowish or white, or sometimes blue or purple, 12-20 mm long, 2-lipped, the palate bearded with whitish hairs; sterile filament yellow-bearded; pollen sacs glabrous, ovate, becoming opposite; capsules 6-8 mm long.

Open or wooded slopes at about 5000 feet.

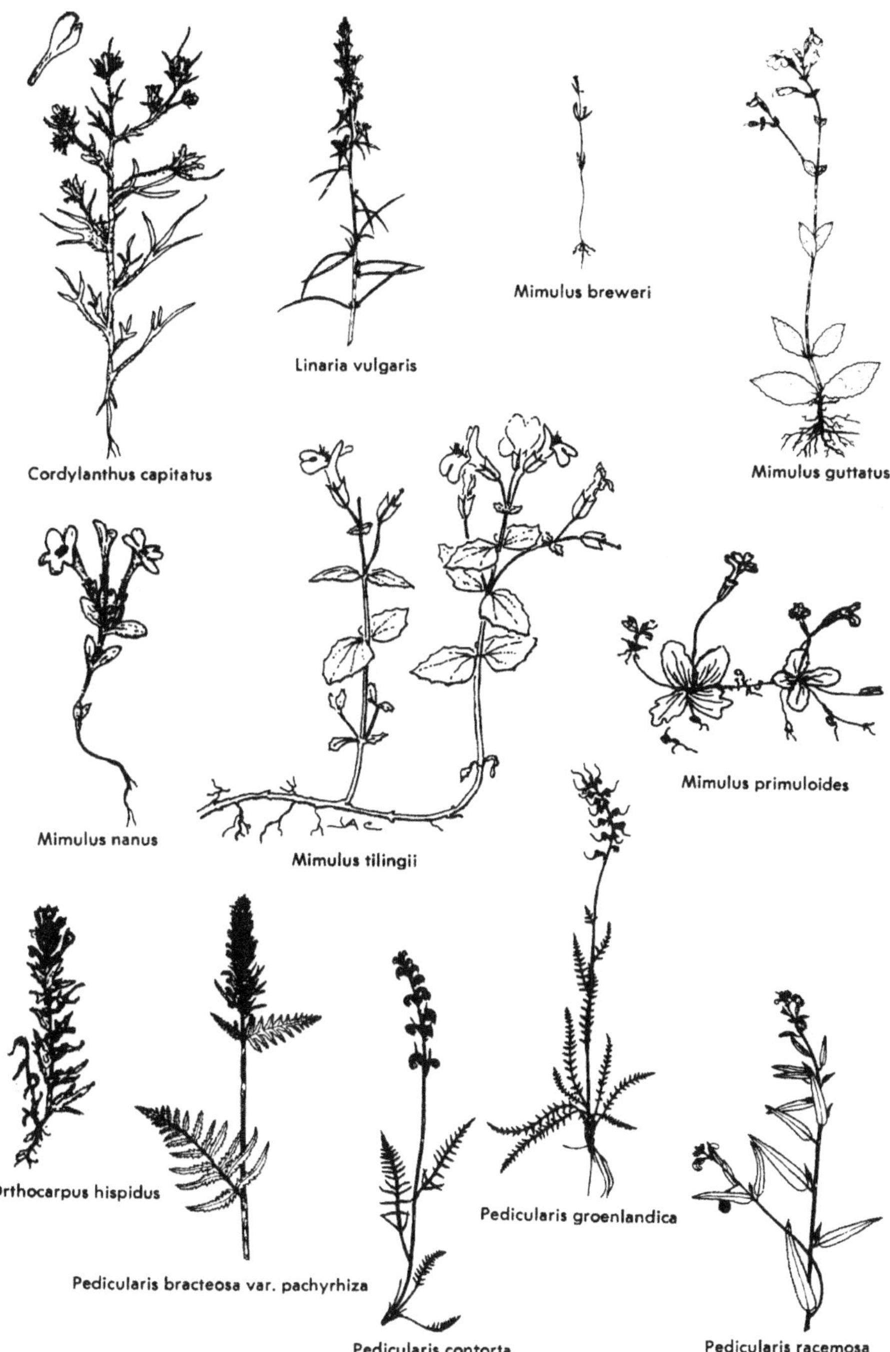

Mimulus breweri
Linaria vulgaris
Cordylanthus capitatus
Mimulus guttatus
Mimulus nanus
Mimulus tilingii
Mimulus primuloides
Orthocarpus hispidus
Pedicularis bracteosa var. pachyrhiza
Pedicularis contorta
Pedicularis groenlandica
Pedicularis racemosa

Penstemon deustus Dougl.   Hot-rock Penstemon
   Plants woody at the base, glabrous or glandular-pubescent; stems in clumps, stiffly erect, 20-60 cm tall; leaves oblanceolate to elliptic, bright green, opposite or scattered, toothed or entire, up to 6 cm long, short-petioled to sessile or clasping; inflorescence glabrous or somewhat glandular, narrow, often loose; calyx 2.5-6 mm long; corolla nearly tubular, glandular, pale dull whitish with some purplish lines, 8-20 mm long, the upper lip much shorter than the lower; anther sacs orbicular, 0.5-0.9 mm long, glabrous, opening all the way, the tips spread away from each other.
Dry open rocky places at about 4500 to 5000 feet.

Stems shorter; leaves mostly narrow and finely toothed, glabrous, glaucescent; corolla glabrous within, somewhat glandular on the outside; sterile filament very short, not bearded; dry cliffs at about 5000 feet............................var. **heterander** (T. & G.) Cronq.

Penstemon fruticosus (Pursh) Greene   Shrubby Penstemon
   Plants shrubby at the base, forming wide clumps, glabrous or finely puberulent up to the inflorescence, 10-40 cm tall; leaves firm, green, elliptic to oblanceolate, entire or toothed, 1-5 cm long, larger and more crowded below, reduced upward; inflorescence a short, dense, few-flowered, glandular-hairy raceme; calyx 7-15 mm long; corolla bright lavender-blue, 25-38 mm long, glabrous on the outside, the throat bearded within with long white hairs along the ridges; anthers densely long-woolly; pollen sacs opening all the way and becoming opposite; sterile filament shorter than the fertile stamens, long-yellow-bearded at the tip; capsules 8-12 mm long.
Rocky slopes in open coniferous woods, 4500 to about 8500 feet.

Penstemon globosus (Piper) Pennell & Keck   Globe Beard Tongue
   Tufted plants from a woody base, glabrous or nearly so, 20-60 cm tall; leaves thin, bright green, 5-18 cm long, oblanceolate to elliptic or ovate, the upper clasping; flowers in a single dense cluster, or sometimes in 2 to 4 smaller clusters, the upper more crowded than the lower; calyx 5.5-8 mm long, the segments scarious-margined and erose, with a pointed tip; corolla bright blue or blue-purple, 15-20 mm long, the palate bearded; pollen sacs elliptic or oval, becoming opposite but not opening completely through the partition nor to the pouched far ends, the margins denticulate-ciliolate; sterile filament densely bearded half its length with yellow hairs; capsules 6-7 mm long.
Moist or dry bogs, meadows or open rocky slopes, 5500 to about 8000 feet.

Penstemon humilis Nutt.   Lowly Penstemon
   Tufted plants 10-30 cm tall; herbage grayish, finely puberulent almost throughout; leaves firm, mostly entire, oblanceolate to elliptic or ovate, up to 12 cm long, the upper ones reduced and sessile; inflorescence glandular-pubescent, of 3 to 6 scarcely separated few-flowered clusters; calyx 2.5-6 mm long; corolla glandular-hairy, blue-purple, 10-17 mm long, the palate bearded; pollen sacs ovate, glabrous, opening fully and becoming opposite; sterile filament densely bearded at the tip with golden hairs and less densely for $\frac{1}{3}$ its length.
Dry rocky slopes at low elevations.

Penstemon payettensis Nels. & Macbr.   Payette Penstemon
   Glabrous plants forming clumps; stems 15-60 cm tall from a short woody crown;

leaves thick, entire, the lower oblanceolate and long-petioled, up to 18 cm long, the upper cauline lance-ovate to ovate, sessile, broad-based and clasping; inflorescence of several to many clusters; calyx 4.5-8 mm long; corolla bright purplish-blue, 20-27 mm long; pollen sacs 1.1-1.9 mm long, becoming opposite, opening nearly or all the way to the far ends but not through the partition, often dentate along the margins; sterile filament short-bearded toward the tip or nearly glabrous.

Sandy or rocky soil, often on exposed ridges and slopes, 6000 to about 9600 feet.

Penstemon procerus Dougl.   Tall alpine Beard Tongue
   ? P. confertus var. *procerus* Cov.; *? P. tolmiei* ssp. *formosus* (Nels.) Keck

Tufted plants, woody at the base, glabrous throughout or the sepals puberulent; stems slender, 5-70 cm tall; leaves thin, deep green, entire, the basal when present oblanceolate, up to 10 cm long, the cauline few, narrowly oblong, sessile and reduced; inflorescence of 1 to several very dense clusters, the flowers sometimes declined; calyx lobes glabrous or puberulent, 1.5-6 mm long, entire, with a long caudate tip, scarious-margined, often blue or purplish-tinged; corolla blue-purple or sometimes pale yellow in var. *tolmiei*, 6-11 mm long, the palate lightly or heavily bearded; pollen sacs nearly oval, becoming opposite, opening all the way and through the partition; sterile filament yellow-bearded at the tip, or sometimes glabrous in var. *formosus*; capsules 4-5 mm long.

Dry slopes, 5000 to about 9700 feet.

Calyx mostly 3-6 mm long; basal rosette usually not well developed; plants mostly 10-70 cm tall and usually with more than 1 flower cluster to a stem; corolla blue; dry open or wooded slopes from 5000 to about 8000 feet..var. **procerus**
Calyx mostly 1.5-3 mm long; basal rosette usually well developed; dwarf alpine and subalpine plants mostly 5-15 cm tall with short broad basal leaves; inflorescence usually a single cluster; flowers blue; dry slopes mostly above treeline, 8400 to 9675 feet..var. **formosus** (A. Nels.) Cronq.
Basal rosette usually well developed; plants mostly 5-15 cm tall, mostly with 1 cluster of flowers to a stem; corolla blue or sometimes ochroleucous; middle to high elevations..var. **tolmiei** (Hook.) Cronq.

Penstemon rydbergii A. Nels. var. **varians** (A. Nels.) Cronq.   Rydberg's Penstemon
   Plants from a woody base, the basal rosette often well developed, glabrous throughout except sometimes along the stem and in the inflorescence, 20-120 cm tall; herbage bright green; leaves thin, oblanceolate to elliptic, the basal 3-15 cm long, sometimes poorly developed, the few cauline ones sessile and reduced; inflorescence narrow, of 1 to 6 many-flowered clusters, the flowers spreading, not declined; calyx 3-9 mm long, the segments pointed, sometimes erose; corolla 10-13 mm long, blue-purple, the palate bearded; sterile filament usually yellow-bearded halfway or only at the tip, rarely glabrous; pollen sacs ovate, opening all the way through the partition and becoming opposite; capsules 5-6 mm long.

Moist or dry meadows and open rocky slopes, 4500 to 9300 feet.

Penstemon spatulatus Pennell   Wallowa Penstemon
   Stems clustered from a woody base, 10-25 cm tall, the basal rosette developed, glabrous below the glandular-hairy inflorescence or finely puberulent on the stems, often mat-

forming; leaves firm, entire, 2-6 cm long, the basal elliptic to oval, the cauline few, oblong-lanceolate; inflorescence of 1 to 4 rather crowded, dense clusters; calyx 2.5-5 mm long, the margins scarious, sometimes erose; corolla violet-blue with guide lines inside, glandular-hairy on the outside, 10-13 mm long, the palate bearded; pollen sacs glabrous, ovate to elliptic, boat shaped, opening all the way or nearly so, becoming opposite; sterile filament densely bearded at the tip with stiff yellow hairs.
Moist or dry open or wooded slopes, in and above the coniferous forest, 5600 to about 8100 feet.

Penstemon speciosus Dougl.   Showy Penstemon
Perennial plants 20-90 cm tall, glabrous or often finely puberulent, somewhat glaucous; leaves entire, thick, oblanceolate to narrowly lanceolate, the basal up to 15 cm long, the cauline reduced, sessile, sometimes clasping the stem; inflorescence elongated, of many showy flowers, sometimes 1-sided; calyx 4-8 mm long, the segments erose, broadly scarious-margined, the tip short; corolla bright blue-purple, 25-38 mm long, glabrous; sterile filament glabrous or rarely bearded at the tip; pollen sacs spreading apart, somewhat twisted, glabrous but dentate on the margins, opening $\frac{2}{3}$ of the way from each end but not through the partition; capsules 9-12 mm long.
Dry brushy or open slopes, 6000 to about 8000 feet.

Penstemon venustus Dougl.   Elegant Penstemon
Shrubby perennial 30-80 cm tall, glaucous and glabrous except often for lines of puberulence on the stem; leaves numerous, reduced near the base, sessile, 2-12 cm long, lanceolate to broadly oblong, sharply serrate to rarely nearly entire; inflorescence a continuous, narrow, spike-like panicle; calyx 2.5-6.5 mm long, the segments erose-toothed and scarious-margined; corolla lavender, bright blue to violet-purple, 20-38 mm long. the lobes ciliate on the margins, the palate usually glabrous but sometimes bearded; fertile and sterile filaments white-bearded toward the tip, somewhat exserted; pollen sacs opening $\frac{1}{3}$ to $\frac{1}{2}$ their length, across the partition and becoming horseshoe-shaped. the suture margins dentate-ciliolate.
Dry rocky slopes, 5000 to about 6500 feet.

Penstemon wilcoxii Rydb.   Wilcox's Penstemon
Stems clustered, herbaceous near the base, 30-100 cm tall, glabrous or sparsely puberulent below; leaves pale to bright green, usually glabrous, lanceolate to broadly ovate, 4-20 cm long, sharply toothed to nearly entire, the cauline often larger than the basal ones; inflorescence open, of several large loose clusters; calyx 2.5-5.5 mm long; corolla bright blue to bluish-purple, the tube lighter, 13-23 mm long, glandular-puberulent on the outside, the lower lip longer than the upper, the palate bearded; pollen sacs opening all the way and through the partition, becoming opposite, glabrous except for the dentate-ciliolate margins; sterile filament strongly yellow-bearded.
Dry rocky open or wooded slopes, 5000 to 6000 feet.

Scrophularia L.
Large perennial herbs with 4-angled stems and opposite toothed petiolate leaves: flowers small, numerous, in an elongate terminal inflorescence; calyx deeply 5-cleft, the sepals almost free; corolla greenish-yellow or -purple to dark maroon, the tube in-

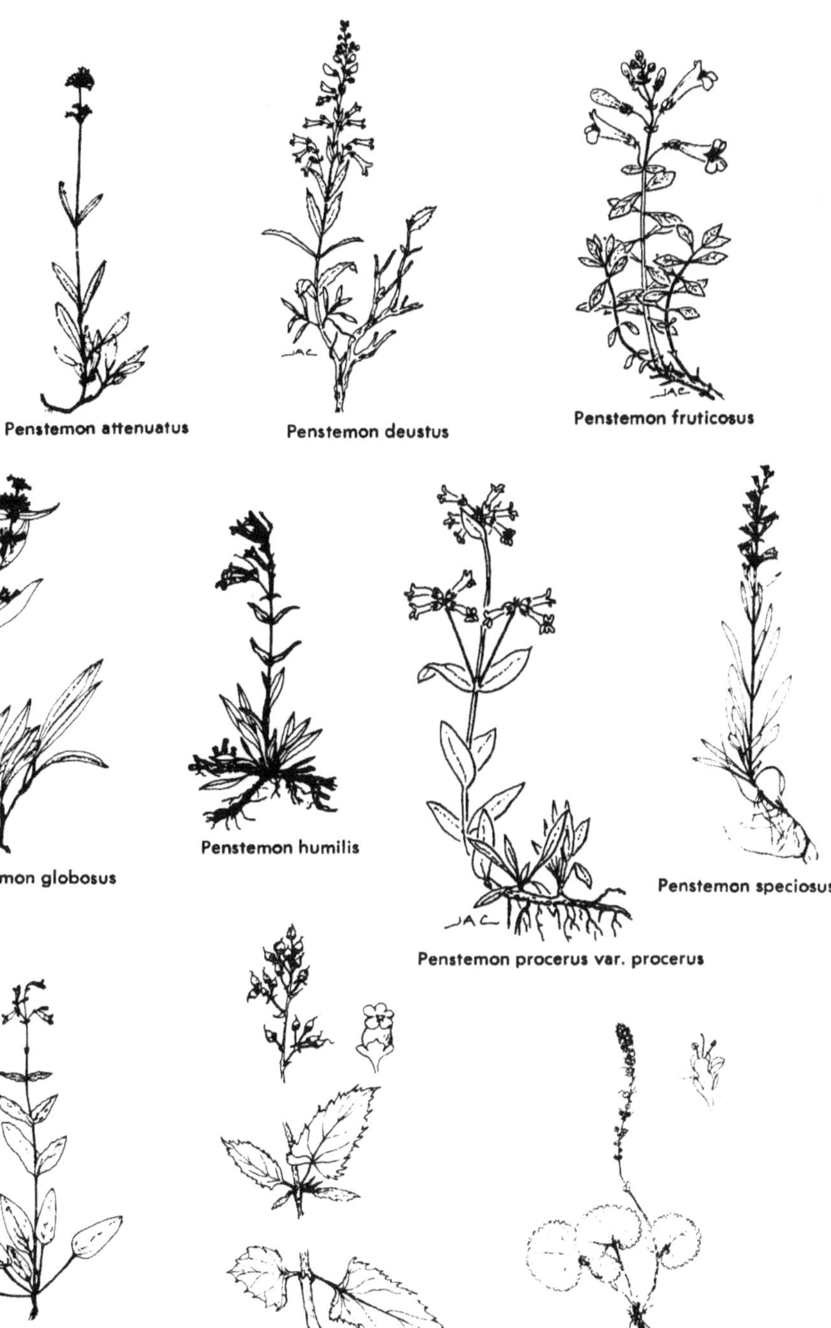

Penstemon attenuatus

Penstemon deustus

Penstemon fruticosus

Penstemon globosus

Penstemon humilis

Penstemon procerus var. procerus

Penstemon speciosus

Penstemon wilcoxii

Scrophularia lanceolata

Synthyris missurica

flated, 2-lipped, the upper lip 2-lobed, horizontal, the lower lip 3-lobed, the middle lobe deflexed or recurved, the 2 side ones upright; fertile stamens 4, the pollen sacs spreading; sterile 5th filament scale-like; capsules septicidal; seeds many.

Scrophularia lanceolata Pursh   Lance-leaved Figwort

Stems clustered, from thick roots, minutely glandular-pubescent or -puberulent, 50-150 cm tall; leaves all cauline, short-petiolate, 9-12 cm long, the blades triangular-ovate to -lanceolate, the tip acute, the base truncate, cordate or rounded, conspicuously once or twice sharply toothed; inflorescence usually long and narrow, minutely glandular or glabrous; calyx 2-4 mm long; corolla 9-14 mm long, light maroon above, yellowish-green on the lower surface; sterile filament yellowish-green; capsules ovoid-conic, 6-8 mm long.

Moist or dry forest clearings, meadows and streambanks, 4800 to about 6600 feet.

Synthyris Benth.

Fibrous-rooted perennial herbs with petiolate basal leaves and flowering stems longer than the leaves, naked or with several small alternate bracts below the narrow terminal racemes; sepals 4, not united; corolla campanulate to rotate, blue or violet-blue, occasionally pink or white, unequally 4-lobed, the upper lobe the largest; stamens 2; stigma capitate; capsules flattened, loculicidal; seeds few to many.

Synthyris missurica (Raf.) Pennell   Western Mountain Synthyris

Perennial from a short thick rhizome, glabrous throughout or the inflorescence brownish-puberulent, 10-60 cm tall; leaves basal, long-petiolate, the blades cordate-orbicular, 2.5-8 cm wide and nearly as long, palmately-veined, the margins lobed or toothed once or twice, all around; raceme rather dense, 6-18 cm long; sepals entire or erose; corolla small, nearly rotate, deep blue, the upper lobe the largest; capsules 5-7 mm wide and nearly as long.

Moist or dry shady places, often among rocks in the forest, 4500 to 9300 feet.

Verbascus L.

Tall biennial or perennial herbs; leaves basal and cauline, alternate, sessile and sometimes clasping; flowers in terminal racemes or crowded spikes; sepals 5, not united; corolla rotate, nearly regular, mostly yellow, occasionally white, deeply 5-lobed; stamens 5, some or all of the filaments densely hairy; stigma capitate; capsules septicidal, ellipsoid to globular; seeds many.

Leaves and stem woolly; flowers in a thick spike-like inflorescence..*V. thapsus*
Leaves and stem nearly hairless; flowers in long open inflorescences on the stem and branches..*V. blattaria*

Verbascum blattaria L.   Moth Mullein

Taprooted biennial, densely glandular above, especially in the inflorescence, otherwise glabrous; stem solitary, 40-150 cm tall, growing out of the previous year's rosette of basal leaves; lower leaves 5-15 cm long, toothed and often lobed, the upper elliptic to ovate, clasping, toothed, becoming smaller and sessile; raceme glandular, loose and open, long, the pedicels longer than the bracts; sepals 5-8 mm long; corolla yellow or white, often rose-tinged, 2-3 cm wide; filaments purplish-hairy; capsules 6-8 mm long. Roadsides and dry places, about 4500 feet.

Verbascum thapsus L.   Common Mullein

Biennial, densely woolly with branched hairs; stem usually 30-120 cm tall, growing out of the previous year's rosette of basal leaves; lower leaves oblanceolate, 10-40 cm long, entire, the cauline numerous, reduced upward, becoming sessile and clasping the stem; inflorescence very dense, long and narrow, the flowers sessile or nearly so; sepals 7-9 mm long; corolla bright yellow or rarely white, 1-2 cm wide; filaments densely yellow-hairy or glabrous; capsules 7-10 mm long.
Roadsides and waste places at low elevations.

Veronica L.

Annual or perennial herbs; leaves opposite, or alternate in the inflorescence, entire or toothed; flowers in axillary or terminal racemes or spikes, or solitary in the upper axils; sepals 5 or 4, not united; corolla nearly rotate, irregularly 4-lobed, the upper lobe the largest, the lower lobe the smallest; stamens 2; stigma capitate; capsules flattened, loculicidal; seeds few to many.

1. Leaves toothed or lobed, appearing alternate sometimes
    2. Leaves toothed but not lobed; stems erect or nearly prostrate on the ground, sometimes branched, 5-30 cm long..*V. arvensis*
    2. Leaves with 5 lobes mostly; stems erect, usually branched from the base, 5-12 cm tall...*V. triphyllos*
1. Leaves not conspicuously toothed or lobed, usually all opposite
    3. Flowers blue or blue-violet; style 1-10 mm long
        4. Inflorescence narrow, single, at the top of the stem, elongating with maturity; plants perennial
            5. Style inconspicuous, 1-3 mm long; plants variously hairy
                6. Capsules longer than wide; hairs of stems, and sometimes the leaves, long and loosely spreading ....*V. wormskjoldii*
                6. Capsules wider than long; hairs very short and fine.................*V. serpyllifolia*
            5. Style conspicuous, 5-10 mm long; plants of upper mountain elevations....*V. cusickii*
        4. Inflorescences several, open, from the axils of the leaves; plants hairless, usually growing in wet places..*V. americana*
    3. Flowers white or whitish, inconspicuous; style obsolete; plant an annual.............*V. peregrina*

Veronica americana (Raf.) Schwein.   American Brooklime

Glabrous perennial with creeping rhizomes; stems often branched and rooting at the base, 10-100 cm long; leaves opposite, short-petiolate, serrate to nearly entire, lanceolate or elliptic to ovate-lanceolate, acute, 1.5-8 cm long; racemes axillary, 10- to 25-flowered, peduncled; sepals 4; corolla blue, rarely pink, 5-10 mm wide; fruiting pedicels 5-14 mm long; style 2.5-3 mm long; capsules turgid, 3-4 mm long, oval, notched above. Wet or moist bogs, meadows and streambanks, up to about 6100 feet.

Veronica arvensis L.   Corn Speedwell

Taprooted annual, pubescent throughout; stems erect or nearly prostrate, 5-30 cm long; leaves opposite, ovate, sometimes subcordate at the base, 0.5-1.5 cm long, crenate-dentate, sessile or short-petiolate; inflorescence a spike-like often elongate terminal raceme with alternate bracts and very short pedicels; corolla blue-violet, 2-2.5 mm wide;

capsules 3 mm long, obcordate, ciliate, pubescent, deeply notched above; style up to 1 mm long; seeds several in each locule.
Roadsides, fields and waste ground, 4500 to about 5000 feet.

Veronica cusickii Gray   Cusick's Speedwell
Perennial from shallow rhizomes; stems erect or curved at the base, 6-20 cm tall, finely glandular-pubescent; leaves opposite, elliptic to obovate, 1-2.5 cm long, glabrous, sessile and entire; flowers in terminal racemes, the bracts small and alternate, the pedicels glandular-pubescent, becoming 3-9 mm long; sepals 4, glandular-pubescent, 3 mm long; corolla 8-13 mm wide, deep blue-violet, rarely red or rose-pink; filaments 4-8 mm long; style conspicuously exserted, 5-10 mm long; capsules finely glandular-pubescent, deeply or shallowly notched, 4-6 mm long and nearly as wide; seeds numerous.
Meadows, bogs, streambanks, lake borders and moist rocky open slopes, 7000 to about 8500 feet.

Veronica peregrina L. var. **xalapensis** (H. B. K.) St. John & Warren
Erect annual, or sometimes curved at the base, the stems 3-30 cm tall, often widely branching from the base; leaves opposite, glabrous, 5-30 mm long, linear-oblong to oblanceolate, obtuse, dentate to entire; inflorescence terminal, lax, mostly glandular-pubescent; calyx lobes unequal; corolla white or changing to pale lilac, about 2.5 mm long, the lobes much longer than the tube; capsules sharp-edged, wider than long, shallowly notched above.
Damp ground at about 4500 feet.

Veronica serpyllifolia L.   Thyme-leaved Speedwell
Perennial from creeping rhizomes; stems 10-20 cm long, branched, creeping and rooting below, finely puberulent; leaves opposite, broadly elliptic to ovate, mostly 1-2.5 cm long, glabrous or nearly so, entire or short-petioled; flowers in a loose elongate terminal raceme, the upper bracts alternate, the pedicels finely puberulent, becoming 4-5 mm long; sepals 4, the rounded lobes subequal; corolla 4-8 mm wide, pale blue or whitish, the upper lobes with violet lines; style 2-3.5 mm long; capsules finely glandular-puberulent, obcordate, 4 mm wide and a little shorter, the notch wide and shallow; seeds numerous.
Moist shady coniferous woods, about 5600 feet.

Stems and pedicels with longer mostly spreading hairs; plants usually larger; corolla wider, pale violet or bright blue; inflorescence more hairy than the rest of the stem; pedicels with some spreading glandular hairs; capsules 4-5 mm long; stems creeping and rooting below; moist or wet shady woods, 4500 to 7500 feet....var. **humifusa** (Dickson) Vahl

Veronica triphyllos L.   Three-leaved Speedwell
Erect annual finely glandular-pubescent throughout; stems usually branching from the base, 5-12 cm tall; lower leaves mostly 5-cleft or deeply lobed, sessile, 5-12 mm long, the upper 5-lobed; bracts 3-lobed; pedicels 5-10 mm long; calyx about 4.5 mm long; corolla deep blue, 6-9 mm wide; capsules deeply emarginate, 5-6 mm long; seeds hemispheric.
Gravel bars and shady woods, usually near streams, 4500 to about 5000 feet.

Veronica wormskjoldii Roem. & Schult.   American Alpine Speedwell

Perennial from shallow rhizomes; stems 10-25 cm tall, loosely long-spreading-hairy; leaves elliptic to ovate, mostly opposite, 1-4 cm long, long-soft-hairy like the stem or often glabrous, obtuse to acute, dentate to entire, sessile; inflorescence densely soft-hairy and somewhat viscid or glandular; flowers in short dense terminal racemes, the upper bracts usually alternate, the pedicels becoming 2-5 mm long; sepals 4, obtuse, densely glandular-pubescent; corolla deep blue-violet, 6-10 mm wide; filaments and style very short; capsules glandular-pubescent, 7 mm long, a little higher than wide, broadly notched; seeds numerous.

Moist or wet meadows, bogs, streambanks and shady coniferous woods, 5700 to about 8200 feet.

OROBANCHACEAE   Broomrape Family

Herbaceous root parasites without chlorophyll; stems yellowish or purplish; leaves scale-like, alternate; flowers perfect, solitary or in terminal spikes or racemes; calyx 4- or 5-cleft or split to the base on 1 or both sides; corolla tubular, rather irregular, 2-lipped, 5-lobed, usually with a pair of bractlets; stamens 4, didynamous, often with a vestigial 5th borne on the corolla tube; filaments glabrous or hairy; anther sacs parallel; ovary superior, 1-celled; style often with a 2- to 4-lobed stigma; fruit a 2- to 4-valved capsule; seeds many, small.

Orobanche [Tourn.] L.

Glandular-pubescent yellowish, brown or purplish root parasites with stems sometimes subterranean, simple or branched; leaves scale-like; flowers yellowish or purplish, solitary or in spikes, corymbs or panicles, subtended by a pair of bractlets; calyx 4- or 5-cleft into acute lobes, or divided to the base on 1 or both sides; corolla tubular, 2-lipped, 5-lobed; stamens 4, the anther sacs mucronate at the base; ovary ovoid; stigma entire or lobed, peltate to funnelform.

1. Flowers 1 to 12 on long pedicels (stalks) ; stems mostly 1-15 cm tall
    2. Pedicels 1-3 cm long, very much longer than the scarcely developed short stem; flowers 1 to 4; calyx lobes much longer than the tube..*O. uniflora*
    2. Pedicels 4-10 cm long, about equaling the well developed, elongated stem; flowers 3 to 12; calyx tube and lobes about equal in length..*O. fasciculata*
1. Flowers many more than 12 in a dense inflorescence; pedicels short when present; stems 10-40 cm tall
    3. Calyx 5-8 mm long, the lobes about equaling the tube; stems much branched in the inflorescence..*O. pinorum*
    3. Calyx 10-20 mm long, the lobes much longer than the tube; stems unbranched or sometimes with a few branches..*O. corymbosa*

Orobanche corymbosa (Rydb.) Ferris   Many-flowered Broomrape

Glandular-pubescent plants, 5-12 cm tall from thickened bases; cauline scales ovate; inflorescence a compact corymb 2.5-5 cm long, the pedicels 3-10 mm long, subtended by a bract; calyx 10-20 cm long, the lobes much longer than the tube, subtended by a pair of bractlets; corolla purplish, 2-3 cm long, the upper lip dark, shallowly-lobed, the lower lip lighter, deeply cleft, 0.5 cm long; anthers long-woolly; stigma peltate.

Exposed rocky slope at about 7000 feet. No other plant near it.

Orobanche fasciculata Nutt.   Clustered Broomrape
Glandular-pubescent plant; stem 3-15 cm long, mostly underground, the bracts few; flowers 3 to 12, without bracts; pedicels 2-20 cm long, about equaling the stem, the lower usually longer than the others to form a loose flat-topped inflorescence; calyx 5-cleft, 5-10 mm long, the lobes acuminate, about equaling the tube; corolla yellow or purple-tinged, 2-lipped, 1.5-3 cm long, the upper lip 2-lobed, the lower with 3 spreading longer lobes; anthers pubescent; capsules broadly ovoid.
Dry open slopes about 5800 feet. Parasitic especially on *Artemisia tridentata*.

Orobanche pinorum Geyer   Pine Broomrape
Finely glandular-pubescent perennial 10-30 cm tall with a thickened tuber-like base and 1 to few stems short-branched above to form a large loose many-flowered panicle; flowers sessile, or on pedicels up to 3 mm long, subtended by a bract; calyx with a pair of bractlets at its base, 5-8 mm long, the lobes equaling or a little shorter than the tube; corolla yellowish or tinged with brownish-purple, 13 to 20 mm long, the lips much shorter than the tube; capsules broadly ovoid.
Parasitic on *Pinus* and *Pseudotsuga*, 5000 to about 5300 feet.

Orobanche uniflora L.   Naked Broomrape
Glandular-pubescent plant; underground stem very short (1-5 cm long) with 1 to 3 slender pedicels 3-10 cm tall; flowers without bractlets; calyx 3-12 mm long, the lobes narrow, attenuate, much longer than the tube; corolla creamy-purplish, 1-3 cm long, the upper lip 2-lobed, the lower 3-lobed, the lobes broadly ovate, finely ciliate-fringed; anthers nearly glabrous.
Wet stony slope at about 5300 feet. Parasitic on many species, especially *Sedum*, and members of the Saxifrage and Composite families.

LENTIBULARIACEAE   Bladderwort Family

Aquatic or terrestrial annual or perennial insectivorous herbs of wet soils with well developed basal leaves; flowers single at the ends of the long scapes; calyx 2- to 5-lobed; corolla 2-lipped, the lips lobed, the lower lip prolonged into a straight spur; stamens 2: ovary superior, style short or obsolete; stigma 2-lobed; fruit a capsule opening by 2 or 4 valves; seeds small and numerous.

Plants growing submerged in water; corolla large, yellow; leaves dissected and often bearing bladders...*Utricularia*
Plants growing on land (wet to moist or mossy) ; corolla violet; leaves not dissected, usually in a basal rosette...*Pinguicula*

Pinguicula |Tourn.| L.

Fibrous-rooted insectivorous perennials of mountain bogs; acaulescent; leaves succulent, slimy, basal; flower solitary; corolla 2-lipped, the upper lip shorter than the lower: capsules 2-valved.

Pinguicula vulgaris L.   Butterwort
Insectivorous perennial; leaves 2-5 cm long in a basal rosette, slimy above; scapes 4-11 cm tall, glandular above; calyx purple, 3-4 mm long; corolla about 2 cm long

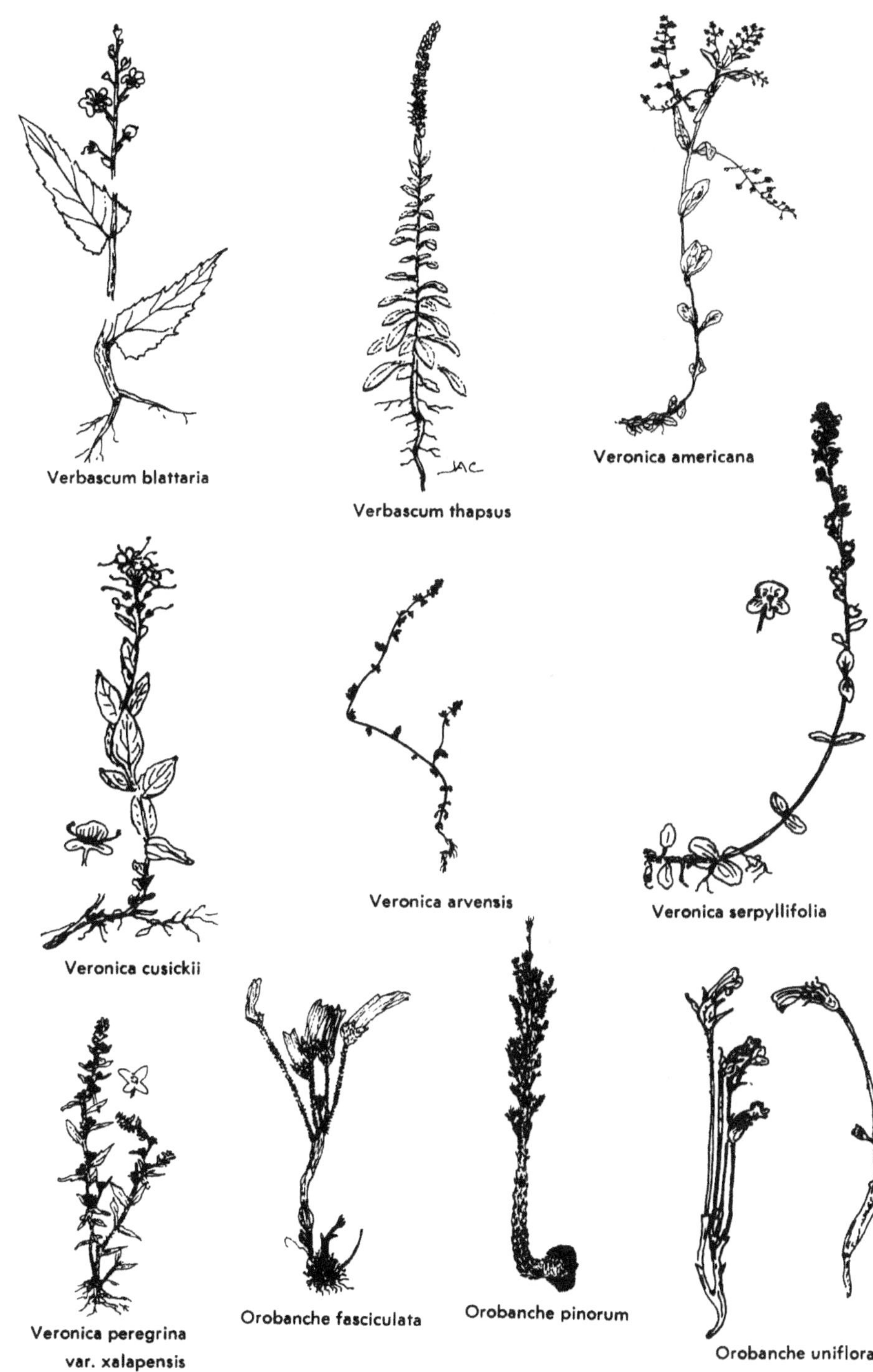

Verbascum blattaria
Verbascum thapsus
Veronica americana
Veronica cusickii
Veronica arvensis
Veronica serpyllifolia
Veronica peregrina
var. xalapensis
Orobanche fasciculata
Orobanche pinorum
Orobanche uniflora

including the spur, deep violet-purple, trumpet-shaped, the upper lip 2-lobed, the lower 3-lobed, longer, with a spur; capsule longer than the calyx.
Mossy bogs, meadows, lake borders and mossy streambanks, 5500 to about 8200 feet.

Utricularia L.

Seemingly fibrous-rooted aquatic or bog herbs; leaves alternate or whorled, much dissected into linear divisions, at least some of them with bladders; flowers solitary or in a raceme, the scapes naked or with a few scales; pedicels axillary; calyx 2-lobed, persistent; corolla 2-lipped, the lips entire or lobed, the tube prolonged into a spur or sac; capsules few- to many-seeded; seeds peltate, the margins sometimes winged.

Utricularia vulgaris L. Common Bladderwort

Submersed free-floating plants with leafy stems; winter buds 1-2 cm long; leaves crowded, alternate, 1-5 cm long, 2-parted at the base and then dichotomously divided repeatedly into very narrow segments; bladders about 3-4 mm long, borne on the leaves; scapes stout, 3-30 cm long; flowers 6 to 20 in a lax raceme, the pedicels reflexed in fruit; corolla yellow, 1-2 cm long, the lips about equal, the upper nearly entire, the lower slightly 3-lobed, the spur 6-8 mm long, curved, shorter than the lower lip; capsules globose.
Marshy outlet from Duck Lake, 5600 feet.

PLANTAGINACEAE   Plantain Family

Annual or perennial herbs, rarely stoloniferous; leaves mostly basal, simple, entire or toothed, alternate or opposite, parallel-veined; inflorescence a dense, bracteate, terminal spike or head, or the flowers rarely solitary; flowers small, mostly regular, perfect or sometimes imperfect, ordinarily 4-merous, or the stamens rarely only 1 to 3; calyx lobes overlapping, persistent; corolla lobes scarious, persistent; stamens borne on the petals; ovary superior, 1- or 2-celled or falsely 3- or 4-celled; style solitary; fruit a circumscissile capsule with 1 to several seeds in each cavity, or an indehiscent nutlet.

Plantago [Tourn.] L.

Acaulescent or rarely leafy-stemmed herbs, the scapes arising from the axils of the basal, ribbed, alternate leaves; inflorescence an elongate, long-peduncled spike; flowers inconspicuous, white or greenish, perfect or sometimes unisexual; calyx-lobes 4, all alike or sometimes 2 of them larger; corolla salverform; stamens 4 or 2, the filaments long-exserted; fruit a capsule with 1 to several seeds in each locule.

1. Leaf blades narrowly longer than wide
    2. Plants conspicuously long-white-woolly-hairy; annual..*P. patagonica*
    2. Plants sometimes inconspicuously tan-woolly only at the leaf bases; leaves often
      wider than *P. patagonica*; plants perennial..*P. lanceolata*
1. Leaf blades conspicuously broader, mostly 1 to 2.5 times as long as wide; plants hairless,
  perennial...*P. major*

Plantago lanceolata L. English Plantain

Fibrous-rooted perennial with a short caudex and a taproot, tan-woolly at the leaf bases; leaves narrowly lanceolate, 3- to 5-ribbed, 4-40 cm long, the blade usually entire.

the petiole winged; scapes several, mostly hairy, 10-60 cm tall; spikes dense, elongating at maturity; bracts longer than the calyx; sepals ovate, the 2 outer ones usually united; corolla glabrous, brownish; capsules oblong, obtuse, 2-seeded.
Roadside weed, 4500 to about 5000 feet.

Plantago major L.   Common Plantain
Essentially glabrous perennial sometimes hairy at the bases of the leaves but not woolly; leaves ovate, 5-30 cm long, horizontally spreading, entire or irregularly toothed, the blade about 1 to 2.5 times as long as wide, 3- to several-nerved, the petiole winged; scapes curved or decumbent, 8-40 cm long; spikes dense, narrow; bracts and sepals ovate; corolla lobes reflexed; stamens 4, exserted; capsule circumscissile near or below the middle; seeds angled.
Roadsides and moist ground, 4500 to about 6600 feet.

Plantago patagonica Jacq.   Woolly Plantain
White-woolly-long-hairy annual, 5-30 cm tall; leaves narrowly linear to oblanceolate, 3-12 cm long, essentially entire, minutely callous-tipped; scapes usually longer than the leaves, 8-16 cm tall; spikes 3-8 cm long, dense, cylindric, narrow; bracts firm, linear; corolla lobes spreading, white with a brownish spot below; stamens 4, about equaling the corolla; capsules ellipsoid; seeds 2, dark brown.
Dry open places in the foothills, about 5000 feet.

RUBIACEAE   Madder Family

Trees, shrubs or herbs (ours) with mostly 4-sided stems and opposite or whorled simple, entire, stipulate leaves; flowers regular, small, perfect or sometimes imperfect, gamopetalous, epigynous; calyx lobes entire or toothed, or obsolete, the tube adnate to the ovary; corolla 3- to 5-lobed; stamens 3 to 5, epipetalous; ovary inferior, 1- to 10-celled; style simple or lobed; fruit a capsule, berry, drupe, drupelet or nutlet; seeds 1 to many in each cell.

Leaves opposite, with small stipules; corolla funnel-shaped..*Kelloggia*
Leaves all or some of them whorled around the stem; corolla small, the lobes spreading.............*Galium*

Galium L.
Annual or perennial herbs with angled, erect, lax or spreading stems; leaves and leaf-like stipules entire or in whorls of 2 to 8 (opposite above in *G. bifolium*); flowers small, perfect or unisexual, in terminal or axillary cymes, or solitary; calyx lobes obsolete; corolla mostly rotate, white, greenish or purplish-red, 3- to 5-lobed; ovary 2-celled; stamens 4 or 5; styles 2, short; fruit indehiscent.

1. Leaves 2 to 4 to a whorl around the stem
  2. Leaves mostly 4 to a whorl, not 2 or 3; hairs on the fruit usually straight, not
    hooked; plants perennial
      3. Flowers white, perfect, in a dense, branched, conspicuous inflorescence at the
        top of the leafy stem..*G. boreale*
      3. Flowers yellowish or greenish, imperfect, numerous, but not in a conspicuous
        inflorescence; branches from the plant base ....*G. serpenticum*
  2. Leaves 2 to 4 to a whorl, very unequal, the upper opposite; flower solitary from the
    leaf axil; fruit with hooked hairs...*G. bifolium*
1. Leaves 4 to 8 to a whorl

4. Leaves very narrow, several times longer than wide, the blade scarcely wider at the middle; leaves usually 6 to 8 in a whorl, rarely 4 or 5
    5. Hairs on the fruit hooked at the tip; leaves 5 to 8 in a whorl, 1-5 cm long; plant annual..*G. aparine*
    5. Hairs on the fruit straight, or the fruit hairless; leaves 4 to 6 in a whorl, 7-12 mm long; plant perennial..*G. trifidum*
4. Leaves not so narrow, the blade rather wider at the middle than at the ends; leaves 5 to 8 in a whorl, sometimes 4, 1-5 cm long
    6. Flowers greenish, 1 to 3 from the leaf axils; leaves 5 or 6 in a whorl; fruit with hooked hairs..*G. triflorum*
    6. Flowers white, 3 or more to a leaf axil, in an irregularly-branched, widely-spreading inflorescence; leaves 6 to 8 in a whorl, very unequal; fruit with straight or hooked hairs..*G. asperrimum*

Galium aparine L.   Cleavers; Goose grass

Annual; stems weak, erect or usually spreading over other vegetation, 10-150 cm long, seldom branched, retrorsely hispid; leaves in whorls of 5 to 8 or rarely 4, narrowly oblanceolate, 1-5 cm long, hispid on the upper surface, margins and midribs; flowers in 1- to 5-flowered cymes in the upper axils; corolla greenish-white, very small, on straight widely-spreading pedicels, 2-20 mm long; fruit mostly 1.5-3 mm long, covered with hooked bristles.
Riverbanks and open woodlands, 4500 to about 6600 feet.

Galium asperrimum Gray   Tall Rough Bedstraw

Perennial from creeping rhizomes; stems 20-80 cm long, erect or partly supported by other vegetation, hispid; leaves unequal, 1-4 cm long, in whorls of 6 to 8, rarely 4, narrowly lanceolate, hispid on the margins and midrib, otherwise glabrous; inflorescence terminal, leafy, many-flowered, the pedicels capillary; corollas white, 2-4 mm wide: fruit covered with short straight or hooked bristles.
Shady woods, 4500 to about 6000 feet.

Galium bifolium Wats.   Low Mountain Bedstraw

Annual; stems erect, 5-40 cm tall, simple or branched, glabrous; leaves lanceolate, glabrous, 1-2.5 cm long, the upper ones opposite, the lower unequal, in whorls of 3 or 4: flowers solitary on axillary peduncles that elongate and become divaricate or nodding in fruit; corolla white, minute; fruit 2.5-3.5 mm broad, covered with slender hooked hairs.
Open coniferous woods and meadows, 5000 to about 6000 feet.

Galium boreale L.   Northern Bedstraw

Perennial with creeping rhizomes; stems 20-80 cm tall, erect, leafy, glabrous or some-times roughened on the angles and below the nodes; leaves in whorls of 4, lanceolate. glabrous or sometimes ciliate-margined, 1.5-4.5 cm long or smaller on axillary sterile branches; flowers faintly fragrant, in a many-flowered, large, dense inflorescence: corolla white, mostly 3 or 4 mm wide; fruit glabrous or thickly covered with short incurved or straight hairs.
Moist open woods, 4500 to about 6000 feet.

Galium serpenticum Dempster   Many-flowered Bedstraw
  G. multiflorum Kell.

Glabrous (ours) perennials with creeping rhizomes; stems clustered, sometimes woody at the base, 15-40 cm tall, freely branching and glabrous; leaves in whorls of 4, lanceolate to ovate, 5-15 cm long; inflorescence of many small clusters at the ends of the branches or on short axillary peduncles; corolla inconspicuous, pale greenish-yellow; fruit densely covered with long white bristles; staminate flowers with no ovaries, or abortive if present.
Dry open rocky meadows or slopes and ridges; 4500 to about 8400 feet.

Galium trifidum L.   Small Bedstraw
Perennial with slender rhizomes and weak stems 15-50 cm long, glabrous or rough on the angles; leaves in whorls of 4, 5 or 6, linear-lanceolate, 7-12 mm long, obtuse, usually scabrous-margined and on the midribs, otherwise glabrous; flowers 1 to 3 together, terminal or axillary, on capillary pedicels which become curved in fruit; corolla small, whitish, mostly 3-lobed but sometimes 4-lobed; fruit glabrous, globose.
Wet meadows, about 7200 to 7500 feet.

Galium triflorum Michx.   Fragrant Bedstraw
Perennial with sweet, vanilla-scented leaves and creeping rhizomes; stems lax, 20-120 cm long, glabrous or somewhat scabrous; leaves mostly in whorls of 6 or sometimes 4 or 5, narrowly elliptic to oblanceolate, cuspidate, 1.5-4.5 cm long, scabrous on the margins and midribs, otherwise glabrous; inflorescence a 3-flowered cyme, terminal or on axillary branches; corolla small, greenish-whitish, 4-parted; fruit covered with hooked bristles.
Shaded moist woods and mossy banks, 4500 to about 6800 feet.

Kelloggia Torr.

Perennial herbs with opposite, stipulate leaves and small flowers in a loose terminal cyme; calyx tube bristly; calyx teeth 4, short; corolla funnel-shaped, 4- or 5-parted; stamens 4 or 5, exserted; ovary 2-celled, each cell with one ovule; fruit covered with hooked bristles.

Kelloggia galioides Torr.   Kelloggia
Glabrous perennial with woody rootstocks and slender stems 10-60 cm tall; leaves lanceolate, 1-5 cm long, obtuse; flowers long-pedicellate in a loose inflorescence; corolla 4-8 mm long, pink or white, pubescent on the outside, the lobes about equaling the tube; fruit about 4 mm long, covered with hooked bristles.
Dry woods and open sandy slopes, 5000 to about 8000 feet.

CAPRIFOLIACEAE   Honeysuckle Family

Trees, shrubs, vines or perennial herbs with opposite, simple or pinnately compound leaves and perfect, regular or irregular flowers; inflorescence mostly cymose; calyx 3- to 5-lobed; corolla mostly 5-lobed, sometimes 2-lipped; stamens usually 5, alternating with the corolla lobes, (only 4 in *Linnaea*); ovary inferior, 1- to 6-locular, ovules 1 to

329

several in each locule; style slender; stigma capitate or 2- to 5-lobed; fruit a berry, drupe or capsule.

1. Plants evergreen herbs creeping along the ground; flowers pinkish, long-stalked, bell-shaped, paired____*Linnaea*
1. Plants shrubs or vines climbing on trees, none evergreen; flowers not always paired, usually short-stalked
    2. Leaves divided into 5 to 11 leaflets; inflorescence large and many-flowered______________*Sambucus*
    2. Leaves not divided at all into leaflets; inflorescence smaller and few-flowered
        3. Corolla either 2-lipped or with a spur at the base, or both; flowers yellow to reddish-orange; fruit a red to blue or black berry_________________________________*Lonicera*
        3. Corolla regular, without a spur, not 2-lipped; flowers pinkish to white; fruit white____*Symphoricarpos*

Linnaea [Gronov.] L.

Creeping evergreen herbs with opposite leaves and perfect 5-parted flowers paired at the ends of long naked peduncles; corolla funnel-shaped to campanulate, pink or pinkish; stamens 4, the pairs unequal, attached near the base of the corolla; ovary 3-loculed, only 1 functional; style elongate; stigma capitate; fruit small, dry; seed solitary.

Linnaea borealis L. ssp. longiflora (Torr.) Hulten   American Twinflower

Stems slender, woody, creeping, hairy and often glandular, often over a meter long, producing short erect leafy branches up to 10 cm long, each with a slender solitary peduncle; leaves evergreen, short-petioled, orbicular to obovate, entire or shallow-toothed, 1-2 cm long; peduncles with a pair of minute bracts at the top and usually forking into a pair of pedicels each with a pair of bractlets and a short-pedicellate nodding flower at the end; calyx pubescent; corolla 12-15 mm long, pinkish; fruit ovoid, enclosed by glandular-pubescent bractlets.

Cool moist shady woods, 5000 to about 6000 feet.

Lonicera L.

Erect shrubs or woody vines with opposite leaves; flowers regular or irregular, 5-merous, often showy, in pairs or short clusters subtended by bracts and bractlets, these separate, united or missing; corolla tubular or funnel-shaped, often with the tube swollen or spurred at the base; stamens 5; ovary 2- or 3-loculed; stigma capitate; fruit a several-seeded berry.

1. Plant an erect shrub; flowers usually paired, yellow or yellowish
    2. Flowers bright yellow; fruit surrounded by large red-black bractlets______________*L. involucrata*
    2. Flowers cream, pale yellow or white; berries bright red, the bractlets small or missing____*L. utahensis*
1. Plant a climbing or twining vine; flowers yellowish-orange-red ___________________*L. ciliosa*

Lonicera ciliosa (Pursh) DC.   Orange Honeysuckle

Twining vine, often up to 7 meters long; leaves mostly elliptic, 4-10 cm long, ciliate-margined, otherwise glabrous, glaucous beneath, sessile or nearly so, the upper 1 or 2 pairs on the flowering branches united around the stem; flowers showy, sessile, in 1 to 3 terminal whorls or clusters; corolla reddish-orange, 2.5-4 cm long, the tube much longer than the lips; fruit bright red, nearly 1 cm thick.

Moist woods, 4500 to about 4700 feet.

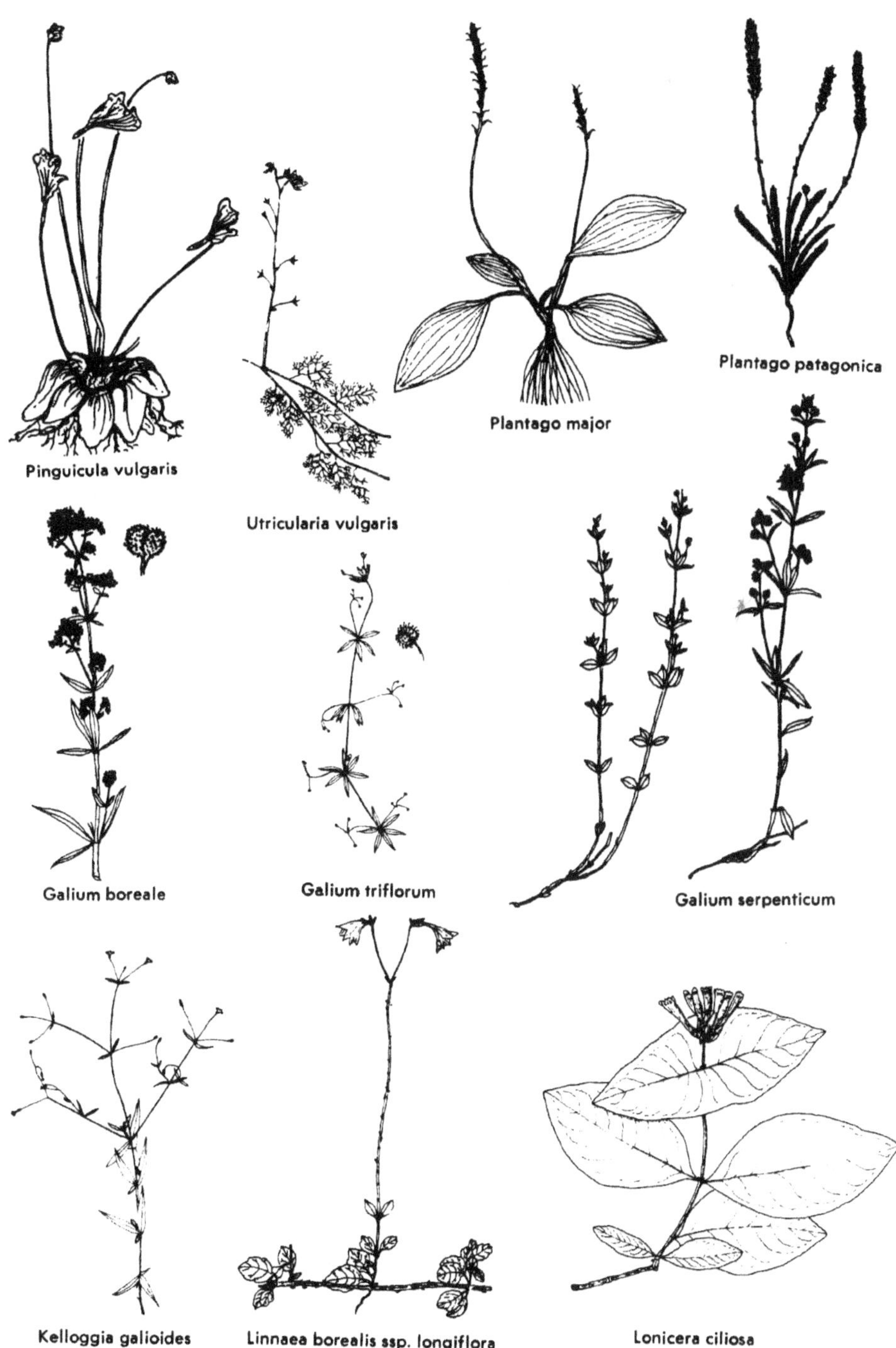

Pinguicula vulgaris
Utricularia vulgaris
Plantago major
Plantago patagonica
Galium boreale
Galium triflorum
Galium serpenticum
Kelloggia galioides
Linnaea borealis ssp. longiflora
Lonicera ciliosa

Lonicera involucrata (Richards.) Banks   Black Twin-berry
Erect shrubs 0.4-5 meters tall; leaves ovate, elliptic or oblong, short-petioled, 3-10 cm long, glabrous or pubescent, especially beneath, ciliate-margined; flowers in pairs on axillary peduncles subtended by 2 pairs of bracts which enlarge, surround the fruit and become bright purplish- or blackish-red; corolla yellow, sometimes red-tinged, glandular-pubescent, mostly 1-2 cm long; berries black.
Moist woodlands, thickets, lake borders and streambanks, 4500 to about 8200 feet.

Lonicera utahensis Wats.   Rocky Mountain Honeysuckle
A low bushy shrub 1-2 meters tall; leaves oblong, oval or elliptic, 2-5 cm long, thin, glabrous or a little pubescent beneath, short-petioled; peduncles axillary, 1-2 cm long; flowers paired; bractlets minute or obsolete; corolla pale yellow or creamy white, 1-2 cm long, funnel-shaped, hairy within; berries bright red, globose, slightly united.
Moist wooded slopes and streambanks and lake margins, 4500 to about 8000 feet.

Sambucus [Tourn.] L.

Shrubs, trees or coarse herbs with large opposite pinnate leaves and serrate leaflets; flowers small, numerous, white or pinkish, in large terminal compound cymes; calyx 3- to 5-parted; corolla rotate, deeply 3- to 5-lobed; stamens 5; ovary 3- to 5-parted; stigmas 3; fruit berry-like with 3 to 5 small stones or nutlets, each enclosing a seed.

Inflorescence flat-topped, large; fruit black with a dense whitish "bloom"____*S. cerulea*
Inflorescence rounded or pointed at the top but not flat-topped; fruit purplish or black but
    without a "bloom"____*S. racemosa*

Sambucus cerulea Raf.   Blue Elderberry
    S. glauca Nutt.
Large shrub or small tree 1-7 meters tall with erect stems sprouting freely from the base, the twigs glaucous; leaves 15-60 cm long, petiolate; leaflets 5 to 11, sharply serrate, 5-15 cm long, glabrous or nearly so, lanceolate, often asymmetrical at the base; flowers white or creamy in a broad, compound, flat-topped cyme; fruit bluish-black under the dense waxy white bloom.
Coniferous and mixed woods, 4500 to about 5300 feet.

Sambucus racemosa L. var. **melanocarpa** (Gray) McMinn.   Black Elderberry
    S. melanocarpa Gray
Shrub 1-3 meters tall; leaves petiolate; leaflets mostly 5 to 7, ovate to lanceolate, 5-17 cm long, dark green, serrate, pubescent to glabrate; inflorescence pyramidal or convex, about as broad as high; flowers white or creamy; fruit globose, usually purple-black, without a bloom.
Dry or moist woods along streams, 4500 to about 7000 feet.

Symphoricarpos Duhamel

Shrubs with opposite simple leaves and small perfect white or pink flowers in axillary and terminal clusters; calyx and corolla 4- to 5-merous; corolla campanulate, bearded within; stamens adnate to the corolla; ovary 4-locular, 2 of the locules functional with 1 fertile ovule each, the others abortive; stigma capitate or 2-lobed; fruit a 4-celled, 2-seeded berry-like drupe, white or greenish, or sometimes even red or black.

1. Plants erect branching shrubs; common in our area
   2. Corollas 3-5 mm long, the lobes about as long as the tube which often swells up after flowering..*S. albus*
   2. Corollas 7-9 mm long, the lobes definitely shorter than the tube which never becomes swollen...*S. vaccinioides*
1. Plants trailing shrubs; rare in our area...*S. mollis*

Symphoricarpos albus (L.) Blake   Snowberry
    S. rivularis Suksd.

Erect branching shrub up to about 3 meters tall; leaves oval to elliptic, entire or irregularly-toothed, 1.5-5 cm long, glabrous or often sparsely pubescent beneath and on the margins; flowers 1-2.5 cm long, solitary or in terminal and axillary racemes; corolla bell-shaped, rose-pinkish to white, the lobes and the tube about equal or the lobes half as long as the tube; fruit white, globose, 6-10 mm broad.
Open woodlands, about 4500 to 6000 feet.

Symphoricarpos mollis Nutt.   Creeping Snowberry
    S. acutus Dieck

Low shrub, trailing, spreading or prostrate, 30-100 cm tall, the young twigs puberulent; leaves elliptic to ovate, 1-4 cm long, entire or shallowly- to deeply-lobed, ciliate on the margins and long-hairy on both surfaces or becoming glabrate above; flowers in few-flowered racemes on the upper part of the stems; corolla campanulate, slightly hairy within, white or purplish; fruit white, 5-6 mm broad.
Open woodlands and brushy places, about 5000 feet.

Symphoricarpos vaccinioides Rydb.   Mountain Snowberry
    S. oreophilus Gray

Low branching shrub 80-150 cm tall; leaves oval to elliptic, mostly 1-2.5 cm long, short-petioled, pubescent or nearly glabrous; bracts, pedicels and the calyx puberulent; flowers in short racemes, white, pink or yellowish; corolla bell-shaped, the tube often hairy within; fruit white, ellipsoid, about 1 cm long.
Dry meadows and open woods and slopes, 4500 to about 5500 feet.

VALERIANACEAE   Valerian Family

Annual or perennial odoriferous herbs with basal and opposite, simple or pinnately compound leaves; flowers small, perfect or imperfect, regular or irregular; calyx limb expanded and pappus-like in fruit, or inconspicuous, or obsolete; corolla tube often spurred or gibbous, the limb usually 5-lobed; stamens 1 to 4, borne on the petals; ovary inferior with 1 fertile 1-ovuled carpel, the other 2 sterile, sometimes obsolete; fruit a nutlet.

Valeriana |Tourn.| L.

Strong-scented perennial herbs with simple to pinnatifid basal and cauline leaves; flowers small, usually numerous in a corymb, panicle or thyrsoid inflorescence; sepals inrolled and inconspicuous at first, spreading and becoming plumose after flowering; corolla funnel- or saucer-shaped, gamopetalous, 5-lobed; stamens 3; ovary with 1 fertile and 2 vestigial carpels; fruit a 1-seeded, nerved nutlet.

Basal leaves thin, divided into mostly 3 to 9 leaflets; inflorescence small..............................*V. sitchensis*
Basal leaves thick, sometimes slightly lobed but not divided into leaflets; inflorescence
large...*V. edulis*

Valeriana edulis Nutt.   Tobacco Root

Robust glabrous perennial with a thick taproot and stems 10-120 cm tall; leaves mostly basal, long-petioled, linear to obovate or oblanceolate, 7-40 cm long, entire or often some with a few lobes; cauline leaves 2 to 6 pairs, smaller, mostly pinnatifid, becoming sessile and reduced upward; inflorescence compact at first, becoming large and expanded after flowering; flowers small, white or pinkish, pistillate on some plants, perfect or staminate on others; sepals 9-13 mm long, plumose; corolla rotate; fruit ovate to ovate-oblong, 2.5-4.5 mm long.
Moist pasture-grasslands and in Ponderosa pine woods, about 5000 to 5300 feet.

Valeriana sitchensis Bong.   Mountain Heliotrope

Fibrous-rooted perennial with an unpleasant odor, from a thick rhizome, glabrous, 35-120 cm tall; lower leaves and the basal when present petioled, mostly with 3 to 9 ovate to obovate, entire to dentate segments, or undivided; cauline leaves mostly 2 to 4 pairs, becoming smaller and sessile upward, the leaflets narrower, entire or toothed; inflorescence compact at first, more expanded and open after flowering; flowers ordinarily all perfect; corolla white or pink-tinged, the lobes half as long as the tube; calyx segments plumose, 12-20 mm long; fruit glabrous, 3-6 mm long.
Moist meadows, bogs and shady coniferous woods, 5000 to about 8000 feet.

CAMPANULACEAE   Bluebell Family

Annual or perennial herbs (ours), sometimes trees or shrubs, with milky juice and alternate simple leaves; flowers perfect, nearly regular; calyx lobes 3 to 5, the tube joined to the ovary; corolla 3- to 5-lobed, regular, gamopetalous; stamens 3 to 5, alternate with the corolla lobes; style 1, the stigma lobes usually as many as the carpels; ovary 1- to 5-celled; ovules numerous to few; fruit a capsule (ours) opening by valves or pores, or a berry; seeds minute, numerous.

Campanula [Tourn.] L.

Annual or perennial herbs (ours) with alternate leaves; flowers showy, solitary, perfect and regular, in racemes or panicles; calyx 5-lobed, the tube joined to the ovary; corolla 5-lobed, blue or white, bell-shaped or rotate; stamens 5, free from the corolla, the filaments usually dilated at the base; ovary inferior, 3- to 5-locular; stigma 3- to 5-lobed; fruit a capsule opening by 3 to 5 pores on its sides.

1. Flowers large and showy, deep blue, several on the rather thick stems; plants large, well
   developed, mostly at low elevations near valley gardens...................................*C. rapunculoides*
1. Flowers smaller and less showy, lighter blue, usually 1 to few on the delicate, slender
   stems; plants small, from low to high elevations in the mountains
   2. Flowers and capsules nodding; plants not hairy...*C. rotundifolia*
   2. Flowers and capsules erect; plants bristly pubescent.......................................*C. scabrella*

Campanula rapunculoides L.   Valley Bluebell

Large, well-developed plants of the valley and foothills, probably garden escapes; leaves well-developed, lanceolate to subcordate, crenate, thick, short-petioled; flowers

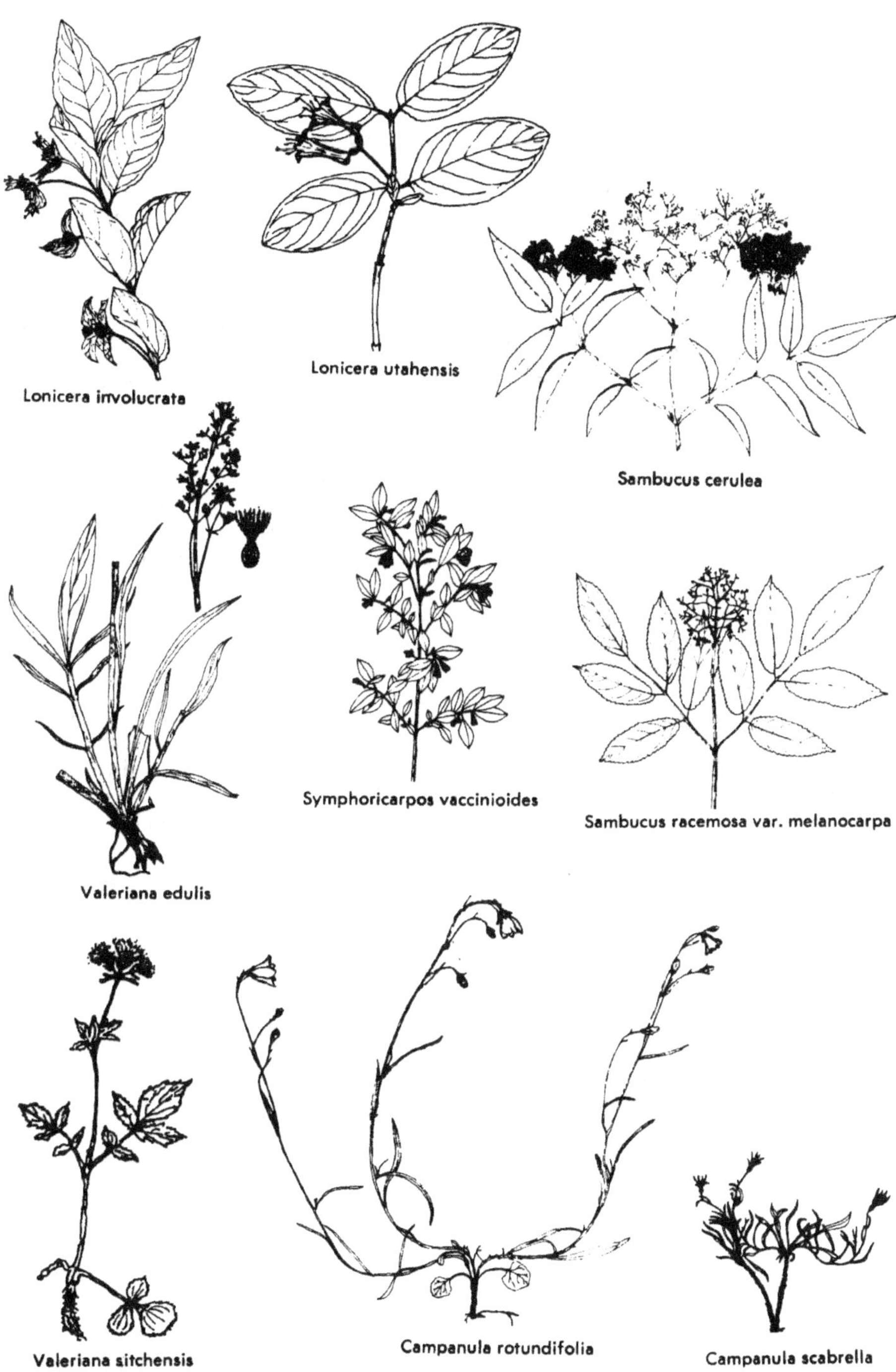

Lonicera involucrata
Lonicera utahensis
Sambucus cerulea
Valeriana edulis
Symphoricarpos vaccinioides
Sambucus racemosa var. melanocarpa
Valeriana sitchensis
Campanula rotundifolia
Campanula scabrella

deep blue, 1.5-3.5 cm long, numerous, showy, scattered in an elongate inflorescence.
mostly 1-sided; calyx lobes turning black.
Introduced Bellflower, often cultivated. Roadside at about 4500 feet.

Campanula rotundifolia L.   Scotch Bluebell

Glabrous perennial with slender spreading or decumbent elongated rootstocks; stems
simple, slender, 10-100 cm tall; basal leaves long-petioled, broadly ovate to subrotund,
mostly toothed, often missing; lower stem leaves short-petioled, oblanceolate, becoming
entire, narrower and sessile upward; flowers solitary or few in loose panicles, erect or
nodding; calyx lobes spreading; corolla blue, 1.5-3 cm long, the tube longer than the
lobes; capsule nodding, opening near the base.
Dry to moist rocky meadows, woods, streambanks, gravel bars, sandy places and rocky
slopes; 5300 to about 9600 feet and possibly higher. Our common bluebell.

Campanula scabrella Engelm.   Rough Harebell

Perennial from a taproot, minutely but densely short-bristly-pubescent throughout:
stems clustered, 3-12 cm tall; leaves 2-5 cm long, thick, entire, oblanceolate and clustered
near the base, becoming lanceolate, narrower and smaller upward; flowers solitary and
terminal, or 2 to 5; sepals subulate; corolla light blue, 6-12 mm long; capsule ellipsoidal
to obconic, opening near the top.
Talus slopes and exposed ridges and cliffs, mostly above 9000 feet. Rare.

COMPOSITAE   Sunflower Family

Annual or perennial herbs or shrubs; leaves opposite or alternate, entire or dissected;
flowers usually borne in a head on a receptacle and encircled by an involucre of bracts
or phyllaries in 1 or more series; receptacle naked or chaffy with small scales, bristles
or bracts among the flowers; heads one to many, mostly of 3 kinds: (a) all the corollas
strap-shaped (rays or ligules) and the head ligulate; (b) all the corollas tubular, 5-lobed,
and the head discoid; or (c) the corollas of both kinds with the ray-flowers surrounding
the central disk of tubular corollas, and the head radiate; corollas perfect or imperfect:
stamens usually 5, borne on the corolla tube and alternating with the corolla lobes, the
elongated anthers united into a tube; ovary inferior; style usually 2-cleft; fruit an achene,
with or without a pappus of scales, teeth, awns or bristles.

1. Petal-like ray-flowers present, white or colored, completely forming the head or only
encircling the central usually yellow disk
  2. Heads without a central disk, composed entirely of perfect ray-flowers, the corollas
5-lobed at the tip, yellow or white
    3. Leaves mostly basal or nearly so, the flowering stems leafless or nearly so
      4. Achenes beaked at the tip; pappus of white or whitish capillary bristles
        5. Heads solitary on the leafless stalk
          6. Achenes spiny near the top, 4- or 5-angled, the beak slender;
final leaf lobe usually quite large..*Taraxacum*
          6. Achenes not spiny near the top, 10-nerved; final leaf lobe
not usually large, though often long ....*Agoseris*
        5. Heads several on the flowering stem; pappus early deciduous, of
whitish or brownish capillary bristles or awns..*Crepis*
      4. Achenes without a beak; pappus of scales or bristles; involucral bracts
unequal

7. Pappus of up to 30 scales, each tipped with a bright white, soft, long, feathery awn; outer involucral bracts much shorter than the inner, usually hairless; heads nodding in bud................................*Microseris*
7. Pappus of many fragile whitish or brownish bristles; involucral bracts blackish-hairy and with gray star-like hair clusters....*Hieracium gracile*
3. Leaves mostly alternate on the stem, often with some also at the base
  8. Heads large, solitary on the branches; flowers yellow; pappus of white or golden feathery bristles forming a round globe; achenes with a thick beak; leaves sometimes cobwebby near the base................................*Tragopogon*
  8. Heads small, on slender stalks in an open inflorescence; flowers yellow or white; pappus of whitish to brownish capillary bristles; achenes without a beak................................*Hieracium*
2. Heads with a central yellow disk surrounded by petal-like ray flowers; disk flowers tubular
  9. Rays mostly yellow or orange, 2- and 3-toothed at the tip; pappus conspicuous or poorly developed or none
    10. Involucral bracts equal, in 1 "fence-like" series around the head
      11. Plants whitish-cobwebby-hairy; receptacle naked; pappus inconspicuous if present................................*Eriophyllum*
      11. Plants green, sometimes hairy but not cobwebby; pappus various
        12. Involucral bracts glandular, surrounding and enclosing the ray achenes; pappus inconspicuous................................*Madia*
        12. Involucral bracts not glandular, usually narrow, often brownish or blackish at the tip, not enclosing the achenes; pappus conspicuous, of many capillary bristles................................*Senecio*
    10. Involucral bracts in more than 1 series, unequal, not strictly "fence-like," the outer ones often larger than the inner ones and leaf-like
      13. Heads small, often numerous in the inflorescence, rarely few or solitary; pappus of capillary bristles
        14. Leaves basal, narrow; flowering stems essentially leafless............*Erigeron*
        14. Leaves numerous on the flowering stems, often toothed, the basal mostly early deciduous................................*Solidago*
      13. Heads medium-sized to large, mostly solitary to few; pappus of capillary bristles, or none (or a crown in *Anthemis tinctoria*)
        15. Plants rather coarse, large, the flowering stems mostly over 30 cm tall
          16. Leaves mainly basal, those on the flowering stems few and reduced
            17. Rays 25-40 mm long; basal leaves triangular or heart-shaped at the base of the blade, often whitish-hairy....*Balsamorhiza*
            17. Rays inconspicuous, usually not over 12 mm long; basal leaves elliptic, tapered at the base of the blade, usually green................................*Haplopappus*
          16. Leaves mostly on the flowering stems though some often basal as well
            18. Leaves toothed and petiolate; pappus of 2 or more deciduous scale-like awns; heads usually more than 1................................*Helianthus*
            18. Leaves not toothed, the petioles very short or missing; pappus of 2 short persistent awns with scales in between; head usually solitary................................*Helianthella*
        15. Plants smaller, not so coarse, mostly under 30 cm tall
          19. Leaves opposite; pappus of whitish or brownish capillary bristles................................*Arnica*
          19. Leaves alternate
            20. Pappus of numerous white to brownish bristles

21. Plants shrubs or woody-based herbs; pappus
bristles unequal but all in one series................*Haplopappus*
21. Plants herbs; pappus of 2 series, the outer much
shorter than the inner..*Chrysopsis*
20. Pappus poorly developed, of membranous scales, or
a short crown or not developed (see also *Anthemis
tinctoria*)
22. Pappus of several nerveless scales joined at the
base and forming a ring; densely glandular-hairy
perennial plants..*Hulsea*
22. Pappus of small knobs at the top of the achene;
resinous plants, not hairy or glandular; involucral
bracts conspicuously curved................................*Grindelia*
9. Rays white, pink, blue, purple or red but not yellow or orange; disk flowers
tubular; pappus well or poorly developed, or missing
23. Pappus developed on some or all the achenes
24. Pappus of the disk flowers partly or entirely of capillary bristles
25. Involucral bracts mostly unequal, curved outward and overlapping, with green tips and often whitish bases, or green and
leaf-like throughout; central disk often small
26. Plants with a taproot..............................*Machaeranthera*
26. Plants with rhizomes or fibrous roots.........................*Aster*
25. Involucral bracts about equal, often green but not definitely
leaf-like, not whitish at the base; central disk usually larger
27. Rays very short and narrow, about equaling the pappus.........*Conyza*
27. Rays narrow or wider but mostly longer than the pappus
of the disk flowers..*Erigeron*
24. Pappus of the disk flowers of about 10 or more flattened bristle-like
scales; involucral bracts closely fringed........................*Townsendia*
23. Pappus none, or poorly developed and inconspicuous
28. Rays very large, 1.5-5 cm long, white or creamy; leaves not lobed.......*Wyethia*
28. Rays smaller; leaves usually toothed or lobed
29. Leaves dissected into many lobes or narrow segments; rays
white
30. Rays 10 or more, 5-11 mm long; annual with an unpleasant
odor..*Anthemis*
30. Rays only 3 to 5, less than 5 mm long; plant a perennial.......*Achillea*
29. Leaves sometimes toothed but not lobed.................*Chrysanthemum*
1. Petal-like ray-flowers missing or poorly developed
31. Pappus well developed on some or all the achenes, of capillary bristles, sometimes
with additional outer scales
32. Receptacle with some bristles among the disk corollas, or the leaves spiny and
thistle-like, or both
33. Leaves thistle-like with spiny margins; plants mostly of dry sunny places....... *Cirsium*
33. Leaves not thistle-like or spiny; involucral bracts unequal, pale with dark
tips and margins, the outer shorter and wider than the inner; plants of
moist meadows and bogs..*Saussurea*
32. Receptacle without bristles among the disk flowers; leaves not spiny
34. Involucral bracts thin, dry, membranous, translucent, colorless or whitish
or slightly tinged with pink sometimes; leaves and stems often woolly-hairy
35. Plants with a taproot; outer flowers numerous and pistillate, the inner
few and with both stamens and pistils.................................*Gnaphalium*
35. Plants fibrous-rooted, often with rhizomes or stolons
36. Pappus bristles of the pistillate flowers united at the base and
falling off as a ring; basal leaves well developed, persistent, often
tufted...*Antennaria*

36. Pappus bristles not united, falling separately; basal leaves early
   deciduous; flowering stem quite leafy________________*Anaphalis*
34. Involucral bracts green, at least partially, sometimes whitish at the base;
   leaves and stems not evidently woolly-hairy
   37. Plants shrubby or woody at the base
      38. Involucral bracts arranged in several series, in vertical rows;
         leaves very narrow________________*Chrysothamnus*
      38. Involucral bracts in several series but not in vertical rows; leaves
         narrow or wider
         39. Head mostly solitary; involucre 15-30 mm high________*Haplopappus*
         39. Heads usually several; involucral bracts striped, the involucre
            10-20 mm high________*Brickellia*
   37. Plants herbaceous, not woody-based usually
      40. Plants annual; involucral bracts unequal, in more than 1 series,
         mostly overlapping________*Conyza*
      40. Plants biennial to perennial; involucral bracts in 1 or more series
         41. Involucral bracts equal and in 1 series, sometimes "picket
            fence-like"
            42. Leaves opposite; heads medium-sized________*Arnica*
            42. Leaves alternate or basal; heads small________*Senecio*
         41. Involucral bracts usually in 2 or more series, often over-
            lapping
            43. Involucral bracts striped; flowers cream-colored________*Brickellia*
            43. Involucral bracts not striped
               44. Pappus in 2 or more series, the outer much shorter
                  than the inner
                  45. Bracts unequal, not conspicuously
                     overlapping________*Erigeron*
                  45. Bracts clearly overlapping________*Chrysopsis*
               44. Pappus in 1 series, the bristles not always equal in
                  length
                  46. Pappus bristles unequal in length________*Haplopappus*
                  46. Pappus bristles all about equal, sometimes with
                     a few short ones also, at the top of the achene
                     47. Involucral bracts clearly overlapping
                        48. Involucral bracts unequal, conspicu-
                           ously overlapping, the green tips curved
                           and spreading, the base whitish____*Machaeranthera*
                        48. Involucral bracts with straight tips,
                           the base not whitish; plants with a
                           sweet odor________*Eupatorium*
                     47. Involucral bracts not clearly overlapping,
                        the base mostly green________*Erigeron*
31. Pappus inconspicuous, poorly developed, of a crown or border of small scales, or
   missing; rays none or vestigial
   49. Inflorescence large with many small heads; leaves lobed or toothed, or entire
      50. Involucral bracts spiny; pappus missing________*Centaurea diffusa*
      50. Involucral bracts not spiny; pappus a short crown or missing; plants
         usually aromatic________*Artemisia*
   49. Inflorescence smaller with 1 to few small to medium-sized heads; leaves toothed
      or lobed or dissected
      51. Receptacle cone-like, pointed at the itp
         52. Plant with an odor of pineapple, the leaves much dissected; receptacle
            green________*Matricaria*
         52. Plants without pineapple odor, the leaves large, toothed; receptacle
            brownish-black________*Rudbeckia*

<pre>
51. Receptacle not cone-like; leaves lobed or toothed
    53. Flowering stems appearing leafless, the leaves mostly basal, wavy-
        margined, white underneath; flowers white.........................Adenocaulon
    53. Flowering stems leafy; flowers pinkish or yellow
        54. Involucral bracts conspicuously curved and downward-spreading,
            the involucre thick; flowers yellow; leaves toothed...............Grindelia
        54. Involucral bracts erect, not curved or spreading; flowers pinkish;
            leaves lobed...Chaenactis
</pre>

Achillea L.

Perennial herbs with alternate, nearly entire to pinnately dissected leaves and small heads of flowers in a terminal corymb-like inflorescence; involucral bracts scarious, in several series; ray flowers white or pinkish, pistillate and fertile; disk flowers perfect; receptacle chaffy, conic or convex; achenes flattened, glabrous, callous-margined; pappus none.

Achillea millefolium L. Common Yarrow

Aromatic woolly-villose perennial from rhizomes; stems 5-70 cm tall; leaves deep green, pinnately dissected, the cauline sessile and auriculate, the basal petioled; heads numerous, radiate, in a flat- to round-topped inflorescence; rays 3 to 8, white or pink; disk flowers 10 to 40.

Dry rocky slopes, grasslands and talus, 4500 to about 9600 feet.

Plants 5-40 cm tall; heads few; margins of involucral bracts dark brown or nearly black; on rocky slopes, talus and exposed places, mostly over 8000 feet elevation...var. **alpicola** (Rydb.) Garrett

Plants 30-100 cm tall; heads numerous; margins of the involucral bracts pale to brownish; grassy slopes and open ground from low to middle elevations...var. **lanulosa** (Nutt.) Piper

Adenocaulon Hook.

Annual or perennial herbs with large alternate leaves and small heads; corollas tubular, the 3 to 7 outer ones pistillate, the inner staminate; involucral bracts 10, green; receptacle naked; pappus none; achenes large and glandular.

Adenocaulon bicolor Hook. Pathfinder

Perennial 30-90 cm tall; leaves long-petioled, mostly near the base, 3-15 cm wide, the blades large, thin, triangular to ovate, glabrous above, white-woolly beneath; inflorescence paniculate, the peduncles glandular; heads very small, discoid; flowers whitish; involucral bracts 4 or 5, spreading or reflexed in fruit; receptacle naked; achenes glandular above; pappus none.

Moist shady woods and thickets, 4500 to about 5000 feet.

Agoseris Raf.

Acaulescent annual or perennial herbs with milky juice and a taproot; leaves in a basal rosette, entire to pinnatifid; scapes 1 to several, usually longer than the leaves; heads mostly solitary, ligulate, yellow, pinkish or burnt orange; involucre bell-shaped, the bracts (phyllaries) in 2 to 5 series; receptacle naked or chaffy; achenes about 10-

nerved, usually distinctly long-beaked when mature (beakless in one variety of *A. glauca*); pappus bristles silky-white to dull tan-ish, longer than the achene.

1. Petal-like outer corollas of the head (rays or ligules) burnt orange or pinkish; plants perennial..*A. aurantiaca*
1. Petal-like ligules yellow; plants annual or perennial
    2. Plants slender annuals; hairs of the involucre long, twisted, sometimes purplish and glandular...*A. heterophylla*
    2. Plants stronger perennials; involucre hairless or with short fine tangled hairs
        3. Flower heads large, 2.2-4 cm high; beak of the achene 2 to 4 times as long as the body of the achene..*A. grandiflora*
        3. Flower heads usually less than 2 cm high; beak from nearly undeveloped to about half as long as the achene body...*A. glauca*

Agoseris aurantiaca (Hook.) Greene   Orange-flowered Agoseris

Perennial 18-40 cm tall, glabrous or villose; leaves variable, basal, linear-lanceolate to oblanceolate, entire or toothed, or with a few oblong lobes; heads few-flowered, burnt orange or pinkish, conspicuously white-woolly at the base; involucral bracts narrow and pointed, sometimes purple-spotted; achene 5-9 mm long, the beak from half as long as the achene to slightly longer; pappus silky-white to tan-ish.
Woodlands, often near water, 4800 to about 8000 feet.

Agoseris glauca (Pursh) Raf.   Short-beaked Agoseris

Slender perennial, sometimes glaucous, 10-70 cm tall, with a long heavy taproot; leaves lanceolate to oblanceolate, 5-35 cm long, mostly glabrous, entire to somewhat toothed or lobed, usually much shorter than the scapes; heads yellow, often drying pinkish; involucral bracts 1-3 cm high, often purple-spotted; achenes 5-12 mm long, gradually tapering into a thick, striate beak up to about half as long as the achene (rarely nearly beakless); pappus 10-16 mm long.
Meadows and open woods, 5000 to about 8400 feet.

1. Plants glabrous; leaves not lobed or toothed...var. **glauca**
1. Plants hairy at least in and below the involucre; leaves various
    2. Plants mostly over 25 cm tall; outer involucral bracts pinkish in part...var. **agrestis** (Osterh.) Q. Jones
    2. Plants mostly less than 25 cm tall; involucral bracts not usually pinkish..var. **monticola** (Greene) Q. Jones

Agoseris grandiflora (Nutt.) Greene   Large-flowered Agoseris

Perennial 20-60 cm tall; leaves variable, linear to oblanceolate, entire to deeply and irregularly pinnatifid; scapes coarse, ribbed, somewhat pubescent; heads large, many-flowered, 2.2-4 cm high; involucral bracts tomentose, in 4 or 5 series, the outer ciliate, broader and shorter than the inner ones; corollas yellow, shorter than the involucre, often drying pinkish; achenes spindle-shaped, about 4-7 mm long, tapering to a filiform nerveless beak 2 to 4 times as long as the achene body; pappus 8-12 mm long.
Open grassy places at about 5000 feet.

Agoseris heterophylla (Nutt.) Greene   Annual Agoseris

Slender annual, 6-20 cm tall, crisp-hairy, often appearing to be caulescent; leaves oblanceolate, entire to denticulate or lobed, sometimes developed above the basal rosette;

scapes several, glabrous or pubescent, glandular-pubescent beneath the heads; involucral bracts in 2 series, 1-2 cm long in fruit, villous with twisted many-celled hairs, some of them purplish and glandular; flowers closing by afternoon, yellow, often turning pinkish in drying; achenes 2-5 mm long, 10-ribbed or the ribs missing; beak slender, about 2 or 3 times as long as the achene body.
Dry open grassy woods, 4500 to about 5800 feet, or so.

Anaphalis DC.

White-woolly perennials with running rootstocks; leaves entire, alternate, the lower ones often deciduous; heads numerous, many-flowered, imperfect, in small cymose panicles; involucral bracts white and papery, in several series; receptacle naked; staminate flowers tubular with undivided style; pistillate flowers tubular and filiform with 2-cleft style; pappus bristles capillary.

Anaphalis margaritacea (L.) Benth. & Hook.   Pearly Everlasting

White-woolly perennial with running rootstocks; stems solitary, 20-100 cm tall; leaves numerous, linear to oblanceolate, sessile, usually tomentose beneath but green and nearly glabrous above, the margins often rolled under; heads many in a rounded cymose panicle; involucre 5-10 mm high, woolly at the base, the bracts white and papery, sometimes with a blackish-brown spot at the base; achenes small, stiff-hairy.
Meadows, open woods, and along streams and lakes, about 5000 to 8200 feet, and possibly higher.

Antennaria Gaertn.

White-woolly dioecious perennials, often forming mats; leaves mostly entire, alternate, the basal more abundant, the cauline reduced upward; heads discoid, small, many-flowered; involucral bracts in several series, scarious at the tips, often woolly below, white or colored; receptacle naked; staminate flowers with undivided style, scanty pappus and with the tips of the bristles often dilated; pistillate flowers with bifid style and pappus of many capillary bristles united at the base and falling in a ring; achenes nearly terete.

1. Heads many in the flower cluster
    2. Leaves green on the upper surface, conspicuously hairy underneath; inflorescence not crowded, the heads on slender glandular stalks ....*A. racemosa*
    2. Leaves white-cobwebby-hairy on both sides
        3. Plants stoloniferous and with many rosettes of spreading basal leaves, forming mats
            4. Tips of the outer involucral bracts brownish or blackish-green; stem leaf tips with a brownish, membranous appendage
                5. Tips of the involucral bracts blackish-green, usually sharp-pointed....*A. alpina*
                5. Tips of the involucral bracts brownish, usually blunt...............*A. umbrinella*
            4. Tips of the outer involucral bracts white or deep pink; stem leaves without an appendage at the tip..*A. rosea*
        3. Plants not with runners, and without rosettes of leaves matted at the base, though sometimes very leafy at the base
            6. Involucre sometimes hairy at the base and on the outer bracts, the inner ones not hairy; stems often more than 1 from a woody branching leafy base ....*A. luzuloides*
            6. Involucre densely hairy at the base and on some of the inner bracts; flowering stem usually solitary, the base not so leafy

<pre>
   7. Involucre greenish or whitish; plants 20-50 cm tall; lower leaves
       6-15 cm long, 3- to 5-nerved; stigma equaling the pappus........A. anaphaloides
   7. Involucre blackish; plants mostly under 20 cm tall; lower leaves
       2-6 cm long, 3-nerved; stem leaves with a brownish appendage at
       the tip; stigma shorter than the pappus........................A. lanata
1. Head solitary on the stem; plants very small, stems up to 4 cm tall; stolons long and
   thin ....A. flagellaris
</pre>

Antennaria alpina (L.) Gaertn.   Alpine Everlasting

A. media Greene

Low, mat-forming stoloniferous perennial, gray-tomentose; stems 1-10 cm tall; basal leaves mostly oblanceolate, up to 2.5 cm long, usually apiculate, loosely gray-tomentose on both sides or becoming glabrate and glandular-puberulent; cauline leaves few, linear, pubescent, small, with a dark brown appendage 1-2 mm long at the tip; heads few in a dense cluster; involucral bracts sharp-pointed, very dark greenish-black or -brown, the tips sometimes striate, white or tan; achenes mostly papillose; pappus of the staminate flowers dilated at the tips.

Moist meadows at about 7000 to 9000 feet.

Antennaria anaphaloides Rydb.   Tall Everlasting

Tomentose perennial with slender rootstocks; stems usually solitary, 20-50 cm tall; leaves lanceolate, lanate on both sides, 3- to 5-nerved, the basal petioled, the cauline few, nearly sessile, reduced upward, the tips sometimes scarious-appendaged; heads several to many in an open inflorescence; involucre whitish, 7-8 mm high, the tips rounded, white, pinkish or brownish and usually with a small dark spot at the base; achenes glabrous; tips of the staminate pappus bristles dilated.

Grassy open woods and slopes, about 4500 to 5000 feet.

Antennaria flagellaris Gray   Dwarf Spreading Everlasting

Dwarf, silky-tomentose slender plants; stems solitary or clustered; stolons filiform, purplish, naked, erect at first, later spreading or prostrate, each bearing a terminal leafy propagative bud; leaves gray-tomentose, linear, 1-3 cm long; heads solitary on very short erect stems; pistillate involucres greenish-brown or reddish-tinged; staminate involucres blackish-brown; pistillate achenes papillate; staminate pappus barbellate upwards.

Dry stony open slopes and woods, at about 6000 to 6100 feet.

Antennaria lanata (Hook.) Greene   Grayish Everlasting

Densely gray-tomentose perennials; stems leafy, mostly 10-20 cm tall; basal leaves oblanceolate, tufted, 2-10 cm long, 3-veined; cauline leaves narrower, reduced upward, the upper ones often with a brownish scarious appendage at the darkened tips; heads in a small compact cyme; pistillate involucres 5-8 mm high, the staminate smaller; involucral bracts dark brown or blackish-green and tomentose near the base, the tips pale or whitish; achenes glabrous; staminate pappus-bristles dilated at the tips.

Meadows, often near water, and open rocky slopes, 7200 to 9600 feet and probably higher.

Antennaria luzuloides Torr. & Gray   Woody Everlasting

Gray-tomentose perennial, woody at the base; stems 10-70 cm tall; leaves 3-nerved,

4-8 cm long, linear to oblanceolate, nearly sessile, the upper reduced; heads small, several to many in a close inflorescence; involucres glabrous except at the very base; bracts scarious, pale greenish or brownish, the tips sometimes white, rarely pink; tips of the staminate bristles dilated and serrulate.
Moist rocky hillsides, 4500 to about 7000 feet.

Antennaria racemosa Hook.   Slender Everlasting

Perennial with slender creeping leafy stolons; stems 10-60 cm tall; leaves elliptic to obovate, green and glabrous above, tomentose beneath, the lower ones petioled, 2-10 cm long, 1- to 3-nerved, the upper ones narrow and sessile; heads on slender glandular peduncles, usually in an open raceme; involucres nearly glabrous, 4-8 mm high, the bracts greenish or brownish with whitish tips; achenes glabrous; stigma equaling or longer than the pappus.
Mountain slopes and open woods near streams, 4700 to about 6800 feet.

Antennaria rosea Greene   Rosy Everlasting

Low mat-forming perennial with creeping leafy stolons, floccose-tomentose throughout; stems 7-35 cm tall; lower leaves spatulate, 1-nerved, 1-3.5 cm long; cauline leaves numerous, the upper ones with colored tips; heads several in a small close inflorescence; pistillate involucres 4-7 mm high, the staminate shorter; involucral bracts greenish or brownish at the base, the scarious tips pale or deep pink or white; achenes glabrous; tips of the staminate pappus bristles dilated.
Moist to dry open woods and meadows, 4500 to about 9200 feet.

Antennaria umbrinella Rydb.   Brown Everlasting

Cespitose stoloniferous perennial, gray-tomentose; stems 6-15 cm tall; lower leaves oblanceolate or spatulate; cauline leaves narrow, the tips tapered or with a colored appendage; heads 2 to 5 in a close cluster; pistillate involucres 4-6 mm high; bracts greenish, brownish or blackish-green, woolly at the base, the tips striate, brownish to white; staminate involucres shorter, brownish or white; staminate pappus bristles dilated at the tips.
Moist to dry grassy meadows and steep rocky slopes, 5200 to about 9800 feet, or so.

Anthemis L.

Annual or perennial aromatic herbs; stems leafy; leaves alternate, pinnatifid; heads solitary at the ends of the branches; rays white or yellow; involucral bracts dry, scarious, in several series or sometimes about equal; receptacle chaffy; ray flowers pistillate; disk flowers perfect; achenes ribbed, ellipsoid; pappus a short crown, or none.

1. Petal-like rays (ligules) white
     2. Rays 10 to 15, rounded or notched at the tip; plant with a strong odor......................... *A. cotula*
     2. Rays 15-20, 2-cleft or straight across at the tip; plant without an odor above the
        root..*A. arvensis*
1. Petal-like rays yellow..*A. tinctoria*

Anthemis arvensis L.   Field Chamomile

Leafy annual, the root with an unpleasant odor; stems often decumbent, 10-60 cm tall; leaves 3-5 cm long, bi-pinnatifid; heads solitary at the ends of the branches; involucral bracts hairy-tomentose; receptacle chaffy top to bottom, the bracts awn-tipped;

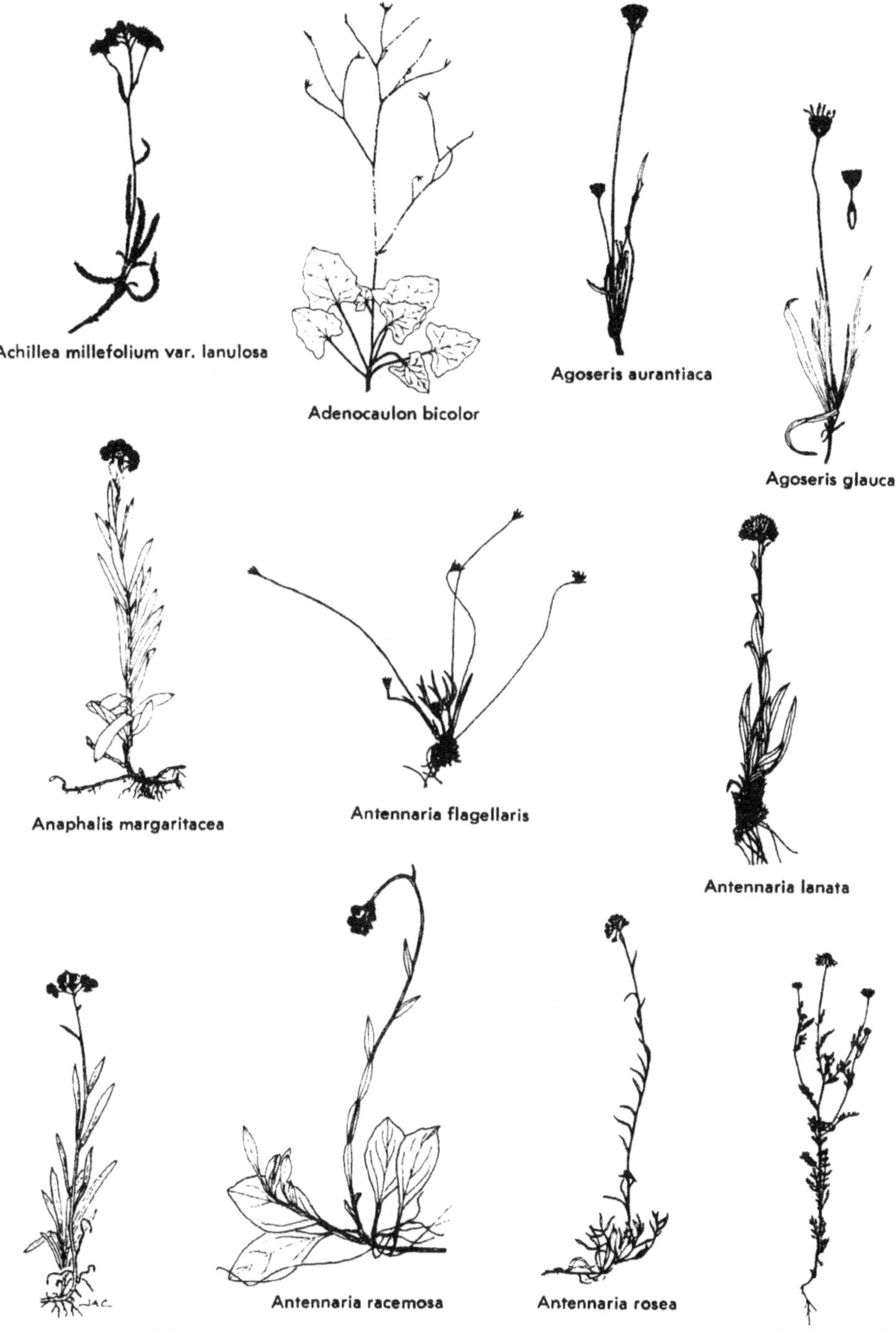

Achillea millefolium var. lanulosa
Adenocaulon bicolor
Agoseris aurantiaca
Agoseris glauca
Anaphalis margaritacea
Antennaria flagellaris
Antennaria lanata
Antennaria luzuloides
Antennaria racemosa
Antennaria rosea
Anthemis arvensis

rays white, pistillate, fertile; achenes smooth and quadrangular; pappus a minute crown, or none.
Campground, 4900 feet.

Anthemis cotula L.   Dog Fennel

Leafy annual with a strong unpleasant odor; stems 10-60 cm tall; leaves pinnatifid, 2-6 cm long; heads numerous on short peduncles at the ends of the branches; rays white, sterile, 6-10 mm long; receptacle scaly only above the middle; achene ribs tuberculate; pappus none.
Introduced weed at campgrounds and roadsides, about 5000 to 5600 feet.

Anthemis tinctoria L.   Yellow Chamomile

Perennial, 30-90 cm tall; leaves 2-5 cm long, pinnatifid, the rachis winged; heads solitary, large, on long peduncles; involucres villose-tomentose; rays yellow, pistillate, fertile; receptacle chaffy, the bracts awned, yellow-tipped; achenes quadrangular, smooth or striate; pappus a short crown.
Garden escape. Collected near the Power House, 4600 feet.

Arnica L.

Perennials; leaves mostly opposite; heads 1 to several, large, mostly radiate (discoid in *A. parryi*) ; ray-flowers few, pistillate and fertile; disk-flowers perfect and fertile; corollas yellow or orange; involucral bracts in 1 or 2 series, about equal in length; receptacle naked; achenes slender, 5- to 10-nerved; pappus of white or brownish capillary bristles, barbellate to subplumose.

1. Heads with petal-like rays around the central disk
    2. Stem leaves mostly 5 to 12 pairs
        3. Leaves toothed; stems solitary or few..*A. amplexicaulis*
        3. Leaves usually not toothed; stems many..*A. longifolia*
    2. Stem leaves mostly 1 to 4 pairs
        4. Pappus brownish, feathery
            5. Rays about 8, or about 13; middle leaves usually the largest, with broad
               petioles..*A. diversifolia*
            5. Rays mostly 12 to 18; lower leaves petioled, usually the largest, the
               middle ones smaller, without broad petioles..*A. mollis*
        4. Pappus white or whitish, not feathery
            6. Lower leaves broad, conspicuously toothed, long-petioled, faintly few-
             nerved
               7. Lower leaves usually heart-shaped; involucres long-hairy at the
                  base; common in the woods..*A. cordifolia*
               7. Lower leaves seldom heart-shaped; involucres with few or no long
                  hairs at the base; not common in the woods..*A. latifolia*
            6. Lower leaves narrow, scarcely petioled, toothless or sometimes slightly
             toothed, conspicuously several-nerved
               8. Heads large, rays 10 to 23; species of low elevations..*A. sororia*
               8. Heads smaller, rays usually 7 to 10; usually at higher elevations....*A. rydbergii*
1. Heads with a yellow disk but without ray-flowers; leaves few; stems often purplish at the
  base..*A. parryi*

Arnica amplexicaulis Nutt.   Clasping Arnica

Perennial, glandular and usually hairy; stems clustered, 30-80 cm tall; cauline leaves 4 to 10 pairs, elliptic, sessile, little reduced upward, toothed, mostly 4-12 cm long; heads

1 to 5 on long peduncles; involucre 9-15 mm high; rays 8 to 14, pale yellow, 1-2 cm long; achenes slightly hairy and sometimes glandular; pappus brownish, subplumose. Moist woods and sheltered stony places near water, 5900 to about 8000 feet.

Arnica cordifolia Hook.   Heart-leaved Arnica

Glandular-pubescent to white-hairy perennial; stems usually solitary, mostly 10-60 cm tall; basal leaves clustered on short shoots; cauline leaves mostly 2 to 4 pairs, the lower larger, petioled, cordate, unevenly toothed, 4-12 cm long and 3-9 cm wide, the upper smaller and sessile; heads 1 to 3; involucres mostly 13-20 mm high, glandular and white-hairy especially toward the base; rays bright yellow, mostly 10 to 16, sometimes missing, 1.5-3 cm long; achenes short-hairy or glandular, or both; pappus silvery-white, barbellate, longer than the achene.

Moist meadows, lake shores and shady woods, about 5500 to 8200 feet.

Dwarf perennial of higher elevations, mostly under 25 cm tall; leaves narrower, often entire, scarcely cordate, 2-5 cm long; achenes glandular; exposed places at about 8400 to 9200 feet..var. **pumila** (Rydb.) Maguire

Arnica diversifolia Greene   Varied-leaved Arnica

Glandular-puberulent to nearly glabrous perennial thought to be a hybrid; stem solitary or in loose tufts, 15-40 cm tall; cauline leaves 2 to 4 pairs, blades ovate to elliptic, irregularly toothed, 4-8 cm long and 2-6 cm wide, the middle pair of leaves usually the largest, the petioles winged or the leaves sessile; heads usually several, narrow, turbinate, the disk-flowers few; involucres 10-14 mm high, glandular and sometimes also sparsely hairy; rays light yellow, usually about 8 or about 13, 1.5-2 cm long; achenes pubescent; pappus straw-colored to pale brownish, subplumose.

Base of cliffs and among granite rocks and boulders, often near water, 6900 to about 9000 feet.

Arnica latifolia Bong.   Mountain Arnica

Glandular-pubescent to nearly glabrous perennial; stems 10-60 cm tall, solitary or few together; cauline leaves 2 to 4 pairs, glandular and hairy to nearly glabrous, sessile or petioled, lance-elliptic or broader, toothed, sometimes cordate, 2-14 cm long and 1.5-8 cm wide, the middle pairs the largest or as large as the lower ones; heads 1 or 3 or more, the peduncles glandular; involucres 7-18 mm high, glandular; rays about 2 cm long; achenes generally glabrous but often hairy and glandular; pappus white, barbellate.

Plants 10-60 cm tall, of moist woods and meadows at lower to middle elevations in the mountains..var. **latifolia**
Plants 10-30 cm tall, tufted; heads small, narrow, often up to 9, densely and finely glandular in the involucre; leaves rarely over 2.5 cm wide....var. **gracilis** (Rydb.) Cronq.
                                              (*A. gracilis* Rydb.)

Moist mossy cliffs and other rocky places, 4500 to about 9000 feet.

Arnica longifolia D. C. Eat.   Long-leaved Arnica

Plants in large dense patches; stems clustered, the flowering ones 30-60 cm tall, the sterile ones shorter; leaves all cauline, 5 to 12 pairs, 2-15 cm long and 1-2 cm wide, nearly entire, narrowly lanceolate, the upper sessile and clasping, the lower often reduced, short-

petioled and sheathing; heads 3 to many; involucres 7-10 mm high, glandular-puberulent, sometimes also with some long hairs; rays 8 to 13, light yellow, 1-2 cm long;
achenes glandular and hairy, or glabrous; pappus brownish.
Among rocks and boulders of cliffs, rock slides, seeps, meadows and moist banks, 5000
to about 8000 feet.

Arnica mollis Hook. Fragrant Arnica

Glandular-hairy perennial; stems 20-60 cm tall; cauline leaves 3 to 5 pairs, irregularly
toothed or nearly entire, ovate or elliptic to oblanceolate, the lower ones usually the
largest, all sessile or the lower ones short-petioled; basal leaves often well-developed;
heads solitary or few, the disk sometimes up to 3.5 cm wide; involucres 10-16 mm high,
long-hairy at the base, glandular above; rays 12 to 18, light yellow, 1.2-2.5 cm long;
achenes sparsely pubescent; pappus brownish, subplumose.
Moist cliffs, rock slides and banks of streams and lakes, about 4500 to 9200 feet.

Arnica parryi Gray Nodding Arnica

Perennial, glandular above, woolly-villous below; stems solitary, 20-60 cm tall;
cauline leaves mostly 2 to 4 pairs, much reduced upwards, lanceolate or lance-ovate,
glandular and soft-hairy, the lower ones with sheathing petioles; heads mostly 3 to 9,
nodding in bud, erect later; rays none; involucres 10-14 mm high, glandular-hairy;
achenes glabrous, pubescent or glandular; pappus brownish.
Moist shady woods and slopes, 5600 to about 9000 feet.

Arnica rydbergii Greene Subalpine Arnica

Perennial; glandular and short-hairy or nearly glabrous; stems often clustered, 10-30
cm tall; leaves mostly lanceolate, crowded near the base, 3- to 5-nerved, 3-10 cm long,
nearly entire, the cauline 3 to 4 pairs sessile, reduced upward, the lower ones petioled
and sometimes also on separate short shoots; heads solitary or few; involucral bracts
9-12 mm high, glandular and long-hairy to nearly glabrous, the margins ciliate or scabrous; rays about 8, 1-2 cm long; achenes densely hairy; pappus white or yellowish.
Dry rocky open places, 7000 to about 8500 feet and probably higher.

Arnica sororia Greene Twin Arnica

Slender, glandular-hairy perennials; stems 20-60 cm tall; leaves nearly entire, 3- to
5-nerved, elliptic to oblanceolate, 3-12 cm long, sometimes white-woolly in the axils, the
basal petioled, the 2 to 4 cauline pairs far apart, becoming reduced and sessile upward;
heads 1 to 3; involucral bracts mostly about 1 cm high, the tips acute; rays 10 to 23;
pappus white.
Moist to dry open rocky places, about 4500 to 7000 feet.

Artemisia L.

Herbs or shrubs, usually aromatic; leaves alternate, entire to dissected; heads discoid,
small, clustered, arranged in spikes, racemes or panicles; involucral bracts dry, overlapping, scarious; receptacle naked or with many long hairs; flowers all perfect or
sometimes the marginal ones pistillate and the central flowers either fertile or sterile;
achenes ovoid, usually glabrous; pappus none.

1. Plants shrubs, woody at the base
    2. Leaves deeply divided into 3 to 5 very narrow leaflets; heads without stalks................*A. rigida*
    2. Leaves not deeply divided, but mostly with 3 shallow teeth at the tip (rarely 5 teeth) ; at least some of the heads with a short stalk................................*A. tridentata*
1. Plants herbs, not woody usually (sometimes in *A. absinthium*)
    3. Leaves mostly narrowly oblong, not toothed or lobed, numerous on the stems; disk-flowers sterile..*A. dracunculus*
    3. Leaves wider, mostly lobed; disk-flowers fertile
        4. Leaves dissected into very many narrow lobes
            5. Receptacle with long hairs between the flowers; plants sometimes woody at the base; inflorescence large with very many nodding heads............*A. absinthium*
            5. Receptacle without hairs; plants not woody-based
                6. Leaves with 1 or 2 pairs of small, stipule-like lobes at the base; inflorescence open; plants of low elevations................................*A. vulgaris*
                6. Leaves without stipule-like lobes at the base; inflorescence long and narrow; plants of high elevations................................*A. michauxiana*
        4. Leaves with fewer wider lobes, or not lobed at all
            7. Involucre longer than broad; leaves often grayish-hairy................*A. ludoviciana*
            7. Involucre shorter than broad, purplish or green; leaves usually green and shining on the upper surface................................*A. tilesii*

Artemisia absinthium L.   Absinthe; Wormwood

Fragrant perennial herb, sometimes woody at the base; stems 40-100 cm tall; leaves silky-canescent, the lower 3-12 cm long, petioled, rounded-ovate, 2 or 3 times pinnatifid into obtuse lobes, the upper smaller with fewer, more acute lobes; heads many, nodding, in a large panicle; involucres 2-3 mm high and much wider; marginal and inner flowers all fertile; receptacle with many long hairs; achenes cylindric, glabrous.
Dry fields and open woodlands, about 4500 feet.

Artemisia dracunculus L.   Tarragon; Dragon Sagewort

Perennial herb, strongly aromatic to nearly odorless; stems 50-150 cm tall; leaves mostly linear, 2-8 cm long, entire or a few cleft, sessile, glabrous to silky-canescent; heads many, nodding, in a large leafy panicle; involucre hemispheric, 2-3 mm high and about as wide; outer flowers pistillate and fertile, the disk-flowers sterile; receptacle glabrous; achenes glabrous.
Dry rocky open places and streambanks, 4500 to about 5100 feet.

Artemisia ludoviciana Nutt.   Prairie Sagewort

Aromatic perennial herb; stems 30-100 cm tall; leaves 3-10 cm long, white-tomentose on both sides or becoming green and glabrate on the upper surface, lanceolate to oblanceolate or elliptic, entire or the margins lobed and toothed especially near the base; heads many in a dense narrow elongate panicle, sometimes more open; involucre 3-4 mm high, 2-3 mm wide, usually tomentose; receptacle glabrous; achenes glabrous.

Leaves densely pubescent on both sides, without stipules; heads larger, involucres 3.5-4.5 mm high and with 17 to 45 disk-flowers; dry open sunny places at 4500 to about 6000 feet................................ssp. **candicans** (Rydb.) Keck (var. *latiloba* Nutt.)
Leaves less pubescent, greenish or even glabrate, smaller, more dissected, stipulate or with stipule-like appendages; heads smaller, involucres mostly 2.5-3.5 mm high with 15 to 30 or so disk-flowers; moist to dry open to shady meadows and slopes, 5000 to about 8000 feet................................ssp. **incompta** (Nutt.) Keck

Artemisia michauxiana Bess.   Michaux's Sagewort

Perennial herb, sometimes taprooted; stems often several, 20-40 cm tall; leaves green above, white-tomentose beneath, the lower ones 2-5 cm long, bipinnately dissected into short divisions which are often toothed, the upper leaves reduced and sometimes entire; inflorescence narrow, elongate; involucre 3.5-4 mm high, glabrous or nearly so; flowers all fertile; receptacle glabrous; achenes glabrous.
Talus and rocky slopes, 8500 feet to 9600 feet and probably higher.

Artemisia rigida (Nutt.) Gray   Scabland Sagebrush

Low rounded aromatic shrub; stems up to 40 cm tall, densely tomentose when young or glabrate and yellowish, becoming dark gray with shredding bark later; leaves deciduous, silvery-tomentose, narrow, 1-4 cm long, deeply divided into 3 to 5 narrow segments, or the upper often entire; heads solitary or clustered in the upper leaf axils; involucre bell-shaped, 4 or 5 mm high, grayish-tomentose; flowers all fertile; receptacle glabrous; achenes glabrous.
Dry rocky hillside, about 5000 to 5800 feet.

Artemisia tilesii Ledeb.   Shining Sagewort

Perennial with spreading rhizomes; stems 30-150 cm tall; leaves 5-15 cm long, variable in shape, green and shining above, tomentose beneath, deeply lobed and toothed near the base, entire in the inflorescence; heads in a narrow, spike-like, open panicle; involucre mostly 3-5 mm high and 4-8 mm broad, the bracts sometimes with dark margins; receptacle glabrous; achenes glabrous.
Dry open rocky places and riverbanks, about 4500 feet.

Artemisia tridentata Nutt.   Sagebrush

Branching aromatic woody shrub, usually 30-300 cm tall, often with shredding bark; leaves 1-2 cm long, silvery-canescent, usually wedge-shaped, with 3 to 9 blunt teeth or lobes but sometimes linear to oblanceolate and entire; heads sessile, paniculate; involucre 3-5 mm high, 2 mm wide; flowers perfect and fertile; receptacle glabrous.
Dry open rocky ground, 4500 to about 6500 feet.

Artemisia vulgaris L.   Common Wormwood

Aromatic perennial herb mostly 50-180 cm tall; leaves green and glabrous above, densely white-tomentose beneath, mostly 5-10 cm long, obovate or ovate, deeply cleft into acute toothed segments and with 1 or 2 pairs of stipule-like lobes at the base; inflorescence open and leafy; involucre about 4 mm long, tomentose; flowers fertile; receptacle glabrous.
Dry ground, about 5500 feet.

Aster L.

Perennial herbs (ours); leaves simple, alternate, entire or variously toothed; heads showy, sometimes solitary but usually several to numerous; involucral bracts in 2 or more series, usually overlapping and either herbaceous throughout or more often scarious at the base, the outer bracts sometimes larger than the inner and leaf-like; receptacle naked, flat or convex; ray flowers pistillate and fertile in varying shades of blue, purple, pink to white, or sometimes missing; disk-flowers perfect and fertile, yellow, sometimes white, red or purplish; achenes 2- or more-nerved, hairy or glabrous; pappus of capillary bristles, sometimes with a few short outer ones.

1. Flower heads usually solitary on the stem; plants small, mostly at upper mountain elevations; leaves narrow, not obviously toothed
    2. Plants with spreading roots; flowering stems leafy
        3. Leaves all about the same size; tube of the disk-corollas longer than the lobes..*A. sibiricus* var. *meritus*
        3. Leaves at the base larger than those above; tube of the disk-corollas shorter than the lobes; involucral bracts often purplish on the margins ...*A. foliaceus* var. *apricus*
    2. Plants with a vertical taproot; flowering stems nearly leafless; ray-flowers violet....*A. alpigenus*
1. Flower heads 1 to several; plants of low to high elevations with fibrous roots or creeping rhizomes; leaves wider, sometimes toothed
    4. Leaves 2.5-8 cm broad, sharply toothed, without petioles, the lower ones soon deciduous; inflorescence glandular, the heads few to many.............................*A. conspicuus*
    4. Leaves mostly less than 2.5 cm broad, sometimes toothed
        5. Lower leaves either with a usually long petiole, or definitely larger than the middle and upper ones or missing; stems often reddish
            6. Inflorescence glandular; heads large ....*A. integrifolius*
            6. Inflorescence not glandular; heads mostly smaller; achenes usually hairy
                7. Outer bracts of the involucre usually yellowish or brownish at the base, the lower margins thin; leaves usually toothed....................*A. subspicatus*
                7. Outer involucral bracts whitish or greenish-tinged at the base, the margins not conspicuously different; leaves usually not toothed
                    8. Outer involucral bracts as long or longer than the inner ones, often enlarged and leaf-like, crowding the corollas; leaves often 1 cm wide or more, sometimes toothed, expanded at the base and clasping the stem...*A. foliaceus*
                    8. Outer involucral bracts not leaflike, usually narrower and smaller than the inner ones; leaves mostly under 1 cm wide, not usually toothed or expanded or clasping
                        9. Flowering stems branched, the heads numerous; leaves abundant; ray-flowers usually white or pink...........*A. eatonii*
                        9. Flowering stems not much branched, the heads few; ray-flowers blue to purplish or violet; leaves fewer, often clasping the stem.............................*A. occidentalis*
        5. Lower leaves not petioled, not noticeably larger than the others; inflorescence glandular
            10. Leaves thickish, 2-10 mm wide..*A. campestris*
            10. Leaves thin, 10-40 mm wide..*A. modestus*

Aster alpigenus (Torr. & Gray) Gray — Alpine Aster

Dwarf perennial, often taprooted; flowering stems nearly leafless, 3-30 cm tall, decumbent or sometimes prostrate, solitary or few; basal leaves entire, linear or oblanceolate, tufted, 2-25 cm long, 1-15 mm wide; stem leaves few and reduced; heads solitary; involucre 5-13 mm high, the bracts in 2 or 3 series, often purplish; rays 10 to 40, 6-15 mm long; achenes ribbed; pappus bristles barbellate.
Sandy cliffs and slopes, open meadows and lake borders, about 7000 to 8000 feet.

Plants smaller, mostly under 15 cm tall; leaves linear-elliptic to linear-lanceolate, acute; mostly 8000 feet to about 9800 feet and probably higher....var. **haydenii** (Porter) Cronq.

Aster campestris Nutt. — Western Meadow Aster

Stems several from slender stoloniferous rootstocks, 10-50 cm tall, glandular-puberu-

lent or nearly glabrous; leaves linear to linear-spatulate, 2-6 cm long, scarcely reduced, entire, sessile and often clasping; heads 1 to many; involucral bracts in 3 series, glandular-puberulent; rays 20 to 30, violet or purplish; pappus brownish.
Dry open meadows, 5300 to about 5400 feet.

Aster conspicuus Lindl. Showy Aster
Stoloniferous perennial; stem usually solitary, glandular and sometimes hairy, 30-100 cm tall; leaves large, ovate, elliptic or obovate, 8-17 cm long and 2.5-8 cm wide, sessile, sharply toothed, scabrous on both sides, the lower ones soon deciduous; heads few to many, 1.5-4 cm wide; involucre bell-shaped, 7-10 mm high, the bracts in several series (up to 6), densely glandular, ciliate with a papery base and spreading or recurved green tips; rays violet or pale blue, 1-1.5 cm long.
Brushy openings in shady coniferous woods, 4500 to about 5500 feet.

Aster eatonii (Gray) Howell Whitish Aster
Perennial from creeping rootstocks; stems often much branched, 30-100 cm tall; leaves linear or lanceolate, 5-15 cm long and 4-20 mm wide, sessile, usually entire, glabrous or scabrous, the lower ones usually soon deciduous; heads numerous in a long, narrow, leafy inflorescence; involucre 5-8 mm high, the bracts nearly equal, leaf-like, loose or rolled outward, the outer ones broad, green or green-tipped and spreading; rays violet, lavender, pinkish or white, 5-12 mm long; achenes hairy.
Shady woods, mostly near streams, 4500 to about 5100 feet.

Aster foliaceus Lindl. Leafy Aster
Stems clustered, reddish, 30-100 cm tall, from creeping rootstocks; leaves entire or inconspicuously toothed, glabrous or finely puberulent, the blades lanceolate, oblanceolate to obovate, the margins scabrous, the lower ones petioled and often deciduous, 12-20 cm long and 16-24 mm wide, the middle ones sessile, clasping, 5-12 cm long and 1-4 cm wide; heads 1 to several; outer involucral bracts sometimes equaling the inner ones but often much larger, green and expanded and leaf-like; rays 10 to 50, rose-purple, blue or violet, 10-17 mm long; pappus brown to purplish.
Dry to mostly moist rocky meadows, woods and streambanks, 4500 to about 9000 feet.
Plants 25 cm tall or less, pubescent above; heads mostly solitary; involucral bracts usually purple-tipped or -margined; 7500 to about 9300 feet................var. **apricus** Gray
Plants 60-100 cm tall; the lower and the middle leaves similar in length; outer involucral bracts green, expanded and leaf-like; with the species..........var. **cusickii** (Gray) Cronq.

Aster integrifolius Nutt. Sticky Aster
Fibrous-rooted perennial, glandular-pubescent above, glabrous below; stems 20-70 cm tall; leaves entire, the basal and lower ones oblanceolate to obovate, petioled, 5-25 cm long, the others reduced upward, elliptic to lance-linear, sessile and clasping; heads several; peduncles glandular; involucral bracts in 3 series, green or sometimes purplish-tinged, glandular, 1-3 mm wide, the outer wider than the inner ones; rays 10 to 27, deep violet to purple, 10-15 mm long.
Drier rocky meadows, open woodlands and granitic slopes, 4500 to about 8100 feet.

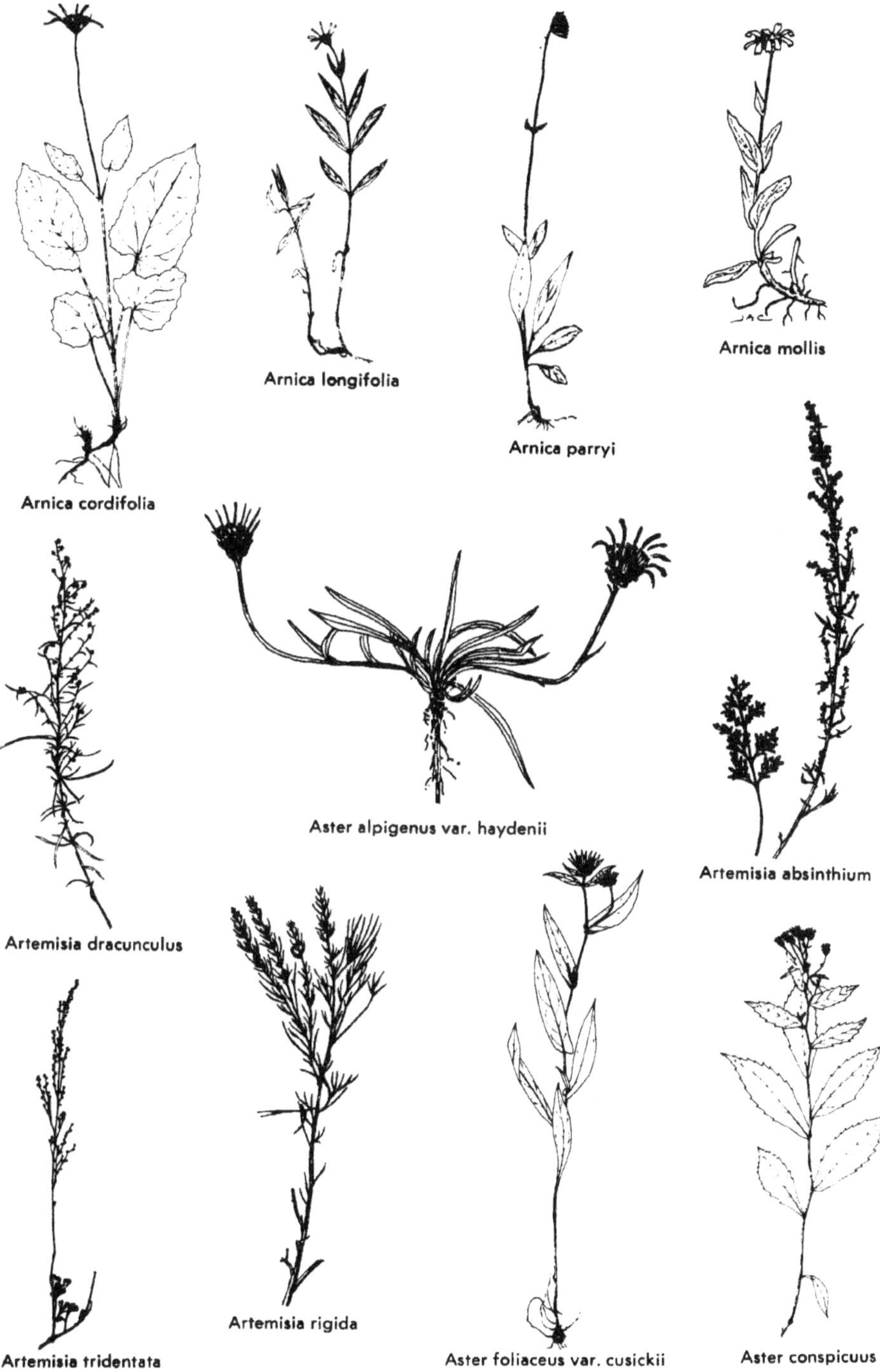

Arnica longifolia
Arnica mollis
Arnica parryi
Arnica cordifolia
Aster alpigenus var. haydenii
Artemisia absinthium
Artemisia dracunculus
Artemisia tridentata
Artemisia rigida
Aster foliaceus var. cusickii
Aster conspicuus

Aster modestus Lindl.   Great Northern Aster
Perennial with creeping rhizomes, 30-120 cm tall; stems and often the leaves stipitate-glandular at least above and sometimes spreading-hairy also; leaves lanceolate, mostly 5-15 cm long, 1-3 cm wide, thin, glabrous or hairy, entire to sharply few-toothed, sessile and clasping; heads 1 to many in a leafy inflorescence; involucre 7-11 mm high, glandular, the inner bracts often purplish, the outer green; rays 20 to about 45, purple or violet. Moist shady woods, mostly at about 6000 feet.

Aster occidentalis (Nutt.) T. & G.   Western Mountain Aster
Perennial with creeping rootstocks; stems 20-80 cm tall, usually pubescent above in lines or all around, glabrous below; leaves mostly glabrous and entire but the margins often ciliate or serrulate, the lower leaves oblanceolate and petioled, the upper ones linear-lanceolate and sessile; heads usually few; involucre about 6 mm high, the bracts narrow, appressed and ciliolate, often green to the base; rays 20 to 50, blue to purplish or violet, 6-15 mm long; achenes hairy.
Moist woods, meadows and streambanks and other wet or boggy places; 4500 to about 8000 feet.
Plants small, simple, up to 50 cm tall; inflorescence of 1 to 10 heads, few-leaved; mostly over 5000 feet..var. **occidentalis**
Plants larger, more branched; inflorescence of several to many heads, conspicuously leafy-bracted; usually below about 5500 feet...............................var. **intermedius** Gray

Aster sibiricus L. var. **meritus** (A. Nels.) Raup.   Arctic Aster
Perennial with slender spreading rootstocks, usually about 10 cm tall; stems 1 to several, often clustered, usually purplish and puberulent; leaves oblanceolate to oblong-elliptic, 2-7 cm long, firm, entire or with a few small teeth, sessile or short-petioled near the base, often hairy beneath; heads solitary, few or many, 2.5 cm wide; involucre 6-9 mm high, the bracts in several series, often spreading, purplish with whitish base and often green tips; rays 12 to 25, blue, purple or violet, 8-12 mm long; pappus brown, purplish-tinged.
Dry open rocky slopes, 7000 to about 9800 feet and probably higher.

Aster subspicatus Nees   Spike-like Aster
A. douglasii Lindl.
Slender perennial with branching rootstocks; stems clustered, 30-100 cm tall, pubescent in lines above, glabrous below; leaves abundant, oblanceolate to lance-linear, mostly clasping, somewhat crowded, glabrous, rough-margined or usually toothed toward the tips; heads few to many, 2-3 cm wide; involucre 5-10 cm high, the bracts loose, green throughout or green-tipped and yellowish or brownish at the base; rays 20 to 40, blue-purplish or violet, about 1 cm long.
Moist shady woods and streambanks, 4500 to about 5200 feet.

Aster perelegans Nels. & Macbr.   Elegant Aster
This species does not appear to have been collected since 1909 but may be growing in our mountains. It is a fibrous-rooted perennial with several stems 30-60 cm tall, puberulent and sometimes glandular; leaves numerous above the vestigial lower ones, sessile, entire, linear-oblong to lanceolate, 2-5 cm long, 3-10 mm wide; rays 5 or 8.

deep violet, 7-12 mm long; involucre purplish-tipped, 6-9 mm high, the bract villous-ciliate, often fine-hairy, keeled, acute, overlapping.
Dry mountain slopes to about 6000 feet or so.

Balsamorhiza Hook.

Perennials with thick fleshy roots and several stems; basal leaves large and broad, the cauline much reduced; heads large, radiate, mostly solitary on the stems; involucre in several series, the bracts mostly green, the outer ones sometimes large and leaf-like; receptacle flat or convex, chaffy, the scales clasping the achenes; ray and disk flowers fertile; pappus none.

Balsamorhiza sagittata (Pursh) Nutt.   Arrow-leaved Balsamroot

Perennial with woody roots; stems few, 20-80 cm tall, white-tomentose; basal leaves large, long-petioled, the blades triangular-oblong to cordate-sagittate, entire, up to 30 cm long and 15 cm wide, often glandular, silvery-tomentose when young becoming glabrate above later; heads large, usually solitary; involucre densely white-tomentose, the outer bracts longer than the inner ones; rays 8 to 25, yellow, 2-4 cm long; achenes glabrous.
Grasslands and open woods and hillsides, about 5000 to 6400 feet.

Brickellia Ell.

Herbs or shrubs, mostly fibrous-rooted; leaves simple, alternate or opposite, resin-spotted; heads discoid, solitary or in panicles; involucral bracts stiff, ribbed, in several overlapping series; receptacle flat and naked; corollas white, ochroleucous or purplish; achenes 10-ribbed; pappus of few to many scabrous white bristles.

Leaves toothed, triangular-shaped, petiolate...*B. grandiflora*
Leaves narrow, not toothed or petiolate...*B. oblongifolia*

Brickellia grandiflora Nutt.   Large-flowered Thoroughwort

Perennial with long thick roots; stems 20-70 cm tall; leaves mostly alternate, petiolate, the blades deltoid-ovate or -lanceolate to nearly cordate, toothed except near the tip, glandular beneath, 2-11 cm long, 1-6 cm wide; heads discoid, solitary or in small clusters, nodding or erect; involucre 7-11 mm high, puberulent, glandular; corollas creamy; achenes sparsely hairy.
Dry rocky slopes and slides, creek beds and other rocky places, 4800 to about 7000 feet.

Brickellia oblongifolia Nutt.   Narrow-leaves Brickellia

Woody perennial; stems 10-60 cm tall, clustered, glandular-puberulent; leaves alternate, elliptic, narrow, mostly entire, sessile or nearly so, pubescent, 1.5-4 cm long; heads discoid, 1 to many, usually clustered at the ends of the branches; involucre 10-20 mm high, glandular-puberulent, the outer bracts spreading; corollas purplish or ochroleucous; achenes glandular.
Dry rocky open slopes at about 5600 feet.

Centaurea L.

Herbs with entire to pinnatifid leaves; heads discoid, the corollas all perfect or the marginal ones sterile; involucral bracts in several series, the tips spiny or fringed or appendaged; receptacle bristly; corollas purple, blue, yellow or white; achenes compressed, usually smooth and shining; pappus of several series of bristles or scales, or sometimes reduced or none.

Centaurea diffusa Lam.   Tumble Knapweed

Taprooted biennial, scabrous, pubescent or tomentose; stems 10-80 cm tall, angled; basal leaves pinnatifid, oblanceolate to oblong, up to 20 cm long and 5 cm wide, short-petiolate, often deciduous; cauline leaves sessile, reduced upward becoming entire; heads 1.5 cm long, solitary to few at the ends of the branches; involucre 8-10 mm high, the outer bracts conspicuously spiny-ciliate and tipped with a definite spine; flowers usually white, sometimes pinkish or purplish; achenes 2.5 mm long, brownish; pappus none. Roadsides and dry forest clearings, 4500 to about 5000 feet.

Chaenactis DC.

Annual, biennial or perennial herbs with alternate, pinnately dissected (ours) leaves; heads discoid, terminal at the ends of the branches, the flowers all perfect; involucres turbinate or campanulate, the bracts nearly equal, in one series, green; receptacle flat, mostly naked; flowers white or pinkish (ours), the marginal ones sometimes enlarged; achenes dark; pappus of 4 to 20 unequal hyaline scales.

Plants stemless, the flower stalk rising above the basal rosette of leaves to about 10-15 cm;
  alpine..*C. alpina*
Plants with 1 to several stems, mostly over 15 cm tall; plants of elevations mostly below
  about 8000 feet..*C. douglasii*

Chaenactis alpina (Gray) Jones   Alpine Chaenactis

Dwarf alpine floccose-tomentose perennial with thick woody roots; stems 4-15 cm tall; leaves 2-6 cm long, thinly tomentose to nearly glabrous, with several pairs of pinnae which usually are again cleft into short teeth or lobes; peduncles 2-8 cm long, finely glandular-puberulent, axillary, leafless; heads 40- to 50-flowered, white or rose-colored; involucre 10-12 mm high, the bracts unequal, purplish, glandular; corollas flesh-colored; pappus of about 10 unequal rose-purplish scales.
Exposed rocky or sandy ridges and slopes, between about 6900 to 9600 feet.

Chaenactis douglasii (Hook.) H. & A.   Hoary Chaenactis

Biennial or perennial herbs, 15-60 cm tall, tomentose and sometimes glandular below the inflorescence; leaves 2-12 cm long, pinnately dissected, tomentose, glandular-pitted. the many segments contorted and curled so the leaf looks thick; upper leaves sessile. reduced, less dissected, the lower ones petiolate, often tufted; heads usually several. white or pinkish; involucre 7-16 mm high, the bracts narrow, glandular-pubescent; achenes 6-9 mm long, densely pubescent; pappus of 9 to 16 unequal wedge-shaped scales. Dry open sandy or rocky places, 4500 to about 7000 feet.

Involucre stipitate-glandular; leaves greener than the species; stems much branched: flowers consistently pink; with the species......................................var. **glandulosa** Cronq.

Chrysanthemum L.

Annual or perennial herbs with alternate, entire, toothed or pinnatified leaves; heads solitary or clustered, radiate, usually long-peduncled; involucre hemispheric, the bracts in 2 to 5 series, scarious; receptacle naked, flat or convex; ray flowers pistillate and fertile, white (ours) or yellow or rose; disk-flowers perfect and fertile, yellow; achenes angled or roundish; pappus a short crown, or none.

Chrysanthemum leucanthemum L. Ox-eye Daisy

Perennial with creeping rhizomes; stems 20-80 cm tall, simple or forked above, glabrous or sparsely hairy; basal leaves oblanceolate, 4-15 cm long including the petiole, cleft, lobed, toothed or merely wavy-margined; cauline leaves reduced and becoming sessile, toothed to nearly entire; heads radiate, 3-5 cm wide, long-peduncled; involucre about 1 cm high, the bracts very unequal, narrow, brown-margined; receptacle flattish; rays 15 to 30, white, about 2 cm long; disk-flowers yellow; achenes dark with white ribs; pappus none.
Moist shady foothills, 4800 to about 5500 feet.

Chrysopsis [Nutt.] Ell.

Annual or perennial pubescent herbs with alternate, entire leaves; heads radiate or discoid, large or medium-sized; involucral bracts green, overlapping; receptacle flat, naked; all flowers yellow and fertile; achenes rather flat, often twisted; pappus usually double, brownish, the inner of many capillary bristles, the outer when present of short scales or bristles.

Chrysopsis villosa (Pursh) Nutt. var. hispida (Hook.) Gray Hairy Aster

Taprooted perennial, woody at the base, 10-60 cm tall; stems and leaves greenish-gray with spreading hairs or the hairs replaced by glands; leaves abundant, the basal deciduous, the cauline alternate, evenly distributed, sessile, 2.5-5 cm long; heads mostly several, sometimes solitary, yellow; involucre campanulate, 5-10 mm high, the bracts glandular or spreading-hairy, regularly overlapping; rays about 10 to 25; achenes villous; pappus brownish.
Dry sandy or gravelly places, 4500 to about 5300 feet.

Chrysothamnus Nutt.

Low leafy branching shrubs; leaves alternate, narrow, entire, sessile; heads numerous, discoid, narrow, yellow; involucral bracts stiff, overlapping, in 5 vertical series; flowers perfect; pappus of many capillary bristles.

Chrysothamnus nauseosus (Pall.) Britt. Rabbit-brush

Shrubs 30-200 cm tall, often with an unpleasant odor; stems erect, spreading or nearly prostrate; leaves alternate, linear to filiform, tomentose to nearly glabrous; heads in rounded or elongate clusters; involucre 6-13 mm high, the bracts in 3 or 4 series, sometimes glandular; florets usually 5, yellow, 7-12 mm long; pappus white.
Dry rocky places and forest openings on mountainsides, 4500 to about 7000 feet.

Cirsium [Tourn.] Adans.

Annual, biennial or perennial spiny herbs with alternate toothed or pinnatifid leaves; heads solitary to several, discoid, many-flowered; involucral bracts spine-tipped, overlapping in several series; receptacle densely bristly; flowers all tubular and perfect or the flowers imperfect by abortion; corollas white, yellowish, reddish or purple, with slender tube and long narrow lobes; achenes oblong, flattened; pappus bristles deciduous as a ring.

Heads small; involucre 1-2 cm high..*C. arvense*
Heads large; involucre 2.5-4 cm high..*C. vulgare*

Cirsium arvense (L.) Scop.   Canada Thistle

Perennial with creeping roots; stems 30-150 cm tall; leaves mostly glabrous or white-tomentose beneath, usually very spiny, 10-15 cm long; heads more than one, unisexual, usually one kind on a plant; involucre 1-2 cm high, the bracts sometimes with weak spines; flowers pink-purplish or white; achenes narrowly oblong, about 4 mm long; pappus pale brownish, up to 2 cm long.
Roadsides and other dry places, 4500 to about 6000 feet.

Cirsium vulgare (Savi) Airy-Shaw   Bull Thistle

Biennial weed, 30-160 cm tall; stem spiny-winged, hairy to tomentose; leaves pinnatifid, very spiny, lobed and toothed, up to 30 cm long and 10 cm wide, the upper surface spiny, the underside thinly hairy; heads several, large, purple or white; involucre 2.5-4 cm high, the bracts all spine-tipped; achenes 3-3.5 mm long, brownish with black lines; pappus 2-3 cm long.
Campgrounds and roadsides, about 5000 to 5100 feet.

Conyza L.

Annual or perennial herbs; leaves alternate; heads very many, small, disciform or minutely radiate, whitish or purplish; pistillate flowers many, the tubular corolla equaling or shorter than the pappus; disk flowers few, 5-toothed; involucral bracts in about 2 overlapping series; receptacle flat, naked; achenes compressed; pappus of few fragile capillary bristles.

Conyza canadensis (L.) Cronq.   Horseweed

Annual, usually branched, mostly 20-100 cm tall, pubescent to nearly glabrous; leaves many, linear to oblanceolate, entire or toothed or ciliate toward the base, the lower ones petiolate and often deciduous, the others becoming sessile; heads small, abundant, in an elongated panicle, or sometimes only a few; involucre 3-4 mm high, the bracts overlapping, glabrous or nearly so; rays white, inconspicuous, short; pappus brownish-white.
Mostly near streams but often in dry open places, 4500 to about 6000 feet.

Stems glabrous or nearly so; more common than the species in our
area..var. **glabrata** (Gray) Cronq.

Crepis L.

Annual or perennial herbs; leaves chiefly basal, alternate, entire to toothed or pinnatifid; heads 1 to many; involucre cylindric or campanulate; bracts in 1 to 3 series, the inner longer than the outer ones; receptacle nearly flat, usually naked; flowers all ligulate, perfect, yellow or sometimes white or pink; achenes cylindric or fusiform, 10- to 20-ribbed; pappus bristles in more than 1 series, white to brownish, persistent or deciduous.

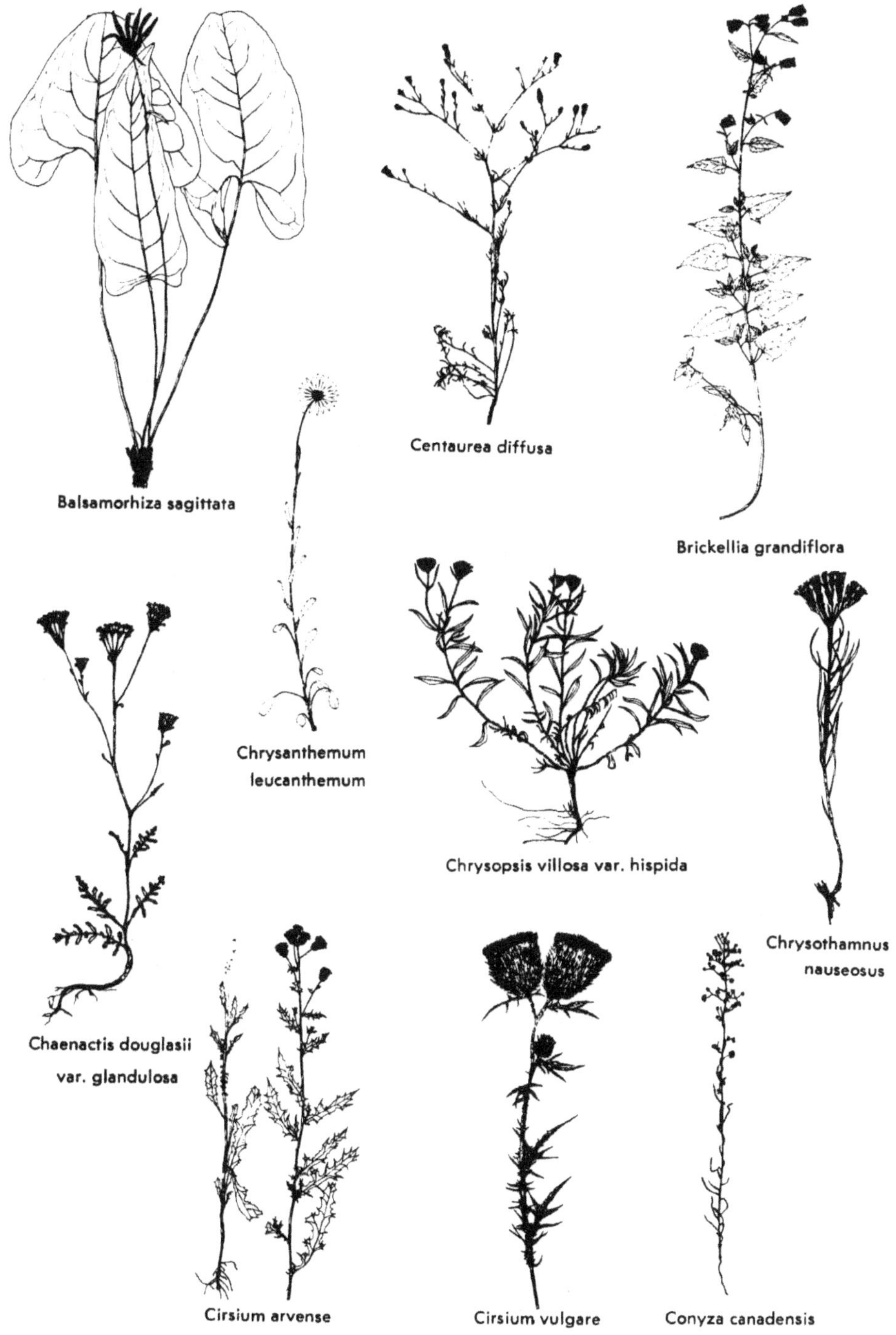

Balsamorhiza sagittata

Centaurea diffusa

Brickellia grandiflora

Chrysanthemum
leucanthemum

Chrysopsis villosa var. hispida

Chaenactis douglasii
var. glandulosa

Chrysothamnus
nauseosus

Cirsium arvense

Cirsium vulgare

Conyza canadensis

1. Plant a dwarf alpine mostly under 10 cm tall; leaves often purplish, rarely with a few
   teeth...*C. nana*
1. Plants 10-70 cm tall, of low to upper elevations; leaves usually grayish-hairy, toothed or
   lobed, not purplish
      2. Heads few, 2 to 25, each with 12 to 30 flowers...*C. occidentalis*
      2. Heads usually more, 20 to 100 or more, each with 5 to 12 flowers........................*C. acuminata*

Crepis acuminata Nutt.   Long-leaved Hawksbeard

Taprooted perennial 20-70 cm tall; herbage gray-tomentose or eventually nearly glabrous; basal leaves 12-40 cm long, pinnately lobed, the lobes entire or toothed or cleft, the petiole winged; stem leaves few, reduced, sessile; heads 20 to 100 or more, each with 5 to 12 flowers; involucre 8-16 mm high, nearly glabrous; corollas 10-18 mm long; achenes yellow or brownish, beakless, equaling the pappus.
Dry rocky soil in meadows and on slopes in coniferous forest, 5500 to about 7800 feet.

Crepis nana Richards.   Dwarf Hawksbeard

Taprooted tufted perennial 2-10 cm tall, glabrous and glaucous; leaves mostly basal, up to 8.5 cm long including the petiole, spatulate to obovate, often purplish; heads several or sometimes many, 9- to 12-flowered, borne on short stalks among the leaves; involucre 7-13 mm high, the inner bracts about 10, mostly twice as long as the outer ones; achenes golden brown, sometimes with a very short beak.
Dry talus slopes and other loose gravelly sandy places, 7000 to about 9600 feet and probably higher.

Crepis occidentalis Nutt.   Western Hawksbeard

Perennial 10-40 cm tall; leaves and stems gray-tomentose or nearly glabrous with age and sometimes also glandular-hairy above; leaves lanceolate to oblanceolate, toothed or deeply cleft into toothed lobes, becoming reduced and sessile upward; heads 2 to 25, mostly 12- to 30-flowered; involucre 11-19 mm high, often with gland-tipped black bristles, the inner 8 to 13 bracts longer than the outer ones; achenes light to dark brown.
Dry rocky or sandy open places, 4500 feet and at 8000 feet, possibly in between also.

Erigeron L.

Annual, biennial or perennial herbs; stems leafy or scapose; leaves alternate or sometimes all basal; heads solitary to many, hemispheric to turbinate, radiate or discoid or a few species with rayless pistillate flowers and the heads disk-shaped; involucral bracts narrow, equal or overlapping, herbaceous in part or throughout but not expanded and leaf-like; receptacle flat or nearly so, naked; pistillate marginal flowers when present usually numerous with narrow, white to pink, blue, yellow or purple rays; disk-flowers yellow, abundant; achenes 2- to many-nerved; pappus of few to many capillary bristles with or without an outer ring of minute bristles or scales.

1. Leaves at the base and on the stem all alike, very narrow, not lobed or toothed or divided;
   heads solitary to many
      2. Flowering stems leafless or nearly so, 3-15 cm tall; leaves mostly at the base; rays
      sometimes missing, short when present, yellow
         3. Hairs of the stem and leaves usually spreading; rays up to 1 cm long when
         present..*E. chrysopsidis*
         3. Hairs of the stem and leaves not spreading, usually whitish, flat on the
         surface; rays usually missing; disk often red...*E. bloomeri*

2. Flowering stems leafy, 5-50 cm tall; rays usually present, white to colored, mostly over 1 cm long
    4. Heads, and often the flowering stems, very many; plants grayish-rough-hairy and sometimes glandular..*E. pumilus*
    4. Heads few, mostly 1 or 2 on the flowering stem; plants hairy or not
        5. Rays blue to yellow; heads small; stems and leaves smooth................*E. linearis*
        5. Rays white to pink; heads larger; stems and leaves rough-hairy; plant purplish at the base..*E. eatonii*
1. Leaves at the base and on the stem not always all alike, those at the base often much longer, or petiolate, or missing at flowering time, all with a more widened blade than above and sometimes toothed, lobed or divided into segments
    6. Leaves toothed or lobed or cleft
        7. Leaves toothed but not otherwise lobed
            8. Involucral hairs with black crosswalls near the base; rays usually white..*E. coulteri*
            8. Involucral hairs without black crosswalls; rays very narrow and numerous, pink to white or blue..*E. philadelphicus*
        7. Leaves lobed or dissected; rays not so narrow or numerous
            9. Plant conspicuously hairy; leaves crowded on short stems, mostly with 3 short, broadly-rounded lobes; rays usually present, spreading, white or pink..*E. vagus*
            9. Plant not so conspicuously hairy; leaves 3-cleft or dissected into narrow lobes; rays white, pink or blue, often missing................................*E. compositus*
    6. Leaves not toothed or lobed or dissected
         10. Flowering stems nearly leafless; basal leaves well developed, numerous; flowers mostly solitary, not yellow
            11. Involucre and often the stem conspicuously long-woolly-hairy; plants of high elevations, rarely over 20 cm tall..*E. simplex*
            11. Involucre and the stem glandular and sometimes inconspicuously fine-short-hairy, but not woolly; plants often purplish-red at the base................*E. ursinus*
        10. Flowering stems leafy; basal leaves present and well developed, or missing; flowers various
            12. Basal leaves numerous, well developed, often with long petioles, the stem leaves gradually reduced upward but still well developed
                13. Rays very narrow, numerous, about as long as the disk flowers; involucre glandular or hairy or both, but not woolly-hairy
                    14. Involucre glandular; heads mostly 1 or 2 on stalks that are often arched or curved or glandular..*E. acris*
                    14. Involucre hairy but not glandular; heads usually more than 1 or 2, the stalks usually erect, not curved or arched................*E. lonchophyllus*
            13. Rays wider, well developed, not short and narrow, often spreading; plants usually erect, Aster-like
                15. Rays mostly 2-3 mm wide, mostly colored; upper leaf blades rounded at the base, the lower tapering into the petiole; common species..*E. peregrinus*
                15. Rays narrower, about 1 mm wide, mostly white or pink
                  16. Hairs of the involucre with black crosswalls near the base; involucre 7-10 mm high..*E. coulteri*
                    16. Hairs of the involucre without black crosswalls; involucre 5-7 mm high..*E. eatonii*
             12. Basal leaves either few and poorly developed, or withered, or deciduous; stems leaves numerous, well developed though sometimes reduced upward
                17. Stems and leaves conspicuously spreading-hairy, at least below; leaves long and strap-like; rays blue, purplish or pink................*E. subtrinervis*
                17. Stems and leaves not conspicuously spreading hairy; leaves shorter; rays mostly blue, rarely white..*E. speciosus*

Erigeron acris L. var. **debilis** Gray   Bitter Erigeron
Biennial or perennial, 2-30 cm tall, the stem often curved at the base; stems and leaves glabrous to spreading-hairy and often also glandular; basal leaves entire, oblanceolate, the cauline mostly narrower and becoming sessile; heads 1 or few, the peduncles arched or spreading, often glandular; involucres 5-12 mm high, glandular and often also coarsely hairy, the bracts nearly equal, green or purplish; rays numerous, erect, incon- spicuous, white or purplish, the inner pistillate flowers rayless; achenes 2-nerved, sparsely hairy; pappus of about 30 bristles, sometimes also with a few short outer setae. Rocky mountainsides, 6000 to about 7000 feet.

Erigeron bloomeri Gray   Scabland Erigeron
Perennial 5-15 cm tall; stems scape-like, clustered on a woody branching base; herbage finely appressed white-hairy; leaves mostly in basal clusters, linear, 2-9 cm long; heads solitary on the peduncle; involucre 5-10 mm high, long-hairy, the bracts green; ray-flowers none; disk corollas yellow, 4.5-7 mm long; achenes 2-nerved, hairy above; pappus bristles unequal.
Exposed ridges, sandy passes and dry stony soils mostly in the open, 7200 to about 9700 feet and probably higher.

Erigeron chrysopsidis Gray   Dwarf Golden Daisy
Perennial with a taproot and branching caudex; stems closely tufted, 3-16 cm tall; herbage spreading hairy; leaves linear-oblanceolate, entire, up to 9 cm long and 1-3 mm wide, mostly in basal clusters; heads solitary; involucre hemispheric, 5-8 mm high, hairy and sometimes glandular; pistillate flowers when present 20 to 50, the rays bright yellow; pappus of 15 to 25 bristles, the outer setae few, short and inconspicuous.
Sandy or stony open woods, 5000 to about 6000 feeet.

Plants smaller and more compact; heads smaller; pubescence partly appressed; moist to dry cliffs, slides and slopes in coniferous forest, 6000 to 9500 feet..var. **brevifolius** Piper

Erigeron compositus Pursh   Dwarf Mountain Erigeron
Perennial with simple or branched caudex; stems scape-like, 10-25 cm tall; herbage nearly glabrous to densely glandular and spreading-hairy; basal leaves ternately dis- sected; cauline leaves mostly entire, few and reduced; heads solitary; involucres 5-10 mm high, glandular and pubescent, the bracts sometimes purplish; pistillate flowers 20 to 60, white, pink or blue, or the rays reduced, or none; pappus simple, of 12 to 20 bristles.
Rocky and sandy places and often on exposed ridges and cliffs, 4500 to 9800 feet and probably higher.

Erigeron coulteri Porter   Coulter's Erigeron
Fibrous-rooted perennial with a caudex or a rhizome; stem leafy, 10-60 cm tall, long-hairy at least above; leaves oblanceolate, hairy, mostly entire, petiolate near the base, becoming sessile upward; heads usually solitary but sometimes up to 4; involucre 7-10 mm high; involucral bracts equal, green, covered with hairs that have black cross- walls near the base; rays 50 to 100, white, up to 1.5 cm long; pappus of about 25 bristles.
Grassy moist woods, meadows and streambanks, 5000 to about 6500 feet.

Erigeron eatonii Gray var. **villosus** Cronq.   Eaton's Daisy

   Taprooted perennial; stems clustered, 5-30 cm tall, usually purplish and curved at the base; herbage closely hairy; leaves 1- to 3-nerved, linear to narrowly oblanceolate, mostly basal, petiolate, reduced upward; heads solitary or up to 7; involucre 5-7 mm high, conspicuously long-white-hairy, often purplish and glandular; rays 20 to 50, white or light blue, 7-11 mm long; pappus bristles about 20, the few outer setae inconspicuous. Sandy or rocky places in open woods and exposed ridges and slopes, 4500 to about 8400 feet.

Erigeron linearis (Hook.) Piper   Yellow Daisy

   Perennial with a branching caudex and a thick root; stems 5-30 cm tall; herbage finely rough-gray-hairy; bases of stems and lower leaves rather hard, enlarged and yellowish or purplish; leaves mostly basal, linear, 1.5-9 cm long; heads solitary or few; involucre 4-7 mm high, pubescent and sometimes finely glandular as well; rays 15 to 45, yellow, 4-11 mm long; disk corollas 3.5-5.3 mm long; pappus of 10 to 20 bristles and a few short outer setae.
Dry rocky open places, 5000 to about 6000 feet.

Erigeron lonchophyllus Hook.   Low Meadow Daisy

   Biennial or short-lived perennial with weak roots; stems 2-60 cm tall; herbage long-hairy or the leaves nearly glabrous; leaves entire, often ciliate-margined, the basal oblanceolate, up to 15 cm long including the petiole, becoming sessile and reduced upward but sometimes elongate; heads solitary or several, often with long subtending leaves; involucre 4-9 mm high, long-hairy but not glandular, the bracts unequal, overlapping, light green with purple tips; rays very narrow, numerous, about 2-3 mm long, white or sometimes pinkish; disk corollas 3.5-5 mm long; pappus of about 25 short white bristles.
Moist meadows, shady bogs, gravel bars and other rather moist places in shady woods, 4500 to about 7000 feet.

Erigeron peregrinus (Pursh) Greene   Wandering Daisy

   Perennial with short heavy fibrous rootstocks; stems leafy or nearly leafless, 20-70 cm tall; leaves glabrous to long-hairy, ciliate-margined, the basal oblanceolate and petiolate, the cauline reduced upward, ovate to linear and often clasping; heads solitary or few; involucre 7-11 mm high, the bracts about equal; rays 30 to 80, white to purple, 8-24 mm long; disk corollas mostly about 5 mm long; pappus of 20 to 30 long bristles; achenes usually 5, several-nerved.
Moist meadows, bogs, streambanks and open woods, 5000 to about 9500 feet or so.

Involucre densely glandular, sometimes also with long white hairs; peduncles thickly long-hairy; rays deep rose-purple..........................ssp. **callianthemus** (Greene) Cronq.

1. Plants mostly under 20 cm tall, of high elevations; flowering stems often nearly leafless...var. **scaposus** (T. & G.) Cronq.

1. Plants larger and taller, up to 70 cm tall, not confined to alpine elevations; flowering stems leafy, the leaves mostly ovate, not reduced much; basal leaves wider...var. **callianthemus**

Erigeron philadelphicus L.   Philadelphia Fleabane
   Fibrous-rooted biennial or short-lived perennial with a simple caudex; stems 20-70
cm tall; herbage long-hairy to nearly glabrous; basal leaves oblanceolate or obovate,
toothed or lobed or sometimes entire, up to 15 cm long and 3 cm wide, the petioles
winged; cauline leaves not much reduced but becoming sessile and clasping; heads 1
to many; involucre about 5 mm high, the bracts with broad hyaline, occasionally purplish, margins; rays 150 to 400 or so, very narrow, deep pink to white, 5-10 mm long;
pappus of 20 to 30 short delicate bristles.
Moist open woods and grassy streambanks, 4500 to about 5000 feet.

Erigeron pumilus Nutt. ssp. **intermedius** Cronq.   Shaggy Daisy
   Perennial with a taproot and a caudex; stems 5-50 cm tall; herbage conspicuously
spreading-hairy and sometimes a little glandular; leaves all narrowly oblanceolate, up
to about 8 cm long; heads 1 to several; involucre 4-7 mm high, hairy and glandular;
rays mostly 50 to 100, narrow, 6-15 mm long, usually blue or pink; disk corollas 3.5-5
mm long, often puberulent at the base; pappus double, the inner bristly, the outer of
short setae; achenes hairy.
Dry open mostly sandy places, 4500 to about 6000 feet.
Stems over 1.5 mm thick near the base; heads 5 to many......................var. **intermedius**
Stems thinner, plants smaller and more delicate; heads seldom as many
as 5 ....var. **gracilior** Cronq.

Erigeron simplex Greene   Alpine Daisy
   Perennial with a caudex and fibrous roots; stems few or solitary, 2-20 cm tall, viscid-
hairy; leaves oblanceolate, mostly basal, up to 8 cm long and 13 mm wide; head solitary; involucre 5-8 mm high, the bracts white-woolly with flattened multicellular hairs,
the crosswalls sometimes reddish-purple; rays 50 to 125, blue, pink, or rarely white, 7-11
mm long and up to 2.5 mm wide; pappus double, the inner ring of 10 to 15 bristles, the
outer of several short setae.
Open rocky slopes and exposed ridges, 8000 feet to about 9700 feet.

Erigeron speciosus (Lindl.) DC.   Showy Daisy
   Perennial with a woody caudex; stems clustered, leafy, 15-80 cm tall, mostly glabrous;
leaves oblanceolate or spatulate to lanceolate, glabrous or nearly so, ciliate-margined,
the lower petiolate and early deciduous, the upper ones shorter and sessile; heads 1 to 3;
involucre 6-9 mm high, hairy and glandular; rays 65 to about 150, blue or rarely white,
9-18 mm long; disk corollas about 4 mm long; pappus of 20 to 30 bristles and some
short outer setae.
Open woods, moist meadows and rocky mountainsides, 4500 to about 7000 feet.
Leaves rather narrow, lanceolate above, usually ciliate-margined and hairy on the
surface; involucre long-hairy..var. **speciosus**
Leaves a little wider, ovate above, not thickly ciliate-margined or hairy; involucre
without hairs..var. **macranthus** (Nutt.) Cronq.
With the species.

Erigeron subtrinervis Rydb.   Three-nerved Daisy
   Perennial with branched caudex; stem leafy, 15-90 cm tall; herbage pubescent with

long spreading hairs, sometimes restricted to the leaf veins and margins; leaves 1- to 3-nerved, entire with ciliate margins, the lower ones oblanceolate and wing-petiolate, the others lanceolate to ovate and sessile; heads solitary to few or several; involucre 6-9 mm high, glandular and conspicuously pubescent with long spreading hairs; rays over 100, blue or purplish, 7-18 mm long.
Open woodlands and meadows, 5200 to about 7800 feet.

Erigeron ursinus D. C. Eat. Purplish Erigeron

Fibrous-rooted perennial with slender shallow caudex; stems 5-25 cm tall, curved and purplish at the base, hairy; leaves glabrous, ciliate-margined, oblanceolate at the base, reduced upward; head solitary; involucre 5-7 mm high, glandular, spreading-hairy; rays 30 to 100, blue to pinkish, 7-15 mm long; disk corollas 3.2-4.5 mm long; pappus of 10 to 20 bristles and some outer setae.
Wet meadows at high elevations in the mountains, 6000 to about 8000 feet.

Erigeron vagus Payson Loose Daisy

Low perennial from a branching caudex; herbage and involucre spreading-hairy and glandular; leaves crowded at the base on short stems, mostly 3-lobed; heads solitary on the peduncles; disk 8-16 mm wide; involucre about 6 mm high; rays about 30, white or pink, 4-7 mm long; pappus of about 20 bristles.
Woodlands, moist rocky slopes and loose talus, 5000 to about 9600 feet and probably higher.

Eriophyllum Lag.

Annual or perennial herbs, shrubby or herbaceous, with woolly herbage; leaves mostly alternate, entire or usually lobed, toothed or divided; heads radiate or sometimes discoid; rays few, pistillate, fertile, usually yellow, rarely white or bluish; involucre of firm, erect keeled bracts which partly surround the ray achenes; receptacle naked, flat or curved; disk flowers perfect, yellow; achenes 4-angled; pappus of scarious paleae, or none.

Eriophyllum lanatum (Pursh) Forbes var. **integrifolium** (Hook.) Smiley
Woolly Sunflower

Tomentose perennial from a woody base; stems thick, mostly 10-25 cm tall; leaves mostly alternate, 1-8 cm long, usually woolly beneath, glabrate to glabrous above, entire or 3-lobed at the tips; heads few to many; peduncles long and thick; involucre 6-20 mm high, the bracts not united; rays 8 to 12, yellow; achenes angled, about 3-4 mm long.
Dry open rocky places, 4500 to about 7200 feet, probably higher also.

Eupatorium L.

Herbs or shrubs; leaves usually opposite, sometimes alternate or whorled, petiolate, toothed or entire, often glandular; heads discoid, small; involucre of 2 or more series, the bracts overlapping or nearly equal; receptacle flat or convex, naked; corollas pink, blue, purple or white; achenes 5-angled, glandular (ours); pappus of rigid capillary bristles.

Eupatorium occidentale Hook. Western Eupatorium

Perennial with several puberulous stems 15-80 cm tall; leaves numerous, ovate, mostly

1.5-6 cm long, alternate as well as opposite, petiolate, toothed, conspicuously veined, glandular beneath; heads 9- to 12-flowered, small, clustered at the ends of the branches; involucre 3-5 mm high, the bracts nearly equal; corollas reddish, pink, purplish or white; achenes glandular, 3 mm long; pappus bristles dull-whitish.
Dry open granitic slopes, 6400 to about 6800 feet.

Gnaphalium L.

Annual or perennial herbs, densely tomentose and often aromatic; leaves alternate, entire, sessile; heads small, disk-shaped, in cymose clusters or glomerules; flowers yellow or whitish, all tubular, the outer pistillate, the inner perfect; involucral bracts scarious, white or colored, overlapping; receptacle flat and naked; achenes nerveless, small; pappus of capillary bristles, free or united.

1. Inflorescence roundish, head-like, with leaf-like bracts; involucre 2-4 mm high................*G. palustre*
1. Inflorescence not head-like, mostly in open, broad clusters, the bracts not leaf-like; involucre 4-7 mm high
    2. Plants conspicuously loosely-cobwebby-hairy; leaves clasping the stem; involucres yellowish, often densely clustered..*G. chilense*
    2. Plants not so cobwebby-hairy; leaves not clasping the stem; involucres white to tan, in many small clusters..*G. microcephalum*

Gnaphalium chilense Spreng.   Cotton-batting plant

Annual or biennial, 10-80 cm tall, densely though loosely tomentose throughout, usually aromatic; leaves spatulate to oblong or linear, the lower ones 2-9 cm long, auricled and clasping the stem, the upper ones reduced and often running down the stem; heads in 1 or more dense clusters, yellow or whitish, with 150 to over 200 tubular flowers; involucres 4-6 mm high, white to yellowish or brownish.
Moist disturbed ground, about 4700 feet.

Gnaphalium microcephalum Nutt. var. **thermale** (E. Nels.) Cronq.

                      White Everlasting
Perennial with a woody base, white-tomentose throughout, sweet-scented or odorless, mostly 20-40 cm tall, or more; leaves numerous, alternate, entire, linear to oblanceolate near the base, sometimes running down the stem; heads numerous in small clusters forming a broad, open inflorescence; involucre 4-7 mm high, the bracts white to tan, woolly only at the base if at all; pappus bristles falling separately.
Dry sandy open place in coniferous forest, about 6500 feet.

Gnaphalium palustre Nutt.   Lowland Cudweed

Low spreading branched annual, loosely floccose-tomentose especially above, 2-30 cm tall; leaves sessile, oblanceolate or oblong, 1-3 cm long; heads in small clusters at the tips of the branches and in the leaf axils; involucres 3-4 mm high, the bracts brown with whitish tips; pappus bristles falling separately.
Moist meadows, open woods and streambanks, 4800 to about 5800 feet.

Grindelia Willd.

Annual, biennial or perennial coarse herbs, sometimes woody at the base; leaves alternate, stiffish, resinous; heads radiate or sometimes discoid; rays mostly 10 to 45, yellow, fertile; disk flowers usually perfect; involucre resinous or gummy; receptacle flat or

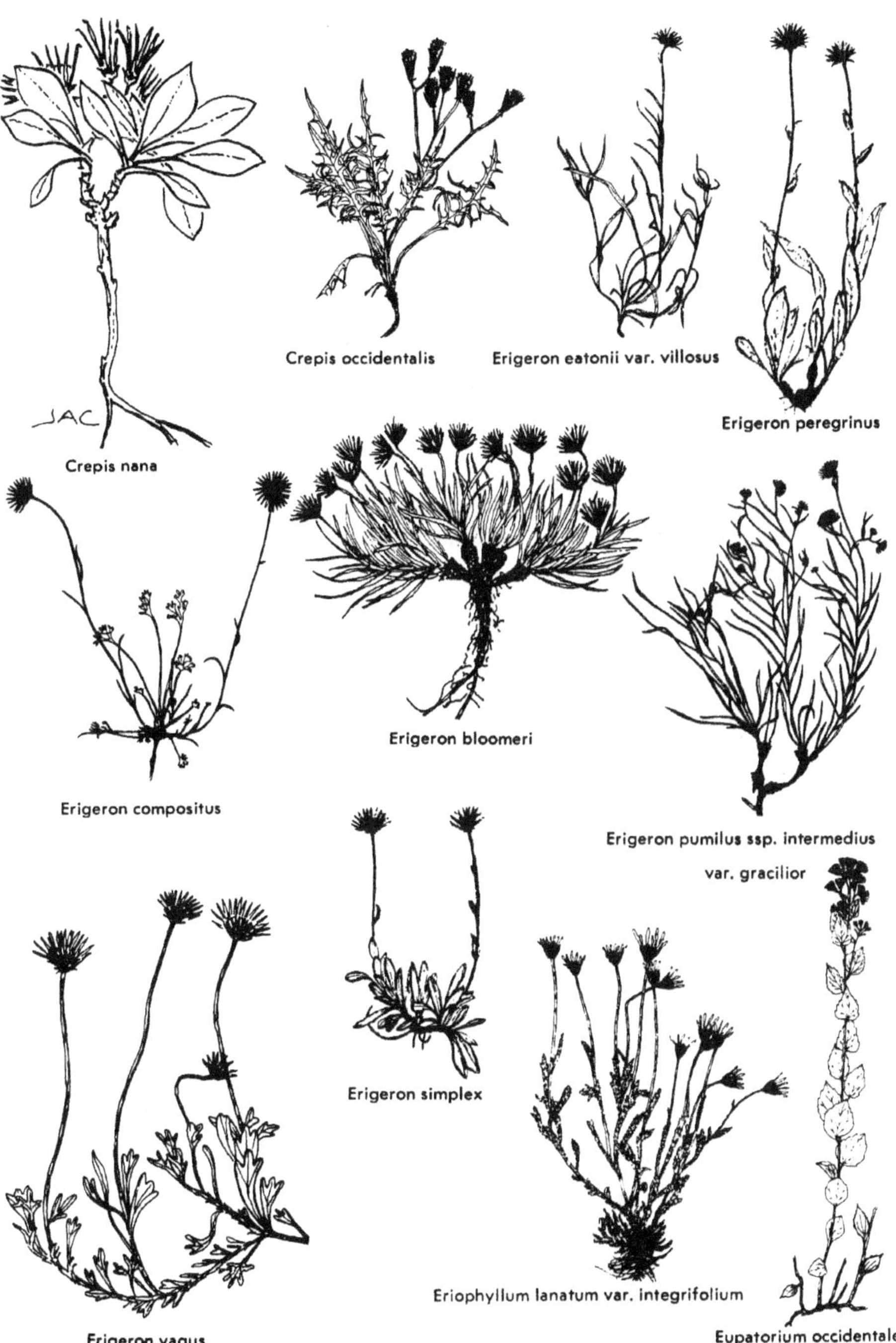
Crepis nana
Crepis occidentalis
Erigeron eatonii var. villosus
Erigeron peregrinus
Erigeron compositus
Erigeron bloomeri
Erigeron pumilus ssp. intermedius
var. gracilior
Erigeron simplex
Erigeron vagus
Eriophyllum lanatum var. integrifolium
Eupatorium occidentale

convex, naked; achenes glabrous, somewhat angled; pappus of 2 to several deciduous awns.

Grindelia nana Nutt. Resin-weed; Gum-plant

Glabrous perennial, usually branched, 20-80 cm tall; leaves spiny-toothed to entire, the lower oblanceolate, up to 15 cm long, petiolate, the others reduced upward and clasping; heads 1 to several; involucre 8-12 mm high, viscid, the bracts strongly curved outward and downward, the tips green; disk mostly 8-25 mm wide; rays mostly 12 to 25, yellow, 5-15 mm long; pappus usually of 2 long awns; achenes with 1 to 3 short knobs at the top.
Grassy slopes and open woods, 4500 to about 5200 feet.

Haplopappus Cass.

Taprooted herbs or shrubs usually resinous and often glandular; leaves alternate, entire to bipinnatifid; heads solitary to many, radiate or discoid, yellow or rarely creamy; involucre cylindric to hemispheric, the bracts variable, dry and colorless to green and leaf-like; receptacle naked, flattish; ray flowers pistillate or neutral, yellow, many to few or none; disk flowers numerous to only a few, mostly yellow, sometimes white or purplish; achenes roundish or angled, glabrous to silky-hairy; pappus of unequal capillary bristles.

1. Plants shrubby with many woody branches from the base; plants of upper mountain elevations; stems leafy
    2. Heads rather large, 20- to 40-flowered; leaves tending to curl along the margins; glands with stalks; involucre 10-16 mm high..*H. suffruticosus*
    2. Heads smaller, mostly 10- to 20-flowered; leaves not curled; glands without stalks; involucre 8-12 mm high...*H. greenei*
1. Plants not shrubby though the base sometimes woody and often with many tufts of leaves; plants of low to high elevations
    3. Heads large; rays inconspicuous or none; disk corollas 10-14 mm long; involucre 15-30 mm high...*H. carthamoides*
    3. Heads mostly smaller; rays present, usually conspicuous; disk corollas about 5 mm long
        4. Leaves toothed; heads mostly more than 1 on the stems; plants rough-hairy.......*H. hirtus*
        4. Leaves not usually toothed; heads mostly solitary; plants smooth
            5. Plants cobwebby-grayish-hairy, tending to form mats at the base; involucre 10-12 mm high...*H. lanuginosus*
            5. Plants green, glandular, sometimes fine-hairy, with creeping roots but not forming dense mats; involucre 6-12 mm high.....................................*H. lyallii*

Haplopappus carthamoides (Hook.) Gray Large Bristleweed

Taprooted perennial 10-60 cm tall, the stems few, puberulent or nearly glabrous, curved at the base; leaves few or many, the basal clustered, oblanceolate to oval, 10-40 cm long, petioled, entire or spiny-toothed, the outer bracts leaf-like; rays up to 30 or none, inconspicuous; disk corollas numerous; achenes glabrous; pappus stiff, brownish. Dry rocky hillsides, about 4900 to about 6000 feet.

Plants smaller, the stems decumbent; heads more turbinate, smaller; involucral bracts narrow, loose, seldom overlapping or whitish-margined; 6000 to about 9000 feet...var. **cusickii** Gray

Haplopappus greenei Gray   Brittle Bristleweed
Low broad shrub 10-30 cm tall; herbage tomentose to nearly glabrous, resinous or glandular especially above; leaves abundant, oblanceolate to linear, 2-3 cm long; heads 1 or more at the ends of the twigs; involucres 8-12 mm high, the outer bracts leaf-like the others in 3 or 4 series, about equal to overlapping; rays showy, 1 to 7; disk flowers mostly 7 to 20.
Open and wooded rocky slopes and sandy forest openings, 5000 to about 9200 feet.

Haplopappus hirtus Gray   Hairy or Sticky Bristleweed
Taprooted perennial 10-40 cm tall; herbage villous-tomentose with multicellular hairs and glandular at least in the inflorescence; leaves oblanceolate to oblong, irregularly toothed, 3-20 cm long, the basal tufted and petiolate, the cauline reduced and becoming sessile and clasping; heads mostly several; involucres 5-15 mm high, the bracts green with loose tips, stipitate-glandular and long-hairy; rays 13 to 25; achenes hairy; pappus yellowish.
Open rocky wooded slopes, 5800 to about 6200 feet.

Haplopappus lanuginosus Gray   Woolly Haplopappus
Densely cespitose shrub or subshrub, 7-20 cm tall, usually mat-forming, with a much-branched caudex and fibrous roots; herbage floccose-tomentose to nearly glabrous and glandular; leaves numerous, narrowly oblanceolate to almost linear, 2-10 cm long, entire, in basal tufts, fewer and reduced on the flowering stems; heads solitary; involucres 10-12 mm high, the bracts mostly about equal, scarious-margined; rays 7 to 20, showy, 7-12 mm long; achenes short-pubescent; pappus whitish.
Dry rocky or sandy soils on exposed slopes and ridges, 8000 to about 8500 feet.

Haplopappus lyallii Gray   Lyall's Haplopappus
Perennial with a branched caudex and often with long creeping rhizomes as well, sometimes forming small mats; stems few to several, leafy, 3-15 cm tall; herbage and involucres densely stipitate-glandular; leaves oblanceolate to oblong, mostly 1.5-7 cm long, entire; heads usually solitary; involucres 6-12 mm high, the bracts herbaceous, nearly equal, often purplish, in 2 or 3 series; rays 13 to 35, 6-11 mm long; achenes nearly glabrous; pappus white.
Talus, rocky or sandy slopes and other exposed rocky, sandy places, 7000 to about 9800 feet.

Haplopappus suffruticosus (Nutt.) Gray   Ruffled Haplopappus
Low shrub 15-40 cm tall; herbage glandular and fragrant; leaves numerous, narrowly oblanceolate to oblong, 1-3.5 cm long and up to 7 mm wide, entire, the margins wavy or crisped; heads solitary or up to 4 in loose clusters, campanulate; involucres glandular, 10-16 mm high, the outer bracts often longer than the inner; rays 3 to 8, showy, up to 2 cm long; disk corollas 17 to 40, about 1 cm long; achenes flattened, hairy; pappus straw-colored.
Open gravelly, sandy or rocky slopes, mostly at or just above treeline, 8000 to about 8400 feet.

Helianthella T. & G.

Coarse taprooted leafy-stemmed perennial herbs; leaves alternate or opposite, entire;

heads solitary or few, medium to large, radiate; involucral bracts in 2 to 4 series, nearly equal or overlapping, herbaceous, often a few outer ones enlarged and leaf-like; receptacle flat or convex, chaffy, the bracts partially surrounding the achenes; rays few, yellow, neutral; disk flowers abundant, yellow, fertile; achenes flatly compressed or thickened; pappus of 2 persistent awns and a crown of short scales.

Helianthella uniflora (Nutt.) T. & G. var. **douglasii** (T. & G.) Weber False Sunflower

Perennial with a branching short caudex; stems several, 20-100 cm tall, mostly spreading-hairy or puberulent becoming glabrate below; leaves scabrous, alternate and opposite, lanceolate or elliptic, the middle cauline ones largest, 3-nerved, 8-20 cm long, the others reduced, short-petiolate or sessile; heads mostly solitary on long peduncles, the disk mostly 2-2.5 cm wide; involucre 12-18 mm high, the bracts ciliate-hairy, the outer ones rarely enlarged; rays 11 to 20, mostly 13, 3-4 cm long; receptacle bracts firm; achenes flat, ciliate and pubescent; pappus of 2 unequal awns and some short scales. Dry hillsides, mountain open woods and grassy slopes, 5000 to about 6400 feet.

Helianthus L.

Coarse annual or perennial herbs; leaves simple, usually petiolate, opposite at the base but the upper ones sometimes alternate; heads solitary to a few, radiate and large; involucral bracts herbaceous, in 2 series; receptacle flat, chaffy, the bracts surrounding the achenes; rays large, yellow, neutral; disk flowers perfect, the corollas yellow, brownish, or tinged with reddish-purple; achenes moderately compressed, 4-angled, nearly glabrous; pappus of mostly 2 deciduous awns and rarely with some short scales.

Helianthus annuus L.   Common Sunflower

Coarse annual 30-200 cm tall or more; herbage harshly pubescent; leaves alternate above, petiolate, mostly toothed, ovate or wider, the lower ones often cordate, 7.5-40 cm long and 3-40 cm wide; heads large, the disk 2.5-4 cm wide, reddish-brown or rarely yellow; involucral bracts ovate or ovate-lanceolate, glabrous or pubescent on the backs, ciliate on the margins, the tips acute; rays 8 to 20, 2-3 cm long; receptacle flat or nearly so; achenes about 4 mm long.
Dry roadsides, barely reaching our area at about 4500 feet.

Hieracium [Tourn.] L.

Fibrous-rooted perennial herbs with a thick rhizome or slender stolons; herbage and involucre sparsely stellate-hairy; leaves alternate or all basal, entire or toothed in most of ours, the lower sometimes early deciduous, the others persistent, few and reduced; heads solitary to several, small or large, few- to many-flowered; flowers all ligulate and perfect, yellow, white or orange-red; involucres cylindric or bell-shaped, the bracts in 1 to 3 graduated series; receptacle naked; achenes ribbed and grooved; pappus of white to brownish stiff capillary bristles.

1. Flowers white; plant without star-like hairs..*H. albiflorum*
1. Flowers yellow; star-like hairs on the involucre and often on stems and leaves as well
    2. Leaves conspicuously hairy or glandular, or both
        3. Involucre evidently glandular-hairy; leaves and stems hairy or nearly hairless;
          pappus pale yellow or brownish...*H. cynoglossoides*

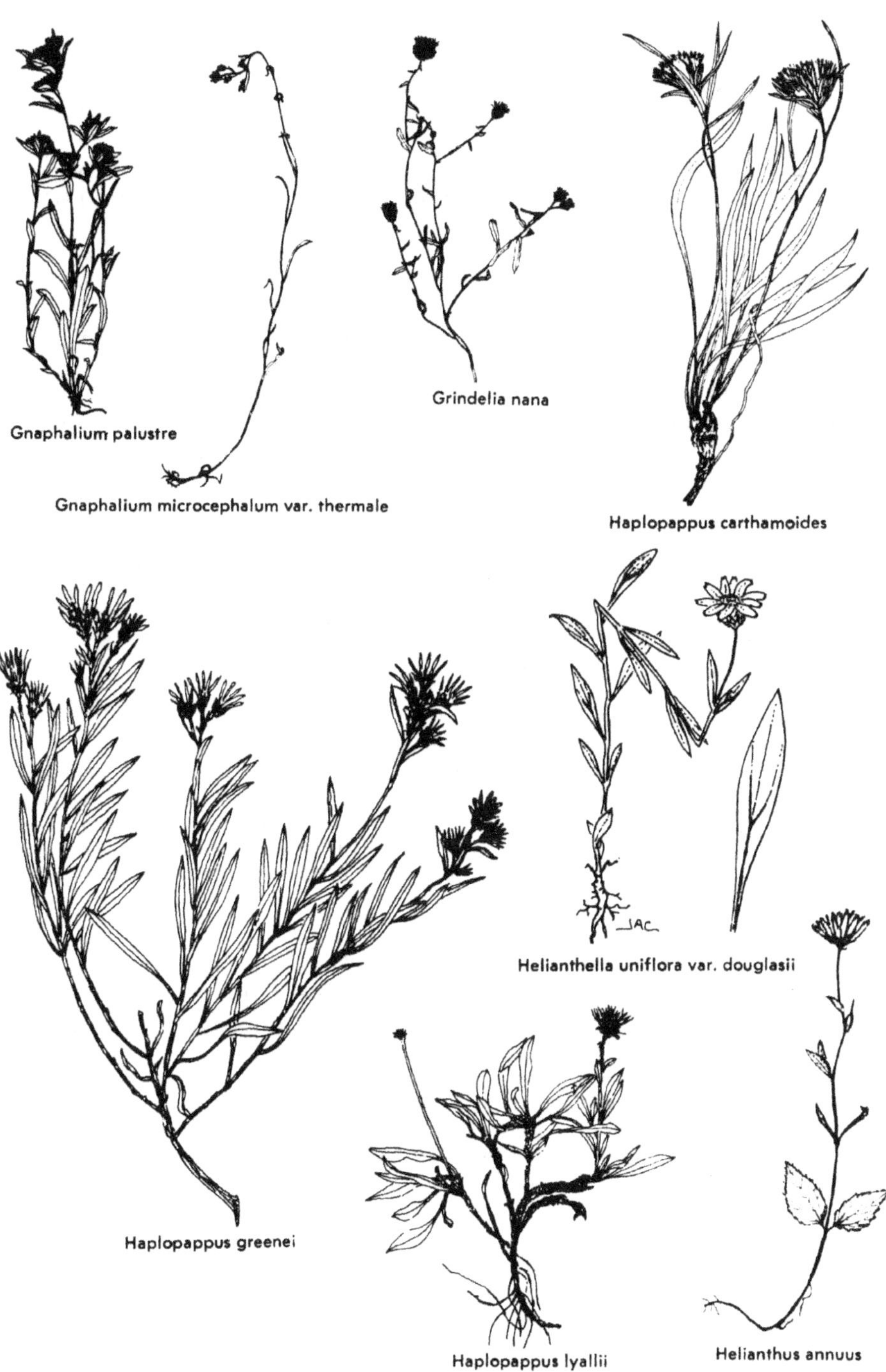

Gnaphalium palustre
Gnaphalium microcephalum var. thermale
Grindelia nana
Haplopappus carthamoides
Haplopappus greenei
Helianthella uniflora var. douglasii
Haplopappus lyallii
Helianthus annuus

> 3. Involucre not conspicuously glandular; leaves and stems very densely and
> conspicuously long-hairy; pappus whitish..*H. albertinum*
> 2. Leaves hairless or sometimes with a few short hairs; plants small, slender.................*H. gracile*

Hieracium albertinum Farr.   Woolly Hawkweed

Coarse perennial with thick rootstocks; stems mostly solitary, 20-120 cm tall; herbage sparsely or densely hairy with long white or yellowish hairs and sometimes some stellate hairs especially above; basal and lower leaves lanceolate or oblanceolate, 8-25 cm long, nearly entire, narrowing into a winged petiole, the middle and upper leaves much reduced, farther apart and sessile; heads yellow, few to many; involucre 7-12 mm high, the bracts slightly to densely covered with long hairs black at the base, some stellate hairs and rarely some glands as well; achenes ribbed; pappus whitish.
Dry rocky meadows and coniferous woods, 6400 to about 7000 feet.

Hieracium albiflorum Hook.   White-flowered Hawkweed

Perennial, 30-120 cm tall, with a woody root and short caudex; stems usually solitary, almost leafless, long-hairy near the base, becoming glabrous upward; leaves mostly basal, 4-18 cm long, oblong to oblanceolate, petiolate, long-hairy, entire or toothed, the middle and upper leaves sessile, lanceolate, reduced, sparsely hairy and farther apart; stellate hairs missing from herbage and involucre; heads several or many, on slender peduncles up to 7 cm long; involucre 6-11 mm high, blackish-green, sparsely hairy to glabrous, often sparsely glandular with pale or black hairs; flowers usually white or creamy; pappus white or brownish.
Moist or dry open or shady woods, 4600 to about 7200 feet.

Hieracium cynoglossoides Arv.-Touv.   Hound's-tongue Hawkweed

Perennial with horizontal rootstocks; stems 25-70 cm tall; herbage hairy to nearly glabrous, scarcely if at all stellate; leaves mostly below the middle, 8-20 cm long, lanceolate to oblanceolate, entire or low-toothed, reduced upward; inflorescence glabrous or short-bristly and sometimes slightly glandular, the heads few- to many-flowered; involucre 8-10 mm high, glandular-pubescent with short yellow or sometimes blackish gland-tipped hairs and sometimes also finely stellate and with some long bristles; pappus pale yellowish or brownish-tinged.
Dry woods, 4500 to about 4600 feet.

Hieracium gracile Hook.   Low Alpine Hawkweed

Slender perennial with short caudex and horizontal rootstocks; stems 10-30 cm tall, few to several, nearly leafless, glabrous to finely stellate-puberulent, especially upward; leaves 1-10 cm long, mostly basal, spatulate to oblanceolate, essentially glabrous, petiolate; heads yellow-flowered, solitary or several in a raceme; involucres and peduncles generally with black or whitish usually gland-tipped bristles and also often gray-stellate-pubescent; pappus light brown to white, longer than the achene.
Rocky or sandy dry to wet open meadows, talus, ridges and slopes at and above treeline. 8000 to about 9000 feet.

Hulsea T. & G.

Annual, biennial or perennial, aromatic, glandular and long-hairy herbs; stems leafy to nearly leafless; leaves alternate, entire to pinnatifid; heads radiate, many-flowered;

involucral bracts herbaceous, in 2 or 3 series; receptacle flat, naked; ray flowers pistillate and fertile, yellow or purplish; disk flowers perfect, fertile, yellow; achenes hairy; pappus a ring of 4 or more hyaline scales.

Flowering stems without leaves; basal leaves with short blunt lobes; plant mostly under 10 cm tall..*H. nana*

Flowering stems with some or many leaves; basal leaves sometimes toothed but not lobed; plant 10-40 cm tall..*H. algida*

Hulsea algida Gray   Alpine Hulsea

Perennial with a caudex and thick taproot; stems 10-40 cm tall, succulent, densely glandular-puberulent; leaves many, oblanceolate to linear or oblong, up to 15 cm long, nearly entire to toothed, mostly at or near the base; heads large and solitary; involucre 13-20 mm high, glandular-pubescent and sometimes woolly-long-hairy; rays deep yellow, 7-15 mm long; achenes about 7 mm long; pappus scales fringed, in 2 unequal pairs.
In scree, talus, granitic sand or gravel and on steep rocky slopes, usually among rocks, 8500 feet to about 9600 feet.

Hulsea nana Gray   Dwarf Hulsea

Perennial with slender branched rootstocks, glandular-long-hairy; stems 4 to about 10 or 15 cm tall; leaves many, clustered at the base, on short stems, oblanceolate to oblong, 2-6 cm long, glandular and sparsely to densely woolly-long-hairy, the blades with short blunt lobes up to half the width of the blade, narrowing into long flat petioles; heads large, solitary on nearly leafless stems; involucre 10-12 mm high, glandular, purplish and woolly-villous at the base; rays yellow, 7-12 mm long; pappus pairs about equal, deeply fringed.
Talus and granitic sand or gravel on exposed places, 8000 to about 9600 feet.

Machaeranthera Nees

Taprooted annual, biennial or perennial herbs; leaves alternate, spiny-tipped or -toothed, pinnatifid to pinnately parted to entire; heads solitary to few to many, often large; involucre graduate, in several series, the bracts thin, or thick and leathery with green or leaf-like tips; ray flowers pistillate and fertile; rays purple or white or rarely none; disk flowers perfect; achenes glabrous to woolly-long-hairy; pappus of unequal barbellate bristles, often brownish.

Involucral bracts rather broad, in 3 series, purplish; stems 5-20 cm tall ....*M. shastensis*

Involucral bracts narrower, in 6 to 8 series, green; stems 15-60 cm tall....................*M. canescens*

Machaeranthera canescens (Pursh) Gray   Hoary Aster

M. viscosa Greene; *Aster canescens* Pursh

Taprooted biennial or short-lived perennial, 15-60 cm tall, grayish-hairy, often glandular in the inflorescence; leaves entire to usually with spiny teeth or tips, the basal ones petiolate, oblanceolate or spatulate, up to 10 cm long and often deciduous, the upper ones smaller, often linear, sessile; heads many in an open cyme or panicle; involucre 6-10 mm high, grayish, glandular, the bracts in 6 to 8 series, the tips short, green, spreading or reflexed; rays bright bluish-purple; pappus bristles unequal, brownish.
Dry open slopes and hillsides, 4500 to about 6000 feet.

Machaeranthera shastensis Gray   Shasta Aster

Aster shastensis Gray; *Aster glossophyllus* Piper

Taprooted biennial or short-lived perennial, 5-20 cm tall; herbage finely grayish-puberulent, often glandular in the inflorescence; leaves entire or few-toothed, spatulate or oblanceolate to linear, the basal 1-6.5 cm long, the cauline usually entire and reduced upward; heads solitary or few to many; involucre about 7 mm high, the bracts in 3 to 5 series, grayish-hairy and rarely glandular, purplish and usually with spreading green tips; rays blue-violet, about 8 or about 13, neutral or sometimes pistillate; disk corollas often purple; achenes pubescent; pappus brownish.
Dry open sandy or rocky places, 5000 to about 9000 feet.

Leaves narrow, the lower mostly linear-oblanceolate, sometimes toothed; plants usually erect or stiffly ascending, up to 40 cm tall, nearly or actually without a caudex; 5000 to about 8000 feet..var. **glossophylla** (Piper) Cronq. & Keck

Leaves broader, the lower mostly oblanceolate or broader, mostly entire or nearly so; plants with a taproot and a caudex, 10-20 cm tall, decumbent or ascending; 8000 to about 9000 feet, and probably higher....................var. **latifolia** (Cronq.) Cronq. & Keck

Madia Mol.

Annual or perennial herbs usually glandular and smelling of tar; leaves entire or slightly toothed, opposite or alternate; heads radiate; involucre angled, the grooved bracts completely enclosing the ray achenes; receptacle flat or convex with a series of bracts between the ray and disk flowers; ray flowers pistillate and fertile, yellow; disk flowers perfect, sometimes sterile; ray achenes usually compressed and ridged; disk achenes similar or abortive; pappus usually none, or sometimes a short crown or a few scales.

1. Involucre 2-4.5 mm high, the bracts united around the solitary fertile disk flower; plants
   seldom over 30 cm tall
   2. Upper leaves mostly opposite (sometimes all the leaves opposite), 1-2 cm long.......*M. minima*
   2. Upper leaves mostly alternate, 1-4 cm long..*M. exigua*
1. Involucre 5-12 mm high, the bracts not united, each one enclosing an achene; fertile disk
   flowers usually more than 1
   3. Heads broadest at or near the base but below the middle; rays 6 to 15..................*M. gracilis*
   3. Heads usually narrowed at the base; rays none, or up to 5.................................*M. glomerata*

Madia exigua (J. E. Sm.) Gray   Little Tarweed

Slender annual, 5-30 cm tall or more, branched above; herbage rough-hairy, glandular and aromatic; leaves linear, 1-4 cm long, mostly alternate above the middle; heads small on long naked peduncles; involucre 2.5-4.8 mm high, the bracts falling with the fruit; ray flowers 5 to 8, the rays very short; achenes beaked; disk achenes fertile.
Open woods and grasslands, 4500 to about 6000 feet.

Madia glomerata Hook.   Mountain Tarweed

Slender hairy annual, glandular and with a strong unpleasant odor; stems leafy, 10-80 cm tall, simple or branched above; leaves linear, sessile, entire, 3-9 cm long; heads in small dense clusters; involucres 6-9 mm high, ovate or tapered at both ends; ray flowers 1 to 5, or none, the rays inconspicuous, greenish-yellow to purplish; disk flowers 1 to 10.

yellowish; ray achenes compressed; disk achenes 5-sided; pappus none.
Dry grassy open woodlands, 4500 to about 6000 feet.

Madia gracilis (Smith) Keck   Slender Tarweed; Gum-weed
Slender annual, simple or branching from the middle, 10-100 cm tall, mostly rough-hairy toward the base, glandular above with stalked glands; herbage with the fragrance of resin; leaves linear, 2-11 cm long; heads in panicles or racemes, not clustered; involucre 6-11 mm high, ovoid or broadly urn-shaped, glandular; ray flowers 5 to 13, usually 8, less than 1 cm long; disk flowers fertile; ray achenes compressed and incurved; disk achenes straighter.
Moraines and dry ground in open coniferous woods, 4500 to about 5200 feet.

Madia minima (Gray) Keck   Woodland Tarweed
Slender branching annual 2-15 cm tall, long-hairy, stipitate-glandular above; leaves 1-2 cm long, linear, opposite or clustered at the nodes; heads 2-3 mm high, solitary or in small clusters on the branches and in the forks of the stem; involucre 2-4 mm high, the 3 to 5 bracts broadly rounded on the back and glandular; rays inconspicuous; achenes black, incurved.
Dry openings in coniferous or mixed woods, 4500 to about 5500 feet.

Matricaria [Tourn.] L.

Annual or perennial herbs, often aromatic, with alternate pinnatifid or pinnately dissected leaves; heads many-flowered, radiate or discoid, at the ends of the branches; involucre saucer-shaped, the bracts in 2 or 3 series, scarious-margined; receptacle naked, hemispheric or long-conic; ray flowers when present pistillate and fertile with white rays; disk flowers yellow, perfect, fertile; achenes 3- to 5-ribbed on one side, smooth on the other; pappus a short crown, or none.

Matricaria matricarioides (Less.) Porter   Pineapple Weed
Pineapple-scented nearly glabrous annuals 10-40 cm tall; leaves 1-5 cm long, dissected 1 to 3 times into short narrow segments; heads numerous, rayless, conical; involucre about 3 mm high, the bracts oval with broad scarious margins; disk flowers yellowish-green; receptacle conical, hollow, pointed; achenes with 3 or more nerves; pappus a minute crown.
Moraines and roadsides, 4500 to about 5200 feet.

Microseris D. Don

Annual or taprooted perennial herbs; leaves entire to toothed or pinnatifid, glabrous or puberulent; heads many-flowered, solitary on long leafless peduncles; outer involucral bracts shorter than the inner ones; receptacle naked or with black hairs; corollas all ligulate, yellow-orange, yellow or white; achenes not beaked, smooth or scabrous, ribbed, the outer often densely white-hairy; pappus of several scales tipped with plumose or capillary bristles, or sometimes the scales nearly obsolete.

Microseris nutans (Hook.) Sch.-Bip   Nodding Microseris
Glabrous or scurfy caulescent perennials with fleshy taproots; stems 10-70 cm tall, usually few, branched and leafy; leaves variable, linear to spatulate, entire or with

slender teeth or lobes; heads nodding in bud, 10- to 75-flowered; outer involucral bracts unequal and shorter than the inner ones; corollas yellow to yellowish-orange; achenes columnar or tapering above; pappus of 10 or more scales each tipped with a bright-white plumose bristle.
Moist open mixed and coniferous woods, meadows and grasslands, usually near water, 4600 to about 8000 feet.

Rudbeckia L.

Large coarse annual or perennial herbs; leaves alternate, entire to pinnatifid; heads large and showy, solitary or few, radiate or discoid; rays neutral, yellow or with purple-brown base, sometimes orange or crimson; disk hemispheric to conic, purplish-brown to greenish-yellow; involucre of unequal herbaceous bracts, spreading or reflexed; receptacle conic to columnar with short chaffy bracts; disk corollas usually dark purplish, 5-toothed at the tip; achenes angled, glabrous (ours); pappus none or of 2 to 4 minute teeth.

Rudbeckia occidentalis Nutt.   Western Chocolate-cone
Coarse, nearly glabrous perennial mostly 50-200 cm tall; leaves ovate or elliptic, up to 25 cm long, entire or toothed, sometimes lobed, long-petiolate near the base, sessile or short-petiolate above, usually scabrous; heads discoid, 1 to 4 on long peduncles, the disk black or purple-brown, roundish at first but elongating in fruit to as much as 6 cm and becoming cone-shaped; involucral bracts very unequal, herbaceous, reflexed in age; achenes oblique at the base; pappus a short irregularly-toothed crown.
Moist or boggy meadows, streambanks and drier places but near streams, 5000 to about 7000 feet.

Saussurea DC.

Perennial herbs; leaves alternate, entire, toothed or pinnatifid; heads small, solitary or in corymbose clusters, discoid, the flowers all tubular and perfect; involucral bracts overlapping, in several series; receptacle flat or convex, naked or chaffy; corollas blue or purple; achenes oblong, often angled; pappus single or double, the inner a ring of plumose bristles and mostly deciduous, the outer shorter, not plumose and sometimes missing altogether.

Saussurea americana D. C. Eaton   American Saw-wort
Coarse fibrous-rooted leafy perennials 30-150 cm tall, or more; herbage sparsely puberulent or tomentose and slightly glandular, especially on the lower leaf surface; leaves thin, ovate to lanceolate, toothed, the lower up to 15 cm long and petiolate, the upper reduced and sessile; heads in a corymbose cluster; involucre 10-14 mm high, the bracts mostly ovate, overlapping, in many series, frequently tinged with purplish black or dark brown; receptacle naked or fringed; corollas violet-purple or rarely white; achenes angled, turgid or flattened, glandular or glabrous; outer pappus bristle-like and deciduous, the inner plumose and persistent.
Boggy or moist mountain meadows and slopes, usually in rocky places near a creek, 5000 to about 7000 feet.

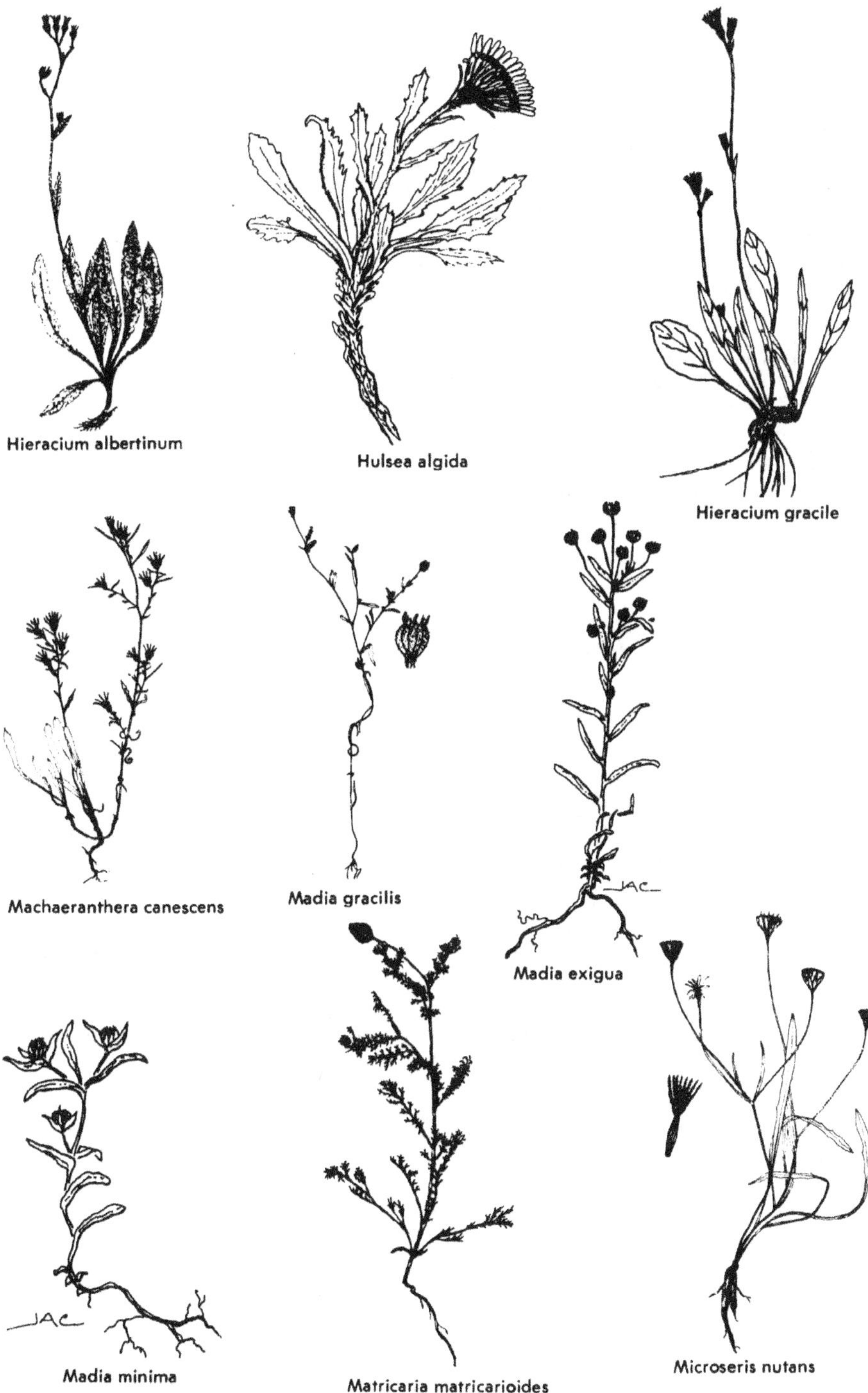

Hieracium albertinum
Hulsea algida
Hieracium gracile
Machaeranthera canescens
Madia gracilis
Madia exigua
Madia minima
Matricaria matricarioides
Microseris nutans

Senecio L.

Perennial herbs (ours) ; leaves alternate or all basal, entire to toothed or cleft; heads solitary to many, small to medium-sized, cylindric to hemispheric, radiate or discoid; rays pistillate and fertile, mostly yellow but sometimes orange, reddish or white, or missing; involucral bracts equal, essentially in one series but often with a few smaller outer ones; receptacle naked, flat or convex; disk flowers perfect and fertile; achenes 5- to 10-ribbed; pappus of many capillary bristles.

1. Stems quite leafy, the upper ones well developed, only slightly smaller than the lower
ones
  2. Plants dwarf, about 10 cm tall; stems mostly sprawling on the ground................*S. fremontii*
  2. Plants much taller, up to 150 cm or more; stems erect
    3. Leaves triangular, sometimes heart-shaped at the base.................................*S. triangularis*
    3. Leaves broadest at or near the middle, usually tapered at the base of the blade..... *S. serra*
1. Stems with few leaves, the upper ones conspicuously smaller and less developed than the
lower ones; plants often with a basal tuft of leaves
  4. Leaves and stems hairy at flowering time, sometimes only at the base, the
pubescence cobwebby and often whitish, especially on young plants
    5. Stems mostly solitary
      6. Leaves usually toothed and often lobed as well
        7. Hairs loosely curled and long, to rather cobwebby; stems and
leaves thick...*S. integerrimus*
        7. Hairs softer, more dense and entangled, usually short and fine;
stems and leaves more slender...*S. pauperculus*
      6. Leaves only slightly short-toothed if at all, not usually lobed; pubescence
fine and soft; leaves thin, mostly green on the upper surface........*S. sphaerocephalus*
    5. Stems usually more than one, branched from the roots, one flowering the
others not; leaves whitish...*S. canus*
  4. Leaves and stems usually not hairy
    8. Heads nearly always solitary; plants of higher elevations
      9. Head on a leafless stalk; leaves kidney-shaped, the margins wavy; rare
in our mountains..*S. porteri*
      9. Head on a stalk with 1 or more leaves; leaves roundish, the margins
sometimes toothed; common in wet meadows and lake borders..... *S. cymbalarioides*
    8. Heads usually more than one
      10. Blade of the basal leaves broad or heart-shaped at the base, sharply
toothed on the margins; upper leaves lobed at the base
        11. Heads without rays, or if radiate, heads only 1 or 2; bracts of the
involucre usually tipped with reddish-purple...........................*S. pauciflorus*
        11. Heads radiate; leaves thin..*S. pseudaureus*
      10. Blade of the basal leaves tapering into the petiole, not broad or heart-
shaped at the base; upper leaves toothed or lobed; heads radiate
        12. Leaves thick and firm, the basal elliptic to roundish.............*S. streptanthifolius*
        12. Leaves thin, the basal mostly elliptic, not roundish................. *S. pauperculus*

Senecio canus Hook.   Gray Woolly Butterweed

Perennial herbs with 1 or more stems from the caudex, 10-40 cm tall, white-tomentose throughout, except sometimes the upper leaf surface glabrate; leaves mostly clustered near the base of the plant, entire to toothed or lobed, ovate to narrowly oblanceolate, 1-8 cm long on long petioles, the cauline few and reduced upward becoming sessile and bract-like; heads several; involucre 4-8 mm high, the bracts in one series; disk 6-13 mm wide; rays mostly 6-13 mm long; achenes glabrous; pappus of capillary bristles. Dry rocky open slopes, forest openings and dry rocky meadows, 4600 to about 9000 feet.

Senecio cymbalarioides Buek.   Alpine Meadow Butterweed
(Formerly known as *S. subnudus* DC.)
Glabrous fibrous-rooted perennial with a short rhizome; stem solitary, nearly leafless, 5-30 cm tall; leaves few, the lower ones obovate to orbicular, wavy-margined, the blade up to 2.5 cm long; cauline leaves 1 or 2, narrower, pinnatifid, much reduced upward to nearly bract-like; heads mostly solitary, the disk 8-15 mm wide, yellow; involucre 5-8 mm high, sometimes purplish; rays conspicuous, 7-14 mm long; achenes glabrous. Wet meadows and swampy ground near lakes and streams, 5700 to about 9000 feet.

Senecio fremontii T. & G.   Dwarf Mountain Butterweed
Glabrous perennial with branching caudex and a taproot; stems branched, 10-15 cm tall, often sprawling; leaves thick and succulent, toothed or lobed, obovate to spatulate, 1-4 cm long, the lower ones reduced and wing-petiolate, the upper ones larger and sessile; heads few, terminal on the many branches; involucre about 7-12 mm high; rays 6-10 mm long, bright yellow; achenes usually glabrous.
Talus, exposed cliffs, rocky slopes and ridges, 7600 to about 9100 feet.

Senecio integerrimus Nutt. var. **exaltatus** (Nutt.) Cronq.
Single-stemmed Butterweed
Stout, fibrous-rooted perennial with a short caudex and a single stem 20-70 cm tall; herbage hairy to tomentose, becoming nearly glabrous with age; leaves entire to toothed, the basal oblanceolate to ovate, petiolate, 6-25 cm long, the cauline progressively reduced upward and becoming sessile; inflorescence short and crowded or more open and longer, of 5 to 35 heads, the peduncle of the terminal head shorter and thicker than the others; involucral bracts black-tipped, 5-10 mm long; rays yellow, 6-15 mm long.
Dry or moist open woods or forest clearings, 4500 to about 6500 feet.

Senecio pauciflorus Pursh   Small-flowered Butterweed
Fibrous-rooted glabrous perennial with a simple or branched caudex; stems 15-40 cm tall; leaves thick and succulent, wavy-margined, toothed or pinnatifid with blunt lobes, the basal petiolate, elliptic-ovate to rounded and abruptly narrowed to the truncate base, the cauline reduced and becoming sessile; heads 2 to 6, sometimes more, orange or reddish, discoid or with short rays; involucre about 7 mm high with 13 or 21 bracts usually reddish-purple-tipped; disk 1-1.5 cm wide; achenes glabrous.
Dry rocky woods, about 8000 feet.

Senecio pauperculus Michx.   Showy Butterweed
Fibrous-rooted perennial sometimes with some short stolons; stems clustered or solitary, 10-70 cm tall; herbage glabrate or tomentose at the base of the stems and in the leaf axils; lower leaves oblanceolate-elliptic, nearly entire or the margins wavy or sharply cut, petiolate, the upper ones conspicuously reduced, pinnatifid, becoming sessile and entire; heads several; involucre 6-10 mm high; rays showy, deep yellow, 5-10 mm long, rarely none.
Rocky streambanks and shady boggy places, 5000 to about 5500 feet.

Senecio porteri Greene   Porter's Butterweed
Glabrous fibrous-rooted perennial with long rhizomes; flowering stem 3-8 cm tall, leaf-less or with 2 or 3 small bracts; leaves kidney-shaped or roundish, petiolate, crowded

near the base of the plant, the blades thick, wavy-margined, up to 2.5 cm wide; heads solitary; involucre about 1 cm high, purplish.
Apparently collected only once in our mountains at Ice Lake, elevation about 8000 feet, and reported as "very little seen." (W. C. Cusick 2308)

Senecio pseudaureus Rydb.   Streambank Butterweed
Fibrous-rooted perennial floccose-tomentose when young, soon becoming glabrous; stems 30-70 cm tall; leaves thin, the basal long-petiolate, the blade mostly ovate, cordate to truncate at the base, the margins serrate, the cauline leaves few, pinnatifid toward their bases, reduced upward and becoming sessile and clasping; heads several to many; disk about 8-13 mm wide; involucre 5-8 mm high; rays about 6-10 mm long.
Streambanks, wet meadows and moist shady woodlands, 4500 to about 5000 feet.

Senecio serra Hook.   Tall Butterweed
Fibrous-rooted perennial, glabrous or fine-hairy near the base; stems leafy, clustered, 50-200 cm tall; leaves oblanceolate to lanceolate, sharply toothed to nearly entire, 7-15 cm long, the lower ones short-petiolate and deciduous, the others becoming sessile but not much smaller upward; heads numerous, almost cylindric; disk about 3-7 mm wide; involucre about 7 mm high, the bracts often black-tipped; rays about 5 or 8, 4-8 mm long.
Moist meadows, streambanks and other open places, 4500 to about 5500 feet.

Senecio sphaerocephalus Greene   Mountain-marsh Butterweed
Fibrous-rooted perennial from a short horizontal rhizome, thinly tomentose when young and often glabrate later; stem mostly solitary; leaves entire or slightly toothed, the lower ones oblanceolate or elliptic, petiolate, 5-25 cm long, the others few, becoming reduced upward and sessile; heads about 3 to 25 in a compact cluster; involucre 4-8 mm high, the bracts black- or brown-tipped; disk 8-15 mm wide; rays 6-10 mm long.
Swampy streambanks, shady bogs and wet meadows, 4500 to about 6000 feet.

Senecio streptanthifolius Greene   Rocky Mountain Groundsel
   (Formerly known as *S. cymbalarioides* Nutt.)
Nearly glabrous fibrous-rooted perennial; stems clustered, 10-50 cm tall; leaves glabrous, rather thick and succulent, the basal long-petiolate, the blades elliptic to ovate, toothed or shallowly lobed or entire, the cauline few, reduced, becoming sessile, often cleft and toothed near their bases; heads several or many; involucres about 6 mm high; rays bright yellow, 6-12 mm long.
In thin sandy soils of mostly exposed steep slopes, but also moist meadows and lake borders, 7500 to about 9500 feet.

Senecio triangularis Hook.   Arrowhead Butterweed
Coarse perennial, mostly 30-150 cm tall, tomentose when young, usually becoming glabrate later; stems leafy, clustered; leaves numerous, neither tufted at the base nor conspicuously reduced upward, the lower ones triangular with cordate or arrow-shaped bases, the petioles long, the upper ones narrower and more lanceolate, becoming sessile; leaf blades generally 4-20 cm long, toothed; heads few to many in a short, flat-topped inflorescence; involucre 6-10 mm high, the bracts often black-tipped; rays 5 to 10, 7-13 mm long.

Streambanks, moist meadows and near lakes, 6000 to about 8500 feet and possibly higher.

Solidago L.

Perennial herbs with fibrous roots or rhizomes; stems erect and leafy; leaves alternate, entire or toothed; inflorescence usually a large panicle, raceme or cyme or a number of small radiate yellow heads (ours); involucral bracts overlapping in several series, usually with green tips; receptacle naked; ray flowers pistillate and fertile, the rays short; disk flowers perfect and fertile; achenes short and ribbed; pappus usually of many white capillary bristles.

1. Basal and lower stem leaves conspicuously fringed with hairs (ciliate) at least on the petiole, otherwise glabrous; plants usually at high elevations............*S. multiradiata* var. *scopulorum*
1. Basal and lower cauline leaves not or scarcely ciliate-margined; plants usually at low to middle elevations; stems often reddish-purple toward the base
    2. Stem leaves numerous, crowded; basal leaves missing or reduced; stem fine-hairy at least above the middle; rays about 13.................................*S. canadensis* var. *salebrosa*
    2. Stem leaves fewer, smaller, not crowded; basal leaves usually well-developed, up to 30 cm long, persistent; stem and leaves hairless or nearly so throughout; rays about 8 mostly, but sometimes 13.................................*S. missouriensis*

Solidago canadensis L. var. **salebrosa** (Piper) Jones   Meadow Goldenrod

Perennial from creeping rhizomes; stems leafy, clustered, 30-200 cm tall, sparsely pubescent except near the base where glabrous; leaves 5-12 cm long, 1-2 cm wide, crowded, lanceolate, sessile, 3-nerved, entire or sharply serrate, scabrous on veins and margins, pubescent on both sides or glabrous, the lower ones early deciduous; inflorescence a large, dense broad panicle 5-20 cm long, the heads small, sometimes 1-sided on the spreading or curved lower branches; involucre 3.5-5 mm high; rays 10 to 17, 1-3 mm long.

Streamsides and sunny open woods, 4500 to about 5500 feet.

Solidago missouriensis Nutt.   Missouri Goldenrod

Perennial mostly 20-50 cm tall, glabrous or sometimes pubescent in the inflorescence; stems solitary from long rhizomes or clustered from a caudex; basal leaves mostly persistent, 8-15 cm long, oblanceolate, petiolate, entire or serrate; cauline leaves few, reduced, entire, becoming sessile upward; panicle oblong, rhombic or pyramidal, the heads often 1-sided; involucre mostly 3-4 mm high; rays 7 to 13.

Dry rocky meadows and open mixed or coniferous woods, 4500 to about 6000 feet.

Solidago multiradiata Ait. var. **scopulorum** Gray   Northern or Alpine Goldenrod
S. corymbosa Nutt.; *S. cusickii* Piper; *S. ciliosa* Greene; *S. scopulorum* (Gray)
A. Nels.

Perennial with mostly short rootstocks, crisp-pubescent at least in the inflorescence; stems 5-50 cm tall; basal and lower leaves oblanceolate to elliptic, 2-10 cm long, glabrous, toothed or entire, the leaf blades and petioles ciliate-margined; upper leaves spatulate to lanceolate, few, sessile and somewhat clasping, the margins ciliate toward the base; heads few to many in a loose or dense terminal corymb, the pedicels white-long-hairy; involucre 4-7 mm high, usually shortly ciliate; rays usually 13, 2-6 mm long.

Moist or swampy meadows and lake borders and rocky wooded slopes, 5300 to about 9600 feet.

Taraxacum Wiggers

Taprooted perennial herbs; leaves entire, toothed or pinnatifid in a basal rosette; heads large, solitary on leafless, hollow, erect scapes; flowers all ligulate, perfect, yellow; involucre of 2 series of bracts, the outer usually shorter than the inner and often curved outward; receptacle naked; achenes oblong or spindle-shaped, ribbed, round or angled, roughish, prolonged into a beak above; pappus of many soft unequal capillary bristles.

Taraxacum officinale Weber   Dandelion

Scapose perennial, tomentose when young, later glabrous; leaves 5-40 cm long, oblanceolate to oblong, pinnatifid or lobed, the lobes pointing downward, the terminal lobe largest; scapes 5-50 cm high, usually several; heads solitary, large; outer involucral bracts shorter than the inner and curving downward; achenes grayish or greenish-brown, rough at the top, the beak 2 or 3 times as long as the body of the achene; pappus white. Moist grassy open woods, streambanks and gravelly roadsides, 4500 to at least 6100 feet.

Townsendia Hook.

Taprooted annual, biennial or perennial herbs; leaves alternate or all basal, entire; heads few or solitary, radiate, medium to large and showy, the rays pistillate and fertile, white, pink, blue or violet; involucral bracts overlapping, green-striped with scarious margins; receptacle flat, naked; disk flowers perfect, yellow or reddish; achenes flattened, 2-nerved, sometimes triangular; pappus a single series of barbellate bristles or small scales.

Plants dwarf, stemless, seldom over 5 cm tall...*T. montana*
Plants larger, the stems up to 30 cm tall..*T. parryi*

Townsendia montana M. E. Jones   Mountain Townsendia
    T. alpigena Piper
Acaulescent perennial with a taproot and branching caudex, 2-6.5 cm tall; herbage

Ri   cidentalis

Saussurea americana

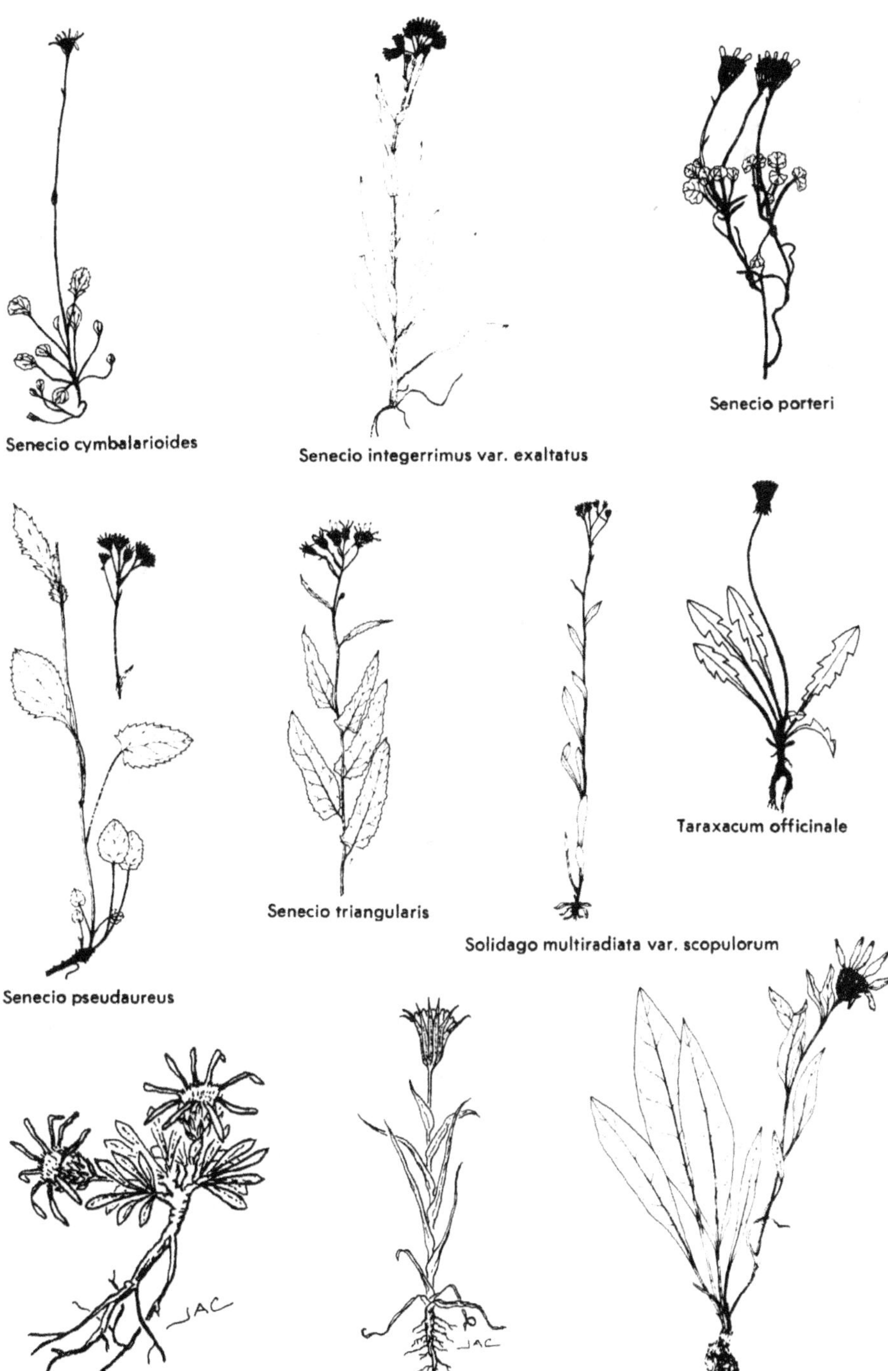

Senecio cymbalarioides
Senecio integerrimus var. exaltatus
Senecio porteri
Senecio pseudaureus
Senecio triangularis
Solidago multiradiata var. scopulorum
Taraxacum officinale
Townsendia montana
Tragopogon dubius
Wyethia helianthoides

rough-hairy when young, mostly glabrate later; leaves mostly crowded at the base, 1-3.5 cm long, oblanceolate; heads sessile, solitary on naked scapes up to 6.5 cm long; involucre 6-12 mm high, the bracts in 3 or 4 series, ciliate and purplish on the margins; rays mostly blue or violet, 5-10 mm long; achenes nearly glabrous except for a few hairs; pappus about 5 mm long.

Sandy or gravelly open places and among rocks on exposed cliffs and ridges, 7500 to about 9800 feet.

Townsendia parryi D. C. Eaton   Parry's Townsendia

Grayish-hairy stout perennial 5-30 cm tall with 1 or more stems; basal leaves crowded, oblanceolate, 1-6 cm long including the petiole, thinly pubescent or glabrous; cauline leaves few and small; heads solitary, large and showy; involucre 9-16 mm high, the bracts in about 5 series, long-pointed, the margins ciliate and scarious; rays 40 or more, violet or bluish purple, 1-2 cm long; pappus of barbellate bristles.

Dry sandy talus slopes and ridges, 7000 to about 8500 feet and possibly higher.

Tragopogon [Tourn.] L.

Taprooted annual, biennial or perennial herbs; leaves alternate, clasping, grass-like; heads large, long-peduncled, solitary; flowers all ligulate, perfect, yellow or purple; involucral bracts in 1 series; receptacle naked; achenes rounded or angled, ribbed, beaked or beakless; pappus a single row of unequal plumose bristles united at the base.

Tragopogon dubius Scop.   Yellow Salsify

Taprooted biennial, or sometimes annual, 30-100 cm tall; leaves linear, entire, clasping, 12-15 cm long, floccose when young, becoming nearly glabrous and glaucous later; peduncles conspicuously inflated beneath the heads; flowers all ligulate, perfect, the rays pale or greenish-yellow; involucral bracts longer than the rays, 2.5-4 cm at first but elongating in fruit to 4-7 cm long; achenes slender, 2.5-3.5 mm long, beaked; pappus of whitish, interwebbed plumose bristles.

Dry meadows, grassy moraines and rocky roadsides, 4500 to about 5200 feet.

Wyethia Nutt.

Fragrant, thick-rooted perennials; stems clustered; basal leaves large, the cauline reduced and alternate; heads large, solitary to few, radiate (ours), the rays pistillate, fertile, mostly yellow but sometimes white; involucre in 2 to 4 series, the bracts nearly equal or the outer enlarged and leaf-like; receptacle flat or rounded, the bracts clasping the achenes; disk flowers perfect, yellow; achenes 3- or 4-angled with intermediate nerves; pappus a crown of united scales, sometimes awned.

Wyethia helianthoides Nutt.   Mule Ears; Rough Dwarf Sunflower

Perennial with a thick carrot-shaped caudex and root; stems 15-40 cm tall, thick but not stiff, stipitate-glandular and loosely hairy especially above; leaves rough-hairy, entire or nearly so, ciliate-margined, the basal 9-35 cm long and wing-petiolate, the cauline smaller, becoming nearly sessile; heads usually large, showy and solitary; involucre wider than high, the bracts woolly-ciliate on the margins; rays white or cream (ours), often drying yellowish, 2.5-4.5 cm long.

Wet grassy meadows in open pine woods, 5800 to about 6100 feet.

SELECTED REFERENCES

Abrams, LeRoy, 1940-1960. Illustrated Flora of the Pacific States, Vol. I-IV. Stanford University Press.

Baldwin, E. M., 1959. Geology of Oregon. University of Oregon Co-op Book Store.

Barneby, Rupert C., Atlas of North American Astragalus, Parts I and II. 1964. Memoirs of The New York Botanical Garden, Vol. 13. Bronx, New York.

Davis, Ray J., 1952. Flora of Idaho. Wm. C. Brown Co., Dubuque, Iowa.

Head, S., 1959. Study of the Wallowa Mountains. Ph.D. Thesis, Oregon State University.

Hitchcock, C. L., A. Cronquist, M. Ownbey and J. W. Thompson, 1955-1969. Vascular Plants of the Pacific Northwest, Parts 1-5.

Horner, J. H. and G. Butterfield, 1953. Spring Wild Flowers of Southeast Washington and Northeast Oregon. Walla Walla College Publication, Vol. 3, No. 1.

——————————, 1949. Wallowa, the Land of Winding Waters. Compiled and Published by Horner and Butterfield, Joseph, Oregon.

Lowell, W. R., 1940. Glaciation in the Wallowa Mountains of Oregon. M.A. Thesis, University of Chicago.

Miller, Mabel C., 1915. A Comparison of the Flora of the Wallowa Region with that of the Blue Mountains in Regard to their Geological Relations. B.A. Thesis, Eastern Oregon College.

Peck, Morton E., 1947. Certain Plant Species of the Canyon of Hurricane Creek, Wallowa County, Oregon. Madrono, Vol. IX, Number 1.

——————————, 1961. A Manual of the Higher Plants of Oregon. Second Edition. Binfords & Mort and Oregon State University Press.

Ross, C. P., 1938. The Geology of Part of the Wallowa Mountains. Bull. 3. Oregon Dept. Geol. and Mineral Indust.

St. John, Harold, 1963. Flora of Southeastern Washington. Edwards Brothers Inc.

Smith, Warren D., 1929. Wallowa Mountains, Mazama, Vol. 5, No. 3.

——————————, 1928. Physical and Economic Geography of Oregon, Chapter 8, The Wallowa Mountains and County. Commonwealth Review of the University of Oregon, Vol. 10, No. 4.

Smith, W. D., J. E. Allen, L. W. Staples and W. R. Lowell, 1941. Geology and Physiography of the Northern Wallowa Mountains, Oregon. Bull. 12. Oregon Dept. Geol. and Mineral Indust., Portland.

Stevens, Louise F., 1932. Certain Dike Effects Due to Contact Metamorphism at Aneroid Lake, Oregon. University of Washington B.A. Thesis.

Stevenson, Elmo N., n.d. Nature Rambles in the Wallowas. Metropolitan Press, Oregon.

Steward, A. N., L. D. Johnston, H. M. Gilkey, 1960. Aquatic Plants of the Pacific Northwest. Oregon State College Press, Corvallis, Oregon.

Stovall, J. C., 1929. Pleistocene Geology and Physiography of the Wallowa Mountains with Special Reference to Wallowa and Hurricane Canyons. M.A. Thesis, University of Oregon.

Wagner, N. S., 1955. Summary of Wallowa Mountains Geology. The Ore-Bin 17(5) : 31-35. (Pub. by Oregon Dept. Geol. and Mineral Indust., Portland).

Weber, William A., 1967. Rocky Mountain Flora. University of Colorado Press, Boulder.

Wilson, Ralph R., 1964. Illustrated Fundamentals of Tree Identification. The Litho Printing Co., Pocatello, Idaho.

GLOSSARY

Aborted: parts not formed or incompletely formed.

Acaulescent: without a stem.

Achene: a small, hard, dry fruit which remains closed at maturity.

Acuminate: having a gradually tapering point.

Adherent: the union of a part or organ to another.

Adnate: attached the whole length.

Aggregated: collected together.

Acute: sharply pointed but not tapering to the point.

Alternate: said of leaves when arising singly from each node, as opposed to arising in pairs from each node, when opposite.

Ament: a catkin; a spike of flowers.

Androgynous: descriptive of a spike in which the staminate flowers are above the pistillate ones in the same spike, as in some species of *Carex*.

Angiosperms: plants with their seeds enclosed in an ovary.

Annual: plants which finish their cycle of life within one year.

Annulus: a ring; the elastic band on fern sporangia which breaks at maturity and releases the spores.

Anterior: indicating a position in front of an organ or the front part of an organ.

Anther: the portion of a stamen which produces and contains the pollen.

Apex: the tip of an organ or part.

Appendage: a part added to another, as the small part added to the tip of the leaf of certain species of *Antennaria*.

Appressed: lying flat for the whole length of the organ or body.

Aquatic: living in water.

Arachnoid: like a cobweb; descriptive of an entanglement of fine whitish hairs.

Ascending: directed upward, as the branches of a plant.

Asexual: descriptive of a taxon without staminate or pistillate organs; neuter.

Attenuate: narrowed, tapered.

Auricle: a small lobe or ear, as an appendage to a leaf.

Awl-shaped: narrow and tapering to a point.

Awn: a bristle-like appendage, as that at the tip of glumes or lemmas in the grasses.

Banner: the upper petal of a pea-like flower; also called a standard.

Barbed: with short firm points directed backward or downward.

Basal: at the base of a plant or any particular plant part.

Beak: a prolonged slender tip or projection.

Beard: a tuft of hairs.

Berry: a pulpy fruit.

Biennial: a plant which lives two years, flowering and setting seed only in the second year.

Bipinnate: said of a leaf when both primary and secondary divisions are pinnate.

Bipinnatifid: said of a leaf when the divisions of a pinnatifid leaf are in turn pinnatifid.

Blade: the expanded portion of a leaf or petal.

Bloom: a whitish or waxy covering on some fruits, as the plum.

Blunt: not pointed; the rounded shape at the tip of some plant parts as opposed to a pointed tip.

Bract: a modified or much-reduced leaf.

Bristle: a stiff hair.

Bulb: a modified bud with fleshy leaves and a short stem, usually underground.

Bulbil: a small bulb, usually in a leaf axil.

Callus: a thickened or hardened part.

Calyx: the outer set of parts of the flower, generally green, composed of a number of sepals.

Canescent: grayish-hairy.

Capillary: thin or hair-like.

Capitate: head-like, or formed like a head; a dense or compact cluster.

Capsule: a dry dehiscent fruit composed of 1 or more carpels.

Carpel: a simple pistil, or one part of a compound pistil.

Catkin: a deciduous spike of flowers without petals, as in *Salix.*

Caudex: the short woody basal portion of some perennials.

Caulescent: having an evident stem above ground.

Cauline: on the stem, as leaves arising from nodes of the stem.

Chaff: small membranous scales or bracts, as in the heads of some Compositae.

Chartaceous: papery or tissue-like, usually not green in color.

Chlorophyll: the green coloring material in plants.

Ciliate: fringed with marginal hairs.

Cinereous: ashy gray.

Circumscissile: splitting around at the middle.

Clavate: thicker at the top than at the base; club-shaped.

Claw: the narrowed base of a floral part, such as a petal.

Cleft: cut half-way down.

Cleistogamous: closed, as the late-season flowers of some Violets.

Cluster: a group, as flowers gathered together.

Cobwebby: slender threads entangled with each other.

Collar: an encircling membrane.

Colored: any tint except green.

Colorless: pale, hyaline.

Column: the single central organ formed by the union of stamens and styles in the Orchid Family.

Coma: the tuft of hairs at the end of some seeds.

Commissure: the face by which two carpels adhere.

Compound: said of a leaf divided into 2 or more leaflets; of a pistil with 2 or more carpels; of an inflorescence when it has secondary inflorescences.

Compressed: flattened.

Concave: hollowed out as a saucer is hollowed.

Cone: a cluster of scales attached to a main axis.

Confluent: running together, as the terminal lobes of some leaves.

Congested: crowded.

Conical: cone-shaped.

Coniferous: referring to trees which produce cones.

Connate: united, whether at first or later.

Connective: the tissue which connects the two cells of an anther.

Constricted: contracted; drawn together.

Contorted: twisted or bent.

Contracted: narrowed or shortened; not spreading much.

Convex: having a rounded or arched surface.

Cordate: heart-shaped; with rounded lobes separated by a deep sinus at the base of an organ or plant part.

Corm: a bulb-like fleshy stem or base of stem, usually underground.

Corolla: the set of petals in a flower whether united or separate from each other.

Corrugated: wrinkled.

Corymb: a flat-topped cluster of flowers with pedicels or unequal length.

Costa: a rib, a midrib or middle-nerve.

Cotyledon(s): the first leaf or leaves of the embryo.

Creeping: running along or under the ground and rooting at intervals along its length.

Crenate: scalloped or with shallow rounded teeth.

Crest: a toothed ridge or outgrowth.

Crisped: curled.

Culm: the stem or stalk of grasses and grass-like plants.

Cuneate: wedge-shaped.

Cyme: a rather flat-topped flower cluster in which the central flower develops first.

Deciduous: falling after maturity, as the leaves in the autumn.

Declined: curved or bent downward.

Decompound: several times divided or compounded.

Decumbent: lying on or close to the ground but the tips raised.

Decurrent: running down and adnate to the stem; descriptive of leaves prolonged below their point of insertion.

Deflexed: bent outward; reflexed.

Dehiscing: splitting into definite parts.

Dentate: toothed with sharp spreading teeth directed forward.

Denticulate: minutely toothed.

Depressed: sunken or flattened from above.

Descending: tending downward.

Diadelphous: having the stamens in two groups or bundles.

Dichotomous: forked; parted by pairs.

Dicotyledoneae: class of plants having two seed leaves.

Diffuse: descriptive of an inflorescence which is widely spreading, loosely branched, or the flowers scattered.

Dilated: expanded; widened.

Dimorphic: having two different forms or shapes.

Dioecious: having the staminate flowers on different plants from those with pistillate flowers.

Disc: a development of the stem around the base of the pistil; the central part of the flower-head in Compositae.

Discoid: indicating flower heads composed entirely of perfect tubular disk flowers only, as some flowers in Compositae.

Disk: the central part of the head of some Compositae.

Dissected: deeply divided, or cut into many segments.

Distal: some distance away from the place of attachment of an organ or plant part.

Distinct: free; separate; not united.

Divaricate: spreading widely outward from the axis or rachis.

Divided: a condition in which a part or organ has lobes or segments cut nearly to the base or midvein.

Dormant: not actively engaged in life activities.

Dorsal: the back; the surface away from the plant axis; the under-surface of leaves.

Down: fine soft hair, as the pappus in some plants.

Drooping: tending downward.

Drupe: a stone fruit; an indehiscent fruit containing a solitary seed within a softer outer part.

Ebracteate: without bracts.

Egg-shaped: ovate; ovoid; narrower at the tip than at the base.

Elliptic: oval in outline, with regularly rounded ends and widest at or about the middle.

Emarginate: shallowly notched at the tip.

Emersed: raised above and out of the surface of the water.

Entire: applied to leaves and other parts when the margin is even, without toothing or other division.

Equitant: said of leaves which overlap or fold around or in each other in two ranks, as the leaves of *Iris*.

Erose: unevenly-margined; jagged, as though gnawed or bitten or chewed.

Exfoliating: said of bark peeling off in layers.

Exserted: protruding beyond or sticking out, as the stamens from a perianth.

Falcate: sickle-shaped.

Farinose: covered with mealy patches.

Fascicle: a close cluster or bundle, as of roots, leaves or flowers.

Feathery: plumose.

Fertile: able to produce fruit or seed.

Fibrous: with fibers or woody thread-like endings, as in roots or leaves.

-fid: meaning deeply cut when placed at the end of a word, as pinnatifid.

Filament: the thread-like stalk supporting the anther of a stamen.

Filiform: long and slender or thin, as a thread.

Fimbriate: fringed.

Fistulose: hollow.

Flabellate: fan-shaped.

Flaccid: withered, limp.

Fleshy: succulent, thick, soft and juicy as the edible portions of fruit.

Flexible: able to bend but also able to return to the original state.

Floccose: with locks or tufts of soft hair or wool.

Floret: a small individual flower, one of a cluster, as in the grasses.

Foliaceous: leaf-like in shape, color or texture.

Foliose: closely covered with leaves or leaflets; leafy.

Follicle: a dry fruit of a single carpel which splits at maturity along one side only.

Fornices: small scales, as appendages in the corolla tube of some flowers.

Fovea: a small depression or pit.

Free: not united or joined or adhering.

Frond: leaf of ferns.

Fruit: the mature ovary, with or without the associated parts which have matured with it.

Fusiform: swollen in the middle but tapering toward each end.

Fusion: complete union.

Galea: a helmet-shaped structure, as in the corolla of *Castilleja*.

Gamopetalous: with petals united by their edges.

Gamosepalous: with sepals united into a whole.

Geminate: in pairs or doubled.

Geniculate: abruptly bent or twisted, as the elbow-joint.

Gibbous: the pouch-like swelling on one side at the base of an organ or flower part.

Glabrate: becoming nearly without hairs.

Glabrous: without hairs.

Gladiate: swort-shaped.

Gland: a structure able to produce a secretion.

Glandular: having glands.

Glaucescent: becoming slightly bluish-green.

Glaucous: bluish-green or whitish, as some leaves; the whitish bloom of some fruits, as plums.

Globose: nearly spherical.

Glomerule: a small dense cluster of flowers or heads.

Glume: one of the pair of sterile papery bracts at the base of the grass spikelet.

Granular: composed of grains or small particles.

Gymnospermae: the group of plants having naked seeds.

Gynaecandrous: descriptive of a spike in which the pistillate flowers are above the staminate in the same spike; associated with certain species of *Carex*.

Hastate: arrow-shaped but with the basal lobes turned outward.

Head: a close dense cluster of sessile flowers on a peduncle, as in Compositae.

Herb: a plant with a stem which dies at the end of the growing season.

Herbaceous: not woody.

Herbage: leaves and stems of plants.

Hirsute: with long coarse or stiff hairs.

Hispid: with rough or stiff hairs or bristles.

Hoary: with minute grayish hairs.

Hyaline: colorless, translucent, transparent, thin.

Hypanthium: a cup or tube surrounding the ovary and bearing the sepals, petals and stamens.

Hypogynous: with stamens and petals attached below the ovary and surrounding it.

Imbricated: overlapping as the shingles on a roof.

Immersed: entirely under water.

Imperfect: a flower with either the staminate or the pistillate part undeveloped.

Incised: cut sharply or slashed irregularly into the margin, as of a leaf.

Inclined: bent downward.

Indehiscent: said of pods or other fruits not splitting at maturity by valves or along regular lines.

Indurated: hardened.

Indusium: an outgrowth which covers the sori of many ferns.

Inferior: said of an ovary which is below the attachment of floral parts.

Inflorescence: the cluster of flowers of a plant.

Insectivorous: said of plants which capture insects, as *Drosera*.

Internerves: the portion between nerves of the glume, lemma or palea of grasses.

Internode: the portion of the stem between nodes.

Introduced: said of plants which have been brought from another country.

Involucel: a circle of bracts under a secondary umbel, as in the family Umbelliferae.

Involucre: a ring of bracts surrounding several flowers or their stalks at the base, as in *Eriogonum*.

Involute: with the edges of the leaves rolled inward.

Irregular: when applied to a flower indicating that one or more petal(s) or sepal(s) are in some way different from the others in that set; example: the spur in violets.

Keel: a dorsal rib, ridge or crease; the structure formed by the fusion of petals in some species of Leguminosae.

Lacerate: mangled; torn or irregularly cleft.

Laciniate: slashed.

Lanate: covered with woolly and inter-grown hairs.

Lanceolate: narrow, tapering to each end.

Lax: loose; distant.

Legume: the unconstricted fruit (pod) of some species of the family Leguminosae.

Lemma: one of the pair of bracts which usually enclose the grass floret.

Lenticular: lens-shaped or disc-shaped.

Ligule: a little tongue; the expanded strap-shaped portion of the ray-flowers in Compositae, or the flowers themselves; also a membranous appendage or projection of the leaf sheath of grasses.

Limb: the expanded upper portion of a tubular corolla.

Linear: narrow, several times longer than wide.

Lip: one of the two divisions of a 2-lipped corolla or calyx; also the fifth (odd) petal of the orchids.

Lobe: any division of a plant part which is larger than a tooth but cleft less than halfway to the midline or the base.

Locule: cell or compartment of an ovary or other floral part.

Loculicidal: splitting or dehiscing on the back, between the partitions, into the cavity.

Loment: a fruit which is constricted between the seeds and breaks apart at the constrictions at maturity into 1-seeded segments, as in *Hedysarum*.

Lunate: half-moon-shaped.

Lyrate: lyre-shaped; pinnatifid but with the lobe at the tip larger than the lower smaller lobes.

Macro-: prefix meaning large or long.

Marcescent: withering without falling off.

Matutinal: said of flowers which are open and functional during the morning.

Mealy: granular-scaly.

Mega-: prefix meaning large.

Megasporangium: a sporangium producing megaspores.

Megaspore: a large spore from which the female gametophyte develops.

Membranaceous, membranous: skin-like; thin, transparent, flexible.

Membrane: a thin delicate skin of tissue.

-merous: suffix indicating parts; as tetramerous, meaning having four parts in each of the floral whorls.

Micro-: prefix indicating small.

Microsporangium: a sporangium producing microspores.

Microspore: a small spore from which the male gametophyte develops.

Minute: very small; inconspicuous.

Mixed forest: a forest of several genera and species of trees.

Monadelphous: stamens united into one group only.

Mono-: prefix indicating one.

Monoecious: stamens and pistils in separate flowers but borne on the same plant.

Mucro: a sharp terminal point.

Mucronate: leaves tipped with a minute, abrupt, sharp point.

Muricate: rough, with short and hard tubercular projections.

Naked: without a covering, as flowers without a perianth.

Nectary: a gland capable of secreting nectar.

Nerve: an unbranched vein or slender rib.

Netted: net-veined.

Nocturnal: plants which open or are active at night and close during the day.

Node: the place on the stem where a leaf is attached, or has been.

Nodding: hanging down.

Notched: nicked.

Nut: a hard and indehiscent one-seeded fruit.

Nutlet: a small nut.

Ob-: a prefix meaning in the opposite or inverse position or direction, as obovate, meaning inverted ovate.

Obcordate: upside down heart-shaped, that is, notched at the tip rather than at the base.

Oblanceolate: broadest above the middle and tapering to the base.

Oblique: slanting.

Oblong: longer than broad, but not broader at one place than another.

Obovate: reverse of ovate, that is, broadest at the top than below.

Obsolete: so small as to be almost invisible.

Obtuse: blunt or rounded at the end.

Ochroleucous: pale, yellowish-white, buff.

Ocrea: a sheath or tube formed by a pair of opposite stipules on the stem just above the leaf base of some species in the family Polygonaceae.

Odd-pinnate: said of a leaf having a single terminal leaflet.

Opposite: paired organs or parts, as leaves arising across from each other on a stem.

Orbicular: a circular-shaped or nearly circular flat body or organ.

Oval: broadly elliptic.

Ovary: the part of the pistil containing the ovules.

Ovate: egg-shaped; broader at the base than at the top.

Ovule: young undeveloped seed.

Palate: a projecting portion of the lower lip of a 2-lipped corolla which partially or completely closes the throat.

Palea: an inner bract which, with the lemma, encloses the grass flower.

Palmate: like the palm of the hand; having several nerves, veins, lobes etc. radiating from the same place or point.

Panicle: an inflorescence usually many times branched and having pedicellate flowers.

Papilionaceous: butterfly-shaped, as the flower of the sweet pea.

Papillate: having soft short rounded protuberances; warty or pimply.

Pappus: the modified outer perianth series of the Compositae, composed of hairs or bristles or scales or various mixture of these, and borne on the ovary.

Parasite: a plant which is attached to another and absorbs food and water from it.

Parted: cleft, but not quited to the base.

Pedicel: the support or stalk of a single flower in a flower cluster.

Peduncle: the stalk of a flower cluster.

Peltate: shield-shaped, as is a leaf attached to its stalk or petiole by the lower surface instead of at the margin.

Pencilled: marked with fine distinct lines, as in the violets.

Pendent, pendulous: hanging down from its support; drooping.

Perennial: a plant which lives more than two years.

Perfect: a flower with both stamens and pistil.

Perianth: the floral envelope; the calyx or the corolla, or both, of a flower.

Pericarp: wall of the fruit or the ripened ovary.

Perigynium: the inflated sac-like bract around the achene of the species *Carex.*

Perigynous: calyx, corolla and stamens united into a basal structure surrounding but not beneath the ovary, usually free from it but sometimes adnate to it as in some species of *Saxifraga.*

Persistent: remaining attached after maturity.

Petal: a unit of the floral whorl, usually colored and attractive to pollinators.

Petaloid: petal-like.

Petiole: the stalk of a leaf.

Phyllary: a bract, as one of the segments of the involucre of a flower head in Compositae.

Pilose: having long straight soft distinct hairs.

Pinna: a primary division or leaflet of a pinnate leaf.

Pinnate: feather-structured; with leaflets of a compound leaf arranged on either side of a common stalk or rachis.

Pinnatifid: deeply cut or cleft pinnately rather than palmately.

Pinnule: a secondary pinna or leaflet of a leaf which is pinnately compound two or more times.

Pistil: the female organ of a flower, consisting of ovary, style and stigma.

Pistillate: having pistils, but without functioning stamens.

Plumose: like a plume; feathery; with fine hairs.

Pod: a dry and many-seeded dehiscent fruit.

Pollen: the powdery material (young male gametophytes) produced by the anthers of seed plants.

Pome: a fruit with a core, as an apple.

Prickle: a small, weak, spine-like outgrowth of the bark or epidermis, as of the rose.

Procumbent: lying along the ground but not rooting.

Prostrate: generally meaning flat on the ground.

Pruinose: with a waxy powdery secretion on the surface, as a plum-like bloom.

Puberulent: with minute loose fine hairs.

Pubescent: with hairs of any kind.

Pulvinate: cushion-like.

Punctate: dotted with small pits which may be glandular or translucent.

Pungent: piercing, as the sharp pointed tip of a Juniper needle; also when applied to an odor or a taste which is sharp or penetrating or acrid.

Pustular: with little blisters or pustules.

Raceme: an elongated unbranched inflorescence with pedicellate flowers which develop from the bottom upwards.

Rachilla: the axis of the spikelet in the grasses and some other plants.

Rachis: the main axis of an inflorescence or of a compound leaf.

Radiate: spreading outward from a common center; in the family Compositae referring to heads with the ray-flowers surrounding the tubular flowers of the disk.

Ray: a branch of an umbel; the strap-shaped, petal-like flower in some Compositae.

Receptacle: the portion of the flower which supports the sepals, petals. stamens and pistils.

Recurved: curved backward or downward.

Reflexed: abruptly bent or turned downward or backward.

Regular: when associated with a flower

indicating that the parts in each set are similar in size, shape and arrangement.

Remote: scattered; separated from each other by some distance.

Reniform: kidney-shaped.

Reticulate: netted, forming a network.

Retrorse: bent or directed backward or downward, as some prickles.

Retuse: with a shallow notch in a blunt or rounded tip.

Revolute: rolled backward; with the margin rolled toward the lower side.

Rhizome: a creeping underground stem or branch which roots at the nodes; root-like but different in that it possesses nodes, buds and scale-like leaves.

Rib: a main vein.

Rigid: stiff, inflexible.

Rootstock: rhizome, caudex, or underground stem.

Rosette: a cluster of leaves or other organs in a circular arrangement.

Rotate: saucer-shaped, open and rather flat or wheel-like; used to describe the arrangement of petals in some flowers.

Rotund: full and round or rounded.

Rough: scabrous; sometimes used to describe surfaces covered with stiff coarse hairs.

Rudimentary: imperfectly developed and non-functional.

Rugose: wrinkled.

Runcinate: saw-toothed, with the teeth pointing toward the base.

Runner: a long portion of the stem lying on or close to the ground and able to root and produce new plants.

Saccate: bag-or sac-shaped; pouched.

Sagittate: shaped like the head of an arrow, with the acute straight lobes in line with the body (not directed outward).

Salverform: shape of a flower with flat abruptly spreading petal blades above a slender flower tube.

Samara: an indehiscent winged fruit, usually one-seeded.

Saprophyte: a plant living on dead organic material and usually not green.

Scabrous: rough to the touch.

Scale: a small flat, bract-like or leaf-like structure, membranous as in *Carex* or woody as in the pine cone.

Scape: a leaf-less flower stalk arising from the ground.

Scarious: thin, dry, not green.

Scorpioid: descriptive of an inflorescence in which the flowers are 2-ranked, developing alternately from opposite sides.

Scurfy: scaly.

Secund: one-sided.

Sepal: the segment of a calyx.

Septa: partitions or crosswalls.

Septate: having septa or partitions.

Septicidal: dehiscing along or into the partitions, that is, not opening directly into the locule.

Sericeous: silky-haired.

Series: a row or sometimes a whorl.

Serrate: with sharp forward-pointing teeth on the margin, as of a leaf.

Sessile: without a stalk.

Seta: a bristle.

Sheath: an encircling structure of some length, as the cylindrical tube surrounding the stem of a grass.

Shrub: a woody perennial which is usually smaller than a tree and has more than one shoot or trunk from the base, as opposed to a tree which is usually larger and has only one trunk.

Silicle: a short fruit which is usually not more than twice as long as it is wide.

Silique: a long fruit which is several times longer than it is wide and consists of 2 valves separated by a partition (replum) to which the seeds are attached.

Simple: undivided, as a leaf without lobes or leaflets.

Sinuate: deeply wavy-margined.

Sinus: the space or cleft between 2 lobes or divisions.

Spatulate: like a spatula; oblong but with the basal end narrowed.

Spermatophyta: plants with true seeds.

Spicate: arranged in a spike.

Spike: an elongated, usually unbranched, inflorescence bearing flowers without stalks or nearly so.

Spikelet: a cluster of 1 or more flowers subtended by a common pair of glumes, as in the grasses.

Sporangium: a spore-case.

Spore: a reproductive cell capable of developing into a new individual.

Spur: a hollow tubular or sac-like projection of the calyx or the corolla, sometimes secreting nectar.

Squarrose: spreading or recurved at the tip, as the involucral bracts of some Compositae.

Stalk: any support or stem of an organ, as the pedicel of a flower.

Stamen: the pollen-bearing organ of a flower, consisting of an anther usually supported by a stalk, the filament.

Staminate: descriptive of a flower, spike, cone or plant having stamens but no functional pistil or pistils.

Staminode: a modified sterile stamen which is incapable of producing pollen.

Standard: the broad upper petal of a pea-like flower; sometimes called a banner.

Stellate: star-shaped or with radiating points like a star.

Stem: the main axis of a plant, normally rising above ground and with nodes, leaves and often flowers.

Sterile: not functional.

Stigma: the upper portion of the pistil or style which receives pollen.

Stipe: a stalk in certain plants, as in *Eriogonum*.

Stipule: an appendage at the base of the petiole of a leaf, and sometimes leaf-like itself, as in *Galium*.

Stolon: a slender runner or shoot, usually above ground, able to take root.

Stomata: breathing mouths or pores on stems and leaves of most of the higher plants.

Strap-shaped: long and narrow like the ray-flowers of Compositae; ligulate.

Striate: having fine longitudinal lines or rows.

Strigose: having sharp-pointed appressed straight stiff hairs.

Strobile: the cone-like inflorescence of certain plants, like *Equisetum*.

Style: the stalk connecting the ovary with the stigma at its tip.

Stylopodium: an enlargement at the base of the style in Umbelliferae.

Sub-: a prefix indicating slightly, rather. under or below.

Submersed, submerged: growing under water.

Subtend: to extend or lie directly under or below some other body or organ. as a bract subtends a flower.

Subulate: awl-shaped; tapering toward the tip.

Succulent: fleshy; juicy; with sap.

Suffruticose: somewhat shrubby or woody.

Sulcate: grooved or furrowed.

Superior: growing or placed above, as an ovary that is free from the stamens, petals and sepals attached below or around it.

Suture: a seam, groove or line of opening or dehiscence.

Symmetrical: balanced or regular in the number of parts and in shape, as in the whorls of a flower.

Taproot: the primary root.

Tendril: a slender outgrowth of leaves or stem which serves to support the plant by grasping or clinging to another.

Terete: round in cross section.

Ternate: in 3's.

Tetra-: prefix indicating 4, as tetramerous meaning with 4 parts.

Thorn: a sharp-pointed woody branch which did not continue development.

Throat: the opening into the top of the tube of a tubular corolla or perianth.

Tomentose: densely covered with often tangled wool or short hairs, usually matted.

Torulose: twisted or knobby or unevenly cylindric due to swellings of enclosed seeds.

Trailing: prostrate on the ground but not rooting.

Tri-: prefix indicating 3 or 3 times, as trifoliate (three-leaved), trifoliolate (with three leaflets).

Trifid: deeply 3-cleft.

Truncate: abruptly cut off or cut across.

Tubercle: a short thickened growth, as at the top of the achene of *Eleocharis*.

Turbinate: shaped like a child's top; cone-shaped.

Turgid: swollen.

Turion: a scaly young bulb-like sucker or shoot from the ground, as in *Epilobium*.

Type: the original specimen on which a botanical name is based.

Umbel: an often flat-topped inflorescence with pedicels spreading outward from the same point, nearly like the ribs of an umbrella.

Umbellet: a small umbel.

Unarmed: without prickles or bristles or sharp points.

Uncinate: hooked.

Uni-: indicating one.

Unilocular: with 1 locule or cell.

Unisexual: of one sex, as a flower with stamens only or pistils only.

Utricle: an achene-like fruit, usually indehiscent, thin-walled, one-seeded, with a membranous sac surrounding the fruit proper.

Valve: one of the portions of the ovary wall into which the capsule splits at maturity.

Vascular: indicating the presence of conducting tissues in plants.

Ventral: the side facing the main plant axis; the upper surface of a leaf.

Verticillate: arranged in whorls.

Villous: shaggy; bearing long, soft or weak, unmatted hairs.

Viscid: sticky; greasy.

Whorl: a circular arrangement of organs around an axis, as the leaves of *Galium*.

Woolly: with long soft rather matted hairs.

INDEX TO COMMON AND SCIENTIFIC NAMES

Names of families are printed in CAPITALS; names of genera and species are printed in roman type; names printed in *italics* are synonyms.